BEYOND THE GHETTO INSIDE & OUT

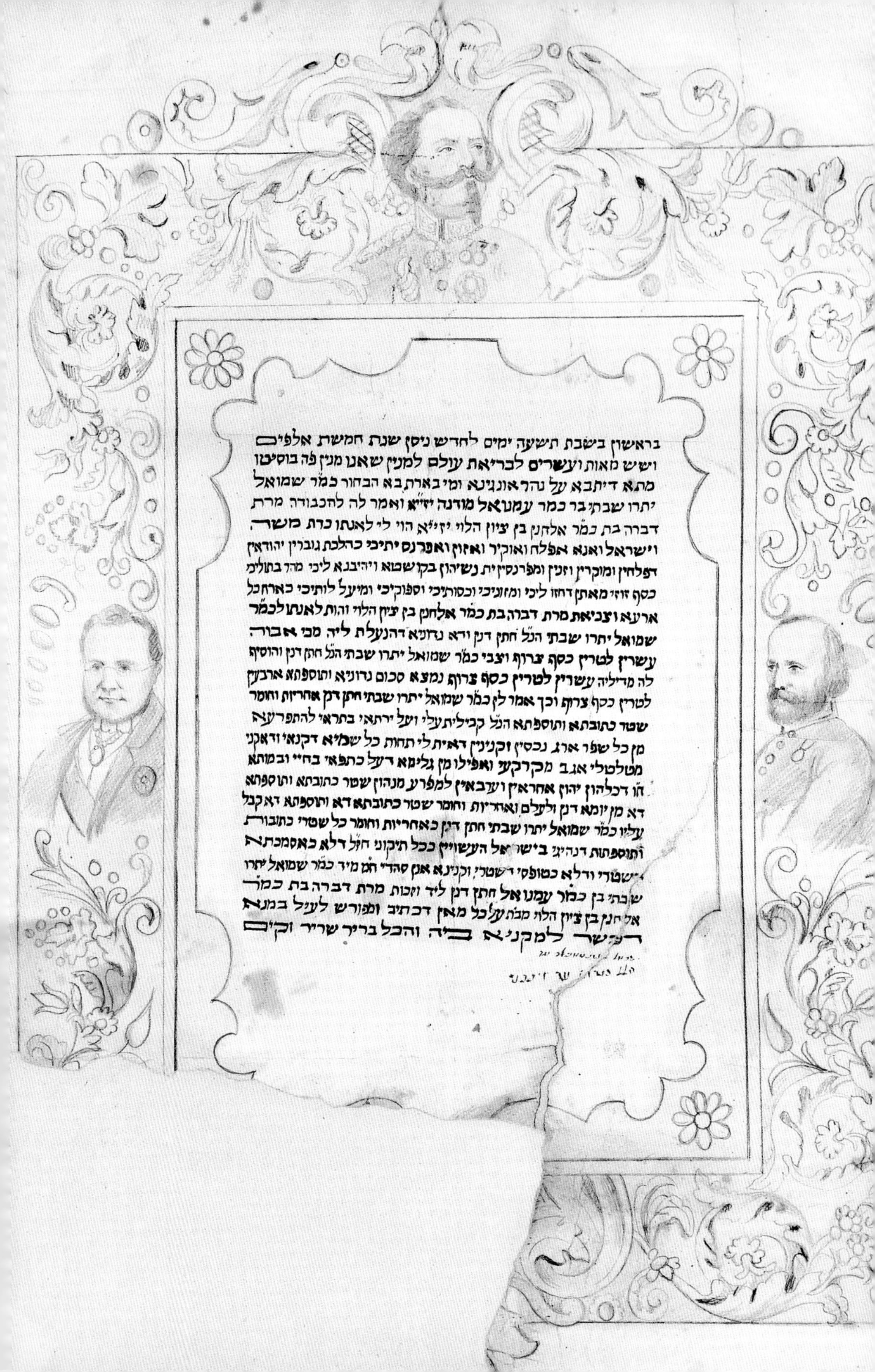
בראשון בשבת תשעה ימים לחדש ניסן שנת חמשת אלפים
ושש מאות ועשרים לבריאת עולם למנין שאנו מונין פה בוסיטון
מתא דיתבא על נהר אונגינא ומי בארת, בא הבחור כמ״ר שמואל
יתרו שבתי בר כמר עמנואל מודנה יז״א ואמר לה להכבודה מרת
דבורה בת כמ״ר אלחנן בן ציון הלוי יז״א הוי לי לאנתו כדת משה
וישראל ואנא אפלח ואוקיר ואזון ואפרנס יתיכי כהלכת גוברין יהודאין
דפלחין ומוקרין וזנין ומפרנסין ית נשיהון בקושטא ויהיבנא ליכי מהר בתוליכי
כסף זוזי מאתן דחזו ליכי ומזוניכי וכסותיכי וספוקיכי ומיעל לותיכי כארח כל
ארעא וצביאת מרת דבורה בת כמ״ר אלחנן בן ציון הלוי והות לאנתו לכמ״ר
שמואל יתרו שבתי הנ״ל חתן דנן ודא נדוניא דהנעלת ליה מבי אבוה
עשרין לטרין כסף צרוף וצבי כמ״ר שמואל יתרו שבתי הנ״ל חתן דנן והוסיף
לה מדיליה עשרין לטרין כסף צרוף נמצא סכום נדוניא ותוספתא ארבעין
לטרין כסף צרוף וכך אמר לן כמ״ר שמואל יתרו שבתי חתן דנן אחריות וחומר
שטר כתובתא ותוספתא הנ״ל קבילית עלי ועל ירתאי בתראי להתפרעא
מן כל שפר ארג נכסין וקנינין דאית לי תחות כל שמיא דקנאי ודאקני
מטלטלי אגב מקרקעי ואפילו מן גלימא דעל כתפאי בחיי ובמותא
הן דכלהון יהון אחראין וערבאין למפרע מנהון שטר כתובתא ותוספתא
דא מן יומא דנן ולעלם ואחריות וחומר שטר כתובתא דא ותוספתא דא קבל
עליו כמ״ר שמואל יתרו שבתי חתן דנן כאחריות וחומר כל שטרי כתובות
ותוספתות דנהיגי בישראל העשויין ככל תיקוני חז״ל דלא כאסמכתא
דשטרי ודלא כטופסי דשטרי, וקנינא אנן סהדי ה״מ מיד כמ״ר שמואל יתרו
שבתי בן כמ״ר עמנואל חתן דנן ליד וזכות מרת דבורה בת כמ״ר
אלחנן בן ציון הלוי מבת על כל מאי דכתיב ומפורש לעיל במנא
דכשר למקניא ביה והכל בריר שריר וקים

BEYOND THE GHETTO
INSIDE & OUT

edited by
Andreina Contessa, Simonetta Della Seta,
Carlotta Ferrara degli Uberti, Sharon Reichel

SilvanaEditoriale

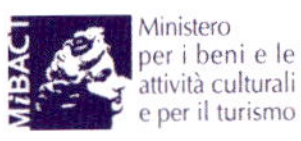

Minister
Dario Franceschini

General Secretary
Salvatore Nastasi

Director General of Museums
Massimo Osanna

Regional Secretary for Emilia-Romagna
Corrado Azzollini

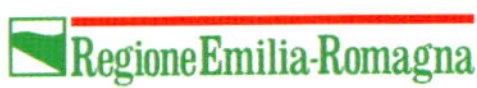

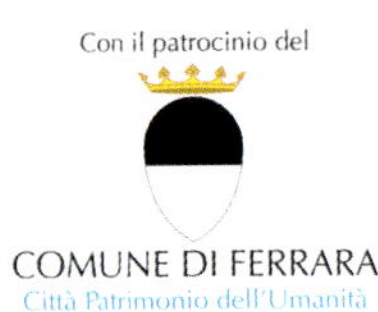

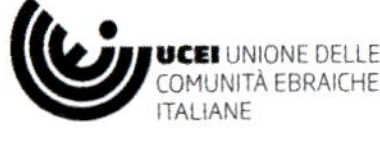

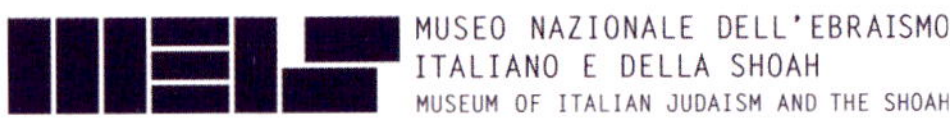

Chair
Dario Disegni

Board of Directors
Gloria Arbib
Massimo Mezzetti
Giovanni Franco Pernisa
Daniele Ravenna

Board of Auditors
Fabio Giuliani, *Chair*
Francesco Badia
Riccardo Bauer

Scientific committee
Shaul Bassi
David Bidussa
Saverio Campanini
Francesca Cappelletti
Alberto Cavaglion
Tania Coen-Uzzielli
Andreina Contessa
Claudia De Benedetti
Simonetta Della Seta
Anna Foa
Gadi Luzzatto Voghera
Saul Meghnagi
Bice Migliau
Liliana Picciotto
Anna Quarzi

Director
Amedeo Spagnoletto

Conservator, Registrar
Sharon Reichel

Technical Manager, staging and systems
Giulia Gallerani

Administration
Nicola Novelli

Organization
Donatella Buonfrate
Alessandra Roncarati

Press Office
Rachel Silvera

Webmaster
Stefano Furin

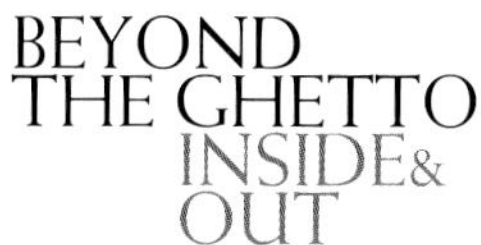

Exhibition presented by the
National Museum of
Italian Judaism and the Shoah

Under the patronage of
Ministry of Cultural Heritage and Activities and Tourism
Emilia-Romagna Region
Ferrara City Council
Union of Italian Jewish Communities
Jewish Community of Ferrara

Ferrara, MEIS
March 5 – September 12, 2021

Exhibition curated by
Andreina Contessa
Simonetta Della Seta
Carlotta Ferrara degli Uberti
Sharon Reichel

Layout and staging
Studio GTRF
Giovanni Tortelli Roberto Frassoni Architetti Associati

Management and coordination of works
Giovanni Tortelli
with Francesca Ferlinghetti, Erika Oliboni and Davide Piazza

Graphic design, reconstruction drawings, recompositions
Studio GTRF
Giovanni Tortelli Roberto Frassoni Architetti Associati
with Daniele De Santis, Rocco Pagnoni, Alessandro Polo

Security coordinator in the project phase
Elisabetta Mancini

Security coordinator in the execution phase
Stefano Marsili

Multimedia design and implementation
Umberto Saraceni, Amalia Zeffiro
Archivio Fotografico della Fondazione CDEC, "TUTTI ITALIANI" installation

Catalogue
Silvana Editoriale

Communication and marketing
Lara Facco

Translations and editing
Eileen Cartoon
Irene Groffsky Wernik (editorial assistance)

Supply and assembly services
Amisura
Archi&Media
Capatti&Bressan
C.S.I.
Graphic Report
Italvideo Service
Visual Lab

Process technical support
Andrea Conci

Security Manager
Stefano Bergagnin

Legal consultancy
Maria Letizia Govoni

With the support of

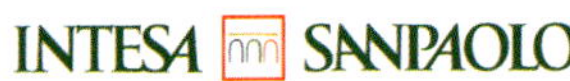

THE DAVID
BERG FOUNDATION

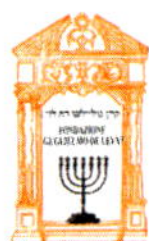

Thanks to
FONDAZIONE CDEC
and Ambassador
Giulio Prigioni

Lending institutions
Abbazia di Praglia, Teolo (PD)
Alberto Di Castro Collection, Rome
Alberto Mortara Family Archive
Archivio della Comunità Ebraica di Mantova, Mantua
Archivio di Stato di Torino, Turin
Archivio Ebraico Terracini, Turin
Archivio Storico della Città di Torino, Turin
Archivio Storico della Comunità Ebraica di Livorno
Archivio Storico della Comunità Ebraica di Roma "Giancarlo Spizzichino", Rome
Biblioteca Queriniana, Brescia
Biblioteca Nazionale Centrale, Roma
Centro Bibliografico UCEI, Roma
David and Cindy Sofer Collection, London and Jerusalem
Complesso Monumentale della Pilotta, Biblioteca Palatina, Parma
Comunità Ebraica di Livorno, Museo Ebraico, Livorno
Domus Mazziniana, Pisa
"Fausto Levi" Museum and Synagogue, Soragna
Fondazione Musei Civici di Venezia, Biblioteca del Museo Correr, Venice
Uffizi Gallery, Florence
Uffizi Gallery, Gallery of Modern Arte in Palazzo Pitti, Florence
Gallery of Modern Art, Rome
Intesa Sanpaolo
Jay and Jeanie Schottenstein Family Collection of Judaica
Museo Civico "Giovanni Fattori", Livorno
Museo d'Arte e Storia Antica Ebraica, Casale Monferrato
Museo Ebraico di Roma, Rome
Gallerie d'Arte Moderna e Contemporanea, Ferrara
Museo Storico e il Parco del Castello di Miramare, Trieste
Palazzo Madama - Museo Civico d'Arte Antica di Torino, Turin
Palazzo del Quirinale, Rome
William Gross Collection, Tel Aviv

We would like to thank all the private collectors who lent their works.

Catalogue edited by
Andreina Contessa,
Simonetta Della Seta
Carlotta Ferrara degli Uberti,
Sharon Reichel

Texts by
Michela Andreatta
Francesca Bregoli
Marina Caffiero
Tullia Catalan
Alberto Cavaglion
Andreina Contessa
Emanuele D'Antonio
Simonetta Della Seta
Serena Di Nepi
Riccardo Di Segni
Cristiana Facchini
Carlotta Ferrara degli Uberti
Raniero Fontana
Alessandro Guetta
Pier Cesare Ioly Zorattini
Dora Liscia Bemporad
Gadi Luzzatto Voghera
Elèna Mortara
Marcella Pellegrino Sutcliffe
Mauro Perani
Ariel Rathaus
Sharon Reichel
Edward Reichman
Shalom Sabar
Francesca Sofia
David Sorkin
Amedeo Spagnoletto
Francesco Spagnolo
Mario Toscano

Entries edited by
Andreina Contessa
Simonetta Della Seta
Carlotta Ferrara degli Uberti
Sharon Reichel
Rachel Silvera

Acknowledgements

Cristina Ambrosini
Marcella Ansaldi
Jack Arbib
Margherita Ascarelli
Beatrice Bentivoglio-Ravasio
Loredana Brancaccio
Laura Brazzo
Donatella Calabi
Tania Coen-Uzzielli
Emanuele Colorni
Claudia De Benedetti
John Dickie
Giovanni Ferrara degli Uberti
Pietro Finelli
Giovanni Grasso
Sergio Guarino
Alfredo Guerra
Ari Kinsberg
Antonio Lampis
Gisèle Levy
Gadi Luzzatto Voghera
Olga Melasecchi
Maria Vittoria Marini Clarelli
Daniela Porro
Claudio Procaccia
Daniele Ravenna
Marcella Ravenna
Patrizia Rusciani
Marcello Sacerdoti
Eike Schmidt
Ada Vittorina Segre
Guido Servi
Elisabetta Rattalino
Talitha Vassalli
Simone Verde
Stefano Visintin
Federica Zalabra
Giacomo Zarfati

The exhibition, which was due to open on April 3, 2020, was conceived and organized under the direction of Simonetta Della Seta and has been postponed until 2021 due to the Covid-19 pandemic.

Contents

10 **Jewish Culture is Part of Us**
Dario Franceschini

12 **A New and Important Accomplishment**
Dario Disegni

14 **Looking through the Window**
Amedeo Spagnoletto

15 **Inside and Out**
Andreina Contessa, Simonetta Della Seta, Carlotta Ferrara degli Uberti, Sharon Reichel

18 **The Perennial and the Ephemeral. Material Culture and Artistic Production in the Age of the Ghettos**
Andreina Contessa

36 **Objects Reveal: The Life Cycle and Its Rituals**
Shalom Sabar

48 **Silver Ceremonial Objects in Italian Synagogues**
Dora Liscia Bemporad

52 **Within the Walls and Beyond. Three and a Half Centuries of Italian History**
Serena Di Nepi

64 **Jewish Education in the Ghetto**
Amedeo Spagnoletto

68 **The Del Monte Family**
Marina Caffiero

72 **The Origin and Development of the Italian Liturgical Tradition**
Riccardo Di Segni

78 **From *Musica Hebræorum* to *Musica Sacra*. Musical Encounters in the Italian Synagogue (Seventeenth-Nineteenth Centuries)**
Francesco Spagnolo

84 **Epithalamia and Other Occasional Poetry**
Ariel Rathaus

90 **Medicine and the Jews. Training and Practice in Late Renaissance Italy**
Edward Reichman

96 **The Confraternities in the Sociocultural Fabric of the Communities**
Michela Andreatta

104 **Italy without a Ghetto: The Jewish Community of Livorno**
Francesca Bregoli

112 **Marrano and Sephardic Culture in the Early Modern Period: The Case of Italy**
Pier Cesare Ioly Zorattini

116 **Schools of Thought in Jewish Italy from the Fifteenth to the Eighteenth Centuries**
Alessandro Guetta

124 **The Universalism of Elia Benamozegh**
Raniero Fontana

126 **"Know Before Whom You Stand." The Synagogue from the Age of Ghettos to Emancipation**
Sharon Reichel

138 **The Tombstone Speaks**
Mauro Perani

144 **Jewish Emancipation in Europe**
David Sorkin

150 **Jewish Citizens**
Carlotta Ferrara degli Uberti

166 **Mazzini's Jewish Entourage**
Marcella Pellegrino Sutcliffe

170 **Jews and Freemasonry**
Francesca Sofia

172 **Italian Jewish Periodicals 1845–1915**
Carlotta Ferrara degli Uberti

174 **The Catholic Church and the Jews in Italy from the Early Modern Period to the Twentieth Century**
Cristiana Facchini

182 **The Facts and Lesson of the Mortara Case**
Elèna Mortara

196 **The Jews of Hapsburg Trieste: Social Inclusion, Emancipation, and Integration (1719–1914)**
Tullia Catalan

202 **Italian Zionists, between Italian Nationalism and Jewish Nationalism**
Simonetta Della Seta

210 **The Jewish Question in Cesare Lombroso's Science**
Emanuele D'Antonio

214 **Jews and Public Life in Liberal Italy**
Gadi Luzzatto Voghera

224 **Mirror Effects. Jews and Literature**
Alberto Cavaglion

226 **Italian Jews and the Great War**
Mario Toscano

234 **Museum and Exhibition Design**
Studio GTRF
Giovanni Tortelli Roberto Frassoni
Architetti Associati

239 CATALOGUE OF WORKS
edited by Andreina Contessa, Simonetta Della Seta, Carlotta Ferrara degli Uberti, Sharon Reichel, Rachel Silvera

323 **Bibliography**

Jewish Culture is Part of Us

Dario Franceschini
Minister of Cultural Heritage and Activities and Tourism

Beyond the Ghetto. Inside&Out is the evocative title of the third MEIS exhibition on Italian Judaism: an important piece of Italy's history and, at the same time, a crucial theme that prompts us to tackle important questions, today more than ever.

Based around the central theme of the Jewish identity in Italy, this modern exhibition guides us across the centuries, through the vicissitudes of the Italian Jewish experience, taking in both the dark chapters characterized by segregation, made real by the establishment of the ghettos (the first in Venice, in 1516, followed forty years later by Rome), and a number of significant positive turning points, such as the extension to Jews of all civil and political rights, with their immediate participation in the process of the Risorgimento and in the construction of a united Italy.

Jewish culture is part of us; indeed, it constitutes an important, profound piece of Europe's root. In Italy, in particular, we are talking about an uninterrupted presence that stretches back twenty-one centuries, making it the most longstanding Jewish presence in the West. For this reason, it is incumbent upon us to renew our awareness of just how valuable and fertile the contribution by Italian Jewry to the cultural, religious, social and political history has been. Italy, and Europe as a whole, are now becoming increasingly multicultural and multi-faith. In the face of the re-emergence of the poisonous seeds of fear of the other and of difference, intolerance, xenofobia and antisemitism, it seems urgent to promote culture as an antidote, and to forcefully affirm the value of diversity.

The new exhibition confirms the National Museum of Italian Judaism and the Shoah's ability to work in concert with all of the national museums in Italy and to be granted access to major works on loan from institutions both within and outside the country. In this regard, to prove the point it is sufficient to cite just a few of the paintings on display in this exhibition: *Esther before Ahasuerus* by Sebastiano Ricci (1733) comes from the collection of the Quirinal Palace, no less; *Interior of a Synagogue* by Alessandro Magnasco (1703) is on loan from the Uffizi Gallery; the *Portrait of Victor Emmanuel II* (painted between 1850 and 1899) comes from the Museo Storico e il Parco del Castello di Miramare in Trieste; and *The Kidnapping of Edgardo Mortara*, by Moritz Daniel Oppenheim (1862), was sent from the United States of America.

I am also delighted that in just a little over two years since its opening to the general public, MEIS is displaying objects from its collection: busts, documents, photographs and personal items of Jewish families. Indeed, how could we fail to notice the growth of this esteemed national museum? With the *Beyond the Ghetto* exhibition, it completes its offer, and in Ferrara visitors can now dive into an all-encompassing experience of the Italian Jews' history and culture, from the time of ancient Rome right up to the creation of the united Europe. I would like to applaud MEIS's President, Dario Disegni, and Simonetta Della Seta, under whose direction this important exhibition was conceived and organized, for reaching this ambitious goal.

A special thanks should go to the curators of the exhibition – Andreina Contessa, Carlotta Ferrara degli Uberti, the museum's curator Sharon Reichel and the aforementioned Simonetta Della Seta – and to the designer Giovanni Tortelli, the various prestigious loaning bodies, the institutional and private sponsors and, last but not least, all those who have contributed to this new part that enriches the museum's offer. Albeit still under construction, MEIS is already attracting students and tourists from around the world.

A New and Important Accomplishment

Dario Disegni
President
National Museum of Italian Judaism and the Shoah

Beyond the Ghetto. Inside&Out represents an important accomplishment for the National Museum of Italian Judaism and the Shoah. This third great exhibition prefigures the last segment of the MEIS permanent museum display that was first inaugurated in December 2017 with the exhibition *Jews, an Italian Story. The First Thousand Years,* curated by Anna Foa, Giancarlo Lacerenza and Daniele Jalla, and that continued with *The Renaissance Speaks Hebrew* curated by Giulio Busi and Silvana Greco.

After shedding light on the earliest documentation attesting to the presence of Jews in Italy, presenting a selection of over two hundred unique objects and archaeological finds on loan from prominent Italian and international museums, and after having revealed the osmotic relationship between Renaissance and Hebrew language via the study of illuminated texts and paintings by artists such as Andrea Mantegna and Vittore Carpaccio, today *Beyond the Ghetto* draws attention to a crucial period in the history of Italian Judaism: the time span from the institution of ghettos in 1516 and the gradual extension of civil and political rights for Jews living on the Italian Peninsula, to their ardent participation first in the Risorgimento uprisings, then in the economic, political, social and cultural spheres in a united Italy.

This exhibition project offers viewers the chance to discover the traces and the character of two thousand years of Italian Judaism – a consistent narrative documenting the seasons of dialogue and exchange as well as those of conflict and persecution, through a variety of displays including liturgic objects, every-day items, works of art, as well as multimedia and music installations.

The *Beyond the Ghetto* exhibition also marks an important evolution in the Museum's exhibition project development, since the two esteemed scholars Andreina Contessa and Carlotta Ferrara degli Uberti have worked side by side with the former Director of the Museum Simonetta Della Seta and Curator Sharon Reichel.

I wish to underline one further significant aspect: this exhibition, whose design has been realized by the Studio GTRF Giovanni Tortelli Roberto Frassoni, has provided the occasion for an effective and fruitful collaboration between MEIS and many Italian Jewish Communities that have loaned some of the extraordinary objects on display.

One of the institutional objectives of MEIS is to present the multifaceted cultural contribution of Italian Judaism, stemming from the unique identity and exclusive artistic voice that each Community has developed over the centuries. Mantua, Venice, Turin, Livorno, and Casale Monferrato are but some of the centers having a place in MEIS's narratives.

Also significant has been the choice of giving space to the history and evolution of Judaism in the city of Rome: from the ghetto instituted in 1555, with its afflictive and sorrowful restrictions, to the choice of the Jews of Rome to fight strongly for peace, culture, and their hard-earned freedom, and to participate in the making of the Capital of Italy.

This exhibition at MEIS represents an extraordinary occasion to admire unique paintings such as Sebastiano Ricci's *Esther before Ahasuerus* on loan from the Quirinale; Ulvi Liegi's *Interior of The Synagogue in Livorno* (1935) and Vittorio Corcos's *Portrait of Giuseppe Garibaldi (1882)* from the Museo Civico "Giovanni Fattori" in Livorno; Alessandro Magnasco's *Interior of a Synagogue* (1703) from the Uffizi Gallery; and Moritz Daniel Oppenheim's *Kidnapping of Edgardo Mortara* (1862), which was auctioned a few years ago at Sotheby's and that is publicly displayed here for the first time: all circumstances that I believe attest to the growth of MEIS on the Italian and international cultural scene.

MEIS and I myself personally are very grateful for the contribution of the illustrious curators, lenders, private collectors, designers, authors, catalogue publishing house and all the professionals and artisans who participated in the making of *Beyond the Ghetto*.

I also wish to express once again my deepest gratitude to the Ministry of Cultural Heritage and Activities and Tourism, which provides MEIS with the fundamental resources to carry out its activities, and that, thanks to Minister Dario Franceschini's committed and constant support, continues to acknowledge the fundamental role our Museum plays in our country's culture and society.

A heartfelt thanks also goes to the City of Ferrara and to Regione Emilia-Romagna. From the Museum's foundation they have always welcomed MEIS with great interest and openness, sharing its growth and consolidation step after step.

Also of great importance has been our fruitful and beneficial collaboration with the Union of Italian Jewish Communities, based on an ongoing dialogue and exchange on the historical and cultural heritage of Italian Judaism.

This exhibition would never have been possible without the generous contribution of its private partners, first and foremost Intesa Sanpaolo, that has supported MEIS and its projects since its first opening exhibition, as well as other Italian and international supporters. A special mention goes to the David Berg Foundation of New York.

Against the complex backdrop of our current historical period, in which antisemitism, racism, and intolerance have risen to unsettling levels, MEIS, by recounting the history of the Jews of Italy – a narration that continues in this third essential exposition and will hopefully inspire further reflections and exchanges –, intends to reconfirm its role of a great cultural and educational center where all visitors can look to the future with awareness, without forgetting or mystifying the past.

Looking through the Window

Amedeo Spagnoletto
MEIS Director

The exhibition *Beyond the Ghetto. Inside&Out* may rightly be considered the latest, prestigious result of the efforts that all the members of the MEIS team have put in over recent years.

I gratefully acknowledge the input of all concerned, from the previous director of the museum, Simonetta Della Seta, who is also among the curators of this exhibition, alongside Andreina Contessa, Carlotta Ferrara degli Uberti and Sharon Reichel, to the president Dario Disegni and all of my other colleagues, to whom I offer my heartfelt thanks.

A number of scholars, albeit aware of the paradoxical nature of what they are positing, have claimed that they can trace the roots of the ghetto far further back than the shared chronological limits.

Jacob's 70-strong family, having made their way to Egypt to escape the harsh famine gripping the land of Israel, chose a distinct region in which to settle. "Please let your servants dwell in the land of Goshen" (Genesis 47:4) – this is what Joseph proposes that they request from the Pharaoh. It was a place that, on the one hand, enabled them to conserve and develop their identity, but on the other soon became a byword for the years of odious slavery that the populace was to undergo.

For centuries, the Italian ghetto – an enclosure within which the Jews suffered a long, tortuous segregation – represented a narrow, shadowy space, albeit always fitted with symbolic windows that only rarely afforded any access to the outside world. The ghetto functioned as a cultural and physical filter that molded every facet of Jewish life, deeply affecting the social and domestic spheres, modeling the lexicon and rendering certain aspects of religious life more resistant than elsewhere, but also suffocating the energy that under conditions of liberty would have blossomed more vigorously in myriad fields.

This exhibition describes the complex interpretations that can be given to this experience. It covers not only the delicate relations between the Jewish communities and the local government, but also family stories, anecdotes and regional traditions, as well as the cultural and artistic activities that, despite everything, still managed to flourish within such a restricted dimension.

Emancipation, which came later to Italy than to other European countries, was welcomed by the Jews as a form of liberation and, at the same time, an auspicious opportunity to demonstrate to themselves and to others their passion for, loyalty towards and pride in their Italian homeland.

The exhibits on display here collectively constitute a key chronological map for gleaning an understanding of the subtleties of a bimillennial tradition and for giving consideration to the more recent history of the Jews.

Inside and Out

Andreina Contessa, Simonetta Della Seta,
Carlotta Ferrara degli Uberti, Sharon Reichel

All European citizens of today live "inside and outside" a country, a culture, a language. Each of us is part of one group interacting with a plurality of other groups. Today more than ever, we often work and study in a context different to the one in which we were born. We meet people raised in cultures that are different from ours, we interact with these cultures, sometimes as part of a minority, sometimes as part of the majority. The globalized world has erased monolithic identities, and despite all difficulties, Europe as a union encourages its citizens' multiple identities, while also safeguarding the different roots and individual specificities that are part of this complex mosaic.

The condition of Jews in Europe, who over the centuries resisted and grew within their own culture always trying to establish a dialogue with the society around them, even when limitations and barriers were put in place, is a condition common to many today. Ghetto and integration issues have made a comeback.

At MEIS we believe that the history and the lives of the Jews of Italy and Europe hold universal values providing tools that can be still useful today. From this reflection – one of the mainstays of the Museum's mission – stems the spirit that underpins our third historiographical exhibition on Italian Judaism.

March 2021 will in fact see the inauguration of a third great exhibition studying, prefiguring, and preparing the final section of the Museum's permanent display. *Beyond the Ghetto. Inside&Out* sets out to complete the museum's experience, and has been especially conceived as a journey across the various stages of Jewish identity in Italy and in Europe, where after being confined to ghettos, Jews eventually and gradually integrated into general society, firmly believing in and joining all movements of national liberation, and fighting in World War I. The present exhibition is the result of a rigorously historical and artistically mindful approach, in keeping with the rest of the Museum's experience, paired with a research covering sociological dynamics, documenting intimate individual choices, personal stories, and issues that are still very relevant today.

The myth of Queen Esther who hid her Jewish lineage from her husband, Persian King Ahasuerus, only to reveal it to save her fellow Jews from the councilor Haman's plans to exterminate them, is certainly a myth of modern relevance. This Biblical story was first revived by the *conversos* – the Spanish and Portuguese Jews forced to convert to Christianity – who saw in Queen Esther, who hid and protected her religion to the very end, a heroic figure to look up to. A myth that eventually spread to the Italian ghettos too, also because it allowed Jews, who could not relate to Christian theatrical subjects, to develop a heroic narrative integral to their culture and inside the ghetto walls (Contessa).

Because inside the ghetto, the "inside" becomes an "outside." And the "outside" – through painting, beauty, music (Spagnolo) and arts of the late Renaissance – is brought "inside" combined with the intimate Jewish world, beautifying and enriching it, making it habitable despite its restrictions (Liscia Bemporad). Inside ghettos, the synagogues, which had to remain invisible from the outside, morphed into precious spaces where Jews could pray, study and gather, surrounded by liturgic objects forged and decorated in keeping with the taste of the "outside" world (Di Segni, Sabar, Reichel).

Paradoxically, as pointed out by Andreina Contessa, "the liminality of the ghetto provided the Jews with a safe space for material and cultural growth." "The period of the ghettos was also one of immense typographical creativity and here we need to keep in mind the materiality of book production, which required typographic composition, designing and engraving decorations and illustrations, binding together quires and finally putting it all together." Ghettos were also home to educational initiatives, such as those in Rome described by Amedeo Spagnoletto, and saw the flowering of Hebrew poetry (Rathaus), medical studies (Reichman) and above all the consolidation of community life (Andreatta).

The issue of identity in the inside-and-outside-the-ghetto relation is a recurring and multifaceted phenomenon. As Serena Di Nepi explains, the ghetto is a complex notion emanating from political choices. It is no coincidence that the word *ghetto* has survived generations and is still used today to define all types of past and present segregation.

If on the one hand, from a historical standpoint, the ghetto is a Catholic and Italian invention and a manifest form of anti-Judaism functional to segregating and controlling Jewish minorities, on the other there have been many other forms of intolerance that have accompanied this structured separation of Jews from the rest of the population (Facchini), such as forced conversions, trials, prohibitions, book burnings, humiliations, houses of catechumens, courts of the inquisition, informing, children's kidnappings (Caffiero). As late as 1858 for instance, there was a case of kidnapping in Bologna – at the time still under the rule of the State of the Church, while Jews in the Kingdom of Sardinia had already been granted civil and political rights – six-year-old Edgardo Mortara was secretly baptized by the family housemaid and then kidnapped by the Guards of the Pope to be raised in Rome to become a Cardinal. His case, precisely documented by his descendent, scholar Eléna Mortara, was a scandal in many European countries. But the child's destiny was written and eventually he did become a Cardinal.

The "inside" and "outside" dynamics can coexist inside a closed perimeter, as in the State of the Church, as well as in an open one. This was the case of Livorno, for instance, where Jews were among the minorities the Medici summoned to promote the development of a city open to the world for the benefit of the Grand Duchy of Tuscany.

The so-called *Livornine* were a set of privileges emanated to attract to Livorno "merchants from whatever nation, Levantines, Ponentines, Spaniards, Portuguese, Greeks, Germans, and Italians, Jews, Turks, Moors, Armenians, Persians and others" assuring religious freedom and protection from Inquisition. Thanks to these laws, many Sephardic Jews – about 1500 – expelled from Spain and Portugal found refuge and freedom "inside" and "outside" the new free port (Bregoli, Zorattini).

The lengthy process of Jewish emancipation in Italy should be read, as David Sorkin explains, against the backdrop of the many other political processes that were occurring in Europe at the time. In those years the most oppressive of ghettos was being established in Rome (1555), while the Jews of Eastern and Western Europe (in Poland, Bordeaux, and

Hamburg) were beginning to enjoy the same rights as those granted to Christian merchants. A similar process was also underway in Livorno and even in the Venice ghetto. Sorkin also points out that in 1590 the Jews of Amsterdam and London started to see their rights brought on a level with those of general society. Therefore, there were different forms and types of emancipation and of Jewish emancipation (Sorkin believes that today Jewish emancipation still cannot be entirely taken for granted). So how did this process of civil rights extension to Jews of Italy come about? Where? And in what ways? This long chapter about "inside" and "outside" the ghetto is described in all its aspects by Carlotta Ferrara degli Uberti who explores the Jews' enthusiasm towards gradually opening up to the surrounding society – participating first and foremost in the Risorgimento uprisings towards the creation of the Italian nation (Pellegrino Suttcliffe) – as well as the difficulties and the pitfalls of this process.

Individuals and communities; families and individual professionals; community educational institutions and schools of thought (Guetta, Fontana); cultural renaissance and media debate (Ferrara degli Uberti, Cavaglion): the (numerically) small population of Italian Judaism joining the Carboneria secret revolutionary society and masonic lodges, undertaking liberal professions and academic, political, and military careers, in a context of social advancement, love for homeland Italy, and in some cases drawn to Jewish nationalist Zionist positions (Sofia, Luzzatto Voghera, Toscano, Della Seta); the *scola*-synagogues where Jews used to pray and study far from sight, redesigned with great domes that could be spotted from a distance (Reichel). But to what extent did this immersion in general society safeguard the survival of Jewish identity and culture?

Over the course of one generation the Jews of Italy trained to become and found a role in society as servicepersons, lawyers, engineers, scientists, judges, mayors, ministers. Italy even had a Jewish Prime Minister (Luigi Luzzatti, in office from March 1910 to March 1911). Resilience, integration, participation, assimilation, cultural dialogue, desire for equality, preserving differences. The sixteenth- to nineteenth-century history of European Jews, of Italian Jews in particular, is a journey of hope and disillusion, inspiring reflections that are still topical today. A journey across a variety of solutions, depending on place, culture, education, and wealth. A mosaic of individual faces tracing a common narrative based on a drive to improve one's personal condition, contribute to the development of society and progress of the country, and participate in the growth of Italy and of its people. A sweeping fresco of common and sometimes less-common people looking forward to the new century with hope. The exhibition at MEIS goes as far as 1914, a year that would turn out to be crucial for the small but dynamic universe of Italian Judaism: World War I had begun in Europe and would spread to Italy in 1915 (Toscano). In less than 25 years, Fascism would label Italian Jews as citizens who had to be expelled from society work, rights, and life.

The Perennial and the Ephemeral. Material Culture and Artistic Production in the Age of the Ghettos

Andreina Contessa

It is difficult to determine to what degree the long period in the ghetto influenced the essence of Jewish culture in Italy. Starting with the institution of the first ghetto in Venice in 1516, then followed by the one in Rome and all the others, the Jews were obligated to contend with this ambivalent place, which simultaneously included and isolated them within the urban space, constraining them to live in an isolated, clearly demarcated area of the city. This closed, peripheral corner within the wider world was the seat of Jewish life where the family-related and private aspects of everyday life were unfolded and the space within which the Jewish identity developed for nearly three centuries.

More than 500 years since its institution and more than a century and a half after its gates were destroyed, the concept of the ghetto still reverberates through history and raises issues about migration and identity in our own time. Considering Jewish history beginning with the institution of the ghetto means examining the circularity of the itinerant history of the Jews, between expulsions and migrations, and the polarity established since that time between temporary and permanent residence.

It is indicative that the word ghetto no longer refers solely to the inhospitable urban island that was demarcated in almost every city as a refuge and forced residence for the Jews, having become the symbol of all segregation and commonly used to describe situations of physical, social and conceptual marginalization. While the ghetto became a universal symbol of segregation and degradation, at the time of its founding it was probably considered an important concession to the Jews, for whom it meant gaining a permanent home inside the city.

The Venetian ghetto contained in embryonic form all of the basic elements of the future ghettos, becoming clearly evident in cities such as Rome, Ferrara and Mantua. It hosted a mixed Jewish community, including Jews of Italian, Ashkenazic and, later, Sephardic origin, the latter migrating from Spain, Portugal and the Levant. Shrewd Venice might have been the first to note the potential for the economic growth of its immigrants, and in particular the Jews, who were recognized for their business acumen and vast network of cultural resources and financial connections. At the same time, the Venetian government wanted to find a remedy for the intrinsic danger of a cultural clash deriving from the coexistence of religious credos and different customs and traditions, which could have easily given rise to intolerance. From the perspective of the local governments, the cruel discrimination and segregation of the Jews in the stark, mixed living spaces of the ghetto was a necessary measure for the protection of the citizens and needed to function in both directions, inside and outside the ghetto gates. It guaranteed the Jews a certain degree of self-government and organizational freedom, adherence to religious precepts and community and family traditions. The cosmopolitan communities of the ghettos were able to develop a rich cultural life, scrupulously practice their religion, produce wondrous religious objects and create different forms of social assistance and reciprocal solidarity.

The ghetto gates were closed at night and watched over by Christian guards paid by the Jews, but the space of the ghetto was not sealed and the gates functioned in both directions, permitting continuous osmosis between inside and outside.

Identity and narrative in liminality

Paradoxically, the liminality of the ghetto provided the Jews with a safe space for material and cultural growth, the fruit of which circulated well beyond the confines of the ghetto and government regulation. Starting in the early sixteenth century and continuing through the beginning of the seventeenth, the spirit of Jewish creativity permeated the ghetto walls. Cultural exchange could not be held back by gates and walls.

The first ghetto, the one in Venice, was already a hotbed of intellectual activity, inhabited by a multitude of figures, including the scholar Leone da Modena, the kabbalist and poet Mosè Zacuto, the rabbi Simone (Simcha) Luzzatto, the linguist, physician and philosopher David de Pomis, the poet Sara Copio Sullam and the painter Mosè del Castellazzo.

The identity issues intrinsic to the relationship between the inside and outside of the ghetto clearly emerge in two of the most important books on Judaism that surfaced from the overlapping of city and ghetto. Written in Italian so that they would be accessible to non-Jewish readers, both volumes were published in 1638 by Giovanni Colleoni: the *Historia de' riti Hebraici* written by the renowned polymath rabbi Leone da Modena (1571–1648), and the *Discorso circa lo stato de gl'Hebrei*, written by his younger colleague Simone (Simcha) Luzzatto (1583–1663).

In their books, Modena and Luzzatto formulated a new way of presenting the concept of Jewish collective identity and explained the role of the Jews within Christian society – and this in a period of unbending religious division. Modena's book in particular was an attempt to portray the Judaism of his time, while, however, also transmitting an ideal vision of Judaism as it ought to be perceived and understood by the outside world.

What is extraordinary and extremely new in Modena's book (cat. 3), and distinguishes it from the genre of books on rites, *sefer minhagim*, addressed to an "internal" readership, is its consideration of the outside world, explaining the rituals and traditions, formulating an updated narrative of its most intimate self and at the same time providing the image and attitude that it would like the other to have of and towards it.

In the subsequent century, a similar work, however expressed through prints, introduced the reader to the rites and holidays of the Jews through drawings by Francesco Novelli – inspired by the ones by Bernard Picart – printed in 1727 under the title *Costumi degli ebrei di Venezia nel XVIII secolo* (Customs of the Venetian Jews in the eighteenth century).

The need to render the Jewish cultural universe visible through book illustration was expressed between the seventeenth and eighteenth centuries in the creativity that was applied to a vast range of publications: from Bibles to scientific tomes and even religious ones, like an Ashkenazic Jewish prayer book printed in Venice in 1749 at the Bragadin printing house and filled with illustrations of holidays and preparations for Shabbat.

Throughout the sixteenth and seventeenth centuries, Venice was the theatre of unique encounters between Christians and Jews. The Venetian publishing houses and printers became meeting places for intellectuals, typographers, poets, artists, scholars and theologians. Protestants and Catholics were returning at that time to the original texts and wanted to study the Bible in Hebrew. Books were printed in Hebrew and Jews were therefore sought out by non-Jews as teachers and translators, consultants, editors and proofreaders for Hebrew texts and the Bible. The publication of numerous books on Hebrew grammar, dictionaries and encyclopedic works demonstrate the interest in Hebrew and Biblical studies that characterized the age of the ghettos.

One example of the spirit of collaboration generated by the intellectual encounters between poets, artists and scholars from different cultures and religions is the work of the multifaceted artist Francesco Grisellini, the work of whom is known but little about his biography. We know that he was born in Venice in 1717, where he was a member of numerous academies, including those of London, Bern, Gorizia, Florence and Bologna. Between 1739 and 1741, he drew and engraved a series of twelve Biblical scenes that were used to illustrate a Hebrew Bible printed by Bragadin for Isacco Foa, for whom he also designed the family crest, a palm flanked by two heraldic lions (U. Nahon Museum of Italian Jewish Art, Jerusalem, inv. ON 1284 A-C).

We do not know precisely when he engraved the decorative image designed by Avraham Calimani to be hung in a *sukkah* (hut) for the festival of Sukkot (Gross Family Collection Trust, Tel Aviv, inv. 038.011.008)

The small, elegant, delicately watercolored medallion bears a Hebrew inscription flanked by the figures of Moses and Aaron and surrounded by clipei with scenes linked to the festival according to the cult of the Temple of Jerusalem. The inscription was drawn from Psalm 76 (75), 11, "Surely the wrath of man shall praise Thee; The residue of wrath shalt Thou gird upon Thee." Among Grisellini's collaborations with Venetian Jewish publishing, the most striking example is the long series of engravings illustrating the Esther scroll, printed on parchment (Contessa 2016), as we shall see shortly. Grisellini was an intellectual with varied interests and worked in the areas of geography, theatre, botany and politics. In 1768, he began publication of the two-volume *Dizionario delle arti e de' mestieri*, and edited the *Giornale d'Italia*, in which he published various scientific articles.

The period of the ghettos was also one of immense typographical creativity and here we need to keep in mind the materiality of book production, which required typographic

1. *Megillah* ("scroll") of Esther. Biblioteca Palatina, Complesso Monumentale della Pilotta, Parma (cat. 9)

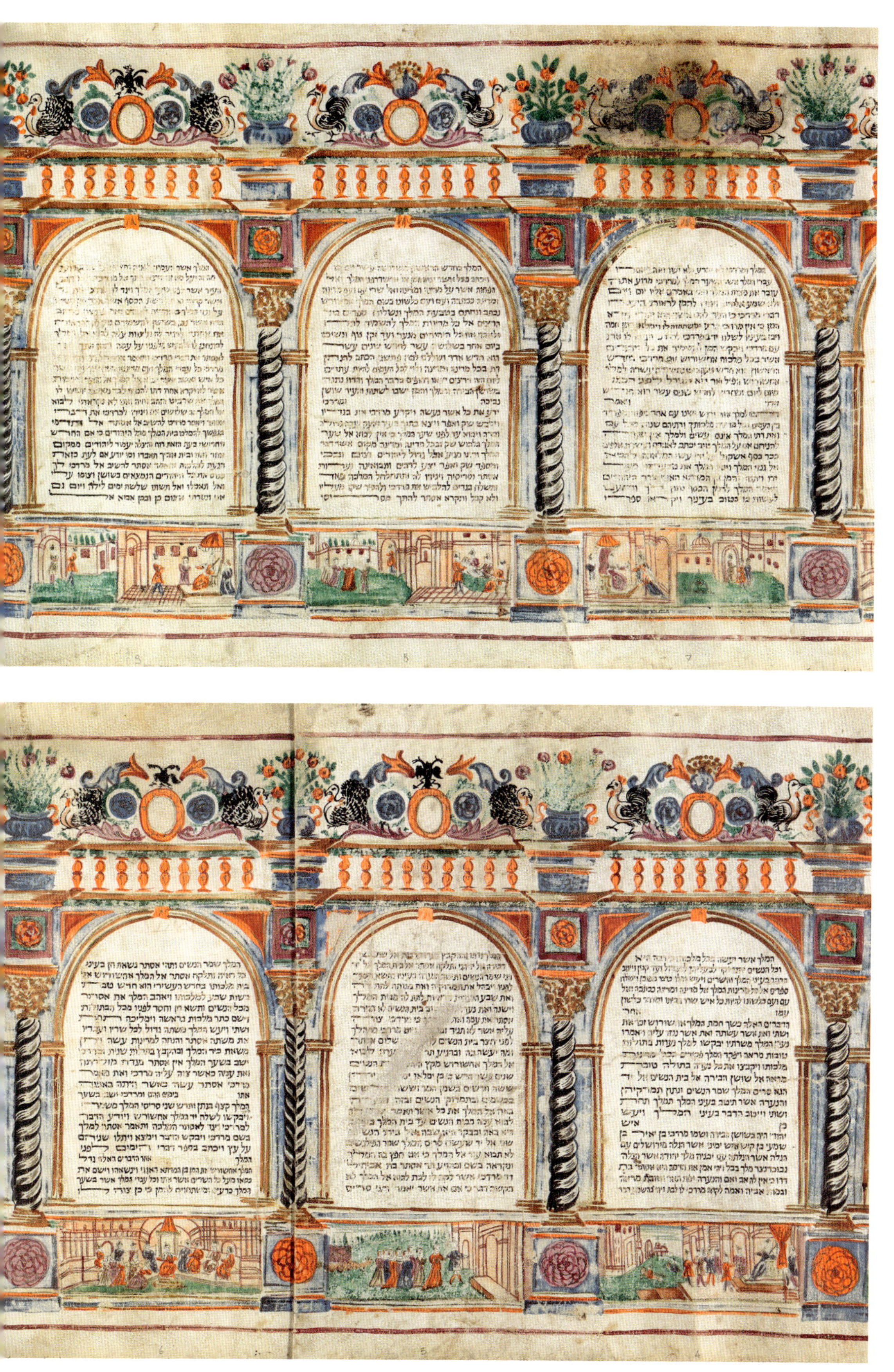

composition, designing and engraving decorations and illustrations, binding together quires and finally putting it all together. The most successful of these projects was the modern reworking of the illustrations for the Pesach *Haggadah*. The printer Israel Zifroni di Guastalla was the figure behind the edition of the Pesach *Haggadah* (cat. 4) with an entirely new series of illustrations, which was specially printed at Giovanni di Gara's printing house in Venice. In this volume, the text of the *Haggadah* was in the middle of the page and flanked by an image and commentary written in one of the three vernacular languages: Judeo Italian, Judeo Spanish or Judeo German. Each of these languages was transcribed into Hebrew characters, but the fact that three different editions were prepared, each with captions in a language that reflected the three main Jewish communities that were living in Venice was in and of itself extraordinary, including from the publishing perspective.

From its first appearance in 1609, the Venice *Haggadah* was a huge success and had a long-lasting influence on all future illustrations of the *Haggadah*. The original wooden blocks were used multiple times to print new editions of the book. They were later carefully

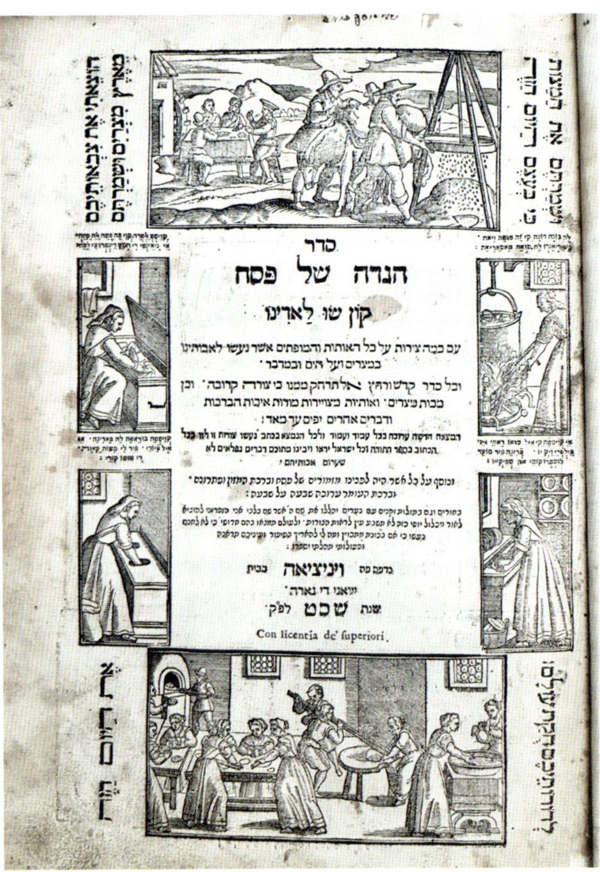
סדר
הגדה של פסח
קון שו לאדינו
עם כמה צירות על כל האותות והמופתים אשר נעשו לאבותינו
במצרים ועל הים ובמדבר׳
נדפס פה ויניציאה בבית
יואני די גארה׳
שנת שסט לפק׳
Con licentia de' superiori.

2. Pesach *Haggadah* with Ladino translation.
David and Cindy Sofer Collection, London (cat. 4)

copied and printed in hundreds of editions over the subsequent 200 years. In the nineteenth century, when a new pocket edition of the *Haggadah* was being prepared in Livorno, the printers carefully copied the Venetian illustrations and adapted them to the new, smaller format. It was not until the publication of the Morpurgo *Haggadah*, printed in Trieste in 1864 with new illustrations in the nineteenth-century style, that the artistic and editorial domination of the *Haggadah* of the Venetian ghetto came to an end (Contessa 2013[b]).

The illustrations for the Esther scrolls were probably conceived and created between the sixteenth and seventeenth centuries. One of the oldest scrolls is a *megillah* written in Ferrara between 1616 and 1618 by Moshe ben Abraham Pescarolo (c. 1560–c. 1640). The decoration of the *megillot* frames the columns of text with a series of arches in different designs and hues that were further embellished in the early seventeenth century with narrative scenes illustrating the whole cycle of the story of Esther.

Starting in the late seventeenth century, engravings were made and the illustrations and decorations of the Esther cycle were printed on parchment and then colored by hand,

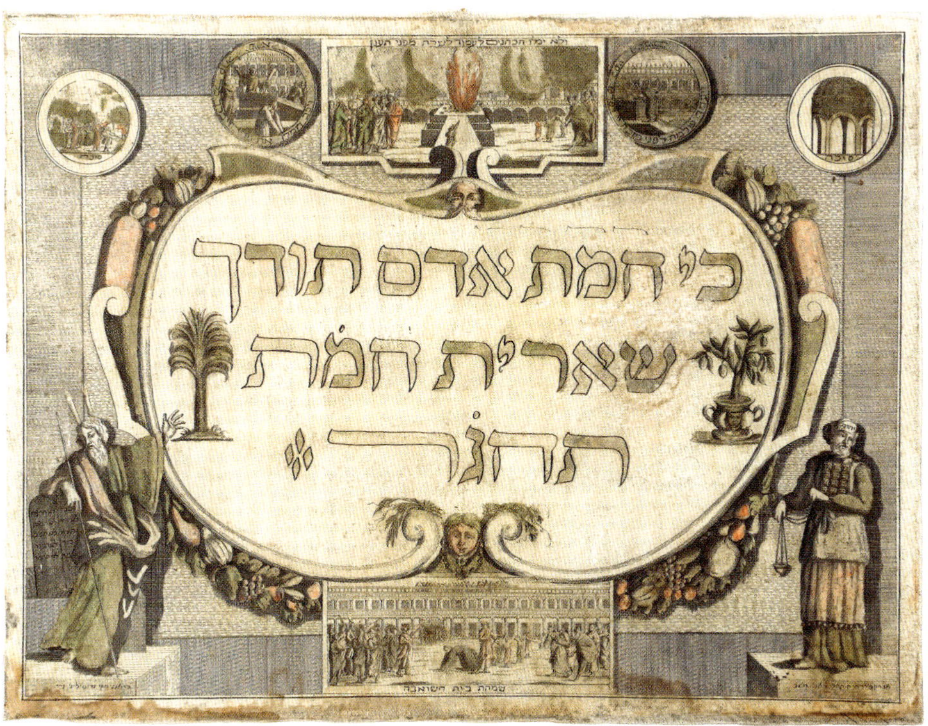

3. *Sukkah* decoration plaque. Gross Family Collection Trust, Tel Aviv (cat. 31)

after which the text was added, written by hand in accordance with synagogal prescription. In addition to the decorations by Andrea Marelli (a Christian Italian engraver active in Rome from 1567 to 1572 and author of a repertoire of Mannerist borders filled with garlands, masks, grotesques and animals), the narrative cycles also circulated in the Venetian sphere and enjoyed great success throughout the entire seventeenth century.

The above-mentioned *megillah* by Grisellini was of undoubted artistic and iconographic importance. The decoration comprises a series of elegant arches supported by columns of various design set on high pedestals and topped with a lavish balustrade embellished with large paterae holding splendid flowering branches and pairs of birds. The scenes from the Biblical story of Esther are contained in rectangles in the lower register and reflect the theatrical late-Baroque style of the time (Budzioch 2016; Sabar 2012).

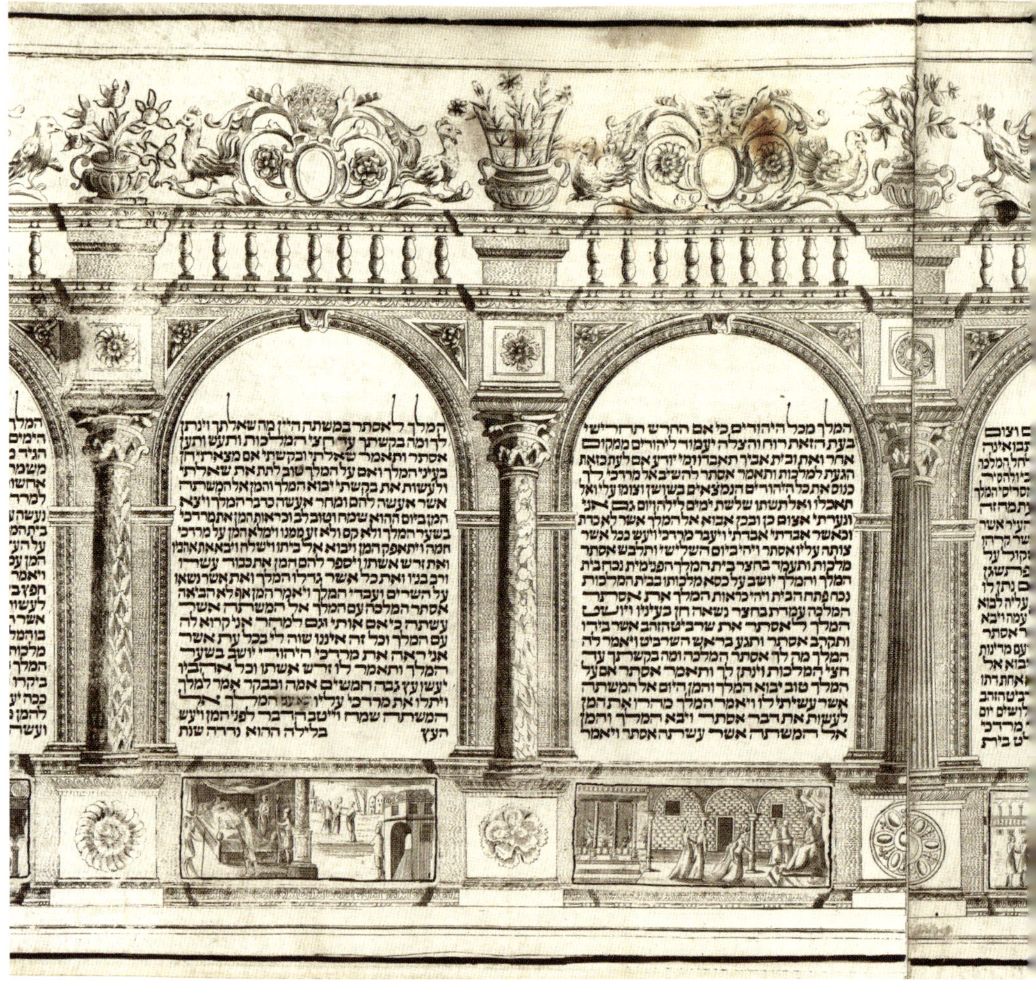

4. *Megillah* of Esther, Venice, mid-eighteenth century. U. Nahon Museum of Italian Jewish Art, Jerusalem, ON 0501

Esther, biblical heroine in the age of the ghettos

The fashion for decorating and illustrating Esther scrolls came at a time when the figure of Esther was of particular cultural prominence, and new attention was being devoted to the Biblical heroine in theatre, poetry and the visual arts. During the age of the ghettos, Esther seems to have become emblematic of mediation between the Jewish minority and power, symbol of a wise policy of responsibility that preserved the Jews as a people.

Circumstances had forced Jews to navigate the world since ancient times as a minority that could not exercise political power. The enduring legacy of the Hebrew Bible had permitted Jews to hold onto the collective concept of themselves as a people for millennia, in spite of the loss of political sovereignty, exile and diaspora.

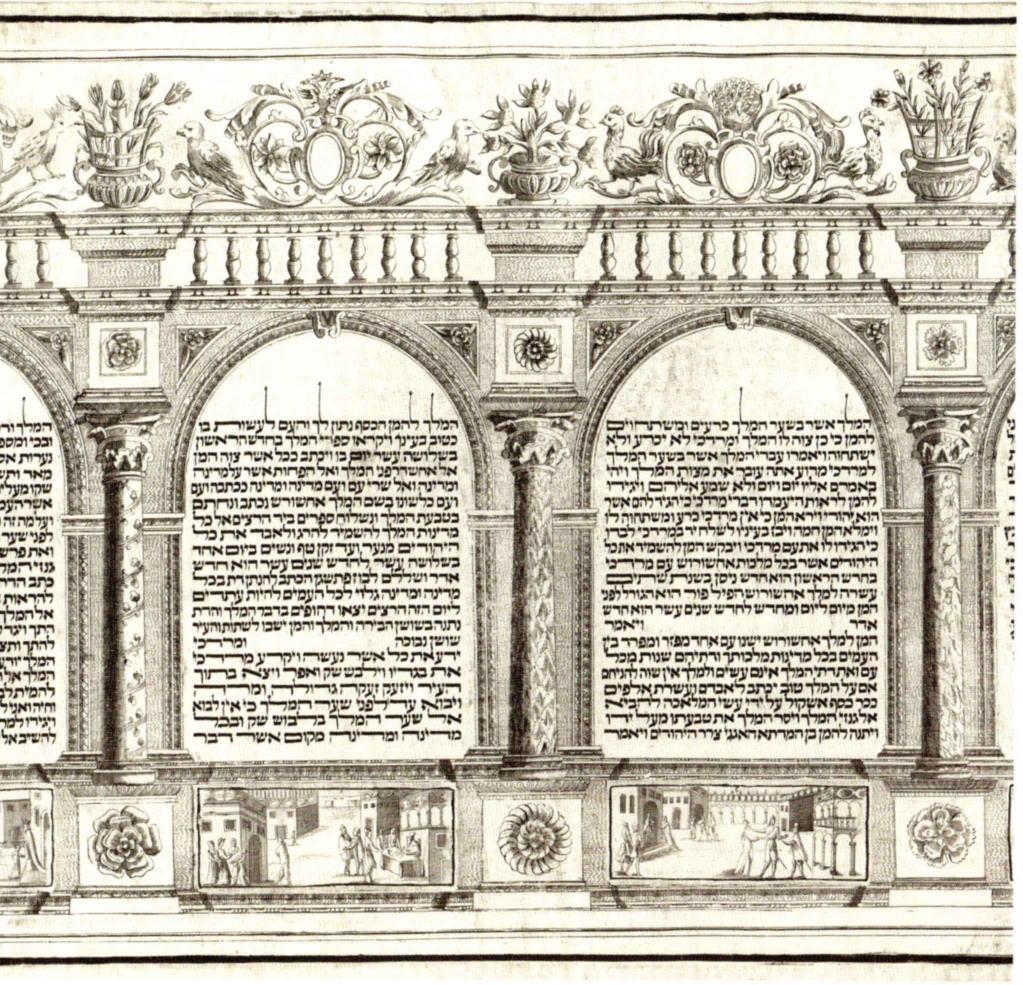

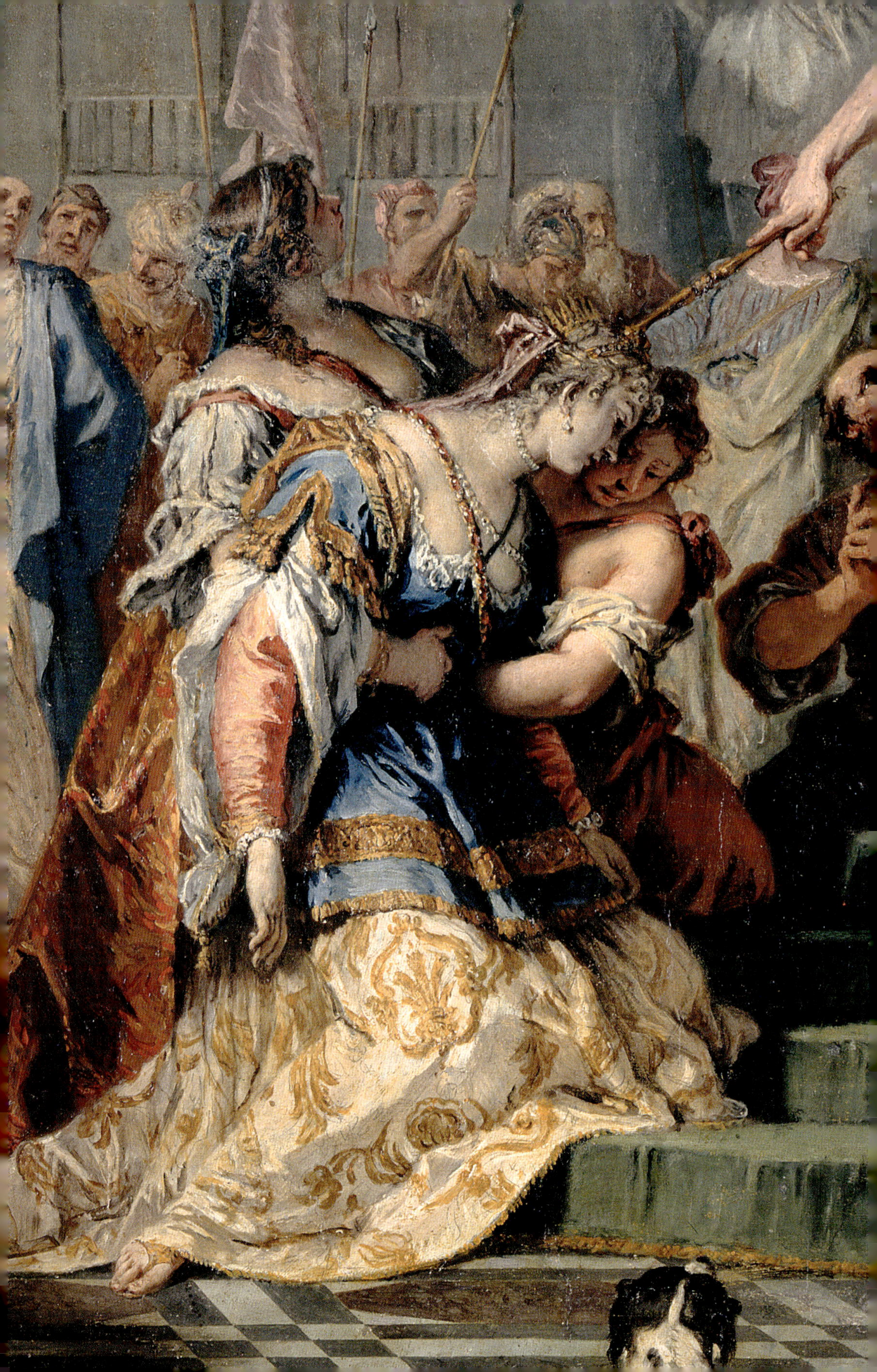

The story of Esther had never been at the center of illustrated Christian Biblical cycles much less that of theological reflection, due to the marginality of the book within the Christian canon, its liturgical irrelevance and the difficulty of giving it an exegetic reading in Christological and typological terms, as attempted by St Bernard and St Bonaventure in the twelfth and thirteenth centuries. Nor was there a clear female parallel with the Virgin or the symbology of the Church, even if occasionally found in the sources and art, examples including the *Biblia pauperum* and the *Bible moralisée*, where the scene of Esther supplicating the king for her people served to prefigure Mary interceding with her Son for the salvation of humanity. Esther's concealed Jewish identity, her role as a favourite in the harem, able to bend the royal will of her husband Ahasuerus, overturning the false decree and winning revenge against the Persians impede a typological relation between Esther and the Virgin.

Although surviving examples are rare, the situation is different in the Jewish tradition, with evidence of the depiction of the Esther cycle dating back to the middle of the third century, in the synagogue frescoes of Dura Europos.

The heart of the liturgy for the feast of Purim, the book of Esther is clearly etched in the popular Jewish imagination. It is no surprise, therefore, that the book of Esther has been the focus of many Jewish scholars and the subject of much commentary. The vivid representation of court life and the vital role played by the Biblical heroine in saving her people from imminent ruin must have touched a sensitive chord in the hearts of Jews throughout history. Frequently finding themselves prey to persecution in and expulsion from the various countries of their exile, the Jews had to maintain relations with power, often thanks to the good offices of a courtier, indispensable to the well-being of the community. The Jews of the diaspora could have seen themselves reflected in the book of Esther in multiple ways, finding it a source of comfort and inspiration over the centuries.

The Biblical story of Esther seems to provide Jews with a possible model for minority politics in relation to Gentile political power. The book tells of the clash between Mordecai, a Jewish member of the court and close to the Persian king Ahasuerus, and Haman, his powerful advisor. Mordecai's refusal to prostrate himself before Haman provoked the latter's wrath, who then formulated a plan to destroy all of the Jews of Persia, then approved by the king. Mordecai's refusal not only put his own life at risk, but also that of all the Jews in Persia. Esther, Mordecai's cousin and adoptive daughter, who was a member of Ahasuerus's harem when the king rejected his queen for disobedience, was chosen as the new queen and found the courage to save Mordecai and all of the Jews of Persia from extermination. In order to do this, Esther had to risk her own life, violating Persian law, according to which no one could present themselves before the king unless called, on pain of death. Esther revealed her hitherto hidden religious/national identity to the king, laying bare Haman's plan to destroy her people and, consequentially, herself as well. Ahasuerus ordered Haman to be hung on the gallows that the latter had prepared for Mordecai. And Esther convinced Ahasuerus to permit the Jews to defend themselves against those preparing to implement his previous genocidal decree. The story ends with Mordecai rising to the powerful role of Ahasuerus's trusted advisor. The Jews defeated their aspiring persecutors in battle and were free to practice their religion in peace.

5. Sebastiano Ricci, *Esther before Ahasuerus*, detail.
Palazzo del Quirinale, Rome (cat. 1)

The book of Esther was the subject of numerous commentaries during the Medieval European diaspora, from Saadiah Gaon, whose commentary on Esther survives in only fragmentary form, to Rashi, Samuel ben Meir, Joseph Kara and many others, including in the Sephardic tradition, culminating in the work of Abraham Ibn Ezra. But it was at the end of the fifteenth century that commentary on the book of Esther proliferated, simultaneously expanding in length, a trend that continued into the sixteenth century, which saw an explosion of commentary on the Esther scrolls (Walfish 1993).

These commentaries are packed with references to courts and reigns from different times and in different places, the role of Jewish courtiers and relations between Jews and Gentiles. The commentary of rabbis on court life reveals active interest in relations with a dominant institution and profound awareness of their importance for Jewish survival. The book of Esther offered exegetes an opportunity to reflect upon the position of the Jew in the court of the time and the figures of Mordecai and Esther served as a model for good Jewish behavior.

It is not surprising, therefore, that the sixteenth and seventeenth centuries marked the apex in Italy of the art of *megillot*, parchment scrolls decorated with the story of Esther. In these scrolls, the Biblical story is illustrated scene by scene, and set in a late Baroque context that imagines ancient Persia as a contemporary Italian city, with grand piazzas, streets and gardens.

The court context characterizing the book of Esther might explain its particular popularity among aristocratic women, with Esther cycles appearing in the decoration of private residences and on the elegant painted chests used to store the dowries of young brides while at the same time providing them with a model of female virtue.

It was precisely in the sixteenth and seventeenth centuries that the figure of Esther began to spread in Italian painting, in particular the scene portraying her meeting with Ahasuerus, often painted according to the apocryphal version, in which Esther faints upon the appearance of the august king.

The importance of this Biblical heroine is evidenced in the paintings by Paolo Veronese (1528–1588) on the ceiling of the church of San Sebastiano and others by Tintoretto, Ludovico Carracci, Guercino, Orazio Gentileschi, Domenichino, Leonello Spada, Artemisia Gentileschi as well as a number of less famous artists. An especially monumental work is *Esther before Ahasuerus* by Sebastiano Ricci (1659–1733), one of the leading figures in late-Baroque Venetian painting.

Esther also provided a model for the relationship between Jews and the reigning power in the ghetto context moving in the opposite direction. One example is found in the period during which the papacy installed itself in areas of northern Italy famously lenient and favorable with respect to the presence of Jews, a time when Cardinal Magalotti, bishop of Ferrara and founder of the ghetto in that city in 1627, indeed commissioned Guercino to paint a version of *Esther before Ahasuerus* in celebration of his "clemency" towards the Jews of Ferrara (Perlove 1989).

Similar to what we see in the Italian painting of the time, Esther, the Biblical heroine whose story is set in the third year of the reign of Ahasuerus, king of Persia, is portrayed in the *megillot* as a noblewoman living in a magnificent Baroque palace with a large atrium, elegant dining rooms, sumptuous courts and Italian-style symmetrical gardens. Her court is made up of aristocrats who dress, speak and gesture in the manner of artistic conventions at the time. A great deal of importance is placed on the representation of architectural spaces that serve as background both for the text and the pictorial narration. The handwritten text of these scrolls is framed by a decorative, architectural border made up of arcades, columns, balustrades and flower-filled urns. The scenes from the story of Esther within the architectural arches reveal that the illustrators were familiar with contemporary painting and, in representing the scenes, sometimes drew inspiration from the famous models of the time.

The illustrators also described the celebration of Purim, with dances and masks, and drew inspiration from popular stage adaptations of the story of Esther, which influenced the visual narrative of the Esther scrolls. This explains the set-like framing of the scenes, the sophisticated clothing and the gestures of the figures depicted on the scrolls. The first Jewish play with the title *Esther* (cat. 11) was written by Solomon ben Abraham Usque (c. 1530–c. 1596) and staged in Venice in 1559 and 1592. The presence of the Esther theme in Venice during that time is also attested by the tragedy *Ester*, which was inspired by the *Writings*, or *Hagiographa*, written by rabbi Leone da Modena and published in 1619. Leone da Modena's idea to write a tragedy that met the criteria of the time seems to have been part of a much broader cultural plan to break through the boundaries of the ghetto, as he had done circulating Jewish culture beyond the walls with his *Historia de' riti Hebraici*, writing a play on a biblical episode that proposed mediation between and the intertwining of the two cultures. His play was performed for the first time in 1531 and then again in

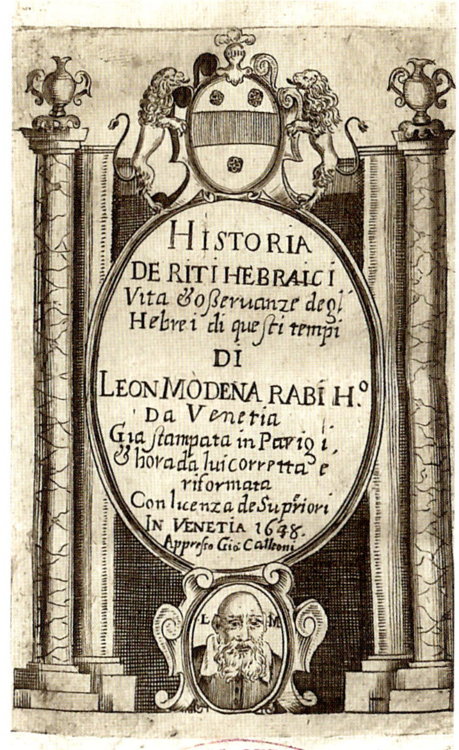
HISTORIA
DE RITI HEBRAICI
Vita & oßeruanze degl'
Hebrei di questi tempi
DI
LEON MODENA RABI H.°
DA Venetia
Gia stampata in Parigi,
& hora da lui corretta e
riformata
Con licenza de Superiori
IN VENETIA 1638.
Appresso Gio: Calleoni

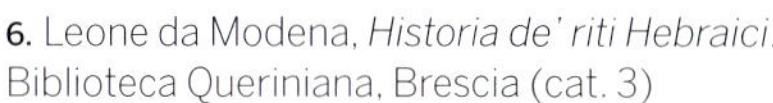

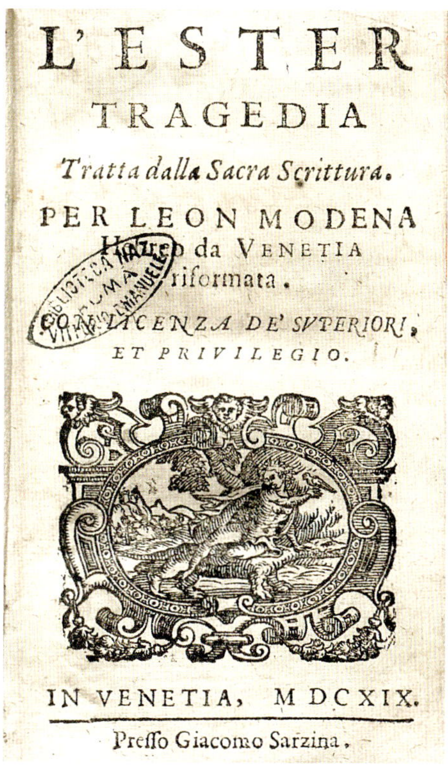
L'ESTER
TRAGEDIA
Tratta dalla Sacra Scrittura.
PER LEON MODENA
Hebreo da VENETIA
riformata.
CON LICENZA DE' SVPERIORI,
ET PRIVILEGIO.
IN VENETIA, MDCXIX.
Presso Giacomo Sarzina.

6. Leone da Modena, *Historia de' riti Hebraici*. Biblioteca Queriniana, Brescia (cat. 3)

7. Leone da Modena, *L'Ester, tragedia tratta dalla Sacra Scrittura (Esther, a tragedy drawn from Holy Scripture)*. Biblioteca Nazionale Centrale, Rome (cat. 11)

1559 and 1592. To the above examples we can also add Vincenzo's *Amano* (1614), Federico della Valle's *Ester* (published in 1627) and Ciro di Pers's *L'umiltà esaltata ovvero Ester regina* (published in 1664 and again in 1689).

The relationship with power and ephemeral production

Visual evidence of the relationship between Jews and the reigning power is quite rare in the period of the ghettos. Examples include the ephemeral works that decorated the ghetto area during sovereigns processions. A series of large decorated panels preserved in the Archivio Storico della Comunità Ebraica, Rome, documents the Jewish contribution to the Roman ceremony that marked the establishment of a new papacy and paid reverent homage to the new pope, to whom all Jews were subject.

Jewish participation in what was known as the "Solenne Possesso," a lavish ceremony during which, from the Middle Ages to Italian Unity, the popes and bishops of Rome processed from their residence to St John Lateran, is documented in these rare tempera panels (unique of their kind and extraordinarily for having avoided destruction), which were prepared by the Jewish Community of Rome to decorate the path of the "Solenni Possessi" of the eighteenth-century popes. The Jews, as a recognized community, were allowed to attend the ceremony, occupying the stretch of the procession route between the Arch of Titus and the Colosseum, and displaying "signs" lavishly embellished with text, painted symbolic figures and mottoes in Latin and Hebrew praising the pope (Di Castro 2010[a]).

These homages of the Roman Jews to the election of new popes reveal the ambivalence of their participation, divided between the effort to be included in celebrations that involved the whole city and loyalty to their different cultural and religious traditions.

The decorations included human figures, animals and objects of various kind, mottoes, citations from the Psalms and the Pentateuch written in ornate Hebrew and magniloquently translated into Latin and allegorical figures praising the pope. All elements that document the participation of the Jews from the ghetto in the joy over the election of the new pope as a religious minority, but also as full Roman citizens.

Another very rare example documenting the relationship with political power is a sketch of a temporary structure made by Leonardo Micheli (cat. 28) for the first visit of the archduke Ferdinand Charles of Hapsburg to Mantua in 1771, a document that has never been displayed to the public and is preserved in the Archivio della Comunità. It was the sovereigns' custom to occasionally visit their dominions, and these visits were marked by great pomp, including a procession through the city, packed with cheering crowds. The city had temporary decorations made for the occasion, which were set up along the entire procession route, and the Jews were also expected to properly decorate their area of the city, creating a temporary backdrop (Contessa 2017).

For the archduke's visit to Mantua, the Jews did their utmost to properly welcome the new sovereign, preparing displays of various kind and decorating the area of the ghetto their procession would pass through with temporary "machinae."

8. Leonardo Micheli, Sketch for temporary decoration. Archivio della Comunità Ebraica di Mantova, Mantua (cat. 28)

9. Temporary decoration, detail. Archivio Storico della Comunità Ebraica di Roma "Giancarlo Spizzichino," Rome (cat. 21)

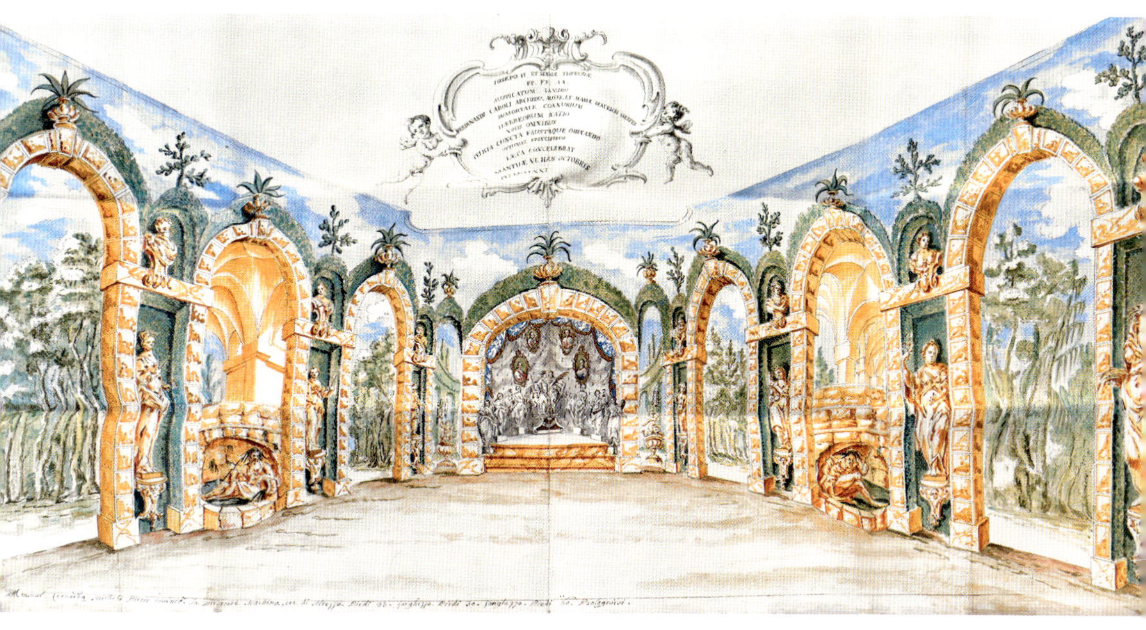

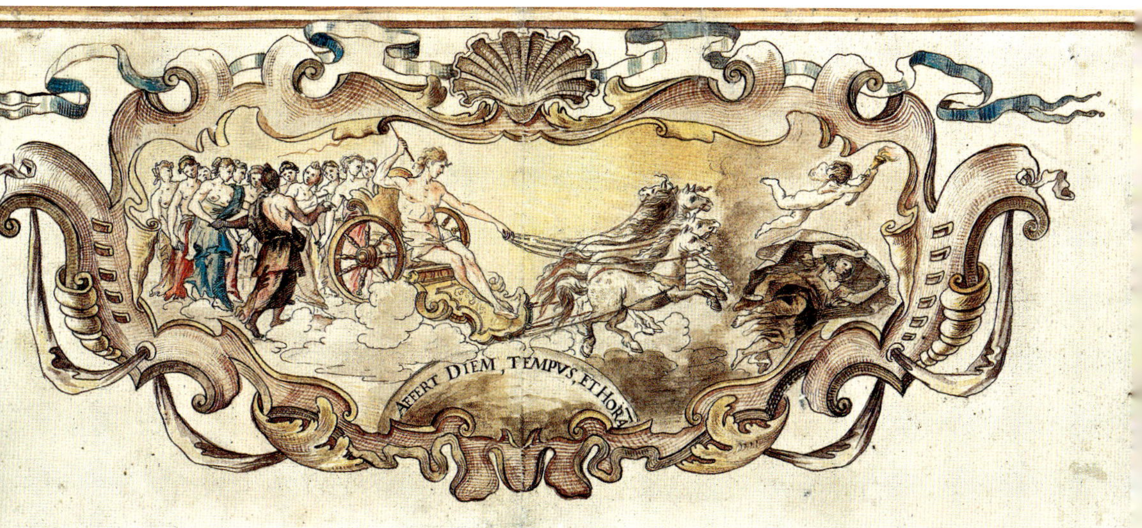

Structures of this kind were kept and probably reused for the visits of other sovereigns, perhaps after some touch-ups and repairs. The preparations in honor of the sovereign also included music and lighting as well as a "spontaneous" monetary gift.

The sketch depicts a series of airy decorated arches populated with personifications. The painted bower-roofed pavilion decoration and niches filled with personifications of rivers closely recalls the Sala dei Fiumi in the Palazzo Ducale of Mantua, which was completely redecorated in the eighteenth century with allegorical representations of Mantuan rivers, traditionally identified as the Po, Oglio, Mella, Chiese, Mincio, and Secchia.

Portraits of the sovereigns Joseph II and Maria Theresa Hapsburg dominate the niche in the sketch, beneath whom are portraits of the archduke and his young bride surrounded by personifications of the virtues of the good sovereigns' rule.

The iconography of the sketch made for the Jewish community celebrating the virtues of "good government" perfectly reflects an artistic language that pays homage to power and circulates a political message pleasing to the Empire and its model of hierarchical society, which was tightly organized around the sovereign, supreme regulator of social order. In the Latin text at the top of the image, within a cartouche held up by two winged putti, the Jewish community expressed its joy over the recent marriage of Ferdinand Charles Hapsburg Lorraine and Maria Beatrice d'Este, daughter of Ercole III d'Este. The archduke Ferdinand was designated by his mother Maria Theresa ruler of Lombardy and, in 1771, when he came of age, he began to personally carry out the functions of governor and captain general.

Artistic production and material culture in the ghettos

The ghetto and its binding rules and laws influenced the daily life of Jews and had material repercussions on their activity and artistic and craft production. Jews had limited work options, being for the most part excluded from the guilds, but this probably did not exclude them from working in Christian workshops. It is very rare to find the name of an artisan inscribed on metal or wood, an exception being the eighteenth-century ark of San Daniele del Friuli, on which the name Nathanel is carved in Hebrew among the decorative rosettes on the pediment. The names that we do know are mainly from the fields of publishing and manuscript production, book production being one of the areas in which Jews continued to invest, even during the period of the ghettos (Contessa 2013[a]; Friedman 1988).

Exclusion from the Christian guilds was in force almost everywhere in Europe. Jews were not granted full access to most professions until 1797, when Napoleon ordered the opening of the ghetto gates.

Besides the traditional occupations that Jews were permitted to practice, such as moneylending, they were more or less directly involved in various types of trade, production and commerce, in particular those connected to textiles, parchment and jewelery. Other Jews, with degrees from the prestigious University of Padua, practiced medicine or were tailors, and played an important role in the everyday activities of Italian cities. Towards the middle of the seventeenth century, Jews played an important role in the management of most of the foreign trade of many Italian cities. Many of the businesses were family businesses, partially run by women, who contributed significantly in the areas of tailoring, dressmaking, mending and bookbinding. Over the centuries, Jewish women created extraordinarily beautiful pieces made by hand for collective or personal use, as evidenced by rare surviving fabrics embellished with hand embroidery and lace decoration. Embroidered prayer shawls and Torah binders for the synagogue, fabulous tablecloths for the home decorated with rare golden lace, richly embroidered pillows and lace personal decoration reveal that they took inspiration from contemporary trends. Exclusion from guilds did not influence the work of Jewish women, who used their talents to sew and embroider textile objects for synagogue use (Cassuto 1988; Liscia Bemporad 2007).

One of the activities Jews were permitted to practice was the second-hand fabric and garment trade, *strazzaria*, which literally means rag collection and involved buying, selling and giving new life to used fabric and clothing, often costly pieces, such as precious brocades and embroidered silks that were transformed and reused. The contribution of women in the area of *strazzaria* can be appreciated in a few objects made for use in the synagogue, such as refined silk brocade *mappot* for the Torah scroll and *parochot* made out of stitched together strips of old fabric.

Even works with a sumptuous appearance reveal themselves to be made from pieces of different fabrics, assembled and reused in a completely new context. One example is a *mappah* (cat. 26) preserved at the Museo Ebraico, Rome, donated to the Scola del Tempio by the Della Torre family in 1730, as one gleans from the inscription embroidered in gold threat on velvet and the embroidered family crest depicting a tower flanked by two rampant lions (Yaniv 2009; *Tutti i colori* 2019, pp. 46–53). In order to reach the necessary length, two irregular pieces of seventeenth-century silk lampas were stitched onto the embroidered velvet, the former with a pattern of tiny flowers, pinecones and leaves on a gold ground typical of ornate clothing. And yet the overall effect is extremely elegant and opulent. The straightened circumstances and poverty of the ghetto were kept at arm's length from the pomp of the synagogues and their furnishings, the ritual, the daily prayer, and the solemn prayers for Shabbat and feasts (Weber 1997-1998; Nashman-Fraiman 2006). Indeed, while the exterior of the synagogues, located on the upper floors of homes in the ghetto, was spare and almost imperceptible, the interior was in contrast like a treasure chest of silk brocades, carved wood, gilding and precious silver. Every silver or silk object was donated by a family, as we see from the inscriptions and dedications incised on the objects or embroidered on the fabric gifts (Di Castro 2010[b]).

The reuse of objects from the past was put into practice on different levels and in different contexts. One interesting case is that of a *ketubah* (marriage contract) originally cre-

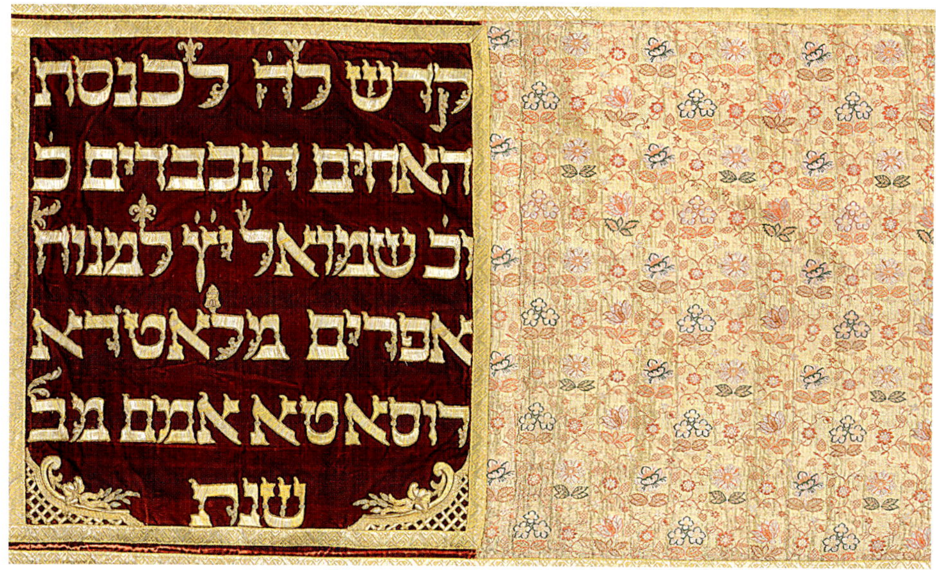

10. Della Torre *Mappah*, detail. Museo Ebraico di Roma, Rome (cat. 26)

ated for the Cohen-Sullam wedding in Mantua in 1733. Richly decorated in the Venetian style, the document was probably considered a precious family heirloom when it was used almost 100 years later, in 1820, for the Cohen-Franchetti wedding, removing the original text and replacing it with a new one (cat. 6). Different decorative and iconographic traditions can also coexist in an Esther *megillah*, created for personal use copying Grisellini's eighteenth-century architectural decoration, but drawing on a seventeenth-century source for the narrative scenes (cat. 9).

While the life of the residents of the ghetto was marked by a series of events and correlated objects that accompanied each individual from birth to death (see the essay by Shalom Sabar), time was marked by Jewish feasts, prayer, rites linked to the cycle of life and community gatherings.

The illustrations of the Esther *megillot* also describe the festivities for Purim, with banquets, gift exchanges and masked balls. The first images relative to the Jewish holiday in the Venetian *Haggadah* of 1609, and in the various subsequent copies, are of special value for capturing in images a few moments tied to the feast of Pesach. The illustrated pages of the *Haggadah* offer us a look inside a Jewish home and a glimpse of family life and traditions. One scene takes us into a kitchen, where preparations for the Jewish Easter are underway. Another shows us the dining room where everyone is seated for the Seder meal, dressed in festive, fashionable clothing.

A rare decorated plate of a *sukkah* allow us to imagine the construction of the temporary habitations for the festival of Sukkot, or the Huts, from Praglia. With its Biblical origin in Leviticus (23:42–43), the festival of Sukkot commemorates the period when God provides protection for the Israelites as they crossed the desert after leaving Egypt. The *sukkah* has therefore always been a temporary dwelling loosely covered with branches where the Jews partially reside for a week to commemorate the exodus. However, in Europe, with its colder climate, huts began to be built with wooden panels, which were then dismantled and used again the following year. These panels – which were meant to be temporary and so were only rarely preserved – were sometimes painted, as evidenced by a few extremely rare examples in the U. Nahon Museum of Italian Jewish Art in Jerusalem, dated to about the middle of the eighteenth century, in the Jewish Museum of Venice and in the abbey of Praglia.

The ten wooden panels in Praglia, probably dating to the late eighteenth century, are painted with Biblical subjects and accompanied by Hebrew text: Melchizedek blessing Abraham, Isaac bringing Rebecca into the tent of Sarah, Jacob meeting Rachel at the well, Joshua stopping the Sun, David returning victorious, Elijah taken up to Heaven. Some of the panels seem to evoke the Jewish feasts: Moses on Mount Sinai (Shavuot), Jewish Easter (Pesach), the construction of the *sukkah* (Sukkot), the Triumph of Mordecai (Purim).

The images were painted inside the *sukkah* and opened up a series of imaginary windows onto the Biblical world, where the figures of Isaac, Moses or Rachel lived again, almost creating a kind of passageway between the Biblical narrative and the world of the ghetto, past and present, identity and integration, inside and outside. Without forgetting that the *sukkah*, commemorating the long period spent by the Israelites in the desert after their liberation from Egypt, had become an icon of uncertainty and faith, but also of liberation, a place for projecting the visions and hopes of the residents of the ghetto, the gates of which were finally reopened just a few short years later.

11. *The Construction of the Sukkah*. Abbazia di Praglia, Teolo (Padua) (cat. 5)

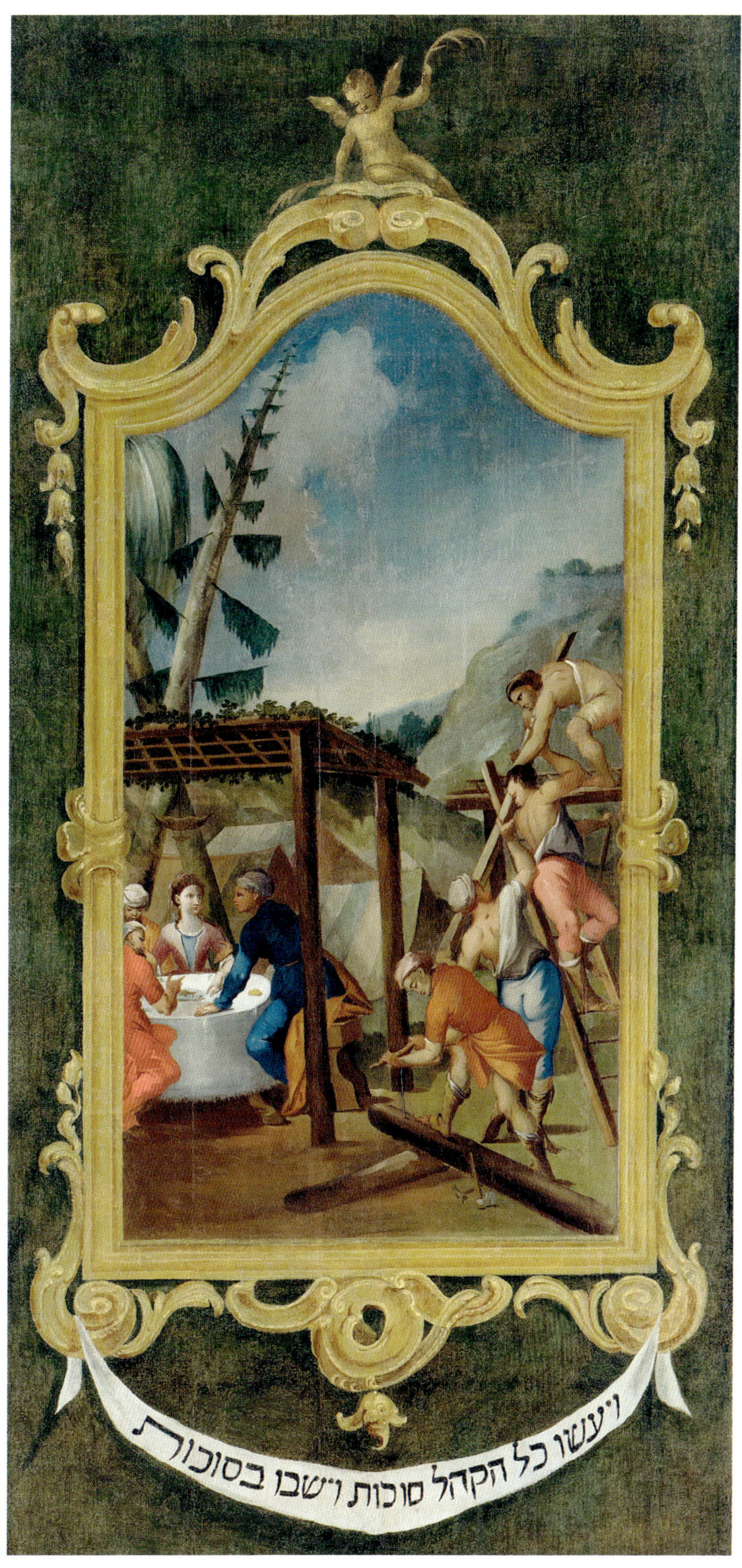
ויעשו כל הקהל סוכות וישבו בסוכות

Objects Reveal: The Life Cycle and Its Rituals

Shalom Sabar

Rituals and ceremonies in the life cycle of traditional societies are marked by a series of events performed on special occasions that individuals commonly encounter progressively in their lifetime, from pregnancy and childbirth to coming of age, betrothal and marriage, and death and burial. Defined as "rites of passage," these rituals serve in the eyes of cultural anthropologists a substantial role in strengthening the link between the individuals and their respective communities, presenting them in their new status in society. Thus, for example, the marriage ceremony solidifies the symbolic passage of a pair of youngsters from the environment of their parents and family into a new life as a husband and wife, about to establish its own identity and family.

In order to have the required impact and symbolize the change effectively the rites of passage have to be powerful and memorable. This goal is naturally achieved differently in various societies and cultures. In general, the more human senses are evoked in the ritual process the more effective it is. Accordingly, characteristic features of many a life cycle ritual include, for example, eating special foods, reciting particular prayers and blessings, playing specific music and songs, dressing up with suitable and carefully selected items of clothing – the purpose of all these is to reinforce the psychological and cultural power of ceremony and make it unforgettable and usually also irreversible. No less significant and effective is the role of items of material culture and artistic objects. The distinct items for each ritual, commonly handmade in the past, become significant symbols of the ceremonies for which they are prepared, and their design and ornamentation serve to enhance and deepen the experience of the participants.

Living as a religious minority, the Jews of Italy developed their own system of rites of passage that defined their status as a homogeneous and distinct group active within the larger Christian host society. These rituals shaped their cultural and social identity and played a decisive role in the course of their life cycle, associating them with the larger Jewish ideas and ideals as they developed over the ages. At the same time, life under the strong influence of the rich Italian culture left indelible marks on various components which guided the way they celebrated the Jewish ceremonies on Italian soil. This is especially noticeable in the realm of material culture and the visual arts. The objects created for the life cycle rituals of Italian Jewry are imbued with the designs, styles and artistic tastes of the time, making them characteristic of this particular Jewish community and set its visual culture as a separate cultural phenomenon in comparison to that of their coreligionists whether elsewhere in Europe or the Islamic East.

An important factor influencing the rituals in the life cycle of Italian Jewry and by extension its visual culture during the seventeenth to nineteenth centuries concerns its composition of various Jewish subgroups. Though the mutual life in the ghettos naturally led to influences and borrowings, the customs brought by the *Ponentini* (Sephardim) from the Iberian Peninsula or the *Levantini* significantly differed from those of the *Tedeschi* (Ashkenazim from Germany in particular), or those of the *Italiani* (indigenous Italian Jews) – as noted also by contemporary writers (e.g., in the important guidebook for rituals and customs by rabbi Leone da Modena [1571–1648], *Historia de' riti Hebraici: Vita, & osservanza degl'Hebrei di questi tempi* [Venice, 1637]). Local traditions that developed in the course of the centuries likewise defined many customs and shaping of items, and the Judaic objects of Venice, for example, have their distinct characteristics and aesthetics, markedly different from those of Rome. While these differences should be kept in mind, the limited space here does not allow for elaborating on these issues, and actually a comprehensive study of the topic is still wanting.

Pregnancy and childbirth

"Be fruitful and multiply" (Gen. 1:28) – the first commandment in the Bible – is considered a fundamental and principle *mitzvah* (commandment) in rabbinic sources, often overriding other laws and practices. From the moment a couple was married everyone around them expected the woman to get pregnant and bear an offspring as soon as possible. Any delay would cause fears and worries of barrenness and considerable grief among the family members and their immediate community. These worries did not stop during pregnancy period and were now replaced by fear of miscarriage or loss of the child during childbirth. Customs such as giving charity during the pregnancy, visiting tombs of past family members and righteous rabbis, and even fasting became common, especially in the last weeks before the expected childbirth. Special prayers were composed by rabbinical authorities for women, expressing hope and faith for a healthy pregnancy and a safe delivery of her unborn baby. It was not unusual in Italy of this period to inscribe such prayers in specially commissioned small prayer books for women, handwritten and at times colorfully decorated. In some rare cases, these books are accompanied by figurative imagery, depicting such scene as the woman lighting a typical Italian Shabbat lamp or other scenes related to the commandments of women.

Childbirth called likewise for measures of safeguarding. The possibility that either the mother or her newborn would not survive the traumatic event was a fact of daily life. To overcome the large mortality rate in this period, contemporaries – whether Jews or

Christians – employed a wide range of protective amulets and charms and took other measures believed to protect the mother and ensure safe delivery. One custom reported by rabbi Isaac Lampronti (1679–1756) of Ferrara was to bring a Torah scroll from the synagogue and put it at the entrance of the room where the woman was delivering the infant. More common was the usage of amulets made of various materials, including precious metals. Commonly, pieces of papers or parchment would be inscribed with conjurations and names of angels who are believed to protect the mother and the newborn from Lilith, the demon who is depicted in Jewish folklore as the evil spirit preying on pregnant women and infants. These would be hung on the four walls of the delivery room, and sometimes the scribes added the name of the woman in childbed. While such handwritten amulets were common in other Jewish communities, the Italian examples stand out in their calligraphic Hebrew script and other decorative features, in particular delicate micrographic script shaped in attractive designs.

Specifically, Italian-Jewish object in this category is the amulet case called Shaddai – "the Almighty" or "The Powerful One" – an appropriate name for an object intended to protect the baby and his mother from evil spirits. Unlike the common paper amulets of the Ashkenazim in Europe or the protective jewelry of the Jews in Islamic lands, Italian Jewish families preferred to invest in making ornamental silver (at times even gold) cases, usually produced by Christian silversmiths. Sometimes the cases housed miniature inscribed scrolls, or the case itself was used as an amulet hung on the baby's crib. The ornamental cases were often decorated with the Temple implements and priestly vestments, such as the Menorah, Tablets of the Law, and the blessing hands of the priests – all believed to provide protection by their sacredness. The amulets commissioned by wealthy families were at times decorated with their respective coats of arms and passed in the family from one generation to the next.

Circumcision

Most rituals and specific objects made for the newborn concentrated around the birth of an infant boy. Preparations for the coming circumcision day took place immediately after the birth of a male son. The tension and worries in the days preceding the biblical ritual culminated in the night before circumcision. Called *mishmara* or *veglia* in Italian, this ritual served to guard the newborn in the night considered most dangerous – the one preceding the successful completion of the change in his status. This was a sleepless night for the family, relatives and friends who gathered in the house of the newborn, enjoying foods and drinks. The main activities during this night in the sixteenth century (e.g., in Padua, Ancona, Cremona) were in the spirit of merrymaking and amusement, including even mixed dancing and gambling, to keep the participants awake throughout the night. However, the rabbinical authorities gradually encouraged their congregants to shift the focus to more spiritual matters – mutual learning and recitation of blessings, which became the standard features of the eve of circumcision till modern times.

1. *Ketubah*, marriage contract.
Private collection, Mantua (cat. 6)

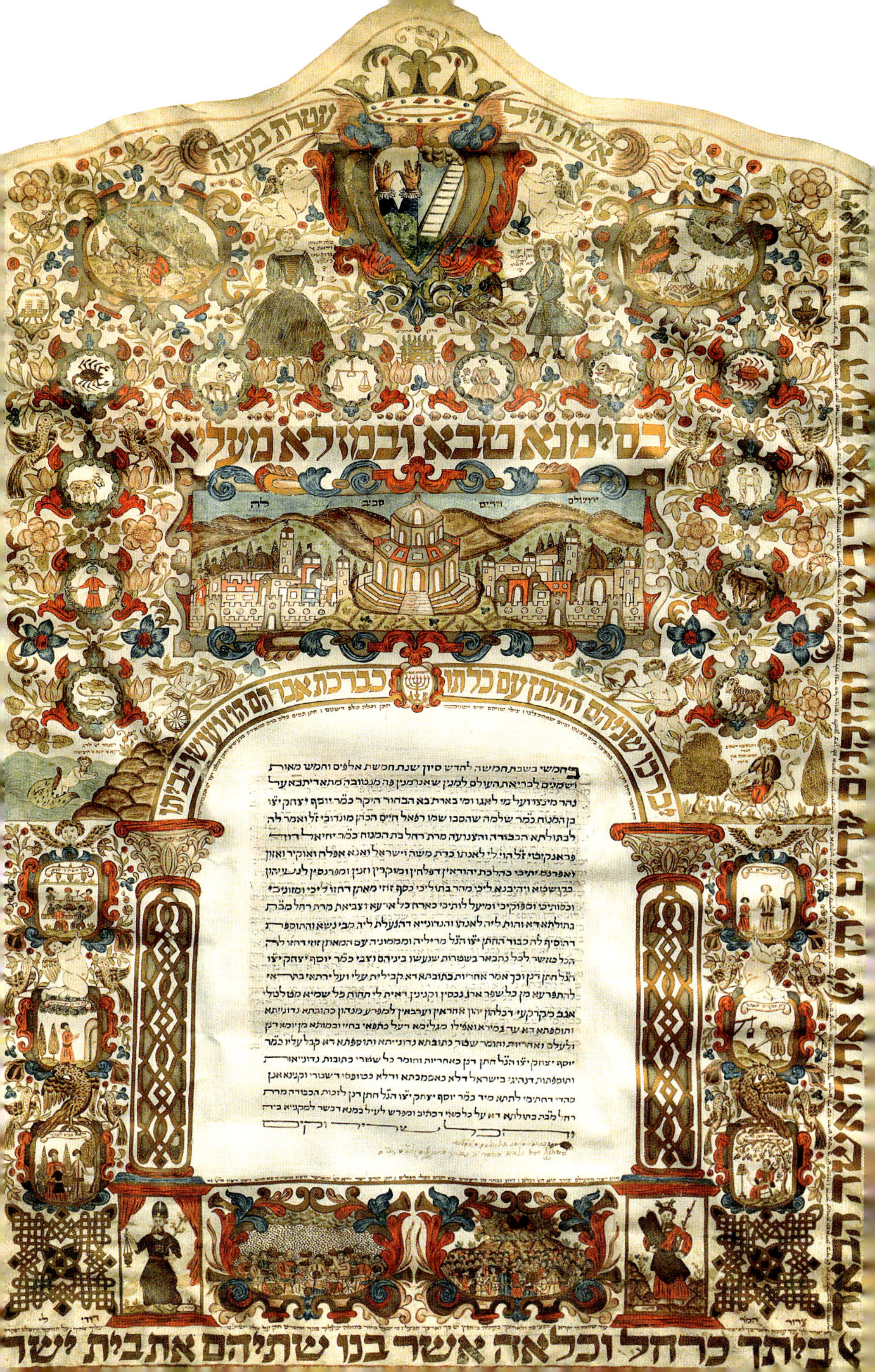
אשת חיל עטרת בעלה
בסימנא טבא ובמזלא מעליא
ביתך כרחל וכלאה אשר בנו שתיהם את בית ישר

The circumcision ceremony took place either in the synagogue or the family home. The intensive preparations for the ceremony included dressing up the baby with specially made festive clothes, including a tiny *tallit* (*talled*). A trained *mohel* (circumciser) would arrive early on with the traditional set of implements required for performing the ritual. The set was usually kept in a specially made decorative wooden case, at times illustrated with a scene of circumcision or another episode. Chief among the silver implements (e.g., silver trays, clip, pointer, silver flask, a spice vessel) is the circumcision knife. The intricately decorative wooden handle of one exceptional Italian knife (seventeenth or eighteenth century) is comprised of the scene of the Binding of Isaac, closely inspired by Lorenzo Ghiberti's influential panel depicting this topic.

Much attention was paid to the shaping of the traditional chair of Elijah used in the ceremony. As mentioned by rabbi Leone da Modena, in Venice (and other communities) two chairs were commonly used – one that remained unoccupied for the Prophet Elijah, "the angel of the covenant," who, according to tradition is obliged to visit every Jewish circumcision ceremony to testify the observance of the covenant (*berit*), and the other for the companion of the baby (*sandak* in Hebrew) who holds him in his lap during the ritual. In Rome and its sister communities, only a single chair was commonly used – which became the norm in modern times. In addition, rather than one *sandak*, the custom in Rome has been to give the honor to a second one (*compadrino*). The Italian Elijah chairs stand out for their expert craftsmanship and beauty. A noteworthy example is the sumptuous Elijah chair in the synagogue of Siena, exquisitely decorated with inlay work. One from Rome is decorated with the Temple implements and the lighted golden Menorah from the vision of prophet Zechariah (Ch. 4), while another from Venice depicts a circumcision scene as well as a surprising realistic image of the Bridge of Sighs with a gondola and gondolier passing underneath – both scenes delicately carved in wood.

The birth of a baby girl was celebrated more humbly, or, as rabbi Leone da Modena reports, "there is no ceremony used at all about her." At the same time, he continues, when the mother goes to the synagogue for the first time 30 days after birth (in Rome 40 days), commonly on the first day of the Hebrew month, the baby girl would be blessed publicly and her name announced. This ceremony is commonly known in Hebrew as *Zeved ha-bat* (naming ceremony for girls) and the baby girl is dressed elegantly. Following the ceremony in the synagogue, the parents invited the guests for a festive meal.

Education and Bar / Bat Mitzvah

A Jewish child during the "age of the ghetto" went through several successive stages that eventually prepared him to celebrate the next major rite of passage in his life, namely the Bar Mitzvah ceremony. Learning to read passages of the Torah in Hebrew commonly started at early age, at times as soon as or shortly after the boy started to talk. Subsequently, the child learned to translate the text into Italian (or Ladino or Yiddish). In the next level of the child's Jewish education he was taught the sacred texts along with the commentaries of the classic commentators, primarily Rashi, enhanced by an introductory chapter of Jewish law written by medieval authorities, such as Maimonides. Classes in Hebrew grammar followed this stage and the child also learned to master reading without the diacritical signs (*niqqud*).

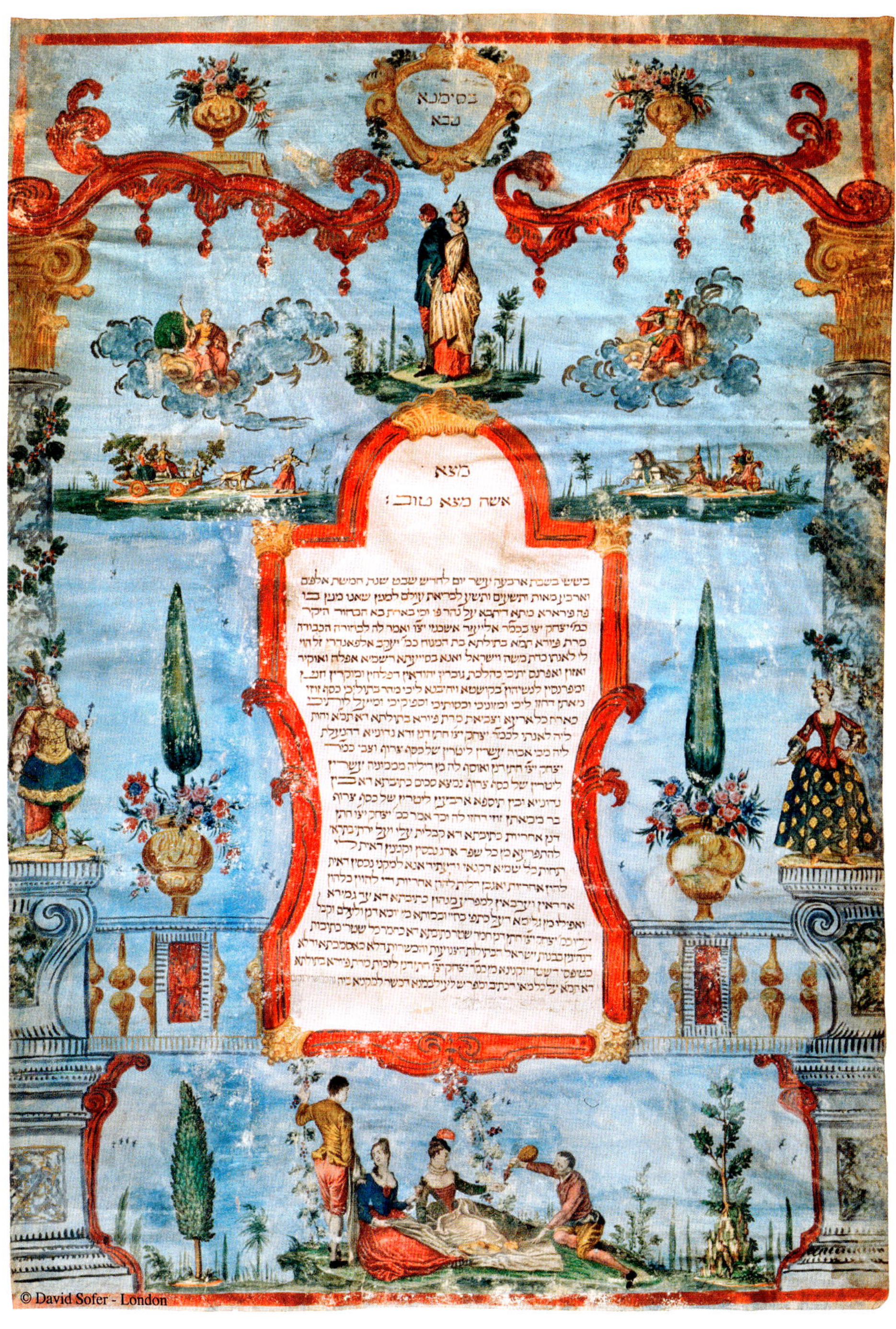

2. *Ketubah*, marriage contract. David and Cindy Sofer Collection, London (cat. 10)

The importance of learning Torah, the basic commandments, and reciting Hebrew correctly is illustrated in a popular educational Hebrew alphabet chart, variations of which were printed mainly in Venice and Livorno, and hung on the walls of the classrooms. The center of the pedagogical broadside is occupied by multiple lines in which appear the 27 Hebrew letters (regular 22 and 5 in final form), with all the vocalization possibilities, developing the ability of the children to identify the different sounds of Hebrew. The sides panels present essential blessings and prayers, selected Psalms (and other biblical quotes), and rabbinic aphorisms. This school chart is commonly illustrated with a moralistic woodcut depicting a school scene – an angel bestowing sweets on the "good" or diligent pupils who sit respectfully around the school table, while one unruly pupil receives disciplinary lashes by his teacher.

By the time the boy reaches the age of 13, he is, in the words of Leone da Modena, "accounted a *Man,* and becomes bound to the Observation of All the *Precepts of the Law:* and therefore he is now called, *Bar mitzvah* – although others say '[entrance] into the *minian*' ([*enter*] *the minian)* – that is to say, a Son of the Commandment." The Bar Mitzvah ceremony developed in medieval Ashkenaz, gradually spread to neighboring communities and reached its consolidated form in Italy of the late sixteenth – early seventeenth centutier. According to the account of the Jewish convert to Catholicism Giulio Morosini (*Derekh emunah - Via della*

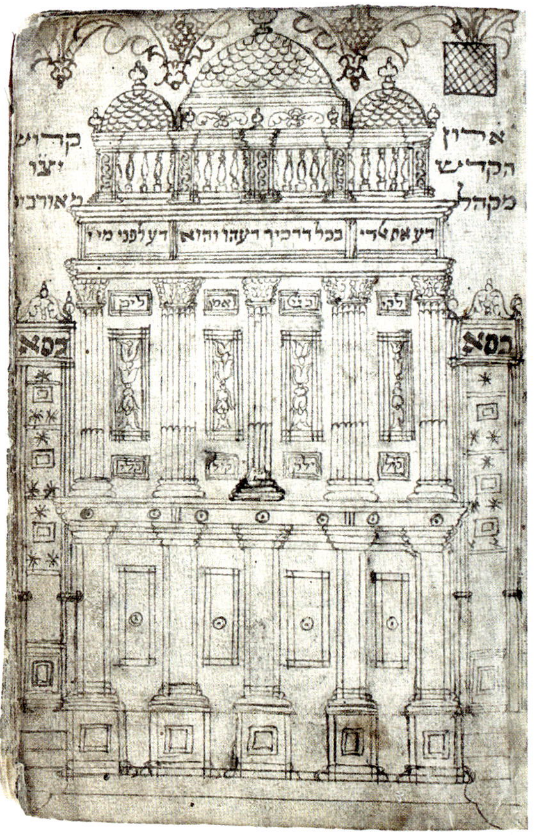

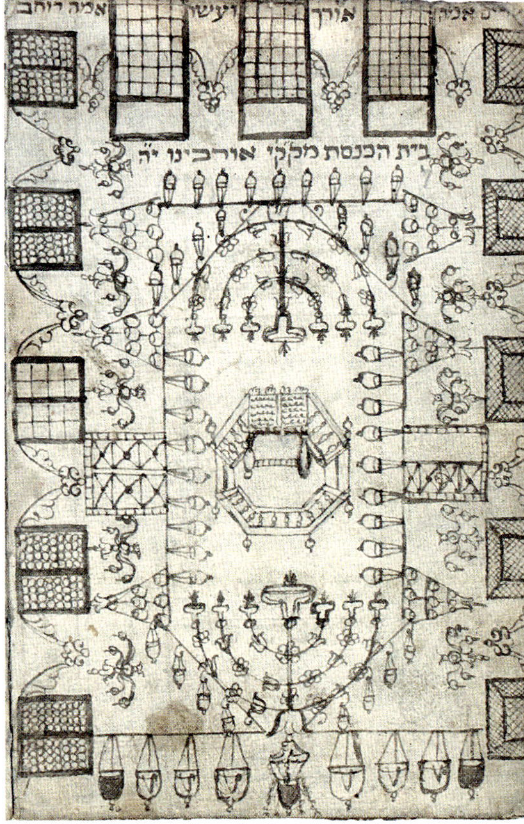

fede, Rome, 1683), the 13-years-old child came on Shabbat to the synagogue with his father, greeted by everyone, and then he was called to recite publicly for the first time his portion of Torah; subsequently, he would recite the appropriate blessings, announce some donations, and upon descending the Bimah he would kiss the hands of his father and his teacher.

Unlike other rites of passage, very few ceremonial objects were created specifically for this ceremony, testifying to its "late introduction" into Jewish life in Italy and lack of traditional objects related to its celebration. A primary object would be a handmade white silk *tallit* along with its bag, often of delicate brocade fabric. Though created to be used for the first time on this occasion, these items would be then used ordinarily in the years to come. A unique manuscript that is associated with the ceremony is *Sefer ha-Maftir* of Urbino, 1704. The 34 pages small codex, containing various blessings and prayers recited on Friday night and *Shabbat mincha* (Shabbat afternoon service), was presented by a grandfather to his grandson, apparently on the occasion of his Bar Mitzvah and reading the haftarah in the synagogue. The richly decorated codex, including images of the Urbino synagogue interior and its impressive Torah ark (*heikhal*), testifies to the importance of the ceremony in the eyes of contemporary Jews.

When a Jewish girl reached the age of 12 – halakhically the majority age for girls – no public rituals and celebrations were held in Jewish communities of the past. It was actually in some towns in Italy that a ritual for 12-years-old Jewish girls was introduced around the 1840s. This is relatively late in the period covered here, undoubtedly reflecting the process of modernization in European society of the time and its impact on Jewish culture. The girls prepared for the day of their Bat Mitzvah by learning basic Hebrew and Jewish precepts, and the ceremony would take place in the synagogue on a weekday for a group of them together, ideally around the Shavuot holiday. Dressed in pure white and covered with white head veils, symbolizing their purity, they recited some blessings and the rabbi would bless them in front of the open *heikhal*. It should be noted that while most communities in Italy followed this practice some rejected it because it reminded too much the Catholic confirmation ritual.

Betrothal and wedding

The Jewish wedding was a major theme in Hebrew illuminated manuscripts of Renaissance Italy (fifteenth century). The elaborate miniatures often depict the ritual of placing the ring on the bride's index finger, preceding the wedding. Many details reveal how sumptuous were the weddings of the elite of Italian Jewry at the time: extravagant costumes made of choice textiles – especially those of the bridal couple, luxurious interiors and settings, the bride riding a noble horse, a fashionable musical group. Moreover, the miniatures show mixed dancing, whether of the bride and groom or of apparently married couples – largely forbidden in other Jewish communities of the time. The image of the wedding rituals emerging from the ghetto period is different but still shows that marriage was a primary occasion to show one's wealth and status.

3. *Sefer Ha-Maftir di Urbino*, Urbino, Italy, 1704.
U. Nahon Museum of Italian Jewish Art, Jerusalem

Unlike other rituals in the life cycle, the planning and preparations for the wedding were long and constituted of many stages. As early as a girl was born her mother started preparing the bed linen her daughter would need for her wedding. Finding a fitting match for her was primarily a family issue and the parents of both sides played a decisive role in this process. Factors such as social standing, economic status, and lineage were principal in making the final decision. Once an agreement was reached, the conditions, primarily financial, were written down and other arrangements were discussed between the families – the dowry and its contents, the groom's voluntary increment, the expenses for the wedding, and the date for the event. Relatives and friends were invited to celebrate with the families the conclusion of this stage (equivalent of *erusin* or "engagement") and in the period passed to the wedding (according to Modena – between a year to two), gifts were exchanged and the families visited each other.

Ethnographic details about the wedding in this period, such as the quantity of the foods served, number and type of pieces of jewelry, number of guests, dance regulations between males and females, are found in the *pragmatiche* – enactments issued by the community authorities from time to time against luxury and ostentation (e.g., in Mantua, Rome and Venice). Works of art depicting the wedding, such as that of a Sephardic wedding in Venice (school of Pietro Longhi, circa 1750, the Israel Museum), show the ceremony taking place in the interior of a home (bride's or groom's), a fixed Sephardic Huppah, lavishly dressed and wigged participants, servants, musical band, lighted torches, two cups of wine, etc. The wedding day for first marriages would be set to either Wednesday or Friday and to the first 15 days of the Hebrew month when the moon is waxing – a good sign of fertility. Preferred days were eve of holidays – in particular Sukkot and Pesach – which allowed for the seven day celebration of the families (especially when the families were not from the same town). Only in the course of the nineteenth century these prevalent customs started to fade – Sunday became gradually a more common wedding day and the place of the wedding switched to the synagogue.

Of the many artistic objects associated with the Italian-Jewish wedding, including, for example, opulent jeweled wedding rings, sumptuous silver book bindings given as wedding gifts, colorfully (or printed) illustrated riddles and wedding poems distributed during the ceremony – the most attractive and versatile is undoubtedly illustrated *ketubah*. It was in Italy that the decoration of Jewish marriage contract reached the height of its artistic development during the seventeenth and eighteenth centuries. From Venice to Rome, every major Jewish community developed its own typical style and set of motifs for decorating this document. Families vied each other over whose *ketubah* was more attractive and in a number of cases the authorities had to put a limit on the amount one might spend on this costly item. This visual tradition did not originate in Italy itself during the Renaissance as was thought in the past – evidence shows it was actually imported to Italy from the Iberian Peninsula by Sephardic immigrants. The earliest extant examples, produced by the Sephardim on Italian soil (late seventeenth – early seventeenth centuries), show obvious Spanish designs, but a generation later, when the *tedeschi* and *italiani* followed suit and adopted this practice, Baroque Italian decorative arts influenced more and more the appearance of the *ketubot*. Moreover, the Jewish makers of the splendid parchment contracts and their advisors invested many efforts to produce colorful, attractive and thoughtful folk artworks that reflect high Jewish ideas and ideals, deeply intertwined with and inspired by the local culture. The illustrations thus open a wide window to many rich cultural topics concerning Jewish life in Italy at the time hardly available or matched in other sources.

Death and burial

At the request of the *Hevrah Kaddisha* (burial society) of the Mantua community, rabbi Aaron Berechiah of Modena (died 1639) was invited to write a book, which he entitled *Maavar Yabbok* – a treasury of prayers and instructions on the proper conduct for sick and dying people and the dead, and the rules for their treatment. Similarly, the "Society for Visiting the Sick" of Verona, asked the rabbi Hezekiah Mordechai Bassan (circa 1632 – 1703) for the proper rituals they should be conducting around the deathbed. Despite the moralistic tone of these books, they contain invaluable information, which along with other resources recreates the beliefs, rituals and practices on the final stage in the life cycle of Italian Jews at the time. A special conduct developed for people about to die of what we might call natural causes. It was considered very important to visit the dying person and extend any assistance to help the family. Family, friends, the rabbi, and representatives of the various beneficial Jewish societies, would commonly gather around the bed of the person nearing death. Prayers were recited, and the dying person was urged to deliver a *viddui* (confession), the purpose of which was to alleviate any misconduct that the dying person may have caused and to seek forgiveness, promising that by the merit of the confession the soul will have a place in the World-to-Come (the full version of the prayer is in *Maavar Yabbok*).

One of the requests of the dying person – often also included in the will – was that his family would recite the Kaddish prayer in his memory, to observe the *Yahrzeit* (*il giorno dell'anno*), and pay for the oil that will be used for a personal memorial light lit in the synagogue throughout the first year and then also annual memorial services in the coming years. A special metal memorial plaque inscribed with some details on the deceased was prepared and placed next to the lamp. In Modena, Mantua and perhaps other locations, the custom was to prepare a small memorial decorative parchment tablet, which was trimmed into attractive designs and inscribed with calligraphic and telling texts. The contour and design of the cutout parchments is at times reminiscent of the designs of typical tombstones, associating the tablets with funerary art.

Funerals and burials were handled by the beneficial societies, accompanied by many relatives and friends. Clean white shrouds and a small hat were prepared by women of the community, and, in case of a man, also his personal *tallit* was put over the death cloths. The body was placed between two white sheets in a coffin, which was commonly carried by the rabbis and learned men of the community. In some towns, the coffin was followed by men carrying kindled torches or lighted candles, while other men recited devoutly psalms. The funerals in Venice necessitated leading the coffin from the narrow ghetto streets to the cemetery on the Lido in gondolas or boats, as shown in some extant images. At the cemetery, prayers were read and the rabbi or others said eulogies, which were much longer if the deceased was an important person of the community. The coffin was then lowered to the grave and customarily the person's son was the first to throw dirt on the cover, followed by others. Before leaving the cemetery, everyone used to pick a piece of soil with some grass or plants in it and then threw it behind the back – a symbolic folk belief said to be associated or derived from the Psalmist words about resurrection "May the crops flourish… and thrive like the grass of the field" (Ps. 72:16). The meal served to the mourners after the funeral (called in Rome, for example, *pasto di avelut* ['mourning' in Hebrew]) included, as in other Jewish communities, symbolic foods such as hard-boiled eggs and olives, which are symbols of the cyclical time (due to their shape) and rebirth and regeneration (implied by the nascent life that might emerge from them).

The Jewish cemeteries of Italy represent the multifaceted traditions of the communities that gathered on the Peninsula. From the upright tombstones of Ashkenazic immigrants to the horizontally positioned Sephardic graves, often tent-shaped (e.g., in the Lido cemetery), to the nineteenth century grand figurative monuments (e.g., Vercelli). The epitaphs show likewise a great variety, including the selection of languages (mostly Hebrew in the early period but also Spanish, Portuguese, Italian, Latin and in some cases also Yiddish). The texts range from simple and short to elaborate poetic texts in erudite and poetic Hebrew, at times composed by leading figures of the time (in his autobiography rabbi Leone da Modena of Venice wrote that one of his professions was composing poems for gravestones). Engraved on the stones is a varied array of motifs and symbols, taken from both the Jewish visual culture and that of the host society – often familiar from other Judaic objects such as the *ketubot*. Chief among these in many cemeteries are family emblems commonly set in heraldic shields. The emblems are generally located in the tympanum or upper part of the stones, proudly representing the deceased, his family and lineage. Thus, appearing on objects such as *Shaddai* amulets, marriage contracts, and tombstones, these escutcheons accompanied Italian Jews from childbirth to the grave, making the distinctive artifacts in their life cycle so rich, attractive and meaningful.

4. *Ketubah*, marriage contract.
Private collection (cat. 61)

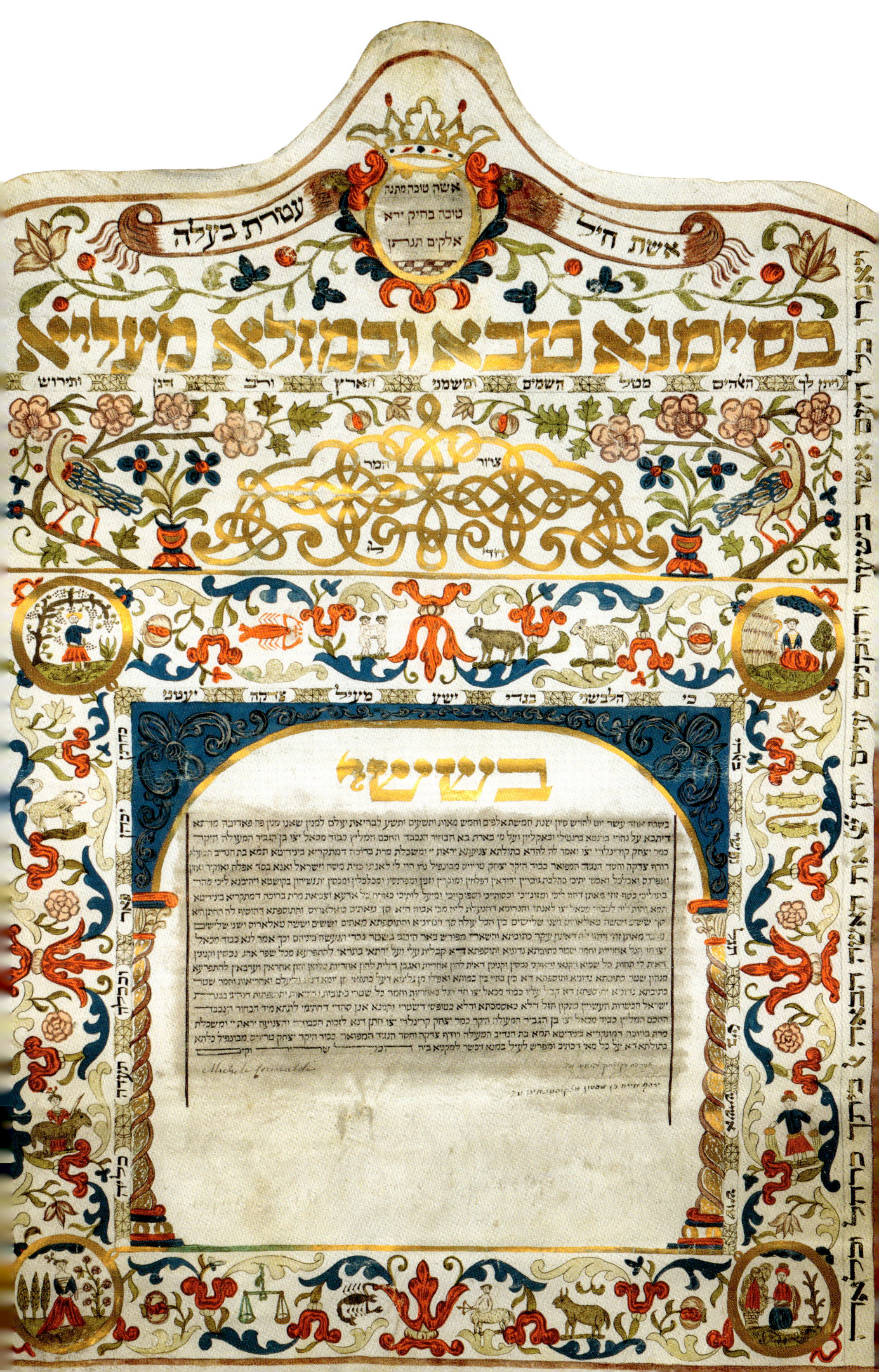

אשה טובה מתנה
טובה בחיק ירא
אלקים תנתן
אשת חיל
עטרת בעלה
בסימנא טבא ובמזלא מעליא
ויתן לך האלהים מטל השמים ומשמני הארץ ורב דגן ותירוש
כי הלבישני בגדי ישע מעיל צדקה יעטני
בששי

Silver Ceremonial Objects in Italian Synagogues

Dora Liscia Bemporad

The features of the silver ceremonial objects used in Italian synagogues are the consequence and fruit of the heterogeneous structure of the communities. After the *gherush,* the expulsion from Spain in 1492, Sephardic culture became dominant, in some cases filtered through extended periods in the regions of the "Levant," understood in the broad sense, that comprised the Ottoman Empire. We do not know if the Jews were able to bring their ritual objects with them, but, even if not, they certainly brought the memory of them, which they were able to use to define their commissions from the Christian silversmiths, the only ones authorized to work with precious materials.

The ritual objects cannot, therefore, be traced to a single model, since the peninsula, due to its history and geographic configuration, embraced multiple influences: Italian, of course, but also more generically European as well as that of the countries in the Mediterranean basin, with which the communities developed very close ties. One should not leave aside detailed analysis of the objects city by city, rather than analyze them as a whole, although in the case of Jewish silver, as with ecclesiastic and secular (the silversmiths being the same for all types), there was a unique substratum that we can trace to the classical model of Italian art. And this in spite of the undeniable differences deriving from the different origins of the various ethnic groups. The *tik*, for example, that is the openable cylindrical case for Torah scrolls, often covered in precious metal, topped by pinnacles and sometimes a crown, had been a quite common object since the arrival of the Jews in Italy from the Levant, but only a few exemplars have survived, in Venice and Ancona. We learn from one document that, in Pisa, when the Jewish community was reconstituted after the promulgation of the *Lettere Patenti* in 1591, then amended in 1593, a *sefer* in its case was carried in procession from the old synagogue in Palazzo Da Scorno to the new one, located on the other side of the Arno, where the current one is today. We imagine that, where relations with the Middle East were more strongly preserved, use of the *tik* was dominant, whereas the mantle (*meil*) made of fine or embroidered fabric was used elsewhere, and more frequently, complete with silver ornament, both *rimmonim*, which is to say the finials attached to the end of the two rods that the parchment is rolled around, and the crown, or *atarah*. There were definitely no *tas*, which is to say the plaque that hangs down the front of the *meil*, since it came to Italy quite late.

The history of Italian Judaism has often been equated with that of Rome, the oldest Diaspora community, and with that of its residents. Unfortunately, the demolition of the ghetto at the end of the nineteenth century, along with its five surviving synagogues, left an irremediable mark on the development of research on the papal city's Jewish art, nor were these losses compensated by the erection of the stunning synagogue in 1904 in a Neo-

Assyrian style diametrically opposed to the classical, Renaissance and Baroque tradition that Roman Jewish art is steeped in. The 'Scole', present in Rome before and after the establishment of the ghetto in 1555, the year of the promulgation of the Bull *Cum nimis absurdum*, reflected the varied composition of the Jewish population. The solid substratum of Jews of very old Roman origin was joined by Sicilian, Catalan, Aragonese and German Jews, who might have initially furnished their places of worship with objects similar to those they had left behind in their places of origin. As in other cities, even if more slowly than elsewhere, the differences gradually faded away and, by the early seventeenth century, the unique features of the individual groups were lost, if not in terms of subtleties.

Nor are the archival documents of any help, even though they are relatively numerous. At the current state of research, we are unable to determine who introduced the 'mace'-shaped *rimmonim*, which is not found in any other city. The strong presence of Iberian Jews might have favored this shape, since Spanish *rimmonim* seem to have borrowed their features from the processional mace.

An important example is a Florentine *rimmon*, the oldest known object from the time of the ghettos, the only one remaining of a pair (the other was lost during World War II), made in about 1580 and comprising a smooth, thin rod topped with a small central-plan building that cites some of the Tuscan city's buildings. However, objects made at other manufactories were used in Florence as well, as elsewhere. Venice in particular laid down the law, since the ceremonial objects produced in its workshops comprise a special chapter in the already fascinating history of Jewish art, marked by such unmistakable features that they have often been equated with all Italian production. We should note straightaway that their characterization owes its success to a perfect balance between structure, decoration and iconography, independent of the workshops where they were made, workshops that are known through the numerous brands stamped onto the objects. The *rimmonim* are generally in the shape of three-story towers hexagonal in plan, with symbols of the Temple and the High Priest inserted in niches that are repeated on the crown. These objects were extremely popular, to the point that there are not only exemplars in all of the Italian communities but also others clearly inspired by them that were made, for example, in the Netherlands. There are exceptional pieces in Ancona, Rome, Florence, Pisa, Livorno, Modena and Ferrara. Perhaps because of their success, they still had Baroque stylistic features at the end of the eighteenth century. In Piedmont, and Turin in particular, the same models were interpreted in terms of local taste. Among other things, at the end of the eighteenth century, Jews under the Savoy could join the association of goldsmiths and register their own brands, an opportunity unique in Italy and quite late.

In other cities, although Jews had enjoyed greater freedom since the time of Napoleonic domination, liberties that were definitively confirmed with Italian Unity, they never worked on the production of liturgical objects. There was an attempt to update what had by that point become standardized forms by using different models. Just as the synagogues were inspired by a reworked Moorish style, in virtue of the fact that the Jewish population had Middle Eastern roots, the objects, especially in Livorno, imitated the ones coming from Tunisia, which had very close ties with the Tuscan port. In the end, however, this was a short-lived chapter: the emergence of monumental synagogues led to a crystallization of structures and forms that halted the renewal of Jewish heritage, incapable of adapting itself to new styles and contemporary taste.

1. *Rimmonim* Efrati. Museo Ebraico di Roma, Rome (cat. 19)

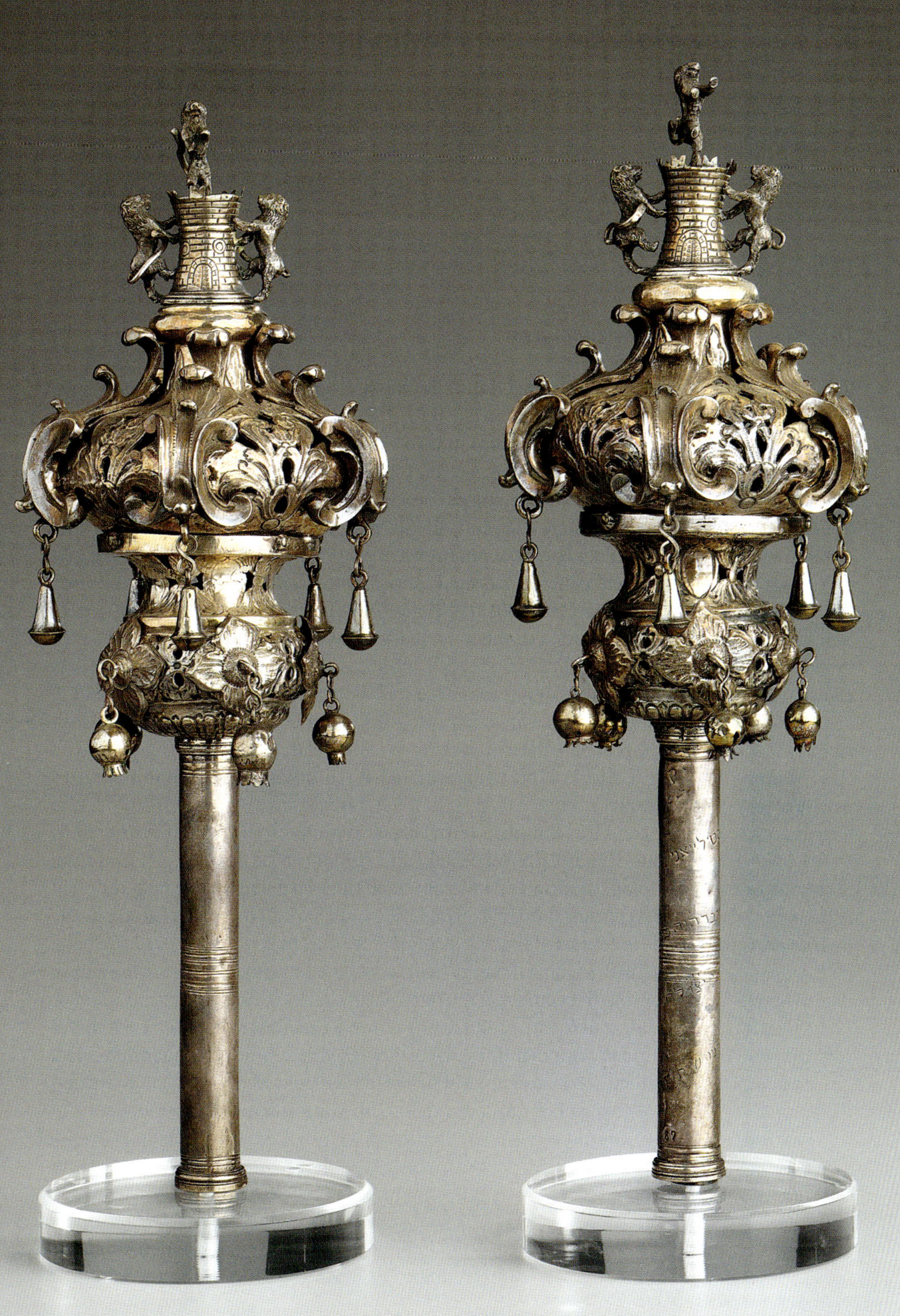

Within the Walls and Beyond. Three and a Half Centuries of Italian History

Serena Di Nepi

Three hundred and fifty-four years of history

On March 29, 1516, the Senate of the Republic of Venice made an important decision. From then on, all Jews of Venice were to live in the San Girolamo neighborhood – "*tutti abitar unidi in la corte de case, che sono in Ghetto appresso s. Girolamo*" – in a walled area with guards at its gates who were to be paid by the Jews themselves. This measure was somewhat of a revolution for the Republic: with this regulation Venice, on the one hand, was imposing a time-based segregation – during the day the gates were left open and the inhabitants were free to come and go as they pleased – while on the other it was formally giving Jews the unprecedented authorization to reside in a central area regardless of census or trade (Calabi 2016; Ravid 2018). During the following weeks Venetian Jews unenthusiastically complied with the new orders and the ghetto was put into effect. Over the years, other cities, each with its specificities, followed Venice's example: Dubrovnik established its ghetto in 1546 (the Balkans were, and traditionally had been, an area of strong Venetian influence), followed by the State of the Church in 1555. Gradually, from then on, all northern and central Italian states – from the largest to the smallest – that had not yet expelled Jews during the sixteenth century established their ghetto.

The last ghetto was – one might say tardily – installed in 1782 in Correggio in the region of Emilia and specifically intended for poor Jews (Caffiero 2014). At a time when the rest of the world was coming to terms with the extraordinary events that had initiated in Philadelphia in 1776 with the Declaration of Independence, and when the Enlightenment debate on the rights of individuals was spreading in every European circle, a small town on the Po Plain inaugurated the peninsula's last enclosure, whose gates would have been taken down only fourteen years later.

The Jacobine surge, followed by Restoration and the Risorgimento movement, put an end to the season of segregation, and in 1870, in Rome, the walls of the last ghetto and of the Papal State were taken down. Three hundred and fifty-four years had gone by since the Venetian deliberation: a very long time that inevitably left a deep mark in Italian history. To understand why, we need to look back to the crucial events that were part of this story by putting into focus the happenings of around 1516 when ghettos were first established as well as those that took place during the following centuries, all the way to emancipation.

Why a ghetto, of all things?

For over three hundred years ghettos regulated Jewish-Christian relations throughout half of the Italian peninsula by instituting a – to some extent – unprecedented model of partial urban segregation. The ghetto was Venice's answer to a longstanding and difficult question: what could or should a state do with a minority that was stubbornly convinced of its alterity, a minority whose alterity also proved functional to that same state? The regulation of Jewish presence within Christian societies had been a millenary challenge, a lengthily debated problem, to which many other solutions had been offered in the past.

The terms of this question had already been set in the second century BCE, in correspondence with the earliest traces of Jewish presence found on the Italian Peninsula, in settlements and communities in Rome and elsewhere. The Jewish-Roman wars, the uprisings in Palestine, and the Jews' not yet subdued nationalistic ambitions were all factors that made the integration of Jews into the bustling and cosmopolitan Imperial society difficult. Rome in those years sought to impose peace across its dominions and among the populations under its rule. Even within the plural first-century Roman society, where minorities were not thought of in terms of integration or assimilation, those strange Jews, who did not accept military defeat and practiced unknown rites, were looked upon with suspicion (as well as curiosity). With the Christianisation of the Empire, the handling of Jewish communities took on new symbolic and eschatological meanings, and the very existence of said communities started to be read in ways that exceeded traditional political patterns and customary miscomprehensions. Augustine's and then Pope Gregory I's famous positions introduced a contradictory logic into the discussion about Jews: repulsion, precariousness and acceptance, could coexist with the idea that the survival of the Jewish minority could be considered a necessary evil.

On a conceptual level we detect two main arguments: on the one hand, the truthfulness of the Gospels and the waiting for the second coming of the Saviour required the existence of the population into which Christ was born; on the other hand, the substitution theory and the spread of apocalyptic predictions regarded the conversion of the Jews as a necessary and instrumental prelude to the return of the Messiah. Christian thought on this aspect tried to incorporate positions in favor of the elimination of Jewish alterity via assimilation with those that on the contrary believed this alterity had to be kept in place. The unending oscillation between these fairly incompatible opposites translated into the construction and implementation of systems of progressive social and economic discrimination and into the complete exclusion of Jews from all ambits dedicated to political administration and decision-making. Furthermore, public opinion and intellectual discussion contributed to the marginalization of the group and to the perception of its extraneousness to the community of believers and hence to society. Recurrent anti-Jewish revolts, expulsions, prearranged acts of violence, and more or less sudden aggressions were the reflection of a process heavily marred by inconsistencies and that from within its specific theoretical framework was unable to reach a synthesis (Stefani 2004; Todeschini 2018).

Throughout the age of the Communes and Principalities, a solution to these matters had been the *condotta*, a temporary license that was discretionally issued by the local government and associated with the practice of one specific trade (pawnbroking), which allowed the widespread formation of very small Jewish communities while also guaranteeing prolonged and considerable individual and familial mobility. At the close of the fifteenth century, that longstanding condition of indeterminacy eventually came to an end with the Iberic expulsions and the initiation of the French-Spanish struggle for supremacy over the Italian Peninsula. The seventy-seven years between the Alhambra Decree (1492) and the Peace of Cateau-Cambrésis (1559) were a crucial time of pivotal decisions, when the world, Europe, and the ways in which until then Christian society had defined and understood itself, changed forever. And it was against this background of extraordinary transformations that we should read the birth of the ghetto structure, taking into account the evolutions of anti-Jewish Christian theology and practices – as historiographical studies have powerfully proved from a variety of standpoints (Caffiero 2014; Stow 1977) – as well as the equally important political events of that period. The first one of course being the expulsion of 1492.

The sixteenth century and its divides

The drastic Spanish expulsions, which directly affected Sicily and other Italian states, followed by the forcible baptizing of Jews in Lisbon in 1494, produced consequences that were felt throughout the peninsula. For Italian courts, the concession or the denial of entrance permits to Jewish refugees soon took on political and diplomatic connotations, overriding the economic argumentations that had traditionally accompanied negotiations regarding the settlement of Jewish groups. Granting or denying access to Jews could have been read as a sign of favor to or of hostility against the Spanish crown, just as the death of Lorenzo de' Medici made the peninsula's precarious political balance even more fragile. In 1493, despite official remonstrations from the Catholic Monarchs, Alexander VI – the Spanish Pope from the Borgia family – settled the matter by informally admitting into the holy city the Jewish fugitives encamped outside the gates of Rome. Against such a politically and military complicated backdrop, the Pope's initiative clarified that the position of the Church did not coincide with that of the Spanish crown (Esposito 1995).

The Italian Wars, which broke out when Charles VIII of France marched into Naples, were of consequence even for Jewish communities living in those Italian states from which they had not yet been expelled.

This prolonged conflict affected Jews first of all because they resided in areas the armies happened to cross, and also because they were looked upon as a troublesome minority that was very unpopular with the Spanish forces. The Jews living in the area of the

Venetian *terraferma*, for instance, suffered the attack of the Holy League, and during the Battle of Agnadello in 1509, like many other people living in that area, Jews sought refuge in the capital. When Venice had to cede its *terraferma*, as defined by the Peace of Noyon (1512), Jewish refugees found themselves living in Venice with no official permit. Those were difficult and unpredictable times, with some preachers praying for the adoption of the Spanish solution and others maintaining that the admission of the Jews might prove useful to the Republic of Venice in times of emergency. The institution of the ghetto represented an acceptable compromise: while being physically separated from Christians and recognizable at first sight – these measures were supposed to silence anti-Jewish complaints – Jews would have continued living and working in the Laguna by virtue of specific regulations and forms of protection (Ravid 2018).

The conflict with the Turks in the Mediterranean and the advent of the Protestant Reformation further complicated the extant scenario. The Sack of Rome in 1527 was a blow to the heart of the Church which seemed to pave the way to Italy becoming part of the Spanish Empire. Spain was at the height of its power in Europe, while France was surrounded

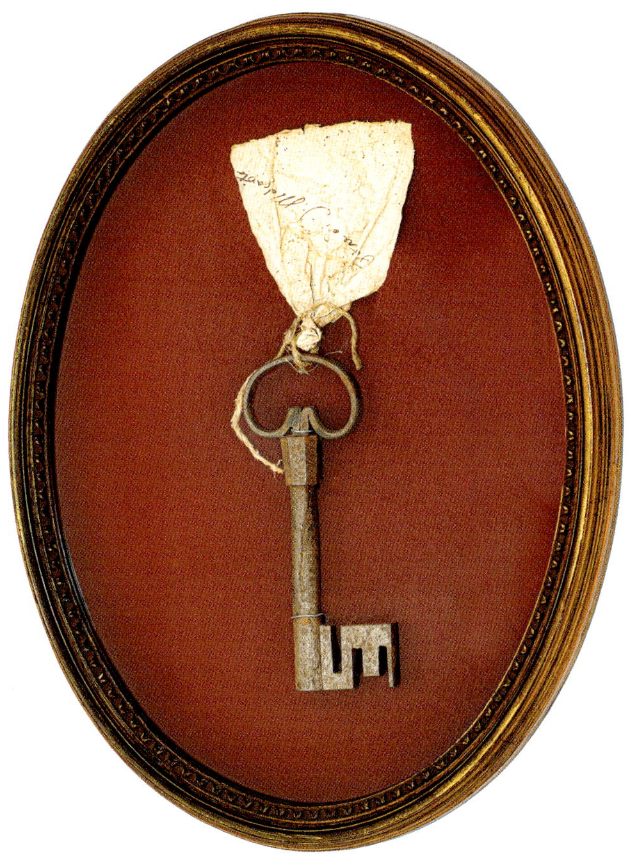

1. Key to one of the gates of the Ferrara Ghetto.
Private collection (cat. 2)

and finally ready to wage war on Christianity's real enemy, the infidel Sultan of Istanbul. In 1534, the election of Paul III Farnese, the Pope of the Roman Catholic comeback, initiated a new chapter in what had already been a decades-long conflict, further worsened by the explicit mutual dislike between the new Pope and Charles V (Bonora 2014).

The Jews witnessed these events with consideration and concern, as the areas where their communities could live gradually shrank. Explicit signs indicated that a new season of restrictions was about to begin. In 1541, the Kingdom of Naples issued a decree of expulsion that completed the process of Jewish banishment from southern Italy that had first begun almost fifty years earlier with the expulsion from Sicily. This decision clearly indicated (to anyone willing to read the signs) that, should the Empire prevail in Italy, similar measures would be adopted even in the rest of the peninsula. The anticipated deliberation was

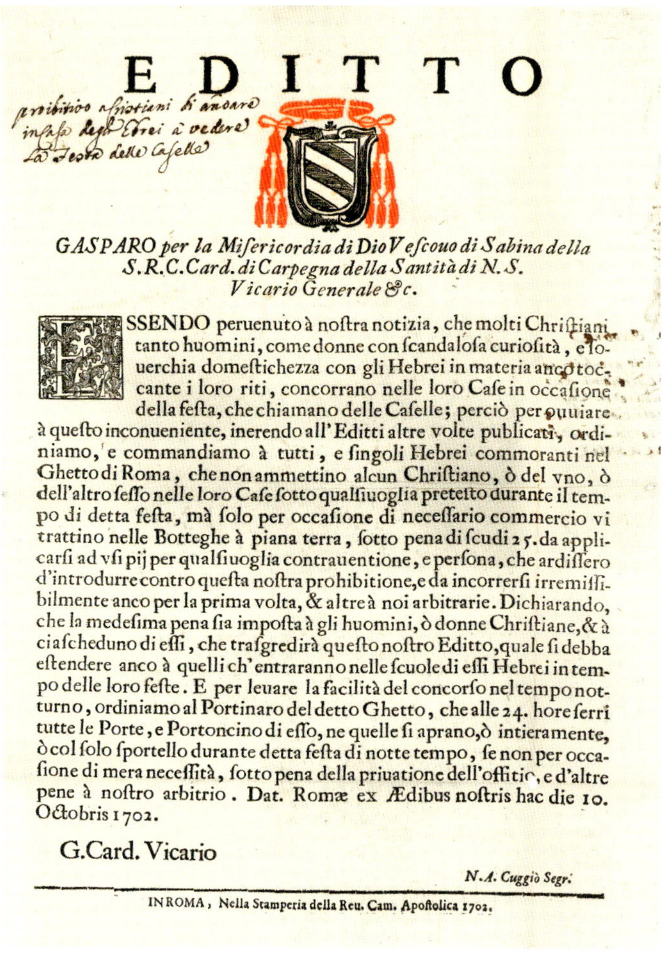

EDITTO

prohibitione christiani di andare in casa degli Ebrei à vedere la Festa delle Caselle

GASPARO per la Miſericordia di Dio Veſcouo di Sabina della S.R.C. Card. di Carpegna della Santità di N.S. Vicario Generale &c.

ESSENDO peruenuto à noſtra notizia, che molti Chriſtiani tanto huomini, come donne con ſcandaloſa curioſità, e ſouerchia domeſtichezza con gli Hebrei in materia anco toccante i loro riti, concorrano nelle loro Caſe in occaſione della feſta, che chiamano delle Caſelle; perciò per ouuiare à queſto inconueniente, inerendo all'Editti altre volte publicati, ordiniamo, e commandiamo à tutti, e ſingoli Hebrei commoranti nel Ghetto di Roma, che non ammettino alcun Chriſtiano, ò del vno, ò dell'altro ſeſſo nelle loro Caſe ſotto qualſiuoglia preteſto durante il tempo di detta feſta, mà ſolo per occaſione di neceſſario commercio vi trattino nelle Botteghe à piana terra, ſotto pena di ſcudi 25. da applicarſi ad vſi pij per qualſiuoglia contrauentione, e perſona, che ardiſſero d'introdurre contro queſta noſtra prohibitione, e da incorrerſi irremiſſibilmente anco per la prima volta, & altre à noi arbitrarie. Dichiarando, che la medeſima pena ſia impoſta à gli huomini, ò donne Chriſtiane, & à ciaſcheduno di eſſi, che traſgredirà queſto noſtro Editto, quale ſi debba eſtendere anco à quelli ch'entraranno nelle ſcuole di eſſi Hebrei in tempo delle loro feſte. E per leuare la facilità del concorſo nel tempo notturno, ordiniamo al Portinaro del detto Ghetto, che alle 24. hore ſerri tutte le Porte, e Portoncino di eſſo, ne quelle ſi aprano, ò intieramente, ò col ſolo ſportello durante detta feſta di notte tempo, ſe non per occaſione di mera neceſſità, ſotto pena della priuatione dell'offitio, e d'altre pene à noſtro arbitrio. Dat. Romæ ex Ædibus noſtris hac die 10. Octobris 1702.

G.Card. Vicario

N.A. Cuggiò Segr.

IN ROMA, Nella Stamperia della Reu. Cam. Apoſtolica 1702.

2. *Edict of the Cardinal Vicar of Rome*. Gianfranco Moscati Collection, MEIS (National Museum of Italian Judaism and the Shoah), Ferrara (cat. 17)

issued as Charles V embarked on an expedition against the Ottoman pirates in Tunis, and Francis I of France stipulated an anti-Spanish alliance with the Sultan himself. Once again, the Italian states had to decide the destiny of Jewish refugees: take them in or reject them?

Meanwhile in Rome, between 1542 and 1543, the inauguration of the House of Catechumens confirmed once more to the world (and to Charles V especially) the Papacy's position regarding the Jews and their destiny: inflexible evangelising was definitely in order, but physical violence and forced expulsions were not. The Council of Trent (1545) was inaugurated soon after the opening of the House of Catechumens and the reorganisation of the Roman Inquisition, at a time when the debate on the purity of faith and on the boundaries of orthodoxy inevitably affected the Jews, a minority that had always refused to embrace Christian religion in whatever form.

A few years later, again in Venice, the commercial dispute between Marcantonio Giustiniani and Aloise Bragadin, owners of the two most important typographies specializing in Jewish publications that had almost simultaneously printed Rambam's *Mishneh Torah,* made Jewish concern increase even more. This Jewish-Christian controversy in fact led to a ruling issued by the Roman Inquisition proclaiming the publication of Jewish texts illegitimate and ordering all volumes of the *Talmud* to be burned. The verdict was promptly applied in Rome on Jewish New Year of 1553 before a speechless crowd, and then in multiple other cities over the following weeks. The Jews were scared. They feared that the Pope who had attacked books so suddenly could take one further step and order their expulsion from the State of the Church, finally complying with Spanish policy, thereby imposing this solution to the rest of the Catholic world (Caffiero 2012).

The Papal election of Grand Inquisitor Gian Pietro Carafa in 1555 somehow contributed to settling the matter. One of the new Pope's first deliberations was the publication of the bull *Cum nimis absurdum* (1555) that ordered the institution of ghettos in the Papal State, and the initiation of the investigation campaigns that in turn led to the trials of the *Marranos* of Ancona (1556). In the meantime, in Germany the Peace of Augsburg and the famous *cuius regio eius religio* principle marked the end of religious homogeneity in Europe and the (temporary) interruption of religious conflicts in the German area.

In 1556, the abdication of Charles V and the division of the Hapsburg dominions between Austria and Spain constituted the last step in the ever-tense relations between the Pope and the Emperor. By passing on to his son the arduous task of finding a definitive agreement also for Italy, the Emperor essentially acknowledged the end of his vision of political and material hegemony, a project he had tenaciously pursued for so many years. Even the clash between the Pope, the Hapsburgs, France and Venice entered its final stages, and in 1559 the signing of the Peace of Cateau-Cambrésis defined Italy's political and geographical fragmentation a condition that would last for centuries (Di Nepi 2019).

The destiny of the Jews in Italy was to be decided in this new season. Following the agreements, Italy was divided into three areas: the south, where there were no Jews; the northern and central Italian states with Jewish communities of all sizes; and lastly the Papal State and Venice where Jews lived in ghettos, each with its own set of rules. In 1595 in Milan the last Spanish expulsion in Italy was carried out, exemplifying once again Spain's approach to this long-standing matter (Cassen 2017). Whichever reading we might choose to give to the period that saw the birth of ghettos, we can all agree on the fact that the ghetto solution was a popular one during the sixteenth century. Ghettos have marked the existence of Italian Judaism and this is why it is worth trying to give a general reading of this experience, regardless of the countless variations it experienced throughout its long history of segregation.

Ghettos in (half of) Italy

In the seventeenth and eighteenth centuries, Jews continued to live in cities across northern and central Italy, adhering to the various rules imposed by the single states that gradually adopted the ghetto solution: the obligation to wear a sign of identification, exclusion from specific trades, separate magistrates for institutional relations, limited autonomy in community-related decisions (taxes for instance), ecclesiastic interference, Roman Inquisition inspections, the pressure of Catholic proselytism were but some of the aspects and rules that characterized and were enforced in the various contexts that adopted ghetto segregation (Ioly Zorattini 1980–1999; Maifreda 2014). Despite the very varied range of specific situations, by analyzing the basic structure of the ghetto enclosure, its role in the organization of urban spaces, and its effects on the communities living inside them, we are able to clearly define what the Early Modern Period ghetto in Italy was, differentiating it from its later remodulations (Bonfil 1991; Malkiel 2001).

The two essential elements of this segregation system were the forced enclosure of Jews inside one single walled guarded area inside the city and the opening of its gates during the hours of daylight (Ravid 2018). The ghetto came with a precise set of rules clearly stating that Jews did not belong to the urban space and univocally defining where Jews could and could not reside and practice their religion (Cooperman 2018). During the day, Jews could circulate freely around the city, in the streets, markets, courts, ports, private homes, taverns, and often even beyond the city walls for either personal or professional reasons (such as family meetings or fairs for instance). But at night Jews had to return to their houses inside the ghetto where there were also authorized synagogues. Non-resident Jews would also go to the city ghetto to find accommodation, and had to identify themselves to the local Jewish authorities (rabbis, usually).

From this standpoint, even Livorno and Pisa – two Tuscan cities where a ghetto was never established by explicit order of the Grand Duchy (although Tuscany was one of the first states to adopt the Roman model, in Florence in 1571) – can be considered part of the system. The *Patenti livornine* of 1593 assured merchants "from any nation" who moved to the Tyrrhenian coast protection from Inquisition inspections and freedom of cult (with strong limitations for Protestants). Sephardi Jews in search of a place to settle immediately seized this opportunity. All these guarantees were due to the fact that Livorno was a free-trade port, meaning this tolerant approach was not valid outside its territory nor in the rest of the State (Frattarelli Fisher 2008). Pisa, which also had no ghetto, was home to the Inquisition court, while in Florence the House of Catechumens (Marconcini 2016) and the ghetto (Siegmund 2006) worked at full capacity. Jews knew well that what was allowed in Livorno would not be acceptable in the rest of the state, almost as if that whole city were one large ghetto, only slightly more tolerant and comfortable than the others.

The intermittent and irregular establishment of ghettos led Jews to base their behavior on an attitude of cautious adaptation. Jews moved from one Italian state to another, and the various communities kept in touch, via familial and trade networks, which sometimes overlapped the greater international networks of the Sephardi diasporas. The Jews who travel led across the northern and central Italian states, regardless of their provenance and destination, knew the general context was one of discrimination with local specificities that determined who they had to respond to, where they could stay, and what behavior they were to adopt.

The Church of Rome was a key player in this scenario. As we have said, the ghetto was a solution functional to teleological, diplomatic, political, and social needs. Among these was of course the ultimate objective of Jewish conversion and the adaptation of the thesis of a Jewish nation's economic utility. Rome was adamant about the first point. Unsurprisingly, the ideological preamble to the 1555 Papal Bull *Cum nimis absurdum* explicitly referred to the Baptism of Jews as the purpose of the regulation itself, which apart from reorganizing urban spaces, simply implemented a set of pre-existent norms dating back to the 1215 Council, if not earlier. In other contexts, such as in Venice and in Tuscany in 1593 for instance, the focus was on other matters considered to be of public interest, such as commerce.

At all times all Jews could leave the ghetto. That option was always available. Baptism guaranteed full acceptance into the predominant society. Close daily contacts with members of the Christian society were a constant reminder of how conversion would have been a simple and convenient choice. Jews were continuously reminded that their condition was a direct consequence of their decision to remain faithful to their discriminated religion: there were sermons (in Rome, Jews were forced to attend weekly lectures), recurrent violent anti-Jewish teleological protests, plus all of the day-to-day activities Jews necessarily had to carry out with Christians. Initiatives towards Jewish evangelizing were constant, supported and promoted in all ways possible. The House of Catechumens' fierce pressure to celebrate as many Baptisms as possible, at all costs, the hunt for voluntary/reported Jews across half of Italy, ghetto perquisitions to track down banned Jewish books (which were regularly found despite censorship), and supervision over Jewish religious practices were common and extremely vexatious aspects of the entire period we are examining (Caffiero 2004). The fear of children being kidnapped and of secret Baptisms was still alive in Rome even after the city was named capital of the Kingdom of Italy: people avoided a particular road of the Monti neighborhood where for centuries Jews had been enclosed before their voluntary, or more often forced, conversion. The Jews who night after night returned to their ghetto were making a deliberate choice: they were choosing a life of discrimination over an apparently more convenient existence that for many reasons was considered unacceptable.

The indissoluble connections between the Jewish communities throughout the peninsula and those around the world allowed Jews living in the ghettos to participate in the great events of Jewish history of the time. The city of Padua, with its University (partially) accessible to Jewish students specializing in medical sciences, become an international point of reference where Jewish youths from different and far away communities could meet and connect (Ruderman 2010). Italian Jews also joined the Sabbatean movement, contributed to the most current debates, and set up great libraries. These and many other elements attest their effective integration into the international Jewish circles of the time: questions, interests, answers, ideas, and objects traveled beyond walls assuring the cultural and physical survival of the Jewish communities living inside the Italian ghettos.

Beyond walls

During daytime hours the gates of the ghetto were left open: Jews could leave and Christians could enter for all sorts of everyday business, commerce, and personal reasons. In general, as a rule, Jews could not own real estate property (an old restriction that was still in effect) and were forced to reside inside the ghetto: these two requirements were the cause of the Jews' definitive departure from rural contexts and small centers. Despite the many differences between the various local regulations, commerce and pawnbroking were the cornerstones of the economy of all ghettos, contributing to the definition of a common framework.

The formula *sola arte stracceria seu cenceria* – restricting Jewish trade to second hand rags and fabrics – which was included in the Papal Bull of 1555, set a limit to the number of professions Jews could undertake even outside the State of the Church. Reusing textiles was a common practice in pre-industrial society when new objects were rare and even members of the upper classes used to adapt and reuse old clothes and linens. Textile commerce was carried out on many levels and could range from cheap worn out textiles to exclusive silks and velvets in the latest fashion. Yarns of all prices circulated and traveled across the borders of the *naçao* together with precious stones and exotic products, arriving in Venice, Livorno, and also Ancona, and from there distributed far and wide (Trivellato 2016). During the eighteenth century, the Jewish merchants of Rome, for instance, worked at the city customs and in Civitavecchia where they imported Levantine fabrics as well as occasionally trading coffee, tobacco, and other luxury goods with relatives and acquaintances living elsewhere. The Jews' specialization in the textile sector was present in all ghetto social strata, but most Jews were tailors, peddlers, and small shopkeepers (Di Nepi 2013).

Pawnbroking, a business that had developed on the basis of the *condotte* issued during the previous centuries, remained an important activity also during this period. Jewish usu-

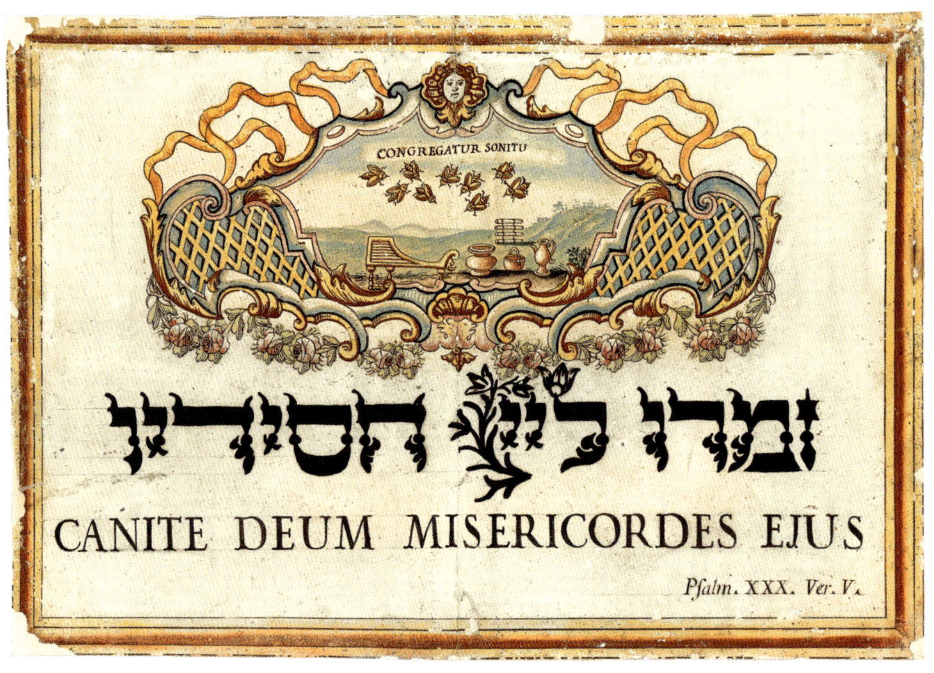

3. Temporary decoration. Archivio Storico della Comunità Ebraica di Roma "Giancarlo Spizzichino," Rome (cat. 22)

rers however worked on a local scale and never reached the level of political and financial influence that banking institutions had been enjoying since the fifteenth century. Jews were obviously excluded from the inner patronage and family courtly circles that favored the extraordinary careers of the members of the Chigi, Medici, and Fugger families. On the other hand, it should be noted how these forms of discrimination proved instrumental in the construction of modern states, which came about via the continuous erosion of privileges held by small groups, power centralization, and restricted access to the decision process, establishing *modern* forms of government that could not handle specific negotiations as were those that led to the *condotte* (Todeschini 2016). However, as rabbi Simone Luzzatto remembered in his famous 1638 *Discorso circa lo Stato degli Hebrei et in particolar dimoranti nell'inclita città di Venezia,* Jewish effort (and money) in commerce could and should contribute to the success of those states like the illustrious Republic of Venice that proved capable of carving a space for Jews within their plural societies (S. Luzzatto 2019). But that space in any case remained a marginal one, where the economic players, kept at a distance from politics, were forcibly segregated, in compliance with the principle of impossible acceptance that characterized all Christian-Jewish relations.

The social and cultural dialectics occurring inside Jewish communities responded to the multiple stimuli reflecting both the evolution of relations with the outside world and inner ghetto dynamics. Professional success in the world *outside* the ghetto and good rela-

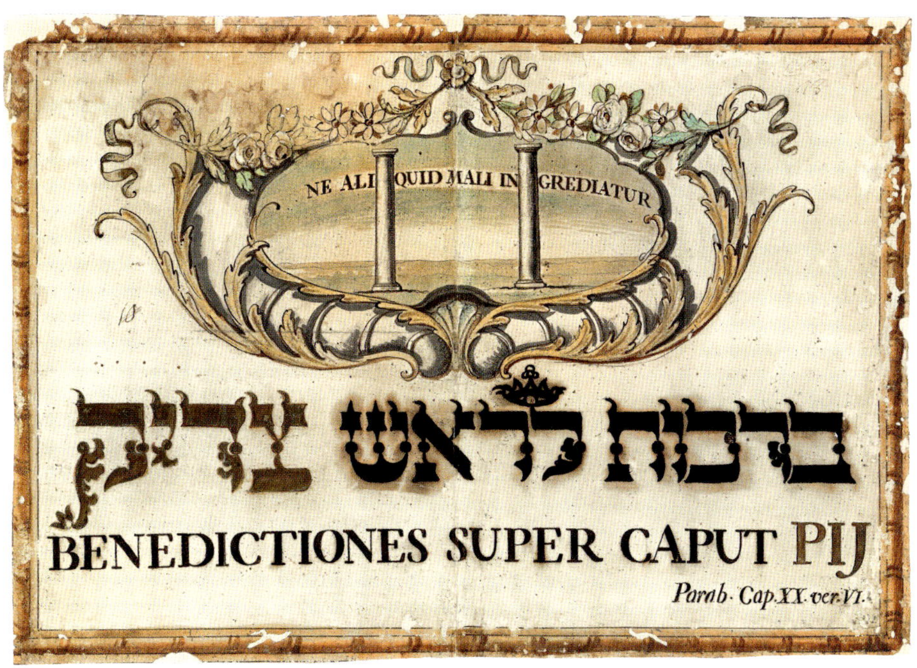

4. Temporary decoration. Archivio Storico della Comunità Ebraica di Roma "Giancarlo Spizzichino," Rome (cat. 23)

tions with members of the Christian upper class were inevitably connected to the achievement and preservation of prestigious positions *inside* the ghetto. Against the backdrop of a complex pattern of relations and connections, the representatives of Jewish institutions were necessarily educated, rich, esteemed Jews and the positive results they reaped and the important and personal connections they established reinforced their political position. The magnificent liturgic decorations that the most prominent and wealthy families donated to the Synagogues certified and celebrated a twofold message: on the one hand, these splendid, exclusive, costly objects confirmed the patron's prestige; on the other, they reminded their fellow Jews inside the Synagogue of the religious choice that offering confirmed, a choice that hopefully would be renewed generation after generation (Di Castro 1994; *Tutti i colori* 2019).

Most Jews living in the ghettos however did not fall into this category. The few rich Jewish merchants lived amongst a multitude of indigent Jews, in obedience to the forced unity imposed on the discriminated group – yet another aspect of the ghetto system. Many times, Sephardi Jews in London and Amsterdam tried to reject poverty-stricken, ignorant, and misbehaving Jews, but this could not have happened in the Italian Peninsula, where rules were made by Christian authorities for whom the only element that mattered was a person's faith (Kaplan 2000).

Towards unification

Jewish and Christian coexistence was never a neutral fact. Relations between the two groups were marred by frequent forms of vexation, by a slow but steady stiffening of anti-Jewish doctrinal prescriptions, and by equally important reformulations of political and juridical thought within institutional ambits. Contacts between the prevailing group and the discriminated minority never ceased since, as we have seen, these contacts were integral and instrumental to the ghetto logic. A feeling of mutual hostility was the undertone of all forms of contact, based on the awareness of a reciprocated and inevitable alterity. Jews chose to remain Jews and refused with determination to join the majority group, protecting their difference with strength, aware of the consequences this position entailed. But these very circumstances were what made those continuous contacts possible: everybody knew who was who, everybody had a vague yet plausible idea of the rules of the counterpart's life, and everybody was aware of the juridical and theoretical framework that legitimized and delimited those contacts. This precarious balance assured that the Jews' alterity remained only partial and clearly distinct from other conditions of substantial alienation, such as those imposed on slaves and foreigners.

At one point, however, this structure experienced a setback as the debate on citizens' individual rights reached the ghetto walls, questioning the essence of this system founded on religious intolerance. The Patent of Toleration issued by Joseph II (1781) and then the opening of the ghetto of Trieste (1785) marked the beginning of a new era (Catalan 2000; Dubin 1999). The effects of the French Revolution and the so-called Sister Republics did the rest and Jews were finally free from life in the ghetto. Restoration soon reinstated all limitations, but the dice had been cast, and with the outbreak of the Risorgimento uprisings and the Jews' emancipation in Piedmont (1848) the discussion on the Jews' destiny started taking on a new, different, and increasingly explicit political import. Ghettos became the symbol of an old and deplorable past. The imposition of conditions of urban blight, poverty, and ignorance perpetuated in the name of faith were evils of the Ancient Regime, that the new order had to dispel once and for all. In 1858 the international scandal caused by Edgardo Mortara's kidnapping once again turned the spotlight on the violence and unfairness of anti-Jewish discrimination that was still practiced in Rome and the Papal States (Kertzer 2005). All the parties involved interpreted Pope Pius IX's rigid and repressive policy as the symbol of resistance to the push for unification led by the Kingdom of Piedmont-Sardinia. And so, when on September 20, 1870, at dawn, the Jewish Captain Giacomo Segre ordered to open fire at Porta Pia – working around the excommunication the Pope had imposed over whoever dared to order an attack against the holy city – everybody understood the innermost and personal significance of that action: Segre was unhinging the gates of Rome making way for a new world, for the country, and for the King. And the Jews were as ready as ever to be among the protagonists of that incoming season (Ferrara degli Uberti 2012).

Jewish Education in the Ghetto

Amedeo Spagnoletto

According to the Jerusalem Talmud, the first great revolution took place at the time of Shimon ben Shatach, a century before the destruction of the Temple, with the establishment of a public education system, "in order that all children may attend school." Of no less importance is the testimony that appears in the Babylonian Talmud, according to which the scholastic reform completed by the eminent man of the cloth Yehoshua ben Gamla in the first century was considered essential. He is recalled as the person who prevented "the Torah being forgotten from Israel," and who widened out the network of schools to the entire country – with children starting from the age of six or seven – in order to assist those who could not afford private tutors (Botticini, Eckstein 2012; Greenberg 1960). The Jews' high level of literacy was, then, the result of the determination with which the Biblical prescriptions that imposed the study of the Torah and traditional rabbinical literature, in every context and at every level, were implemented.

It should come as no surprise that, at the same time as the foundation of the communities in the fifteenth and sixteenth centuries, a relatively complex public management infrastructure was being established. It was intended to meet the need to provide children with a Jewish education. Even in the smaller cities, steps were taken to ensure that the community benefited from the presence of at least one paid teacher – who was often the rabbi himself – to assist the less well-off families, whereas their more affluent counterparts recruited personal tutors, who worked for various families, or specialists employed to educate the children of a single, wealthy family (Bonfil 1991). It is no accident that, given its dual purpose as a place of prayer and a place of study, the synagogue in Italy, as elsewhere, was called the *scola*. Until the seventeenth century, when the Jewish population was still fragmented into relatively small settlements, it was common practice for a young man to leave his home and to learn Jewish doctrine and Hebrew at a private college. It was not in the least rare that the fundamentals began to be learned from the age of three, in groups of boys and girls together, where play was the vehicle through which they started to memorize the everyday precepts in short prayers and to familiarize themselves with Hebrew letters.

The splitting up of males and females occurred for the most part around the age of six, with the diversification of the respective programs. Although most girls were not expected to undergo a thorough course of study similar to that designed for boys, thanks to the network of tutors they nevertheless acquired a basic education that enabled them to pick up at least the rudiments of the sacred texts and the precepts intended for them. Moreover, it would be wrong to conclude that the road to higher education was entirely barred to them, despite the barriers they faced due to the cultural environment and to the difficulties of interpreting the sacred texts. It was through the teachers themselves that we found out about the existence of numerous cases of youngsters whose marked aptitude for study was repaid with the planning out of courses that rewarded their genuine interest and made the most of their specifically female skill sets (Weinstein 2007). This program, which was geared towards the young ladies who were already growing up and were expected to start a family in the relatively near future, found success in Italy, as did similar schemes in northern Europe, and was implemented numerous times over the course of the seventeenth and eighteenth centuries. The "Precepts to be learned by Jewish women," written in Yiddish by Binyamin Aharon Slonik in the late sixteenth century and translated into Italian by Jacob Alpron, who had accumulated a great deal of experience as an instructor in Jewish houses, declared on the frontispiece his intention to "demonstrate the way of living in accordance with the *dat yisrael* (the law of Israel), and to rule the household and bring up the *Israelim* (Jewish) children with the fear of God (Settimi 2017).

We know in more detail about the study program designed for boys that was delivered on two distinct levels almost everywhere in order to prepare the young men for their entry into society through the rite of passage of the *Bar Mitzvah* at the age of 13. The *Talmud Torah* (study of the Torah) – this was the generic name by which school was known – was *de rigueur* in every Jewish institution, no matter how small. There, the boys learned first of all how to read and write in Hebrew characters and would very often also learn Italian, regardless of the community from whence they came: German, Spanish-Portuguese or Italian. Great importance was given to the reading of prayers and the Torah, in order that the fundamentals would be acquired very thoroughly and in such a way that they would accompany the young man throughout the remainder of his life.

The legal form that the institution would take varied from one place to the next, and in certain cases it would be part of the system of fraternities that guaranteed services to the members of the community. In Rome, as far back as 1602 the Talmud Torah had its own legal personality as an association, and from the regulatory framework of the late eighteenth century we can discern the existence of a library for use by the students (Ferrara, Franzone 2011). In Livorno, with the *haskamah* 65 of 1664, the influential figures decided to make it compulsory to attend the public school made available by the community and to outlaw, with no exceptions, the private provision of primary education through tutors (R. Toaff 1990). Secondary school offered a higher level of education but was attended only by a minority of young men. The name by which it was known, above all in northern Italy, was *esger*, denoting a sort of boarding school, where the old-

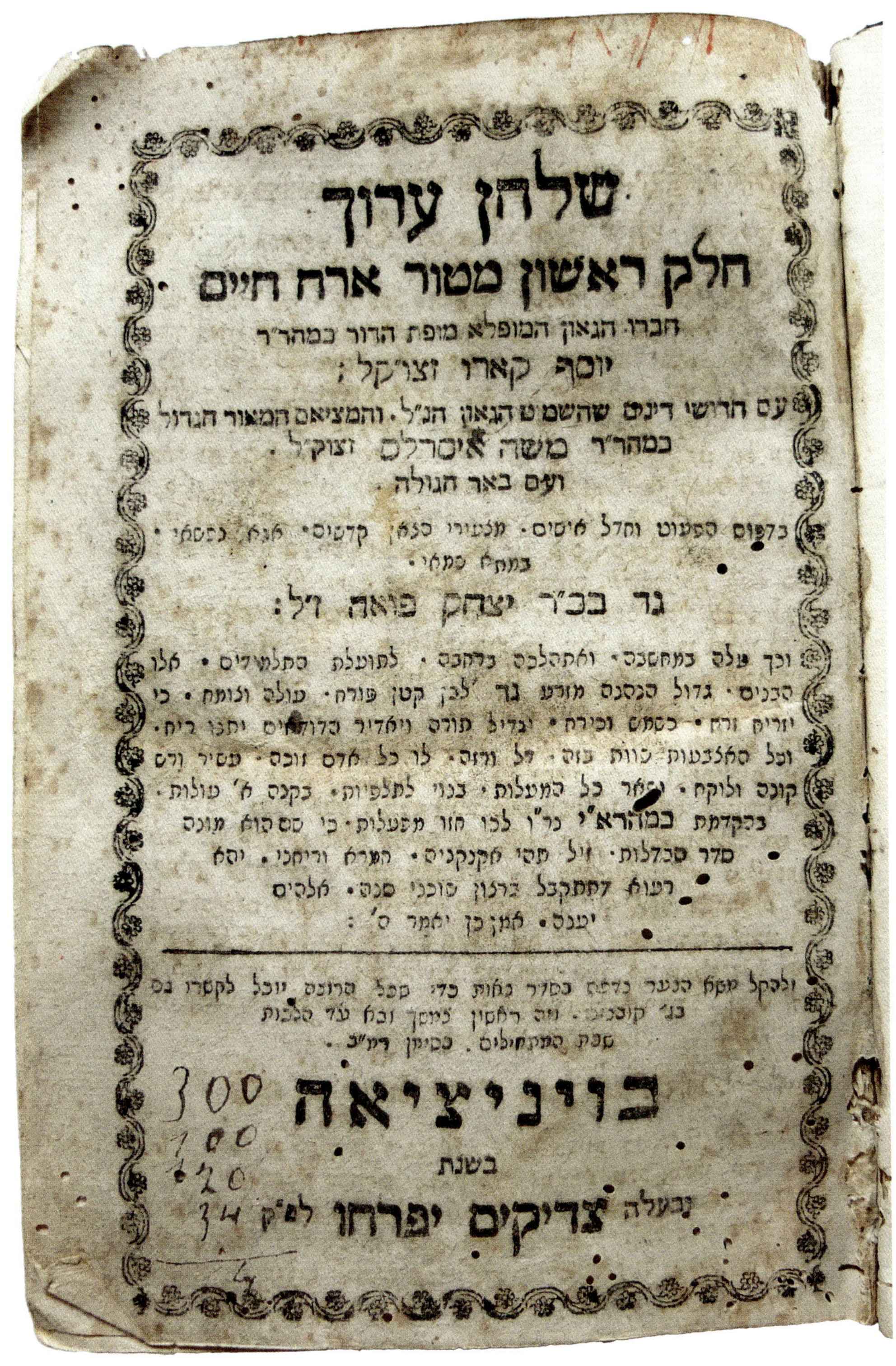
שלחן ערוך
חלק ראשון מטור ארח חיים
חברו הגאון המופלא מופת הדור כמהר"ר
יוסף קארו זצוק"ל ;
עם חדושי דינים שהשמיט הגאון הנ"ל. והמציאם המאור הגדול
כמהר"ר משה איסרלש זצוק"ל.
ועם באר הגולה.
גד בכ"ר יצחק פואה ז"ל:
בויניציאה
בשנת
וכעלה צדיקים יפרחו לפ"ק

er children received lessons throughout the entire day, and overnight accommodation was sometimes available. The most deserving of the poorer students not only had their boarding costs covered but also the cost of their clothes and other services. The array of subjects taught at the various levels was wide-ranging. Students were given a grounding in the Talmud and its commentaries. They learned the content of other books of the Bible and of the main exegetical works, and they were introduced to the Jewish legal codes – Maimonides' *Mishneh Torah*, above all, as well as Yosef Caro's *Shulchan Arukh*. This was the preferred route for those who wanted to continue their education at the *yeshivot* or academies that led to the studies which then made it possible to become ordained as a rabbi. In Rome, in the early eighteenth century, the school founded by Tranquillo Vita Corcos used as its model the institutes already operating in the north and included, alongside the development of the students' expertise in Hebrew language and grammar, the study of the *halakhah* (rituals) and of the *kabbalah*, as well as an ordered approach to the arts of the *trivium* and the *quadrivium*, with an effort being made to enable the students to overcome the cultural limits imposed by the conditions of life in the ghetto (Caffiero 2019; Sermoneta[a] 1989).

In this last type of academic institution, age was not the requisite principle that afforded access; what was more important was the capacity to take full advantage of the lessons – with or without the ambition of ending up as a rabbi – and the intention to continue refining one's own knowledge and putting into practice the model of life-long learning that marks out Jewish culture (Bonfil 1991).

1. Yosef Caro, *Schulchan Arukh*. MEIS (National Museum of Italian Judaism and the Shoah), Ferrara

The Del Monte Family

Marina Caffiero

The Del Monte family was one of the most eminent and prominent in the Roman community. An important house of the ruling class of Roman Jews, it was allowed to share the crest of a pope (Sixtus V, Felice Peretti, cardinal of Montalto, 1585–1590: Roth 1967) and the surname of another pope (Julius III, Giovanni Maria Ciocchi Del Monte, 1550–1555). During the seventeenth century, various members of the family held the important post of land agent, as recorded in the Registers of the Jewish community of Rome, where we find the names Barukh in 1650, Yaakov in 1659 and then Yaakov di Barukh in 1670 and 1674. We also have documentation of other members of the Del Monte family receiving the post of treasurer. Since the group of families who headed the community comprised a rather small circle, together forming the Council or Congregation of the Sixty, it is certain that the Del Monte family was a member. The Museo Ebraico, Rome (Davanzo Poli, Melasecchi, Spagnoletto 2016, pp. 132-133, cat. 52, pp. 210-211, cat. 109, p. 213, cat. 110) preserves various finely embroidered textiles that were donated by the family to the Scola del Tempio and the Scola Siciliana. Specifically, a *mappah* of 1755, depicting Mount Sinai with the Tablets of the Law at the summit along with three small mountains (the Del Monte crest) embroidered in gold and silver thread, and side inscriptions explaining that it was a gift from the "magnificent" Barukh, son of Shabetai Del Monte, to celebrate his children Manoakh and especially Anna, who escaped an attempted forced baptism. The Biblical verse embroidered on the cloth, Isaiah 1:27, is a clear reference to the triumph of the religion of Anna's forefathers and her safe return to the ghetto.

Manoakh (Tranquillo) Del Monte, son of Barukh, was an eminent member of the family, holding the prestigious post of Community Land Agent on many occasions between 1776 and 1802, after having often served as a member of the Congregation of the Sixty. A member for more than thirty years of the two key political and administrative bodies of the Roman ghetto and the Jewish university, he was witness, always while holding important posts, to the international developments that saw the French invasion of the Church State, the collapse of the pope's secular power, the proclamation of the Roman Republic of 1798–1799 and, finally, the first restoration of the Papal States in 1800. And yet we do not have a biography for him.

Besides his political role, Tranquillo Del Monte also made an important contribution to Jewish culture and literature and continued the attempt of the rabbi and physician Hizqiyah Manoakh Hayyim ben Yitzhaq (Tranquillo Vita Corcos, 1659–1730) to initiate cultural reform within Roman Judaism (Caffiero 2019), authoring a long poem on the celebrated story of Esther and the feast of Purim (Milano 1966). Furthermore, while telling the story of the "prodigious" rediscovery of the diary written by his sister Anna about her imprisonment, he also reported finding, among the newly unearthed family papers, an operetta written for his marriage to Ester Zevi, probably in connection with his association with the literary academy of Corcos. Finally, Tranquillo was in all likelihood the author, in 1793, of the chronicle of the attack on the ghetto during the anti-French revolt of the Roman population and assassination of the diplomatic agent Hugon de Bassville. This event was critical for the community, since it made the Jews a target of anti-French hatred, being considered complicit in and supporters of the Revolution. During those terrifying days for the Roman community, Tranquillo worked with the church authorities and obtained the end of the attack on the ghetto and the attempt to set it on fire (Sereni 1935, pp. 112–122). To commemorate that day, after their escape from danger, the Roman Jews instituted a feast of Purim.

The family's name and renown are, however, linked to a dramatic episode of attempted forced conversion involving the young Anna Del Monte, Tranquillo's sister, in the middle of the eighteenth century. What makes this episode exceptional is, first, that we have a very precise account of it in the form of Anna's diary, where she wrote in detail about her imprisonment (the aim of which was to force her to convert) and her victorious resistance (Caffiero 2008; Sermoneta 1989[b]). The fact that the diary was presumably written, or at least dictated, by a woman further increases its importance, since first person narratives, chronicles and autobiographies written by women are rare in both the Jewish and the Christian worlds. The mystery surrounding the diary derives from the fact that it is not autograph, having been transcribed by her brother many years after the event. The manuscript, comprising about 100 numbered recto-verso sheets, was written in Italian with interspersed Hebrew words and sentences, and opens with a title page, written and richly decorated by hand, with the title, the year it was written and the Del Monte family crest: three small mountains beneath a half moon (Caffiero 2008; Roth 1967). The codex, the original of which is lost, is composed of various parts and was written by a single hand. It begins with an introduction by Tranquillo Del Monte ("To the perpetual memory of the Event / To the Benevolent Reader"), including the story of the lucky discovery of the young woman's diary, many years after her death. This is followed by a "faithful" copy of the original, titled "Faithful copy of my sister's rediscovered manuscript," also copied out by Tranquillo, and a long 126-stanza poem in ottava rima on the episode by rabbi Sabato Mosé Mieli, completed by Tranquillo. The transcription of the manuscript can be dated between 1793 and 1795, or shortly after (Caffiero 2008).

In his introduction to his transcription of the diary, Tranquillo briefly tells of his sister's kidnapping and her "prodigious" return to their parents. He adds that, after returning to her home in the ghetto, she "set her hand to writing in detail about what had happened to her over those days." Later, however, still upset and exhausted by what had happened to her, she no longer wanted to talk about it, at all, nor write about it, to the point of fainting any time she was reminded of the episode. The family therefore decided to let her be, and it was only after Anna's death that they started to look, in vain, for the diary among the family papers. But, as in every story of the lucky rediscovery of lost manuscripts, the text reappeared years later, unexpectedly and almost miraculously, having wound up in the hands of a junk dealer who gave it back to the family along with other papers. That was when Tranquillo, rereading the dramatic text, decided to faithfully transcribe Anna's account "to preserve the memory of it at home" (Caffiero 2008; Sermoneta 1989[b]).

But let's turn to Anna's dramatic story. Eighteen years old, the daughter of Benedetto Del Monte and Belfiore Zevi, she was dragged from home on 6 May 1749 by two papal guards – who, weapons in hand, threatened to arrest her parents if they objected – and locked up in the House of Catechumens. The "abduction" – as it came to be called by the Jews, and indeed that was the title of the diary – followed a formal statement, made before a notary and two witnesses, by the neophyte Sabato Coen who, immediately after converting, had "offered" the young woman to the Catholic religion, claiming that she was his promised bride.

The, often arbitrary or even false, offers and statements made by Jews, unbeknownst to the person named and motivated by revenge and interpersonal or family grudges, resulted in the victim being closed up in the House of Catechumens for twelve days, in order to verify their desire to convert. But the abuse perpetrated by the directors of the House of Catechumens often prolonged the imprisonment many days beyond the agreed number, in order to have more time to secure conversions, even extending to forty or more days of detention (Caffiero 2004).This was made possible by sidestepping church regulations and asserting that the extrajudicial, but decisive, argument of *favor fidei*, the interest of the religion, prevailed over all legal arguments. However, unlike minors, adult Jews who were reported or offered could resist catechisation and return to the ghetto, as Anna was able to do, managing to return after thirteen days.

The diary is in fact noteworthy for the account of her active resistance. She reported her experience on multiple fronts. First and foremost, the physical and psychological: shouting, crying, praying and defending herself, but also dealing with the prison, darkness, insomnia, solitude, pain (including physical) and fear. Alternating stubborn silence and apparent calm with firm, decisive answers, sometimes harsh, sometimes "joyful," but always focused on stressing loyalty to her faith. Speaking with a low voice and patiently listening to prayers, even for three consecutive hours, making sure to never say the word "yes," which, said in any context, could have meant her ruin since it would have been taken as consent to her conversion. She kept her wits about her to the point of coming up with a clever system for not losing her sense of time: she asked to be given two eggs a day, one of which she put aside "for me to use to count the days," as we see in the precise numbering of the days in the diary. As one understands from subsequent passages as well, the young woman knew how long she could legally be kept in the House and evidently wanted to keep track of the days in order to check the duration. Careful to not make a mistake or lose her footing, prudent and wary, dignified and able to give decisive, sharp answers, even to the vicar of the Roman diocese, who was pressing her to "save her soul," Anna was fighting a battle of vigilance and survival: "I was always mindful of not saying anything that could damage my soul, and so I endeavored to say little, and balance my speech to avoid endangering myself." She was alone and sometimes "there were ten of them": she needed to be clever and not fall into traps, but also to forcefully claim her rights, freedom, choice and most importantly free will.

Anna's frequent reference to the modern principle of "free will" and voluntary, unconstrained choice is astonishing coming from the mouth of a young person and a woman, but it also partly reveals the cultural and intellectual world she belonged to. It especially reveals the most remarkable aspect of this diary: the young woman's ability to keep her wits about her, responding to theological arguments designed to show her the false nature of her faith and that Christianity was the one true faith with appropriate doctrinal arguments of her own. In this dramatic episode, the battle waged by the ecclesiastics for souls and their salvation at any cost, even against an individual's will, stands in contrast to the young woman's tireless and fully cognizant struggle to avoid the "abduction of her soul" and to firmly maintain her personal and family choice. And in fact, she was released on May 16, 1749.

Two visions of religious membership seem to be opposed in the diary. On the one hand, the modern principal of free religious choice and of the awareness necessary to make this choice. On the other hand, its rejection by the Catholic Church since this principle questioned the operative, performative capacity of baptism, beyond all individual awareness and personal freedom of choice. Indeed, the fact that it was the theologians and canonists most expert in Judaism that were brought in to convert Anna confirms that they were aware of dealing with an educated, well-trained young woman and member of one of the most cultured and important families in the Roman community.

Beyond her presence of mind, courage and ability to refute the Catholics' reasoning on the level of doctrine, Anna's strength consisted above all in her constant, insistent, tireless affirmation of her personal identity and her membership in and loyalty to her original religion. "Jewish I was born and Jewish I want to die"; "I would first die a thousand deaths rather than change my God, my Holy Law and my Parents"; "I have no other belief than the one shared by my Parents"; "I will never leave my Law, Nation and Parents, I would rather die one hundred times"; "I want to die as I was born."

While the subject of baptizing Jews offers an important opportunity for reflection on the processes of identity construction, this is not limited to studying the choices, behavior and ideology of converts, which is to say those who changed their identity, taking on another one or finding ways for the old and the new ones to coexist, but also analyzing those who rejected conversion to the end, resisting in every way possible in order to remain faithful to their original identity. Anna's diary is a stylistically powerful narration of an episode of the oppression of personal liberty and conscience in which the individual was nevertheless able to fight back, and carries with it a positive message of the force of reason and of possible reciprocal respectful acceptance.

In the subsequent century, the family's renown was increased by Crescenzo Del Monte (1868–1935), a poet and the greatest writer working in the Judeo Roman language. In his sonnets, he portrayed the Jews before and after the transition from the ghetto to emancipation, which is to say the attainment of civil and political rights after the capture of Rome in 1870. He was the first scholar to work in the Judeo Roman language, into which he translated a few medieval and sixteenth-century texts and works by Dante and Boccaccio (Procaccia,Teodonio 2007).

The Origin and Development of the Italian Liturgical Tradition

Riccardo Di Segni

When the Bible was translated into Greek in Alexandria by the "Seventy" scholars, commissioned by Ptolemy II Philadelphus (first half of the third century BCE), the word "liturgy" was used to render the Hebrew term *avoda*, "cult" or "service," with reference to the cult practised at the time in the Temple of Jerusalem. The "service" that was held outside the Temple, in the synagogues, was at the time a small affair compared to the one in the Temple. When the Temple was destroyed by the Romans in 70 CE, only the external part of the liturgy was left and it gradually developed as a consequence. The core always remained the same, but the geographic dispersion and predominance of local masters, called upon to decide how to behave in controversial cases, fostered the development of local traditions. This led to the emergence of the *minhaghim*, plural of *minhag*, "use" or "rite," which indicate the liturgical practices of individuals, families and especially entire communities who share the same origin. The *minhag* had, at least initially, a geographical base, a place where it gradually developed and became progressively stronger. But when historical pressure intervened, forcing groups and entire communities to move, they brought their *minhag* with them, to another place. It therefore was and still is often the case that communities and synagogues in the same city have different rites, handed down and maintained by families of different origin. These rites often take the name of their place of origin, even when transplanted elsewhere (as it might be for the classical denominations of Sefarad, Spain, and Ashkenaz, Germany and their later branches, like Levantine and Ponentine for the Sephardic, and *Ashkenaz,* Germany, and *Polin*, Poland, for the Ashkenazic. Or they take the name of the city where they settled, even if they came from far away: such as the ancient rite of the northern French communities, maintained by the exiled communities in Asti, Fossano and Moncalvo (all in Piedmont) and known by the name *minhag APaM*, which is a Hebrew acrostic of the names of the three cities.

The differences between the rites concern a variety of aspects: first and foremost, the text of the prayer and the ways it is recited, but also, more generally, different interpretations of the ritual norms, supported by generations of masters who belong to or influence a group. Other elements can relate to clothing, cooking, folklore and spoken language.

There were two main Jewish settlements at the historical origin of the division of the rites: the Land of Israel (where organized and authoritative Jewish life was possible until the fifth century CE) and Babylonia (where Jews prospered and were dominant, with respect to the rest of the Jewish world, for the entire first millennium). Hence, following a basic outline that scholars have shown to be overly simplistic, there were two initial large liturgical groups that originated two distinct families. In fact the story is far more complicated or perhaps even simpler, since all rites passed through Babylonia, where they were organized into a common order, the ninth-century *Seder Rav Amram.* The circulation of that text fueled a process called by some scholars "Babylonisation." Undoubtedly some strong local tradition resisted this and the result of this encounter is the presence in many places, including Italy, of vestiges of the distant past, the identification of which falls to specialist scholars.

Classification into two main groups, whatever their origin, seems appropriate, since it gathers together the resemblances and distinguishes the differences. Very schematically, the group of rites described as deriving from the Land of Israel includes the Greek rite (or the Romaniote one), which until recently survived only in Corfù, the Italian one, the one of the northern French communities that moved to Piedmont (*minhag APaM*, noted above) that no longer exists, and the German one, which is further divided into a western branch (*Ashkenaz*) and an eastern one (*Polin*). The Babylonian group instead originated the Sephardic rite, with numerous variants (north African, *Edot mizrach*, eastern from Syria to Iraq, Iberian Catalan-Aragonese, Spanish and Portuguese), the Provençal rite and the Yemeni one. Very roughly, the historical circulation of the main groups went, at least in the beginning, through the Babylonian-Ashkenazic branch in the Christian world and through the Land of Israel-Sephardic one in the Muslim world.

Beyond this classification, the actual presence of the rituals in the communities was always variable. Today, the vast majority of the Jewish population identifies as either Sephardic or Ashkenazic, groups that are in turn divided into various branches, whereas the other *minhaghim* have either entirely disappeared or are limited to small minorities, often unknown to the general public. This is the case for the Italian *minhag*. One of the most common questions people ask Italian Jews is if they are Sephardic or Ashkenazic, and the answer, which reveals an unknown world, leaves the asker astonished.

A person or an entire community with origins in one tradition does not necessarily follow the original *minhag*. In some cases, local prevalence can smother the differences: in Livorno, one was either Sephardic or was not. In some cases, the construction of monumental synagogues, like in Rome or Florence, leveled some of the differences. In other cases, the shift was determined by cultural factors: due to the influence of the mystics who privileged the Sephardic liturgical text, eighteenth-century *Hasidism* introduced the *Nùsach* (formulaic) *Sefarad* into the Ashkenazic world.

The differences in the *minhaghim* are not limited to the prayer text. Italian and Ashkenazic (Germanic) ritual texts are very similar, but attending the respective services is like experiencing two different worlds, from words' pronunciation to the melodies, even in the case of the oldest identifiable melodies, as well as the style of the response recitation between officiant and congregation. The close relationship between Italy and Ashkenaz can be traced to the early medieval origins of German-Jewish settlements, which, at least in the case of the ruling classes, we know passed through Italy from Puglia, to Rome and to Lucca.

Italy was a place of Jewish transit and settlement for twenty-two centuries. From inscriptions in the Roman catacombs, we know that there were numerous synagogues in ancient Rome and that they were even further divided by origin, such as the one of the Jews from Tripoli, and it would not be out of place to imagine that there were already differences at the time. Italy received streams of exiles in various epochs (from France, the Iberian Peninsula, Germany) and was the site of internal migration (usually from South to North, such as after the expulsion from southern territories under Spanish rule) and external migration in all directions. A standard rite would therefore be inconceivable, but we do find the (not terribly peaceful) coexistence of different traditions. Starting with the original Italian one.

The Italian rite has different names, such as *minhag kahal kadosh* ("rite of the sacred community of the") *Italians* and *minhag loez* o *loazim* (literally: "of those who speak a foreign language," probably Latin or an original vulgate) and *minhag benè Roma* ("of the sons of Rome"), indicating the original centrality of Rome. It is currently present in some Italian communities either exclusively (as in Turin, Padua and Bologna) or along with numerous other rites (as in Milan); but in many Italian communities it has disappeared, a victim of demographic depletion, succumbing to the pressure of rites with more representation (as in Venice and Florence). There were once Italian synagogues in Thessaloniki and Safed and there still is an Italian synagogue in Istanbul, but it follows the Sephardic rite. Today, there is a thriving Italian-rite synagogue in Jerusalem (where the rite is also called *italki,* an ancient Hebrew adjective meaning "Italian", probably derived from *italicus*) and another that is rigorously of Roman rite. Elsewhere in Israel, groups of Italian origin and following the Italian rite are emerging.

It might be surprising that such a small world could be even further divided between "Italian" and "Roman." But this is where the weight of the history lies. No *minhag*, even if defended by its followers with all their might, is immune to influences that slowly change it. For a variety of reasons. One is the orality of tradition. If you take a melody sung in a synagogue today and compare it to a score from 150 years ago, you will find that it is not exactly the same, because listeners and singers have gradually changed it. The other is outside influence. Every day, someone shows up who has heard a beautiful melody or has seen a slightly different behavior, and tries, with varying success, to introduce it. Today, a time marked by globalization and an immense focus on communication, the pressure keeps getting stronger. Sometimes, the introduction comes through authoritative channels: influential rabbis, not originally Roman (there has not been a Roman head rabbi in Rome for more than 160 years), who introduced things that hadn't existed before, not without some opposition or grumbling. Again in Rome, the monumental synagogue, drawing the majority of the faithful even though the Spanish synagogue continued to be autonomous, had to make some compromises. And so, the Torah is read with typically Spanish cantillation (imported directly from Spain), whereas the original Italian chant, which is based on entirely different criteria, is almost forgotten. The Italian rite has its fundamental texts, handwritten and printed, for both prayer and rule. But if we check what each community does with these texts and rules, we find a lot of diversity. Finally, modernity has carried quite a lot of weight, one example being the introduction of the organ into synagogues, where it still remains, although its use is limited (weddings, celebrations except those on Saturdays and holidays). The presence of the organ stimulated new liturgical styles and the introduction of music quite different from that of the past.

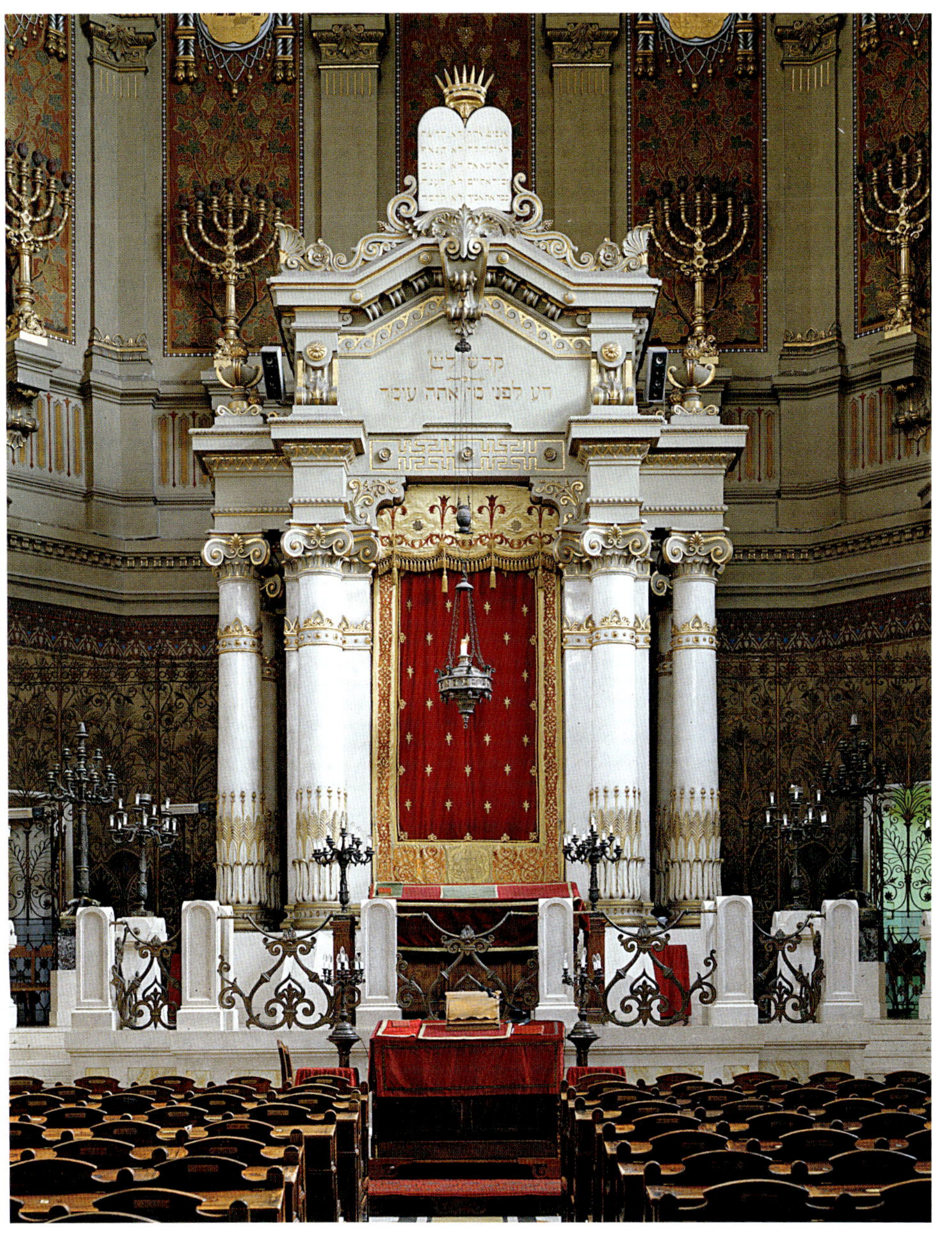

1. Interior of the Great Synagogue of Rome

As for the history of Italian specificity, we have some very old sources. The oldest is in the Talmud, where it recounts the custom, introduced in Rome by Todòs, of consuming a whole roasted kid on the evening of Pesach, the same way that it was prepared in the Temple of Jerusalem. Doing this outside of Jerusalem was potentially sacrilege and of debatable lawfulness, but Todòs was not cast out. We do not know how long ago the Roman Jews have stopped practicing this tolerated sacrilege, but what is certain is that on the evening of Pesach they eat roast kid, cut into pieces, which is not permitted in many other communities in the world.

The Italian rite was, however, consolidated in the Middle Ages through a centuries-long process. The problem was no longer the fundamental structure of the texts, but the additions that had come to expand the liturgies, especially those for holidays. A great poetic tradition developed all over the world, and each group had to decide what to include and what to exclude. The initial relative freedom of choice was gradually limited and structures hardened. The Italian rite includes poems by Spanish, Ashkenazic and Italian authors, in many cases local. Whereas the Ashkenazic rite uses poems written in Puglia (such as *Ezkera E-loqim wehemaya*, by Amitai di Oria, late ninth century, in the prayer of *Neila* di *Kippur*) that are unknown in the Italian formularies.

Scholars have determined that the process of organizing the Italian rite was nearly complete in the thirteenth century. The work of Roman rabbis, it spread from Rome all over Italy, as testified in numerous manuscripts. The authority of the tradition is evidenced by the fact that the first complete volume of prayers (*machazor*) to be printed was the one for the Italian rite (Soncino-Casal Maggiore 1485–1486).

Jewish Italy is not, however, only Italian rite. Twentieth-century immigration brought many Sephardic and Ashkenazic Jews to the peninsula. When they found themselves in the minority, they chose the existing synagogues. When they were able to organise, they built their own. Like Persian Jews in Milan, or the more numerous Jews of Libyan origin, who maintain their original rites. Libyan Jews use the *nusach* of Livorno for prayer, which is to say the formulaic that was controlled and selected by the rabbis of that city (especially the *Chida*, Chaym Yosef David Azulai 1724–1806) and circulated throughout the Mediterranean basin by the Livorno printers. But their way of praying is much different from that of the traditional Italian Spanish synagogues, like the ones in Livorno (in the past) or Florence or Venice. One then notes, through Livorno, the global importance of Italian Sephardic influence, which is now at odds with other emerging Sephardic models. As for the recently arrived Ashkenazim, their presence was felt in the decades around the Shoah and then gradually weakened. Today, the Ashkenazic temple in Rome is Chabadic and its congregation mostly young people of Libyan origin.

More recent immigration has only partly influenced the original Italian non-Italian rite groups. A few historical Ashkenazic groups disappeared (for example, Casale Monferrato and Venezia, where they were, however, revived by the presence of Chabad and tourists), and others are in periodic rotation (in Trieste). The Sephardic tradition, however, remains firm, resisting the demographic drop. Tourists (often not very cultivated) find it hard to believe that what they are hearing in Florence or Venice is Sephardic. However, it is none other than the rich, elegant Sephardic tradition of Europe, which flourished in Italy. As for Rome, the original Spanish synagogue is an island with respect to its Italian sisters in the north, with its unique mix of Castilian, Catalan (once clearly separated), and Sicilian components, and preserves an invaluable treasure of liturgical traditions.

Liturgical tradition is not limited to the prayer text recited in the Synagogue. It expands to domestic practice and various aspects of everyday life. The coexistence of so much diversity in the heart of Italian Judaism is reflected in the development of models of Jewish behavior that are different from one another but in some ways homogeneous with respect to other nations. Italian Jewish cooking varies from city to city, but it is always Italian; liturgical art developed in different ways in different times and places, but Jewish art objects of Italian origin are easily identified; the spoken language (which is disappearing today) is not strictly Judeo-Italian, because it is always and in any case a mix of Hebrew and local dialect. In short, study of the Italian Jewish liturgy reveals an extremely rich world, to be protected and passed down, that is dissimilar and composite and yet strangely Italian in spite of all the differences.

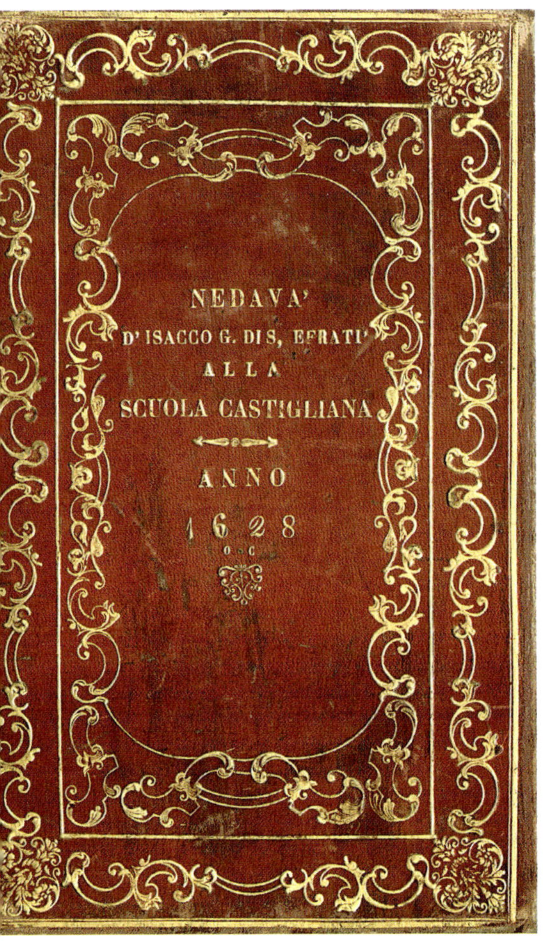

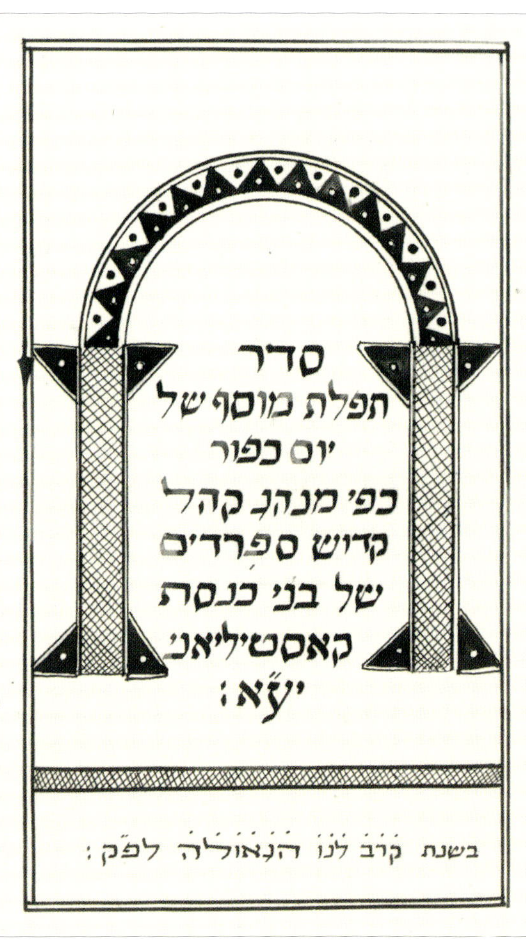

2. *Musaf Kippur*, Nedavah (offering) made by Isacco G. Di S. Efrati to the Scola Castigliana. Archivio Storico della Comunità Ebraica di Roma "Giancarlo Spizzichino," Rome (cat. 15)

From *Musica Hebræorum* to *Musica Sacra*. Musical Encounters in the Italian Synagogue (Seventeenth-Nineteenth Centuries)

Francesco Spagnolo

Introduction

The historical development of Jewish musical practices is best understood within the broader context of synagogue life, namely, the daily activities of prayer, study, and assembly, which are in turn based on a wide variety of cultural and artistic endeavors. These include literature in many languages (Hebrew, Aramaic, and local vernaculars), music (improvised according to the local canons of oral tradition or formal compositions performed on the basis of written musical notations), architecture, visual culture, applied arts, as well as an array of material cultures ranging from the body language and choreography of ritual to food consumption.

This article focuses on the role of music within Italian synagogue life between the seventeenth and the nineteenth centuries by examining the main primary sources that have been handed down to us in written and oral form. These sources help understand the core areas of musical interaction within the synagogue and beyond, as well as the principal modes of musical representation of Jewish life and culture over time. During these three centuries, Italian Jewish life underwent a series of dramatic changes, marked by local and global migrations, the emergence and then decline of the Jewish Ghetto as an Italian urban institution, the evolution of the political status of Italian Jews from alien residents to citizens, and the gradual contraction of the impact of Italian Jewish culture on a global scale. By virtue of its close relationship with many key aspects of Jewish life, liturgical music often mirrors social change through sound. The styles, genres, and repertoires of public ritual performance are closely related to shifts in economic and social status, inter-generational dynamics, gender roles, and aesthetics, as well as in the relationship between history and memory across time and space.

In musical terms, the period under consideration can be framed by the emblematic activities of two intellectuals and Jewish community leaders. At the beginning of this period, in the early seventeenth century, the publication of Salamone Rossi's groundbreaking collection of polyphonic vocal compositions on Hebrew texts, *Ha-shirim asher li-shelomoh* (Venice, 1622–1623; Harran 1999; 2003), was made possible by the cantor and rabbi Leone da Modena (1571–1648). Framing the other side of this time period, at the end of the nineteenth century, the unique blend of tradition and modernity epitomized by Livorno's synagogue life reached the United States with the founding of the Jewish Theological Seminary of America (New York, 1887) by another Italian cantor and rabbi, Sabato Morais (Livorno, 1823 – Philadelphia, 1897; Kiron 1992). The range of musical ideas and liturgical perspectives that emerged in the Italian synagogue between these two framing events is staggering, and can only be surveyed here through salient examples. Among these, two main notions of "Jewish music" stand out, and appear to still gain currency to this day, far beyond the geographic boundaries of the Italian Peninsula. On the one hand, the notion of synagogue music as an immutable biblical *musica hebræorum* ("music of the Hebrews"), shaped through the experience of Christian synagogue goers since the seventeenth century, continues to inform the value attributed to synagogue song by Jews and non-Jews alike. On the other hand, the establishment of the synagogue as a public space of intercultural and "interfaith" encounters, centered around Jewish ritual sounds as a *musica sacra* ("sacred music") accessible to all, still echoes in today's understanding and public celebration of Jewish culture, in Europe and beyond.

The study of the musical materials and of the development of musical practices during these three centuries presupposes a multi-disciplinary understanding of the synagogue as a place *both* of intimate negotiation of Jewish ritual identity, and of public display of ritual performance before a broader audience, made of Jews and non-Jews alike. The multi-cultural texture of Italian Jewish society caused by the successive waves of immigration from the Middle East, Central Europe, and the entire Mediterranean Basin allowed for distinct Italian, Ashkenazic and Sephardic ritual identities to be preserved within individual synagogues (often named after the ritual identities themselves: *tedesca*, *spagnola, italiana*, etc.), and also to be negotiated among Jews of different cultural backgrounds who found themselves sharing the same synagogue spaces. Ritual negotiations were often very "private," and for the most part unintelligible to the outside world: they took place within a circumscribed space, the *bimah* (Heb., "elevated place"), the platform in the synagogue on which the Torah is read and prayers are sung. At the same time, synagogues also became public spaces of intercultural dialogue between Jews and Christians. The latter often attended synagogue functions, brought there by personal and professional connections, curiosity, intellectual and higher learning agendas, the performance of new rituals inspired by Kabbalah (Jewish mystical), and political functions (Ravid 2008; Spagnolo 2018). In this latter function, the *bimah* also acted as a *bamah* (Heb., "stage"), a platform on which Jewish cultures and identities could be performed and presented before an interfaith audience.

Sources

The sources of Italian synagogue music that were handed down to us from the seventeenth to the nineteenth centuries can be divided into three distinct typologies: a) musical materials preserved by means of oral tradition and documented through archival field recordings;

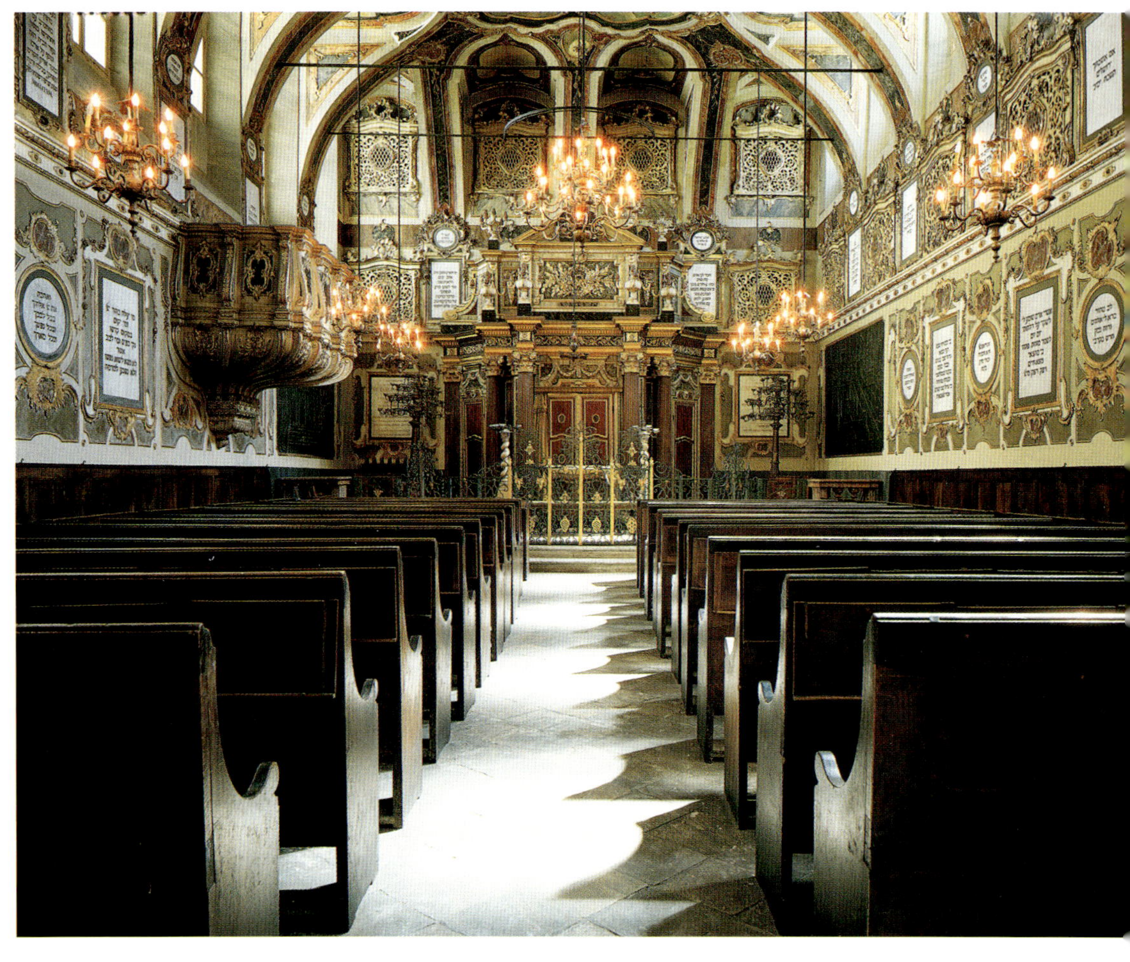

1. Synagogue of Casale Monferrato

b) written musical notations in manuscript and printed form; and c) literary descriptions of musical and liturgical practices and ideas. These sources can be ascribed to both Jewish and non-Jewish "musicians" – a variety of agents in active contact (as professionals or amateurs) with the world of sounds, including composers, performers, publishers, copyists, editors, printers, and writers – and often are the direct result of the encounter and collaboration between Jews and non-Jews around the topic of synagogue music.

A) ORAL TRADITIONS

Oral sources, preserved in archival recordings and in the memory of living culture bearers (often, but not exclusively, professional synagogue cantors and rabbis), document the development of local oral traditions of liturgical song in the many Jewish communities scattered throughout the Italian Peninsula. Local variants of Italian, Ashkenazic, Sephardic and French liturgical customs (Heb., *minhagim*) that were part of the tradition progressively disappeared over time along with the communities that had preserved them or in merging with one another, creating new musical hybrids. A statistical survey carried out in the middle of the nineteenth century attested to the existence of 108 synagogues (or sites of worship) located in sixty-six different Italian centers. By 1901, only 35 locations were chronicled (Servi 1865[b]; 1866; 1903).

All sound recordings documenting the oral traditions of the Jewish communities of Italy (and of those communities in Southern and Northern Europe, North Africa, and the Middle East that were historically impacted by Italian Jewish synagogue culture) were made in the twentieth century, since the technology to create them did not exist before then. However, some of these recordings succeeded in capturing a direct musical knowledge that dates back to the second half of the nineteenth century. Several informants, recorded as early as the 1930s and then during the 1950s by Leo Levi (1912–1982), were the bearers of musical practices that dated back to the Jewish Emancipation and to Italy's unification process (Spagnolo 2005; 2018).

B) WRITTEN MUSICAL SOURCES

Italian Jewish music manuscripts up to the first decades of the nineteenth century have been fully described by Israel Adler (I. Adler 1966; 1989), while an overwhelming number of documents dating from the 1840s onwards remain uncharted. The Eduard Birnbaum Collection at HUC (Klau Library), and the Jacob Michael Collection at the Music Department of the National Library of Israel, along with Jewish and public archives across Italy, hold invaluable and yet to-be-explored music manuscripts originating from a host of Italian communities.

Jewish musical notations include documents created by synagogue cantors, such as Avraham Segre of Casale Monferrato (before 1670), who used his acquired skill in notating music to commit to paper an orally transmitted repertoire; by Christian scholars, like Giulio Bartolocci (1616–1687) in Rome (1675–1693), who, in researching the "music of the Hebrews," wished to notate what he had heard from the oral repertoires of Italian Jews he had encountered; and by Jewish and non-Jewish musicians including the above-mentioned Salamone Rossi, and Benedetto Marcello (1686–1739), who published eleven transcription of Venetian synagogue melodies in *Estro poetico-armonico: Parafrasi sopra li salmi* (Venice, 1724–1727). An even broader musical framework is handed to us by the scores, librettos, and historical descriptions of the Kabbalistic ceremonies for the day of *hosh'ana rabbah* (the last day of the holiday of Sukkot) in Venice (a *Cantata Hebraica in Dialogo* written before 1682 by the Christian composer Carlo Grossi, 1634–1688), and in Casale Monferrato (three Hebrew cantatas, presented respectively in 1732, 1733, and 1735), as well the Kabbalah-infused liturgy for the inauguration of the Synagogue of Siena (1786) (I. Adler 1966; 1986).

These materials vary greatly in scope, content, and format. Their production alternatively aimed at documenting cantorial practices and passing them on to a new generation of synagogue musicians (Segre); at researching synagogue liturgy in order to identify the historical roots of Christian liturgical music (Bartolocci); at creating a new corpus of polyphonic music based on Hebrew texts (Rossi, Grossi, and the compositions for the synagogues of Casale and Siena); and at regenerating a musical "sacred bridge" between Jews and Christians in modern times (Marcello). Formally, they included both manuscripts and printed music, which in turn experimented with how to balance the graphic relationship between Hebrew texts (written from right to left) and musical notes (typically written from left to right).

With the nineteenth century, written musical production for the synagogue increased exponentially. A survey of manuscript sources from Piedmont alone, for example, unearthed over 700 musical compositions for the synagogue, now in communal and university archives in Italy, Israel and the United States. The archives of other Italian Jewish communities, including Rome, Venice, Florence, Padua, Mantua, Reggio Emilia, and Trieste, are currently being inventoried. These written sources are essential to the understanding of the degree to which the Emancipation prompted Italian Jews to innovate their liturgical "sound" by commissioning amateur and professional musicians (both Jewish and non-Jewish) to write for the synagogue, and by collecting Jewish liturgical works by other European composers – like Salomon Sulzer (1804–1890), Emile Jonas (1827–1905) and Samuel Naumbourg (1815–1880) – who were often connected with the Reform movement.

The musical content of nineteenth-century scores allows us to reconstruct a synagogue sound reminiscent of several non-Jewish musical worlds: melodies evoking Opera (and operetta), the liturgy of the Catholic Church, and the hymns of the Risorgimento (Italy's unification wars) were sung by small choirs of children and adults (at times also including women), and accompanied by the organ or, depending on the space and the resources made available by each synagogue, by the harmonium. The names of the composers, and often of the performers, appear together with the scores. They are too many to accompany them with biographical details (Seroussi 2002; Spagnolo 2007; Troìa, 2013).

c) LITERARY SOURCES

Liturgical texts such as Hebrew Prayer Books, rabbinic *responsa* (rulings on matters of Jewish law) and commentaries, communal records (*pinqasim*), personal papers, correspondence, etc., dating from as early as the sixteenth century, help in understanding the context (and at times the minute details) of synagogue performance practices. As in the case of music manuscript sources, these materials have been painstakingly researched and documented by Israel Adler up to the year 1800 (I. Adler 1975). These documents range in scope from philosophical investigations about the role of music in Jewish thought and religious life to the records of diatribes on matters such as the permissibility of repeating words of the Hebrew text of the prayers (to allow liturgical text to accommodate new musical materials), or the possibility of introducing polyphony and secular music in the liturgy itself. Of particular relevance are, in this realm, Leone da Modena's *responsa* about music, which were also published as part of the introductory materials to Salamone Rossi's *shirim* (Harrán 1989, 1992).

In the nineteenth century, literary sources are complemented by the addition of the Italian Jewish press. The pages of the *La Rivista Israelitica* (Parma, 1845–1847), *L'Educatore Israelita* (Vercelli, 1853–1874), *Il Corriere Israelitico* (Trieste, 1862–1914), *Il Vessillo Israelitico* (Casale Monferrato and Turin, 1874–1922), and *La Rassegna Mensile di Israel* (since 1925) contain a treasure trove of information, ranging from the dates and details of many synagogue performances, establishment of choirs, special liturgical ceremonies, to full-fledging debates about the role of music in synagogue life, the impact of the Reform, the role of ethnography in maintaining (or reconstructing) older musical traditions, and the involvement of Jewish musicians in the Italian and European music scene.

Conclusions

Taken as a whole, oral, written and literary sources are essential for grasping how synagogue music has been practiced, and understood, by those who were exposed to it. Two different, and eventually overlapping, attitudes to the sounds of the synagogue seem to have emerged between the seventeenth and nineteenth centuries.

The earlier studies by Christian Hebraists refer to synagogue music as *musica hebræorum*, the "music of the Hebrews" across a host of publications written in Latin. By virtue of being transmitted orally around the text of the Hebrew Bible, synagogue music was deemed worthy of being listened to and studied as a "portal" into musical (and biblical) antiquity. Hebrew music was appreciated for its historical and academic value, sought after by curious listeners as exotic knowledge (often connected with modern Kabbalah), or fostered by Jews themselves (including, in the seventeenth century, Leone da Modena and Salamone Rossi) as a cultural and political asset. Its performance spun new compositions, which gained traction as a new synagogue genre. In the course of the eighteenth century, the practice of performing musical compositions set to Hebrew texts inside synagogues was adopted by other European communities through a Spanish-Portuguese network that connected Italy to the Netherlands and beyond (I. Adler 1966; Seroussi 2002).

Between the end of the eighteenth and the early nineteenth centuries, a new concept, that of *musica sacra*, emerged among Italian Jewish musicians and intellectuals. While echoing the antiquity of Biblical sounds, this expression implicitly encompassed the new sounds of choral music and instrumental accompaniments created at the time of the Emancipation. Liturgical in nature, *musica sacra* was intended for public synagogue celebrations attended by both Jews and non-Jews together. Its aesthetics bridged Jewish, Catholic, and secular worlds, and its sound was the common denominator that unified both communities (Spagnolo 2018).

This syncretic and dynamic relationship between "old" and "new" music, musical antiquity and musical modernity, biblical sounds and their modern intelligibility, characterized the exporting of Italian Jewish musical lore from the Peninsula across the Mediterranean, and all the way to the United States (via Sabato Morais), in the course of the nineteenth century, and continues to act as a conduit for the musical encounters inside the Italian synagogue today.

Epithalamia and Other Occasional Poetry

Ariel Rathaus

In answer to a singular question from his nephew, Mantuan rabbi Moshe Provenzali (1503–1576) permitted him to compose, mentally, "measured and weighed" regular prosodic poetry on Saturdays (Provenzali 1988–1989, pp. 74–75, no. 46). Beyond its halachic-historical eccentricity, this episode can be taken as symbolic of the spirit of the times and, more specifically, of the rise of a unique socio-literary phenomenon: question and answer are not abstract theory, in late-Renaissance Jewish Italy, they have, in some way, something to do with real life.

Hebrew poetry, under the name of occasional poetry, was increasingly widespread among Italian Jews. The number of authors who wrote it grew, as did that of the patrons who used it, and it came to be one of the most typical cultural features of Italian Jewish community life until at least the early nineteenth century. By "occasion" what we mean here is a specific, unique event celebrated in homage to the individuals, families or community institutions that are either its subjects or organizers. We are therefore in the world of what has sometimes been defined "ceremonial" poetry (Matvejevitch 1971, pp. 87–88). But more than ceremony, since it was not necessary for there to be one (for example in the case of poetic prefaces to books), it would be more accurate to speak here of social function of encomium/homage/commemoration and also, evidently, subordination – although in quite different measure – of the material and content of the text to this function.

Already in Spain, with the flourishing of the greatest Jewish school of poetry of the Middle Ages, the courtly status of the poet had created ample space for celebratory poetry tied to events of the life of the Jewish potentate, the author's patron (Pagis 1976, p. 18). In Italy it was instead, as noted above, in the sixteenth century that clear signs began to emerge of a form of occasional writing in verse as a large-scale phenomenon that influenced the community's social customs.

The earliest signs included poetic epitaphs for tombstones, the most famous of which are the ones in Venice (Berliner 1881; Bernstein 1935) and, thanks to recent detailed research, the ones of the Jewish cemeteries in Padua (Malkiel 2013; 2014). The important Hebrew-Spanish precedents for the poetic epitaph date to the fourteenth century, although one also needs to consider humanist interest in the Greco-Roman epigram and epitaph.

In the 1570s, Azariah De' Rossi discussed this funerary/literary usage, which had become popular, in the final chapter of his *Meor Enaym* ("Light of the Eyes," Mantua, 1573–1575) and justified and legitimized it, including the text of his own future poem/epitaph that he had written for himself and the one written for the tomb of his grandson (Malkiel 2014, pp. 46–55).

A few decades later, in the *Diwan* ("songbook") of the Venetian rabbi and multifaceted writer Leone da Modena (1571–1648), occasional poems would appear to be the fulcrum or pillar of the author's activity as a poet and stand out for the varied range of social circumstances for which they were composed (L. Modena 1932). Besides numerous epitaphs, there are also many epithalamia and elegies, but also poems for circumcisions, for completing study of a Talmudic treatise or finishing a degree in medicine, for the installation of a new Torah scroll in an oratory, and rhymed prefaces to books with praise for the author. Modena practiced the "poet's trade" in the lucrative sense of the term, as also declared in his famous list of professions that he had tried without success, and this might explain so much abundance. But at the same time, it is an index of the magnitude of the demand for and the importance of a socio-literary practice that had by that point become open to a wide range of "occasions" and was at the time already quite rooted among the Jews (in Venice and in general north-east Italy).

The seventeenth and eighteenth centuries were the period of the most intense affirmation and popularity of this practice, in part in the wake of what was happening in, first, Baroque and, then, Arcadian Italian literature. Writing occasional poetry "in praise of," nourished since the Renaissance by the patronage of princes and nobles and by the sprouting up of cultural/literary academies in Italy, the members of which cultivated versification and rhetorical practice ("academies" of this kind also sprung up among the Jews), received a considerable boost during this period. The "collections," little books of laudatory poems by different authors, the first examples of which date to the sixteenth century, became common in the eighteenth century (for weddings, deaths, professions, graduations), sometimes with the collaboration of such men-of-letters as Vico, Goldoni and Parini (Colagrosso 1908). Among the Jews, the less expensive loose sheet with verse by a single author generally (but not always) replaced the costly bound books of the Italian collections, but the events that were celebrated, excepting the obvious religious differences, were the same.

Nevertheless, the two phenomena are not simplistically assimilable in terms of historical importance within the spheres of their respective literatures. In the gradual, organic development of a majority literature like the Italian/Tuscan, marked by immense poetic production, the laudatory genre can be, rightly or wrongly, ignored. Whereas the texts in the anomalous literary development of a minority, fragmented community with precarious fortunes like that of the Jews have an altogether different importance.

For the Italian Jewish men-of-letters of the seventeenth and eighteenth centuries – shut within the microsociety of the ghetto, where the community aspect had the most weight, and versifying in an unspoken ancient language, understood by few experts at the levels required by poetry and therefore lacking a readership large enough to justify the expense of print – the ceremonial channel was the main tool for circulating new poetry outside the classification of liturgical writing. Whence the importance of this minor production – in which, alongside the classical Spanish quantitative monorhyme poetry, the writers increasingly practiced and mastered Italian strophic forms, the sonnet, the ottava, the sestina, the terzina, the canzone – for the development of Jewish poetry and, one can say, for its very survival in Italy during that period.

The loose sheet that affluent families or institutions involved in the celebrated event often had printed in order to distribute the text among participants, sometimes with remarkable care and rich typographical decoration, ensured the author a real presence, a tangible relationship and a dialogue with their, albeit few, readers/listeners. As has been noted, the lyric poetry by the most important Jewish poets of the seventeenth century (Modena, Moshe Zacuto, the Frances brothers) remained handwritten until the modern editions of their work, whereas their occasional poetry, valuable to community life, was immediately printed and circulated (Bregman 2015, p. 55).

On the other hand, there was also space within the system of occasional production for a literary interest that was not at all occasional. The system was elastic enough to allow the event to be at times mere pretext for the realization of an author's personal project, with tenuous ties to the social function that it explicates. Here, it is the hierarchical relationship between "minor" and "major" work, already in and of itself problematic, that is subverted. The two verse dramas *Migdal Oz (The Strong Tower)* and *La-yesharim tehillah* (*Praise to the Righteous*) by Moshe Hayyim Luzzatto (1707–1747), central works in eighteenth-century Hebrew literature, fall functionally within the "epithalamium" genre. But the text's independence from the event suggests an earlier origin, later adapted to a ceremonial function. The same might be said for the funeral elegies by the Venetian poet Yehoshua Yosef Levi (late seventeenth/early eighteenth century), works dense with theological and philosophical reflections in the form of existential drama and among the most original and stimulating Hebrew poetic texts from that period (Y.Y. Levi 2013).

Epithalamia and elegies were the two main occasional genres, both with deep roots not only in the earlier Spanish Hebrew poetry but also in post-Biblical or even Biblical Jewish culture (David's lament for the death of Saul and Jonathan). Singing the praises of the "beautiful and pious" bride was prescribed by the school of Hillel (*T. B. Ketubbot* 17a) and funeral elegies by wise masters comprise an important proportion of the scant evidence of Hebrew poetry from the first centuries of the common era, preserved in Talmudic literature (*T.B. Mo ed Qatan 25b*).

In this essay, we will not be discussing the enigma-emblems in verse that appeared in Italy in the middle of the seventeenth century, a genre that might have constituted a clever pastime for various events, but were primarily used in the context of weddings (Pagis 1986), but rather epithalamia in the traditional sense of the term, congratulatory verse for the newly-weds and not tests of acumen for the guests. It is clear that highly stereotyped technical and thematic conventions coexisted in the epithalamia with remarkable inventive freedom. Typical clichés included praise of the wise groom, well studied in the Torah, and brides as beautiful as they were modest (as prescribed by Hillel), the similarity of the human qualities and social extraction of the couple, which ensured future harmony, blessings for fertility and happiness and, often, at the end of the text, hopes that the new couple

1. Wedding poem. Gross Family Collection, Tel Aviv (cat. 7)

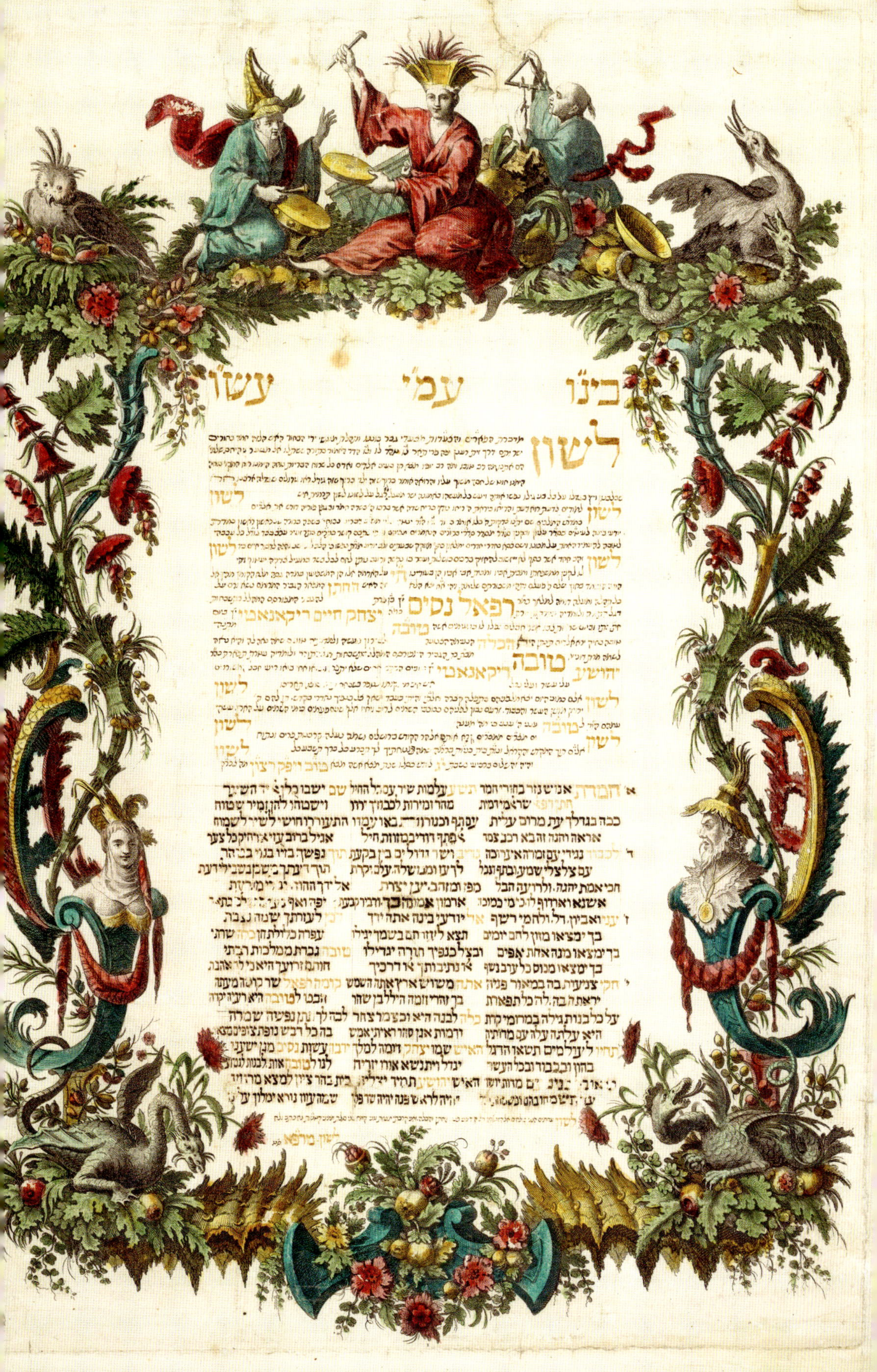

would see the Messiah and the redemption of Israel. But, while respecting these conventions, the central theme of the poem could vary considerably and diverge to a surprising degree not only from the stereotypes but even from the natural thematic boundaries of the genre. Examples include intellectual themes such as the cultural significance of writing (Moshe Levi Muggia) or the nature and value of music (Shelomoh Bassan) or the reworking of the classical literary motif of pastoral life in Hebrew (Itzchaq Hayym Cantarini). Even the most technical and stereotypical laudatory device, the mention of the names of the bride and groom and/or their families, could be a source of thematic/compositional originality. One monumental epithalamium in blank verse by Moshe Hayyim Luzzatto presents a kind of contrast between "land and sea," both entities that aspire as much to supremacy as to beauty, riches and natural resources: all of this in homage to the surnames of the bride (Italia, understood as "Italian mainland") and groom (Marini, "sea"). In this case, a largely specious play on names generated a complex imaginative construction, rich, at its loftiest heights, in poetic afflatus (M.H. Luzzatto 1945, pp. 27–42).

A common theme in epithalamia is the irresistible power of love, sometimes stressed in contrast with the rather anti-sentimental reality of weddings that were of course arranged by the families using intermediaries or matchmakers. Cupid was always working behind the scenes, sometimes making an appearance and saying a few words, as in a long scherzo in ottava by Shelomoh Lustro, which also makes use of the illustrious topos of the "upside-down world" (the newly-weds' love will not end until the "sea dries up," the "river runs backwards," "a donkey flies in the sky" and so on; Benayahu 1978, pp. 130–132). The meeting of the newly-weds was rich in passion and emotion, on the model of Petrarch dazzled by the appearance of Laura, and was to be sung in terms of the amorous Petrarchan tradition in its most recent seventeenth- and eighteenth-century formulations. A clear example is the recurrent motif of the contradictory and paradoxical prison of love, at once both pleasant and oppressive: "In prison relief, salvation!? / And yet you work the miracle Love!" (Shimshon Cohen Modon, *Apirion Shelomoh*; National Library of Israel, Ephemera Collection); "You will delight in the mighty chains, / Since the snares that capture you are sweet" (Yeshayahu Bassan, *'Et lata'at*; NLI, Eph. Coll.).

More in detail, the same theme of the prison of love is translated into a series of refined images steeped in Baroque conceptualism in this stanza of a canzone by Yaaqov Frances (also indebted to the lexicon of Hebrew-Spanish love poetry):

> Great and wondrous is the force of love: / the lover is like a lion, / whose strength blunts on the burning / ember of a fawn's cheek; who can understand / how that gentle gazelle lit up, / with a twinkle of the eye, the breast of a valiant man/ and in her heart she holds close / the soul that seeks an escape that does not exist. / Loosening her hair along her neck, / she would bind his strong heart, he would be a lion / in golden fetters chained to a marble column (Frances 1969, pp. 248–249).

This indulgence in the motif of flirtation and seduction was not expected in the period in question. Medieval Hebrew-Spanish poetry had cultivated the theme of love and, in Italy, Immanuel Romano had highlighted it in his work, often with a degree of eroticism. But the times and ethos had changed, especially after the explicit condemnation of Immanuel by rabbi Yosef Caro in chapter 307 (section 16) of the first part of his authoritative *Shulchan Arukh* ("The Set Table"). Although that condemnation did not stop poets from continuing to write about love in Hebrew (Pagis 1991, p. 69), the epithalamium in any case remained the poetic genre in which it was publicly permissible or even laudable to write about it, even with more or less openly sensual aspects, in the tradition of the Song of Songs: "She is on bedding of fine linen and white wool / and you will embrace her until dawn" (Shelomoh Lustro, *Beyom chatunat ha-bachur*, NLI, Eph. Coll.); "they unite / breast to breast, mouth kissing mouth" (Yeshayahu Bassan, ibid.); "he places his mouth upon her own to placate his desire"; "the young man reaches out his hand, seizes her shawl / to see the light of her breast he raises veil with force" (Yaaqov Frances; Frances 1969, p. 280).

The polar opposite of the epithalamium in terms of tone, mood and imagery, the funeral elegy was dedicated for the most part to more or less illustrious rabbis (more rarely, to other figures) and, more than the epithalamium, which as we have seen sometimes slipped in the direction of unusual themes, adhered closely to its own, naturally mournful and consolatory, sphere.

The development of this genre was also strongly influenced by medieval Spanish poetry. The constitutive elements of the Spanish elegy – the lament, praise for the deceased, consolation, meditation on human destiny and death (Matvejevitch and Levin 1973) – are generally found in the Italian elegy as well. In Italy, this reflection sometimes led to poetry on correlated meditative themes, such as the nature of the soul, theodicy, free will, the human faculty of knowledge (in the above-mentioned elegies by Levi). But it usually especially stressed, sinisterly, the universal domination of death over this earth and, brightly, the joys that await the just in the next life. One example is the contrast between Life and Death penned by Yosef Fiammetta for the death of rabbi Moshe Zacuto in 1697 (Ch. Schirmann 1934, pp. 335–341).

The domination of death seems less absolute in another popular occasional genre, which for understandable historical reasons had no Hebrew-Spanish precedents but only parallels in contemporary Italian laudatory literature: poetry for graduating "in philosophy and medicine" (Rathaus 2012). One of the recurrent points of praise for new graduates in medicine was in fact that of "defeating" death, bending it to his power on the strength of doctrine, even, emphatically, "putting Death to death." The genre developed especially after the influx of Jewish students at the university of Padua in the early seventeenth century, after the power to grant degrees passed from the representatives of the pope to the Collegium Venetum. In 1624, Leone da Modena contributed to this development with the printing of an uncommon "collection" of poetry and prose by various authors, *Belil Chamitz (Miscellany for Chamitz)*, for the graduation of his favorite student Yosef Chamitz (Ruderman 1995, pp. 100–102)

Beyond their mostly modest and mannered literary achievements, Hebrew poems for doctors were bearers of an important and, to say the least, innovative ideological and cultural message. A central theme in this poetry was that of secular science, its value and lawfulness, and the conflict that it generated in relation to tradition, even in a Jewish society open to secular study like the Italian one. In spite of these conflicts, which sometimes led the poet to praise the new doctor while stressing the superiority of the wisdom of the Torah over science, the genre celebrated secular culture overall as well as academic recognition, which is to say intellectual and social achievement outside the ghetto walls.

From this point of view, it anticipated the developments of Jewish history, defining an already modern figure of the Jewish intellectual, which would soon find expression, in Hebrew and in the European languages, in the literature of the Haskalah.

Medicine and the Jews. Training and Practice in Late Renaissance Italy

Edward Reichman

In the Middle Ages and Renaissance there were few professions open to the Jew in Europe. Aside from money-lending, the other major profession permitted to Jews was medicine. In addition, during this period, the Jews were expelled from almost the whole of Western Europe, with one significant exception. As Cecil Roth has noted:

> There was only one country of Western Europe in which Jewish life continued to flourish and to maintain its contact with the general world; thus the inquiry as to the position of the Jews in university life must in effect be very largely confined geographically to Italy, as it is, in point of subject, chiefly to medicine. (Roth 1930)

Italy became the center for medical training and practice for the Jews in the Renaissance period. Though the Jews were permitted to practice medicine, they were generally prohibited from formal training, as the universities were under the auspices of the Catholic Church. Papal bulls, dating back to the 1200s continually declared, with occasional variations, that Jews could not treat Christian patients. One example is the Papal Bull of Pope Gregory XIII, published in 1584, which reaffirmed and expanded the ban on the practice of medicine by Jews and added punishment for Christians who availed themselves of the services of Jewish physicians. Such decrees were common and perpetuated for many centuries, though Popes occasionally granted exemptions. Despite these decrees, many popes had Jewish physicians on their medical staff (Friedenwald 1944, pp. 551–612; Mendelssohn 1991; Pines 1961). The Jews played a key role in the transmission of medical knowledge throughout history by their translation of Greco-Roman and other medical texts, often from Arabic into Latin. As a result, Jews were to some extent considered the bearers of the medical tradition, yet they were the victims of unabashed antisemitism. Raymond Lull, writing in the early fourteenth century, writes, "Jews are universally entrusted by the great with the care of their health. Nor is the Church free of this abomination, for nearly every monastery has its Jewish physician. The custom is accursed" (Bevan, Singer 1965, p. 274). This experience of being simultaneously revered and reviled was the reality of the pre-modern Jewish physician. One of them, David De Pomis (1525–1593), personally experienced this paradox (Friedenwald 1944, pp. 31–53). After the Papal Bull of Pope Paul IV in 1555, which severely restricted Jewish religious practice and relations with Christians, De Pomis was forced to leave his home and medical practice. While this decree was later relaxed, allowing him to treat Duke Nicholas Orsini and the ruling Sforza family, De Pomis spent the rest of his life alternating between periods of oppression and tolerance. Indeed, the Papal Bull of Gregory XIII mentioned above led De Pomis to compose a defense of Jewish physicians, *De Medico Hebraeo Enarratio Apologica* (Venice, 1588), a work defending the character and ethics of the Jewish physician.

Jews also occasionally received papal dispensation to attend universities for medical training. From the diary of Judah Gonzago, an Italian student born around 1700, we have a first-hand account of the trials and tribulations of a Jewish student in medical training (Di Segni 1986; Friedenwald 1944). Judah's early education was confined to Mishna and Torah studies. He later developed an interest in medicine. In order to attend the Sapienza University of Rome, he was required to obtain papal permission. His fees at the university were triple the average student. Though one teacher made accommodations for his Shabbat observance, most were not nearly as forgiving. When time came for final examinations, which were performed on an individual basis, he was required to visit all thirteen examiners to plead his case. One examiner told him candidly that he had passed two Jewish candidates the year before, and there was no need for another as this would set a bad precedent. With much effort and assistance from a local rabbi physician he was able to secure permission for the exams. His last oral exam was on Rosh HaShana, and Judah recounts how he attended the early service, left after *shacharit* (morning prayers), and returned just in time to hear the blowing of the shofar.

The University of Padua and the Jews

In this cultural milieu of systemic discrimination against the Jewish physician both during training and in practice, one university, one of Europe's premier institutions, opened its doors to Jews – the University of Padua. While the relaxation of admission requirements was not specifically intended for Jews, and included other non-Christians as well, such as Protestants (Glasberg Gail 2016), many a Jewish student took advantage of the remarkable opportunity to acquire a formal medical education, something denied them until this point in history (Ciscato 1901; Reichman 2017, Reichman in press; Ruderman 1995).

Jewish students now descended upon Padua from other European countries, such as Germany and Poland (D. Carpi 1986; A. Modena and Morpurgo 1967). This was the first encounter for these Jews with the secular world, having come from insular communities. The contrast was made starker by the fact that Padua was one of the finest institutions in the world. The likes of William Harvey, Galileo, Vesalius, Morgagni, and Fallopius lectured there. The transition must have been traumatic and overwhelming for the average Jewish student, whose technical background for university study was sorely lacking. Some offered training in languages and rhetoric to bring the Jewish students up to par with their Italian peers. Perhaps the most famous of these programs was run by Solomon Conegliano, the teacher of Tobias Cohen (Reichman, 2019; Ruderman 1995). The language of this preparatory instruction was usually Hebrew or Yiddish (Shatzky 1950). This is evidenced by an exceptionally rare manuscript in Yiddish of a digest of the works of Andreas Vesalius.

The Jewish medical students of Padua faced unique problems, such as higher tuition fees. In addition, each community was required to provide bodies for dissection. The Jewish students, who objected to this practice based on Jewish legal grounds, paid large sums of money for the privilege of having the deceased bodies of the Jewish community left untouched. Despite this privilege, non-Jewish medical students often forcibly claimed the bodies of Jews from their burial places (Friedenwald 1921; Reichman 2008).

It is at the University of Padua that Andreas Vesalius practiced and taught. Vesalius intersects with the Jews in a number of ways (Reichman 2008), the most obvious being the presence of Hebrew terms in his anatomy work, *De humani corporis fabrica.* In addition, a remarkable manuscript now housed in the University of Pennsylvania attests to the challenges faced by the Jewish students matriculating into the University of Padua in the sixteenth century. It is a Yiddish translation of the work of Vesalius dating from the late sixteenth century. Jewish students coming from Poland and Germany, who were not fluent in

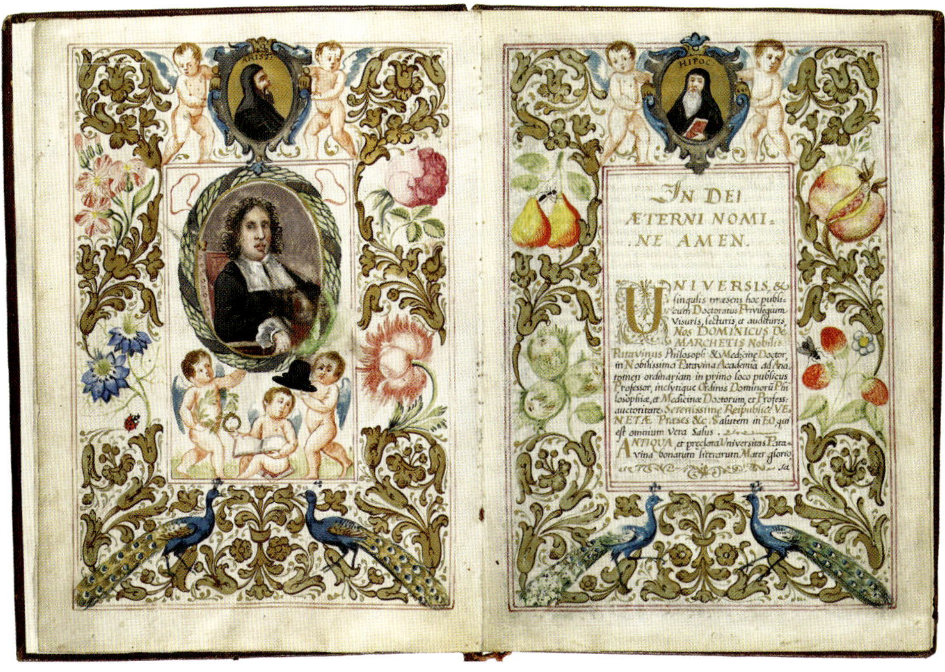

1. Medical diploma of Moyses Tilche.
Gross Family Collection, Tel Aviv (cat. 29)

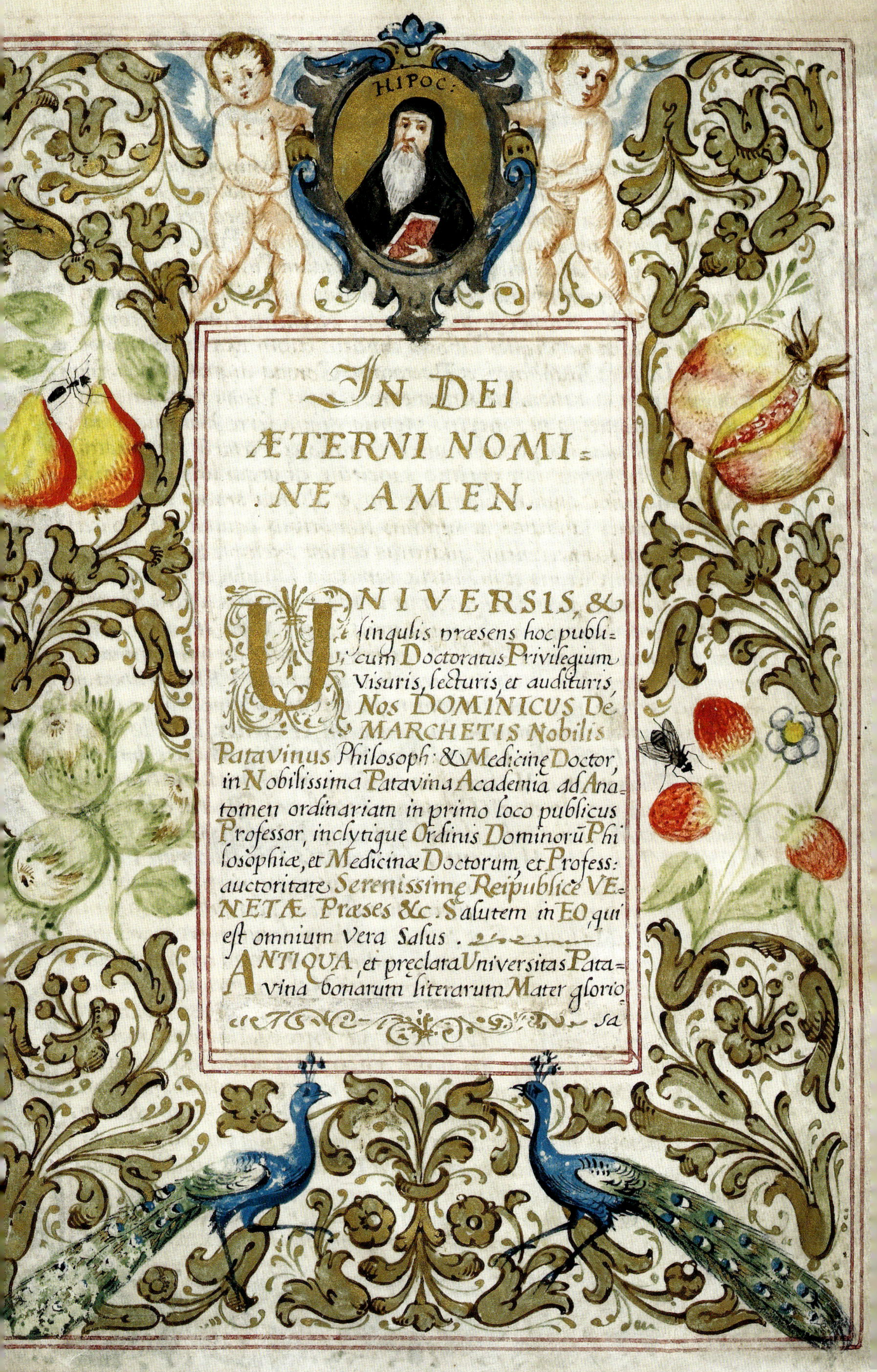
H.IPOC:

IN DEI
ÆTERNI NOMI-
NE AMEN.

UNIVERSIS, & singulis præsens hoc publicum Doctoratus Privilegium Visuris, lecturis, et audituris, Nos DOMINICUS De MARCHETIS Nobilis Patavinus Philosoph: & Medicinę Doctor, in Nobilissima Patavina Academia ad Anatomen ordinariam in primo loco publicus Professor, inclytique Ordinis Dominorū Philosophiæ, et Medicinæ Doctorum, et Profess: auctoritate Serenissimę Reipublicę VENETÆ Præses &c. Salutem in EO qui est omnium Vera Salus.

ANTIQUA, et preclara Universitas Patavina bonarum literarum Mater glorio-sa

Latin or Italian, would have used this to study for their anatomy course (MS UPenn LJS 485).

Despite the challenges for the Jewish medical students in Padua, there were also accommodations made. For example, the Jews at the university were exempted from the obligation of wearing the red hat, which was required to distinguish every Jew from the rest of mankind. They were permitted to wear a black head covering like the other students (Roth 1930).

On occasion, the degrees of Jewish students were supported or promoted by great personalities in the history of medicine and science, such as Fallopius (1523–1562), Girolamo Fabrici d'Acquapendente (1537–1619) and Galileo Galilei. Galilei in particular supported the degree of the Mantuan Jew David Portaleone, nephew of Abraham, the great physician who took care of, among others, the king of Naples Ferdinand II of Aragona, Galeazzo Maria Sforza and Giovanni dalle Bande Nere. Giovanni Battista Morgagni, the founder of modern pathology, served over a number of decades in varying positions at the university. His name appears on the diplomas of a number of Jewish students (Kisch 1949).

Many of the medical students maintained a connection to the rabbis of Padua and nearby Venice and continued their studies of Torah and rabbinic literature. Avtalyon Modena, a brilliant Talmudist and student at the University of Padua Medical School, learned Torah with Meir ben Isaac Katzenellenbogen (1473–1565), known as the *Maharam Mi-Padova* (Fano 1607, pp. 35a and 36b). Rabbi Leone da Modena, another prominent Italian rabbinic figure, also had significant contact with the Jewish medical students of Padua (Cohen 1988). Tobias Cohen, one of the most famous graduates of Padua, emphasized the importance of Jewish learning in the introduction to his classic late Renaissance work, written in Hebrew, Maaseh Tuvia (Reichman 2019):

> It should not enter the mind of any man in all the lands of Italy, Germany, and France to study the art of medicine without first mastering ("filling his belly") the written Torah, the oral Torah, and all its related wisdom…

Some of the Italian Jewish medical students, not exclusively from Padua, later authored important works in Jewish law or related to Judaism and medicine. Examples include Judah Messer Leon (D. Carpi 1972 and 1974; Rabinowitz 1983), Joseph Del Medigo (Barzilay 1997; D.A. Friedman 1942), Isaac Cantarini, Isaac Lampronti (Glasberg 2016), whose Talmudic Encyclopedia, *Pachad Yitzchak*, was the first of its kind, Samson Morpurgo, Jacob Zahalon, author of *Ozar HaChaim*, and Abraham Portaleone, author of the magnum opus *Shiltei Gibborim* on every aspects of the ancient Temple of Jerusalem (Katan 2009). Some even obtained rabbinic ordination (Silvera 2012). Morpurgo's rabbinic ordination, from rabbi Judah Briel, is housed in the National Library of Israel, and his medical diploma can be found in the Umberto Nahon Museum of Italian Jewish Art in Jerusalem.

Upon completion of their medical studies, students were awarded their customary diplomas. Diplomas issued by Italian universities in the Renaissance were elaborate and ornate works of art (Farina 2005) and Padua was no exception (Baldissin Molli, Sitran Rea and Veronese Ceseracciu 1998). Regarding the diplomas of Jewish medical students, however, certain alterations were made to accommodate their religious beliefs. While the standard issue diploma began by invoking the names of the Christian God (*In Christi Nomine*), the text for the Jewish student was amended to read "*In Dei Aeterni Nomine, Amen*" (in the name of the Eternal God). There were other changes, including the omission of religious imagery, the location of the graduation ceremony (held in a secular as opposed to religious venue), the nature of the oath, and even the manner in which the year of graduation was written (*anno currente*, as opposed to *anno Domini*). A number of diplomas of Jewish medical graduates of Padua are extant today (Kisch 1949; Reichman in press).

While in Germany, for example, the Jewish community was less than enthused about the pursuit of medical education (Efron 2001), the graduation of Jewish students from the medical school of Padua was met with great fanfare by the local Italian Jews. From the seventeenth to the nineteenth century, the Jews of Italy often composed occasional poems to celebrate a variety of communal and private events, including circumcisions, marriages and the deaths of prominent personalities (Liberman Mintz 2015). These literary offerings, usually composed in Hebrew (and occasionally in Italian), were authored by some of the most prominent Jewish writers and poets of the period. This poetic literary form was also applied to graduation celebrations for the Jewish medical students of Padua. Indeed, many of the poets were also physicians (Benayahu 1976 and 1978). For example, Solomon Conegliano, a medical graduate from 1660 and the founder of a preparatory school for Jewish medical students, wrote a poem in honor of the graduation of Isaac Cantarini, who would later become a rabbi physician of great renown. Another poem was penned in honor of the graduation in 1734 of Shmuel Lampronti, son of the famous rabbi Isaac Lampronti, also a graduate of Padua's medical school (Liberman Mintz 2015). A collection of poems was published honoring the graduation of Yosef Chamitz in 1624, cleverly titled *B'leil Chamitz* (Leibowitz 1936; Ruderman 1995). This work was edited by Chamitz's teacher, rabbi Leone da Modena, who also contributed a poem to the volume. The now famous rabbi Moshe Haiyym Luzzatto, author of *Mesilat Yesharim*, wrote a number of poems for his students and colleagues who graduated from the medical school (Reichman 2017).

Jews continued to attend the medical school of Padua into the nineteenth century, with a number of families represented over many generations, such as Luzzatto, Lampronti, Cantarini, Wallich, Morpurgo, and Conegliano. For example, from the end of the seventeenth to the early nineteenth century, at least five members of Luzzatto family from San Daniele del Friuli graduated from the Padua medical school (A. Modena, Morpurgo 1967). Samuel David Luzzatto (1800–1865), the great scholar and bibliophile, known as Shadal, reports that on a visit to his uncle Isaac in San Daniele, he was shown the medical diploma of Isaac's father, Raphael (Mirsky 1987). Shadal then commented, "We learn that the poet Isaac was preceded by a Raphael and an Isaac, and was followed by a Raphael and an Isaac, all of them doctors." Isaac Luzzatto was the last of the direct family medical line, graduating in Padua in 1836.

The Confraternities in the Sociocultural Fabric of the Communities

Michela Andreatta

Starting in the last decades of the sixteenth century and increasing steadily over the entire subsequent century up to the end of the age of segregation, the tendency to form associations, which is to say confraternities (*chevrot* or *chavurot*), came to play a predominant role in the internal organization of Italian Jewish communities, broadly conditioning the forms and circles within which Italian Jews socialized. Charity and religious associations had been common among European Jews since the late Middle Ages, but in Italy this activity is better documented starting in the sixteenth century, when, following the process of urbanization triggered by the establishment of the ghettos and the consequential social stratification within them, these groups became more numerous and better organized. From the beginning, these groups were dedicated to helping members of the community in particular in two essential areas of Jewish life: education and burial. Starting in the second half of the sixteenth century, alongside the traditional charitable groups, called *gemilut chasadim*, numerous smaller charitable associations were founded within the walls of the ghetto, with more circumscribed aims and activity limited to specific areas, such as economic assistance for the poor, dowries for less well-off girls, ransom for hostages and liberation of prisoners (Rivlin 1991).

Alongside these groups, the aims of which were chiefly philanthropic, other, essentially religious, associations began to spread among Italian Jews, meeting the needs of the devotional side of community life, an aspect that would later become predominant (Farine 1973–1974; Horowitz 1982, 1985, 1987, 1993, 2000[a], 2000[b], 2001; Rivlin 1989, 1991). The broad success of confraternities of the latter type is evidenced by their wide diffusion and the multiplication over time of groups with similar aims, though with different names. It found justification not only in the need for social organization and protection within the ghetto but most importantly in the particular ways in which the spirituality of the time was expressed. In fact, these groups ensured the continuity of devotional practices that were increasingly central to community life, such as prayer in particular ritual contexts, study of traditional texts and fasting. Where the traditional confraternities put the accent on charitable activities and had an only generically religious character, the new devotional associations tended to specialize in purely spiritual activities and placed emphasis on carrying out particular ceremonies, rather than on assistance. These groups, however, sometimes paired ritual observance with charitable activity of various kind, mostly alms and assistance at the bedside of the sick and suffering.

Like the charitable confraternities, those devoted to study and prayer also had a hierarchical organizational structure on the basis of which members held different posts and, consequently, enjoyed different privileges. Nevertheless, they were generally less elitist. Although the founders were often linked by family ties or intellectual affinities, in most cases members came from the middle class, and membership in the confraternity ensured them a form of collective participation alternative to community institutions, often allocated among the wealthy representatives of the community (Rivlin 1991). Moreover, the number of members in the study and prayer associations was never very high, which ensured greater intimacy in the performance of rituals and ceremonies as well as in interpersonal relations among the associates. The intense emotional engagement deriving from religious inspiration, further stimulated by the ritual practices observed, some of which Kabbalistic, fostered intense bonds of friendship and spiritual brotherhood among adherents and allowed individuals with shared interests to develop friendships and ties of affinity, in some cases overcoming institutional or cultural barriers that would have otherwise separated them. In fact, while some of these groups were distinguished based on rite (Ashkenazic, Sephardic or Italian), others, in particular in the smaller communities, crossed these barriers to unite different congregations (Rivlin 1991).

A variety of factors contributed to the success of study and prayer confraternities and their wide diffusion in Italian communities. First, there was the embrace of mystical theories coming from the Land of Israel and various newly established paraliturgical rituals, many of which penitential in nature (known as *tikkunim*), inspired by those theories. The new rituals from the Land of Israel spread among the Jews of the Diaspora, finding highly fertile soil in Italy, in particular thanks to the activity of special envoys coming from the Palestinian communities and Italian Kabbalah enthusiastic scholars (Bonfil 1987[a], 1987[b]; Idel 1987; Meroz 1987; Tishby 1974).

Another factor, the importance of which should not be underestimated in order to fully comprehend the phenomenon of Jewish confraternities and their impact on the social life of the communities inside the ghetto, was the model offered by Christian confraternities and the centrality, during the period of the Counter Reformation, of the practice of establishing devotional and ritual groups (Angelozzi 1978, Rusconi 1986, Zardin 1987, Black 1989). In early sixteenth-century Venice, there were more than 200 "schools" – between religious confraternities, guilds and associations linked to specific cities or countries of origin – six of which, the Scuole Grandi, were purely devotional in character (Pullan 1971, Ortalli 2001, Vio 2004). In this sense, it is not incidental that Venetian rabbi Leone da Modena (1571–1648) referred to the practice of forming Jewish philanthropic associations in the *Historia de' Riti Hebraici* (Paris 1637), the first compilation by a Jewish author of the customs and traditions observed by Jews, for a non-Jewish readership (Cohen 1972). During his own life, Leone da Modena was in contact, in various ways, with a variety of confraternities active in the Venetian ghetto, and had good reason to see the Jewish practice of forming associations as a point of communality with the surrounding Christian society. A characteristic that perfectly fit the *Historia*'s apologetic aims:

> There are besides, in big Cities, Fraternities or Companies for Works of Charity: for instance, some that take care of the Sick, and Burial of the Dead, which they call *Ghemilud hassadim*: others for Alms only, which they call *Zedacá*: for Redeeming of Slaves, *Pidion secuim*: for Marrying Maids, *Hassi betulod* and several others: which Companies are more or fewer, proportional to the Number of *Jews* which dwell in the Place" (L. Modena, English trans. 1707, p. 59)

As in the case of charitable and philanthropic associations, study and prayer confraternities were named after the main ritual they performed. Organizing and carrying out the related religious ceremonies became a predominant aspect of the members' life. Among the first confraternities to be organized with a well-defined ritual physiognomy there were those devoted to the practice of the penitential dawn vigil, documented from the end of the sixteenth century in the main Jewish communities of Central and Northern Italy, and active until the end of the seventeenth century (Horowitz 1982, 1987, 1989[a]; Milano 1958; Rivlin 1991; Simonsohn 1959–1960, 1977; Shulvass 1944; Tishby 1974; Vogelstein and Rieger 1895–1896). Members met daily, an hour or two before dawn, for sessions of prayer and study that included reciting penitential prayers and reading passages from the Bible or the *Mishnah*. The aim of these rituals was to invoke forgiveness of sins, considered to be the main obstacle impeding redemption and the coming of the Messiah. These groups, whose wide diffusion and range of action made them an actual movement, were known by different names, the most common being *Shomerim la-boqer* (Morning Sentinels).

The custom of staying awake to recite psalms and *selichot* during the last part of the night was already practiced in Italian communities, although limited to specific occasions, such as fasts, the month of *Elul* and *Yom Kippur* (Fleischer 1975). It was probably in the Kabbalistic center Safad that the Sephardic custom of waking daily in the night to recite *selichot* (thus extending a practice characteristic of the month of *Elul* to the whole year) was grafted onto the long tradition of the mystic study and prayer vigil in commemoration of the destruction of the Temple (Robinson 1981, Idel 1987), generating two distinct types of penitential vigil: one that paired the recitation of *qinot* with the study of texts, held in the hours following midnight (*tikkun chatzot*); one that involved the recitation of *selichot* before the morning prayer. In Italian communities, the penitential vigil was practised in the dawn version, and prevailed over the ritual of *tikkun chatzot* for the entire seventeenth century (Horowitz 1982; Scholem 1980).

A rare description of the ritual of the vigil, as it was practised by Venetian Jews around the middle of the seventeenth century, is found in the well-known conversionist volume *Derekh emunah. Via della fede mostrata a'gli Ebrei*, by Venetian Jew and neophyte Catholic Giulio Morosini (1612–1687) (Andreatta 2014; Parente 1983). Illustrating the observant Jew's morning rituals, with which the observant Jew began the day, the author noted four "classes," or turns, of prayer, the first two of which, recited before dawn, involved rituals of devotion, secondary to the obligatory officiation. Those in the first class, described as "highly devout," carry out a ritual corresponding to the *tikkun chatzot* (although the name is not used); those in the second, who gather to recite the *selichot* and *widduyim* and whom the author defines as "less devout," are the *Shomerim la-boqer*:

> Before the time of the oration that is obligatory for all, the Synagogue opens for those who want to appear more devout, and these can be distinguished in multiple classes. The first is of the highly devout, the other of the less devout. Those of the first, who enter the Synagogue one or two hours before dawn, enter in the dark, the only lamp being the תמיד *Tamid*, which is always burning before the Hechal. They sit on the floor barefoot and, with mournful, tearful voices, sing a few verses and songs about the destruction of the Temple and about Jerusalem, which they call קינות *Kinnoth* (lamentations), and are printed in their Offices in the part about the four Fasts [...]
> Then come the devout of the second class, for which there is a company called חברה שומרים לבוקר Chavrà Sciomerìm labbòker (Company of the Morning Sentinels), and maintains a שמש *Sciammàsh*, who is a Servant or Minister, who goes with a hammer or a stick and bangs on the doors, shouting repeatedly שומרים לבוקר שומרים לבוקר Sciomerìm labbòker, Sciomerìm labbòker (Morning Sentinels, Morning Sentinels). And this is from Psalm 130, De profundis, נפשי לאדני משומרים לבוקר: שומרים לבוקר (My soul waits for the Lord more than watchmen wait for the morning, more than watchmen wait for the morning). And those of that Company, who also rise before Dawn, go doing that office of waking, and beating. This same Company maintains, among other things, candles to be lit when those of that Class arrive at the Synagogue for the orations.
> They wait for the wails of those of the first Class to finish, and then with voices quite a bit more cheerful, or less mournful, say a few שליחות [sic] *Selichoth*, which is to say Prayers to obtain forgiveness for their sins, וידוים *Viduim*, which is to say Confessions to God for the same reason [...] (Morosini 1683, 1, pp. 245–46).

As we can infer from Morosini's vivid description, belonging to a confraternity of this type gave its members a context within which to cultivate their religious piety while also ensuring important spiritual benefits, such as, for example, the intercession in prayer. In fact, the member's support and closeness in sickness and mourning were fundamental components of the spiritual brotherhood shared within these groups. And all of the confraternities, just as in the charitable associations and the parallel Christian confraternities, recited prayers for sick and dead members, or dedicated study or prayer sessions to them. Another form of brotherly participation, in this case for a joyful occasion, was the vigil held at members' homes the evening before their son's circumcision (Horowitz 1989[b]). The confraternity also provided an important framework for study and learning: exegetic literature, ethical-devotional works and religious poetry circulated widely in the groups devoted to the study of the Mishnah or Kabbalistic texts as well as in those devoted to prayer. The social aim was also met through the organization of non-religious activities, such as the procession or ritual meal (*seudat mitzvah*) for the anniversary of the confraternity's foundation (Horowitz 2001). Activities of this kind strengthened ties between members of the associations, but also performed a function of public representation within the Community. The role of "cultural agent" that some of these confraternities came to play in the life of their host communities was indeed the reason for the expansion of their field of action into activities that were more artistic and intellectual in nature rather than uniquely charitable or devotional.

In fact, during the period of segregation, study and prayer confraternities were among the main users and patrons of religious music, in particular cantatas and oratorios, compositions meant to be performed in public "for the benefit of the many" on special days in the liturgical calendar or the anniversary of the group's foundation (Adler 1966;

J. Schirman 1979). It was probably for one of the *Shomerim la-boqer* associations of Modena or Venice that the composer Carlo Grossi wrote the *Cantata Ebraïca in dialogo, [per] voce sola e choro*, which was added at the end of Grossi's collection titled *Il divertimento de Grandi*, printed in Venice in 1681. From the Jewish text set to music by Grossi, we can infer that the cantata was commissioned to celebrate the confraternity's annual celebration, which coincided, as for many groups of this kind, with *Hoshana Rabba*, a holiday that marked the end of a long penitential period begun with the month of *Elul* and therefore also known among Italian Jews as "the day of the great seal" (*Yom ha-chotam ha-gadol*). Grossi, who was not a Hebraiser, probably worked on the Hebrew text in collaboration with its author, who, as seems to be the case considering the use in the text of technical expressions typical of the language of the watchers, must have been in some way connected to the commissioning group (I. Adler 1966; Grossi 1965; Pagis 1973). In Casale Monferrato, in the 1730s, the local confraternity dedicated to the ritual of *tikkun chatzot*, which had given itself the name *Zerizim* (the zealous), commissioned the composition of a "cantata–almost-oratorio," titled *Dio, Clemenza e Rigore*. The libretto, written by a local poet who was also probably linked to the confraternity, S.H. Jarach, was adapted to an original score by an anonymous composer, whereas two of the documented overtures were taken from the contemporary Italian repertoire. The cantata, which is one of the most noteworthy products of Italian Jewish musical culture of the period, was performed on the night of *Hoshana Rabba* in 1732 and then again in 1733 (I. Adler 1992).

The space given to poetry in the members' lives was equally notable, for the contribution of the study and prayer confraternities to the community's cultural and intellectual life. Starting in the last decades of the sixteenth century, these groups began to have special hymnals printed, intended to serve as material aid during the members' meetings (Andreatta 2005, 2011; Benayahu 1998[a], 1998[b]). The first confraternities to move in this direction were the ones who observed the dawn vigil. Collections of penitential compositions, adherent to the usage established by each group, started to be gathered for the use of local branches of the watcher associations and to be printed. Between the end of the sixteenth and the beginning of the seventeenth century, around a dozen hymnals were published for the *Shomerim la-boqer* of Venice, Mantua, Modena, and Ancona. Most of these volumes were reprinted, in some cases more than once, and continued to circulate throughout the entire eighteenth century. Some were still in use during the first half of the subsequent century, as we know from notes of ownership in some of the surviving copies. As historical documentation, these hymnals provide extremely useful information for the reconstruction of the *Shomerim la-boqer* confraternities' ritual activity. They also help to shed light on the individuals who supported (and were often the main drivers of) the institution of the ceremonies, as well as on the complex network of relationships that in some cases linked these groups, often in competition with one another to ensure visibility and influence within the community (Benayahu 1971; Rathaus 2001; Tishby 1974). For historians, these compilations are also a fundamental source for reconstructing the development of the dawn vigil's ritual in the various local communities. More generally, they were an important factor in the dissemination of the Kabbalah coming from the Land of Israel and in the popular acceptance of mystical practices and beliefs, a process in which the role of the confraternities of watchers was fundamental.

In addition to their unquestionable documentary value, the hymnals printed for the *Shomerim la-boqer* also offer a privileged window onto the role of modern poetry, both religious and secular, in the members' lives (Andreatta 2005; A.Y. Lattes, Perani 2010–2011;

Pagis 1975). In fact, the first formularies printed for the Venetian watchers, in the 1680s and 90s, already included "old and new" *piyyutim* compositions by classical *paytanim* and medieval Sephardic poets alternated with compositions by contemporary authors, both Italian and tied to the communities of the Land of Israel. The inclusion of modern compositions, especially by Italian, often local, authors, became predominant in the hymnals published starting in the first half of the seventeenth century, confirming that, in the various communities in Central and Northern Italy at the time, the watcher associations provided an important arena for the composition, practice and use of religious – often Kabbalistic – but also occasional poetry. Due to the development of the printing technologies, the confraternities became the chief promoters of modern religious poetry, contributing to the circulation and popularization of compositions by varied contemporary *paytanim* and

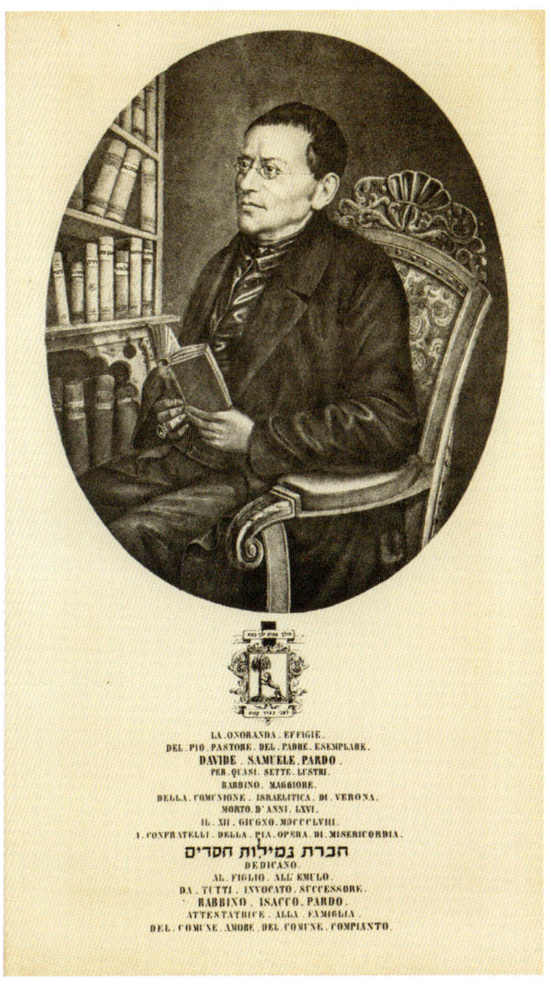

1. *Portrait of Rabbi David Samuel Pardo.*
Private collection (cat. 67)

thus coming to influence not only literary taste but also the religious aesthetic of entire generations (Andreatta 2005).

The cultural promotion role played by the study and prayer confraternities in the ghettos is clearly exemplified by the story of one of the most exquisite and extraordinary texts of Jewish poetry composed in the seventeenth century, the long poem on the fate of the wicked in the Jewish afterlife, *Tofteh Arukh* (Andreatta 2019; Bregman2003, 2012; Hamiel 1949–1950; A.Y. Lattes 2012–2013; Levy 1988, 1989; Meroz 2003; Zacuto 2016). The author of *Tofteh Arukh*, rabbi Moshe Zacuto (circa 1620 – 1697), was not only a talented poet, but also an expert in the Halakha and mysticism. In Mantua, where he lived from 1673 until his death, and where the poem was probably written, Zacuto just "founded" his own confraternity, *Chadashim la-beqarim* (Daily renewal), devoted to the vigil of study and prayer in the hours following midnight, according to the principles of the above-noted *tikkun chatzot* (Simonsohn 1977; Sonne 1936). The members of the confraternity found the text of the poem among Zacuto's papers after his death and, recognizing its clear literary importance and teaching value, started to use it as a text for readings and meditation during the association's meetings, also aided by the Kabbalistic

N. 1 Ancona li 22 56

CONFRATERNITA DI BICHUR KOLIM E. M. L.

OSSIA

SOLLIEVO DEGLI AMMALATI

Si sono ricevuti dal Sig.

Baj. £ 1 · 25 per la corrisposta semestrale

saldo a tutto

Come al Cap. 24 dei nostri Regolamenti.

DicoSc. £ 1 · 25 e Baj.

L' ESATTORE

2. Receipt of the confraternity of Bichur Kolim E.M.L.
Gianfranco Moscati Collection, MEIS (National Museum of Italian Judaism ant the Shoah), Ferrara

inspiration that pervaded the poem. In 1715, the members of the confraternity had *Tofteh Arukh* printed in Venice, accompanied by explanatory notes written by rabbi Aviad Sar Shalom Basilea (circa 1680 – 1749), one of the leaders of the confraternity and one of Zacuto's followers. As stated by Basilea in his introduction to the poem, the members of the confraternity "decided to print the work together with explanation of all of its more difficult terms, so that even younger people and the less educated could read it easily" (Zacuto 1715, c. 2r).

Printed in a portable octavo edition that could even be used by readers less well informed about Kabbalistic studies, *Tofteh Arukh* left the *bet midrash* that once belonged to Zacuto and where the members of the confraternity still gathered, crossing the borders of the Jewish quarter and Mantua, to arrive in Ferrara. There, in 1720, members of a *Shomerim la-boqer* group decided to use the poem for an evocative penitential ritual open to the entire local community. In the summer of that year, every single night during the three weeks between the two holidays on 7 *Tammuz* and 9 *Av*, both devoted to commemorating the destruction of the Temple of Jerusalem, the members of the confraternity held public readings of the poem, alternating portions of the text with singing hymns, presumably *qinot* and *selichot*, with musical accompaniment. According to the organiser of the ceremonies, confraternity member Yaakov Daniel Olmo (circa 1690 – 1757), it would seem that the public poured in and numerous people from the community, including non-members of the confraternity, attended more than once (Zacuto 1744). The success of Zacuto's work and the respect that people held for him were probably what motivated Olmo to compose a sequel not long after, a poem similar in structure and spirit but devoted to the rewards enjoyed by the righteous in Heaven, titled *Eden Arukh*. Published 1744 by the confraternity of Ferrarese watchers, along with a reprint of *Tofteh Arukh*, the two poems thus offered Italian Jews, who were familiar with Dante's *Divine Comedy*, a similar work, but entirely rooted in the Jewish tradition. A work that stands as further confirmation of the study and prayer confraternities' capacity to interpret the deepest cultural needs of its own community and, at the same time, mediate between the Jewish society inside the ghetto and the Christian one outside.

Italy without a Ghetto: The Jewish Community of Livorno

Francesca Bregoli

Introduction

The establishment of the thriving *nazione ebrea* (Jewish nation) of Livorno, the largest and most privileged community on Italian soil in the seventeenth and eighteenth centuries, was a specifically Tuscan instance of a more global early modern phenomenon. Between 1530 and 1650, Jews of Iberian descent and *conversos* (the descendants of Iberian, especially Portuguese, Jews who had been baptized, whether forcibly or willingly) settled in port cities such as Amsterdam, Hamburg, Livorno, London, Recife, and New Amsterdam. They were attracted by mercantilist authorities seeking to control foreign trade, who prized Sephardic Jews and *conversos* as accomplished merchants able to tap into wide-ranging trading networks (Israel 1998). Within just over a century, this process brought about the establishment of Sephardic Jews in most of Western Europe, as well as their arrival in the New World.

Compared to other Sephardic settlements, though, Livorno was unique in several ways. Unlike the Amsterdam and London communities, the *nazione ebrea*'s growth was due to a government edict; for this reason, its administration and internal affairs would be closely monitored and shaped by Tuscan policies. Livornese Jews' history was further entangled with the development of the early modern Tuscan state because they came to populate a previously languishing port-city, whose redesign was to serve as a symbol of the power and aspirations of the Medici house. As opposed to the Protestant ports that received Sephardic Jews in the rest of Western Europe, finally, the Jews of Livorno settled in a deeply Catholic environment in Counter-Reformation Tuscany. Post-Tridentine religiosity could not but affect their daily existence, despite the regime of freedoms they enjoyed.

Thanks to the liberties granted by the Tuscan authorities, the *nazione ebrea* became the second largest community in Western Europe after Amsterdam by 1750, numbering approximately 4300 souls by the 1780s. The density of Livorno's Jewish population was remarkable – 9–12% of the entire population – a percentage unequaled in any other early modern urban center in western Europe. And yet, despite the economic success of its elite, its high level of acculturation, and close daily interactions with non-Jews, Livornese Jewry remained a partially discriminated group well into the nineteenth century (Bregoli 2014; Ferrara degli Uberti 2007). In the following pages we will examine the complex uniqueness of Livorno's enclave in the seventeenth and eighteenth centuries, along with some of the challenges it faced.

The Livornina

The privileges enjoyed by Livornese Jews were extraordinary. These freedoms resulted from the transformations of early modern Tuscany and the growth of its Mediterranean commerce. In 1551, Cosimo I de' Medici, wishing to boost trade with the Ottoman Levant, invited "Turkish Jews" to move to Florence. The Florentine proposal led to a small settlement of Sephardic merchants, who maintained slightly privileged status even after the creation of the city's ghetto in 1571 (Siegmund 2006). Florence would never become an important center of Sephardic life, though. It was first Pisa, and more spectacularly Livorno from the early seventeenth century on, that attracted substantial groups of Jewish traders, thanks to privileges issued by Ferdinand I in 1591.

As other states during the age of mercantilism, Tuscany recognized Sephardic networks' global reach, ranging from the Ottoman Empire to North Africa and from Northern Europe to the colonial world. The Medici promoted the establishment of Jewish communities in Pisa and Livorno as an integral part of the state's strategy of economic expansion, vying with other princes to entice Sephardic Jews and *conversos* with economic and religious freedoms (Ravid 1991). The founding document of the relationship between Livornese Jewry and Tuscany was the charter promulgated by Ferdinand I in 1591, granting extensive concessions to foreign merchants (Cooperman 1976; R. Toaff 1990). The edict, known as *Livornina* after it was reissued with some changes in 1593, was routinely confirmed, retaining its validity almost uninterruptedly until 1861 (Ferrara degli Uberti 2007). Formally directed to "merchants of any nation, Levantine, Ponentine, Spanish, Portuguese, Greek, German and Italian, Jewish, Turkish, Moorish, Armenian, Persian and others," it intended to attract primarily *conversos* and Sephardic Jews. At a time of great political uncertainty and religious unrest, the *Livornina* ensured security for these populations, offered generous economic and fiscal incentives, and set the foundations for broad communal autonomy.

One of the first clauses of the edict (iii) protected from the Holy Office former *conversos* who had returned to Judaism, at a time when the Roman and Venetian Inquisitions actively pursued judaizers. Jewish children under the age of 13 were safeguarded from baptism by zealous Christian servants and wet-nurses (xxvi). Jews were exempted from wearing humiliating distinguishing signs (xxix). The *Livornina* provided Jewish merchants with economic enticements and gave them the same freedoms as Christian traders, including the ability to pursue whatever profession they chose, except for *stracceria*, the retail of second-hand clothes (vii, xxix). Setting the *nazione ebrea* further apart from older Italian communities, the Jewish lay leaders (*massari*) were granted significant jurisdictional autonomy, with the power to settle civil disputes and to adjudicate lower level criminal charges involving Jews (xxv) (sentences issued by the *massari* could still be appealed before the municipal court of Livorno, which oversaw all cases involving Jews and non-Jews). The *massari* had the additional prerogative to impart the status of Tuscan subjects on individuals who legally settled in Pisa and Livorno (xxxi).

Thanks to the *Livornina*, Jews were never confined to a ghetto in Pisa and Livorno. Even though the physical barrier of the ghetto did not actually prevent Jews and non-Jews from mingling in other Italian cities, in Livorno it was easier for Jews and gentiles to socialize and work together, entertain intellectual discussions, or even participate together in criminal activities. It should be emphasized that this sort of socializing did not break down the entrenched socio-cultural structures that kept different ethno-religious groups separate in early modernity; distinct communal boundaries continued to define opportunities and assumptions about the world that Jews and non-Jews lived in, at least until the late eighteenth century.

Jewish space

A small Levantine community already existed in Pisa by 1591, most likely on the basis of the Florentine charter of 1551. Its members increased after the promulgation of the *Livornina*, but the importance and numbers of the Pisa community declined in the seventeenth century. The community in nearby Livorno, on the contrary, experienced a steady growth, from 134 souls in 1601 to around 1250 in 1645, thanks to the port's flourishing economy (Filippini 1997). Initially dependent on the Pisan Jewish leadership, Livorno's *nazione ebrea* established its own autonomous government in 1597. Relationships between the two groups remained tight. Soon, however, Livornese Jewry eclipsed its sister community.

Among the privileges offered by the *Livornina* was the permission to buy real estate (xxix). Although most members of the Livornese *nazione ebrea* resided within a small quarter with four- and five-story buildings located behind the cathedral – away from *piazza Grande* and the city's main street, *via Ferdinanda* – exponents of the Jewish elite purchased properties in more central and fashionable areas, as well as villas and vineyards in the countryside surrounding the port. Jewish landlords rented out apartments to Christian tenants, and *viceversa*. It was not unusual for Jews and Christians to live in the same building, despite the authorities' anxieties about social and physical interactions in domestic spaces (Frattarelli Fischer 2008).

At the center of the Jewish neighborhood was a magnificent synagogue, visited by Christian rulers on their official sojourns in the city (along with the flourishing, Jewish-owned coral factories in the port), as a way to demonstrate their favor. Livorno's synagogue stood as an architectural monument to the community's prosperity and prerogatives, a public display of the *nazione ebrea*'s unity, despite its increasing sub-ethnic diversity. First established in a private home in 1595, the synagogue was replaced with a new building in 1607 and completely remodeled in 1642 along the lines of the monumental Amsterdam synagogue. The building underwent further restorations and embellishments in the eighteenth century. These included the 1742 addition of a lavish marble Torah ark created by Isidoro Baratta of Carrara (1670–1747), who also designed the altar of Livorno's cathedral. In 1745, a new *tevah* (pulpit) designed by David Nunes was inaugurated. Severely damaged during World War II, it was only amidst great controversies that the Livornese Jewish community decided to tear the ancient synagogue down and replace it with a modern building in 1962 (A. Toaff 1955, 1962[b]; Karwacka Codini and Sbrilli 1995).

Society and culture

Jewish merchants were crucial in ensuring Livorno's success, just as the Medici had hoped. By the end of the Thirty Years War (1618–1648), the port had emerged as the chief Dutch and English hub in the Mediterranean and a key center for the distribution of wares from Northern Europe and the American colonies to the Maghreb and the Ottoman Empire, and from the Levant to Amsterdam or London. Sephardic merchants acted as the chief agents for the resale of those goods in North Africa and the Levant (Cassandro 1983; Israel 1998). In the eighteenth century, despite the increasing prominence of Atlantic trade, Livorno did not lose its importance. A high percentage of Dutch and English Mediterranean commerce continued to pass through it, and Livornese Jewish firms dominated the trade of Tyrrhenian coral and Indian diamonds via networks that linked them with the Ottoman Empire, Portugal, and India (Trivellato 2009).

Although a small but visible group of affluent international merchants came to represent the commercial success of the entire community, most Livornese Jews were earning

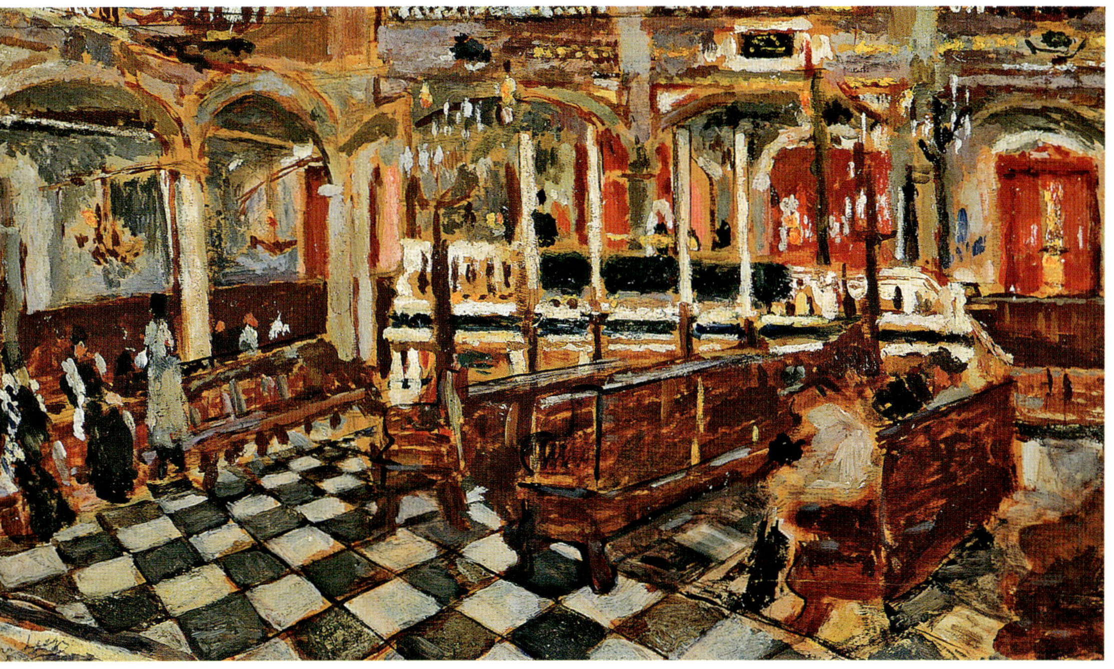

1. Ulvi Liegi, *Interior of the Synagogue in Livorno*.
Museo Civico "Giovanni Fattori," Livorno (cat. 35)

low wages or living in poverty. At the beginning of the nineteenth century, about 42% of the Jewish population worked in professions related to international and local trade. This percentage included not only merchants, cashiers, financial intermediaries, and interpreters, but also a large working class made up of storage, packing, and shipping professionals, and porters. The same data show that about 23% of Jews were petty merchants, grocers, tailors, printers, or second-hand clothes retailers. Another 6% served as rabbis, preachers, teachers, and health care professionals, receiving a salary from the community (Filippini 1997).

As in other sizable Jewish centers, benevolent societies provided Livornese Jews with essential services (R. Toaff 1990). The confraternities known as *Baale teshuvah* ("penitents") and *Malbish arumim* ("clothing the naked") took care of burial needs and distributed clothes and shoes to the poor, respectively. The aim of the *Hebra de Cazar Orfas e Donzelas*, also known as *Mohar ha-betulot* ("dowry for the maidens"), was to provide a dowry for needy girls of marriageable age. Livorno was also a lively center of talmudic and Kabbalistic studies. The community ran a Hebrew school (*Talmud Torah*), which all boys up to 14 were required to attend. Along with it, private studies and oratories formed the backbone of the *nazione ebrea*'s religious life. Yeshivot supported by wealthy patrons often hired prominent foreign rabbis visiting Livorno. One of them was the anti-Sabbatean polemicist Jacob Sasportas (circa 1610–1698) from Oran, who remained in town from 1678 to 1681. Despite the authority he garnered, his sojourn was notoriously marred by harsh disagreements with the *massari* over judicial matters, a symptom of deeper divergences over claims to authority in the Sephardic world (Dweck 2019).

The last decades of the seventeenth and early decades of the eighteenth century represent a time of crisis in Judaism; the *nazione ebrea* was not spared the turmoil. In 1665, when Ottoman Kabbalist Shabbetay Zevi declared himself the messiah, a large portion of Livorno Jewry embraced his message. In time, the port became a center for both Sabbatean teaching and anti-Sabbatean polemics. After Zevi's apostasy to Islam in the fall of 1666, Jewish communities faced deep disappointment and embarrassment. Still, some followers of the failed messiah found refuge in Livorno, from which they spread their ideas to other believers (Scholem 1973). The development of anti-Sabbatean polemics would shape Jewish theology in the following decades, as exemplified not just by the aforementioned Sasportas but also by anti-Sabbatean Kabbalist Joseph Ergas (1685–1730), scion of a prominent Livornese merchant family (Me. Friedman 1966). Among his disciples was Malachi ha-Cohen (1700–1771), prolific author of numerous halakhic opinions and a Kabbalist in his own right (A. Lattes, Toaff 1909).

Between Tuscany and the Sephardic diaspora

Unlike the rest of Tuscany, Livorno's population was mostly made up of immigrants. Initially, the bulk comprised petty merchants and craftsmen from central Italy and the Tyrrhenian basin. When the port's activity took off in the early seventeenth century, international traders from the Levant and north-west Europe increasingly settled in the city, contributing to its diverse character (Fasano Guarini 1978). The foreign groups handling international and internal commerce, including Greek, French, Flemish, British, and Armenian traders, were known as *nazioni* (lit. "nations," a term used to refer to colonies of international merchants). Alongside yet separate from them was the *nazione ebrea*, the largest minority in town.

By the early nineteenth century waves of Jewish emigration to North Africa and the Levant, and of immigration by North African and Italian Jews, had transformed the originally Iberian and Levantine community. An Italian majority (38% of the families) surpassed the Iberian sub-group (35%). The considerable North African presence (11%) was unique in Italy. The remaining 16% was made up of Ashkenazim and other Jews of unidentified descent (Filippini 1998, vol. 1; R. Toaff 1990). The Sephardic enclave retained political preeminence for a long time even after Italian Jews were formally admitted to communal offices (1715), as well as firm control over synagogue rituals and over the languages of preaching, teaching, and legislation (only in 1787 did the Tuscan state order that the records and pronouncements of the Jewish court be kept in Italian). Abraham Isaac Castelli (1726–1789) is emblematic of the prestige that Spanish held in the religious sphere even in the late eighteenth century. This Italian rabbi, originally from Ancona, rose to fame for his Spanish sermons. Still, he not only spoke Italian and Spanish, but also read French, Latin, and Arabic. A pious Jew, he was known as an admirer of Voltaire and the French *philosophes* (Gori 2006; A. Toaff 1937).

The persistence of Iberian languages in communal documents and devotional literature constituted only one side of the multifaceted culture of Livornese Jews. Hebrew was the language of synagogue ritual and legal erudition, mastered by rabbis and cantors

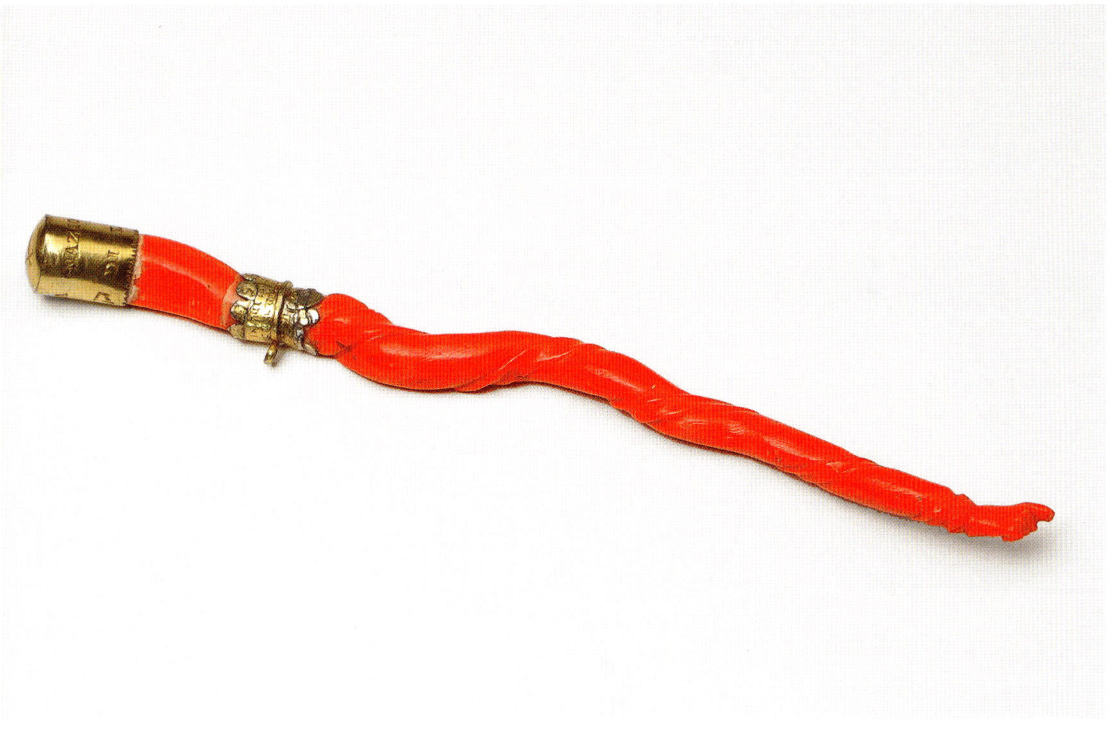

2. *Yad*. Comunità Ebraica di Livorno, Museo Ebraico, Livorno (cat. 33)

but less common among the merchants and the masses. Jews spoke the vernacular on a daily basis with non-Jews. The presence of Italian literary and artistic influences strongly increased from the 1730s, as demonstrated by synagogue epitaphs, ephemeral poems, and eulogies, while prosperous Jews increasingly embraced and consumed the latest Italian, rather than Iberian, cultural fashions (A. Toaff 1933, 1955, 1962a).

Even as the community became gradually "Tuscan," its members maintained vibrant avenues of exchange with other Sephardic centers. Thanks to its location, trans-Mediterranean networks connected the *nazione ebrea* with both the Western and the Eastern Sephardic worlds. The relations between Livornese Jews and Amsterdam, as with Jewish centers in Tunis, Algiers, Smyrna, or Salonika, were not purely commercial. These hubs were linked through systems of cultural exchange, embodied in the flow of people – itinerant rabbis, educators, and fund-raisers for Jewish settlements and academies in Palestine – and of ideas, in the form of correspondence and printed matter (Lehmann 2014; Yaari 1950).

Livornese scholars exemplify the peripatetic life that many Sephardim led. The philosopher and polemicist David Nieto (1654–1728), originally from Venice, rose to fame as a rabbi and physician in Livorno; in 1701 he left to become *chakham* of London's Spanish and Portuguese community. Raphael Meldola (1685–1748), author of the legal collection *Mayim Rabim* (Amsterdam, 1737), moved from Livorno, to Pisa, to Bayonne, and finally back to his home town. Another itinerant rabbi who elected Livorno as his home was Hayim Joseph David Azulai (1724–1806) from Jerusalem, as famous for his fund-raising travels in the diaspora as for his bibliophile interests (Benayahu 1959).

Livornese Jewry's cultural impact in the Mediterranean should also be emphasized. From 1740 on, when Abraham Meldola (a son of rabbi Raphael) established a Hebrew press in Livorno, the port served as one of the main hubs for the publication and distribution of halakhic writings by Levantine and Maghrebi scholars (between 1650 and 1657, Yedidiah Gabbay had operated another Hebrew press in Livorno, but his enterprise faced many obstacles and was short-lived). The flourishing of Livornese Hebrew printing, along with the circulation of customers, editors, and booksellers between Livorno, North Africa, and the Ottoman Empire, facilitated the creation of a cultural bridge between the *nazione ebrea* and other Sephardic communities all the way to the early twentieth century (Boulouque 2018; Bregoli 2007–2008, 2014).

Tensions and paradoxes

The tension between integration and separation, toleration and prejudice was at the core of early modern Livornese Jewish life. Livorno offered unprecedented opportunities for religious and ethnic minorities in Catholic Europe. Still, despite its reputation as a beacon of toleration, it remained a town with a devout Catholic population. Livorno's conservative Christian elite was known to look down on the Jews, and its prejudice could rub off on the lower classes. In a few occasions, hostilities against the Jewish enclave erupted during Christian festivals or in moments of economic or political crisis, with angry mobs attacking the Jewish neighborhood in 1722, 1751, 1790, and again in 1800.

Despite these serious episodes, Livornese Jews generally found that the Tuscan administration was quick to safeguard their legal prerogatives and to defend their lives and homes, according to the framework established by the *Livornina*. At the same time, the privilege-driven, corporatist *Livornina* worked against the best interests of the community when new ideas of toleration and inclusion started circulating in Europe in the 1770s and 1780s. Toward the end of the eighteenth century, members of the Livornese Jewish elite began to demand increased political participation, with mixed success. Despite the favorable disposition of the enlightened Peter Leopold, the Christian conservative patriciate maneuvered to stop a proposal that would have granted each Jewish proprietor access to active citizenship (Gavi 1995; Mangio 1995; Mascilli Migliorini 1997). Instead, a fixed seat of the municipal council was set aside for the inclusion of a single Jewish representative, on behalf of the entire *nazione*. This ruling was based on the idea that Livornese Jewry was a corporate entity, whose members did not deserve rights as individuals, but rather a group privilege as Jews – an idea that had been a cornerstone of Jewish success in the early modern period, but was obsolete in an age of reforms (Bregoli 2014).

In the sixteenth century, thanks to their economic utility Livorno Jews had gained freedoms that Jews elsewhere did not possess. When the European debates over Jewish emancipation emerged in the 1780s, the *nazione ebrea* was still regarded as essential for Tuscan economic development, and thus meritorious, unlike the allegedly unproductive Ashkenazic Jews of France and Prussia. The local Christian majority, however, felt threatened by the *nazione ebrea*'s supposed wealth and power, leading to reactionary responses. The *Livornina* itself paradoxically tied the *nazione ebrea* to outmoded understandings of corporate privileges and turned into a conservative instrument in the hands of both the Jewish oligarchy and the Tuscan authorities. At the onset of "modernity," this factor prevented the full application of reforming and equalizing policies. It was only in 1861, when Tuscany was formally annexed to the Kingdom of Italy, that Livornese Jews were granted full civil emancipation.

Marrano and Sephardic Culture in the Early Modern Period: The Case of Italy

Pier Cesare Ioly Zorattini

The Sephardic and Marrano diasporas in Europe and the Mediterranean area originated in the forced conversion to Christianity in Spain in 1492 and then in Portugal, first in 1497 and again in 1536 with the institution of the State Inquisition on the Spanish model.

The Sephardim were the first to arrive in Italy, initially from Spain and then from the Spanish colonies (Sicily, Sardinia, southern Italy): Spanish-speaking, Spanish-rite Jews whose destinations were papal Rome and Este Ferrara, with quite large numbers heading to the first (Minervini 1994, pp. 133–192, 135–140) and twenty-one families coming from Genoa to the second, thanks to a privilege granted by Ercole I d'Este on February 1, 1493 (Leoni 2000, p. 278; Leoni 2011, I, pp. 25–26). These cities were a magnet for the Marranos, Iberian Jews converted by force, who began to arrive in Venice at the end of the fifteenth century as demonstrated by the edict of expulsion of 1497, which was then reiterated in the same form in 1550 (Kaufmann 1900).

The Sephardim were able to reconstruct a community structure following their ancestral cultural tradition, complete with their own synagogues, schools and institutions, inserting themselves (albeit with some difficulty) alongside the Italian and German Jews. This was not the case for the Marranos and their descendants, who were forbidden access to the texts of the Jewish tradition. The new generations were formally brought up as Christians but orally educated in Judaism in secret, in domestic rites passed down by memory. For them, the language of the religion, Hebrew, was irremediably lost.

The Marranos, divided between irreconcilable worlds, found themselves in situations that forced dramatic choices. A family in some ways emblematic of Marranism (Stuczynski 2010) was that of Gaspar Ribiera, a Marrano condemned for Judaising by the Holy Office of Venice, the life and silences of whom seem to betray a form of indifference or scepticism with respect to both religions. His children followed opposite paths, with Violante adhering fully to Christianity and marrying a noblewoman from Vicenza and João wanting to marry a Jewish woman from the Ghetto (Ioly Zorattini 1987).

Around the first half of the sixteenth century, an increasing number of Marranos chose to return to Judaism and with this came the problem of their re-education. One part of the process was the practice of *milah*, or circumcision of adult males. Few traces remain, but we do know of the clandestine activity in Ferrara of the silversmith Gabriel Henriques, *alias* Yosef Saralvo, extradited to Rome with four other Marranos in 1581 and condemned to death there in the *auto da fè* of February 19, 1583 (Leoni 1991). The second issue concerned the need to obtain the texts necessary for religious instruction for people who did not know the holy language, Hebrew. This opened up a new phase in the production of books for Jews: printing traditional books in vernacular languages. The first to respond to this need was Ferrara, which became the capital of Marrano publishing in the span of just a few years, between 1552 and 1559. Around twenty-one works in Hebrew and eleven in Spanish or Portuguese were published there (Leoni 2011, I, pp. 423–461; Tamani 2003). The most significant example was the translation of the Hebrew Bible into Spanish: the *Biblia de Ferrara* (Leoni 2011, I, pp. 434–441), which appeared in 1553 in an edition dedicated to the duke Ercole II by Jerónimo de Vargas and Duarte Pinel, and in 1555 in an edition dedicated by Yomtob Atias (father of Jerónimo de Vargas) and Abraham Usque to Doña Gracia Naci, patron of the work, the *Señora* who had chosen to openly return to her ancestral religion in Constantinople and an active supporter of the Marrano diaspora (Ioly Zorattini 2013).

The book was therefore the most important intermediary in the development of the Marranos into new Sephardic Jews. At the end of the century, Venice was also the site of flourishing publishing activity addressed to the Marranos. By that point, with the charter of 1589, they could enter the ghetto so long as they presented themselves as Jews, like Isaac *alias* Fernando Cardoso who published his *Philosophia libera* (1673) there, a work written in the ghetto of Verona where he died in 1683 (Yerushalmi 1971). His other work, an argument against Christianity titled *Las excelencias de los Hebreos* (1679), was instead published in Amsterdam. Other liturgical works dedicated to the new Sephardim included the *Haggadah of Pesach*, with a Ladino translation in Hebrew characters printed in 1663 by Girolamo Bragadin for Lorenzo Pradotto (Tamani 2005, p. 111, no. 258). Finally, also in the early eighteenth century, the edition of the *Pirkei Avot* published by the Stamparia Bragadina (1706), in which the Hebrew text alternates with the Spanish translation (*Pirkei Avot* 1706).

Within one century, the Marrano diaspora in Italy had thus given rise to the new Sephardic nation, which developed autonomously alongside the other communities. In Ferrara, however, annexation to the Church State marked its irreversible decline: with the institution of the ghetto in 1620, only one Sephardic synagogue remained (Ioly Zorattini 2012). In Venice, the presence of this wealthy, dynamic group of international merchants fundamentally changed the profile of the ghetto, which was by that point no longer solely the seat of bankers and "*strazzaroli*" (drapers), as attested by travellers passing through Venice struck by the elegance and magnificence of the female Sephardim during religious ceremonies (Coryat 1611). In the Old Ghetto, the elegant, sumptuous Spanish synagogue, rebuilt by Longhena, represented the power and prestige of the Ponentine Nation, elements also reflected in the seventeenth- and eighteenth-century tombs of Portuguese Jews in the *Bet ha-Chaim* of the Lido, which can be to some degree compared to those of the Ouderkerk aan de Amstel, the Sephardic cemetery in Amsterdam (A. Luzzatto 2000). Venice became the model for the large community in Amsterdam, and "Venice" was chosen as the name for the Sephardic quarter in Livorno.

Livorno is a case unto itself. In 1556, the tragedy in Ancona (Ioly Zorattini 2001–2002) opened up new opportunities in Tuscany. In Ancona, in fact, the election of Paul IV had radically changed the situation of the settlement of the *Cristãos Novos*, which is to say the Portuguese Jews who openly practiced Judaism, a settlement that had been possible to build thanks to the privileges granted by Paul III in 1547 and 1549, in particular with the Papal Brief of February 21, 1547, confirmed by Julius III in 1552. With the rise of Paul IV, the Portuguese were no longer considered Jews, but rather apostate Christians and that is why they were tried between July and August 1555. The next year, between April and June, the accused who repented were condemned to the oars on the papal galleys, whereas the unrepentant were condemned to death. According to the sources, twenty-three or twenty-six people went to the stakes overall, to which we need to add the suicide of David Romero. This was unquestionably the most terrible episode of the Roman Inquisition's persecution of the Marranos in the early modern period (Ioly Zorattini 2010, vol. II, p. 526).

Cosimo I de' Medici opened the doors of the grand duchy to these exiles, but it was Ferdinando I who offered, through privileges promulgated between 1591 and 1593 (the "*Livornine*"), merchants from every "nation" the ports of Pisa and Livorno, cities without ghettos. The Sephardic Nation of Livorno was founded on July 10, 1599 and enjoyed considerable demographic growth during the early modern period, increasing from about 100 members in the early seventeenth century to 4,697 in 1806 (R. Toaff 1990, pp. 120, 125).

Livorno became the main centre in Italy for the tobacco and sugar trades and was the only city where a Jew, Iedidia Salomon Gabbai, could run the Jewish printery "*Kaf Nachat*," which published eight books in Hebrew between 1650 and 1657 (Sonnino 1912; Ioly Zorattini 2001). During the seventeenth century, the Livorno community was in profitable contact with Sephardic circles in Amsterdam: the *Academia de los Sitibundos*, founded in Livorno in 1676 and the "first Sephardic academy in the west," which became the model for the more famous academies in Amsterdam, including the *Academia de los Floridos*, founded in 1685 and to which Yosef Penso de Vega (1650–1692) made a critical contribution (Nider 2010, p. 171; Pancorbo 2019).

Livorno preserved Sephardic cultural continuity more than any other Italian community, besides the ritual that has been maintained in Venice up to the present time. At the end of the eighteenth century, Renzo Toaff wrote: "Although there was not much good will between Sephardim and Italians, the Nation was and remained Sephardic. Like it or not, all Sephardim" (R. Toaff 1990, p. 417). Times changed, however, and the Iberian languages were gradually replaced with Italian (Aprile 2012; Massariello Merzagora 1977, pp. 54–61; Minervini 1994, pp. 164–180; Sephiha 1984): in 1787, the grand duke Pietro Leopoldo ended the practice of writing the sentences of the court of the *massari* in Portuguese and, in 1788, the wedding of Salomone Michell and Ester Rodrigues Mercado was celebrated with a collection of epithalamia in Hebrew and Italian (Minervini 1994, p. 169).

Overall, we can conclude that Marranism played a determinant role in forging the Sephardic identity of the New Jews, although in different measure depending on the situation of the settlements in the Italian States of *ancien régime*. The Sephardic legacy in Italy can be perceived most of all in the permanence of the synagogal cult – Spanish, Sephardic and Levantine – that is still practiced in some synagogues, Ancona, Florence, Siena, Genoa, Livorno, Milan, Naples, Rome, Trieste (on weekdays) and, in the typologies of the Sephardic synagogues (including ritual art objects) and in the Sephardic *matzevot* of a few Italian Jewish cemeteries (for example, Ancona, Livorno, Pisa and Venice). Today, however, the sole Italian community to have maintained an authentically Sephardic profile is the Jewish Community of Livorno.

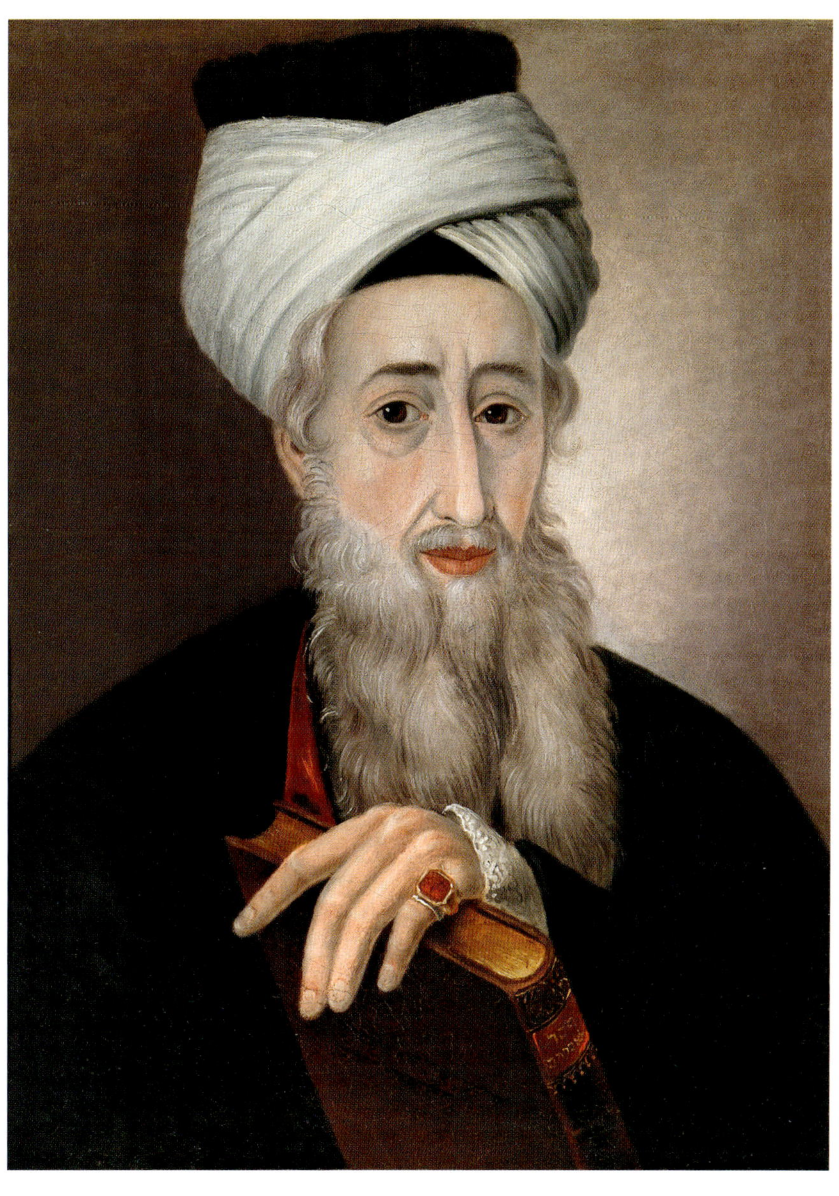

1. *Portrait of Rabbi Abraham Eliezer ha-Levi.*
Alberto Di Castro Collection, Rome (cat. 32)

Schools of Thought in Jewish Italy from the Fifteenth to the Eighteenth Centuries

Alessandro Guetta

In a famous page from his defense of the Jews of Venice, published in 1638, rabbi Simone Luzzatto expressed his not altogether flattering opinions of his coreligionist. Writing in Italian for a Christian audience and for an apologetic purpose – the essay was intended to help convince the authorities of *La Serenissima* not to expel the Jews from the city (Ravid 1978) – Luzzatto described the Jews of Venice as people who had little time for world events, focusing instead on their personal interests, and who were generally ignorant of texts, languages and doctrines other than their own. Those Jews had no lofty ambitions and, indeed, even their mistakes were the result of their narrow-mindedness.

But Luzzatto states that they were also capable of maintaining their faith in a more than a thousand year old religious tradition. They were not inclined to indulge in the sins of the flesh, and they demonstrated empathy and charity towards other Jews, even from far-off regions, as well as respect for those who belonged to another religion. They compensated for their lack of familiarity with high culture (Luzzatto was in all likelihood thinking of both the humanities and the sciences) through their mastery of the Bible and its exegesis – in Hebrew, of course.

The Venetian rabbi then describes the culture of the Jews of the past and of the present, who cultivated the *discipline humane* to the extent that these subjects would enable them to continue studying their sacred texts. Luzzatto then goes on to classify three categories of scholars: the Talmudist rabbis, the theologians (or philosophers) and the Kabbalists. Luzzatto's short but very dense chapter presents the main doctrines of the three groups, doing so with such conceptual and historical precision as to allow us to posit that their author was probably the first modern historian of Judaism and of Jewish thought.

Luzzatto succeeded in observing Jewish culture in the most objective way possible, showcasing its most prestigious authors but also taking the time to cast the spotlight on the lives of more unpresuming people, who had only ever heard of Aristotle but never read him, yet could recite from memory passages from the Bible, along with certain rabbinical formulations. In this essay, we shall endeavor to examine briefly a number of aspects of these two levels, taking in a few major Italian Jewish intellectuals who wrote and taught between the fifteenth and the eighteenth centuries, as well as teachers who have remained outside the main historical narrative but who provide evidence for what would have been the commonplace attitude towards intellectual matters.

But is it really possible to talk about schools, in a group that at no time exceeded one percent of the total population of the peninsula (amounting, therefore, to no more than 30,000 people), and which was for the most part dispersed right across the country, in large and small towns? The answer must be in the affirmative, albeit that the number of students attending the classes of even of the most celebrated teachers will have been very limited; in many cases, we should really be thinking in terms of individual tuition, with a teacher-to-student ratio of one-to-one, or one-to-two, as was often the case of tutors called upon to educate children from wealthy families. In this sense, school was ubiquitous, and in a number of (rare) cases it implied high level and authoritative teaching of original doctrines.

The poet and philosopher Moshe ben Yitzhaq (called Moisè di Gaio in Italian) from Rieti (1388 – before 1466), who was probably the most interesting author of the first half of the fifteenth century, is described in a number of manuscripts as "the great oak," a synonym for "great master." He taught in the *yeshivot* or religious schools in the Umbria and Lazio regions. Indeed, his most ambitious work, *Miqdash Meat* (Small Sanctuary), a Hebrew *terza rima* poem with 5,000 lines, was conceived to allow students to learn the doctrines of the sacred and profane sciences in verse, and thus to retain them more easily:

I set myself a very high purpose:
to put the ancient doctrines of the wise men
In verses that no one imagined.

May they please our God
and the youngsters of my people who search
for beauty and listen to my voice.

The various writings of Moses of Rieti embody an Aristotelianism shot through with Neoplatonic elements, already open to the Kabbalah. But over and above their highly wrought poetic qualities, their originality lies in the recurring idea of the dramatic loss of truth and of the recourse to poetic/philosophical/prophetic momentum to recover that truth, albeit only partially and fleetingly. This attitude can be traced back to the school – in truth, in this case we should use a capital "S," since we are referring to a hothouse in which cohesive new knowledge was developed – of Yehudah Romano, the important fourteenth-century philosopher who had at least two distinguished disciples, the poet Immanuel Romano and Yaaqov ben Shabbetai. We know very little about these philosophical circles, which considered Maimonides to be their fundamental source of inspiration. We do know that they were open to the contributions of Christian scholasticism and that they read and commented upon Dante. We can presume that the influence of Yehudah Romano was significant and enduring, given that an author such as Rieti returned to his themes one hundred years on.

A generation after Rieti, in the second half of the fifteenth century, and in various regions (certain cities of northern Italy, in addition to Naples), one very renowned scholar was Yehudah ben Yehiel, better known as Messer Leon: "Messer" (Sir) because he received the honorific title of "Doctor" from the Emperor Frederick III, while Leon is the common Italian version of the name Yehudah. Yehudah ben Yehiel, "Messer Leon," is the purest – and most prestigious – example of the transposition into the Hebrew orbit of the teachings of the universities. He wrote treatises and commentaries in Hebrew on the Liberal Arts of the *trivium* and the *quadrivium*, returning at the same time to the Arabic-Jewish tradition and the Greco-Roman tradition. One of his most brilliant and original works – and the only one that was printed during the author's life, in 1475 – was the *Nofeth tzufim* (known in English as *The Book of the Honeycomb's Flow*), in which Roman rhetoric, a discipline that was subject to a great deal of renewed interest in that period, was applied to Hebrew. To put it another way: Hebrew and its original text, the Bible, were viewed not simply as the illustration but also as the (albeit implicit) source of rhetoric, which the Jews had forgotten over the course of the centuries in their situation of material and intellectual decadence, and which the Romans had developed following various transmissions from one people to another. For Yehuda ben Yehiel, studying the "foreign science" was, then, a necessary step in the reappropriation of original Jewish knowledge.

If the value of a teacher is judged by that of his or her students, Yehudah ben Yehiel must have been an excellent teacher. At least three leading lights of Jewish culture in the late-fifteenth and early sixteenth centuries studied under him: his son David ben Messer Leon, Yohanan Alemanno and, very probably, Avraham De Balmes. Although they specialised in different disciplines, all three drifted away from the teachings of their mentor in that they enthusiastically embraced the Kabbalistic doctrines of which Yehudah, as a pure rationalist philosopher, had remained suspicious. In David, this shift in perspective was particularly marked and perhaps painful, since it involved breaking away from his father's teachings (Tirosh-Rothschild 1991). As an aside, direct teaching from father to son should be highlighted as one of the modes of the transmission of knowledge in Jewish circles; Moses of Rieti chose as his travelling companion on his literary voyage into the Jewish paradise none other than his own father and teacher. From then on, the Kabbalah – a revealed, non-rational doctrine – would be an established part of the middle- and high-brow culture of the Italian Jews, and would remain so perhaps up until the nineteenth century, contributing to the restructuring of this culture following the gradual, inexorable decline of the intellectual templates of the Middle Ages (Bonfil 2012).

These were also the most intense years of the collaboration between Christian intellectuals and their Jewish counterparts. The former turned to the latter to learn the sacred language, and to better penetrate the secrets of the Bible and the various Kabbalistic texts, considered ancient and therefore thought to embody an original form of knowledge that had then been channeled into the Christian truth. But a number of Jewish intellectuals also worked as translators, from Hebrew into Latin, of medieval philosophical works that, written in Arabic or passing through that language, had been preserved in the Hebrew version alone.

In Florence, Yohanan Alemanno, who was close to Giovanni Pico della Mirandola, was at the center of exchanges with Christian intellectuals on Kabbalistic and magical themes. He was a long-time guest – a sort of "teacher-in-residence" – of the Da Pisa family of Jewish bankers from the city of the same name, and he set out in valuable texts the ideal curriculum for a youngster's studies. De Balmes, who left Naples following one of the expulsions of the Jews from the territories of the Spanish crown, made his home in Venice, translating into Latin a series of scientific and philosophical treatises, and was the author of a rich and original treatise on Hebrew linguistics, written in Hebrew and Latin, the *Miqne Avram* (known as *Abram's Flock* in English, 1523) (Campanini 1997). That this book was supported and published by the Christian publisher Daniel Bomberg is a fact that should not be overlooked – i.e., a high-ranking Jewish intellectual required the assistance of a Christian to fund his linguistic studies. As De Balmes himself wrote in the introduction to his treatise, the young Jews of the Venetian community were very religious, they assiduously attended the synagogue and were generous towards those who shared their faith, but they concentrated most of their energies on business, neglecting "erudition," by which he meant knowledge that was not specifically religious in nature.

This was the same situation that was described one hundred years later, and in relation to the same city, by Simone Luzzatto. But here we witness what was a paradoxical phenomenon: while the average education did not involve rigorous studies of Hebrew grammar, there is no doubt that the Italian Jews were those who, in the Christian world, had the greatest mastery of that language. They were certainly better-versed than their fellow Jews in Germany and Poland, who paid little attention to grammatical correctness and stylistic elegance until much later, towards the end of the eighteen century. Evidently, the close-reading of the texts allowed for an in-depth understanding of Hebrew, even if the teachers themselves were not always equipped with rigorous, systematic knowledge. Moreover, the lexicons and grammar books they used were of questionable quality, as the surviving manuscripts demonstrate, and they produced translations of prayers and of the Bible that, although accurate, were very distant from the standard of the literary language (these were the versions written in so-called Judeo-Italian).

Over the following decades, the most important teacher was Ovadya Sforno (circa 1470 – 1550), who was rightly considered to be the last great representative of Jewish Aristotelianism. He lived and taught in Rome and Bologna. In his philosophical text *Or Ammim* (*Light of the Nations*, 1537, translated into Latin by the author himself with the title *Lumen gentium*), the Jews are seen as the inheritors of the authentic rational tradition, and the theological *quaestiones* are addressed with recourse above all to Aristotle and Averroes, and to a far less extent, to Maimonides. While this philosophical text may not have met with great success, Sforno's biblical commentary has been studied and printed continuously, right up to the present day, and far beyond the Italian Jewish context.

Thanks to the extraordinary discovery of hand-written notes for his lessons, we know that Sforno was in charge of a school, in which he was designated with the exceptionally rare title of *Gaon*, which was attributed to the prestigious religious authorities of Babylonia-Iraq in the post-Talmudic period (Kravitz 2017). As happened to Yehudah ben Yehiel, in Sforno's case, too, the students – or at least one of them, the prolific Elia di Nola – strayed from the master's teachings, complementing his philosophical notions on an increasingly frequent basis with those taken from the Kabbalistic texts, in particular the *Zohar*. To sum it up very succinctly, we can say that the rationalistic universalism of philosophy was replaced by the particularism of the Kabbalah, a prophetic doctrine revealed to the Jews and transmitted in a reserved, exclusive way, and that this closure is associated with the change in the material living conditions of the Jews in those decades. The second half of the sixteenth century and the whole of the seventeenth (the so-called "long seventeenth," which came to an end in the mid-eighteenth century) constituted, in effect, the period of the Catholic Counter-Reformation, marked by the increasing intransigence of the Church of Rome that, combating the Protestant "heresies," also aimed to isolate the Jews socially and to weaken them culturally. This was, after all, the time of the burning of the Talmud, of ecclesiastical censure, and of the ghettos.

But the Kabbalah, which was widely popularized in both its theoretical and practical versions – from the complex theories on the *sefirot* and on the relationships between human action and the world of the divinities, all the way to the use of amulets and magical formulations – also served as the vehicle for an intellectual transformation of a world that was searching for a new frame of reference.

The decades from the end of the sixteenth century to the mid-seventeenth betray some clear tensions. This was the period of repentance: various authors preceded their Hebrew works with the confession that they had sinned by abandoning the way of the *Torah* to "embrace the bosom of the foreigner," meaning that they had dedicated themselves to profane knowledge (the erotic – and therefore sinful – reference was no accident). Their Jewish works were to constitute the expiation of that sin, but at the same time some of these authors did not renounce entirely what they had acquired during their "profane" phase.

One of the most interesting cases is that of the Mantuan physician Avraham Portaleone (1541–1612), a recognized authority in his scientific field, who – after having written a Latin work in an empiricist, sceptical mode, which even included licentious implications on the alleged curative properties of gold – went on, in the wake of his "repentance", to write a voluminous description, in Hebrew, of the ancient Temple of Jerusalem (*Shiltei Ghiborim, Shields of the Mighty*, 1612) (Guetta 2014, pp. 30–61). But this description constituted the backbone of a kind of encyclopedic theatre that made it possible to present the most cutting-edge scientific knowledge. While not being a dyed-in-the-wool Kabbalist, Portaleone declared his admiration for the great Kabbalistic authority in Italy at that time, Menahem Azarya di Fano, who introduced into Italy the texts of the teachers of the Safed School. It can, however, be discerned that the human action on the divine and on the world, as described by the Kabbalah and evoked by Portaleone, does nothing more than retrace the causal pattern that was the cornerstone of empirical science. In other words, the growing rift between science and religion that came after the medieval harmony between physics and theology, and which gave rise for the Jews to ever more frequent references to the prophetic tradition as the only form of truth (i.e., to a form of fideism), also connoted a phase of transition: the forms of science were introjected into the traditionalist doctrine, the frameworks of modern physics were put at the service of the dynamics between man, the divine and the world.

The period of the ghettos, then, was also one of transition towards so-called modernity. It was specifically in the Roman ghetto, deemed by nineteenth-century historiography to have been the most socially and intellectually backward of all of the Jewish communities in Italy, that in those same years straddling the end of the sixteenth century and the start of the seventeenth the most notable manifestation of a more general phenomenon came to pass, as a section of the intellectual elite of Italy's Jews began to contribute to the great wave of vernacularisation, usually taking the form of translations from Greek or Latin into literary Italian or Tuscan, along with a large number of translations from Hebrew. The translators lived in Rome, Mantua and Casale Monferrato. A considerable number of these translations are of Hebrew poems, turned into laudable Italian poetry.

One Hebrew text in particular – a section of Moses of Rieti's *Small Sanctuary* that patently chimed with the sensibility of the time because it contained the declaration of sins and the acknowledgement of human inadequacy before God, the omniscient but compassionate judge – was translated into Italian verses by at least five different authors, all probably Roman. These *terza rima* translations, amounting to a veritable poetic *tour de force*, are for the most part on an elevated literary level, and are entirely unknown to historians of Italian literature. In the period of the ghettos, a shared basis was thus created with the Christians, founded on a common national language.

However, at least until the mid-eighteenth century, the Kabbalah seems to have occupied the entire terrain of Jewish beliefs and to have informed Jewish practices, steering the former towards the vision of Jewish exceptionalism and the latter towards attitudes that the small numbers who still declared themselves to be rationalists viewed as akin to magic. But if we look closely at this reality, the picture is far less uniform.

Aharon Berechiya Modena (1549–1639), known for his *Maavar Yabbok* (*Crossing the Jabbock*, 1626), a book on Kabbalah-inspired rituals and beliefs relating above all to death, brought together in a single manuscript a philosophical lexicon and a Kabbalistic equivalent, both with Italian translations (Montefiore Library 479). And despite his cautious declaration that "light is recognised through darkness," meaning that the truth of the Kabbalah is revealed through the falsehood or inadequacy of philosophy, the explanations that followed abounded in declarations of sympathy vis-à-vis philosophical rationalism, and in certain cases even went so far as to evince a certain dose of scepticism.

The synthesis of scientific form and Kabbalistic content, which had begun to appear in the early seventeenth century, reached its apogee one hundred years later. In this case, rather than a school in the traditional sense, we should refer to a group of scholars who shared the same aspirations and who all recognized an undisputed leader. Moshe Hayyim Luzzatto (Padua, 1707 – Acre, 1746) was the driving force behind a group of young Kabbalists devoted to study and prayer, or rather to a form of studying and reading that served the function of prayer: to intervene on the divine emanations or *sefirot*.

Luzzatto was a highly talented poet and he wrote important texts on various branches of Jewish thought: rhetoric, logic, ethics and, above all, theology. He was at the same time a mystic and a rationalist, he received revelations from a heavenly voice that inspired him to come up with new texts, and he succeeded in giving a systematic, almost geometrical order to the complex doctrine of Yitzhak Luria. He insisted repeatedly on the need for clarity and differentiation in expounding the esoteric doctrines, to such an extent, indeed, that we can speculate on a formal influence of the writings of Descartes, who was well known and much discussed in those years in the Italian universities. The same requirement for explanation and rational comprehension of the Kabbalistic doctrines, without renouncing their revealed origin, can be found in other important Italian Kabbalists of the early eighteenth century, such as Yosef Ergas in Livorno and Aviad Sar Shalom Basilea in Mantua. It was in this way that rationalism penetrated Jewish esotericism, and managed to take its place alongside beliefs, rituals and practices that were very far removed from it.

But to return to the method of Simone Luzzatto, we have to look both at "high-brow" and at "middle-brow", or popular, culture. One way to do so is to turn to the manuscripts of the time, which often feature various types of juxtaposed texts and thus amount to a sort of synthetic library, betraying the choices and interests of a given teacher. We must, then, abandon renowned rabbis and take a look at the teachings of the humble tutors, who are too often overlooked.

A codex written probably at the end of the sixteenth century presents, after the rules of the *shechita* (ritual slaughter), the hundreds of elegant Italian tercets of one of the translations of the *Small Sanctuary*, and a little Hebrew-Italian dictionary (whose author is named as Shelomo ben Moshe Penzo), in addition to an incantation in Italian, written in Hebrew characters, which exhorts the prophet Elijah to act to stop the demonic Lilith, who made her way around the Earth attacking children, drinking their blood, sucking their bone marrow and eating their flesh (Jewish Theological Seminary, ms. 10062). The Italian texts, for their part, were written in Hebrew characters, as was customary well into the seventeenth century. The terror of childhood mortality, against which defense was provided through certain spells (what we would today call superstition), was not evidently seen by the editors or bookbinders of the various textual units of the manuscript as being incompatible with high-minded literature. They were two sides of the same culture.

Other manuscripts were certainly intended for personal use, because they alternated between complete texts and notes, lists, receipts and small balance sheets. In certain cases, they were additions on the blank pages of a codex containing a single work, made by a later owner. A biblical glossary in Judeo-Piedmontese compiled in 1568 by Yaakov d'Olmo at Alba in the Monferrato area, for example, was in the hands, around 1614, of a teacher and administrator of the Ghediglia banking family, who lived initially in Chieri and then in Turin (Jewish Theological Seminary, ms. 838). This unknown person filled the blank spaces with the accounts of the expenditure on the banker's children and on the food purchased from Christian shopkeepers. There is also the receipt for the down payment on the Hebrew lessons given to a friar, who had indicated his willingness to pay more, on condition that he was also taught "the song" (perhaps the sung reading of the *Torah*).

But alongside these documents, the anonymous teacher transcribed an array of different texts that give an idea of his interests. There are brief lexicons, probably intended for teaching purposes: the names in Italian and Hebrew of the compass points, and those of the most common animal sounds in Hebrew. Then there are two texts of a moral-scholastic character: a moral warning to the students and an exhortation to them through maxims arranged in alphabetical order (*Alphabet of a teacher to the student* is the title). Another alphabet of a very different sort is the series of permutations of the Hebrew letters of the *Sefer Yetzirah*, an ancient, acclaimed book that is famously difficult to interpret, in which the letters are considered the constitutive elements of the universe. The same codex contains, in the interstices between the books of the Bible with their translations, a series of precepts of twelfth/thirteenth-century German mystic Yehuda he-Hasid (the pious) on the burying of the dead, in which he addresses the matters of how to prevent access by demons and how to stop the death of innocent citizens in the event of erroneous practices. Alongside these texts, which delineate a culture that was relatively closed in upon itself and inclined towards magical and superstitious rituals, there is however also the Hebrew translation of the first stanza of the nineteenth canto of Ariosto's *Orlando furioso*. Although it is true that this stanza is moralizing in character (it concerns fairweather friends), and that the anonymous Piedmontese teacher perhaps translated it to use it with his students together with other brief moral admonishments, it is also the case that the engagement with a best-selling work that was alien to Jewish culture is somewhat surprising.

The choices made by this teacher reflect the complexity of a period in which Kabbalah, magic, religious ethics and profane poems of love and war accompanied the study of the fundamental texts. It should not be forgotten that the codex on which he wrote his texts is a biblical glossary, an almost complete translation of the Bible to be used for teaching. The contrast – or perhaps what appears that way to us – between various intellectual directions was a common feature of both the upper and lower levels of the culture of the Italian Jews from the fifteenth to the seventeenth centuries. But were these contrasts and this complexity not also an integral part of the Christian culture of that long period?

It is likely that the Jews reproduced in their small communities – with other religious and textual reference points, and in another language – what was happening in the wider Italian culture. And in this sense perhaps Luzzatto had been too strict: after all, were not those who dedicated themselves to the sciences, languages and politics, rather than to their own personal affairs, also a low-ranking minority in the Christian society of Venice? And here lies another difference in perspective: while Luzzatto may have criticized his fellow Jews as having a tendency towards being ignorant in relation to everything outside their religious knowledge, we are today astonished by how such a numerically small group of people was able to produce such a rich, dynamic culture, with the ability to change in line with the evolving sensibilities of mainstream society.

Over subsequent decades, around the middle of the eighteenth century, this culture broke down again and searched for new equilibriums between philosophy and modern science, on the one hand, and religion on the other. The idea started to be developed that the central core of Judaism was ethical in nature, and efforts were made to achieve a synthesis between Jewish particularism and universalism – to use the terms popular in the nineteenth century – or between West and East, Athens and Jerusalem.

But the decline in religious observance, community cohesion and knowledge of Hebrew and of the traditional texts combined to transform the recent history of the Jews in Italy – a history, though, which was not constituted solely by decline and which, in its totality, has yet to be written.

The Universalism of Elia Benamozegh

Raniero Fontana

Elia Benamozegh (1823–1900) was an illustrious teacher of Italian Judaism. He lived his entire life in Livorno. His family origins can be traced back to the traditional Judaism of North Africa. He was schooled by his uncle, Yehudah Coriat, an important Moroccan Kabbalist, but from a young age he had wanted to immerse himself also in Italian and European culture; something he did as an auto-didact. Benamozegh was a genius: in addition to being an original and prolific author – as evinced by the works that he wrote in Hebrew, Italian and French, and equally by the works that he never got around to completing – he was very much a multi-talented figure, at once an erudite rabbi, an educator, a patriot and an apostle for a human race marching towards the One.

Benamozegh's universalism, even before becoming a central theme, was a feature of his desire to contribute to a debate already under way, both within and outside the Jewish world, through his substantial, passionate engagement with the ideas and doctrines of others; a critical engagement, certainly, and one that on occasion betrayed distortions and misunderstandings, but one that was also laden with interweavings and cross-references between epochs and civilizations, between cultures and religions. This put him in the firing line for criticisms from traditionalist colleagues and from exponents of the *Wissenschaft des Judentums*, from the rabbis of Aleppo and Jerusalem and from a respected scholar, the Paduan Samuel David Luzzatto.

His works, such as the biblical commentary *Em la-Miqra* (Livorno, 1862–1863) and the *Storia degli Esseni* (Florence, 1865), are full of brilliant insights; however, they constituted an all-too-easy target on the methodological, historical and doctrinal levels, the last of which was the one that really mattered to him. His legitimate aspiration was to give Judaism an honorable place in mainstream culture via the medium of the Kabbalah, which he considered to be an oral tradition and an esoteric doctrine. Through the Kabbalah, Benamozegh intended to correct the deviations from the right balance between heaven and earth, spirit and letter, ideal and real. Christianity, Spinosizm, Theism and Pantheism were nothing but distorted forms of the teaching contained in the tradition of Israel and in the venerable doctrine. This sums up what he wrote in *L'Origine des dogmes chrétiens* (posthumous publication, Paris, 2011) and in *Spinoza et la Cabbale* (Paris, 1864). The source of the errors of all concerned was, indeed, a distorted use of the *sefirot*, their erroneous reception, not only in the case of Trinitarian dogma and of the Spinozian *res cogitans* and *res extensa*, but also, it should be added, in the case of Hegelian dialectic. Spinoza and Hegel both served as emblems for a modernity of which Benamozegh wanted to critique the outcome. Individualism, rationalism and scepticism were some of the traits of a secularization to which even the Jewish world was susceptible. For him, then, the Kabbalah, was the solution; the ancient knowledge was capable of anchoring becoming to being, the relative to the absolute, the multiple to the one. As doctrine and as tradition, it would anchor humanity *en route* towards that objective content that was to be gradually discovered and developed over the arc of human history. Benamozegh preferred the emanatist monotheism of Jewish mysticism to the doctrine of *ex-nihilo* creation; progression to the ontological leap – progression towards a final synthesis without fusion and without separation, expression of an ultimate vision of harmony and peace, of plurality within unity.

This is also the theoretical assumption behind Benamozegh's most renowned work, the one intended, at least in his mind, for a larger audience: *Israël et l'Humanité* (posthumous publication, Paris, 1914). It was the work in which he put forward his vision of a universal religion and conferred upon Israel the role of humanity's high priest. It was a religious proposal for the whole of humanity, held in store by the tradition of Israel. Benamozegh is deemed to have been the modern architect of Noahidism. Observance of Noahide law constitutes the parameter within which humanity must place itself in order to embrace the universal religion. To do so, however, would require Christianity – with the rejection of a priesthood usurped from Israel – to correct certain essential points of its doctrine. Only in this way could it fall within a Noahide horizon shared with the non-Jewish part of the human family, as one of its myriad religious manifestations. In *Morale juive et morale chrétienne* (Paris, 1867), Christianity had already been subject to a polemical attack on the part of the rabbi appointed to defend Judaism and its values against its detractors, but a proposal of this nature came across as overly doctrinal, especially to those who had to flesh it out. This was the reason why Aimé Pallière subjected it to a highly personal re-reading that was not very consistent with the orthodoxy of his teacher. Alfonso Pacifici, Pallière's Zionist friend, wrote that he was missing "something that could be named, approximately, a limit, a point beyond which it was not possible to adhere […] without finding oneself necessarily in contradiction with one's own faith, which one does not intend to renounce." Whereas Benamozegh gave weight to dogmas and doctrines, formulas and creeds, Pallière focused instead on the *immaterialisation* of their content. Something similar can be said vis-à-vis modernity as not only an epochal experience but also a vital one.

The question of the areas in which Benamozegh can be considered to have been too far ahead or too far behind the *zeitgeist* is still open to debate. What is certain is that he sought its arcane reasons in suggestive sefirotic combinations and ingenious abstractions.

"Know Before Whom You Stand." The Synagogue from the Age of Ghettos to Emancipation

Sharon Reichel

Since the destruction of the Temple of Jerusalem at the hands of the Romans in 70 CE, the synagogue, or *bet haKnesset*, has been a crucial gathering point where Jews could meet to pray and study the Torah.

The synagogue became representative of the identities of Jewish communities, a space where individuals felt acknowledged by society, in the enclosed ghetto as well as in the emancipated society where Jews enjoyed equal rights. Synagogues are the tangible manifestation of Jewish identity, reflecting like mirrors the diverse world of Italian Judaism (Bonfil 1982).

Synagogues have always been the mainstays of the Jewish communities' religious, spiritual and social life and are the outcome of the continuous efforts Italian Jews made to adapt to the surrounding society, in compliance with contemporary laws and evolving values. The present research will focus on the Italian synagogues, also known as *scole*, that were active after the founding of the ghetto, a form of segregation that while limiting the Jews' rights, also contributed to increasing their autonomy and stability and to the development of distinctive behaviors.

We mentioned the need to comply with specific regulations in the edification of synagogues: these were first of all religious prescriptions, according to which Jewish places of worship had to have at least one window following the example of Prophet Daniel who prayed to God inside a room with windows facing Jerusalem (Daniel 6,11). The *Talmud* (Shulchan Arukh, Orach Chayim, cap. 9, 150, 1) prescribes that synagogues are to be situated on the most elevated point of the city and built so that prayers can be directed towards Jerusalem. These norms were accompanied by the laws of the different Italian states that limited the number of synagogues and imposed bare facades prohibiting any element identifying the building as a synagogue. An example of these rules can be found in the Bull *Cum nimis absurdum* issued by Pope Paul IV in 1555. In addition to instituting ghettos in the State of the Church, it also prohibited the construction of new synagogues – a limitation that the various communities cleverly bypassed: the Jews of Rome for instance instituted five synagogues inside one single building known as Cinque Scole (Five *Scole*).

The Jews' compliance with these limitations is still reflected today in the architecture of old synagogues in several cities like Ferrara, Ancona and Casale Monferrato, where an inattentive visitor might not notice the local Jewish synagogue missing the chance to discover authentic treasures of Italian art.

Behind their anonymous facades, the interiors of Modern Period Italian synagogues contain lavish decorations, colorful and gilded furnishings, and valuable silver and other metal ceremonial objects, reminding us of how the notion of a dull and colorless ghetto society is in fact a prejudice far from reality.

Even the synagogue interiors have to comply with the laws of Judaism, therefore every place of worship contains at least one *Sefer Torah* (Torah Scroll) which must be stored in a closet, the *Aron-haKodesh;* furthermore, the Torah must be read from a pulpit that Ashkenazic and German communities call *bimah* while Sephardic, Spanish, and Portuguese Jews call *tevah.*

Apart from the prohibition of anthropomorphic images prescribed by the Second Commandment, there are no further indications on the style that religious architectures should follow, therefore synagogue interiors have been clearly influenced by the predominant artistic styles of the various historical periods. In Italy Baroque and Rococo styles, with their abundance of elaborately carved furnishings, stucco works, and goldwork, were very popular. Synagogue interiors also reflect the various currents of Judaism present throughout the peninsula, each with its traditions, prayer practices, and space organization.

The oratories of German-origin communities required the presence of two closely-positioned focal points situated on the same axis, from where the rituals were officiated: the *aron* on the eastern wall, facing Jerusalem, and the *bimah* at the center of the hall. Usually these spaces contain a gallery reserved for women who had to remain separate from men during religious functions. This spatial arrangement used to be very distracting for worshippers whose attention constantly shifted from one focal point to the other.

A different solution was implemented in Sephardic synagogues such as the Scola Portoghese in Venice, where the problem of the worshippers' loss of concentration, created by the presence of the *bimah* at the center and of the *aron* on the eastern wall was averted by moving the *bimah* onto the western wall. By doing so there were two independent focal points alternatively attracting the followers' attention during the prayers.

Within the Italian context, specifically in a number of eighteenth-century Jewish synagogues in Piedmont – Mondovì, Carmagnola, Cherasco and Chieri – the two-focal-point layout was not adopted due to space limitations and this led to the construction of massive and highly decorated canopy pulpits.

Let's return to the importance of synagogues for the Modern Period Jewish communities, where these edifices offered a space for liturgical practices as well as a location for gatherings, exchanges, and debate between members of the different communities. In these settings Jews could express their identity, and the wealthier classes (a very low percentage of the overall ghetto population) could display their social status and elicit respect, by championing Jewish tradition.

The donation of ceremonial objects to one's own community was a common practice in Jewish society, which was also developed as a reaction to the rigid limitations imposed by the governments of the states present on the Italian peninsula: the only luxury objects Jews could use and produce were ceremonial objects. Dora Liscia Bemporad and Andreina Contessa's contributions to the present catalogue provide an analysis of the different styles and typologies of the objects used in synagogues, which in this study will be considered as tangible forms of Jewish self-representation.

The ownership of ceremonial objects and charitable donations increased a person's prestige, based on the value of the objects and on the magnitude of the benefactor's contribution. The objects are therefore to be considered luxury objects not only because only the upper classes could afford them, but also because their liturgic use gave them an aura of magnificence. Artistic liturgic objects became a way of self-promotion within Jewish communities: their purchase and production were not only prompted by strong religious feelings, since these items were in effect economic investments that would have made a

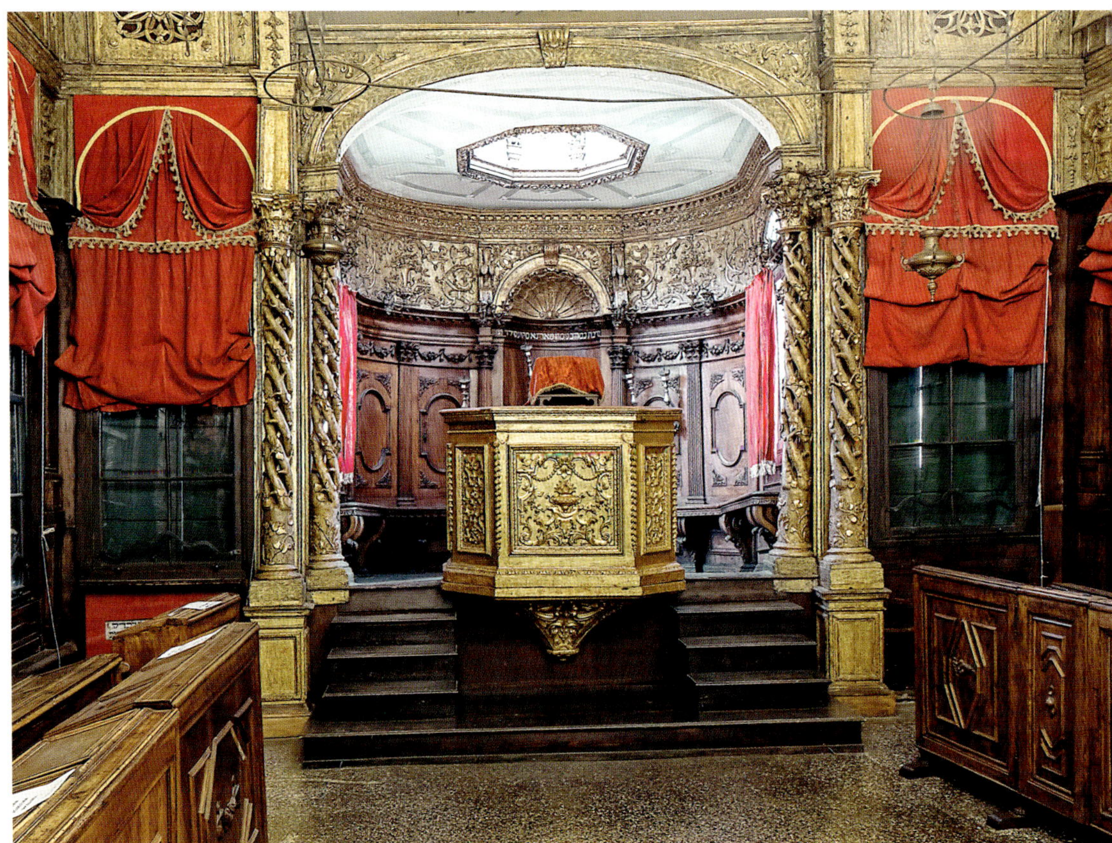

1. *Bimah* of Scola Canton, Venice

profit over the years. Since their economic value was inextricably connected to their sacral purpose, they necessarily had to be used and displayed inside synagogues so that the community could acknowledge the gesture; the synagogues retained the objects, but their ownership remained with the individual families.

In many cases the provenance of these donations is traceable thanks to the Hebrew inscriptions and emblems decorating them, or by studying the bequest papers.

Some examples of these donations can be found today in the collections of the Jewish Museum in Rome. Particularly noteworthy among them is the Del Monte crown (cat. 18) from 1626, the earliest known object thus far. The Museum ascribes the donation to the Scola dei Quattro Capi, named after the bridge by the same name (today known as Ponte Fabricio) across the River Tiber. Some maintain that this *scola* was closed in 1555 when the ghetto was instituted and moved inside the Cinque Scole building (Berliner 1992; Milano 1988). Daniela Di Castro instead believes (Di Castro 2010[b]) it was still active in the eighteenth century. Crafted by an unknown silversmith, this crown features glass paste stones and the emblem of the Del Monte family: two facing lions atop an Italian style trimount. To memorialize the donation of this object to the synagogue, there are four scrolls with Hebrew inscriptions revealing the donor: "Sanctity to the Lord / to the Synagogue of the Quattro Capi; a donation of Yaakov Del Monte / may God spare his life / charges required by law / in year 5386 of the Jewish calendar / in honor of the God of Israel and of His Law" the date of the donation, 1626, and the name of the donor.

Even the pair of *rimmonim* (cat. 19) finials, donated by Mordechai Efrati to the Scola Castigliana in 1730–1731 feature a decoration with the emblem of a Roman family, the Ascarelli, with three lions around a tower (the family also occasionally used a two-lion emblem). These classic eighteenth-century Roman *rimmonim* present a rounded body with an upper narrowing and are adorned by two rows of bells, some shaped as pomegranate fruits. The family emblem crowns the finals and on one of the handles we find the Hebrew inscription "Glory to God at the Scola Castigliana. Offered by the elderly and honored Mordechai Efrati, for the life of his wife, his daughters and son- in-laws. Year 5491."

These objects are the tangible demonstration of the need felt by the members of the community to express their presence and status, and the apposition of the family emblems on these artifacts that adorned the Sefer Torah, the holiest of objects for Jews, further underlines this need for self-representation (Roth 1967; Di Castro 2010[b]).

It is no coincidence that the Community of Rome can boast several liturgic objects. In fact, we know that since 1613 the properties of synagogues were not subject to taxation, while on other properties held by Jews the State of the Church levied a tax of 25% of their value (Di Castro 1994).

Besides the donation of ceremonial objects, community members had several other ways of signaling their presence to their fellow Jews. Among these we can identify two economically distinct traditions.

The first is that of donations to the community and to the synagogue, a method adopted by the most prominent members of the community, whose names were memorialized with visible inscriptions and plaques: inscriptions of this type can be found in synagogues throughout Italy and in some cases appear as actual decorations. An example are the inscriptions found in the Venetian *scole*, such as the lettering on the wooden decoration behind the *bimah* of Scola Canton, which reads: "Exemplary donation of Benyamin Marina di Conselve / יצ"ו (may God protect and preserve him)." In this case, the benefactor's objective was to be remembered by the entire community, and by having his name inscribed and positioned behind the reader of the Sefer Torah he was confident that everybody would have noticed and respected him.

Another, perhaps more democratic donation practice that exposed the contributor to the judgment of the entire community was that of making a donation to the synagogue. Jewish laws forbid the handling of money during Shabbat. In order to insure that the promised donations would be actually made the offering record was introduced, a notice-board where the benefactors' names were inscribed on plaques next to the sum of money they intended to donate. These offerings were therefore conditioned by the community. Some of these items can be found in Piedmont: the Mondovì wooden offering record for instance has the names of the members of the community with leather strings next to them which were drawn out to indicate the extent of the donation. In the eighteenth-century wood and parchment offering record from the synagogue of Carmagnola (cat. 20), today found in the Archivio Ebraico Terracini of Turin, the names of the benefactors are inscribed in Hebrew on the lateral doors, and on the central door there is a corresponding framed section where a small hole was pierced with a needle to indicate the person's intention to make a donation to the community.

So far, we have presented the lively microcosm of the Jewish ghetto communities and the practices the Jewish minority adopted to face the strict segregation policy enforced by the various governments that ruled throughout the Italian peninsula from 1516 to the nineteenth century. We have seen how the lack of tangible forms of representation in the general society contributed to increasing the level of investment in the all-Jewish context of the synagogue; but when the so-called "age of ghettos" came to an end, the history of Jewish communities continued, although radically changed by the process of emancipation that began in the Italian Peninsula in 1848, in the Kingdom of Sardinia, leading to the extension of civil rights to Jews and to the leveling of Jews' juridical status with that of the rest of the population.

Emancipation modified the structure and organization that Jews had given themselves and lived in for centuries, and the opening of the ghetto led to a redefinition of their role within society.

Repercussions were felt both inside the communities and in their relations with the world around them.

The transition between segregation and freedom was not immediate, the ghetto in fact represented both a place of constraint and a refuge, a microcosm where Jews could live a life defined by religious prescripts, where even the poorer inhabitants had the right to have a house.

Synagogues soon became the center of debates on Jewish identity. Now that equality had been obtained, the time had come for Jews to actively participate and be duly recognized

2. Del Monte crown, detail. Museo Ebraico di Roma, Rome (cat. 18)

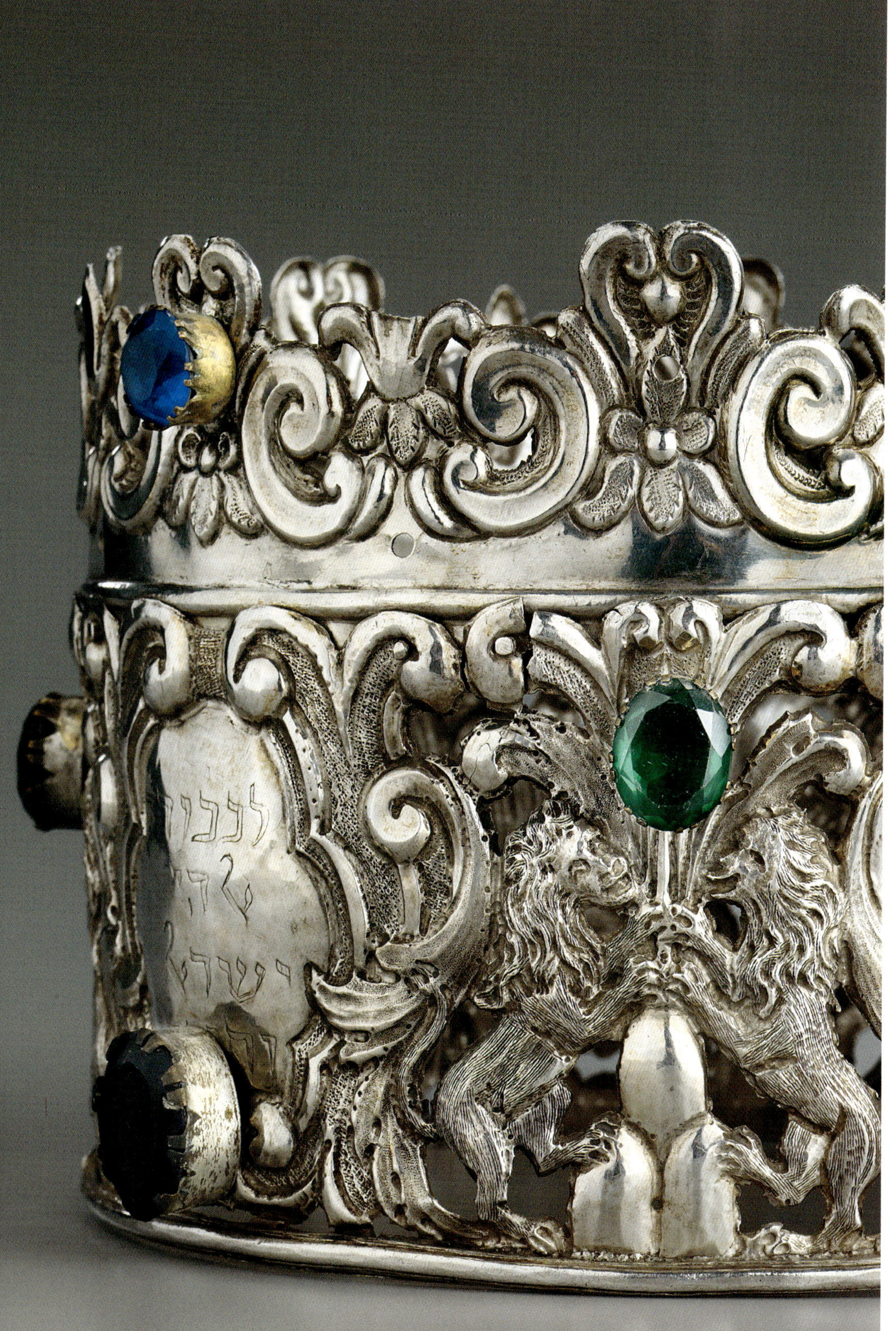

in general society. Against this background, the communities' strong outward drive and need to replace the crumbling synagogue buildings of the ghetto, led to the building of new synagogues, whose architectures were nothing like those that had been built until that day.

As we have seen, until that moment, synagogues manifested their identity only in the interiors, while after emancipation signs expressing Jewish identity could extend to the whole architectural structure, including the exterior of the building.

This change was not easy, since there was no tradition to look back on, and also because initially there were no Jewish architects who could fully understand the nature of the spaces they were to design. Therefore many great temples (this was the name given to the synagogues of the Risorgimento period), almost as if to mark the difference between a more secluded past and a new monumental present, reflected the influence of Christian architecture in their interiors and displayed oriental-inspired features on the exteriors in keeping with the style of the period.

In these synagogues we often find a pulpit in front of the *aron*, replicating the structure of a church altar, a solution that was completely foreign to the Jewish tradition, that still today makes the following of the prayers more problematic.

In the temples built after emancipation decisions were made to unite in the same location the officiation of the different Italian, Spanish and German practices, so as if to create a double equality, outwards towards general society and inwards among the Jews of Italy. These edifices are easily recognizable in the urban setting thanks to the new laws extending civil rights to the Jewish population. In the rabbi's sermons and in the speeches of the community representatives, these new synagogues became the tangible symbol of the Jews' hard-earned freedom. Through their temples, Jews could express the overturning of their previous condition of forced segregation in the ghetto. In some cases, in cities like Modena and Rome, the new synagogues were erected in the old ghetto area, while in other cases, communities found alternative locations for their new edifices of worship.

The construction of new synagogues however did present some complications, difficulties that could be considered a reflection of those experienced by Italian Jews during the process of emancipation.

The most striking case was that of Turin, where Jews were emancipated in 1848 and a project for a new Israelite temple was soon drawn up: a great synagogue meant to become a center for all three practices – Italian, Spanish, and German – and representing the symbol of the new role Jews had carved out for themselves in society.

On March 1, 1859, the Board of Directors of the Jewish Community of Turin approved the construction of a new synagogue, requiring the members of the community to pay a yearly sum to support the initiative. On March 7, the Board appointed a Commission of seven members whose duty was to carry out the surveys, research and propositions for the building. The Commission had concluded its assignment by November of that same year. In the meantime, a Royal Decree accepting the project was issued and in 1860 the land where the temple was to be built was purchased.

Finally, on February 20, 1862, a public call was announced specifying that the required building project had to include a synagogue, plus rooms for the community lay institutions, administrative offices, the Council of the Jewish Community of Turin headquarters, and primary schools. The call allocated 300,000 Lire for the execution of the chosen project. Since all the submitted projects were considered unsatisfactory and incomplete, the community decided to consult the architect Alessandro Antonelli. With an estimated cost of 380,000 Lire, his project was approved by the Community, the King, and the building commission.

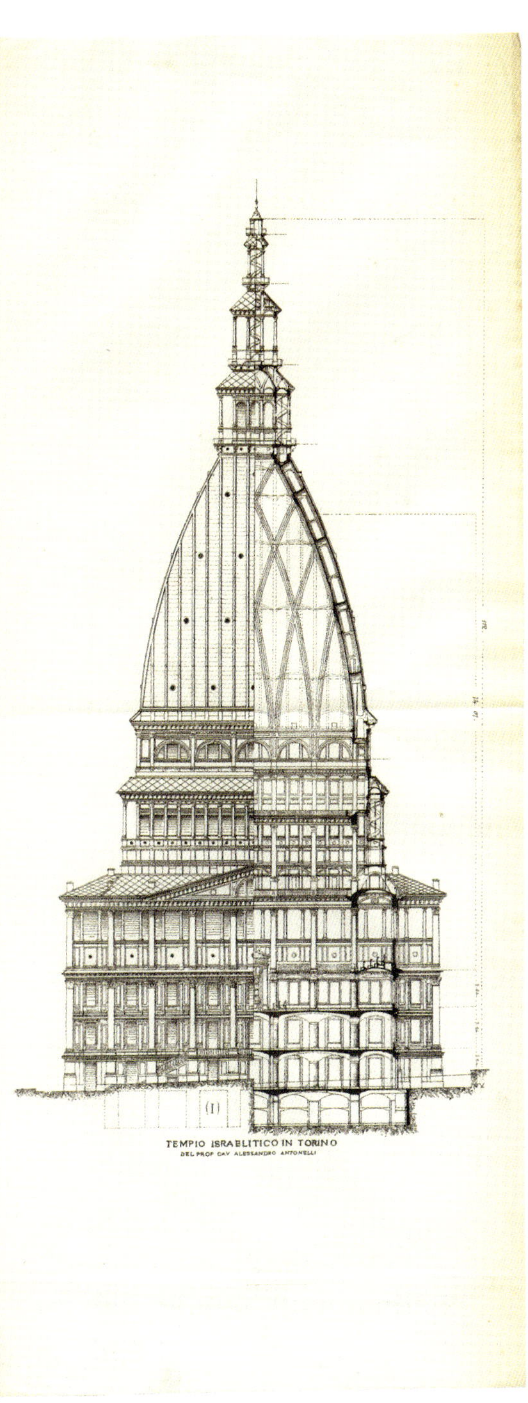

3. Lithograph of the Israelite Temple based on a drawing by Crescentino Caselli and published by Camilla and Bertolero. Archivio Storico della Città di Torino, Turin (cat. 55)

Work started in April 1863 and soon difficulties arose between Antonelli and the Jewish Community of Turin. The critical aspects are listed in a report drawn up by the Board of Directors of the Jewish Community on December 14, 1869 that was sent to the Turin City Council mentioning the almost ten year delay in the work resulting in the expenses inflating up one million Lire.

The purpose of the report was to obtain support from the City of Turin in order to complete the construction of the synagogue. The Università israelitica had in fact come to a crossroads: either suspend the building of the temple or continue without the necessary financial resources. In 1875, faced with the impossibility of finding new funds and due to the difficulties in finishing the project, the Board of Directors decided the building had to be sold.

Despite this decision, the following year the assembly of contributors decided to complete the temple, eliminating parts of the project.

This episode came to a conclusion only in 1877 when, following the City of Turin's offer and a heated vote of the assembly of the Università israelitica's contributors, the Board of Directors approved the sale of the building for 150,000 Lire.

The building (cat. 55) was eventually completed and the Mole Antonelliana, which became the symbol of Turin, was inaugurated in 1889 as seat of the Museum of the Risorgimento.

The Community failed to give itself a temple representative of the new condition of emancipation, and this represented a major setback in the morale and finances of the Jews of Turin. In 1880, once the disastrous experience with Antonelli was over, the Board of Directors bought new land for the construction of a central synagogue. That same year, a new open call was announced, and among the nine submitted projects, the chosen one was by Engineer Enrico Petiti. Building work started on July 9, 1880 and ended four years later with the solemn inauguration of the temple, on February 15, 1884.

Petiti's project envisioned a Moresque building, a style that was fashionable in Europe's post-emancipation synagogue architecture that was also adopted in the temples of Vercelli and Florence. Although we mentioned the initial absence of Jewish architects, the synagogues of Turin, Vercelli, and Florence have in common the figure of the Jewish architect Marco Treves (Vercelli, 1814 – Florence, 1897). He was a consultant for the Temple of Vercelli, a member of the Commission for the synagogue of Turin and one of the authors of the project for the Temple of Florence, which, similar to the Turin synagogue, had a long and troubled history. Even during the years prior to emancipation, the Jewish community of Florence had discussed the need to enlarge their synagogue, but it was only in 1858 that

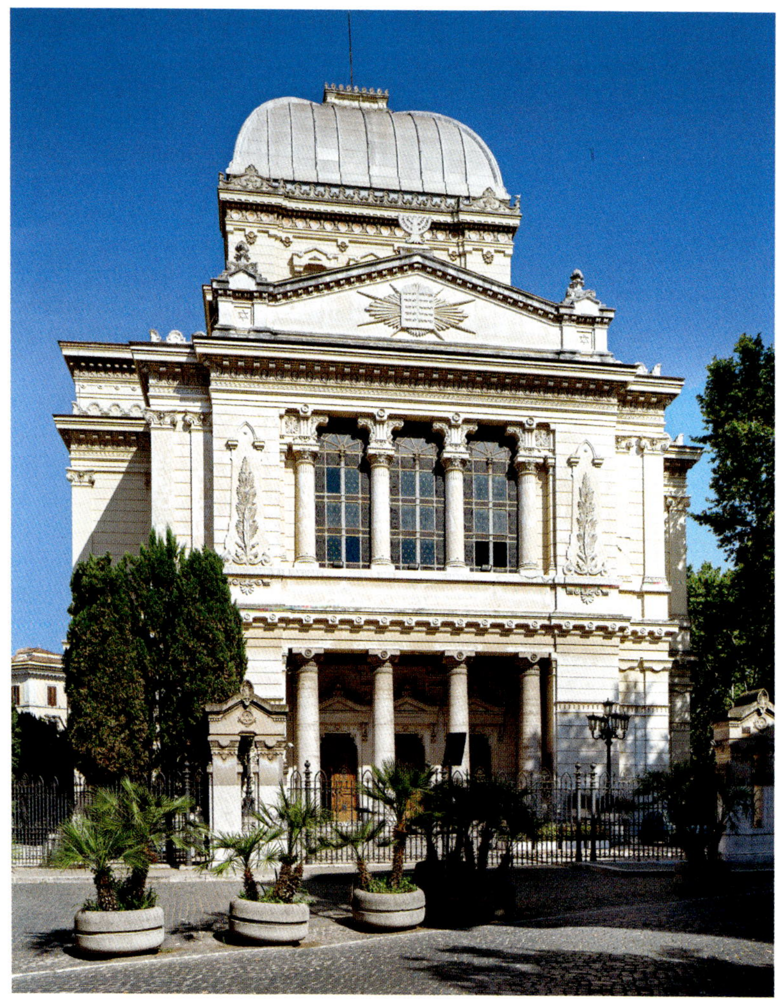

4. Exterior view of the Synagogue of Rome, designed by Osvaldo Armanni and Vincenzo Costa

a program of voluntary public subscription was approved to collect contributions for the building of a new temple (Boralevi 1985).

Two years later, architect Treves was invited to initiate preliminary surveys and research for the construction of a new temple. He immediately made it clear that he would be in charge of the synagogue project. Things did not go quite as he wanted, since Prof. Mariano Falcini and architect Vincenzo Micheli were also involved in the project that came to a conclusion only in 1882. The present contribution will not give an account of all the vicissitudes that led to the inauguration of the Temple of Florence, and will only mention the key fact that made the project possible: Cavalier David Levi's donation. In the wake of the tradition of community donations, Cavalier Levi, who in 1868 was President of the Università Israelitica of Florence, destined his entire patrimony to the construction of a "monumental temple worthy of Florence."

Following Turin and Florence, even in Rome the Jewish community decided to give itself a new temple. In the newly-appointed Capital of Italy, where emancipation had been obtained in 1870, the first steps towards the erection of a new synagogue were only made in 1889, almost twenty years later. This was subsequent to the decision of the City of Rome, in 1887, to expropriate the Jewish community's Cinque Scole buildings (Ascarelli, Terracina 2004).

This decision, which deprived the Jewish communities of Rome of their point of reference, occurred in conjunction with the 1888 epochal end of segregation and the remodulation of the ghetto spaces that led to the demolition of many buildings in the Jewish neighborhood.

In the Roman communities' intentions, the new temple was supposed to have a monumental and severe appearance, breaking all past traditions, detached on all sides, and situated between the Vittoriano, the monument dedicated to King Victor Emmanuel II that was being constructed at the time, and that celebrating Garibaldi (Morpurgo 2010), making the presence of Jews in Rome explicit. Two projects were shortlisted: one by the Jewish engineer Attilio Murgia, and the other by Osvaldo Armanni and Vincenzo Costa. In 1899, ten years after the selection, the project was finally entrusted to Armanni and Costa, also due to Muggia's withdrawal as he had felt offended by the way he had been treated in the second phase of the competition. The first project by Armanni and Costa (cat. 58) is characterized by a strong oriental taste and a style influenced by Babylonian architecture. However, upon its completion in 1904, the building appeared less archaic-looking crowned with a great dome evocative of the Temple of Jerusalem. The result pleased the community that appreciated the new synagogue's monumentality, situated in a location at the center of the Capital where it established a spatial dialogue with the two expressions of Roman power: Saint Peter and the Vittoriano monument.

We conclude this journey inside and outside Italian Judaism and across the evolution of synagogue spaces with an emblematic case that links the ghetto era to that of emancipation: the donation of the Aron-haKodesh of Turin (cat. 54).

In 1884, the Università israelitica of Turin donated to the City and to its Museum two doors of the Aron-haKodesh from the so-called "oldest synagogue" of the ghetto, a denomination which may indicate it came from the Italian Temple situated in the Ospedale di Carità complex, where the Jews of Turin had been forced to reside since 1679. The *aron* dates from the last decade of the eighteenth century and the early nineteenth century, its doors decorated with golden festoons similar to those found in furniture from the same period. The upper part of the doors, also gilded, presents two architectures (most probably inspired by a church or a baptistery) that symbolize the Temple of Jerusalem. On the sides, the structure is framed by two columns whose capitals are missing and by mirrors that originally had the function of reflecting and amplifying the light of the candles inside the synagogue.

The motivations for this donation from the Università Israelitica are stated in the act of donation to the Museo Civico: "[...] in offering it today to the City Museum with much love from his Excellency, the Council believes this destination to be more worthy, as the previous to which it aspired is no longer possible."

Once segregation became a thing of the past, and once equal rights had been acquired, the Jewish minority chose to be represented even in the City Museum, whose mission was to illustrate the history of the city, an undertaking that the present exhibition continues and expands, exploring the various forms of expression of the different communities of the Jews of Italy.

5. Aron ha-Kodesh, double-leaf door.
Palazzo Madama - Museo Civico d'Arte Antica di Torino, Turin, on loan to Synagogue of the Comunità Ebraica di Torino (cat. 54)

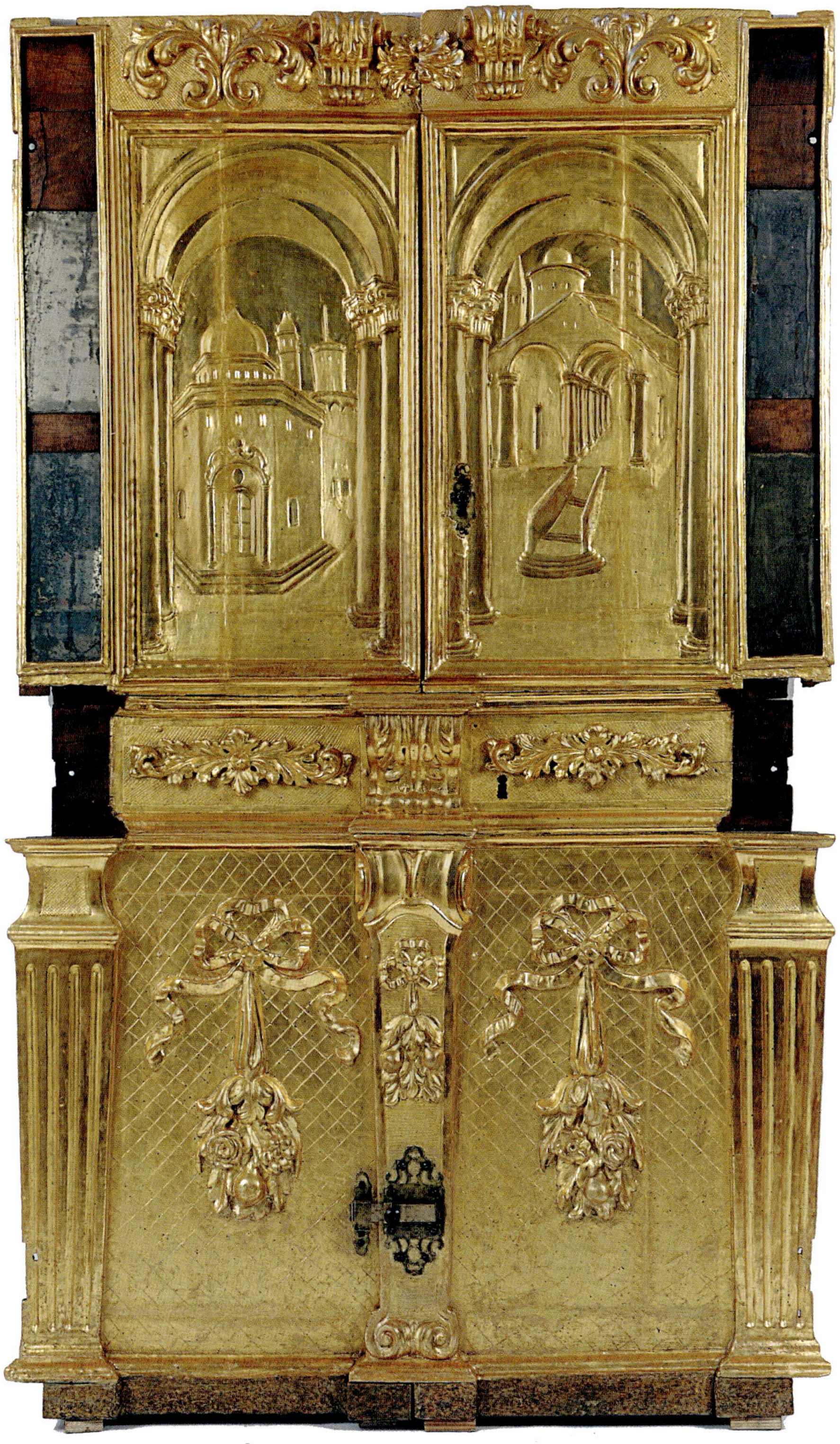

The Tombstone Speaks

Mauro Perani

The Hebrew epitaph between the sixteenth and eighteenth centuries

Italy is home to a Jewish cultural heritage of funerary steles unique in the world in terms of antiquity and extent.

While the evidence from the early centuries almost exclusively concerns Rome and southern Italy, in the sixteenth century the documentation shifts to Jewish cemeteries in central-northern Italy, reaching an apex in the seventeenth century, when the Baroque taste for writing texts in rhythm and rhyme was embraced by the Jews and extended to funerary epitaphs. This tradition continued throughout the eighteenth century and ended in the nineteenth. The use of composing epitaphs that had not only a part in prose containing the personal information, date of death and family relations of the deceased but also a part in poetry, was exclusive to Jewish cemeteries in Italy. This art became a literary genre unto itself, treasured by rabbis and scholars who composed collections of epitaphs that included real ones for people who had died and for themselves but also fictive ones for imaginary people, as mere literary practice. These characteristics made the epigraphs of Italy's Jewish cemeteries a veritable *Diwan* of poetry and a precious *register of people engraved in stone*. The Jewish culture surrounding death, its rituals and its liturgy is enveloped in an air of mystery and vagueness, perhaps due to the fact that the Jew does not talk about or like to discuss the afterlife and does not think about it much, much less dare to imagine and represent it, in stark contrast with the overflowing Christian imaginary relative to the after world, expressed in a mass of literary texts starting with Dante's *Divine Comedy*. For Judaism, the cemetery is an impure place dominated by death, a world that contaminates humans and over which, along with life, they have no power. Death indeed constitutes the highest degree of impurity, since the cadaver marks the victory of the power of death.

The transition of death from natural event to anguished torment in the early modern period

In the ancient texts of the Hebrew Bible, death, while merited by Adam and Eve for their transgression, narrated in the Book of Genesis, was not a distressing or otherwise upsetting event, experienced instead as a natural passage, without reference to eternal life. In Genesis 25.8, we read: "And Abraham expired, and died in a good old age, an old man, and full of years; and was gathered to his people."

On the contrary, starting in the seventeenth century and parallel to the surrounding Christian world, death became an event that agonised, frightened and upset early modern minds. Venetian rabbi Leone da Modena (1571–1648) wrote of it in his *Historia de' riti Hebraici*, printed in Venice in 1637, describing the funerary practices of his contemporaries as follows: "In a great many places they cover the Grave with a Marble, upon which they write an Epitaph, some one way, and some another, in Verse or Prose, with the Name of the Deceas'd, and something in Praise of him; and the Day, Year and Month when he dy'd."

A work devoted entirely to managing fear of death was written by rabbi Leone da Modena's cousin, Aharon Berekyah Modena (date of birth unknown – 1639), a student of the Kabbalist Menahem Azariah da Fano: *Maavar Yabbok* (Crossing the Yabbok), printed in Mantua in 1626. In it, he offered systems and methods, often Kabbalistic in tenor, for managing anxiety about death. The title refers to the crossing of the River Yabbok, narrated in Genesis 23.32, when Jacob needs to cross over the river's ford to reach the Promised Land, the river serving as an allegory for the transition from life to death.

The epigraphs

While many different registers could be used for the funerary texts in this literary genre, it is generally the author of the text who is speaking, although there are also examples where it is the tombstone that speaks and sometimes even the deceased. The first case was the most common and employed various formulas, the most frequent of which were the following.

The speaker is the author of the epitaph or an out-of-frame voice

In the oldest epigraphs, which date to between the eighth and tenth centuries and are documented in southern Italy, in particular the catacomb of Venosa, these formulas were common: *This stone was placed on the tomb of* (הציון הלז הוצב על קבורת) or the similar *This memorial stone was erected on the tomb of* (הציון הלז הוקם על קבר) or the variant *This stone was placed on the head of* (והאבן הזאת הושמה לראש). The same formula appears in the funerary stele of Scarlatta, who died in Aquileia in 1139. The formulas continue in the early-modern tombs in these forms, sometimes with internal rhyme: *This is the memorial stone of a great man from the tribe of Abraham* (ציון איש רם גזע אברם), or *Here lies the lady* (פה נקברת מרת), or *Here in this earth, a woman is buried* (פה באדמה אשה תמה); other variants include *This memorial stone attests to the eyes of the visitor that* (עד הוא הגל הזה לעין אורח). A lovely exemplar with a variation on the terms is that of Aronne Conegliano (or Coneian) who died and was buried in Conegliano on April 9, 1634. His epitaph reads: *This grave is witness to and this tombstone commemorates the death of one who was the splendour of his generation and the light of its eyes* (על מות פאר הדור מאור עינים גל עד ומצבה זאת תהי מזכרת). The powerful words of Job 25.6 were frequently cited, declaring: בן אדמה סופו רמה (*The son of the earth ends with the worms* or, more elegantly, *He who is born of the earth is destined to the worms*).

A fine example drawn from the epitaph of Refael Hiziqiyyah da Forlì, who died and was buried in the cemetery of Lugo in 1592, follows a decasyllabic rhyme scheme in ottava rima, the Hebrew text of which reads:

אדם ילוד אשה קצר ימים[1]
הבט אנוש קם על נכבדי ארץ
איש תם וישר[2] אף נדיב עמים
טוב שב לדל תקוה[3] וגודר פרץ[4]
הובל בקבר זה בשם תמים
עם כל כבוד עשרו[5] כעפרו חרוץ
אין טוב לאיש כי אם לבם רמים
לשא לֶמֶד תכלית אשר לו תרוץ

הנעלה כמה״ר **רפאל חזקיה** זצ״ל
מיפורלי עלה אל האלהים יום
י״א ניסן השנ״ב תנצב״ה

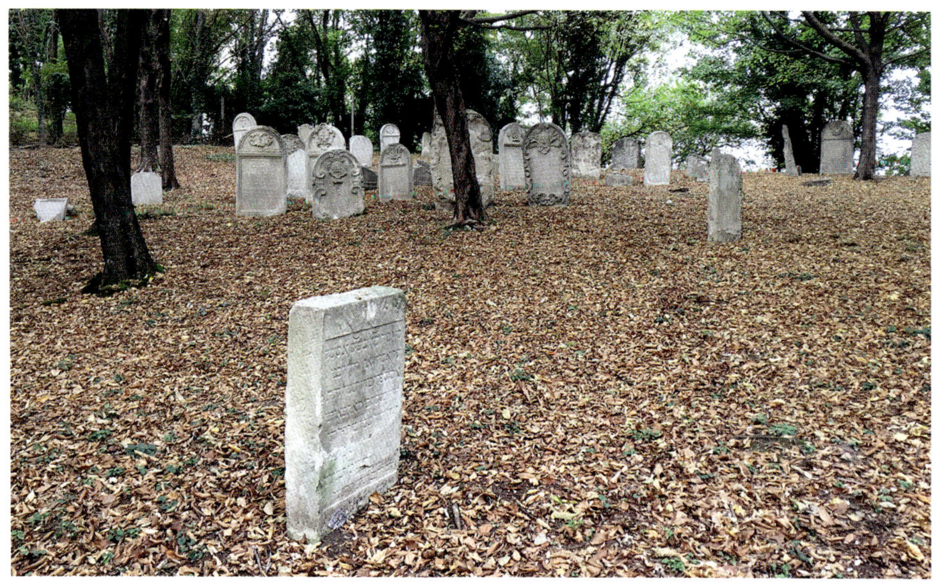

1. View of the Jewish cemetery of Conegliano on the Cabalan hill

And this is the English version of the part in poetry:

1. *Brief is the life of man born of woman* (Job 14.1).
2. See a man who elevated himself above the nobles of the earth.
3. *A whole-hearted and an upright man* (Job 1.8), a *true prince of the peoples* (cf. Psalms 47.10);
4. he was good, *he restored hope to the poor* (Job 5.16) and *repaired the breach* (Isaiah 58.12),
5. placed in this tomb with incorruptible fame.
6. In spite of *glory of his riches* (Esther 5.11), gold is like his powder.
7. *There is nothing good for man* (cf. Kohelet 8.15) except being large of heart,[6]
8. To elevate him to knowledge of the destiny of the end towards which you are running.

Part in prose:

9. The excellent, honoured Refael Hiziqiyyah, blessed be the memory of the just,

10-11. Rose to God from Forlì on Friday 12 Nisan 5352 (March 23, 1592). May his soul be bound up in the bond of life.

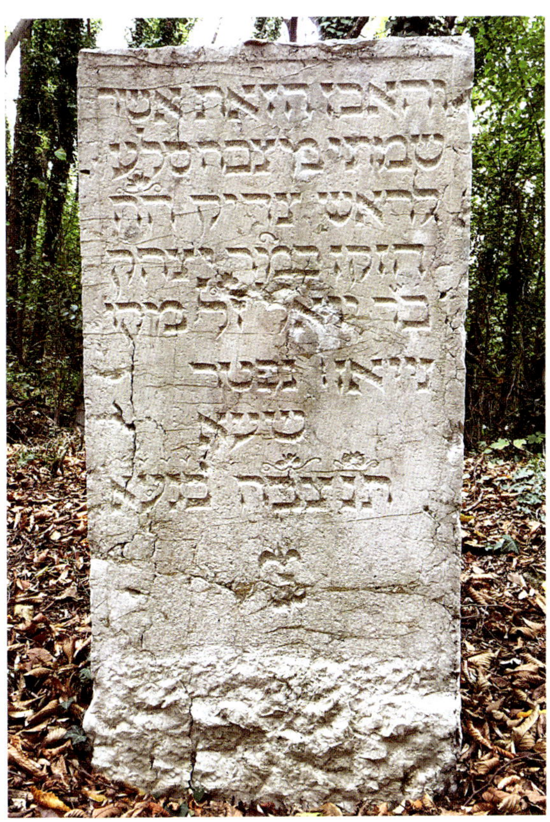

2. Funerary stele of Tishaq ben Yoel from Conegliano, died 1610/1611, in the cemetery of Conegliano

The speaker is the tombstone

Here are a few examples of formulas where the stone itself is speaking to the visitor: *I am the mark of he who is buried here* (אני סימן לפה נטמן), or *Beneath me lies buried the body of a gracious woman* (גוף אשת חן אצלי שוכן); other examples include: *Observe, all of you who pass, that this grave is the mark and emblem of* (הביטו כל עוברי דרך ציון זה הוא אות גם סימן); *The stone shall cry out of the wall* [Habakkuk 2.11] *to the eyes of him who reads it* (אבן מקיר תזעק לעין קורא). And in this interesting example, the stone plays the cicerone who explains to passers-by who is buried in the tomb before them: *To all those who come and who stop here, wondering who it is that lies here, I will answer, saying that…* (לכל הבא ועמד פה והשוכב יהי שואל בקבר זה אני אשי אשיב ואודיעה אשר). In the epitaph of Shemuel ben Shelomoh da Colorno – a forebear of the illustrious Colorni family that came to Mantua from Colorno in the early sixteenth century – who is buried in the city cemetery, the stone speaks, saying: *As a mark, I, stone, a touchstone, was placed here to indicate the body of an upright man* [Job 2.3], *who shared his bread with the hungry* [Ezekiel 18.7 (ציון אבן, אבן בחן יוסדתי פה על איש תמים). From the same old cemetery in Mantua, then brought to the new one in the early nineteenth century, the stone placed on the tomb of Rosa, wife of Eliezer da Rovigo, who died in 1535, speaks and says: *I am the stone erected to celebrate her, placed above the head of Rosa* (אני חומה אשר קמה לרוממה לראש רוסה).

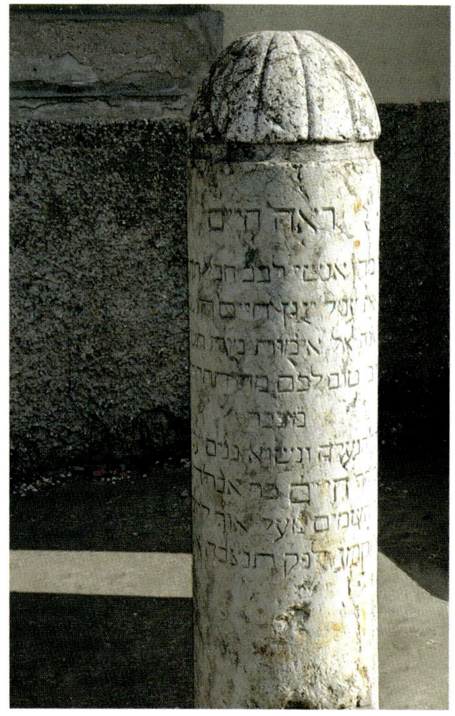

3. Cylindrical memorial stone of Hayyim ben Avraham Norsa, who died in Mantua on January 11, 1783. Cerese

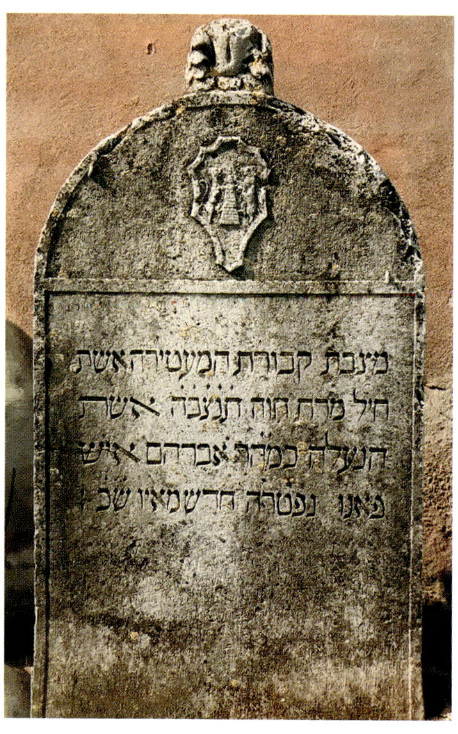

4. Stele of Eva, Avraham Fano's wife, who died in Lugo in 1560. Jewish cemetery of Lugo

The speaker is the deceased

The cases in which the deceased is the speaker in the epitaph are quite rare, but we shall take a look at a few of them regardless. One interesting and significant example is an epitaph in Mantua that is full of Koheletian wisdom bidding the living to enjoy life. It was engraved on the cylindrical memorial stone of an illustrious eighteenth-century Mantuan rabbi and, after it was moved from the old cemetery in the Gradaro quarter to the current site in San Giorgio, it was taken by a non-Jew and placed as ornament with a similar stone on either side of a building that is now in Cerese, in the province of Mantua, whereas the two cylindrical memorial stones are still there. It is the part in poetry, with rhymes always ending in *–u*, of the memorial stone placed to mark the tomb of Hayyim ben Avraham Norsa, who died on the 8th day of the month of Shevat in Jewish year 5543, or 11 January 1783. The text reads:

ראה חיים
עד מה אנשי לבב חבל תחבלו
לתאות עמל גן חיים תשבעו
עד אנה אל אימות מות תשתעו
מנו כי טוב לכם מה תתחלחלו

Enjoy life (Kohelet 9,9). *Until you, men of heart are saddened in mourning, / and fulfilled by the desire to go to the garden of life, / until you look at death with worry and fear, / consider that it is good for you precisely that which is upsetting you.*

The deceased bids the living to consider that their true luck consists in being tormented by life's tribulations, because in any case they are still alive, whereas the speaker is dead. The Hebrew word for life, *hayyim*, is also the name of the deceased, and the person who wrote the epitaph was playing on the double meaning of the word: in the chosen literary genre, it is the deceased *Hayyim* who bids passers-by to enjoy the life *Hayyim*, which opens the part in poetry, citing the words of the preacher or Ecclesiastes, which state: "Enjoy life with the wife whom thou lovest all the days of the life of thy vanity, which He hath given thee under the sun, all the days of thy vanity" (Kohelet 9.9).

[1] Gb. 14,1.
[2] Gb. 1,8.
[3] Gb. 5,16.
[4] Is. 58,12.
[5] Est. 5,11.
[6] Text inspired by Exodus 35.21: "*And all those came who were generous of heart along with all those of noble spirit …*"

Jewish Emancipation in Europe

David Sorkin

What was "emancipation"? "Jewish emancipation" concerns first and foremost the Jews' inclusion and equalization as a distinct religious group. Religious conflict had propelled European polities to engage in destructive wars and systematic persecution for centuries, especially following the Reformation. To endeavor to erect multi-confessional societies, first through various forms of toleration, then through equality, was a historic achievement. The very term "emancipation" came to be widely applied to Jews after Catholic Emancipation Act of 1829 in England. Only in the twentieth century did emancipation come to designate alterations in the Jews' status as a "nation" or a "race" (Grass, Koselleck 2004; J. Katz 1964; Rürup 1975).

Emancipation included civil and political rights. Civil rights comprised residence and occupation, property ownership and freedom of worship, as well as serving as a witness in court, swearing an oath and having juridical standing to bring a lawsuit. Political rights denoted appointment to the civil service, holding elected office and exercising the franchise.

Emancipation designates the acquisition, loss, or recovery of any of those rights. In some countries, the full range of civil and political rights was at stake; in others, exclusively political rights; in still others only one right. Equality requires the ability to exercise all rights; inequality results from the deprivation of even one right.

The story of emancipation is neither a narrative of triumph nor a chronicle of tragedy. Emancipation was inherently ambiguous: the triumphs and tragedies were interlocking. There could not have been triumphs without vicissitudes, tragedies without striking successes.

Jewish emancipation can only be understood through comparison of complex political processes: emancipation belongs to the history of citizenship. The Jews' emancipation cannot be studied in isolation. To cast it as a parochial issue is to misconceive it from the start. We must locate it in its multiple and varied contexts, namely, the individual states in which it developed as well as the transnational patterns that emerged. There were myriad variations across Europe.

I will first offer some general observations about the nature of Jewish emancipation. I will then suggest a schema that distinguishes three patterns of emancipation across Europe. Finally, I will discuss the way Jews lost their emancipation in the inter-war period and with the rise of Nazism.

General observations

Emancipation was recurring and interminable. Emancipation was neither a one-time and chronologically discrete event nor a linear process (Sorkin 2019).

In Italy Jews gained emancipation five times (1796–1799, 1801, 1848, 1861–1870, 1944–1947) and lost it four times (1800, 1813–1815, 1849–1852, 1938). In France Jews gained emancipation six times (1790, 1791, 1818, 1870, 1944, 1961) and lost it twice (1808, 1940). In the German states, they attained rights four times (1800–1813, 1848, 1870, 1945) and lost it three times (1815, 1848, 1933–1941). In Russia Catherine granted privileges in the 1780s that she and her successors rescinded from the 1790s; Alexander III and Nicholas II restricted or overturned (1881–1914) privileges Alexander II had extended in the 1850s to the 1870s; and in the 1920s the Bolsheviks disenfranchised many of the Jews the February 1917 Revolution had enfranchised.

We cannot define emancipation without including the developments of the sixteenth to the eighteenth centuries. Historians' longstanding Germano-centric identification of Jewish modernity with the Berlin Haskalah and Moses Mendelssohn led them to designate events before the eighteenth century "harbingers" and "precursors" (J. Katz 1964; Mahler 1944; Mendes-Flohr, Reinharz 1987). In the abstract there is a clear divide between privileges in corporate society and rights in civil society. In a corporate or estate society privileges were group-specific. Groups held specific privileges through legislated charters that granted them a defined legal status e.g., nobles, priests, burghers. In contrast, the American and French revolutions introduced universal rights predicated on the liberty and equality of the individual. Civil society emerged when group-specific privileges gave way to uniform rights guaranteeing individual equality (Fahrmeir 2007; Poggi 1978).

Privileges in corporate society are conceptually distinct from rights in civil society; historically they were not. Citizenship in civil society emerged from citizenship in corporate society. Parity of privileges in corporate society could lead to equality in civil society.

From 1550, Jews in Eastern (Polish-Lithuanian Commonwealth) and Western Europe (Venice, Livorno, Bordeaux, Hamburg) began to gain extensive privileges bordering on parity with Christian merchants and burghers. In some cases, there was a direct transition from privileges to rights. From the 1590s Jews in Western Europe began to gain civil rights in nascent civil societies (Amsterdam, London).

Emancipation did not end in 1870, or 1917 or 1945. Although the Minority Rights Treaties (1919–1924) that emerged from the wreckage of World War I guaranteed Jews citizenship, the successor states to the Austro-Hungarian Dual Monarchy infringed those rights in the inter-war period. The Nazis put the abrogation of emancipation front and center. Regaining citizenship in Europe after World War II entailed the restoration of rights, the restitution of property and the negotiation of reparations. Some issues of property and reparations are still in play.

The process of emancipation thus continues into the twenty-first century. Jews everywhere, in the Diaspora and in the State of Israel, live in the era of emancipation. Equality and citizenship remain a project rather than a *fait accompli*, a value to be defended rather than taken for granted, a right always subject to infringement or abrogation. Emancipation was, and remains, the principal event of the last five centuries of Jewish history.

Three regions

Two states in Europe created models of citizenship abstracted from birth and religion: the Habsburg Empire by reform, France by revolution (Grawert 1973). These states provided the models for legislation emancipating Jews as well. Other states then adapted that legislation to their own political structures.

Joseph II created the model of conditional or incremental emancipation, meaning partial rights given in reward for utility to the state. Joseph II's legislation was inherently ambiguous. He admitted some Jews "into" estates: some were eligible, for example, to gain the estate specific privileges of guilds. At the same time, he moved Jews collectively "out" of estates by dismantling the Jews' collective corporate privileges. In practice, partial emancipation persisted until 1867 when the new Dual Monarchy resolved the fundamental ambiguity of "into" and "out" of estates in favor of the latter.

France created the model of unconditional emancipation, meaning immediate full and equal rights gained through extraction "out" of estates. This legislation was in keeping with the Revolution's dissolution of estates and corporate bodies. France's practice of emancipation was, however, decidedly ambiguous. Sephardic Jews gained rights through the confirmation of their privileges (1790); Napoleon revived conditional rights (1808); forms of inequality lingered into the 1830s and 1840s (rabbis' salaries; *more judaïco*; state subsidies); and the entire process recapitulated itself in Algeria (1830–1870), although the Mzabi Saharan Jews did not receive citizenship until 1961.

Europe had three regions of emancipation. Emancipation comprised a "complex variegated family of instances," in which the differences between regions, and the variations among countries, were fundamental (Birnbaum and Katznelson 1995).

Western Europe. In Holland, England, and southern France Jews gained civil rights through the circumstances of settlement. Jews had to mobilize only for political rights. Jews in southern France (Bordeaux, Bayonne) gained political rights through the confirmation of their privileges (January 1790). Jews in Holland gained political rights with the creation of the Batavian Republic (August 1796). Jews in England gained political rights piecemeal from the 1830s until the first Jew swore the oath to sit in Parliament (1858). The duration of the struggle for rights was, albeit intense, relatively brief.

Central Europe. From the sixteenth to eighteenth centuries the German states and Habsburg Empire had enacted "Jewry laws" that imposed an inferior legal status, relegating

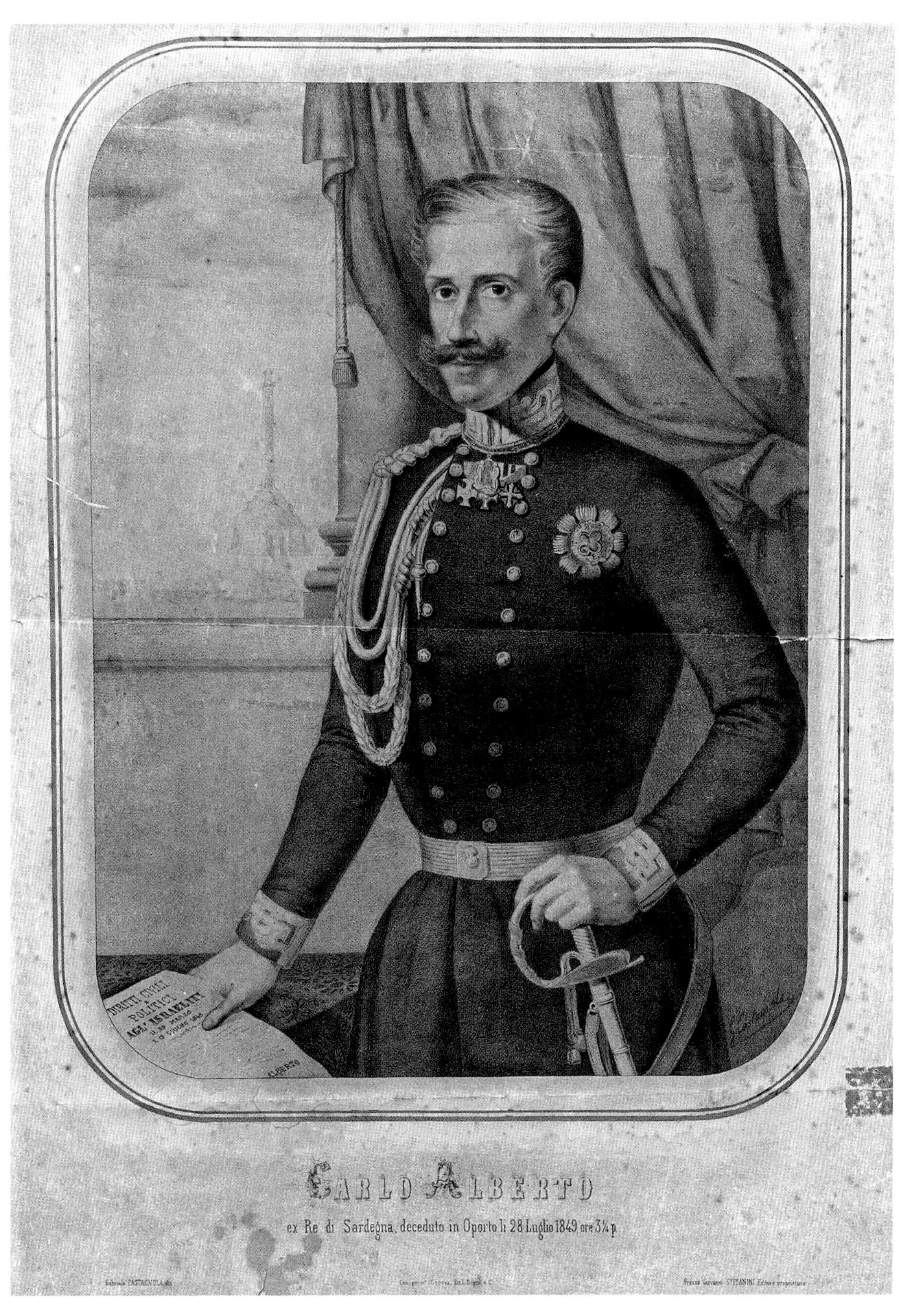

1. Gabriele Castagnola, *King Charles Albert Signs the Emancipation of the Jews*. Museo d'Arte e Storia Antica Ebraica, Casale Monferrato (cat. 42)

Jews to the margins of corporate society and granting privileges according to their ascribed utility. The struggle for rights was broad in scope, encompassing both civil and political rights, and prolonged, lasting for most of a century. Central European states granted conditional or partial emancipation, making additional rights contingent upon *régénération* (Grégoire 1789) or *Verbesserung* (Von Dohm 1781–1783) understood through the ideal of *Bildung*, that is, the restructuring of occupations, education and communal and religious life to promote utility to the state (Fink 2004). The state legislated and supervised that regeneration. States granted rights by moving Jews both "into" and "out" of estates. A definitive policy of "out" of estates came only with the restructuring of the Dual Monarchy (1867) or Germany's unification (1870).

Eastern Europe: Polish-Lithuanian Commonwealth, Russia, Congress Poland. As in Central Europe, the struggle for rights in Tsarist Russia was broad in scope, encompassing civil and political rights, and prolonged, lasting for over a century. It also involved far more Jews: sheer numbers were a significant factor.

Russian legislation followed Central European models of conditional emancipation that made rights contingent upon regeneration. Yet Tsarist policy emphasized coercion over incentives. Moreover, Russian legislation adhered to the policy of moving Jews as individuals "into estates." This was in large part due to the estates' nature: the estates (*sosloviia*) were not direct descendants of medieval or early modern institutions, but an eighteenth-century creation designed to serve Tsarist interests. Finally, in contrast to Western and Central Europe, Jews first gained political rights (Congress Poland, 1861; Russia, 1905) and then civil rights (Congress Poland, 1862; Russia, 1917).

Abrogation

The war and post-war in Eastern Europe crisis impinged directly on Jews' citizenship. The collapse of the Dual Monarchy and Tsarist empires turned masses of Jews into stateless refugees: a half million from Galicia and a half million in Poland and Romania. Many contemporaries regarded the White army's pogroms in Russia as a "reaction to Jewish equality" that aimed to restore "disenfranchisement" (Holquist 2001).

The Paris Peace Conference championed national minority rights. These collided with nationalities-states that aspired to be nation-states, e.g., Poland, Hungary, Romania. The Soviet Union proclaimed itself to be "the incubator of nations" yet disenfranchised a disproportionate percentage of the Jews who had gained rights in 1917 because they pursued occupations deemed inimical to the socialist revolution (Pinkus 1988; Polonsky 2010).

The Third Reich deprived Jews of their citizenship with hundreds of legislative acts. The Nazis peeled away the Jews' rights layer after layer in an almost exact reversal of the emancipation process. Dis-emancipation inverted emancipation's structure (Rürup 1986; Pulzer 1986). The Nazis first attacked the political rights that Jews had acquired most recently (1933); then their citizenship by introducing an inferior status of "State member" (1935); then their civil rights by excluding them from the economy and their residences and expropriating their labor and assets; and finally deprived them of their lives with deportation and mass murder. The Nazis extended this policy to every country they occupied, with varying degrees of intensity and success (Barkai 1989; Dean 2008; Walk 1981).

Italy's racial laws (1938) were indigenous: they were key to a second fascist revolution. The first revolution (1920s) was the consolidation of authoritarian rule; the second (1930s) was shaping a homogeneous nation to support an imperial totalitarian state. Mussolini aspired to transform Italians from a "race of slaves" into a "race of lords" – imperial citizens who were consummate workers and warriors. The antitheses of the new empire and the new fascist man (*uomo fascista*) were the liberal state and the bourgeois spirit: the Jews personified both (F.H. Adler 2005 and 2008; Pavan 2013). Mussolini tried to force Jews to emigrate by depriving them of their occupations and assets (F.H. Adler 2005; Sarfatti 2006).

Vichy France's "national revolution" radicalized the late Third Republic's increasingly hostile policies towards immigrants. Vichy implemented its own, indigenous antisemitic legislation. Its Jewish policy was a "rival" to, not an import from, Nazi Germany (Marrus and Paxton 1995; Mayer 2010). Vichy's "state Antisemitism" (*antisémitisme d'État*) aimed to use the rule of law and juridical procedures to abolish the equality of 1791: the state would regulate Jews for the benefit of all Frenchmen (Marrus and Paxton 1995). The government placed antisemitic activists in positions of power, especially at the Commissariat-General for Jewish Affairs (29 March 1941).

Reinstatement

Restoring emancipation entailed the reinstatement of citizenship, the restitution of property and reparations for resettlement, rehabilitation, forced labor, and "heirless property." In general states promptly reversed de-naturalizations and reinstated citizenship as part of their own reestablishment. In contrast, restitution of property and reparations entailed prolonged and contentious processes, in many cases continuing into the twenty-first century.

The emancipation that began in the sixteenth century continues to this day. It is the principal event of modern Jewish history.

Jewish Citizens
Carlotta Ferrara degli Uberti

The subtitle of this exhibition, *Inside&Out*, evokes a spatial dimension but also a cultural and identity-forming one. Jews moved physically inside and outside the ghetto walls and beyond the confines of the pre-unification states, and this movement was accompanied by the circulation of both material (texts, objects) and immaterial production (ideas, performances, stories, superstitions). Identity, elusive and changeable, is perhaps the most difficult variable to analyze, since intrinsically plural and ambivalent, even when we try to give it a firm definition. Indeed, we are all made up of so many things, and in today's world there is a growing trend to emphasize the value of these different aspects and attribute positive value to choice. Gender, ethnic, national, religious and political identities are decreasingly tied to a presumed material objectively and increasingly linked to the self-presentation of the single individual. The nineteenth century preferred clearer definitions, at least at the level of rhetoric and imagination, since practice is always more complex and multifaceted than theory. It can be described as the century of the idea of nation and of nationalism, although various empires did continue to prosper alongside the birth and development of nation states. This essay explores the intertwining of the Risorgimento, the construction of the Italian nation and the emancipation of the Jews.

The term "emancipation" indicates the attainment of the freedom to act independently, without being subject to a master, in the case of slaves, parents, in the case of children and a husband, in the case of married women. It indicates release from a minority state. Here, we can identify a dual significance. On the one hand, liberty is bestowed upon/granted to the emancipated person. On the other hand, this only happens when a higher authority has determined that an individual or group is worthy of enjoying liberty. In the case of the Jews, this term is usually used to designate the attainment of full equal standing before the law in terms of enjoyment of civil and political rights. The nineteenth century is sometimes described as the century of the emancipation of the minorities (Catholics in the United Kingdom, Protestants in Catholic countries, serfs in Russia, Jews a bit in all directions). As explained by David Sorkin, emancipation is not a single moment but a process, and it is subject to explicit and implicit negotiations over time. Further, it can be partially or fully revoked (Sorkin 2019).

How many, and where

"Italy" is of course too imprecise an indication to be used here without further comment. We shall therefore note what the Italian Peninsula was at the time, where the main Jewish communities were located and the regime to which they were subject. Our first consideration concerns the overall numeric magnitude of Italian Jewry or, as many have argued, Italian Jewries. It is a very small minority, oscillating between 30 and 40,000 individuals between the end of the eighteenth century and today, but distributed very unevenly across the territory. In 1800, there were 34,300 Jews (out of 18 million) resident in the area contained within the Italian borders as they are today, a number that climbed to 43,100 (out of nearly 34 million) in 1900 and then went down to 28,000 (out of just over 45 million) in 1945, as a result of the Shoah. At the end of the eighteenth century, the regions with the largest number of Jews, in absolute terms, were Tuscany, Piedmont, Emilia-Romagna, Friuli-Venezia Giulia, the Veneto and Lazio. There had been almost no Jews south of Rome since the expulsions between 1492 and 1541. Naples again became home to a Jewish community in 1863, through the good offices of the Rothschild family, which inaugurated a branch of its bank there in 1831, opening the way for the return of a number of individuals and families.

Rome has always been at the top of the list of the largest Jewish communities, but the other slots have varied radically. The geography of Italian Jewry changed considerably during the nineteenth century and the first half of the twentieth century, and it is clear that internal migrations were influenced by the political and economic development of the various regions and cities. Two examples will suffice to get an idea of the magnitude of the transformations. In the middle of the nineteenth century, Livorno still occupied second place, with 4,771 Jews registered in the Tuscan census of 1841, while Milan was of utter irrelevance that same year (Luzzati 1986). In the subsequent decades, however, Livorno suffered considerable economic and demographic decline, linked to the reduced importance of its port's economic activity within the new institutional and political framework of unified Italy. The exodus of its entrepreneurs, bankers, merchants and professionals in favor of Florence, Rome and other growing cities was gradual, but it had a profound impact on the city. Milan, on the contrary, slowly became one of the beating hearts of the new state's economic and cultural life, and as the city developed, so did its Jewish community. Its growing importance is also reflected in the current situation (Maifreda 2000).

The Jewish communities scattered across the peninsula were subject to different legal systems, but they had at least one thing in common: they operated as intermediaries between individuals and the state authorities, following a practice typical of the old regime that was not limited solely to Jews. The modern idea of equality, in fact, could not be applied to that political and legal system: indeed, all subjects were placed in categories, groups and bodies that determined their rights, duties and social status (and vice versa); all were un-equal.

The three years of Jacobin rule

The Italian history of Jewish emancipation began with the arrival of the troops of the French Republic established by the Revolution, the bearers of what historians describe as the first emancipation of the peninsula's Jews. This is not merely conventional dating. As is broadly agreed, every reconstruction of the process of Jewish emancipation, as with the origins of the Italian Risorgimento, is rooted in the revolutionary events, which put to the test in political practice, on a large scale, concepts and ways of seeing the world that had been up to that point the preserve of intellectual speculation. I am thinking of the rejection of the divine legitimisation of political power and the attribution of sovereignty to the people (the *nation*); the recognition of the existence of inalienable individual rights and the principle of equality, which must be protected by the state; the breaking up of the intermediary bodies that, in the age of the old regime, had been the mediators between individuals and the central authorities, and the natural holders of rights and duties; the secularization of politics or its sacralization, two only apparently contradictory concepts, and the change in relations between the civil and religious authorities, in particular the Catholic Church.

The Revolution exported its ideals and laws, which included the legal equality of the Jews, sanctioned by the National Assembly in 1790 for the Sephardim and in 1791 for the Ashkenazim (Hyman 1998). The peninsula was almost entirely upended in 1796, with its geo-political configuration completely redrawn for a number of years. The Treaty of Campo Formio, signed on October 17, 1797 by France and Austria, decreed the end of the Venetian Republic, which was ceded to Austria, and the passage of northern Italy under French rule. The Hapsburgs decided against extending the Josephine Edicts to the annexed Venetian provinces. On April 28, 1796, the Kingdom of Sardinia signed the Armistice of Cherasco, surrendering Nice and Savoy to France along with various other territories and guaranteeing the French army passage within its borders. The pope abandoned Rome in 1798. In just a few years, France came to control or directly rule almost the entire peninsula, with the exception of Sicily, Sardinia and the territories ceded to Austria. In 1802, the first Italian Republic was formed, comprising Lombardy, part of the Papal States and the Duchy of Modena, transforming in 1806 into the Kingdom of Italy, with the addition of the Veneto, Istria, Dalmatia and, later, Marche and Trentino.

Not all Jews welcomed these changes. Here, we need to distinguish between the activity of individuals, often enthusiastic about the new course of events and in many cases politically active for the first time, and the official positions taken by community institutions. The latter generally kept a low profile, partly because they feared the repressive repercussions of the "legitimate" sovereigns should the new regime fall; partly because the governing oligarchies were disinclined to cede their own privileges, especially when these were considerable, as was the case, for example, in Livorno (Luzzati 1986; Bregoli in the present volume). There was also a generational element in play, with younger Jews more enthusiastically embracing the cause of liberty and equality. Revolutions, for that matter, are almost always the work of the young.

The revolutionary ferment and new status of the Jews were not welcomed everywhere with calm and enthusiasm. During the three years of Jacobin rule between 1796 and 1799, before the Napoleonic stabilization had its effect, there was antisemitic tumult in Senigallia, Urbino, Pesaro, Monte San Savino, Arezzo, Siena, Pitigliano and Acqui. This was the consequence of the anti-French insurrections (Luzzatto Voghera 1998) and marked the end of the communities in Monte San Savino and Arezzo. Before the French arrived on the peninsula, antisemitic violence was recorded in Livorno in 1790, Mantua in 1792 and Rome in 1793 (Milano 1963). One thing that these violent episodes shared was the equation of the Jews with liberals, Jacobins, anticlericalism, the revolution and, more generally, modernity, which was viewed as dangerous and anti-Catholic.

Napoleon

With the proclamation of the Empire in December 1804, the work of Napoleonic reform and centralization began, part of which was reflection on the situation of French Jews and those living in other imperial territories (Hyman 1998). French Jews had been emancipated just over ten years earlier, but they had not entirely disappeared, blending in with the rest of society, which was interpreted by some as a betrayal of the pact that had been implicitly placed at the foundation of the decree of equality. To clarify the situation, Napoleon decided to convene an Assembly of Notables representing all of the Jews in the Empire, to which the government submitted a list of twelve questions aimed to establish once and for all whether the Jews could be said worthy of the rights of citizenship and whether the labels Jew and French were compatible. The Assembly met in Paris in July 1806. Of the 111 members, thirteen were sent from Piedmont and sixteen from the Kingdom of Italy, out of which only eight were rabbis (Milano 1963). To legitimize the Assembly's answers, a sanction was needed that could be considered binding, and to this end Napoleon actually decided to resurrect a religious and jurisdictional institution of pre-diaspora Judaism: the Sanhedrin. The Grand Sanhedrin, composed of seventy-one members, two-thirds of which rabbis, opened in February 1807. Thirteen rabbis and six laymen came from Italy. This assembly ratified the answers provided by the Notables, adding a clause that permitted Jewish soldiers to abstain from observance of religious precepts should they come into conflict with their military duties. Both the Assembly and the Sanhedrin drew on a recurrent principle in the Talmud: *dinah de-malkutah dinah*, literally translatable as "the law of the kingdom is law" (TB, *Nedarim* 28a; *Gittin*, 10b; *Bava Kamma*, 113b; *Bava Basra*, 54b-55a) (Graf 1985). The preliminary declaration adopted by the Assembly of Notables, which marked out the guidelines for the discussion, is significant in this regard. The French Jews, identified as French citizens practicing the religion of Moses, guaranteed that their religion compelled consideration of the law of the prince as supreme law in civil and political matters (Luzzatto Voghera 1998; Sofia 2008).

The Restoration

For the Jews of the peninsula, the Restoration represented a return to the limitations of the period before 1796, with a few more or less important differences. Almost everywhere, the representatives of the Jewish communities welcomed the legitimate sovereigns with proclamations dripping with joy, relief and adulation. As is always the case when analysing documents of this type, caution is required, since it is very difficult to read between the lines of rhetorical formulas, aimed to protect the minority from the potential reprisals of the central power. Communication with the ruling power is a literary genre unto itself, and the Jewish communities – or more accurately, their elites – had to master it particularly well in order to negotiate their rights and duties in often hostile contexts, over the centuries. Historical research has in fact revealed that Jews were almost never passive in their relations with the ruling power, always at least trying, with varying success, to mediate and negotiate (Biale 1988).

In the Veneto provinces, which returned to Austria after being annexed to the Kingdom of Italy in 1806, the Restoration did not mean returning to the ghetto (in the case of Venice, for example), but nor did it mean the official extension of the Josephine Edicts of Tolerance. The Jews of the Veneto and Friuli were guaranteed important rights such as the right to possess property, to practice a wide spectrum of professions (with the exception of notary and pharmacist) and to enrol their children in the public schools. Exclusion from public office was reconfirmed (D'Antonio 2012). This does not mean, however, that there were no Jews in public positions: numerous exceptions were made, permitting single individuals to construct roles for themselves as public officials.

In Piedmont, the situation of the Jews worsened, at least on paper, due to the restoration of the Royal Constitutions of 1770, with a ban on property ownership and an injunction to transfer ownership of all acquired property. However, contemporary sources mention many cases of Jewish property owners, Jews who had taken advantage of the liquidation of church assets to build property fortunes. Since a return to the situation prior to the French upheaval would have been almost impossible, and potentially bring with it considerable damage to the local economy, the authorities came to terms with the situation as it was, issuing a four-year extension in 1816 for the transfer of property ownership. An additional deferment was granted in 1822 (Luzzatto Voghera 1998).

In the Papal States, the worsening of conditions for the Jews was especially evident and particularly during the papacy of Leo XII (1823–1829) (Caffiero 1997).

In spite of the contradictions of the period between 1796 and the 1820s, we cannot underestimate the importance of those years for the formulation of the idea of an Italian nation, on the one hand, and of the aspiration to Jewish emancipation, on the other.

Regeneration

A word that was very often used in the eighteenth and nineteenth centuries but is relatively unfamiliar to us in the twenty-first century is "regeneration." Then, it expressed a process of rebirth that implied improvement, a transition from a negative condition to a positive one, not only or not so much on the material plane as on the moral one. The obvious opposite is the idea of degeneration, which was very popular in the second half of the nineteenth century, especially after it was theorized by Bénédict-Augustin Morel in 1857. There is a clear tie to the religious lexicon and a progressive conception of history, which, for that matter, permeated the imagination of the leading – Jewish and otherwise – figures of the Risorgimento (Romani 2018). "Regeneration" was used to indicate both the advance of the Italian nation – from Manzoni's "scattered mob with no name" to the self-aware entity that struggles for independence from the foreigner – and a process within the Jewish minority, tied to emancipation. Starting in the late eighteenth century, European debate on the emancipation of the Jews had in fact connected recognition of equality to requirements for improvement that typically involved abandonment of work tied to the manipulation of money in favor of land ownership, agricultural labor and physical activity, but often ended up involving the hope that the final stage of this process would be conversion to Christianity (Luzzatto Voghera 1998). These ideas, with the exception of the final conversion, were also shared by the Jewish elites of the time, who applied them most of all to the poorest levels of the population and used them to promote projects for reform in the heart of the individual communities.

Risorgimento and Emancipation

Between the 1830s and 1840s, various political plans were developed with the aim of creating a new, centralized and federal unified Italian state. The details of these plans are not relevant to our current discussion, but broadly speaking we can identify a moderate monarchic front and a democratic republican front, which were temporarily united by enthusiasm for Pius IX, perceived between 1846 and 1848 as a liberal pope (Veca 2019). Many Jews were involved in the political and cultural activism that characterized these two decades, in particular from the upper middle class, as members of Masonic Lodges (see the essay by Sofia in this volume) and secret societies like the Carboneria or Giovine Italia, founded by Mazzini in 1831. Here, we need to specify that this activity was undertaken by individuals, or, in a few cases, families, and was not an expression of support by the Jewish communities as institutional representatives of Jews living in a given area. A few leading figures postulated an explicit affinity between their own Jewish identity and Italian patriotism, interpreted as liberation from foreign domination or a condition of subjugation. Interpreted, in short, as true emancipation.

1848, a year of upheaval and revolution throughout Europe, is of critical importance to this story (Catalan 2012). Among the numerous sovereigns of the pre-unification states that granted their citizens – more or less reluctantly – a constitution, we find Charles Albert, king of Sardinia, who signed the statute that bears his name, the Statuto Albertino, on March 4. Article 1 read: "The Catholic, Apostolic and Roman Religion is the sole religion of the State. The other existing cults are tolerated in conformity with the law," while Article 24 stated: "All of the citizens of the Kingdom, whatever their title or rank, are equal before the law. All equally enjoy civil and political rights, and may hold civil and military appointments, save for exceptions determined by law." The sovereign had already emancipated the Waldensians on February 17. On March 29, 1848, decree no. 688 was issued, clarifying that the *Israelites* of the Kingdom "will enjoy from this date forward all civil rights and the right to take academic degrees." The final step was decree no. 735 of 19 June, which finally prohibited the limitation of civil and political rights on the basis of religion.

The Piedmontese legislation is worth a close look for two reasons. First, the Piedmont reforms were the only ones to survive the repression of the revolutionary uprisings of 1848/49. All of the other constitutional charters were abrogated, the last being that of Tuscany, in 1852. Second, the statute went on to become the constitution of the Kingdom of Italy in 1861 and remained in force until the Republican constitution was drafted after World War II. In fact, in 1848, Piedmont became the military leader of the process of unification that was accomplished through annexations (by military conquest or plebiscite) to the Kingdom of Sardinia. We can therefore say that, starting in 1848, the fate of the political and military plan for national unification and that of Jewish emancipation were linked, and proceeded together side by side.

This circumstance did not escape the notice of contemporary observers, nor that of their immediate successors. The convergence of events was often interpreted as necessary,

Ebrei 1848.

205

N.° 688.

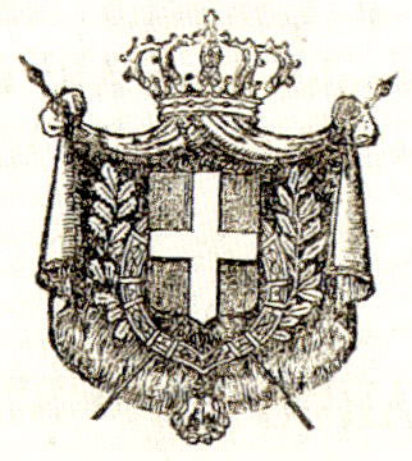

CARLO ALBERTO

PER LA GRAZIA DI DIO

RE DI SARDEGNA, DI CIPRO E DI GERUSALEMME,

ECC. ECC. ECC.

Sulla proposta del Nostro Ministro Segretario di Stato per gli affari dell' Interno abbiamo ordinato ed ordiniamo:

Gli Israeliti regnicoli godranno dalla data del presente di tutti i diritti civili e della facoltà di conseguire i gradi accademici, nulla innovato quanto all'esercizio del loro culto, ed alle scuole da essi dirette.

Deroghiamo alle leggi contrarie al presente.

Il Nostro Ministro Segretario di Stato per gli affari dell' Interno è incaricato dell' esecuzione del presente,

Vol. XVI.

1. Royal Decree of March 29, 1848, granting full civil rights to all "Israelites." State Archives of Turin (cat. 44)

206
che sarà registrato al Controllo Generale, pubblicato ed inserito nella raccolta degli Atti del Nostro Governo.

Dato dal Quartiere Generale in Voghera addì 29 di marzo 1848.

CARLO ALBERTO.

V. Sclopis.
V. Di Revel.
V. Gazelli pel Controllore Gen.

Franzini.

Il Ministro Segretario di Stato per gli affari Interni
Vincenzo Ricci.

Registrato al Controllo Generale
addì 1.° aprile 1848
Reg. 4 Editti a c. 21
Moreno Capo di Divisione.

STAMPERIA REALE.

as if the new Italy were intrinsically tied to this mission of liberty, indeed as if a providential plan bound the destiny of unified Italy to that of the Jews.

Emancipation did not come only as a gracious sovereign concession. In various contexts, Jews and Jewish communities mobilized to call for legal equality, something that had not happened previously. A Special Israelite Committee of Piedmont was instituted in 1845, chaired by rabbi Lelio Cantoni. Its original mission was to investigate the state of the communities, but it soon became instrumental in awakening public opinion and the sovereign to the cause of the emancipation (Arian Levi-Disegni 1998). Collaboration between the different Piedmontese communities was, however, anything but easy, because they were embroiled in deep rivalries. The first meeting of the delegates from all of the communities was held on November 13, 1847. One of the leading figures of this period was David Levi (1816–1898), a Piedmont native born in Chieri, educated at the Collegio Foa of Vercelli and initiated to Freemasonry and to the Giovine Italia in Livorno in 1837 (Grazi 2015). A close associate of Mazzini's, he contributed to the organization of the Bandiera brothers' failed expedition in 1844. He was not only a poet and writer but also a politician, elected to the Parliament of the Kingdom of Sardinia in 1860 and then to the Italian Parliament in 1861. In March 1848, a few days before the Statute was granted, Levi met the King as the representative of the Piedmontese communities, to plead the cause of emancipation. When war broke out between Piedmont and Austria, Lelio Cantoni urged his fellow Jews to support the patriotic effort by enlisting as volunteers. In a letter dated March 22, 1848, preserved at the Archivio Terracini, he celebrated the departure of the volunteers and declared: "I hold it certain that this prelude to our liberation will be felt and put into practice everywhere with equal passion." Between 1847 and 1848, many Jews took up arms in various parts of the peninsula. From a material and symbolic perspective, this was a moment of critical importance, since defense of the homeland is historically tied to citizenship and rights, at least from the second half of the eighteenth century forward. Bearing arms was a right/duty of the (male) citizen.

A civic guard was instituted in the Grand Duchy of Tuscany on September 4, 1847, and after some brief discussion it was clarified that Jews had the right to take part in it, which implicated the revocation of the rules that excluded them from military service. As the jurist Isacco Rignano observed: "Through this virtuous institution, the way has been finally opened for the Israelites to give their lives and resources for the Homeland, and so to fulfill one of the most pressing religious duties, that of loving, serving and sacrificing oneself for one's native land" (Rignano 1847). On September 6, the leaders of the Jewish community of Livorno tasked a committee to formulate a strategy for pleading emancipation before the authorities in collaboration with the other Tuscan communities. In this case as well, rivalry came into play, in particular with Florence, that wanted to take a leading role (Ferrara degli Uberti 2007). Article 2 of the Tuscan statute, promulgated on February 15, 1848, sanctioned the equality of religious minorities.

It would be impossible to map out, in such a short space, a complete picture of Jewish participation in the revolutionary uprisings that shook the various pre-unification states and give an account of its nature and complexity (Catalan 2012). The case of Venice is exemplary. In Venice, the insurrection that cast out the Austrians was led by Daniele Manin (whose paternal grandfather was a Veronese Jew converted to Catholicism), with the support of rabbis Abramo Lattes and Samuele Salomone Olper, the latter a fervent republican and follower of Mazzini, appointed secretary of the provisional government. In 1849, Olper was sent by Manin as an envoy to the Roman Republic and, after the repression of the uprisings, he moved to Florence, then Livorno and finally Piedmont, where he was appointed the successor of Lelio Cantoni as Chief Rabbi. Other prominent figures in Venice were Isacco Pesaro Maurogonato (1817–1892), appointed finance minister by Manin, and Leone Pincherle, minister of agriculture and trade in the provisional government. After unification, Maurogonato was appointed deputy in 1866 and served as vice-president of the chamber between 1874 and 1890.

It is difficult to estimate how many Jews participated in the battles fought during the Risorgimento campaigns. The available lists provide us solely with surnames, which can be, however, misleading. The surname indicates paternity, whereas Judaism is transmitted through the mother (a person is Jewish if their mother is Jewish), and the surname in any case does not tell us whether the person felt any kind of connection with Judaism or descended from people who had converted to another religion generations ago. It is always necessary to cross reference with other sources and carry out more in-depth research. We know, however, that many Jews did fight. One of them was Gustavo Uzielli (1839–1911). The son of Sansone Uzielli (1797–1857), who was a member of the committee for the emancipation of the Livorno community, and Marianna Foà (1808–1882), who was very active in philanthropic activities, both within the community and in the city. Gustavo graduated from the University of Pisa and devoted himself to geography, which led him to become a founding member of the Italian Geographical Society in 1867, along with another Jew, Cesare D'Ancona. He was a friend and patron of the Macchiaioli, with an affinity for their artistic activity as well as their political endeavors in support of the Italian cause. In 1859, he joined the Cacciatori delle Alpi, and then followed Garibaldi, including in his

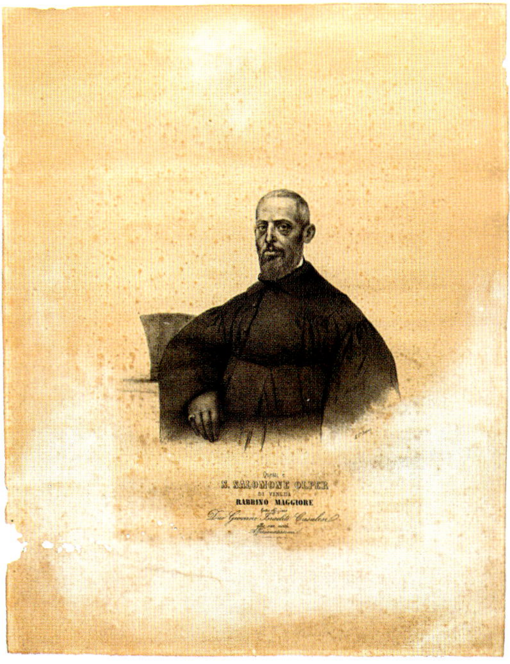

2. E.F. Sotteri, *Salomone Olper*. Museo d'Arte e Storia Antica Ebraica, Casale Monferrato (cat. 43)

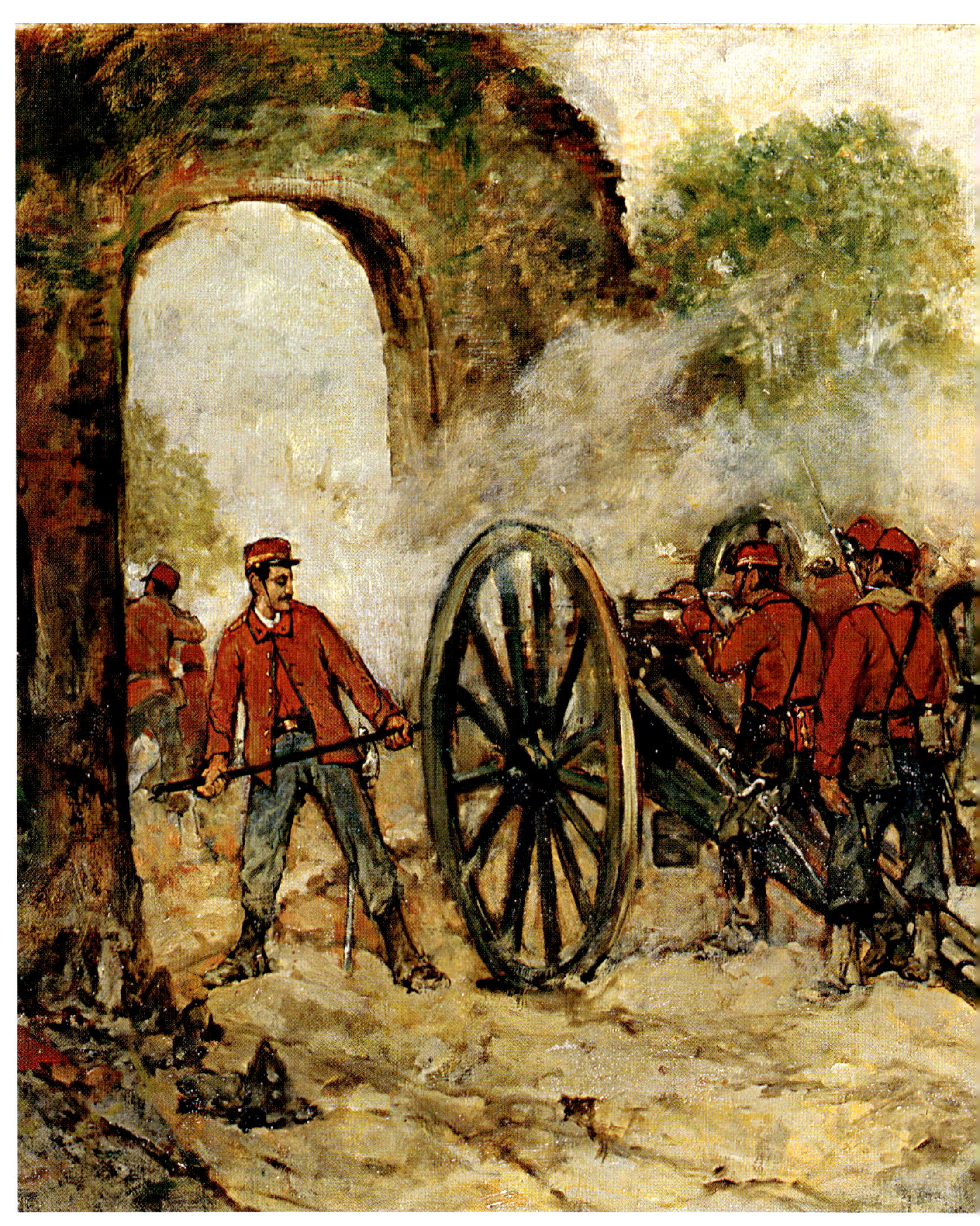

3. Giovanni Fattori, *The Battle of the Volturno*, detail. Gallery of Modern Art in Palazzo Pitti, Uffizi Gallery, Florence (cat. 45)

Expedition of the Thousand, fighting in the Battle of Volturno, that took place between late September and early October 1860. He was decorated with a silver medal for his bravery in battle. This episode, critical in the clashes with the Bourbon army, was immortalised by Giovanni Fattori (1825–1908) in his celebrated painting *The Battle of Volturno*. For the composition of the work, Fattori turned to Uzielli, a friend of his, for his eye-witness testimony and portrayed him in the painting in a position of prominence, legs spread while fearlessly loading a canon under the arch of Porta Capua (Boine 1993; Uzielli 1909).

Among the Macchiaioli, at least two Jews should be noted: Vito D'Ancona (1825–1884) and Serafino De Tivoli (1826–1892), both of whom fought as volunteers in the Battle of Curtatone and Montanara 29 May 29, 1848. Vito was from a prominent Jewish family that was originally from Pesaro but had moved to the area of Florence/Pisa. The nephew of the banker Laudadio Della Ripa, he was the brother of the banker Sansone, the already mentioned Cesare, and the younger Alessandro (1835–1914), the latter an acclaimed literary scholar, specialised in Dante, who taught at the University of Pisa between 1860 and 1900, and served as head of the Scuola Normale di Pisa between 1893 and 1900. Serafino, born in Livorno to a family of merchants but raised in Florence, also participated in the defense of the Roman Republic in 1849. In London from 1862 to 1873, this is where he met Giuseppe Mazzini, of whom he painted a portrait that is now in the Domus Mazziniana, Pisa.

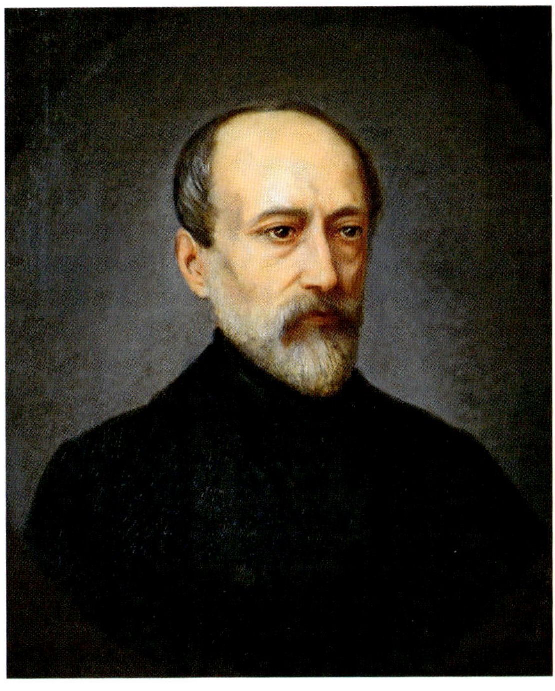

4. Serafino De Tivoli, *Portrait of Giuseppe Mazzini*. Domus Mazziniana, Pisa (cat. 48)

Italians

When the Kingdom of Italy was officially founded on March 17, 1861, the emancipation of the Jewish and Waldensian minorities was a firm fact, merely reinforced by the conquest of Rome on September 20, 1870, with the consequential end of the temporal power of the pope and of the injustices that the Roman Jews had endured under papal domination. Italian Jews, especially those with cultural and economic means, threw themselves enthusiastically into the plan to build a unified state in all of its aspects, both locally and nationally. Purely by way of example, these individuals included Mantuan Tullo Massarani (1826–1905), jurist and politician, appointed member of Parliament in 1860; Giuseppe Ottolenghi (1838–1904), appointed War minister in 1902; Luigi Luzzatti (1841–1927), jurist, economist and scholar of religion, president of the Council of Ministers between 1910 and 1911; Paduan jurist Vittorio Polacco (1859-1926), preceptor of the crown prince Umberto, appointed Senator in 1910; Ernesto Nathan (1845–1921), a Freemason and the mayor of Rome between 1907 and 1913; Lodovico Mortara (1855–1927), son of the rabbi of Mantua Marco, jurist and minister of Justice and Religion between 1919 and 1920, appointed Senator in 1910, and the socialists Claudio Treves (1869–1933) and Giuseppe Emanuele Modigliani (1872–1947). These are just a few of a great many names, to whom we should also add those of the intellectuals, entrepreneurs and individuals – men and women – active in every area of society. How and in what sense were these leading figures in Italian life Jewish? It is impossible to generalize. For some, being Jewish was a fundamental aspect of their individual and family identity and influenced their way of seeing the world. For others, it was instead little more than a family memory, perhaps tied to the survival of a network of friendships. Still others were reminded of being Jewish only when someone labeled them as such. In no way can we think that Jewish politicians and intellectuals worked as a pressure group in favor of some kind of "Jewish" cultural or political project, as also emphasized by Gadi Luzzatto Voghera in his essay in this volume.

How was the identity-forming dynamic between inside and outside reformulated at the moment of integration into national society? An image that was very popular for the entire nineteenth century took a dualistic view, according to which one could remain Jewish (or better, as it was said at the time, an Israelite) within the family and religious spheres (inside), but be Italian like everyone else in the public sphere, or outside (Ferrara degli Uberti 2012). A dichotomy of this kind might work in the abstract, but in practice, inside and outside are in constant relation and impossible to keep clearly separate. Let us, for example, think of marriage. While patriotic enthusiasm is palpable in the numerous examples of tricolor *ketubot* (marriage contracts) and in the beautiful *ketubah* of Soragna of 1860, where Victor Emmanuel II, Garibaldi and Cavour are all portrayed, it is also true that, for those who wanted to defend the survival of the minority, it became increasingly important to support intermarriage and the formation of Jewish couples and families. There was in fact a fear that the new equality might lead to an increase in mixed marriages and, consequently, to the gradual erosion of the already tiny Italian Jewry (Ferrara degli Uberti 2012).

A story titled "Religione e patria," written by Flaminio Servi and published in *L'Educatore Israelita* between 1864 and 1865, clearly expressed some of these issues (on the periodical press, see Ferrara degli Uberti's essay, "Italian Jewish Periodicals 1845–1915," in the present volume). The protagonist of the story is Guglielmo, a fifteen-year-old Jew from Livorno who enlists as a volunteer in 1859. Wounded in the Battle of Magenta, he falls on

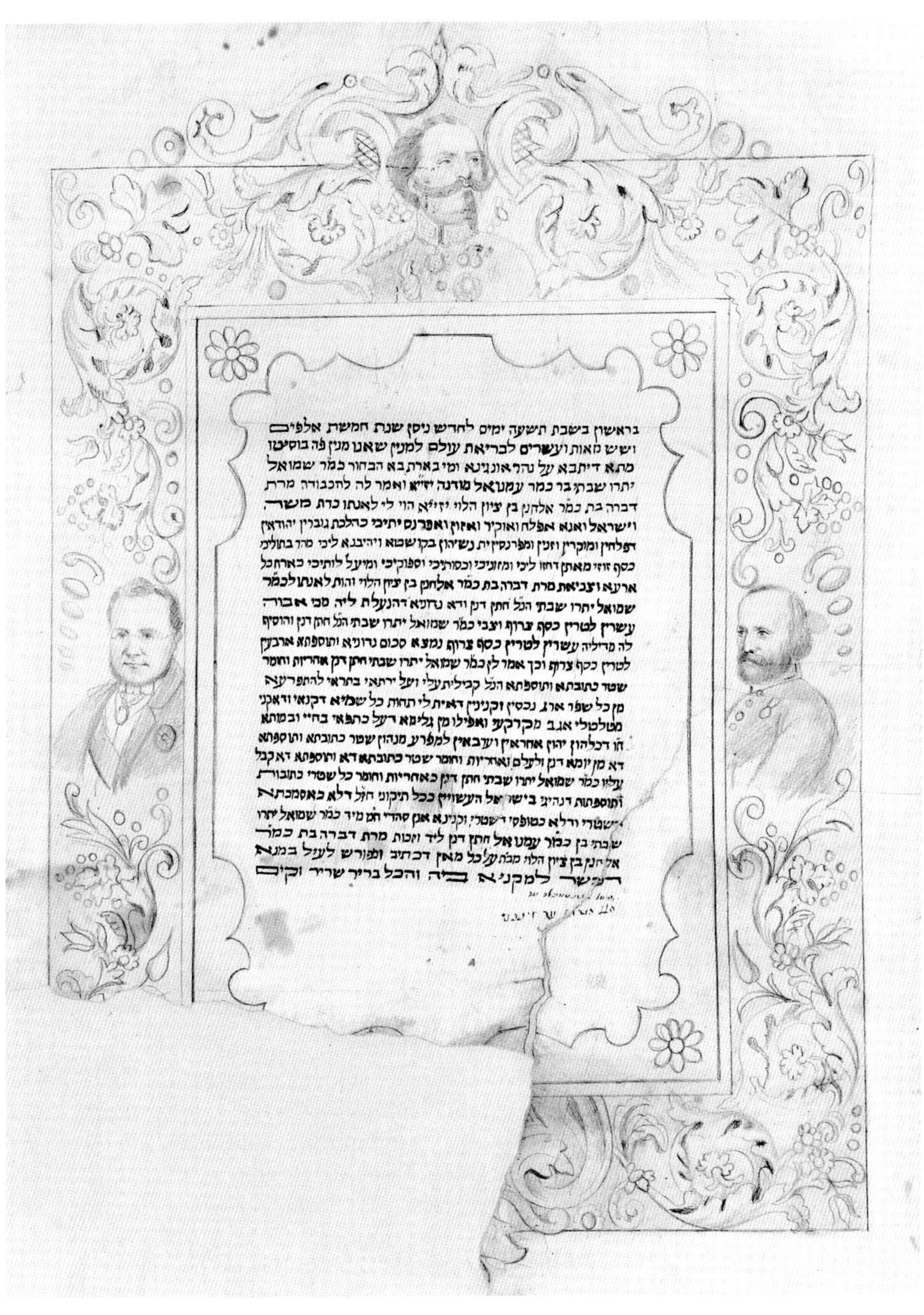

5. *Ketubah*, marriage contract. "Fausto Levi" Museum and Synagogue, Soragna (cat. 52)

the battlefield murmuring *Shema Israel* and is hospitalised in Milan, where he is assisted by a nurse named Giulia. The two young people fall in love, but it is only upon discovering that Giulia is Jewish as well that they can truly imagine a future together. Beyond the plot, the narrative is constructed with continuous references to Jewish citations – especially prayers – and others explicitly or implicitly drawn from Dante, Petrarch, Tasso, Manzoni and Berchet. The Jewish citations and the Italian ones were both an integral part of the author's and his readers' culture and imagination. As for the moral, Servi spells it out in the final remarks, asking: "Do we need to explain why we wrote this story? It was to show the young, in particular, that patriotism and religion can be beautifully paired, with no risk of harm, and should indeed be joined in harmony, where a true citizen is wanted" (Servi 1865[a]). Having Italy as a homeland and being Jewish were not only compatible but indeed reinforced one another and were completed in the formation of a family that was both fully Jewish and fully Italian. This vision can be considered representative of the way that most Italian Jews felt in the second half of the century, and, far from being purely descriptive, it should be read as a program and daily effort. Zionism, which, like the minority movement, burst into the internal debates of Italian Jewry in the 1880s, did not undermine the deep roots of this scenario. Zionists, who were for the most part young, reacted to what they perceived as a dilution of Jewish identity caused by the success of integration, and clamored for the Jewish aspect to be given more prominence, but without putting their Italianness into question.

Equality was, therefore, not only an opportunity but a challenge. Or perhaps it would be more accurate to say that it was a new iteration of an age-old challenge, that of remaining Jewish in a Christian-majority society, and of reinterpreting this plural identity through categories suited to the times. The big change was that, after emancipation, there were no longer external laws that imposed particular behavior on Jews, or that tried to rigidly define what/who Jews and Judaism were or should be.

Resistance

This Jewish history is profoundly Italian, profoundly European. But what was the position of the non-Jews on this key juncture of emancipation? The names of some of the Italian supporters of equality are very well known – Carlo Cattaneo, Niccolò Tommaseo, Massimo and Roberto d'Azeglio – and historians have closely analyzed their arguments, motivations and limits (Luzzatto Voghera 1998). It is important, however, to also keep in mind the resistance and the persistence of prejudice, which was not limited solely to the Catholic Church or the Catholic world proper (see Facchini and Mortara in this volume).

Francesco Domenico Guerrazzi, a patriot and writer from Livorno, described the Jews on many occasions in unflattering terms, although without ever opposing the granting of equality. "Where there is money, there is a Jew." he declared in his *Note autobiografiche*, written in 1833 and published posthumously in 1899. And again: "They cheat with impunity"; "They maintain themselves as Moses made them; whether in Tuscany or Romagna or Poland, everywhere is Egypt for them, every populace, Egyptian. […] They pass through the centuries and people like oil through water." In 1846, Guerrazzi clashed with Sansone Uzielli, who was director of the Banca di Sconto at the time. Getting worked up defending two shareholders against the bank administrators, Guerrazzi compared Uzielli to a "spider at the bottom of a hole lying in wait for a fly, to snatch his portion of usury" (Guerrazzi 1846).

A case well known to scholars is the one involving Isacco Pesaro Maurogonato. When the second Minghetti government was formed in the summer of 1873, Maurogonato's name was on the short list of those considered for finance minister. Veneto deputy Francesco Pasqualigo sent a telegram to the King and publicly declared himself opposed to the appointment. In a letter published in *Il Diritto*, he specified: "I believe that the high offices of minister should only be entrusted to men who are *purely* Italian. It is my view that the Jews scattered amidst other populations, since the time before Christianity, have always constituted and constitute in any case a political-religious association" (Calimani 2016). Maurogonato wrote directly to the King to refuse the post, expressing his conviction that it would have been inappropriate for a Jew to take on the responsibility of imposing of imposing laws on religious bodies, in the context of the clash between the Italian State and the Church, to be assigned to a Jew. The case stirred up broad debate and one of the participants was the rabbi of Mantua Marco Mortara, who wrote a pamphlet titled *Della nazionalità e delle aspirazioni messianiche degli Ebrei* (On nationality and the Messianic aspirations of the Jews) in which he stated that "love for the various homelands and unification with the various nationalities shines perhaps more brightly and vigorously" among the Israelites in all the world (M. Mortara n.d. [1873]).

In 1901, Ferrara nationalist Eugenio Righini published a booklet titled *Antisemitismo e semitismo nell'Italia politica moderna* (Antisemitism and Semitism in modern Italian politics) in which he denounced the over-representation of Jews in positions of power, particularly political ones. Jews, he wrote, "belong to two nations: their own nation, the Jewish one, and the one where they were born and live." Given this alleged fact, which was in his view certain and ineliminable, Righini perceived that there was danger of a sentiment of Jewish solidarity prevailing over the Italian national interest and Jews working as a lobby in pursuit of an autonomous and supranational plan.

These three examples, quite different from one another, show that the persistence of difference, of a plural identity inspired fear even and perhaps actually more after equality, since the restrictive legislation of the past allowed at least some kind of control over the minority. In particular, the existence of a collective Jewish identity – the community, the people – was often erroneously perceived and represented as the threatening presence of a group with interests that differed from those of the majority. While it is true that in nineteenth-century and early-twentieth century Italy antisemitism was rarely used as a tool for political struggle and mobilization of consensus, unlike what happened in other European countries like France, Austria and Germany, various forms of prejudice, mistrust and antisemitism were widely present in Italy as well, at all levels of society.

Formulations of identity move endlessly between inside and outside, minority and majority, family and society, individual and collective, and can be imagined as a game of mirrors and reciprocal influences. Studying Jewish history – e.g. the patriotic enthusiasm and the negotiation of integration – helps us identify important features of the Italian nation building process and of Italian national identity.

Mazzini's Jewish Entourage

Marcella Pellegrino Sutcliffe

What is the purpose of a study on Mazzini's Jewish entourage today? What is the significance of tracing a map of the Italian patriot's connections with the Jews he met during his prolonged exile and of assessing the legacy of these relations? And why carry out this study today? This subject has in fact already been explored (Sofia 2010), yet in the light of the reflections on Mazzini's legacy that have emerged over the last years (Levis Sullam 2010[a]) it is important to understand and newly contextualize the exile's relations with his Jewish friends since it not only furthers our understanding of Mazzini as an individual, but it also sheds light on the meaning of Mazzinian doctrine in its inclusive interpretation of the concepts of "fatherland," "nation," and "people." Therefore, to contextualize Mazzini in the framework of his relations with his loyal Jewish friends, on the one hand provides the opportunity to pay homage to the memory of often forgotten personalities, and on the other serves the purpose of acknowledging the role his Jewish friends played in the definition of his thought and political action towards the unification of the Italian "People," the shaping of a Republican nation, and in bringing Italians to familiarize with democratic citizenship.

In London, where Mazzini lived from 1837 to 1848, and then also after the suppression of the Roman Republic, Mazzini's small entourage included a Jewish family, the Nathans. After marrying Moses Nathan, Sara Levi Nathan – born in Pesaro and raised in Livorno with her cousins the Rossellis – moved to London in 1837, the same year as Mazzini. The two soon met thanks to Angelo Usiglio, a Jew from Modena, also an exiled patriot who after being expelled from Switzerland arrived in London where he shared a house with Mazzini and the Ruffini brothers. A secular and culturally integrated Mazzinian, Usiglio was an important interlocutor for Mazzini who thought very highly of him, defining him as a "honest, conscientious, active and moral [man] above all criticism" (A. Levi 1931). With him Mazzini used to talk about Italy and future projects. Another subject they explored was that of the condition of women: it was during that period that Mazzini developed his reflections on the condition of inferiority women were relegated to and on the need to recognize and encourage the fundamental role women could play in the education of each family and of society as a whole. These ideas found fertile ground in the Nathan family, and in particular with Sara, mother of twelve children, who embodied Mazzini's ideal of motherhood as strictly linked to education.

But let's take things gradually. During his first years in London, Mazzini had to repeatedly deal with the disapproval of his beloved mother who was not supportive of her son's new acquaintance with the Nathan family. In one of his letters to her, Mazzini seems to make fun of his mother's prejudices, ironically reassuring her with these words: "I will eat only after they've eaten. I will have antidotes with me," as if he wanted to dissipate his mother's irrational fears in the face of common Catholic stereotypes.

Mazzini reassured his mother about the Nathan family and cultivated his friendship with them. He recognised the value and patriotic commitment of the Nathans' good nature and of other Jews who had found refuge in London. He knew well that many of them were in exile for the role they played in the insurrection in the Duchy of Modena. Mazzini was adamant about defying the prejudices shared not only by his acquaintances in Italy but also by some of the expatriates he met in London. Before recommending his friend Maurizio Quadrio as tutor for the Nathan children, for instance, Mazzini had to deal with his own friend's reluctancy. He wrote about this matter to his English friend Emilia Hawkes: "I shall decidedly urge Quadrio to accept the 'sons of Israel' [...] And if he surmounts the first impressions he will soon find himself at ease with the Nathans. They are truly excellent people" (Isastia 2010). It is worth underlining how the wording "surmounts the first impressions" is an expression that today might be read as an invitation to overcome wariness towards those we do not know and who belong to a different culture and to defeat fear coming from diversity. In fact, the Nathan household became a place very dear to Quadrio, just as it was for Mazzini who in 1866 wrote to Sara Nathan saying "they were like his family in Italy" ("*consideratevi la mia famiglia in Italia*").

Presumably, first contacts between Mazzini and Sara Nathan were via the Rosselli cousins, Michelangelo and Pellegrino who were friends of Usiglio's. The young exiles used to meet to play music together, the flute and the guitar were their instruments, enjoying each other's company as an antidote to the hardships of their exile. They were young, they shared the same condition, and had the same interests, and this helped them overcome the differences engrained in their different backgrounds. All these aspects in fact became increasingly irrelevant in the relationship between Mazzini and the Nathans that grew closer every day. Suffice it to say, in 1855 – one of the darkest times in Mazzini's life due to the failure of the Milanese insurrection of February 6 – Mazzini was invited to celebrate Purim at the Nathans' where Moses made sure his guest always felt supported (A. Levi 1931).

After Moses' sudden and unexpected death, Sara continued his efforts to provide moral and economic support for Mazzini's republican vision. In 1841 she began collecting subscriptions in favor of one of Mazzini's earliest London projects: the institution of an Italian school for the education and moral training of Italian workers in London. The enthusiasm the young woman poured into this initiative stayed with her throughout her life, even after Mazzini's death when she founded several Mazzinian schools in the newly unified Italy.

In her unwavering commitment towards the education of Italians, Sara embodied the ideal Mazzinian woman, not unlike Giorgina Saffi, Aurelio's wife and Sara's devout friend and working partner. Sara the Italian Jew and British-Italian Giorgina were determined to offer their contribution to the mission of "making Italians" through education, expanding their action beyond the typically female domestic sphere. Sara decided to offer her daughters the same learning opportunities she provided for her sons, and her choice of using the same tutor for all her children confirms this. Mazzini encouraged all the children of the Nathan household. We know for instance that Giannetta, the eldest of the three daughters, was particularly dear to Quadrio and Mazzini for her intellectual curiosity. Mazzini undoubtedly counted on the young Nathans to become future young Mazzinians capable of promoting the Republican cause in Italy and future agents of transformation in the unified Italy. Testifying to the deep bond Mazzini had with this family we must remember that in 1872 Mazzini – who by then was severely ill – stayed in Pisa in the home of Sara's daughter, Janet Nathan Rosselli, in the building that today is home to the Domus Mazziniana, where he died on March 10 of that same year.

Soon after his death, with the support of the trusty Quadrio, Sara, who had by then moved to Rome, dedicated her energies to the foundation of Sala Mazzini, the evening school that aimed to educate the younger generation in Mazzini's ideas, fighting against materialism; later she fought against the disparity between men and women's political and civil rights, in the wake of the emancipation theories promoted by Mazzini himself. Towards the training of a new generation of Italian women, free from obscurantism, ignorance and Catholic superstition, in 1873 Sara started dedicating her energies to the creation of an elementary school for young girls from the poor families of Trastevere. Instead of Catechism classes this school taught principles of civil education based on the reading of a simplified version of Mazzini's *The Duties of Man.* Unsurprisingly these initiatives were greeted with hostility by the priests of the neighbourhood who did not hesitate to spread falsehoods about the school, that was accused of being "in the grip of the devil" (Isastia 2010). But Sara Nathan did not give up, and after her death her daughter Adah continued her work.

Sara Nathan spent her last years in Rome and is buried in the Verano cemetery. Her hometown Pesaro however never forgot her: in 1886 the Republican Association of Pesaro placed a plaque on the house where she was born. A great crowd participated in the event in the presence of the City representatives, the workers' associations, and the children of the Nathan family. Furthermore, Pesaro also entitled one of its roads to Sara Levi Nathan – an important public tribute to a female personality that, as the correspondent for the *English Woman's Review* noted, was a true exception in the Italian context of the time (*Foreign Notes* 1887).

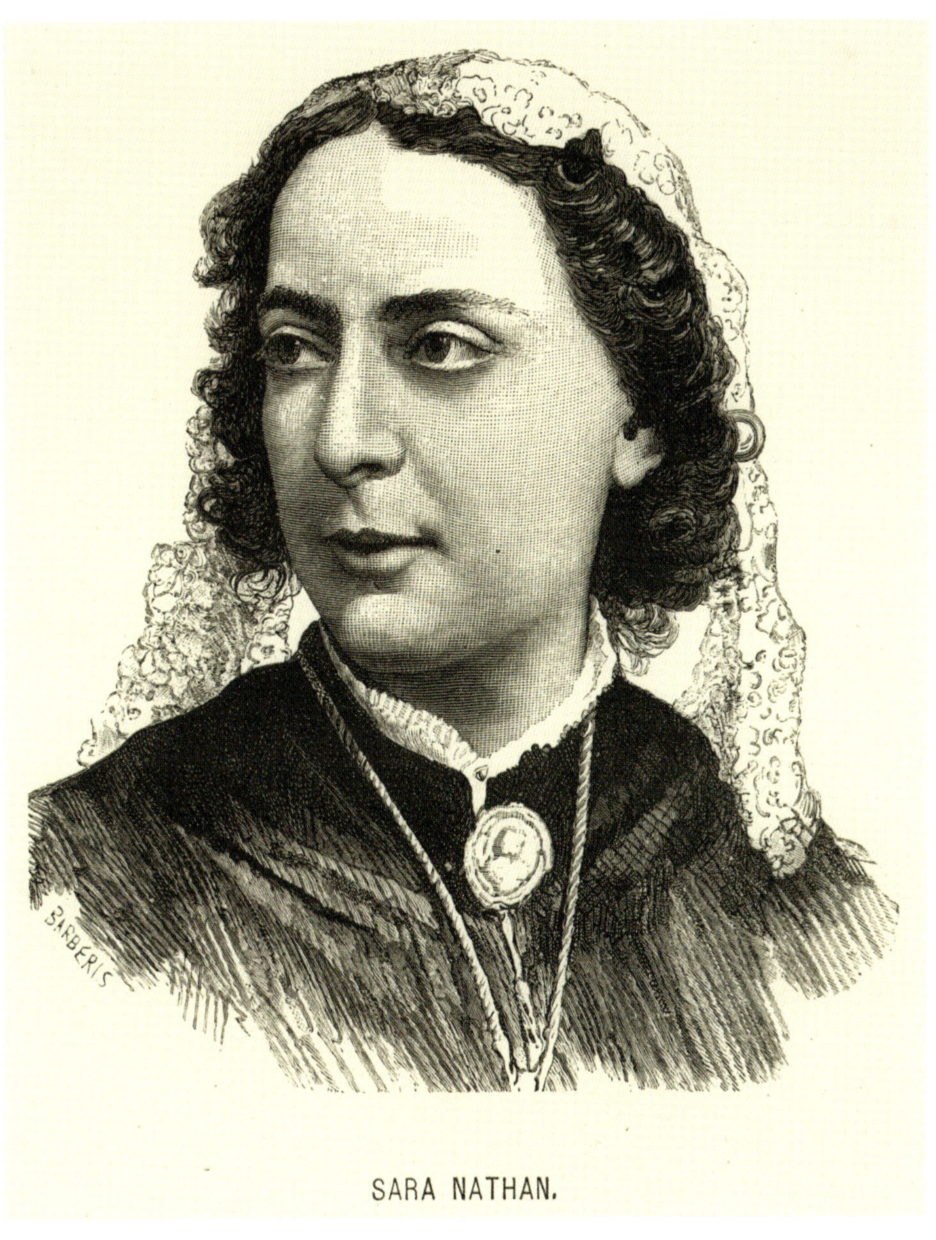

1. *Sara Nathan*. Illustration by Jessie W. Mario for *Della vita di Giuseppe Mazzini*, Milan, Edoardo Sonzogno Editore, 1886

Jews and Freemasonry

Francesca Sofia

If on the one hand the admittance of Jews to Masonic lodges is indicative of their level of integration in society – as pointed out by Jakob Katz (J. Katz 1970) – it must be remembered that in Italy the earliest records referring to Jewish freemasons date back to the 1770s, a few years before Joseph II's *Patent of Toleration* (1781), the act initiating the age of emancipation. The famous response given by rabbi Hayyim David Azulai in 1774 in Tunis about the inappropriateness of sentencing to death fellow Masonic Jews (J. Katz 1967), for instance, refers precisely to a number of "Italian" Jews (probably from Livorno). Jewish presence in Masonic lodges obviously increased after their complete legal emancipation following the arrival of Napoleon's troops in Italy. The Loggia della Perfetta Unione (Lodge of the Perfect Union), for instance, founded in 1796 in Livorno by the officers of the French garrison, was directed by a Jewish merchant from Avignon, Felice Morenas. Jewish presence in this lodge continued to be considerable throughout the years of Napoleonic rule (Bertini 1989).

With the advent of Restoration, many Jews eventually joined secret sects, which often derived from Masonic lodges, to uphold those principles of legal equality and freedom repressed by the reinstated monarchs. This was the case of David Levi, a Jew from Piedmont, who was initiated to Freemasonry in Livorno in 1837 and became secretary of the Grande Oriente d'Italia (Grand Orient of Italy) after the unification. Levi deeply believed in the continuity between Libera Muratoria, the Carboneria, and Mazzini's Giovine Italia, as if these three different affiliations were interchangeable (Sofia 2006 and 2011). A similar course of action was taken by Leone Provenzal, from Livorno: active since 1835 probably in the British lodge of his hometown, he was an active participant in the world of sects, and also became member and honorary master of the Grande Oriente d'Italia (Ascoli 1880). Jews were also an important presence in the lodges after Italian unification, clearly in relation to the percentage of Jewish population in the country that did not surpass 1%. It is documented that some of the most prominent Jewish intellectuals of the time were affiliated to Masonic lodges (the previously mentioned David Levi, as well as Tullo Massarani, Eugenio Camerini, Giuseppe Revere, Giacomo Venezian). But the identification between Judaism and Freemasonry becomes even more marked, especially in the eyes of the

Church, in the years 1896–1904, when the Grande Oriente d'Italia was directed by Ernesto Nathan. It was in these years that the myth of the Judeo-Masonic conspiracy was developed across Europe (Conti 2003).

But why did Jews join the Freemasonry? During the Risorgimento, Jews were probably drawn to Masonic lodges because these organizations upheld principles of democracy and religious equality that were present in the new collective dimension of the Italian nation in the making. After the country's unification, what encouraged Jews to join the lodges were the positions of Italian Freemasonry (widely inspired by the program drawn by David Levi in 1861) on a variety of aspects: their promotion of a patriotic spirit, paired with initiatives encouraging peace in the world, dissemination of culture and of working-class welfare, and commitment to philanthropic initiatives were all causes Jews could easily embrace. An additional aspect that must not be overlooked is the lodges' conspicuous and disorderly assimilation of elements deriving from Jewish culture: the Temple, as a founding myth at the core of Masonic iconography, both in the version of Solomon's Temple built by Hiram, the son of a widow from the Naphtali tribe, and of Zerubbabel's Temple after the Babylonian exile. But there is more: in the Ancient and Accepted Scottish Rite of Freemasonry, which was the most common rite in nineteenth-century Italian democratic entourages, many of the secret ritual words with which initiates confirm their degrees were also of Jewish origin (although not always correctly transliterated) (Cazzaniga 2014). In David Levi's extensive literary production, Masonic and Jewish militancy seem to be connected, as if freemasons were the custodians of the forefathers' ethical and religious principles. But this analogy can also be found in the words written after the Italian Unification by rabbi Elia Benamozegh, whose affiliation to Freemasonry has not yet been confirmed. In his posthumous text entitled *Israele e umanità*, Benamozegh affirmed that "Masonic theology corresponds rather well to the Kabbalah" adding that "in-depth study of the rabbi monuments of the early centuries of the Christian age provides abundant evidence that the *hagaddah* was a popular secret science, whose rites of initiation bear impressive analogies with Masonic institutions" (Benamozegh 1990).

Italian Jewish Periodicals 1845–1915

Carlotta Ferrara degli Uberti

The first half of the nineteenth century saw an unprecedented proliferation of periodicals covering a very diverse range of topics – entertainment, politics, satire, costume – favoured by the increased level of freedom the press had reached in many European countries. The first Jewish periodicals were also founded in this period, providing emancipated Jews, or those in the process of emancipation, a public space where new forms and articulations of Jewish identity could be discussed. To mention just a few of the most important European periodicals of the time: *Les Archives Israélites* and *L'Univers Israélite* were founded in France, respectively in 1840 and 1844; *The Voice of Jacob* and, most notably, the periodical that would become the world's longest running Jewish magazine, *The Jewish Chronicle*, were founded in England in 1841; and the *Allgemeine Zeitung des Judentums* was founded in 1837 in Leipzig.

With regards to Italy, I will offer a brief overview of the most important periodicals that were active between the mid-nineteenth century and World War I. The reader must bear in mind that on the whole the periodicals of that age, often short-lived and with a local focus, but nonetheless very interesting, were far more numerous than those mentioned in this study (Milano 1938).

In 1845 in Parma, then under the rule of Marie Louise of Hapsburg, cultural agitator, captain (later colonel) and patriot Cesare Rovighi (1820–1890) founded *La Rivista Israelitica* with the purpose of educating his coreligionists to modernity, encouraging them to embrace literature, science, the arts and the liberal professions (Di Porto 1999). *La Rivista* was issued irregularly for three years and was permanently closed down during the tumultuous and revolutionary year of 1848.

In 1853 Giuseppe Levi (1802–1874) and Esdra Pontremoli (1818–1888) founded *L'Educatore Israelita* in the Kingdom of Piedmont (Casale Monferrato), that was about to become the leading force in the process of national unification and that had already granted full full emancipation to the Jews in 1848. The aims of this periodical were to support the Jewish minority during the transition to national unification and redefine what it meant to be Jews as well as citizens, Jews as well as Italians (Di Porto 2000, Ferrara degli Uberti 2012). In 1874, when Giuseppe Levi died, Flaminio Servi (1841–1904) took on the role of editorial director and decided to change the magazine's title to *Il Vessillo Israelitico*, maintaining an ideal continuity with *L'Educatore*. Targeting Jewish readers that were already citizens of a unified Italy, *Il Vessillo* set out to promote success stories of integration and defend the Jewish minority from assimilation, intended as the total loss of a separate identity (Ferrara degli Uberti 2012). The periodical closed in 1922 in 1922 having exhausted its programmatic mission that was closely connected to a nineteenth-century liberal mentality.

In 1862 Abram Vita Morpurgo (1813–1867) founded *Il Corriere Israelitico* in Trieste.

Although the city was still under the rule of the Hapsburgs, *Il Corriere* was published in Italian and mostly focused on peninsular Judaism with a certain regard for the German-speaking contexts (Di Porto 2004). Initially similar to the *Vessillo* in its programme, in 1896 *Il Corriere* took on a markedly pro-Zionist position. In 1898 this ideological shift was reinforced by the arrival in Trieste of Dante Lattes (1876–1965) who would remain at the head of the magazine from 1903 to 1915 (Luzzatto Voghera 2005).

Il Vessillo, on the other hand, did not embrace the Zionist movement and this circumstance fuelled a rivalry between the two major Italian Jewish periodicals. Although antagonists, the two magazines shared most of their collaborators. After all, the Jewish minority was so tiny that these disputes necessarily took place in what could be called a "domestic" context. *L'Educatore, Il Vessillo,* and *Il Corriere* represented an important point of reference for a part of the Italian Jewish religious, cultural, and administrative elites, and reflected the effort to create a public space where the challenge of facing modernity, integration and secularization as Jews could be discussed.

Il Corriere wasn't the only expression of Italian Zionism, which was in fact a multifaceted movement including a plurality of voices, although it was supported by a small number of Italian Jews until the second post-war period. Also worth mentioning is *L'Idea Sionnista*, a magazine that was published in Modena from 1901 to 1910, close to the Federazione Sionistica Italiana, the Italian Zionist Federation. Founded by Carlo Conigliani (1868–1901), *L'Idea Sionnista* set out to fight against the growing antisemitism that was affecting especially Eastern Europe by promoting a form of non-religious Zionism based on solidarity: "To show solidarity [...] with our distant brothers, mutually improving them, and ourselves" (*I nostri ideali* 1901, p. 1).

But in the early years of the twentieth century the Italian city that was home to the liveliest literary, artistic, political debates and avant-garde movements was Florence. With regards to the Italian Jewish community, a crucial event in this city was the arrival of Shmuel Hirsch Margulies (1858–1922), who was chief rabbi of Florence from 1890 and director of the Rabbinical College from 1899. Between 1904 and 1915 Margulies personally directed *La Rivista Israelitica,* a periodical that aspired to establish itself as an erudite and international publication, in the wake of *La Revue des Études Juives.* Less directly, the Galician rabbi also deeply influenced *La Settimana Israelitica*, published between 1910 and 1915, whose contents mostly stemmed from the initiatives of Alfonso Pacifici (1889–1981). *La Settimana Israelitica,* which was the first Jewish weekly in Italy, endorsed religious and nationalist Zionism, vigorously promoting a Jewish cultural rebirth, mainly aiming at younger readers. In 1916 *Il Corriere* and *La Settimana* were merged and renamed *L'Israel*, which was the first Italian Jewish periodical that was sold at the newsagent's and not only via subscription.

The Catholic Church and the Jews in Italy from the Early Modern Period to the Twentieth Century

Cristiana Facchini

In his book *Anti-Judaism*, historian David Nirenberg identified hostility to "Judaism" as a central theme of western Christian religious thought, convincingly dealing with a much-debated historiographic subject, that is the difference between "anti-Judaism" and "antisemitism" (Facchini 2010). In his research, Nirenberg acknowledges anti-Judaism and its metamorphoses as a category of political thought inherent to Western culture but, with the exception of the Spanish medieval context, he omits to explore Western Christianity's contribution to the ramifications of such anti-Jewish hostility. In Nirenberg's genealogy, after the Protestant Reformation, the debate on anti-Judaism appears to pass from Reformed to lay contexts, with particular focus on the Enlightenment and the French Revolution (Nirenberg 2013).

The present contribution starts from this omission, without overlooking the problematic and possible interactions with the world of Protestant Reformation, and begins by taking into account the geographical context of the Italian Peninsula that was – and still is – home to the Papal State, and where the demographically limited but culturally lively and relatively stable Jewish presence in some cases dates back to the Roman Empire.

The early modern period

Between the end of the fifteenth and the early sixteenth century, we can single out two events that proved to be crucial in the history of Christian Church-Jewish relations: the first was the "reconquest" of the Iberian Peninsula at the hands of Ferdinand II of Aragon and Isabella of Castile, a struggle that led to the fall of the Kingdom of Granada, to the expulsion of the Jews, to forced conversions, and eventually to the persecution of the *conversos* and the *moriscos* by the Inquisition ecclesiastical courts; the second event was the success of the Protestant Reformation, which radically changed the religious landscape of Latin Christianity. This was indeed a historical phase characterized by a conspicuous presence of refugees and migration fluxes composed of groups forced to leave the country in which they resided, often to escape religious persecution with the hope of finding a new place to settle. Jews were a considerable part of these groups and these resettlements were integral to a long-term process of expulsions and forced emigrations that had first initiated during the Middle Ages. Another factor that further complicated matters in cities that in some cases developed into centers of great religious and economic importance – such as Amsterdam, Livorno and Hamburg – was the presence of the *conversos*, Jews converted to the Catholic faith who were willing (or forced) to return to Judaism (Israel 2002; Bodian 1997).

The Catholic Church with its influence set the standards of religious tolerance across its domains as well as in the other Kingdoms on the Italian Peninsula. One of the most remarkable aspects of this historical period is the ambivalence of Catholic policies in relation to Jewish presence. If on the one hand there was repression, a practice that grew more severe during the years of the Council of Trent, and that continued during the following centuries, on the other there were also alternative approaches based on commercial pragmatism and reason of State.

The attitudes of the Catholic world towards the Jews living on the Italian Peninsula and in the Papal State can be categorized into three typologies.

The first type of approach, which informed policies of refugee acceptance, was based on the principle of economic utility, and was formulated in Spanish and Italian Catholic contexts and widely adopted in Calvinist and Reformed societies. This approach was also to some extent received by the Jewish world, in particular in Simone Luzzatto's works that for a few centuries enjoyed a certain circulation in Europe (Facchini 2011[b] and 2013). In this framework, since the early decades of the sixteenth century, a limited number of Italian cities decided to accept new Christian refugees from Spain, conceding them the right to return to Judaism. These migratory fluxes were therefore connected to the concession of privileges that, as in the case of Ferrara, Livorno, and Ancona, as well as Venice, Padua and Rome itself, allowed Iberic Jews to settle in important cities of the peninsula.

The second type of approach was the previously mentioned forced expulsion: the most conspicuous one was enforced in 1492 in Southern Italy, at that time under Spanish rule; but there were other substantial expulsions in cities belonging to the Papal dominions, where in fact Jews were allowed to reside only in some areas.

The third type of approach, which was also the most prevalent in the Papal dominions as well as in the other pre-Unification Kingdoms, consisted in the institution of a form of urban segregation, a practice that was first inaugurated with the creation of the Venetian Ghetto in 1516 (Calabi *et al.* 1996; Calabi 2016; D.E. Katz 2017). Much has been written about the origin of ghettos and about the "ghetto" in its generally accepted meaning of urban space for marginalized social groups (Wirth 1927, 1928; Duneier 2016). If on the one hand the Venetian ghetto seems to descend from a notion of spatial hierarchy inspired by a combination of "zoning" rules and religious principles, on the other hand the urban segregation initiated by Paul IV with the Bull *Cum nimis absurdum* (1555) was heavily based on theological arguments in favor of the separation of Jews from Christians (Caffiero 2014; Di Nepi 2013; Stow 2001). Segregation was a slow but steady process, and new ghettos were still being established in the eighteenth century (Caffiero 2014; Milano 1963). It can be affirmed that almost all Italian cities with Jewish communities established their own ghetto, responding to either religious or urban-planning purposes, and also that the ghetto is a specifically Catholic and Italian invention (Todeschini 2016). The Early Modern Period was characterized by a strong tendency to regulation, partly as a result of the norms defined by the Council of Trent: the institution of ghettos in fact confirmed this strategy and consolidated the theological principle of acceptance of Jews within Christian society based on the Augustinian and Pauline conception that Judaism was the living testimony of the victory of the Christian *ecclesia*. On the other hand, the ghetto represented the promise of conversion necessary to reach ultimate redemption.

The urban segregation of the Jews was paired with the establishment of new markedly religious institutions: following the burning of the Talmud in Campo dei Fiori in Rome (1553) and two years before the emanation of *Cum nimis absurdum* (R. Segre 1996), the Inquisition was made responsible for the systematic control of Jewish activities and written texts; the houses of Catechumens, on the other hand, were institutions that dealt with the conversion of "infidels" (Jews and Muslims) and Protestants (Al Kalak, Pavan 2013; Caffiero 2014).

Besides being an urban innovation for the marginalisation and control of a religious minority, "ghettos" were also a culturally controversial subject: throughout the nineteenth century and beyond, appeals for the opening or abolishment of ghettos translated ideals of an open society, while for wide swaths of the Catholic Church ghettos remained a functional tool to be conveniently used to achieve a hierarchically ordered society (Taradel and Raggi 2000).

It must be remembered that urban segregation was not enforced everywhere: some cities remained with no ghetto throughout the entire course of the Early Modern Period. This was the case of Pisa and Livorno and smaller rural centers such as those under the rule of the House of Este (Aron Beller 2013).

The Jews and the Catholic world: forms of dialogue and exchange

However, it would be wrong to restrict Jewish-Catholic Church relations only to these ambits. There were further aspects that although marginal were nonetheless significant, especially in the long run. From a religious and cultural standpoint, it is worth mentioning that, since the Renaissance, in the Catholic world emerged religious currents showing particular interest in some aspects of Jewish culture, the Kabbalistic tradition in particular. Exponents of this current were, in the Italian context, Giovanni Pico della Mirandola, the Neoplatonists led by Marsilio Ficino, and also Friar Minor Pietro Colonna Galatino whose *De arcanis catholicae veritatis* (1518) circulated extensively until being accused of plagiarism in the early decades of the seventeenth century. In the German area, analogous activities and interests were cultivated by Johannes Reuchlin and other prominent Hebraists, some of whom, like Sebastian Münster, became Protestant (Frank 1992). It will suffice to mention that these different Christian currents promoted an idea of Christian reformation that was strongly inspired by Millenarian beliefs, envisaging a redeemed society in which, in the framework of universal harmony, "infidels" (Jews and Muslims) and "pagans" (old and new) were admitted. This was a very significant and resilient religious tradition, often hindered and persecuted by the Church because of its eclectic interests, its open approach to non-canonical and heterodox sources, and for its positive views on Renaissance magic, an art that seduced, among others, personalities who were accused of atheism, such as

Giordano Bruno. During the late seventeenth century and the eighteenth century, Christian Millenarian currents diversified: some developed filo-Semitic positions while others became openly hostile to the Jews (Karp, Sutcliffe 2011).

A second aspect that must be considered in the history of Catholic Church-Jewish relations is the approach to the interpretation of the Sacred Scriptures. The conflict over the understanding of extensive parts of the Old Testament was one of the central and most recurrent controversies between the two religions; an aspect that with the Reformation became even more critical due to the major reformers' interest in the sources of Early Christianity and in a study methodology descending from the great philological season of Humanism. It must be kept in mind that in 1523 Martin Luther published *Jesus Christ Was Born a Jew (Dass Jesus Christus ein geborener Jude sei),* a book that was crucial in the development of Biblical criticism and historical theology, as well as for the historical study of Jesus and the general approach to Early Judaism and Christianity. Twenty years later, in 1543, Martin Luther also published *On the Jews and their Lies (Von den Juden und Ihren Lügen)*. The desire to reform Christianity on the basis of a more attentive and exact reading of the ancient sources favoured the development, within the various currents of the Reformed world, of an interest for the history of Christianity and Judaism that encouraged the use and translation of Jewish literature. In this context, Christian Hebraist studies developed, placing Jewish culture at the centre of their field of research (though non without some incorrect representations), and consequently establishing relations with exponents of that world, leading to the creation of remarkable libraries and collections of texts, while also structuring a political discourse on the presence of Jews in the Christian world, a theme that would be much debated over the course of the eighteenth century (Frank 1992; Sutcliffe 2003).

Returning to the Italian context, one particularly significant aspect should be noticed: the historical studies of Early Christianity and Judaism were subject to ecclesiastical censorship. And although Catholic culture in Italy was less productive – compared to other areas in Europe – with regards to the development of a historical discourse on Christianity, the import of studies by major Italian Catholic Hebraists and the abundant production of polemic anti-Christian Italian-Jewish manuscript literature must not be overlooked (Facchini 2019). These aspects, as of today still awaiting thorough study, suggest that regardless of Rome's Catholic censorship, regulation, and control Christian-Jewish relations during the Modern Period were characterized by cultural and religious as well as social and economic interactions.

These topics resurfaced with greater evidence during the Enlightenment, when the Church was faced with new challenges coming from political and religious reform-invoking Catholic circles. The eighteenth century saw the suppression of the Society of Jesus as well as the development of an anti-clerical culture drawing many elements from the modern tradition of libertinism, which found expression among both champions of Deism and those who embraced forms of atheism. Critiques coming from these diverse contexts targeted the nature of the Christian State invoking a separation of its religious and political prerogatives – a subject that had been explored by great late-seventeenth-century philosophers such as Baruch Spinoza and John Locke. Over the course of the eighteenth century, in the wake of the Deist currents, a discourse on religious tolerance also emerged, redefining the prerogatives of a modern state while also reformulating the nature of Christianity, yet without fully assimilating, especially in Western Europe, the reflections on religious plurality that had been developed during the Early Modern Period. Within the Italian context, debate on the tolerance of Jews was often ancillary to conflicts between different Catholic groups, split between religious and political reformers and curial groups (Caffiero 2014).

From the eighteenth to the nineteenth century

In ancient Italian States the relations between Jews and the Church were marked by the conflicts that opposed conservatives and those embracing the principles of Enlightenment. While the tolerant policies promoted by the Hapsburgs – which with regard to the Jews translated into Joseph II's Patents of Toleration (1781) – started to affect Italian territories, the social and economic dynamics anticipated the advent of theories of religious tolerance. This occurred especially in cities with a seaport, where processes of social and economic inclusion allowed a greater integration of Jewish upper middle-class elites (Dubin 1999; Sorkin 2001). In Mantua, as well as in Livorno and Venice, currents of religious Enlightenment emerged, creating spaces of dialogue between Jews and Christians (Bregoli 2014), while from the German area came the first ideas for a reform of Judaism. Throughout the eighteenth century, Rome and other cities under Papal rule continued to adopt policies of repression and control, with forced conversions of Jewish children and accusations of Jewish ritual murder, a canard the Church actively endorsed over the course of the nineteenth century (Caffiero 2004; Facchini 2011[a]; Taradel 2002).

During the so-called Jacobine period, the effects of the French Revolution spread across the Italian Peninsula, creating the conditions for a process of equalization that was arduously defined over the course of the nineteenth century and fully accomplished with the process of national unification. Against this backdrop, the two currents inside the Catholic world continued evolving and interacting: one current more open to liberal principles and the other more inclined to protect itself from the effects of the modern world. This line of thought emerged in the first decades of the nineteenth century in those Catholic circles hostile to the French Revolution, an event they interpreted as a consequence of religious sectarianism (Freemasonry in particular) and Protestant Reformation (Miccoli 1997).

The period that goes from the French Revolution through the Restoration to the revolutionary risings of 1848 was a time of vigorous changes, as well as of representations of Judaism that under the influence of contemporary ideological stereotypes developed both in the secular discourse (whose harsh critiques extended to Catholicism) and in the Catholic circles.

Among Catholics, the works by Vincenzo Gioberti, Antonio Rosmini and Niccolò Tommaseo were partially inspired by filo-Semitic currents. These authors invoked a Risorgimento led by an enlightened Catholicism, and also supported the idea of Jewish emancipation, although it must be said that in their vision Jews and Protestants were only accepted in an eschatological perspective of conversion (Levis Sullam 2010[b]). A specific trait of nineteenth-century Jewish-Church relations in Italy was the alliance between the upholders of a Catholic Risorgimento, who believed in a Unification process under the guide of Pius IX, and Jewish elites in favour of Italian Risorgimento (as well as other national movements throughout Europe), a circumstance that led historians to suggest the notion of "Jewish Neo-Guelphism" (Luzzatto Voghera 1998). Pius IX's conversion to an anti-national attitude implied a radical change in the Catholics' attitude towards modern culture, as detailed in the *Syllabus* (1864), in which the Church distanced itself from liberal thought and its political and cultural models.

Jewish political emancipation was introduced in 1848 with the Statuto Albertino, the constitution that paved the way for the development of the constitutional principle of "a free Church in a sovereign state" allowing for a certain level of religious pluralism (at least in juridical terms).

The conflict with the modern world: the second half of the nineteenth century

In this phase, the contrast with modernizing liberal stimuli that eventually led to Italian Unification was also characterized by explicit anti-Jewish positions that translated into a variety of forms.

Two episodes were particularly significant and took on a symbolic value. The first occurred in 1840 in Damascus, where the disappearance of a Catholic monk was turned into a case of ritual murder that, via press coverage and contemporary debate on the conditions of Jews in Europe, became a case of international relevance (Frankel 1997; Jesi 2007). The second event took place in 1858 in Bologna, where a Jewish child was taken from his family by the Papal Police. The boy was abducted because the Catholic maid who believed his life was at risk had secretly baptized him. Edgardo Mortara, this was the child's name, became a symbol of the backwardness of the Catholic Church (Kertzer 1998). This case ignited another heated debate that spread across Europe.

The advent of Catholic press became a tool used to reinforce the Church's conservative positions. The periodical *La civiltà cattolica* founded in 1850 and directed by the Jesuits soon engaged a systematic campaign of defamation against liberals, Jews, and Freemasons, all accused of having perpetrated another "deicide" by depriving the Church of its political sovereignty (Facchini 2011[a] and 2020; Miccoli 1997).

The crisis of the 1870s, which included the fall of the State of the Church, the demise of the Papal States, the slump of world economy, the *Kulturkampf* conflict in Germany, and

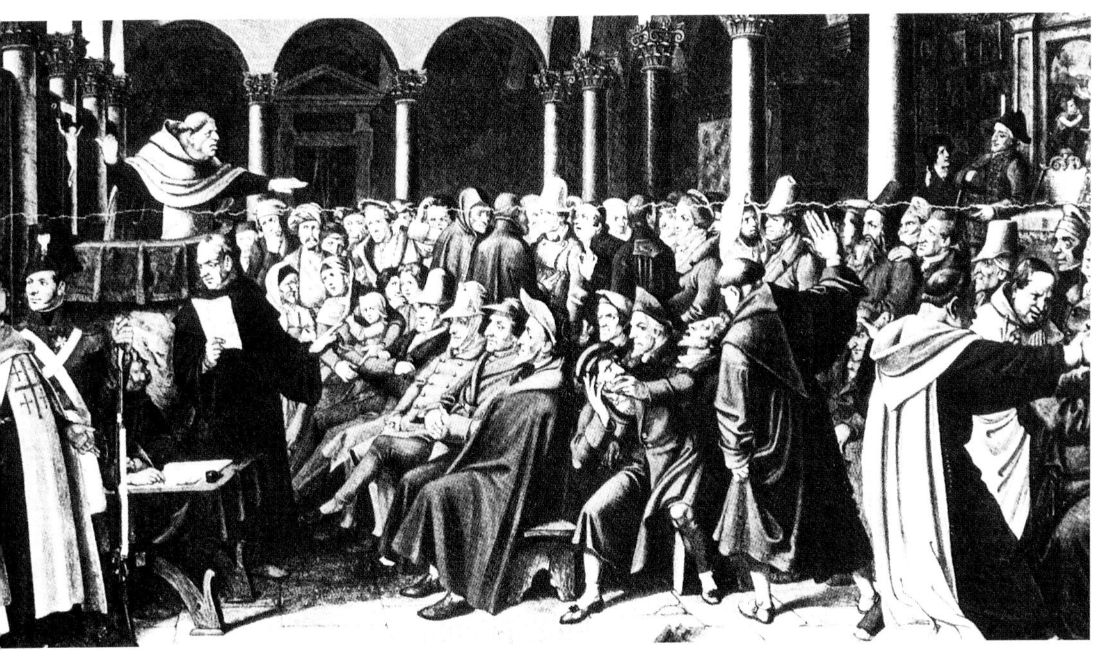

1. *Jews are forced to participate at a sermon*, XVIII secolo. Private collection

the Paris Commune, fueled strong feelings of resentment against Jewish emancipation, reinvigorating various forms of political antisemitism, in which the Catholic component played a significant role, especially in France and the Austro-Hungarian Empire. The most prominent exponents of political antisemitism were the French Édouard Drumont and the Christian Social Party during the years of Karl Lueger's office as mayor of Vienna (Pulzer 1988; Volkov 2006; Germinario 2011).

In Italy the crisis translated into various forms of hostility that appeared very aggressive in the media but curiously more cautious on a political and practical level, also due to the Pope's *non expedit* act that hindered a widespread Catholic participation in the national political life. Furthermore, during the 1880s the Catholic Church carried out a defamatory campaign against Judaism publishing accusations of ritual murder and a new stigmatization of the Talmud (Di Fant 2002; Nani 2006; Wyrwa 2014 and 2016). *L'Osservatore cattolico,* founded in Milan in 1864 and directed by Don Albertario, became a periodical of a certain repute. Part of a galaxy of anti-modern Catholic papers and periodicals, *L'Osservatore* was always aligned with the positions of the Pope although being published in Milan, an urban context with an established liberal Catholic tradition. Albertario's polemical battles voiced the topics aired by the antisemitic currents in Catholic Europe, criticizing the presence of Jews in modern society, especially in the printing business and in journalism, and attacking them for their alleged capacity to occupy power positions. But Don Albertario's main target was by far the blood libel, by which he made a name for himself in European antisemitic circles. In fact, Don Albertario fashioned a narrative that was consistent with the blood libel, establishing a connection between Calvary, the Talmud and ritual murder. In this framework Judaism, understood as a religion and un-civilization, appeared as a criminal system from which Christianity should defend itself (Di Fant 2011; Facchini 2020, in press). The development of a fundamentalist Catholic culture went hand in hand with a systematic denigration of Judaism, always represented as a compact entity out of any historical context. This stance found a partial and always ambiguous corrective in a somewhat cautious approach of the Roman establishment that often manifested its hostility towards political positions promoting mass antisemitism (Miccoli 1997).

Contacts and Interactions

The presence of Catholic positions inspired by liberal principles made contacts with exponents of the Jewish world possible. Among these was eminent economist and constitutionalist Luigi Luzzatti, who believed State and Church had to be two separate entities for the benefit of Catholics (Pertici 2015) as well as being an upholder of an original theory of religious tolerance (Facchini 2016).

In the early twentieth century, exponents of the Catholic world influenced by modern culture, in particular by the spreading of Biblical studies coming from France and Germany, became the promoters of a form of renovation in the Church that was soon condemned and excommunicated (Vian 2012).

The subject of relations between modernism and Jews has not been sufficiently explored yet, but it has so far revealed a series of unexpected contacts and personal and intellectual interactions that somehow complicate the history of Catholic-Jewish relations even more complicated (Botti, Facchini, Zanini 2019). These circles attempted to develop a reinterpretation of Jewish-Christian relations that was harshly repressed by the Church.

Christian fundamentalist currents started to see Jews and modernists as a double threat to Church's doctrinal purity. Worth remembering in this context are the anti-Jewish activities of Monsignor Benigni and the dissemination in Italy of the Protocols of the Elders of Zion at the hands of Giovanni Preziosi.

The advent of Fascism contributed to strengthen the anti-liberal wing of the Catholic Church, whose alliance with the Regime was officially ratified with the Lateran Treaty (1929). There were critical voices that encouraged Catholics and non-Catholics to forms of individual dissent, or exile at times. But they remained a marginal presence, even when racism was overtly embraced by the State, and the Church had to struggle to find a theological and political formula to fight the spreading of racism and antisemitism. In that context, Nazis and Fascists extensively drew from antisemitic history and cultures that various Christian traditions had cultivated over the centuries. And if there were, among both Catholics and Protestants (especially in France, Germany and Austria), attempts to find a theological weapon against state antisemitism, these voices remained an unheard minority up to the Second Vatican Council (Connelly 2012).

The Facts and Lesson of the Mortara Case

Elèna Mortara

The kidnapping and its historical context

What has become known, in both contemporary reports and later historical accounts, as the "Mortara case," or also the "Mortara affair," is the dramatic case of a six-year-old Jewish child from Bologna named Edgardo Mortara (1851–1940), who – having been clandestinely baptized at the age of around one by the family's Catholic maid – in June 1858 was suddenly taken away by force of law from his family, by order of the Inquisition. Bologna was at that time part of the wide Papal States, whose dominion extended across many central regions of the Italian Peninsula, projecting out north-eastwards from Rome to include the Legation of the Romagne, with Bologna as its capital. Bologna was therefore subject to the laws of the Papal State and – given the blurred nature in those days of the lines between religious and temporal power – was governed by a cardinal appointed by the pope, Cardinal Legate Giuseppe Milesi Pironi Ferretti, and was subjected to civil and criminal legislation based on the Code of Canon Law of the Church of Rome. From 1856 onwards, the city's main spiritual authority was the influential archbishop Michele Viale-Prelà, whereas the inquisitor responsible in Bologna for the Roman Inquisition, the institution dedicated to safeguarding the integrity of the Catholic faith against infidels and heresies, had for many years been a Dominican father, Pier Gaetano Feletti. Above all of them, sitting as Head of State on the throne of the Holy Roman Church was Pope Pius IX (born Giovanni Maria Mastai Ferretti, 1792–1878), who became pontiff in 1846.

On June 23, 1858, in the night, the Marshal in the papal *carabinieri*, Pietro Lucidi and Brigadier Giuseppe Agostini, followed by a squad of other papal guards, appeared at the home of Momolo (Salomone David) and Marianna Mortara (née Padovani), at no. 196, Via delle Lame, in a central district of Bologna, with the order to take away with them one of the couple's children – six-year-old Edgardo. "I'm sorry to have to inform you that you are the victim of betrayal," said Marshall Lucidi to Marianna Mortara. "Your son Edgardo has been baptized, and I have been ordered to take him with me" (Kertzer 1998, pp. 4–5; Tribunale 1860). The order, given by the head of the pontifical gendarmerie, Lieutenant Colonel Luigi De-Dominicis, and sent by him to the aforementioned *carabinieri*, came from above, from Father Feletti. The abduction, which was postponed for a day following feverish overnight negotiations with the inquisitor himself, was inexorably carried out the next night, June 24. Torn away from his family and entrusted to Brigadier Agostini, little Edgardo was immediately moved away from Bologna and taken by coach to Rome, and specifically to the *Casa dei Catecumeni* (House of Catechumens) on Via della Madonna dei Monti, the Catholic institution responsible for the indoctrination of "neophytes" who had been converted to Catholicism.

This event marked the start of a family tragedy that would go on to acquire historic importance, extending well beyond a family and a city. The relevance of the kidnapping was not due to the exceptional nature of the episode itself, but to the particular resonance that it had in contemporary public opinion, to the international scandal to which it gave rise, and to the consequences that derived from it.

The kidnapping of a Jewish child who had secretly been converted to Catholicism, unbeknownst to the child's parents and against their will (*invitis parentibus*), and his or her subsequent transfer to the House of Catechumens, was a coercive practice that occurred frequently during the centuries of subjugation of the Jewish minority in the Roman ghetto and in the papal domains. This practice, based on a principle formally sanctioned by the Church for the first time in the sixtieth canon (concerning the Israelites) of the Fourth Council of Toledo in 633, had been questioned numerous times, even within the ecclesiastical hierarchies over the course of the centuries, but it continued to be applied zealously in the regimes still subject to the power of the Inquisition. It was above all in the case of young children considered to be "in danger of death" that, in order to save their souls, it was deemed right and legitimate to baptize them without their parents' knowledge. Once baptized, regardless of the circumstances that had led to the baptism taking place, these youngsters became Catholic, and if by chance they happened to survive, it was necessary to separate them from their families, in order to educate them on the religion to which they were now judged to belong irreversibly.

The astonishment of the ecclesiastical hierarchy in the face of the enormous uproar generated in public opinion not just in Italy but internationally following the revelation of Edgardo's kidnapping is effectively documented by the comment made, after a prolonged silence, in the first article on the Mortara case appearing in the periodical *La Civiltà Cattolica* on October 30, 1858. In this piece, titled *Il piccolo neofita Edgardo Mortara* ("The Little Neophyte Edgardo Mortara"), one evinces bewilderment for the case having become a *cause célèbre* in newspapers across the world. "An event that the world has certainly witnessed before, a very simple one at that and one that in centuries of belief would have passed without arousing attention, let alone surprise, precisely because the minimal faith that is necessary to understand the sense of it was commonplace," observed the editor of *La Civiltà Cattolica*, "that deed, as we may call it, has provoked in this past month of September, and even more so this October, a hornets' nest of journalistic diatribes and declamations, deafening the world." The controversy and the accusation made by the journal – an unofficial voice of the papacy since 1850 (the year of foundation of the Jesuit periodical) – were addressed in particular against those within the Christian world, who in "this century of disbelief, slave to despicable utilitarianism" were blind with respect to the "divine mission of the Church" in favor of "a poor seven-year-old boy, obscure offshoot of a parasitical plant," to whom had been given the gift of grace through baptism: "For this child, an august Sovereign, a Vicar of Christ, a supreme Pontiff must see all of the supposed organs of libertine opinion that are unleashed and quivering with indignation around him as they cry out for diplomatic initiatives, public protests, interventions and who knows what else."

The reaction of the Jewish communities in the Papal States

In "centuries of belief," Edgardo's abduction by the papal guards would have passed over in silence. But, in the new liberal climate of the time, and thanks to the strong reaction of the family, which did not suffer the abuse in silence, the episode no longer appeared so "very simple" and gave rise, on the contrary, to great debate and scandal, which resonated internationally.

From the outset, the driving force behind the struggle for the return of the child to his family was his father, Momolo Mortara, supported by other members of the family and the small Jewish community of Bologna: a community at that time numbering no more than a few dozen members (the Jews had been expelled from Bologna at the behest of the pope in 1593, at the height of the Counter-Reformation, and then had begun to return there only during the Napoleonic period), many of whom, like the Mortara family itself, had recently come from the nearby cities of Modena and Reggio Emilia, forming part of the neighbouring Hapsburg-Este Duchy of Modena and Reggio. With Edgardo now secluded in the House of Catechumens in Rome, it was essential to make the case for the return of the youngster to his family, beseeching no longer only the inquisitor of Bologna but also the pontiff, the Pope-King Pius IX, under whose jurisdiction the kidnapped boy now fell. An initial attempt at direct contact with the papal authority was made on July 4, 1858, when from Bologna two letters were sent, signed by the boy's father Momolo Mortara, one to the inquisitor Feletti in Bologna and the other to the pope in Rome, through the powerful secretary of state, Cardinal Giacomo Antonelli, who in turn was the recipient of an obsequious cover letter (the attempt was destined to remain unanswered). Epistolary contacts were then made with the leaders of the Jewish community – known at the time as the Israelite University – in Rome. This community had a longstanding, albeit often traumatic, tradition of relation with the pontiff, due to its centuries of direct subjection to that power. The Israelite University of Rome had, then, to serve as the go-between with the Holy See in relation to the very difficult negotiations, and it was the university's young secretary, Sabatino Scazzocchio, who in the hectic months following the abduction found himself at the center of the whirlwind of letters and urgent pleas arriving from Bologna and from other parts of the Jewish world, both inside and outside the Papal States, and who tried to manage the negotiation with the pope and his secretary of state, Cardinal Antonelli, striking a delicate balance between the wish to resolve the case and the need not to prejudice relations with the supreme power of the head of state, the Pope-King Pius IX.

From July 1858 onwards, two different struggle strategies began to emerge within the Italian Jewish world. On the one side, there was the approach put forward by the leaders of the Israelite University of Rome, the members of the Vaad [Council], who – while declaring themselves immediately ready to make "any sacrifice" (ASCER, Decrees of the Vaad of the University, July 20, 1858) – tried to handle the predicament by acting in a highly discreet, circumspect way vis-à-vis the outside world. It was through them and through the secretary Scazzocchio that in August Momolo Mortara was able for the first time to be received by the secretary of the Papal States, Antonelli, albeit not by the pope himself. In August and September of that year, Momolo was then afforded the opportunity on several occasions to see his son at the House of Catechumens, though never to spend time alone with him. Moreover, it was a delegation of the Israelite University that, in early September 1858, having been received by Antonelli, sent via him a highly wrought, extremely respectful petition to the pope, composed of a "Promemoria," preceded by a letter from the child's parents, with various appendices, and an erudite "Syllabus" in Latin, containing a compilation of ecclesiastical documents intended to demonstrate the possibility of repealing the decision about Edgardo's kidnapping.

Alongside the route of the secret negotiations supported by the Israelite University of Rome, there was also an alternative approach advocated from the very beginning by the members of the community in Bologna, who in their first letter to Scazzocchio framed the case as a "persecution incompatible with the times" (letter from Angelo Padovani, July 9, 1858) and then at the end of July, exasperated by the slow pace of the negotiations, urged him to mobilise also "the most eminent foreign Jews to interest European public opinion, nations, and governments in the case" (Kertzer 1998, pp. 45, 48).

National and international reactions to the "Mortara case"

News of the abduction spread rapidly, not only amongst the various Jewish communities in Italy but also overseas, and soon began to be featured in the European press. In France, the first account of the case appeared in the daily *La Presse* on July 9, 1858; in Britain, the news was first reported in the *Jewish Chronicle* on July 16. *L'Educatore Israelita*, the only Jewish periodical in Italy at the time, was issued with a supplement dedicated to the "deplorable" event in Bologna (cf. *Il fatto di Bologna*1858); and on August 12, 1858, the representatives of the Jewish communities of Sardinia and Piedmont met in Alessandria, where they signed an appeal to the Jewish national organisations in France and Britain – the Concistoire Central des Israélites de France in Paris and the Board of Deputies of British Jews in London – requesting that, given the pope's insensitivity to the family's petitions, they would involve their respective governments in the protest "against the barbarous act committed in Bologna" (in Anonymous [D. Rabbeno] 1859, p. 76).

Thus, in September, news of the case and of the appeal began to spread more and more in the international press (in France, the *Journal des Débats* published the text in full on September 2, 1858), and it was then that the first public initiatives of protest began. Over the preceding months, two members of the Rothschild family – James Rothschild of Paris in July and Lionel Rothschild of London in August – had sent private letters of protest to Cardinal Antonelli. On September 6, 1858, in response to the appeal of the Piedmontese Jews, the British Board of Deputies decided to set up a special committee, led by the chairman of the board, Sir Moses Montefiore, to deal with the case (Green 2010; Langham 2004). On the same day, in the *Allgemeine Zeitung des Judenthums*, rabbi Ludwig Philippson, founder and editor of this German-Jewish periodical, promoted a petition to the pope, which within a month was signed by more than forty Prussian rabbis (*Allgemeine Zeitung des Judenthums*, September 6 and October 10, 1858). On September 9, numerous British newspapers, including the authoritative *Times*, published the appeal from Turin, along with a summary of the board's decisions; copies of the *Times* article were sent by the board to 1,800 members of the Catholic clergy in Britain (Langham 2004). In France, where the press was to have a particularly strong influence over the debate that was catching fire, on September 22 the *Journal des Débats* included a resonant petition made by the Concistoire Central des Israélites de France, addressed directly to Emperor Napoleon III, requesting that he intervene to assist a family that had been the "victim of an odious violence that was carried out around two months ago now, almost in the shadow of our glorious flag and under the eyes of our brave soldiers" (our translation from the Italian version, in Anonymous [D. Rabbeno] 1859, p. 77).

Starting in September 1858, and with increasing intensity from early October, the scandal over the unresolved case of the Mortara child was spread in the newspapers of Europe. The Bologna episode provoked astonishment, outrage and numerous questions. It was the negation of natural rights and of the rights of the family; an example of barbarity, tyranny and intolerance; a disgrace; a stain; a crime against humanity – such descriptions all appeared in the press of the time, in British newspapers such as *The Times*, the *Daily Telegraph*, the *Daily News*, the *Morning Adviser*, and *The Spectator*. Nor did such arguments appear only in the press of countries with a Protestant majority, more given to criticizing papal power. Especially significant was the case of France, a country with Catholic traditions, where the public debate generated by what would soon become known as "*l'affaire Mortara*" was particularly intense. In this regard, of great interest is the reading of the *Journal des Débats*, which was among the most active newspapers in the diatribe against what had taken place in Bologna, and of the ultra-traditionalist Catholic mouthpiece, *L'Univers*, edited by the antisemite Veuillot, a pugnacious defender of the decisions of the Church of Rome. When *L'Univers*, challenged to break its silence by the exhortations of the *Journal des Débats*, entered the arena of the public debate on October 10, 1858, its pages provided the platform for an explicit exposition of the theory of the inequality of religions before the law; the defence of the existence of a state religion; the superiority of religious law over civil law; and the right-cum-duty to consider Catholic any child of a Jewish family baptized covertly and, as a consequence, to remove that child from the harmful "seductions" of its parents. In this battle *L'Univers* felt isolated in France, having to cross swords not only with the *Journal des Débats*, but also with *La Presse*, *Le Siècle*, *Le Constitutionnel*, and in general with a large part of the media of the time, which were accused by the Catholic newspaper of defending atheism, naturalism and all the "errors" of modern liberal culture.

That the ideological clash was internal to the Catholic world itself was made clear when, a few days later, on October 18, 20 and 29, 1858, issues of the *Journal des Débats* featured three long articles by the Catholic abbot André Vincent Delacouture, known in Italy as the translator of Manzoni's *Observations on Catholic Ethics*, who in the name of religion and using learned theological arguments, criticised Edgardo's kidnapping, defending natural rights over canonical rights. These articles were then expanded and collected by Delacouture in a pamphlet issued in December, titled *Le Droit canon et le Droit naturel dans l'affaire Mortara* (1858); the same publisher Dentu in Paris also released pamphlet in defence of Edgardo's father, *Affaire Mortara: le droit du père* (1858), by the anthropologist Jules Assézat. In April 1859, the pamphlet by Abbot Delacouture was issued in an Italian translation, within

1. Moritz Daniel Oppenheim,
The Kidnapping of Edgardo Mortara, detail.
Private collection (cat. 38)

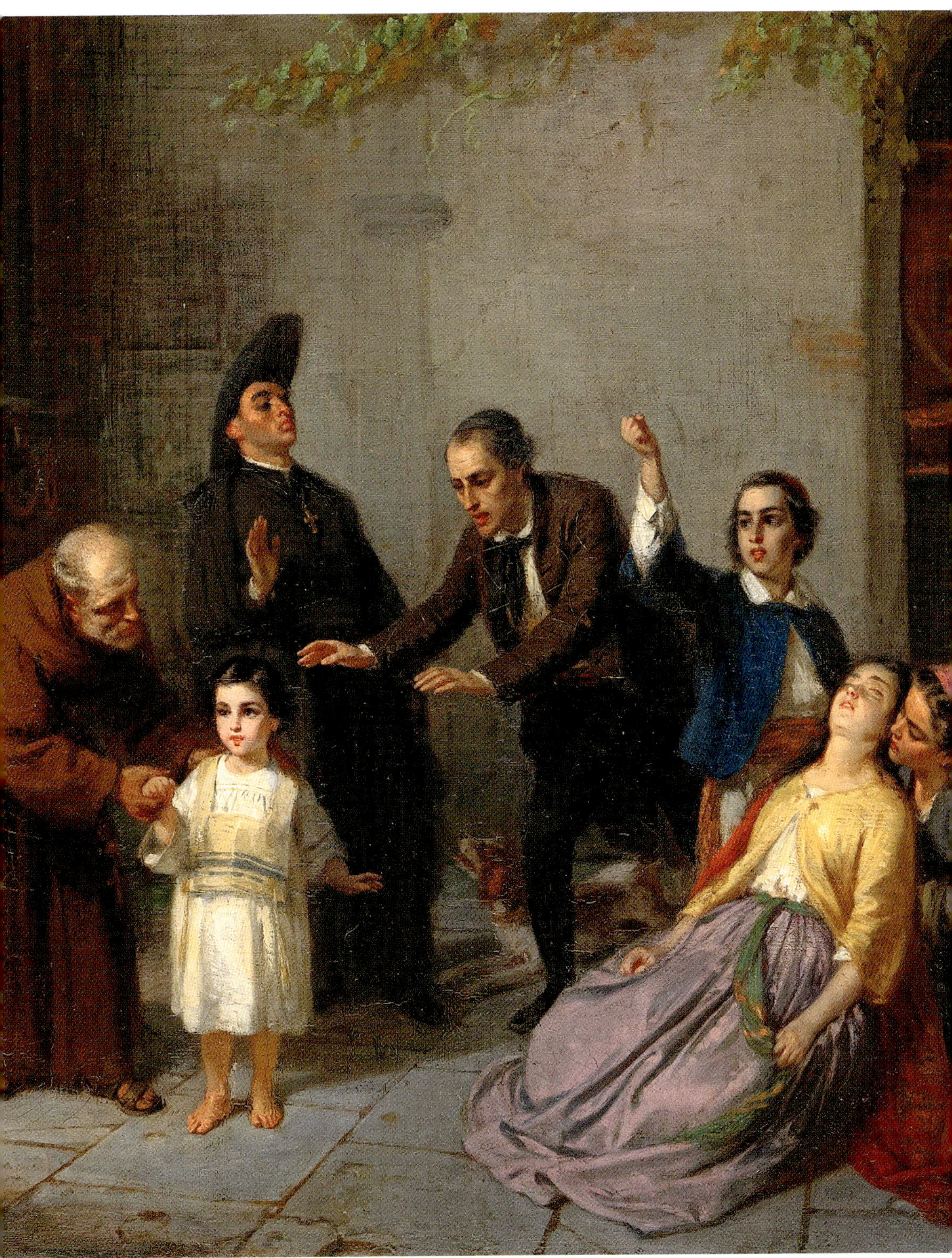

the most important contemporary compendium of documents on the Mortara affair, published anonymously in Turin (but actually put together by the journalist David Rabbeno; cf. E. Mortara 2018), and entitled *Roma e l'opinione pubblica d'Europa nel fatto Mortara*. This title (which translates as "Rome and European public opinion in the Mortara case") was highly significant: as stated in an article in the *Journal des Débats* (September 29, 1858), for that abominable act, those who had perpetrated it were now being prosecuted "in the court of European public opinion." It was in this climate of heartfelt public debate that *La Civiltà Cattolica* provided the channel for the first semi-official pronouncement on the case by the Church, expressing the Church's astonishment in the face of so many criticisms, in the aforementioned article of October 30, 1858. That publication had been preceded, on the 23rd of the month, by the sending of an article by Cardinal Antonelli to the apostolic nuncios across Europe and to the pope's representatives in South America, entitled *Brevi cenni e riflessioni sul Pro-memoria e Sillabo*, in which a summary response was given to the Pro-memoria and the Syllabus submitted by the Mortara family to the pope in September (Archivio di Stato Vaticano [Vatican State Archive]; Kertzer 1998, p. 146).

Alongside the public debate in the press, which had by now reached the other side of the Atlantic, diplomatic initiatives were also under way, as were petitions to the pope, for the liberation of Edgardo. The protest movements in various parts of Europe and America continued throughout the following year and even beyond, given the inflexible refusal of the pontiff to pull back from his decisions. The correspondence dating from July to November 1858 between the Duke of Gramont, French ambassador to the Holy See, and Count Walewski, French Foreign Minister (who in October summoned the apostolic nuncio in France, Archbishop Carlo Sacconi, about this issue), effectively documents the attention paid to the affair by the diplomatic authorities of that country, which was of considerable political and military importance for the pope (Silva 2008, pp. 116–125). Indeed, since 1849, French troops had been stationed in Rome to defend the Papal States. And yet the attempt made in early September by the French ambassador to warn the pope about the disastrous effects that the situation was creating vis-à-vis French Catholic public opinion proved to be in vain. Similarly ineffectual was the trip made, with a view to securing Edgardo's liberation, by the most influential member of the British Jewish community, Moses Montefiore, who as the head of the Board of Deputies and in the name of the "sentiment of unity" of the Jewish people (*Jewish Chronicle*, March 4, 1859), went expressly to Rome with a Memorandum and remained there for that purpose for a month, between April and May 1859, without even being received by the pope, but only, after many days spent waiting, by his secretary of state. The answer – either direct or, as in this case, via Cardinal Antonelli – did not change: *non possumus*.

Aside from the effect of keeping the protest alive, just as unsuccessful was the petition made to the pope in France by the "Alliance Chrétienne Universelle" and the numerous initiatives set in motion by British Protestant organizations, from the "London Society for Promoting Christianity Amongst the Jews," which was preoccupied (as it stated in the October 1, 1858 edition of its periodical *Jewish Intelligence*) about the negative effects of "such examples of injustice and oppression" on the Jews to be converted, to the Protestant Association, the Protestant Alliance, the Scottish Reformation Society, and the particularly active Evangelical Alliance. These initiatives, which arose out of indignation at the cruelty of the case and out of the struggle for religious freedom, included the sending of two Memoranda on the case to the British Foreign Minister, Lord Malmesbury, and culminated in the vibrant Protestant Protest Petition of October 1859, signed by more than 2000 religious and lay notables, in which the procedures implemented through the abduction of Edgardo – "repugnant to the instincts of humanity" and constituting "a dishonour for Christianity" (*The Times*, October 19, 1859; cited in Langham 2004, pp. 99–100) – were roundly denounced. The *Jewish Chronicle* of October 28, 1859 then commented with satisfaction that the protest was "the first public admission by a Christian nation of the fact that the Jews have been wronged in the name of Christianity."

The outrage over the Mortara case reached the United States thanks initially to the hard work of a number of rabbis – Samuel M. Isaacs in New York, Isaac M. Wise and Max Lilienthal in Cincinnati, and Isaac Leeser in Philadelphia – who from the autumn of 1858 published articles and poems inspired by the case in their periodicals, contacted Secretary of State Lewis Cass, and organized mass protest events, attended by both Jews and Christians (of particular importance were those held in New York and San Francisco on December 4, 1858, and January 15, 1859, respectively). In January 1859 a delegation from Philadelphia even met President Buchanan in Washington, in an attempt to convince him to exert pressure on the pope. The Mortara case and the scandal of the kidnapping in the Papal States were by now the subject of a stream of articles in the main newspapers throughout the country (Korn 1957).

It was in the United States that the first pieces of literature inspired by the Mortara case were issued: two long poems by Penina Moïse and Adah Isaacs Menken, which came out respectively in December 1858 and January 1859 in the *Jewish Messenger* and *The Israelite*. But it was in Paris that a play inspired by the Mortara family's tragedy was staged for the first time, causing a sensation: *La Tireuse de cartes* (1859), by American-born writer Victor Séjour, a Catholic, French-speaking "free man of color" from New Orleans, an exile in France, who had become a successful playwright in the great theaters of Paris. The jam-packed premiere of the work, on December 22, 1859, was also attended by the French emperor, Napoleon III, and his wife. Their presence had considerable political significance. When the play was published, the author prefaced it with a long introduction in which he explained that he had written it to defend the Mortara family and that he had done so as a Catholic, in the name of common humanity ("But I am a man …"). With heart-wrenching words, he then addressed the pontiff directly, asking him not to cruelly violate family law and cautioning him on the risks of a similar policy for his own Papal States (reported in E. Mortara 2015, pp. 190–192). Europe was preparing for the Paris Conference, slated for early 1860 (it was eventually never held). So we shall now turn our attention to the political episodes of that tumultuous period.

Historical context and political consequences for the history of Italy and Jewish emancipation

To understand the events fully, it is necessary to widen our view to the entire scene in which the Mortara affair took place, in a crucial period of Italian history and in the history of Jewish emancipation. The start date – the date on which Edgardo was snatched from his family in Bologna – should be borne in mind: June 24, 1858. It will be enough to mention two more slightly later dates of that same summer to get a real sense of how delicate and incandescent the situation in contemporary Europe actually was.

Just one month after Edgardo's abduction, on July 21, 1858, the secret Plombières agreement was signed by Napoleon III, Emperor of France, and Camillo Benso, Count of Cavour. The Italian Risorgimento was in full swing, and one of its issues concerned precisely the future of the temporal power of the pope, the laws of whose states appeared outdated to the liberal Catholics. The breaking out of the Mortara case was nothing but a strident example of this conviction.

The other memorable date of the summer of 1858 concerns specifically the battle for the emancipation of the Jews in Europe, as being fought at the time in Great Britain. It was there, on July 26, 1858, for the first time in the country's history, that a Jew – Baron Lionel de Rothschild – was finally allowed to enter the House of Commons, thanks to the Jewish Relief Act of July 23, 1858. He had been elected to parliament numerous times but had never been allowed to enter due to the obligation to swear in the name of the Christian faith. It was a triumphant moment for the British movement for Jewish emancipation. Against this happy background, the echo of the event in Bologna could not fail to cause alarm and arouse indignation on the part of those who had only just acquired equal rights. We can thus grasp to an even greater extent the reasons for the dismay and the liveliness of the debate aroused by the upsetting news from Italy, and the steadfast commitment of the Board of Deputies of British Jews to the cause of the Mortara family.

The movement for the emancipation of the Jews was then in full flow, and was inextricably intertwined with the struggles for liberation from the old authoritarian power structures and the desperately hoped-for birth of new, modern nations, in which those rights would be affirmed (see Ferrara degli Uberti's and Sorkin's contributions to the present book). This is what lay behind, in the Italian context, the fascination exercised, even on the Jews of the other Italian states, by the Kingdom of Sardinia as the leader of a movement for national emancipation and liberation, since it was there that this religious minority had obtained for itself, along with the Waldensian community, full rights of citizenship, in the revolutionary year of 1848; and it was only there that these freedoms had then been retained, in contrast to what had happened in other states with the Restoration of 1849. The condition of the Jews resident in the Papal States was, in this sense, diametrically opposed: forced for centuries to live a segregated life in the ghettos (on this "amicable segregation," see Foa 2014; Taradel-Raggi 2000) and to be subject, even where there were no ghettos, to a gravely discriminatory form of legislation, during the period from 1846 to 1848 – in the first two years of the papacy of Pius XI – they had experienced a brief liberal season; but, after the parenthesis of the Roman Republic in 1849 and the return of the pope from Gaeta in 1850, a harsh Restoration had been put in place. In no other state within Italy was the conflict between an authoritarian power and the modern world more evident.

The Mortara case was, then, the scandal that made visible to the world a situation of abuses of power permitted by the law but viewed by many as no longer acceptable. It was here that another fundamental factor of the time came into play: the role of public opinion and that of the newspapers in the dissemination of the news and in the generation of that opinion – a role supported by new technologies, in particular the development of the telegraph and a network of rapid postal communications.

While the unresolved Mortara case continued to stir people's consciences and to fascinate the newspapers, 1859 saw the outbreak of the so-called second war of independence. On June 12, 1859, the city of Bologna rose up peacefully against the old papal political power, manifesting the aspiration to join the Kingdom of Sardinia. On that day, Cardinal Legate Milesi Pironi Ferretti, the pontifical governor, left Bologna, while a new temporary governing council was immediately constituted. This marked the end of the temporal power of the Church in that city. In early August 1859, while work was beginning in Zurich on the peace conference between France and the Austrian Empire, in central Italy – where many cities of Romagna and Emilia (including Modena and Reggio, from which Marianna Padovani and Momolo Mortara originally came) had already rebelled against the old authoritarian regimes – the new Governor general of the Romagne sent by the Kingdom of Sardinia, Leonetto Cipriani, in one of his first official acts proclaimed the fundamental principle of the equality of all citizens before the law, "without religious distinction."

On November 10, 1859, the emperors of France and Austria signed the Zurich Peace Treaty. Article 20 of the Treaty decreed that the rebel areas of the Papal States should fall once again under papal domination; the same article, though, also affirmed that the "tranquillity" of those states necessitated "the adoption of a system suited to the needs of the population"; and the two emperors even promised that they would make a joint "effort to obtain from His Holiness an assurance that the need to introduce into the administration of his States the reforms recognized as indispensable will be given serious consideration by his Governor." The Mortara case had certainly reinforced that perception among political authorities and in the wider public opinion.

Despite the terms of the Treaty of Zurich, the former legations of the Romagna did not, however, have the slightest intention of returning under the papal dominion from which they had only just been freed. On November 9, 1859, the Governor general of the Romagne, Cipriani, was replaced by a new Governor, Luigi Carlo Farini, who had also previously served as "dictator" of the provinces of Modena and Parma. Five days after his assignment, on No-

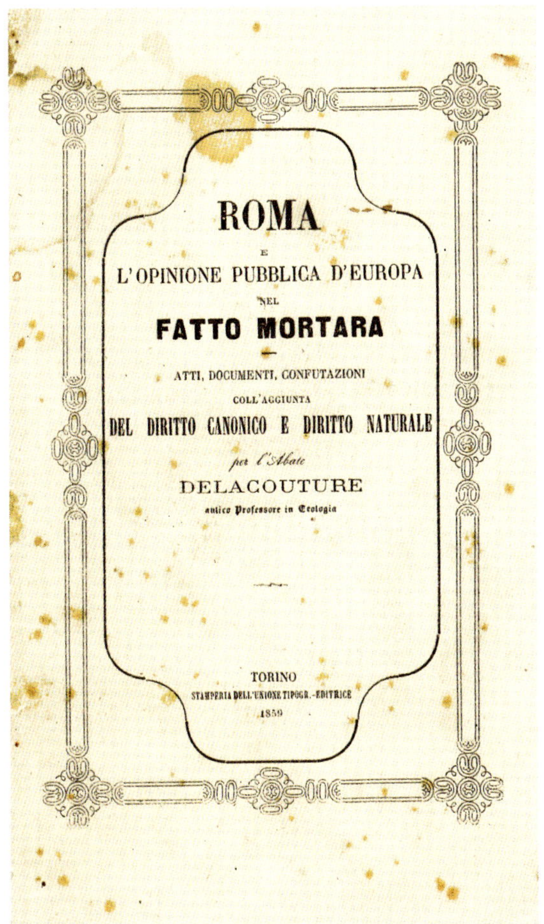
ROMA

E

L'OPINIONE PUBBLICA D'EUROPA

NEL

FATTO MORTARA

ATTI, DOCUMENTI, CONFUTAZIONI

COLL'AGGIUNTA

DEL DIRITTO CANONICO E DIRITTO NATURALE

per l'Abate

DELACOUTURE

antico Professore in Teologia

TORINO

STAMPERIA DELL'UNIONE TIPOGR.-EDITRICE

1859

2. *Rome and public opinion in Europe regarding the Mortara affair. Records, documents, confutations. / Canonical and Natural Law, for Abbé Delacouture, former professor of theology*. Alberto Mortara Family Archives (cat. 39)

vember 14, 1859, Farini decreed for all of the territories under his authority the abolition of the Tribunal of the Inquisition, since – as it stated in the decree – this institution was no longer compatible "either with civilization or with the most common principles of public or civil law" (Mancini 2015, p. 430).

This was the situation in the territories that would soon, in March 1860, vote in plebiscites for the annexation to the Kingdom of Sardinia. But in the heart of the Papal States, in Rome, things were very different. It was in Rome that, since 1858, little Edgardo Mortara had been living, taken care of initially at the House of Catechumens, before being transferred, from December 1858 onwards, to the nearby *Collegio di San Pietro in Vincoli* (College of Saint Peter in Chains), again on the Esquiline Hill, run by the Order of the Canons Regular of the Lateran (Scalise 1997, p. 141). After the initial brief meetings with his father Momolo at the House of Catechumens in August and September 1858, Edgardo had been able to embrace his mother once again for the first time a full four months after his abduction, on October 22 of that year; and he had then seen both of his parents a few times during October and November 1858, always in the same place and under strict priestly surveillance.

Comforted by the myriad protests under way, and after having tried in vain to secure Edgardo's return from Rome, Momolo continued tirelessly to fight to get his son back, and in 1859 he went to Paris and then to London, with the intention of convincing the Board of Deputies to submit a request to the British government to support a new Memorandum on the case, which he intended to send to the representatives at the upcoming peace conference to be held in Paris in early 1860. In the *Jewish Chronicle* of December 16 there appeared a rousing plea to the board to put its weight behind this initiative, signed by 450 members of the Jewish communities of London and the surrounding areas; after a certain amount of hesitation, the board consented, preparing a draft of the memorandum for the forthcoming conference (Langham 2004, pp. 85–86). During those same December days, Victor Séjour's performance of *La Tireuse de cartes* was staged in Paris. The "Italian question" and the related "Roman question," which pivoted around the issue of the temporal power of the Church of Rome, were at the centre of international public attention.

The Bologna trial of the inquisitor Feletti

Then came another turning point in the Mortara case. It all began on the initiative of Simon Levi Mortara, Momolo's father, who sent from Reggio, where he lived, two letters to Governor Farini, the first on October 30, 1859, when Farini was only in charge of Modena and Parma, and the second on December 30 of that year, by which time he had become Governor also of the former papal legations. In the letters, also on behalf of his son (at that time in London), he begged Farini to make use of his powerful intervention "to bring about the longed-for return of my most beloved grandson Edgardo" (Kertzer 1998, p. 185; Volli 1960[b], ed. 2016, p. 29). Farini, who already in response to the first letter had ordered the new Department of Justice to open an investigation, on December 31, 1859, ordered the Minister of Justice to prosecute the perpetrators of the kidnapping. And so it was that the first criminal case of the newly established Royal Government of the Provinces of Emilia had as its subject the abduction of Edgardo Mortara and that, on January 2, 1860, at half-past-two in the morning, the inquisitor Feletti, who had originally ordered the abduction, was sensationally arrested.

One of the great historic results of the trial of the inquisitor Feletti was that it gave an opportunity to all of the main protagonists and eye witnesses of the events of June 23 and 24, 1858, and later episodes, to have their voices heard (and recorded for posterity), on condition that they were present in Bologna during the trial (the records of the trial are now accessible at the Bologna State Archive; Tribunale 1860). The trial on the "violent separation of the young boy Edgardo Mortara from his Jewish family for reasons of forced baptism, which took place in Bologna on the evening of June 24 1858, and his subsequent confinement in the House of Catechumens in Rome" (as the case was described by the investigating magistrate Francesco Carboni, in the indictment of January 18 and in his Report of March 7, 1860), lasted more than three months and included the hearing of the many witnesses as well as of the main defendant. It came to an end on April 16, 1860, with the closing statements by the prosecution and the defense (given respectively by the procurator fiscal Radamisto Valentini and the defense lawyer appointed by the court, Francesco Jussi), and then finally with the sentence, by a jury presided over by the judge, Calcedonio Ferrari. The verdict was one of acquittal; not because the kidnapping "with public force" of the child had not occurred, but because "the removal was done by the Prince." Since the "Prince," or rather, the pope, was outside the jurisdiction of the court, the case could go no further; and, as the sentence put it, "it was not, therefore, and indeed is not appropriate to proceed against the executors of the aforementioned removal" (Jussi 1860, p. 63).

Despite all its ambiguities, the "new Italy" (Druker and Lerner 2018) was in the meantime taking shape in that spring of 1860. Within a year, Italy would be a nation, with its unification and the birth of the new Kingdom of Italy being proclaimed on March 17, 1861.

The outcry and the consequences for the Italian Risorgimento

The question of why Edgardo's kidnapping caused such an outcry, when up until then similar instances of forced baptisms of Jewish children in Italy had elicited no comment, had already been raised in the *Jewish Chronicle* almost two years after the kidnapping (January 6, 1860, p. 4), at a time in which public opinion in Europe and America was still mindful of those events and anxious to know how the situation was developing; and back then the newspaper had already responded that the Mortara case depended not so much on the place or the nature of the crime, but on "the spirit of the age" in which the crime was committed. The fact is that a long tradition of forced baptisms (Caffiero 2004) and anti-Jewish abuses of power on the part of Christians, tolerated for centuries, clashed at that moment with a new culture of widely shared liberal values. These were values of equality that arose out of the Enlightenment, which exploded onto the political scene with the French Revolution and were disseminated by it through the old nations of Europe and the nascent United States of America. By the mid-nineteenth century, these values were imposing themselves as dominant in public opinion, underpinning the birth of the new nations being formed at the time, in which the people's expectations were very much informed by them. The Mortara case highlighted to international public opinion just how backward and inhumane the laws were in what was an authoritarian state, as well as the enormity of the abuse of power and of the injustice to which Jewish people were subject. The resulting discredit for the temporal power of the Church was considerable and bearer of serious consequences.

The texts of the time that document the awareness of the contemporary liberal politicians vis-à-vis the usefulness of the scandal over the abduction of the young Mortara boy for the purposes of the ongoing Italian Risorgimento include the letters exchanged between Cavour and the ambassador of the Kingdom of Sardinia to France, the Marquis of Villamarina, in November 1858. To the ambassador who, in a letter of November 21, had informed him of the great indignation that the kidnapping had engendered both in public opinion and in Napoleon III, of the stormy meeting on the matter between the pope and Gramont, the French ambassador to the Apostolic See, and of how popular resentment was turning French public opinion against the Papal States, Cavour responded on November 25, stressing the "utmost gravity" of the news received concerning the pope's intransigence and confirming the resultant weakening of the Papal States: "The Emperor has been delighted by the Mortara affair (*L'Empereur a été enchanté de l'affaire Mortara*), as indeed he is about everything that can compromise the pope in the eyes of Europe and of moderate Catholics. The greater the protests against the pope, the easier it will be for the Emperor to force him to make the sacrifices necessary for the reorganization of Italy"; "the pope's conduct," concluded Cavour, summing up the message that the ambassador would have to pass on to Napoleon III, "demonstrates the absolute impossibility of maintaining his temporal power beyond the walls of Rome" (Cavour 1926 [1858], letters no. 143 and 149; Martina 1986, p. 35).

For his part, the pope was well aware of the seriousness of the scandal for the temporal future of the Church, and he was not slow to blame his young "protégé" for it. When Edgardo, after years of complete isolation from his family and of intense indoctrination, was made a novice in the order of the Canons Regular of the Lateran in November 1867 with the name of Don Pio, he was "accompanied by the special blessings of Pius IX" (Edgardo Mortara, in Messori 2005, p. 107). On that solemn occasion, that new "father" of his reminded him that "I acquired you at great cost. Because of you, there was a universal eruption of outrage against me, and against this Holy See" (Tesi-Passerini 1879, pp. 140–141).

The core of the Church's temporal power fell apart once and for all in 1870. On the night of October 21, 1870, eighteen-year-old Edgardo – who was still living in San Pietro in Vincoli and had begun the process of entering the priesthood – was gripped with fear over what was happening in the city, now conquered by the Italians. He decided to flee from Rome in the company of another clergyman, both wearing civilian clothing in order to avoid detection. He thus began his life of pilgrimage outside Italy, in the Austrian Tyrol and then in France, Spain and other parts of Europe and America, with occasional returns to Italy. He died at an old age, in 1940, in Belgium, shortly before the Nazi invasion of that country. It was only in 1878 – not coincidentally, after the death of Pius IX – that Edgardo was able for the first time to see his mother again, as well as his brother Riccardo, in France, twenty years after their last meeting at the House of Catechumens; his father, who had battled so hard for his return home, had died in 1872.

The Mortara case and the "Age of Emancipations"

The Mortara case contributed not only to the Italian cause. The scandal also proved useful to the ongoing international struggle for Jewish emancipation, promoting the alliance between the persecuted world and liberal forces, while also encouraging the birth of Jewish national bodies, where they were previously missing, as occurred in the United States in 1859 on the occasion of the protests against the abduction of Edgardo. That period of multiple liberating upheavals on both sides of the Atlantic, which can be collectively defined as the "Age of Emancipations" (where the keyword must necessarily be in the plural), also saw the setting up of the first modern international Jewish assistance organization, the *Alliance Israélite Universelle*, which was established in Paris precisely on the stimulus of the still unresolved Mortara affair. As was stated, using the language of the time, in its important manifesto of May 17, 1860, this still-extant institution was geared towards the "Israelites of the whole world," "scattered across the globe and mixed into the nations." It offered concrete assistance to those "exhausted after twenty centuries of misery, insults and prohibitions," who had been persecuted due to antisemitism and had to be helped to "regain their dignity as human beings, and to acquire their dignity as citizens."

Regaining one's dignity as human beings, acquiring one's dignity as citizens, and being able to do so as Jews, taking pride in one's Jewishness. It was still necessary to fight for these objectives, during that period of transition for the Jewish world around the mid-nineteenth century. And this was even more true for the Italian Jews who, particularly in the territories directly subject to the laws of the Church of Rome, were still struggling to break out of the age of the ghettos, in order to enter as fully fledged members into the wider Italian society, with equal rights and equal duties – like all the country's other citizens.

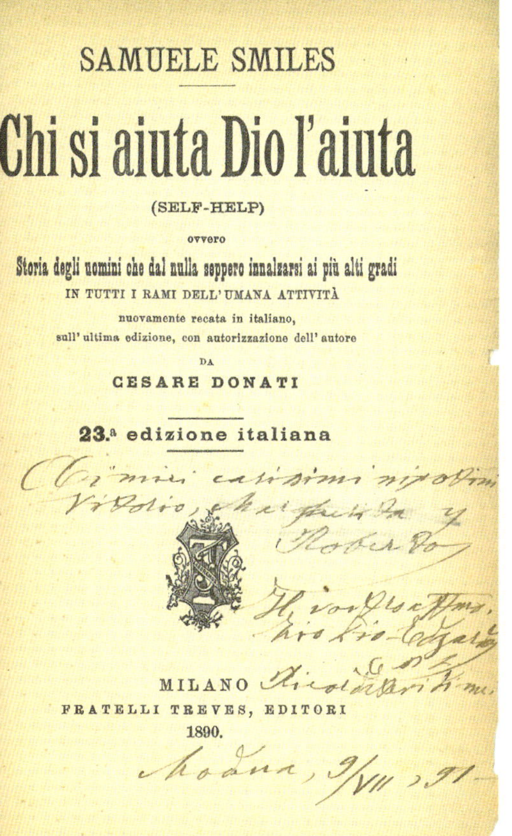
SAMUELE SMILES

Chi si aiuta Dio l'aiuta

(SELF-HELP)

ovvero

Storia degli uomini che dal nulla seppero innalzarsi ai più alti gradi

IN TUTTI I RAMI DELL'UMANA ATTIVITÀ

nuovamente recata in italiano, sull'ultima edizione, con autorizzazione dell'autore

DA

CESARE DONATI

23.ª edizione italiana

MILANO

FRATELLI TREVES, EDITORI

1890.

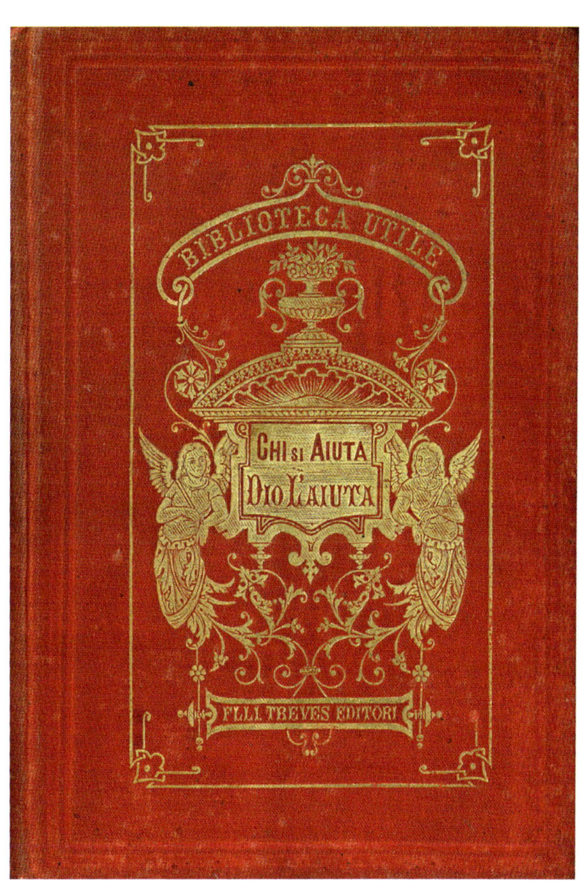

3. Samuele Smiles, *He who helps himself, God shall help (Self-Help), or A history of those men who from nothing were able to raise themselves to the highest ranks in all branches of human activity*, edited by Cesare Donati. Alberto Mortara Family Archive (cat. 40)

The Jews of Hapsburg Trieste: Social Inclusion, Emancipation, and Integration (1719–1914)

Tullia Catalan

From the establishment of the Free Port to civil inclusion

The Hapsburgs' foundation of the Free Port of Trieste in 1719 was a major event in the history of this city on the Adriatic coast and of its small Jewish community, at the time composed of about one hundred people mostly of Ashkenazic descent. Emperor Charles VI literally opened the city to all non-Catholic religious minorities dedicated to commerce, with the objective of rapidly boosting the north Adriatic port of Trieste, which the Hapsburgs believed could grow into a major economic and financial asset (Finzi and Panjek 2001).

Thanks to the privileges and exemptions first given by the Emperor and then confirmed by Empress Maria Theresa in 1771, during the eighteenth century Jews, Greeks, Armenians, Protestants, and Illyrian Serbs, streamed to this new Eldorado of sorts where they could benefit from particularly advantageous commercial and financial regulations, plus freedom of religion with no discriminatory and humiliating taxes, such as for instance the body tax that was levied on Jews in other regions of the Empire. Said privileges were accessible to those who met certain criteria in terms of economic status and could prove they were able to contribute with their own means to the growth of the Free Port. The Hapsburg's relations with the non-Catholic minorities were in fact based on the concept of mutual "utility," a principle that minorities were willing to accept in exchange for commercial advantages paired with higher levels of personal freedom (Catalan 2000; Dubin 1999). To be allowed to live in a city with no particular limitations, buy real estate, and travel and trade freely within the borders of the Hapsburg Empire, was an incentive that made Jews work even harder towards the development of the port. Over a few decades Trieste welcomed Ashkenazic and Sephardic Jews coming from all over Europe, as well as from the Levant, and Africa, attracted by the privileges and the desirable living conditions granted to religious minorities. A considerable number of Jews came from states of the Italian Peninsula and from the Republic of Venice, which by the late eighteenth century was experiencing a strong economic decline.

From a demographic standpoint, during the eighteenth century and especially during the first half of the nineteenth century there was a considerable growth of the Jewish community due to the constant stream of immigration, that was rigorously regulated by police authorities and also by the community leaders who were concerned by the arrival of so many incoming and deprived fellow Jews. Over a few decades, the Jewish population in Trieste passed from 120 individuals in 1748 to 440 in 1775; a significant increase was also registered after Joseph II's 1781 Patent of Toleration. In 1788 the Jewish population had grown to 730, reaching 1082 in 1798 (mostly coming from the former Republic of Venice).

In 1802 it grew to 1247, and soared to 5000 in the 1880s, remaining stable until the Racial Laws of 1938 (Catalan 2000). It should be noted how Jewish immigrants kept in touch with their areas of provenance, especially in those cases when the decision to emigrate to Trieste had not come about to escape anti-Jewish surges but to seize new opportunities of economic development, on a personal, familial, or professional level. Usually the choice to move to Trieste was made by the younger members of merchant and banking families. They eventually settled and married with Jews immigrated from other states, expanding familial and business networks. During the first half of the nineteenth century, an assiduous match-making activity developed within the Jewish community in Trieste. Even illustrious personalities worked as mediators, such as the great exegetist and scholar Samuel David Luzzatto who occasionally accepted to assume this role – with the help of his wife – on behalf of Trieste upper-class families (Catalan 2004). At a time when the Port was significantly expanding, there were very many marriage agents working in the city. The phenomenon is to be linked to the importance of a girl's dowry towards the safeguarding against bankruptcy of companies admitted to the Stock Exchange (Millo 1998).

Jewish immigrants usually kept connections alive with their homeland when they still had relatives living there: this can be inferred from the many bequests that never fail to mention distant relatives who had remained in the motherland, and confraternities of the native community, but also people of Trieste in need, non-Jews included (Catalan 2001). These facts can be read as further signs of the Jewish community's successful process of civil inclusion into the general society. A great contribution towards integration came from the innovative Jewish education system introduced in Trieste following the Patent of Toleration of 1781. Trieste, as well as the nearby Gorizia and Gradisca, were the first communities to implement the educational principles theorised by the exponents of the Berlin Jewish Enlightenment, of whom Moses Mendelssohn was the major representative and supporter. The Jewish school of Trieste pioneered the combination of modern and traditional subjects as early as 1782, thanks to Karl von Zinzendorf's political influence and to the community's close relation with Berlin, validated by the presence in Trieste and Gorizia of representatives of the Haskalah intellectual movement such as Herz Homberg, the author of the *Bnè-Zion* Jewish catechism for children translated into Italian by Leone Saraval and Naftalì Wessely (Catalan 2000; Dubin 1999). The Imperial pronouncement also declared that all Jews in the Empire could have access to public schools, a decision that gave great impulse to integration between Jews and non-Jews; over the years, Jewish schools gradually lost students, to the point that they were attended only by children from poor Jewish families.

The aim of Joseph II's Patent of Toleration was to progressively integrate Jews into general society through civil inclusion. The ghetto, for instance, was permanently closed in 1785: a decision that was much debated within the Jewish community itself since there were some elderly members who still could not fully understand the advantages of such change (Dubin 1999). Also of note is the fact that the issue of the Patent raised concerns even among the community leaders who feared the loss of their long-established privileges (Catalan 2000).

The process of civil inclusion was the distinguishing trait of the port Jews, as Lois Dubin defined them in her important research (Dubin 1999). From the late eighteenth to the early nineteenth century, the Jews of Trieste acknowledged that they could act as single individuals on the basis of the laws of the State without having to rely on the traditional mediation of the community, which gradually lost its political influence especially among the wealthier strata and intellectuals. During the second half of the nineteenth century the community became an institution almost exclusively devoted to religious practices, education, and charitable activities (Catalan 2000).

This higher level of autonomy from the community institutions translated, especially in the local Jewish elite, into the birth of friendships and business partnerships with non-Jewish fellow citizens, based on shared economic and political objectives regarding the management of the city and the port. The framework inside which these friendships and partnerships mostly developed was the Deputation of the Stock-Exchange where contacts with the capital of the Empire were constant: Vienna in fact considered very attentively any request coming from the emergent, multi-confessional and multi-ethnic elites of Trieste (Millo 1998). In a context characterized by a markedly secularist drive and by a well rooted non-religious way of life, port Jews were encouraged to share their professional expertise and their culture with other non-Jewish fellow citizens, in a context of peaceful coexistence (Dubin 1999; Catalan 2011).

It was also thanks to the policies adopted by the House of Hapsburg towards the Jews of Trieste that the three periods of French occupation between 1797 and 1812 did not stimulate strong Francophile feelings in the community. In fact, it was quite the opposite. Apart from a few subjects, members of intellectual circles who enthusiastically embraced the revolutionary principles and the significant political innovation of entrusting a public office of the local administration to a Jew – shopkeeper Aron Vivante –, most Jewish merchants and bankers kept a very low profile, concerned by the economic consequences that the French occupation could have on the port's business. The French pressing demand for money from the wealthiest citizens of Trieste seriously compromised the local economy during the occupation. This was why when the Hapsburgs were reinstated after Napoleon's defeat, they were greeted with joy by most Trieste Jews, even though the French had granted civil and religious equality to all citizens on 27 November 1810 (Catalan 2000).

The French season however left an important political mark especially among some of the most distinguished members of the Jewish intellectual circles, particularly regarding the issue of civil rights that were vigorously reclaimed by the local liberals. In addition, the French had also contributed to the spreading of Masonic Lodges in the Illyrian Provinces. These structures, that were later banned by the Austrians, counted among their members some famed and illustrious Jews such as doctor Benedetto Frizzi (Dubin 1999; Catalan 2000), who with Samuel David Luzzatto was one of the major representatives of Jewish Enlightenment in Trieste.

The years between the Restoration and 1848 were the time when the Port Emporium of Trieste reached its highest development, even though after the French period the Hapsburg rule became more rigid on a political level. However, the local Jewish community was not subject to any restriction, unlike those who lived in the Lombardo-Veneto area. In 1839, thanks to Emperor Ferdinand, the Consiglio Ferdinandeo – a council for the administration of the city – was instituted: three of the forty members were Jews from the local financial elites (Catalan 2000). It was within this framework that gradually the city's multi-confessional and multi-ethnic middle class, as defined by Anna Millo, came into existence. A social group that to avoid multilingualism adopted Italian as its trade language, although maintaining a tradition of linguistic cosmopolitanism until the outbreak of World War I (Millo 1998). Triestine Jews adapted with great flexibility and the use of their mother tongues – Yiddish and Ladino – was limited only to domestic contexts.

In the meantime, the community had changed, seamlessly incorporating Sephardic and Ashkenazic Jews. Unlike other communities living on the Italian Peninsula, Trieste's Jewry was capable of creating the conditions for a harmonious coexistence among all its components, administrating without any particular problem both Sephardic and Ashkenazic oratories. Only in 1912, with the erection of the new monumental Temple did the community officially opt for the Ashkenazic rite. After all, the community had always proved very considerate in the choice of its rabbis, choosing prominent personalities who were not too connected to orthodoxy, considered incompatible with the city's lay spirit. In 1826, upon rejecting the intransigent approach of rabbi Abram Eliezer Levi, the community gave itself a new spiritual leader and chose Abram Vita Cologna, a well-known member of the French Grand Sanhedrin and former president of the Israelite Central *Consistory of Paris*. In 1832 his office was taken over by his former pupil Sabbato Graziadio Treves, a resourceful rabbi who contributed to the gradual renovation of religious practices, never trespassing the boundaries of orthodoxy. The second half of the nineteenth century was the period of greatest transformation from a cultural and spiritual standpoint. The protagonists of this season were rabbi Marco Tedeschi, a personal friend of Cavour's, and rabbi Sabato Raffaele Melli: two men with a great talent for mediating between the various positions within the community (Catalan 2000).

In terms of economic development, the 1830s and 1840s were years of great change with a number of Jewish families of bankers affirming their role in multiple international financial markets. The Morpurgo, Parente, Hierschel, Vivante, Camondo, and Landauer families, by cultivating strong relations with other Jewish families, including the Rothschilds and the Raffalovichs, became part of that Jewish European aristocracy that played a key role in great projects such as the construction of the Suez Canal in 1869, an initiative towards which the Morpurgo gave their active contribution (Catalan 1996).

During the 1830s some of the insurance companies that are still present on the market today, such as Assicurazioni Generali and Riunione Adriatica di Sicurtà were founded in Trieste. Charter members included representatives from all religious minorities, Jews and Greeks in particular, and their presence remained a constant up to World War I and beyond (Millo 1998).

Thanks to the Jewish international networks, the port of Trieste was able to activate a system of relations with Europe's major centers. In exchange for their networking services, the Austrian government assured benefits and advantages to the Jews and after 1848 even dispensed honors and aristocratic titles. Jewish businessmen founded mixed companies, private banks and small insurance companies with non-Jewish partners; they acquired ships and opened branches of their businesses in Odessa, Thessaloniki, Marseille, Livorno, Alexandria and Constantinople. By doing so, the reach of their commerce could grow in size and variety. When "mixed" companies were founded, contracts were always respectful of the different religious festivities of all associates. The most fruitful partnerships where those between Greeks and Jews (Catalan 2001).

1848 was an important year even for Jews, who actively joined the struggles for constitutional rights; some young students volunteered and joined the Risorgimento movement without their families' consent. For these initiatives they were banned and had to leave the Austrian domains (Catalan 2006).

During the second half of the nineteenth century, also following the civil and political emancipation granted by the Hapsburgs in 1867, occasions for Jewish/non-Jewish socialisation multiplied. People used to go to the theatre together, participated in social, artistic, and sport initiatives, attended musical soirees in salons and musical associations regardless of their faith. When sport became popular, Jews and non-Jews went on bicycle tours together or organized trips to the mountains and the seaside. Austria benevolently approved of all this, encouraging social exchanges that led to a spirit of collaboration between the different groups, to the advantage of the development of the Trieste Free Port, until the Congress of Berlin in 1878.

The many occasions for Jewish/non-Jewish socialization led to romantic relationships: starting in the 1870s, to the utter bewilderment of the religious authorities, there were very many mixed marriages, conversions outside Judaism, and even conversions to Judaism that continued until the outbreak of World War I. Also of note were the many *konfessionslos* of Trieste: people mostly from anti-Austrian irredentist families who aspired to join the neighboring anticlerical Italy and share the enviable conditions of Italian Jews. The process of integration of the Trieste Jewish community within the local general society had certainly been a successful one, but in some cases it had translated into entire families turning their back on the Jewish community committing to a radical form of assimilation which also contemplated conversion (Catalan 2000).

During the 1880s and 90s the situation started to evolve due to some significant changes occurring in local and international politics. The gradual increase of hostility in the national conflict between Italian, Slovenian and Germans reached levels of verbal violence that were unthinkable only a few years before. The liberals in favor of Italian irredentism that were at the head of the municipality were mainly *konfessionlos* Jews, such as Felice Venezian, Camillo Ara, Moisè Luzzatto. They were all secretly affiliated to masonic lodges and actively involved in anti-Austrian and anti-Slovene activities. In this period, many Triestine Jews, men and women, joined the irredentist cause, while others remained loyal to Austria, and others embraced the Austrian-Marxist positions of Adriatic Socialism (Catalan 2000).

These political contrasts, also increased by the crisis that followed the closing of the Free Port in 1891, led to a radical change in the internal dynamics within the Jewish community, which encompassed a plurality of conflicting political currents. At the turn of the century, Trieste also saw the spreading of political Zionism, a movement that was strongly supported by the periodical *Il Corriere Israelitico*, founded in 1862. *Il Corriere* rallied for Zionism until the outbreak of World War I also thanks to the unrelenting efforts of Dante Lattes and rabbi Zvi Perez Chajes, director of *Il Messaggero Israelitico*.

In this context however, the entire Jewish community was forced to face, from the 1880s to the early 1900s, the attacks of a small but combative antisemitic group, descending from Christian Socialism and secular positions, that for over a decade via the local press incited antisemitic political positions against Triestine Jews, mainly targeting the Liberal Nationalists that administered the city. In the early twentieth century, antisemitism was stopped by the local socialists (Catalan 2000), while the city was starting to register the arrival of emigrants from Eastern Europe on their way to America, fleeing from the terrible Russian pogroms. The port of Trieste therefore become one of the main centers of this emigration flux, with the organizational support of the local Zionist group (Catalan 1991). Lastly, a significant group of over a thousand Corfiot Jews arrived in Trieste following the 1891 blood libel accusations, and they too were incorporated into the general society with no particular difficulties nor problems (Catalan, Di Fant, Lelli, and Tabor 2013).

The incoming war of 1914 found, on the one hand, a new generation of young Jews ready to desert and fight for Italy and, on the other hand, other young and less young Jews loyal to the Hapsburgs. That was the beginning of a new season for the Jews of Trieste, a city that after World War I in 1919 was to become Italian.

Italian Zionists, between Italian Nationalism and Jewish Nationalism

Simonetta Della Seta

Parallels have often been drawn between the Italian Risorgimento and the awakening of Jewish nationalism (Avineri 2011; Consonni 2015; D.V. Segre 1984). Some of the spiritual fathers of Zionism took their inspiration from the Italian struggle; Moses Hess, for example, in his book *Rome and Jerusalem* (Hess 1861). On closer examination of the application of this concept, we find that the parallels are insufficient in explaining the creation of a Jewish national identity by Italian Jewry.

It is true that the participation of Italian Jews in Italy's national struggle was more than considerable. It is also true that Italian Jews did not play a crucial role in the Jewish national movement, defined as "political Zionism," especially in its first years of activity. In this sense, the participation of Italian Jews in the struggle for Italy's united nationhood had no immediate influence on their developing a Jewish national consciousness.

However, by 1900, something had compelled a small portion of Italian Jewry to rally in support of the Zionist movement. Three years later, in 1903, six hundred Italian Jews had already paid their dues, a *shekel*, to the Sixth World Zionist Congress, and in 1904, the Italian Zionist Federation was founded (*L'Idea Sionnista*, nos. 3, 4, 5, 1904).

Our investigation, then, will focus on the process that prompted a minority among Italian Jews to support a Jewish national movement, and the new political struggle in favor of the establishment of a Jewish national homeland (Herzl 1896). The Zionist movement had been founded at the end of the nineteenth century by some European Jewish intellectuals, led by Viennese journalist Theodor Herzl, in response to the increase in antisemitic acts, both in Eastern Europe – where the Jews had become the target of violent pogroms – and in Western Europe – where a Jewish captain of the French Army, Alfred Dreyfus, had been accused of treachery and condemned on the ground of his origin (Bensoussan 2007; Herzberg 1959; Vital 2001).

To understand this development, we should consider at least three aspects of Jewish life in Italy at the turn of the nineteenth century. First, the general impetus for inclusion that Italian Jews experienced during the struggle for Risorgimento and their emancipation. Second, the Jewish cultural and religious heritage of the two rabbinical schools of Padua and Livorno. Lastly, the growing contact with the Jewish world outside of Italy.

Let us discuss the first aspect

The Jewish minority's contribution to making Italy one renewed nation living in an unified State far exceeded their negligible size, and this was aptly explained by the prominent Italian Jewish historian Arnaldo Momigliano – an interpretation that did not escape the attention of the Marxist thinker and leader of the Italian Communist Party Antonio Gramsci: "The formation of the national consciousness of the Jews of Italy developed in parallel with the formation of the Italian national consciousness of the Piedmontese, or Neapolitans, or Sicilians: it is a specific moment of that same historical process, and characterizes it" (Gramsci 1949; Levis Sullam 2007; Momigliano 1933; Toscano 1998).

The coincidence was first of all chronological: Italian Jewish emancipation was accomplished in several stages, between the years 1798 and 1870. The beginning of the last and decisive step corresponded with the outbreak of Italy's War of Independence (see Ferrara degli Uberti's essay, "Jews Citizen"). The natural link between the two processes – emancipation and Risorgimento – was also facilitated by the juridical structure of Italian emancipation. Emancipation was declared first in the Kingdom of Sardinia with a single decree signed by King Charles Albert. Later, this same decree became automatically effective in all the territories as they became part of the new unified State. This was accomplished without a real debate on the Jewish question. Indeed, the decree found the unanimous support of political parties for whom religious equality was a basis for the national struggle.

For all these reasons, Italian Jews soon felt confident in supporting emancipation, and as a consequence, the magnitude of the Jewish participation in the Italian Risorgimento was extremely conspicuous compared to the small number of Jews in Italy (Della Pergola 1976). A further element that linked the very process of Jewish emancipation to that of the Italian Nation was the fact that modern antisemitism (often different and more articulated than traditional, religious oriented anti-Judaism) in Italy was a much more marginal phenomenon than it was in other European countries (Lindemann, Levy 2010; Poliakov 2013). In fact, the increasing marginalization of the Jews within other European societies, which took place during the second half of the nineteenth century as a result of different waves of antisemitism, certainly did not take the same course in Italy. Here, also due to the small size of the Jewish community, the debate over antisemitism was more limited to the old antisemitic tradition and prejudices of the clergy (see the essays by Cristiana Facchini and Elèna Mortara). Since the new State was mainly secular, none of the antisemitic expressions by the Church resulted in true political pressure, nor did they call for a reaction of the Jews in political terms (see Gadi Luzzatto Voghera's essay), except for the case of Mortara's kidnapping (see Mortara's essay).

The support by a minority of Italian Jews for the new Zionist ideas born in Europe caused no great dilemma. The success of the Risorgimento had offered a very positive picture of nationhood in general, and an impetus to reflect on the condition and self-definition of other Jews who were experiencing problems in other European countries. During the second half of the nineteenth century, new lines of thought on Jewish identity were generated in Italy. We shall mention, for example, names such as Leone Carpi, an economist from Cento, and Giacomo Dina, a journalist from Turin, who voiced the positive contribution of the Jews in many fields of Italian life, such as economics and politics, and demanded from the Jews themselves more active and "noble" participation in the struggle for emancipation (L. Carpi 1956). Another example of a new Italian Jewish position was expressed by Giacomo Venezian – a doctor from Trieste, later a martyr of the Risorgimento – who was convinced of the importance of strengthening Jewish cultural identity. The Jewish revival in Italy was also accompanied by an increase in Jewish publishing and press activity, that took place during the same years (see Ferrara degli Uberti's essay, "Italian Jewish Periodicals (1845–1915)").

The second aspect of Jewish life that we will explore presents a different type of contribution to the shaping of Jewish identity, made by two important Italian rabbis and scholars, Samuel David Luzzatto (known as Shadal, 1800–1865) and Elia Benamozegh (1823–1900) (see Fontana's essay).

Shadal's influence on the growth of a Jewish national consciousness becomes clear through an examination of the development of Italian Zionism. It is notable that interest in Zionism appeared directly within the very same geographical triangle (i.e., the Lombardo-Venetian Kingdom and Emilia-Romagna) in which Shadal had taught and where the Rabbinical College of Padua had educated a great number of students. Furthermore, the most active communities (with several exceptions, such as Livorno and Florence) were those led by rabbis who had studied under Shadal in the Rabbinical College of Padua. To define Luzzatto as a kind of Zionist *ante-litteram* might not be correct. However, "his conceptions were far ahead of those of his contemporaries [...] and such a patriotic Jew was certainly close to being also a Zionist. Shadal loved the people of Israel, the Torah of Israel, and the language of Israel the same way he loved the Land of Israel [...]. He insisted on the everyday ethical precepts as a good orthodox Jew and he loved these not only as religious orders, but also for their social and national meaning" (Klausner 1966). Shadal's historical-national conception of Judaism, and his insistence on the relevance of the Hebrew language paved the way for the modern national Jewish movement.

His teachings found fertile ground, especially among the students of the College that he established in Padua in November 1829 together with another famous rabbi, Hillel Della Torre HaCohen. Even a superficial glance at the list of students, in chronological order, immediately makes us realize that most of the great religious leaders of nineteenth century Italian Jewry came from this institute. Among those were Lelio Cantoni, Abramo Lattes, Eude Lolli, Filosseno Luzzatto, Abramo Mainster, Marco Mortara, Abramo Greco, Samuele Salomoni Olper, and many others (Castelbolognesi 1966).

Most of these teachers caused a Jewish cultural reawakening of their communities. Some of them, influenced by the emancipation and Risorgimento movement, were propagators more of Italian national feelings than of Jewish ones. Others continued to teach a concept of being Jewish which put more emphasis on belonging to a Jewish people, not only to a Jewish culture, and while they were not openly forerunners of modern Zionism, they paved the way for these ideals. Their work was propagated through the new Italian Jewish press, and disseminated abroad when they served as rabbis in other Jewish Mediterranean rabbinical communities. A curious and interesting example of this activity was represented by the contents of the magazine *Mosè* edited in Corfu from 1873 to 1875 by rabbi Giuseppe Levi.

We should also take into consideration the work of the rabbinical school of Livorno, which was particularly fertile in those years thanks to the presence of rabbi Elia

Benamozegh. At that time, the two schools carried on an intense debate – due to the contrasting positions of their two leaders – and these polemics lasted for many years among their students (Colombo 1966 and 1970).

Benamozegh, a kabbalist and mystic, repeatedly expressed the idea of the unity of Israel and the central role of the Holy Land in this context. One example of his conviction was presented at the first congress of all the religious leaders of the Jewish communities of united Italy, held in Ferrara in 1863. His personal battle to convince the assembly of Italian rabbis of the necessity to keep the traditional link with the Jewish "missionaries of the Holy Land," was a demonstration of his ties to the Promised Land. The missionaries, emissaries of the Jewish communities that resided in the four holy cities of the Land of Israel (Jerusalem, Hebron, Tiberias, Safed), traveled periodically throughout Italy to collect the money raised to support their brethren. "The question of the missionaries," explained Benamozegh to the audience, "is not a strictly religious question. There is no religious law which compels us to maintain this tradition. But it is a question of 'religious policy'... You cannot deny that the culture and memory of the Holy Land is a very essential part of our culture as well as a basic condition of our soul when we observe our religious precepts. It is not even a legal religious question, but a moral

„Die Welt"
Redaction und Administration
Wien
IX., Türkenstrasse 9.

Wien, den 9 XII 1903

Mon cher ami Felice,

j'ai l'intention de partir le 25 décembre le soir de Vienne pour Rome. Si vous le voulez je m'arrêterai pour quelques heures à Ferrare pour vous rendre visite, mais il serait peut être préférable de continuer le voyage sans arrêt jusqu'à Florence, si vous voulez monter dans mon train à Ferrare. Nous passerions la nuit du 26 à Florence pour voir le Dr Marguliès et nous irions le 27 à Rome.
Avant tout il faut naturellement que j'aie l'assertion répétée de la part du Dr Marg, que je pourrais voir S. M. immédiatement. À cet effet j'écris aujourd'hui au Dr Marg, parce qu'il me serait impossible de rester longtemps à Rome. Je compte m'arrêter à mon retour chez vous à Ferrare si ce n'était pas en allant à Rome. Veuillez noter mon adresse télégraphique:

Benjamin Wien

parceque probablement vous aurez à me télégraphier.

Bien cordialement mon cher ami je reste votre dévoué

Herzl

1. Theodor Herzl's letter to Felice Ravenna, 1903.
U. Nahon Museum of Italian Jewish Art, Jerusalem

religious attitude of our spirit" (Colombo 1966). Despite the importance of his writings and teachings, Benamozegh was not the head of a large school, as was Shadal, but was, rather, the spiritual guide of a few followers.

The third and last aspect that contributed to the shaping of a national Jewish identity among Italian Jews during the period under discussion was the infiltration of new currents in Jewish thought from other European countries. In the nineteenth century, Italian Jews had several types of contact with world Jewry. Members of the elites were fully integrated into European culture, especially French, and German in the Lombardo Venetian Kingdom and Trieste, so close to Vienna (see the essay by Tullia Catalan). Another channel was offered by the presence in Italy of foreign Jewish personalities, who had moved to Italian cities in order to fulfill duties of religious guidance or social and political leadership. Contacts were also initiated when some of the most important leaders of political Zionism passed through Italy, usually on diplomatic missions, or on their way to northern continental Europe.

One of the important religious personalities, whose work very much influenced Italian Jewry, was rabbi Samuel Hirsch Margulies (1858–1922), a scholar from Galicia who had been the spiritual guide of several German Jewish communities. He was transferred to Florence in 1899 in order to lead the Collegio Rabbinico Italiano that had just been relocated from Rome. The presence of rabbi Margulies marked the acquaintance of Florentine Jewry with new trends of European Jewish thought, and in particular with the new Zionist ideas. Margulies wanted to give Italian Jewry a sense of what it meant being Jewish in a modern and changing world. Towards this purpose, he dedicated himself to educating and

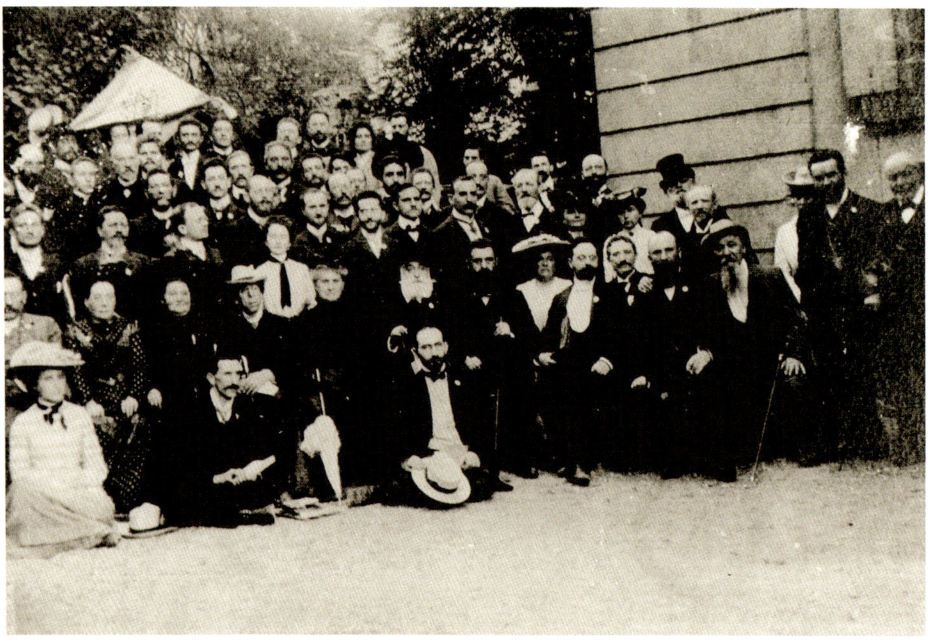

2. Theodor Herzl with some of the participants at the Sixth Zionist Congress in Basel, in 1903, also attended by an Italian delegation (C.Z.A. The Central Zionist Archive)

guiding the young in Jewish studies and ethics, and putting them into direct contact with the Jewish world of Central Europe. Margulies lectured to his students about the Torah and the Talmud, but also about migrations, pogroms, and antisemitism, as well as about Theodor Herzl and Zionism.

Margulies's teachings created a generation of Italian Jews with new conceptions. In fact, among his students were the most important names of twentieth century Italian Jewry, such as Alfonso Pacifici, Umberto Cassuto, David Prato, Elia Artom, Carlo Alberto Viterbo, Angelo Orvieto, and Dante Lattes. This group developed positions that were totally original both in their idea of Jewish identity and of Jewish culture (Airoldi 2015; Toscano 2010).

The work of Margulies was further aided by the arrival in Italy of another important Galician mentor, Hirsch Perez Chajes (1876–1927, the grandson of the Great Rabbi Zvi Hirsch Chajes from Brody), who was appointed lecturer of Jewish history at the Collegio Rabbinico of Florence in 1902. Perez Chajes was another example of the cultured European Jew and devoted Zionist, with an open mind and great enthusiasm, both which he used in educating the young.

Lastly, a completely different case of imported Jewish ideals was exemplified by Joseph Marcou Baruch. Born in Constantinople, a traveler and cosmopolitan, he was a true representative of the revolutionary Jewish national struggle. He arrived in Rome in 1897 and founded the first Italian Zionist group, named Prisoners of Titus, which sent an enthusiastic telegram to the First Zionist Congress in Basel. After further travels up and down the Italian Peninsula, he eventually settled in Livorno and became a close friend of Dante Lattes, who was clearly influenced by this relationship. Baruch died a short time later in Florence, in August 1899, when he shot himself out of personal despair. Italian Zionism actually owes much to this bizarre figure, as he was the first to give Italian Jews direct testimony of the new movements rising within world Jewry, especially the Zionist Movement.

As a result of the presence of all these personalities who brought Italian Jewry closer to other European Jewish communities, when Herzl first visited Italy in January 1904, an Italian Zionist group already existed (Herzl 1960). Furthermore, a few influential Italian Jews were ready to welcome him and support his cause, and helped him arrange the diplomatic meetings with Pope Pius X and King Victor Emmanuel III, which had been the aim of his visit.

The organizer of this trip, as well as the intermediary between Herzl and the Italian authorities, was a young lawyer from Ferrara, Felice Ravenna, who was later the head of Italian Zionism for the first twenty years of the twentieth century. Among those who helped Herzl were also: the Donati brothers in Modena, Angelo Sullam in Venice, and Sabatino Lopez in Milan (Nahon 1960).

Herzl's historic trip to Italy had a great effect on all the Italian Jews of the time. *Il Corriere Israelitico* of Trieste, for example, printed an article by Dante Lattes that applauded the fact that the Zionist Movement had reached the ears of both the King of Italy and the Holy See.

Herzl's mission was reported in detail in *L'Idea Sionnista*. The Italian Zionists applauded the encouragement received from Herzl "to continue our struggle and our propaganda for the noble ideal" and his reassurance that "the whole Zionist Movement will march as a compact body towards the accomplishment of a just solution for the Jewish proletariat."

This statement also shows us that the struggle for Jewish nationalism was very much felt, among Italian Zionists, as a deep sentiment of solidarity with their Jewish brothers who were persecuted in Eastern Europe. In this sense, their Zionism was for many years –

at least until the end of World War I – a philanthropic endeavor to find a solution for other Jews, rather than a search for a home for themselves and Italian Jewry at large.

However, when Theodor Herzl died, a few months after his visit to Italy, in July 1904, all the Jewish communities of Italy officially commemorated his passing, and sent telegrams of condolence to Felice Ravenna. On the same occasion, Italian Zionists deeply felt an integral part of the World Zionist Movement.

It should also be mentioned that Herzl's visit to Italy established a precedent, followed later by such Zionist leaders as Nahum Sokolow, Chaim Weizmann and Vladimir Zeev Jabotisky (D. Carpi, Della Seta 1997).

This is the context in which new expressions of Jewish national identity took shape among the Jews of Italy. However, there was never a point reached where the Italian Jews rejected their identification with the Italian nation. On the contrary, the need to have both aspirations coincide – Italian and Jewish nationalism – was extensively discussed within all trends of Italian Zionism, from the most secular to the most religious. "Without violent intentions, incitement or plans to use bellicose means – Felix Ravenna wrote in his letter to Senator C. F. Gabba, who had attacked the Italian Zionists and accused them of dual loyalty – Zionism wants to achieve its goals peacefully with the consent of Europe and aspires to the superior principle of fraternity" (*L'Idea Sionnista*, no. 13,1905).

Many years later, in the 1930s and already during the Fascist regime, Italian Zionist Raffaele Cantoni, asked about his loyalty to the two homelands, responded that he was unable to give any preference, since it was like speaking about "mother" and "father" (Minerbi 1978).

3. Cover of *L'Idea Sionnista*. MEIS (National Museum of Italian Judaism and the Shoah), Ferrara (cat. 75)

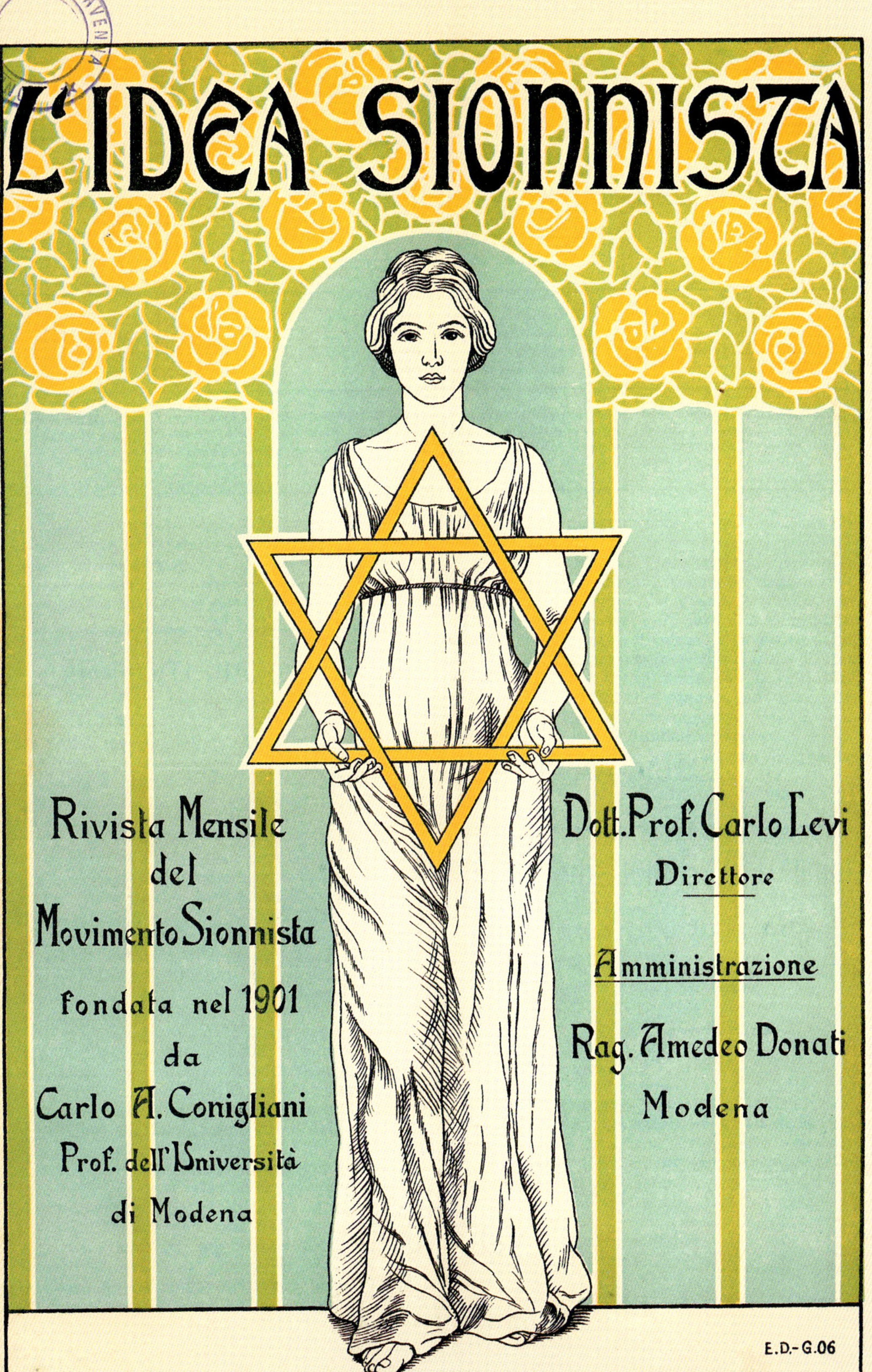

LIT. RABETTI e ROSSI - MODENA

The Jewish Question in Cesare Lombroso's Science

Emanuele D'Antonio

In 1909, the Italian Jewish press celebrated the deceased Cesare Lombroso (Verona, 1835 – Turin, 1909) as a glory of Judaism (Ferrara degli Uberti 2012). The criminologist, intellectual and doctor had gained renown during the Risorgimento, and as an academic of the new Italy and a celebrity of positivism he had been one of the most famous Italian Jews of the period of emancipation. A symbol of the felicitous integration of post-unification Italy, his death did, however, give rise to mixed feelings. The claim that he was indeed Jewish was combined with regret over how far he had strayed from Jewish cultural and religious life. The materialist Lombroso had been a Jew without knowing it, but was deserving of homage for, amongst other things, the courageous – albeit sometimes unwelcome and culturally ambiguous (Finzi 2011) – contributions to the fight against antisemitism in the late nineteenth and early twentieth centuries.

Judaism was an evanescent but not insignificant aspect of Lombroso's character. As a young man, Lombroso – from a family of the Veronese Jewish elite – studied in the climate of renewal that was typical of the scientific, political and cultural milieux of Hapsburg Italy. On the eve of emancipation, his adhesion to positivism and to the *Risorgimento* led him to embrace atheist and assimilationist beliefs: equality called upon Jews and Christians to combine into a single national body, reunited and regenerated from the evils of the past. The scientist nevertheless maintained a relatively solid "ethnic" identity, driven by his sense of belonging to a Jewish family network – that self-identified as Jewish and was perceived as Jewish by outsiders – and this exerted an influence over his private life (Dolza 1990). In 1870, his marriage to the coreligionist Nina De Benedetti confirmed and transmitted his Jewishness to his offspring. His new centrality to the scientific and socio-cultural life of Turin, where he resided from 1876, increased his centrifugal temptations. The boundary between the family and Gentile society was thrown into question by the mixed marriages of his daughters Paola and Gina, but then reestabilished by the endogamic marriage of his son Ugo. The monumental section of the Turinese cemetery, not the Jewish section, hosts the scientist's grave.

Lombroso's bibliography includes a number of socio-anthropological studies on the Jews, in which he comes out strongly in favor of emancipation. From the time of unification, Lombroso responded to anti-Jewish accusations of unresolved separatism made by the dominant cultures (Pavan 2008) through an approach to the Jewish question that endeavored to be scientific. He decided to enter the fray in the wake of the dissemination of the Aryan racial myth in Italian science and culture (Lenz 2014). Anthropological knowledge reaffirmed the fact that the Jews belonged to European civilization. His discourse, while founded on racial culture, accorded to the human races an unlimited capacity for evolution (Montaldo 2018). The Jews of Europe, "robust remnant of the Semitic lineage," offered an admirable example of this process; their survival in a hostile environment, refining their intelligence, had put them on a par with their neighbors, the "arj" (Lombroso 1871). Their psychophysical weakness was not a racial trait, but an inherited defect now on the mend after centuries of political oppression (Lombroso 1867).

The main intervention made by Lombroso on the Jewish question was a response to the challenge posed by the antisemitic movements in Europe at the end of the century. In his *Antisemitismo*, Lombroso – now an intellectual and militant socialist – put forward an authoritative scientific defense of emancipation, delegitimizing its enemies and ideological myths (Lombroso 1894). A political pathology of nationalist-clerical stamp, antisemitism stirred up atavistic hatreds deep-rooted in the European collective psyche. His non-Jewish critics responded putting forward the dominant thesis that antisemitism is a reaction against the alleged Jewish separatism (Bettini 1894; Sergi 1894). For its part, the Jewish world discussed single aspects of that text. His harsh assimilationist critique of Jewish religiosity cost him the respect of many coreligionists (Frigessi 1999), while his diagnosis of a Jewish race weakened by history inspired projects of regeneration in certain Zionists and Jewish socialists (Cavaglion 1988; Levis Sullam 2017). At the turn of the century, Lombroso participated in the mobilization for the defense of Alfred Dreyfus and in the protests against the Russian pogroms; Herzl and his friend Nordau's Zionism, although not entirely convincing, seemed to him to alleviate the dramatic conditions of the *Ostjuden* – an alternative to an emancipation of which he was always a vociferous scientific defender (D'Antonio 2001).

On the following pages
1. Siren letter by Cesare Lombroso for the Ravenna-Pardo wedding. Private collection, Ferrara (cat. 68)

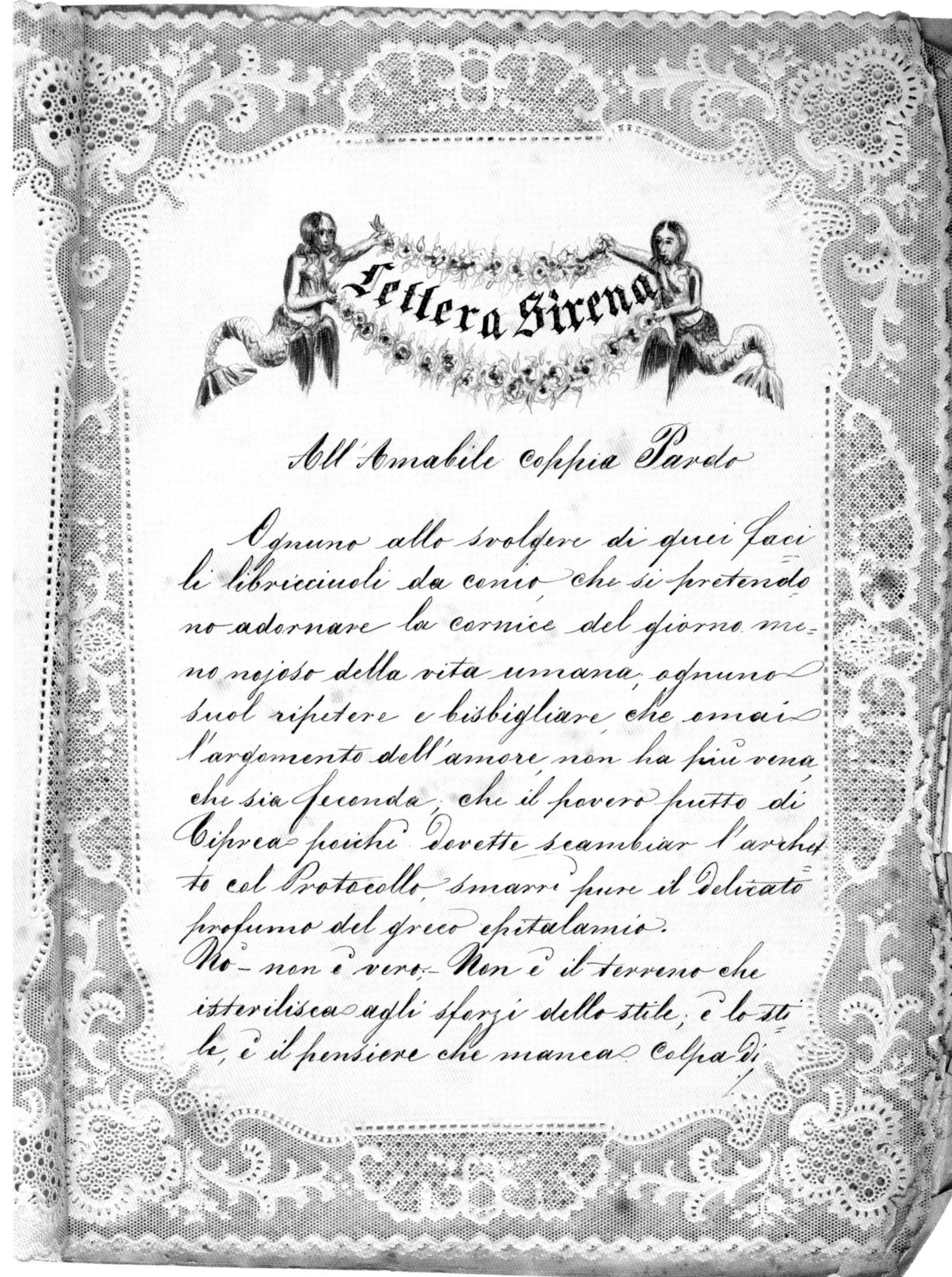

Lettera Sirena

All'Amabile coppia Pardo

Ognuno allo svolgere di quei facili libricciuoli da conio, che si pretendono adornare la cornice del giorno meno nojoso della vita umana, ognuno suol ripetere e bisbigliare, che omai l'argomento dell'amore non ha più vena che sia feconda, che il povero putto di Ciprea poichè dovette scambiar l'archetto col Protocollo, smarrì pure il Delicato profumo del greco epitalamio.
Nò – non è vero. – Non è il terreno che isterilisca agli sforzi dello stile; è lo stile, è il pensiere che manca. Colpa di

coda di pesce, avrò fatto come quei che va di notte =
„Che porta il lume dietro, e a se non giova„
o piuttosto come fanno i più nel mondo e avrò
insegnato senz'apprendere io stesso. – Se non che
io spero che un augurio verace che parte dal cuore
ch'io le offro or ora, come se le fossi dinnanzi e
le stringessi caramente la mano, quest'augurio
le varrà per una slombata perorazione. e se questo
povero bigliettino non avrà la gloria di essere paraninfo, sia almeno della sua gioja non ultima
partecipe e testimonio

Ces. Lombroso

Padova 15 Marzo 1855

Jews and Public Life in Liberal Italy

Gadi Luzzatto Voghera

In nineteenth-century Italy, a series of long-gestating elements came to fruition, forcing a Jewish community undergoing rapid, tumultuous transformation to engage with public life and to participate actively in politics. The myriad, wide-ranging experiences of Jews in Italy during this period saw both individuals and groups committing directly to the realization of a diverse range of political projects.

To better understand these changes, it is worth clarifying a number of dynamics triggered by a complicated, uneven process of legal emancipation that involved most of Central and Western European Jews, associated with a process of generalized secularization that concerned the Jewish world in much the same way as it did the Christian world. Legal, social and women's emancipation also influenced significantly the blossoming of new movements of Jewish national re-birth, which at the end of the century materialized in the Zionist movement.

It is challenging to identify the forms of a politics that we could define as "Jewish" after emancipation. With the gradual acquisition of an equivalence of rights and duties within bourgeois societies, the identification of the Jews as a separate nation fell away, and every autonomous form of Jewish politics – if there had ever been such a thing – began to wither. The very birth of the Zionist movement, and its development leading up to the creation of the state of Israel in 1948, was at best only partially the fruit of independent Jewish political thought. Scholars agree that Zionism was a late manifestation of European nationalism; one that shared forms and modalities with contemporary nationalist movements (Bensoussan 2007; Bidussa 1993).

But it should be stressed that the Jews who populated the political scene at the turn of the century never were, nor did they make any claim to be, representatives of Jewish politics, and it matters very little whether they declared themselves to belong proudly to the ancient religious tradition or whether they were assimilated Jews who were disinterested in their own traditional culture. Precisely because of the lack of hierarchies (including political hierarchies), but also because of the great fragmentation that was a feature of the Jewish turn-of-the-century experience, no Jew who operated in Italian politics demonstrated the tangible aspiration to do so "in the name of" or "as a representative of" their coreligionist. This point must be clear, as it should also be clear that any allegation to the contrary constituted one of the favorite weapons in the antisemitic political dialectic. The epigones of antisemitism were indeed those who posited that a number of Jewish politicians were representatives of a very loosely defined – and indeed, non-existent – "Jewish international," claimed to be behind subversive efforts to destabilize the established order. This is certainly an interesting idea, but it is essentially a metapolitical construct, only vaguely related to the question being addressed here, which concerns the actual, concrete forms in which a Jewish presence in public life developed in Italy.

While it is true that it is rather difficult to identify a form of Jewish politics in the modern era – intended as a theory of government founded on the religious and ethical principles of the biblical and Talmudic tradition – it is also evident that many Jews were deeply involved in the management of the country's social, economic and political life. To illustrate the reasons for this presence, often very visible especially if compared with the numerical weakness of Italian Jewry, it is important to take as our starting point the profound changes that affected this minority over the course of the nineteenth century and into the twentieth.

What had changed compared to previous times? The Italian Jewish experience at the time of emancipation benefited from a very particular set of circumstances with respect to other European situations: a linguistic and cultural integration acquired over centuries, a situation of legal marginalization that was, all in all, less aggressive than in other parts of the old continent, and a tangible predisposition towards integration into non-Jewish society. In this context it is important to underline two important new aspects that would determine to a great extent the transformations under consideration here. First and foremost, starting from the French Revolution, the Jews returned as active players, both individually and as a group, "in history." The famous statement made by Clermont-Tonnerre in 1789 is revealing: "We must refuse everything to the Jews as a nation and accord everything to Jews as individuals" (Clermont-Tonnerre 1789). As a consequence – and this is a second significant element – the Jewish resumed the task of writing their own history, inserting it into the wider context of global history (Myers, Ruderman 1998; Yerushalmi 2011). Moreover, the birth of a new Jewish historiography became a way to shape new forms of collective identity and a means to connect their history to that of the new bourgeois nation; a necessary step to pave the way for an active participation in public life.

But let's take a step back. Already in the first half of the nineteenth century we can identify a group of notable families that we could call, with a certain degree of approximation, the Jewish urban bourgeoisie. These families enthusiastically endorsed the Risorgimento, and at the same time they aspired to be allowed to participate in forms of sociability from which they were excluded for far too long. By contrast, a public image of Jews founded on layers of anti-Judaic prejudices, now reinforced by the emergence of a robust Catholic intransigentism, remained very present in Italian society. In this way a sort of split occurred: on the one side were young professionals from Jewish families who threw themselves with great gusto into various roles in Italian public life – local administrators, directors of chambers of commerce, army officers, journalists and Members of Parliament and Senators. Pitted against them were very large sectors of the Catholic and, at times, liberal leadership, who tried to put the brakes on this phenomenon because they did not understand it and were not ready to accept it.

One of the recurring themes in this regard was that of the necessary conversion of the Jews as a *sine qua non* for their acceptance into the public sphere. This was a significant theme, found also in other European contexts. In Germany, for example, for a long time the Jews were blocked from taking up posts as university lecturers or public administrators unless they first underwent a religious conversion – something that was often expressed in their formal embrace of Protestantism. The constant refrain of the need for conversion can be traced back to two main reasons. First, there was a re-emergence – even in those individuals who were more open and less bound to traditional prejudices – of a purely theological opposition, that led the Christian world to consider the Jewish religion as an error, a deviation from the providential plan, that would inevitably end with re-entry into the bosom of the Church. This position was consolidated by a generalized inability to consider the Jewish world as a universe in itself, which in its internal dynamic was separate from its Christian counterpart. The Jews were for the most part deemed to be a sect – a degeneration that was the fruit of social and moral aberrations arising from historical dynamics that could be corrected precisely through emancipation – rather than a separate group to be respected in its subjectivity and autonomy. The second motivation that lay at the base of the constant call for religious conversion was more deeply associated with the political events of 1848. The necessary unity of action in the political and military fight for the unification of the country and the expulsion of the foreigner from the homeland had led to the identification of Pius IX as the reference point for a wide range of political and ideological configurations (Veca 2018). Pius was considered – whether he liked it or not – to be a reforming pope and a model of the illuminated monarch. At the beginning of his pontificate, he issued a number of humanitarian measures to alleviate the suffering of the inhabitants of the Roman ghetto, which anticipated – according to the polemicists who intervened in the debate – the conversion of the Jews (if not immediate, at least in the foreseeable future). This position, after all, was a feature of all the emancipationist writings of the revolutionary period (Luzzatto Voghera 1998).

The involvement of numerous young Jews in the political and military dynamics of the Risorgimento served as the first step in a direct commitment that would become particularly important in the liberal era. Full emancipation entailed the possibility (often felt to be a duty) of first-hand participation, and indeed there were numerous Jews who saw the national political dimension, the Parliament, as the most appropriate environment in which to exercise the new rights they had acquired. The fundamental value of the Italian parliamentary system was highlighted in numerous speeches by Jewish members of Parliament and senators, and reflected a certain way of interpreting citizenship and its forms of representation. Parliament is a supreme value, regardless of the political orientation of individuals. An echo of this approach can be found in a 1948 speech by Umberto Terracini as he celebrated the revolutionary events of 1848: "It is our great privilege and fortune, as men and as citizens, to have in Rome a constituent assembly representative of the people, freely elected, in the centenary of the start of the fight for the independence and unity of Italy" (Terracini 1948). The association of Italy's "fight for independence" with the work of the "freely elected" constituent assembly signaled the desire to make a connection made between the experience of the Risorgimento and unification movement and the new Parliament, which was about to set in motion the sequence of events that would lead to the formation of the Italian Republic.

The need to establish a historical continuity between the various experiences of the parliamentary system in Italy had already engendered the interest of people who had been deeply involved in the country's institutional life at the time of Giolitti. In 1913, Luigi Luzzatti, the Venetian economist who had already served as the Minister of Finance and the first Jewish President of the Council of Ministers, proposed the study and publication (by the Accademia dei Lincei) of the proceedings of Italian constitutional assemblies from the Middle Ages up to 1831. And a few years before, in 1911, Camillo Montalcini, eminent jurist and, since 1907, first Secretary General of the Chamber of Deputies, had promoted the publication of fifteen volumes with the proceedings of the Assemblies of the Risorgimento, which included documents relating to the Parliaments of Rome, Naples, Venice, Tuscany and Sicily.

Terracini, Luzzatti, Montalcini (to which we could add the names of dozens of other Jewish exponents in Parliament or in other spheres of the public administration) had different political leanings and diverse backgrounds. They shared a commitment to the ideas of citizenship and participation, which they saw as a perpetuation of a long Italian tradition in which the *res publica* was managed by elected bodies, be they Parliaments *per se* or constitu-

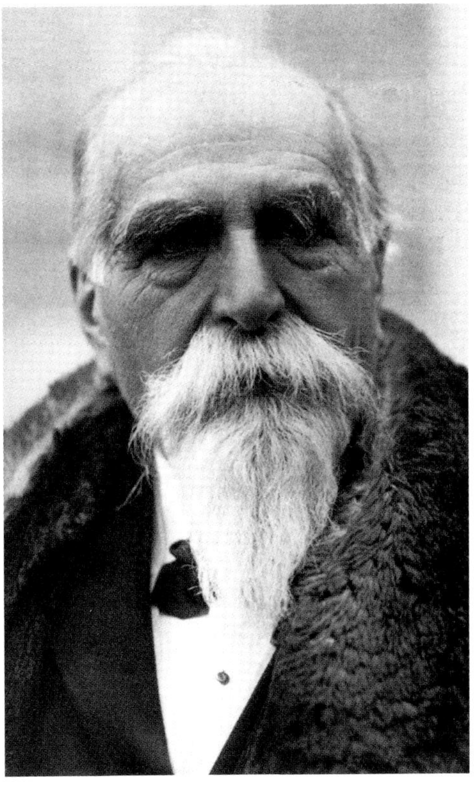

1. Luigi Luzzatti, circa 1920

ent assemblies. It was very much a *Risorgimento*-inspired concept, which entrusted to the citizens (in truth, during the liberal era, only to a certain category of citizens) the destiny of civil society through free debate and the exercise of the democratic vote, which would overcome the estate barriers typical of the *ancien régime*, worsened by the limitations imposed on different religious communities. The Risorgimento – initially with a certain reluctance and later with increasing conviction – had put an end to the civil and political marginalization of the Jews and had accepted them in the new, more inclusive forms of citizenship that many Italian Jews helped develop. But Terracini, Luzzatti, Montalcini and a large number of other people who shared the passion for representative democracy also had another element in common: they were Jews. Not "of Jewish origin," as all too often is written in publications that adopt this ambiguous and subtly equivocal phraseology. They were Jews (at the time, the term "Israelites" was more common), products of a shared family and community experience, and sometimes also active within that religious community.

A number of Jewish MPs and Senators – as in the case of the aforementioned Umberto Terracini and Luigi Luzzatti, but also Claudio Treves, Giuseppe Emanuele Modigliani and Isacco Artom – played a particularly important role in Italian history, and have as a result been the subject of specific, in-depth studies. In contrast, most of the Jewish members of Parliament (who were often high-profile figures) have failed to attract the academic interest they deserve. The reasons for this state of affairs are to be found not in the limited importance of the work done by the individual MPs and Senators, but in the focus that those studying the institutions have thus far had, which has been geared towards revealing any cultural differences in the approach to their institutional duties taken by deputies and senators. The construction of a relatively young nation like Italy required the participation on an equal footing of all of its components in its institutional life, without any of those components asserting their cultural or religious specificities. This type of approach, incidentally, was substantially shared by the Jewish parliamentarians themselves, who in their work and at public events generally avoided placing any emphasis on their Jewish culture or faith.

Despite the numerous books written on Jews in liberal Italy, a specific discussion of Jewish presence in the institutions has not been the main focus of these works. We do not have studies offering an assessment (even solely quantitative) of the extent of Jewish integration in the public administration, the public education system (schools, universities, etc.), in the elected organs of the local administrations and – specifically – of Parliament, an institution in which there was a significant number of Jews. This is not a qualitative judgment: belonging to one religious faith or another as a member of Parliament should not be a source of debate, especially in the case of the Jews who inhabited those Houses of Parliament in the liberal period, when secularization was considered by all (Jews included) as an inevitable destiny. However, the presence of two dozen Jews between the Chamber of Deputies and the Senate, e.g. in the eighteenth legislature 1892–1895, cannot escape the more attentive observer. Such a large number of representatives was completely out of proportion with respect to the Italian Jewish population. This is a historical fact, and as such it is of interest and should be taken into consideration. We must consider that Jews in the second half of the nineteenth century were a predominantly urban population, with a high level of literacy (well above the national average) and with a notable presence of dynamic entrepreneurs who wanted to take on political responsibilities directly. Yet their willingness to be involved in public life and in the ever-challenging parliamentary work still requires further explanation. Other religious groups that were marked out by not dissimilar characteristics – such as, for instance, the evangelical minority – had a far less visible presence in the same period. The historiographic question thus remains and is worth examining in detail.

It is, moreover, complicated to pigeonhole into a single category (that of the Jews), members of Parliament in the liberal period or even in the period before unification; their religious affiliation can, in fact, provide only generic numerical indications and cannot form the basis for interpretations of the institutional history of Italy. In this context, the question of a definition of the Jewish Members of Parliament and Senators becomes decisively important. It is clear that the religious categories (according to tradition, anyone with a Jewish mother is automatically a Jew) cannot be used in the definition; nor does the identification of a parliamentarian on the basis of a (more or less) Jewish surname or their official membership of a community offer much in the way of heuristic value. If we fail to recognize this, we risk making the mistake of associating Jewish politicians with an idea of "otherness," with an identity that is different from that of the majority of the national population. This way

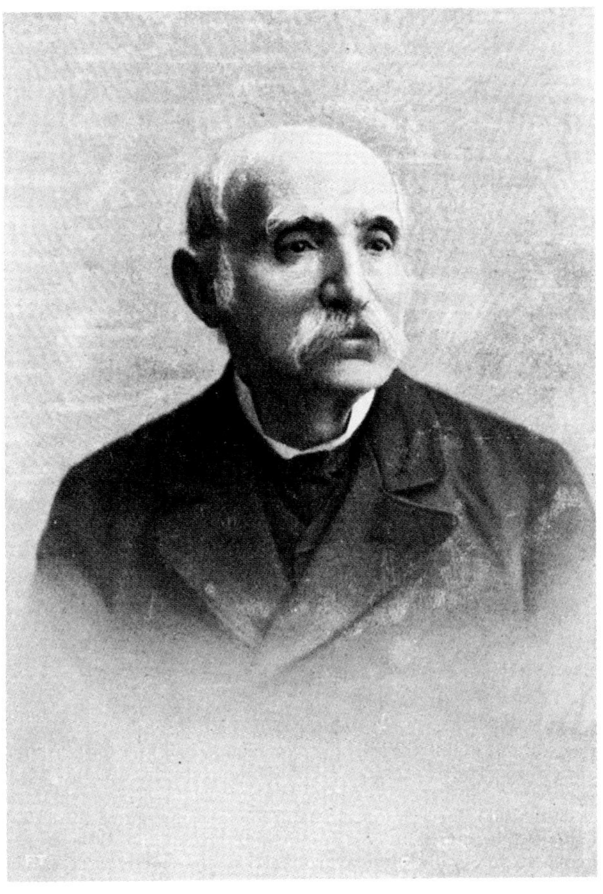

2. Isacco Artom

we would turn the Jews into a sort of ethnic group comparable to certain specific minorities represented – in the Republican Parliament– through the presence of MPs and Senators who directly encapsulated particular linguistic and cultural features, such as the members from the South Tyrol and the Aosta Valley. The Jewish presence in the Italian and European parliamentary institutions would never take on such characteristics, and we are not authorized to create a specific category in which to ghettoize in a relatively artificial manner those people whose personal and family histories, and cultural background, may be associated with the Jewish experience. There is no desire here to seek out a specific Jewish character in the conduct of these individuals. Equally, we are not making any attempt to trace out, artificially, any common course of action in the political and institutional work of individual Jewish MPs and Senators. Any such attempt, in addition to falsifying the historical facts to a considerable extent, would certainly be a betrayal of the intentions of the individual MPs and Senators who, in their institutional and political work, never operated as representatives of the Jewish component of the population. Italian Jews, for their part, never tried to appoint Jewish representatives so that they would promote specifically Jewish causes in Parliament. We must remember that no unified representation of the Italian Jewish communities came into being until much later, in the 1920s, with the establishment of the first Consortium of Israelite Communities, followed by the 1930 law that sanctioned the institution of the Union of Italian Israelite Communities, subsequently overhauled by a new agreement between the Italian state and the Union of Italian Jewish Communities, in 1984.

Having thus delineated the limits inherent to this type of categorization, it is now necessary to clarify in what ways and on the basis of what criteria such a high number of Jewish politicians and professionals became the embodiment on the public stage of that process of emancipation that marked out the journey taken by the Italian Jewish communities during the course of the nineteenth century.

On occasion, over the course of the history of this country, the characterization of a parliamentarian as "Jewish" assumed a value that went beyond the desire of individuals and ended up involving other, more distant categories of thought. Examples of this phenomenon include the MP Pasqualigo, who in the 1870s protested against the possible appointment of Isacco Pesaro Maurogonato to the post of Finance Minister because he was Jewish (Canepa 1975). Or there is the example provided by Flaminio Servi, who at the start of every legislature would use *Il Vessillo Israelitico*, of which he was editor-in-chief, to list with pride the names of the Jews who had succeeded in becoming MPs and Senators. Regardless, it is beyond doubt that on various occasions throughout Italian history, for a Jew, being voted in as a member of Parliament was not something that was completely divorced from their cultural and religious background.

To paint a general picture that would do justice, at least in summary form, to the level of involvement that Italian Jews had in the public sphere after the unification of the country, rather than focusing on the vicissitudes of individual parliamentarians it may be interesting to make reference to the exemplary figure of a woman, also with a view to giving a tangible indication of the genre-based distinctions being made at the time, which in this case had a crucial role to play. We are referring here to Amelia Pincherle Moravia (Venice, 1870 – Florence, 1954), who was a leading figure of both culture and politics, and very much embodied the process of emancipation of Italian Judaism. She gathered around her some of the most important Jewish personalities of Italian public life both in the liberal period and afterwards.

As a young girl from a bourgeois Venetian family, Amelia's imagination was struck by two swords of the National Guard of the Republic of 1848 hanging above the entrance to a house on the Grand Canal, along with a piece of black bread baked during the Austrian siege, and a tattered tricolor flag, all of which she considered admiringly to be "noble signs of our Italianness." To give some idea of the incredible interweaving of personalities who were closely linked to this woman by familial or intellectual connections, and who at the same time had crucial roles to play in the history of the Risorgimento and, subsequently, of united Italy, it is sufficient to map out some of her relatives. Her uncle, Leone Pincherle, was one of the founders of the Assicurazioni Generali insurance company and a driving force behind the Risorgimento uprisings as a minister in Daniele Manin's Venetian Republic. Then there was her husband Joe (Giuseppe Emanuele) Rosselli, who she had married in one of the *Cinque Scole* (five synagogues) of Rome in 1892; it was in the Rosselli family home in Pisa that Giuseppe Mazzini had died, an exile in his homeland, and that family had been one of the main supporters of the father of the Risorgimento both in Tuscany and during his exile in London. Her husband's uncle was Ernesto Nathan, mayor of Rome from 1907 to 1913 and a central figure in Italian politics during the Giolittian era. But as we pan out, even more highly significant people come into focus, including the writer Alberto Moravia (a member of the European Parliament in the 1980s), who was the son of Amelia's brother, Carlo Pincherle. And we also find Laura Capon – wife of the Nobel prize-winner Enrico Fermi – who was the daughter of Amelia's cousin, Augusto Capon.

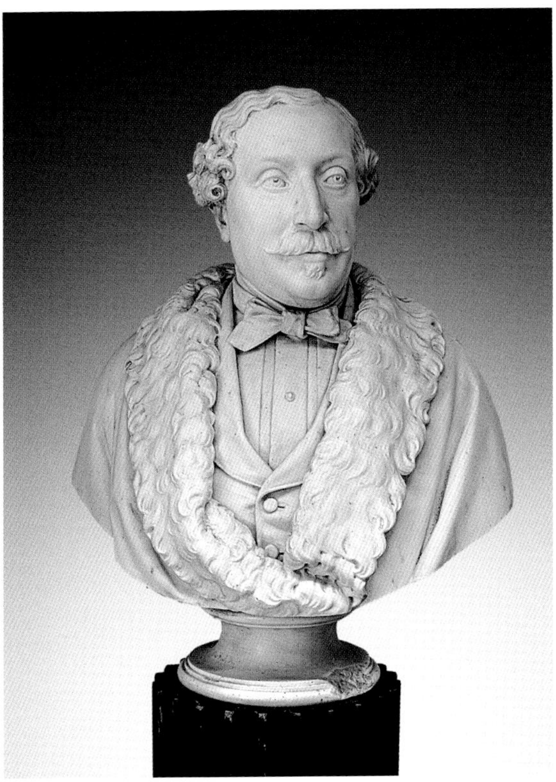

3. Portrait bust of Sansone d'Ancona. MEIS (National Museum of Italian Judaism and the Shoah), Ferrara (cat. 57)

However, the fact that she was related to eminent figures in the country's history is not in itself reason enough to include Amelia Pincherle Moravia Rosselli in the pantheon of the biographies that best illustrate the contribution of Judaism to the history of national unity. The fact is that Amelia was also in herself an esteemed figure, and was a fixture on the cultural, literary and political scenes of the first half of the twentieth century. First and foremost, Amelia was on the cutting edge of the new participation of women in the cultural life of the country – a path that had never been furrowed before but on which there was no going back. After living for ten years first in Rome, then in Vienna, then once again in the Italian capital, following her separation from her husband she moved to Florence, where her salon became the favourite haunt of a large circle filled with representatives of Italian high culture. There, you could run into artists, painters, writers and politicians, and find yourself sitting next to everyone from Eleonora Duse and Ada Negri to Benedetto Croce and Gaetano Salvemini. Ever since the time in which she had lived in Rome, she herself had been an established writer. Indeed, she had written the play entitled *Anima* [Soul], a courageous critique of the self-righteousness of *fin de siècle* society and of bourgeois taboos, for which she was showered with plaudits. And her profile remained high, thanks to essays and speeches concerned with literary criticism, while she also pressed ahead with the writing of new plays, with the job of directing the "*Biblioteca delle Giovani Italiane*" (Young Italian Women's Library) for the publisher Le Monnier, and with her ongoing collaboration with the *Marzocco*, the magazine edited by Angiolo Orvieto, which at the time provided the frame of reference for the Jewish intelligentsia of Florence, as well as for others. She was then, above all, a woman, and an intellectual who toiled to promote the education and liberation of women in the backward Italy of the early twentieth century. And then she was, of course, the mother of Aldo (who died as an officer in the Royal Italian Army in Carnia in 1916), and later of Carlo and Nello Rosselli, two of the leading names in Italian anti-fascism, founders of the "Giustizia e Libertà" (Justice and Freedom) movement and fighters in the Spanish Civil War, who were murdered by order of Mussolini at Bagnoles-de-l'Orne in 1937.

Her Jewishness, as she made clear in her *Memorie* (Rosselli 2001), was of the sort typical of an assimilated bourgeois family, associated with but a few, ever more rarefied family objects and gestures. Her fate was shared with numerous important figures in the history of twentieth-century Italy, from Claudio Treves and Giuseppe Emanuele Modigliani to Vittorio Foa, amongst many thousands of others; Amelia did not deviate from this path. But what is often recalled about her, and not by chance, is the echo of the traditional teachings that she passed on to her children, as summed up by the famous phrase that Carlo Rosselli employed to stress the importance of the war against fascism in Spain, "Today in Spain, tomorrow in Italy", referencing the ancient story of the *Haggadah* of Pesach.

Amelia Rosselli, and the world of personalities that revolved around her in the late nineteenth and early twentieth centuries, seem to epitomize the characteristics of that public role that the Jews wanted to take on – a role that was one of the products of the process of emancipation that would be thrown into crisis by the antisemitic persecutions of the fascist regime, endorsed by an inglorious monarchy and set against a climate of widespread indifference.

4. Giacomo Balla, *Portrait of Ernesto Nathan*, detail. Gallery of Modern Art, Rome (cat. 81)

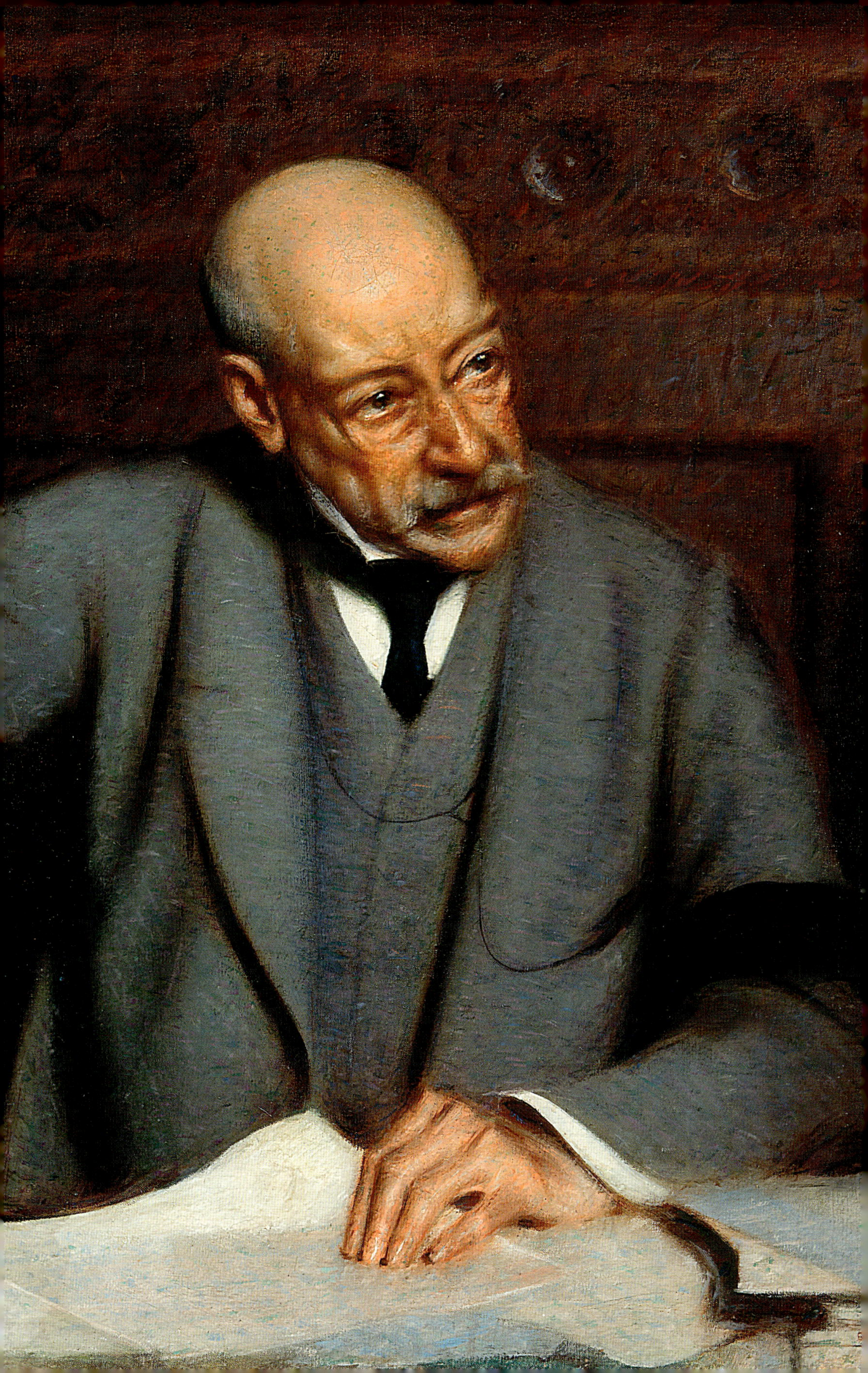

Mirror Effects. Jews and Literature

Alberto Cavaglion

The representation of Jews in Italian literature appears veiled, blurred, often characterized by ambiguity and based on a limited knowledge of the Jewish world. Among the causes of this phenomenon, the numerical exiguity of Italian Jewry.

We can observe the game of mirrors between majority and minority from a double perspective. On the one hand, we have non-Jewish authors describing Jewish characters; on the other, we have Jewish authors and the level and quality of Jewish culture they were able to inject into their narrations. Examples of the first instance, far easier to define, can be found in two radically different works which happen to be two masterpieces of the Italian novella genre: the story of "Abraham the Jew" in Giovanni Boccaccio's *Decameron* (I, 2) and "Goy" (1922), one of Pirandello's *Novelle per un anno* (Pirandello 1994) – two masterworks interestingly both holding an element of ambivalence since they both tell a story of conversion.

The weak presence of Jewish characters in literature certainly derives from a limited knowledge of Judaism, confirmed by the often stereotyped if not caricatural representations of the Jew: this approach reached its peak during the nineteenth century with the myth of the "*la belle juive*," the beautiful Jewess that we find well represented in works of popular literature, such as Rebecca in Walter Scott's *Ivanhoe* (1819) or, in Italy, reworked almost into a caricature in Carolina Invernizio's *Orfana del ghetto* (1887). With regard to the second perspective, although integrating a higher level of complexity, it mostly delivers blurred and inexact representations. How much of Jewish culture were Jewish authors and poets able to infuse into their work?

Jewish literary production such as that found in the Jewish press and deriving from the Jewish communities' cultural activities can be considered of mere testimonial value, documents testifying and promoting traditional values, often against the challenges of modernity. But there were exceptions: one of them is *I Moncalvo* (Castelnuovo 1908), a novel about a Jewish family in Rome. The most emblematic case, however, is represented by Alberto Cantoni's production (1841–1904): in his works, the connection to Judaism is indeed intense, although relegated to a private dimension and never included in his most famous works from which Pirandello drew inspiration for his theory on humor. A further exception is his short story *Israele Italiano*, written in 1903 but published posthumously (Cantoni 2005), containing partial, feeble, and veiled insights into Jewish culture.

In terms of interpretation, this problem was defined very clearly by Giacomo Debenedetti in a famous and today classic essay on Italo Svevo, or more precisely, on the relation between his Zeno-character and his Ettore-Aron-Schmitz-identity. Debenedetti argues that the feeble connection between the Jewish author and his Jewish identity is manifested in his reluctance to attribute such identity to his clearly autobiographical characters (Debenedetti 1971). This aspect is not only relevant to Svevo of course, but to several other protagonists of a literary tradition where Judaism is either absent or transfigured, hence becoming contiguous to caricatural and even anti-Semite representations as in the case of popular literature, or represented as an integral part not of a character's life, but rather of a cemeterial, death-ridden universe. An example of this is the depiction of the Venice Lido Jewish cemetery in Giovanni Prati's lyric epic poem *Edmenegarda* (1841).

In nineteenth- to twentieth-century Italian literature Judaism must be searched for where one would less expect to find it, requiring very laborious textual analyses. Borrowing one of Svevo's effective expressions, we might say that for Jewish and non-Jewish Italian writers, Judaism is a "forbidden love" (De Angelis 2007).

Italian Jews and the Great War

Mario Toscano

On the eve of the outbreak of war in Europe, in the summer of 1914, the Jews in Italy constituted a small minority (Della Pergola 1997), composed for the most part of members of the bourgeoisie and the middle class, albeit with a significant working-class element. The process of integration in the wake of the *Risorgimento* (the movement for the unification and independence of Italy) had taken on the character of an accelerated nationalization. The Jews felt part of the nation, participants in the construction of the State (D.V. Segre 1998), and thankful to the House of Savoy, which had given them equality and freedom. In the liberal era, what had been the totalizing reality of Judaism had gradually been reduced to a mere religious dimension that, in many cases, seemed to offer a less than solid foundation for an identity perceived as fragile in the face of the challenges of secularization and the allure of participation in the political, cultural, economic and social life of the country (Ferrara degli Uberti 2012; Momigliano 1987; Toscano 2003, 2019). The spread of Zionism – viewed initially as a philanthropic movement – encouraged in the early twentieth century a cultural reawakening and triggered a process of rejuvenation and modernization of Jewish identity, but one that involved only a restricted elite of young intellectuals, whose positions gave rise to fierce disputes over the various ways in which the role of Judaism could be interpreted (Toscano 2003).

The war brought with it new reasons for discussion. While individual Jews could participate as citizens in the debates on neutrality and intervention that were tearing the country apart, the rabbis and the Jewish press analyzed the impact of the war on Italian Jewry (Ferrara degli Uberti 2012; Toscano 2016). The two main Jewish periodicals of the time gave voice to this question, each proposing answers aligned with its own perspective: *Il Vessillo Israelitico* supported the primacy of Italianness over a form of Jewishness reduced to a merely religious phenomenon, whereas *La Settimana Israelitica* served as the mouthpiece for an integrated Jewishness and for Zionist ideals. The two journals were in agreement on certain matters: first and foremost, all Jews should fulfill their duties as citizens of their own country, even if the nation issuing the call to arms was hostile and bent on persecution, such as Tsarist Russia; moreover, the periodicals reaffirmed the value of peace as expressed in the Jewish faith and in its traditions; and they augured that the war should lead to the end of antisemitism, which was destroying the lives of many Jewish communities across Europe. But whereas *Il Vessillo* gave priority to the marriage of patriotism and religiousness, *La Settimana* looked to the future and saw in the conflict – deemed to be a specific Jewish tragedy within the general tragedy afflicting humanity as a whole – the opportunity for a reassertion of the right of the Jews to have once again their own nation in the land of their forefathers.

In the months leading up to Italy's entry into the Great War, even the sermons given by the rabbis dealt with the evolution of the Italian Jews' attitudes towards the conflict. In the *Rosh HaShana* and *Yom Kippur* speeches of 1914, prayers for peace predominated, although they also included remarks that mirrored the attitudes taken by the press, denouncing the war as a manifestation of the failure of modern civilization, the idea of progress and dominant religions, and even singling out emancipated Judaism, which was said to have failed to enable humanity "to conquer the ideals manifested by our prophets" (*Il Vessillo Israelitico*, 30 September 1914, p. 521). In Modena, rabbi Cammeo recited every Saturday a prayer he had composed himself, in which he implored that Italy must retain its neutrality (Toscano 2016; *Il Vessillo Israelitico*, 15 September 1914, p. 490). The rabbi of Livorno, Samuele Colombo, in a prayer of his own devising, requested that God "may eliminate war from the world, or that at least he may remove it from the lands and seas of Italy, or that were it to be decreed that also the sons of this land must be deployed in battle, that it be for justice and not for its opposite" (*Il Vessillo Israelitico*, 30 September 1914, p. 518). On the day of *Yom Kippur*, the rabbi of Bologna Alberto Orvieto summarised the plethora of themes that had arisen, recalling that the Jews had been the first to affirm the law of brotherhood, "law of love," and stressing that

> Our deep, devout religious sentiment does not diminish our Italianness; on the contrary, it strengthens and enlivens it with spiritual light […]. We should bear in mind that Italy is our homeland, because we have played our part in its redemption and in its unification, because we have contributed to its greatness […]. While we pray for peace, we shall not be derelict in our duty of brotherhood if we also pray for this Italy that is ours, if we pray for her victory and her greatness, for her constant triumph in the world, in the name of progress and justice. With this prayer, we are not only doing our duty, but also asserting a right, with this prayer we are responding to the most fervent appeal of our heart (*Il Vessillo Israelitico*, 15 October 1914, pp. 539–542).

Over the course of a few months, the developments in the political landscape resulted in significant changes. The speeches given at Pesach (Passover) in 1915 seemed to be riven with anxiety over the horrors and atrocities of the war. The patriotic, *Risorgimento*-inspired tones were reaching a crescendo, forewarning of Italy's imminent entry into the conflict but not canceling out the call to faith and to the practice of the Jewish values, which could offer comfort and guidance. The speeches also lamented the suffering of the Tsar's Jewish subjects and expressed the hope that the hostilities should come to an end as soon as possible. With Italy's entry into the war, Jews "behaved exactly like the other Italians" (Milano 1963), but behind this uniformity it is possible to map out the variety and richness of the experiences and stories of individuals, the interweaving and synthesis of which illustrate the complexity of this sequence of events. For *La Settimana Israelitica* it was *The Moment of Truth*, in which to do one's duty as a citizen, in an awareness of the moral and historical values of one's own Jewishness (*La Settimana Israelitica*, May 28, 1915). For *Il Vessillo Israelitico* it was the moment to give everything "to our fatherland" without asking for anything in return, for the liberation of the unredeemed territories, and for the spread of the "Italic civilization" and its principles of liberty and fraternity, so that the Savoy dynasty "may be crowned with a new wreath of glory" (Toscano 2003: *Il Vessillo Israelitico*, May 31, 1915, p. 261). The Piedmontese journal set itself up as the conduit for feelings that were common amongst the majority of Italian Jews, for whom the war represented the moment of consecration of their process of national integration, to be sealed with blood, as would be illustrated by events, documents and testimonies over the coming days and months.

Over and above the proclamations and rhetoric of the time, Italy's entry into the war gave rise to concrete manifestations of patriotism that animated the Italian Jews and was expressed through individual choices and destinies, whose stories paint a picture with a significance that extends beyond the specific experiences of the conflict, becoming emblematic of the history of the Jews in Italy in the first half of the twentieth century. The small Jewish minority gave a large number of volunteers. While they may have differed in age, profession and condition, they were all united by their genuine sense of belonging to Italy. Amongst the first to head off to war was Giulio Blum, in his late fifties, a private who was promoted to lieutenant for his war service, and who fell in August 1917 on the northern slopes of Mount Hermada; he was the oldest Italian to receive a gold medal, having previously been awarded a silver medal (Briganti 2009; Orsucci Granata 2017). Emanuele Ascarelli, in a letter to a local newspaper, explained how he considered it "my precise duty to enroll as a volunteer for this final battle of Italian independence", into which was also channeled the "desire to pay back, with personal sacrifice, the debt of gratitude that, even as an Israelite, I feel toward my fatherland, the great beacon of freedom beyond any other nation" (*Il Vessillo Israelitico*, July 15, 1915, p. 362). Even Aldo Rosselli, Carlo and Nello's older brother, who came from an interventionist background nourished by the values of the *Risorgimento*, chose to depart for the front (*Epistolario* 1979; Orsucci Granata 2017; Rosselli 2001). The future ambassador Paolo Vita Finzi, at the tender age of seventeen, had been seduced by the idea of enlisting as a volunteer, out of "a good dose of vanity, the thought of being one of the youngest Italian soldiers, and the desire to appear one day [...] dressed in my gray-green finery, before my classmates, including the girls! [...] And out of the idea [...] that [...] you had [...] to grasp, without thinking twice, the extraordinary opportunity to participate in the greatest of conflicts, from which a new world would emerge" (Vita Finzi 1989). There were more than a few Julian irredentists who elected to fight on the Italian side, paying a high personal price (Briganti 2009; Capuzzo 1999; Rigano 2017): in March 1915, Trieste-born Guido Brunner, who had been conscripted into the Austrian army, managed to flee and reached Rome, only to fall in battle on the plateau of Asiago (Catalan 2000; Orsucci Granata 2017).

1. Portrait of Camillo, Eugenio, and Vittorio Artom with Angelo Sullam. Archivio CDEC

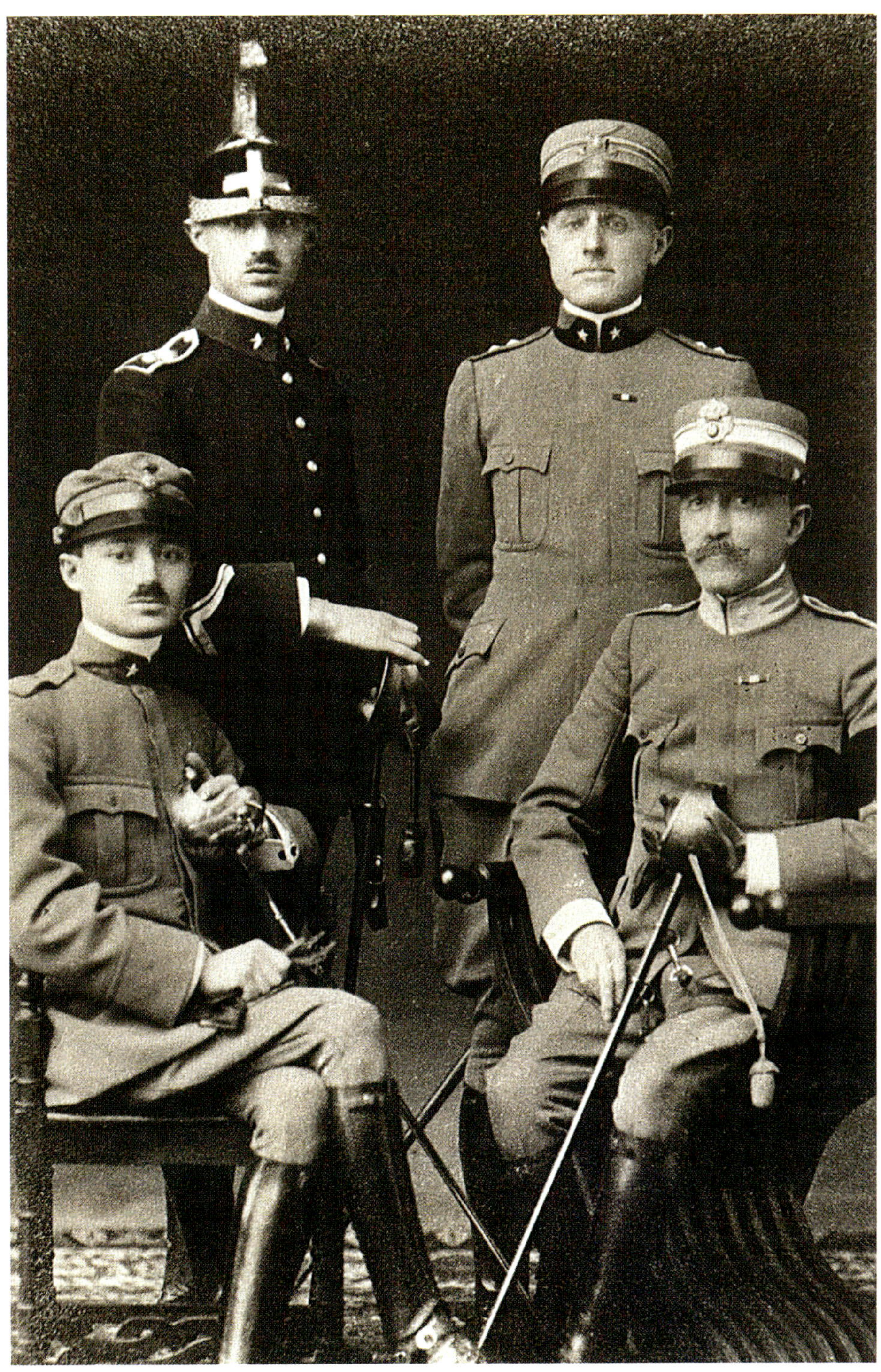

Jews were not the only ones coming from territories outside the Italian border – also answering the call of the fatherland were some who came from "beyond the frontier and over the sea," from Alexandria, Cairo, Thessaloniki, Tunis, Istanbul and Adrianople (Edirne, Turkey). In the description offered by *Il Vessillo Israelitico*, they were for the most part paupers, who spoke poor Italian, "who came of their own volition under the flags of the fatherland," and who were little-known and very underappreciated, but proud of being Italian and aware of their Jewishness. The need to leverage all of the available resources to meet the requirements of total war also extended to women, "a mobilization through which women, Jewish and non-Jewish alike, regardless of their position vis-à-vis female emancipation, shared the experience of work as an opportunity for a new life" (Miniati 2008, 2017). Jewish women operated as Red Cross nurses in the military hospitals in the cities and at the front; those active in the non-Jewish female associations continued their work, while others lent their weight to the new organizations that arose to deal with the impact of the war on the civilian populace. The fields into which they channeled their efforts included assistance to the children of those who had received the call up, whose wives were out at work (in Turin, these children were looked after by Elisa Levi Rignano and other Jewish women, in Bologna by Elena Sanguinetti Ghiron, and in Florence by Bice Cammeo, who had for some time been working with the National Female Union, founded in 1899 by Ersilia Majno Bronzini to support women's emancipation). Other initiatives were launched in Ferrara and Pitigliano, while various forms of collaboration got under way to aid crippled war veterans.

The most significant experiences of Italian Judaism in the years of the Great War certainly included that of the military rabbinate, set up in June 1915 on the initiative of the chair of the Committee of Italian Israelite communities, Angelo Sereni, and the Chief Rabbi of Rome, Angelo Sacerdoti (Toscano 2005). The vicissitudes of the rabbinate are emblematic of the complex, varied Italian Jewish reality during the years of the conflict. Its establishment was intended to overcome not only certain forms of resistance and bureaucratic obstacles but also the diffidence of communities that were often understaffed and lacking in adequate organizational infrastructures. Another issue presented itself in the form of the different reactions of certain rabbis consulted on the matter: there were those who were enthusiastic about the prospect of making "common cause with the brothers of Italy," but others were perplexed in the face of the difficulties that a small number of rabbis would experience trying to take care of Jewish soldiers that, although in small numbers, were scattered throughout the entire army. The military rabbis made their debut while the Jewish press was debating their purpose (were they to serve as chaplains or teachers of the unity of Israel?) and the sudden launch of their mission left open a multitude of problems, from the choice of a uniform that would facilitate their recognition, to their acceptance by the military command, to the problem of respect for the dietary rules on their part and on the part of those soldiers who may submit requests in this regard. On more than one occasion, rabbi Angelo Sacerdoti lamented the consequences of the diet that he was forced to adopt given the lack of kosher food: "Almost every day I eat a soup of cheese and butter, fried eggs and a piece of cheese," he wrote on August 11, 1915, in a letter to Angelo Sereni. He made the same point a week later, adding on that occasion some significant notes on his activities, in which even his description of the landscape revealed the extent of his attachment to Italy:

> I asked to have the car on Thursday to go and find the tomb of Sergeant Verona who died on Mount Nero and of Second Lieutenants Treves and Colombo who died at Plava […] On Thurs-

day morning at 6 the car was outside my house waiting for me. [...] We travelled for 13 hours. First I went to Caporetto. From there I climbed for a while up Mount Nero. You should have seen what a vision it was, *Commendatore* – I felt so much lighter while sweating and struggling to clamber up the mountainside. And it was tremendously satisfying to speak to the tireless Alpine troopers who just wanted to get back to fighting. I came across a fellow Jew, a volunteer, Cantoni from Venice, who was put forward for the valour medal, and I walked with him some of the way.

We returned to Udine to eat, and then we travelled again towards Plava. But I could not get there because after just a few miles we were stopped and ordered to retreat, as the road had been bombed. A grenade exploded not far from me at all.

I stayed for some time to see the phases of the bombing raid, and to contemplate the panorama, and then we turned back. I could see all of the famous Karst Plateau and the mountains to the north of Gorizia, Mount Santo, Sabotino, Podgora, etc. I could even make out the Julian Alps in the distance. I could savour another breathtaking panorama on the way to San Daniele. I could see the Dolomites, which are really marvellous. I began, as you can see, to become as enthusiastic as you are about mountains, and when I got closer to the combat site I was overtaken by a desire to pound my fists, which is not very becoming for a rabbi [...].

I already told you that I saw His Majesty's aide-de-camp, Admiral Capomazza. Yesterday I was at the Café, and as he passed by my table he saw me and turned back to say hello. You cannot imagine the faces of those present, and especially of the many officers, on seeing an admiral, aide-de-camp etc. giving the time of day to a humble captain, and none other than the priest of the Jews at that!

Even finding the Jewish soldiers was no easy task. There were no accurate, up-to-date records, and many Jews ignored the existence of military rabbis, whereas others preferred not to reveal their religious identity, out of fear, weakness, detachment, or perhaps to avoid, especially in the hospitals, any pressure to convert to Christianity. Attempts made in 1915 to celebrate *Rosh HaShana* and *Yom Kippur* with soldiers serving at the front were in great part a failure, due both to inexperience and to organizational difficulties. The drawn-out nature of the war and the associated suffering did, however, render all the more important the efforts made to support and socialize Jewish soldiers on the part of the military rabbis, whose endeavors achieved significant results in terms of the celebrations organized over the subsequent years of the war. Between the 5th and the 7th of October, 1916, hundreds of soldiers came together to celebrate *Yom Kippur* in Padua, which many attended "with their clothes still covered in mud". A great many made their way to Verona, where a very moving atmosphere was generated when the military rabbi "at *nenhilà*, gathered them around himself to give them the *berahà*. At that moment, we saw what was an almost magnetic phenomenon, as even those scattered throughout the temple, even the officers, made their way under the *talèd* of rabbi Lattes, with everyone bowing in the direction of his arms, almost out of fear of being excluded and kept apart from their brothers." More than 700 soldiers, several of whom came from the trenches on the front line, went to Padua in 1917 for *Yom Kippur*. To them, the military rabbi Rodolfo Levi gave a speech that spurred on the fight for the affirmation of Italy's rights, citing the values of human fraternity advocated by Judaism, and exhorted them to support the Jewish national cause. This topic was addressed again the following year, in the wake of the Balfour Declaration and of Italy's agreement in May 1918, at the religious celebrations in Verona, where after the ceremony the Italian

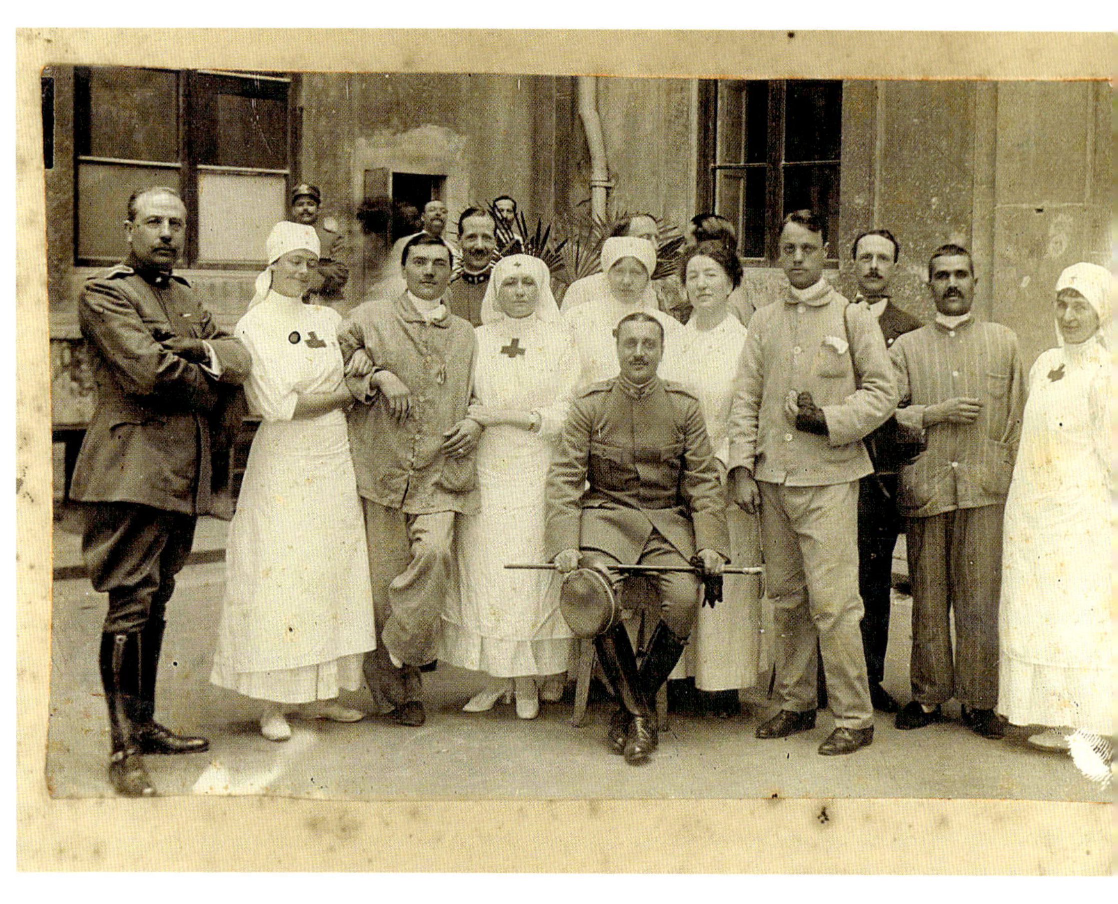

2. Group photo with the Red Cross nurse Matilde Viterbo. MEIS (National Museum of Italian Judaism and the Shoah), Ferrara

and Zionist anthems were sung, and in Ferrara, "where Garibaldi's anthem was heard interwoven with the *atticvà*."[1]

The experience of the military rabbinate, which arose with difficulty in a climate of polemics and uncertainty, came to an end after almost four years of bereavement, pain and hardship, with the consecration of the Jews' Italian nationalization, but also with the reassertion of identity and religious values that had underpinned the establishment of the rabbinate in the first place and that had then drawn sustenance from the assistance provided by rabbis to Jewish Austro-Hungarian prisoners, who were strongly bound to their own traditions and to their faith in Zionism. On the other hand, during the war Italian Jews committed to helping their oppressed Eastern European brothers (Toscano 2017). The press and a number of representatives attempted to raise the public's awareness of these issues, for humanitarian purposes, subsequently inserting them into the debate on the rights of minorities and of peoples fighting for national self-determination, achieving significant results with the creation of *Pro Israele*, a non-Jewish association (1916), and gaining a political boost through the Balfour declaration. These principles were supported by various leading figures of the worlds of culture and politics, especially those with democratic leanings, as illustrated by the speech made by Senator Francesco Ruffini at the conference held in Rome on December 8, 1918 (Toscano 2017). This was another important upshot of this small minority's war experience in the State that arose out of the *Risorgimento*.

The post-war advent of mass politics brought with it changes that resulted in the overturning of existing structures and values, and would go on to disrupt the lives of many of those who fought in the name of Italy and succeeded in escaping death on the battlefields. This is demonstrated by the many exemplary stories of a whole host of different people. Those of the armed forces officers, who were expelled in the name of racial laws (Toscano 2019), such as Ettore Ascoli (who fell in the Resistance), Armando Bachi (deported to Auschwitz) and Adolfo Olivetti (who died in prison before he could be deported) (Rovighi 1999). Those of the people who were forced by the persecutions to emigrate to more hospitable countries, such as Alessandro and Benvenuto Terracini. Those of the people who were deported to the concentration camps, such as Silvio Magrini and the military rabbi Rodolfo Levi. Those of the people who were instrumental in the reconstruction of Italian Jewry after the Second World War, such as Raffaele Cantoni (Minerbi 1992). Those of the people who chose to emigrate to Mandatory Palestine, such as Enrico Salomone Franco, who spent the rest of his life there. And those of the people who, having remained in Italy, chose the Resistance, such as Ferruccio Valobra, Emilio Sacerdote and Mario Jacchia (Orsucci Granata 2017), which was supposed to give rise to a new Italy and a new democratic pact amongst all of its – different but equal – citizens. These are all stories of Italian Jews who fought in the Great War.

[1] For the transliteration of Hebrew terms, the text adopts the rules that were commonly used in Italy at the time: "*nenhilà*" (*Nehilah*) is the fifth and final prayer service of *Yom Kippur*; the "*talèd*" (*tallit*) is a prayer shawl; the "*berahà*" (*berachah*) a blessng; the "*atticvà*" (*haTikvah*, The Hope) is the Zionist anthem [editor's note].

Museum and Exhibition Design

Studio GTRF - Giovanni Tortelli Roberto Frassoni Architetti Associati

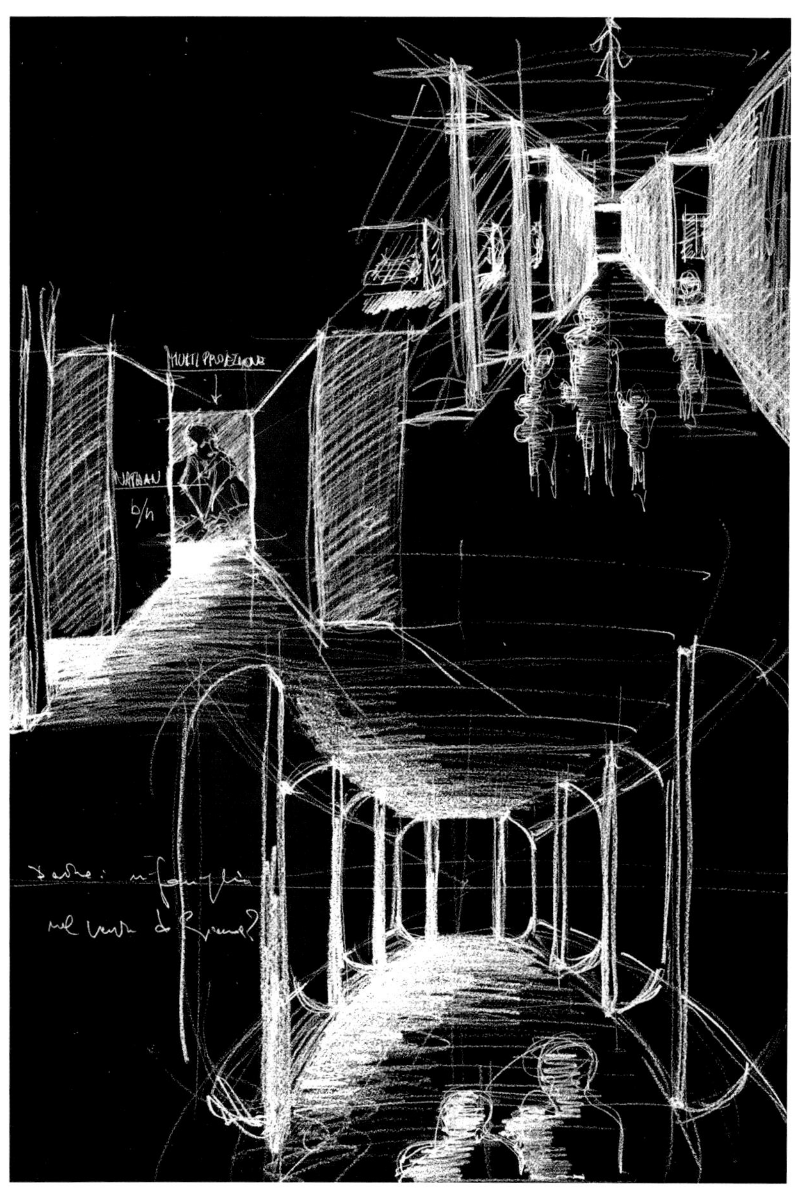

Museum and exhibition design,
Preparatory sketches
(GTRF - Giovanni Tortelli Roberto Frassoni Architetti Associati)

Museum and exhibition design,
Museum map
(GTRF - Giovanni Tortelli Roberto Frassoni Architetti Associati)

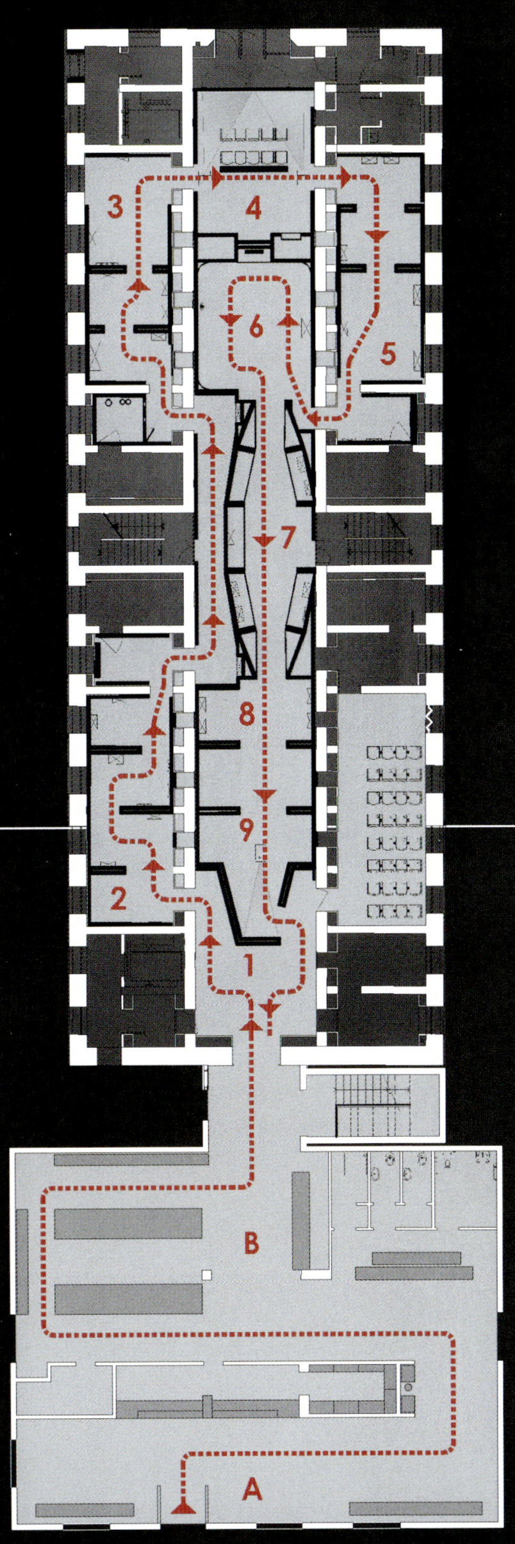

- A Biglietteria
- B Book Shop
- 1 Ingresso
- 2 I ghetti
- 3 Oltre il ghetto
- 4 Antigiudaismo
- 5 Emancipazione
- 6 Fuori, in società
- 7 Dentro: famiglia
- 8 Sionismo
- 9 Tutti Italiani

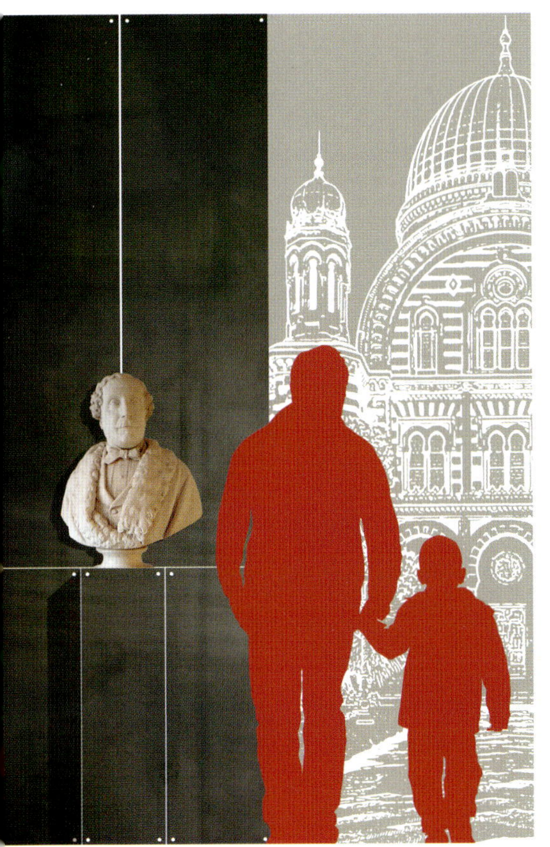

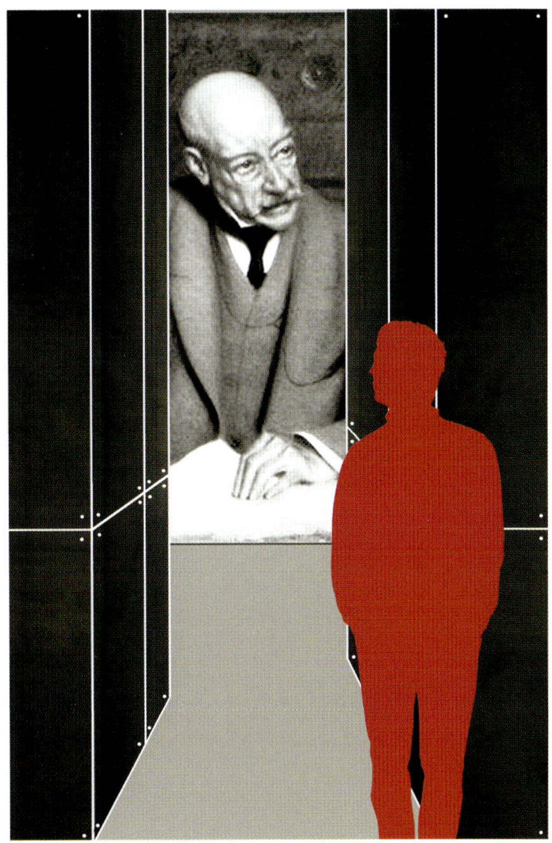

Museum and exhibition design,
Rendering of the back of the synagogue
(GTRF - Giovanni Tortelli Roberto Frassoni
Architetti Associati)

Museum and exhibition design,
The Synagogue of Florence
(GTRF - Giovanni Tortelli Roberto Frassoni
Architetti Associati)

Museum and exhibition design,
Finale: multi-projection
(GTRF - Giovanni Tortelli Roberto Frassoni
Architetti Associati)

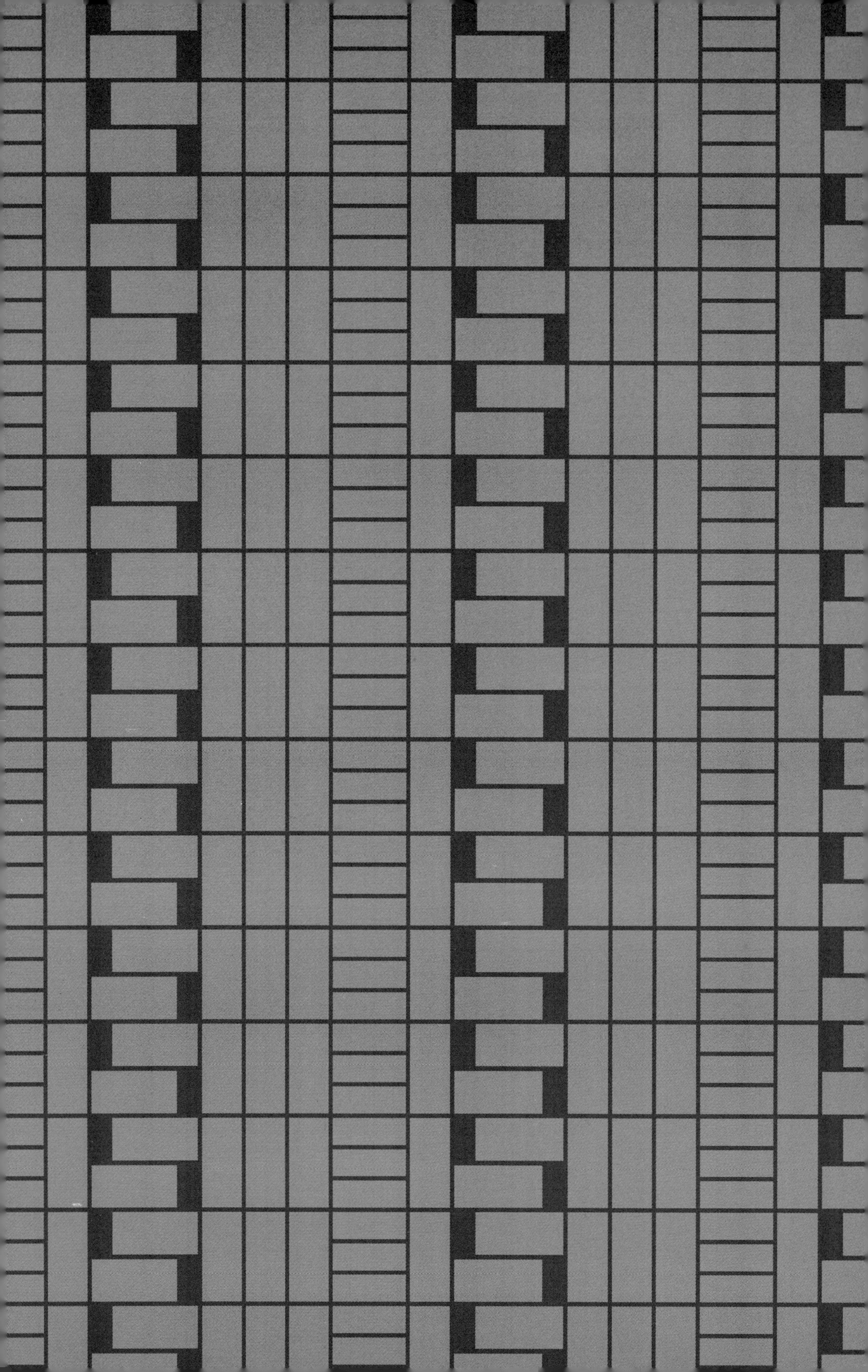

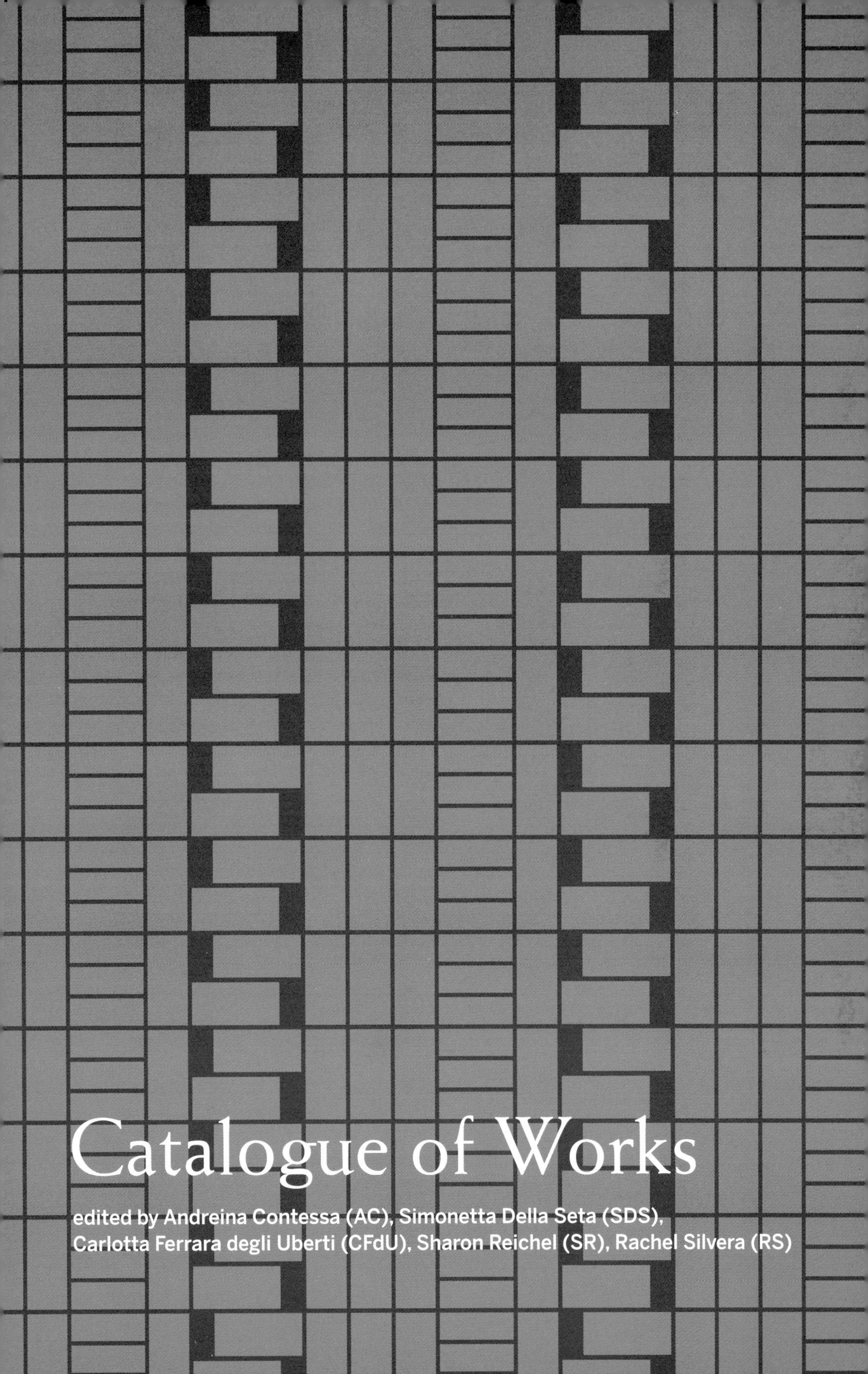

Catalogue of Works

edited by Andreina Contessa (AC), Simonetta Della Seta (SDS), Carlotta Ferrara degli Uberti (CFdU), Sharon Reichel (SR), Rachel Silvera (RS)

1. Sebastiano Ricci, *Esther before Ahasuerus*

Turin (?), 1733
Oil on canvas
211 × 168 cm
Previously Palazzo Reale, Turin
Palazzo del Quirinale, Rome
Inv. PR 17477

Venetian artist Sebastiano Ricci's (Belluno, 1659 – Venice, 1734) monumental canvas depicts Queen Esther as she pleads Ahasuerus to spare her people. In compositional terms, the painting – for which the version at the National Gallery in London is probably a sketch – is elegant and harmonious, with a monochrome, balustraded arcade serving as backdrop to the encounter between Ahasuerus, who is seated on a raised throne, and Esther, who faints in his presence, needing the help of two maids to stay on her feet. The biblical heroine is very much aware that whoever appears before the king uninvited risks execution, but the haughty sovereign rises from his throne and touches her with his golden scepter, granting her permission to speak. The eyes and movements of all the figures seem to converge on Esther, with the exception of the seated man to the king's right. This late work, carried out only one year before Ricci's death, sees one of the key figures of the early eighteenth-century revival in Venetian art – the echoes of which are clearly present in this painting – at the height of his powers.
We know that, following his education in Venice, Ricci moved to the Emilia region in 1680, first to Bologna and then to Parma where he remained – in the service of Ranuccio Farnese – enriching his art through the experience of the great Emilian painting of the seventeenth century. In due course, he was dispatched to Rome, where he was able to expand his artistic horizons even further. His later travels included Vienna, where he painted frescoes in the Schönbrunn Palace, Florence (1706–1707), Venice again, and England (1712–1716). This pan-European perspective and his comprehensive education in visual art are strikingly evident towards the end of his career, when, at the height of his fame, he produced numerous works for the Royal Palace in Turin, from where this majestic canvas has probably come down to us.

AC

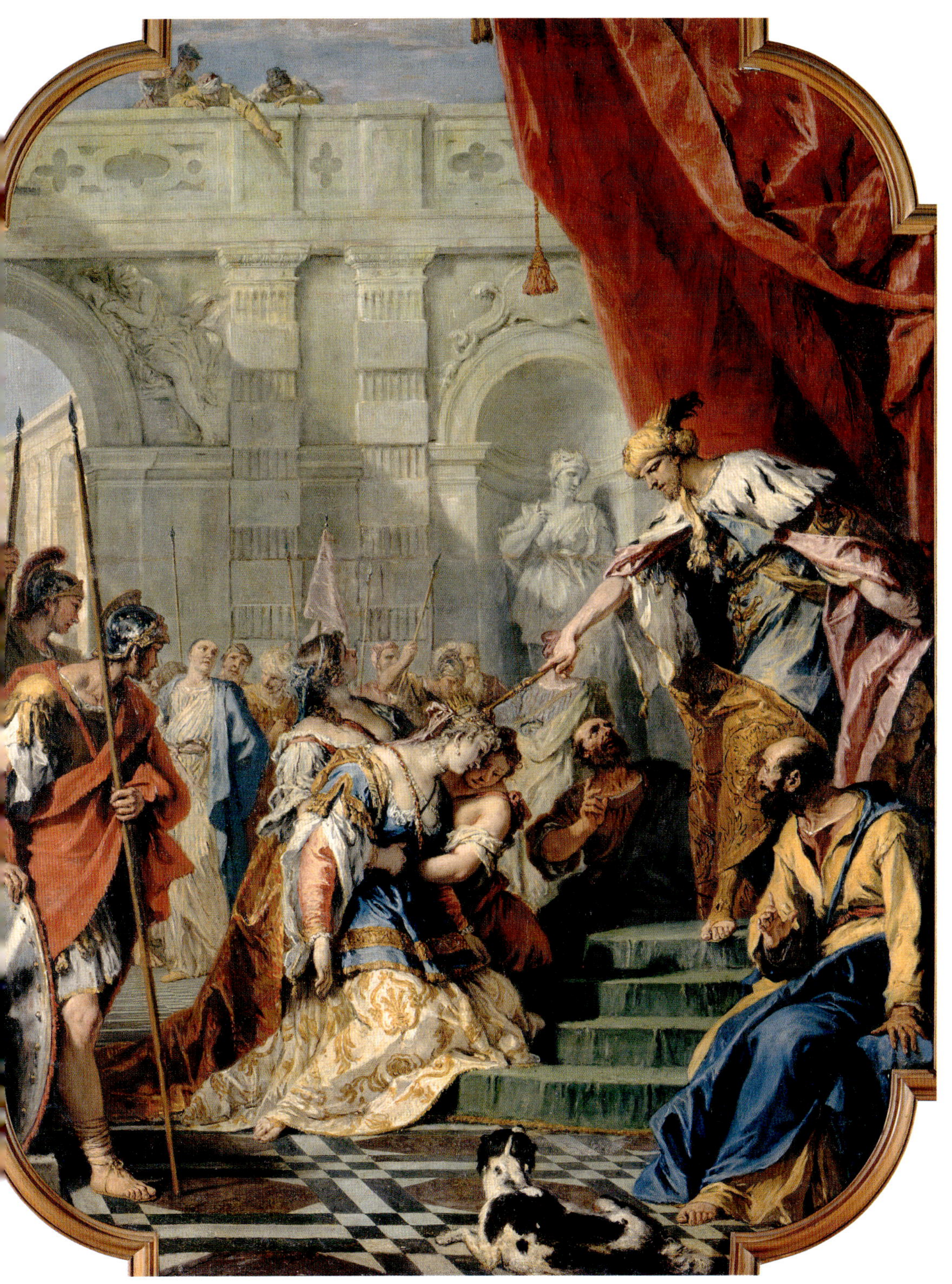

2. Key to one of the gates of the Ferrara ghetto

Ferrara, eighteenth century
Iron
17 cm
Previously Episcopal Palace, Ferrara
Private collection

Specifically, as written on the scroll attached to the key, it is the key to the "*Portone di Santa Margherita*" (Saint Margaret's Gate), which enclosed the ghetto between Via Vignatagliata and Via Contrari, and which was named after the adjacent (and still-standing) church of Santa Margherita, built on Via dei Romei in 1593 by Margherita Gonzaga, third wife of Duke Alfonso II d'Este.

On August 13, 1624, the papal legate to Ferrara issued an edict that formally established the city's Jewish ghetto. It required that the existing Jewish district be isolated by installing five gates, two at the sides of Via Sabbioni, two at the sides of Via Vignatagliata, and one at the end of Via Gattamarcia, today Via Vittoria. The city's Jewish population was definitively restricted to the ghetto three years later, in 1627.

SDS

3. Leone da Modena, *Historia de' riti Hebraici*

Printed by Giovanni Calleoni
Venice, 1638
Print on paper
16 × 11 × 0.8 cm
Biblioteca Queriniana, Brescia
Inv. 10°.A.VI.36

The *Historia de' riti Hebraici* was written by the renowned polymath rabbi Leone da Modena (1571–1648) and published in 1638 by Giovanni Calleoni. The *Riti* is a concise and pocket-sized manual on Jewish rituals, intended to describe the life, customs and beliefs of Jews at that time.
Leone da Modena presented a new concept of the collective identity of Jews and their role within Christian society during times of religious conflict and division. Modena's book in particular was an attempt to portray Judaism as it really was in his time, while conveying an ideal vision of Judaism as it should be.
Da Modena was involved in both the Jewish and the Christian worlds, and was comfortable enough with the spirit of the times to have his own portrait, however small, placed at the bottom of the front page in what was an almost revolutionary act for the Jewish world. Interestingly, the book was published afterwards in many editions and languages, but never again with the author's portrait. While this custom was not unusual in Christian printed books of the time, until this publication such a portrait was unknown in books of Jewish interest.

AC

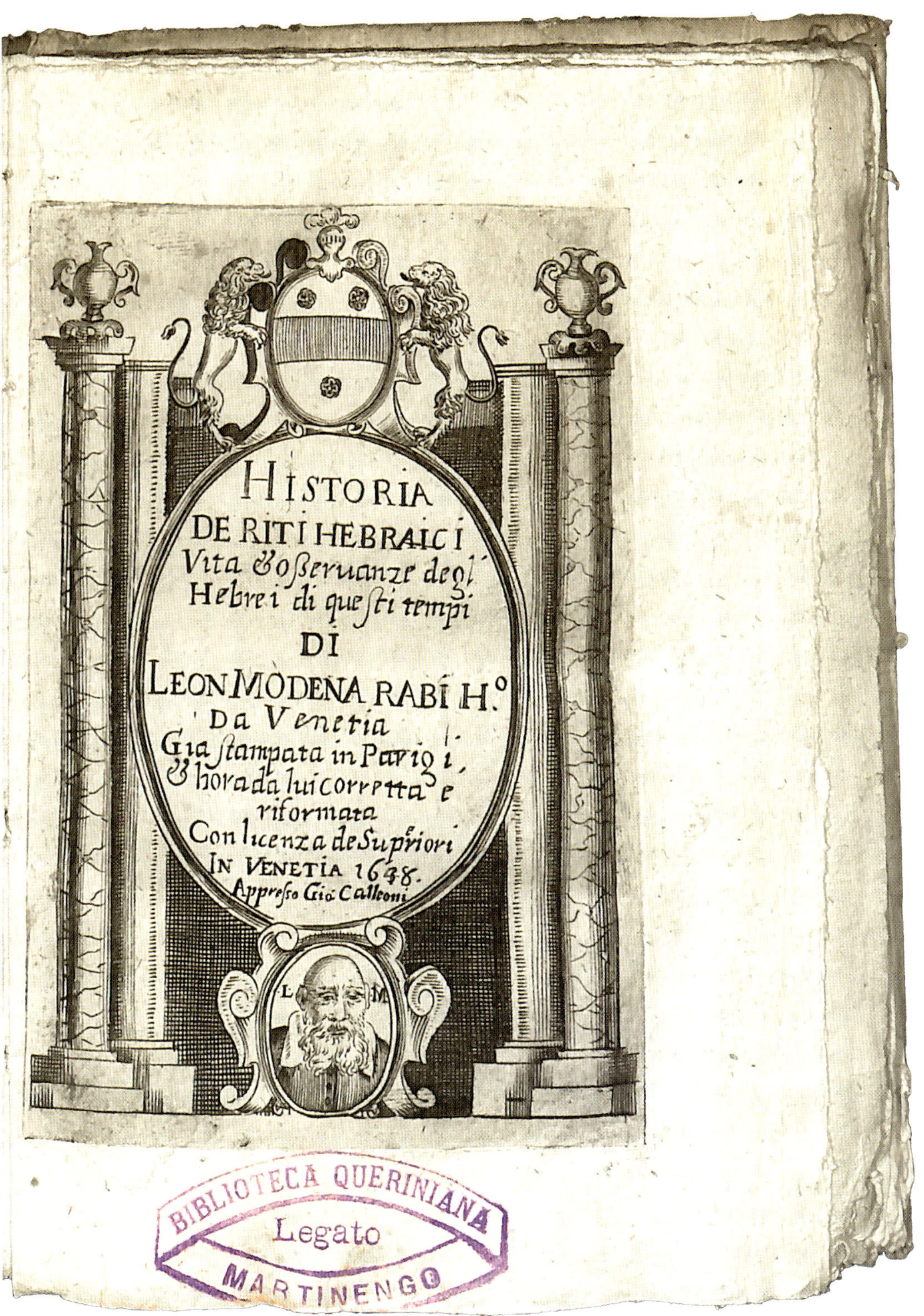
HISTORIA
DE RITI HEBRAICI
Vita & osseruanze degl'
Hebrei di questi tempi
DI
LEON MODENA RABI H.°
DA VENETIA
Già stampata in Parigi,
& hora da lui corretta e
riformata
Con licenza de Superiori
IN VENETIA 1638.
Appresso Giò Calleoni
L M

4. Pesach *Haggadah* with Ladino translation

Printed by Giovanni di Gara
for Israel Zifroni of Guastalla
Venice, 1609
Print on paper
25.4 × 18.4 cm
David and Cindy Sofer Collection, London

In 1609 the printer, Israel Zifroni of Guastalla, was responsible for designing an edition of the Pesach *Haggadah* with completely new illustrations that was printed for him by the printing house of Giovanni di Gara in Venice. The *Haggadah* text, at the center of the page, was flanked by a commentary written in one of the three vernacular languages: Judeo-Italian, Judeo-Spanish (Ladino) and Judeo-German. These were transcribed into Hebrew characters and reflect the three main languages of the Jewish communities living in Venice at the time.

The monumental layout includes a series of Biblical illustrations as well as new illustrations of the "Signs of the Passover Ritual" and the "Ten Plagues," assembled for the first time on one page.

The illustrated pages of the Venice *Haggadah* offer a glimpse into the Jewish home, family life and customs. The interior of a Jewish house is depicted in the midst of Pesach preparation: cleaning of the house and searching for and removing all traces of leaven, as well as cleansing cooking utensils. Preparations for Pesach include making the "*matzah*" dough and baking it. In another scene is a dining room where the whole family – wearing festive, fashionable clothes – sits at the Seder meal.

AC

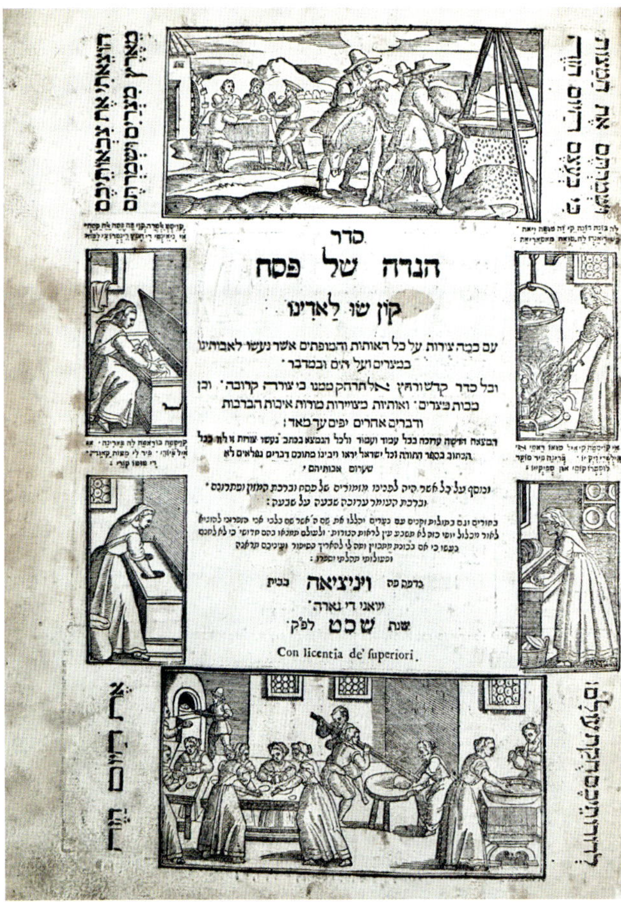

סדר

הגדה של פסח

קון שו לאדינו

עם כמה צירות על כל האותות והמופתים אשר נעשו לאבותינו
במצרים ועל הים ובמדבר ·

ויניציאה

יואני די גארה·

שנת שכט לפ״ק

Con licentia de' superiori.

5. *The Construction of the Sukkah*

Venice (?), late eighteenth or nineteenth century
Painted wooden panel from a *sukkah*
231 × 108 cm
Abbazia di Praglia, Teolo (Padua)

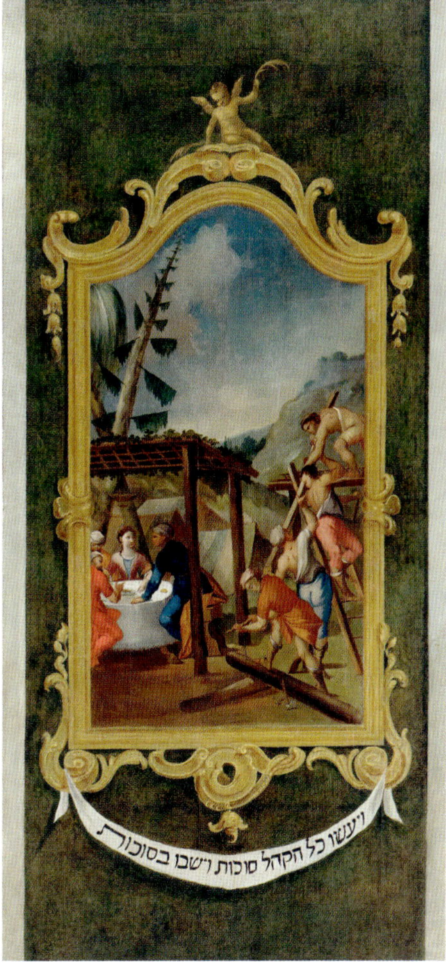

A *sukkah* is a temporary booth constructed for use during the Festival of Sukkot. It is topped with branches, through which one should be able to see the stars, and often decorated with autumnal, harvest or Biblical motifs. The Book of Leviticus describes it as a shelter commemorating the time God provided for and protected the Israelites in the wilderness after they were freed from slavery in Egypt.

The Praglia *sukkah* includes ten wooden panels, painted with biblical subjects and accompanied by Hebrew writings. Some panels seem to evoke the Jewish holidays: Moses receives the Law on Mount Sinai (Shavuot), Passover of the Jews (Pesach), the construction of the *sukkah* (Sukkot), the triumph of Mordecai (Purim). The others illustrate several important biblical personages, such as Abraham, Melchizedek, Isaac and Rebecca, Jacob, Rachel, Joshua, King David, and Elijah.

By the late sixteenth and early seventeenth centuries it was not uncommon to find in Europe, especially in Northern Europe, wooden decorated *sukkot* painted by local artists according to the guidelines of patrons. The panels that compose the *sukkah* were dismantled each year and reassembled the following year. Though many *sukkot* have been dispersed or lost because of their ephemeral and portable nature, this *sukkah* is among the precious few that have survived. For this reason, the images of this *sukkah* can offer fascinating insights into eighteenth-century Italian Jewish ritual customs, art, and cultural tradition.

AC

6. *Ketubah*, marriage contract

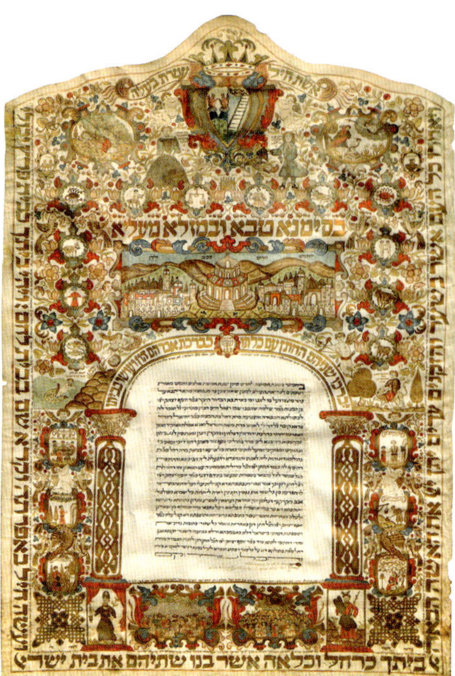

Original text: Mantua, Friday, 12 Av 5493 (1733)
Groom: Avraham son of Tzion son of Isaac Cohen Zedek of Mondovì
Bride: Grazia daughter of Raphael Sullam (?)
Later text: Mantua, Thursday 5 Sivan 5580 (1820)
Groom: Joseph Isaac son of Shelomo, known as Raphael Hayyim HaCohen of Mondovì
Bride: Rachel daughter of Yechiel David Franchetti
Manuscript on parchment
100.7 × 68.1 cm
Private collection, Mantua

This splendid, decorated *ketubah* is proof that even family records could be used a second time. Originally created for the Cohen-Sullam marriage, which was celebrated in Mantua in 1733, we see from the current text – written over the original wording – that it was reused almost a hundred years later, in 1820, for the Cohen-Franchetti marriage. The text is framed by an arch supported by two squared columns. Above the text, but below the arch, we find the arms of the Cohen and Sullam families, flanked by two winged *putti*. From the original text, which is still visible and even legible with the help of ultraviolet photography, it becomes clear why the family emblem represented on the medallion at the top does not match the names in the current text. The Cohen family is referenced by the image of two hands, signifying the blessing of the priests (*Cohanim*), but it is the Sullam family that is represented by the ladder (Sullam means "ladder" in Hebrew). Bride and groom are depicted in elegant eighteenth-century dress to the sides of the respective coats of arms. Each is accompanied by a mythological figure: the groom is presented by a cupid who looks down to the right, while the bride's veil is held up by a female figure above a well.

The lavish Venetian-style decoration – including a rich band with medallions bearing the signs of the zodiac and *clipei* featuring scenes from the Bible – is a perfect example of the golden age of *ketubah* illustration in the Jewish culture of eighteenth-century Italy.
At the center is a symbolic representation of Jerusalem, a reference to the tradition of commemorating the destruction of the Temple on special occasions in the lives of individuals or the wider community.

AC

7. Wedding Poem

Italy, 1799
Groom: Raphael Nissim son of Yitzhak Chaim Recanati
Bride: Tovah daughter of Yehoshua Recanati
Etching on paper
71.6 × 49.9 cm
Gross Family Collection, Tel Aviv
Inv. 034.011.102

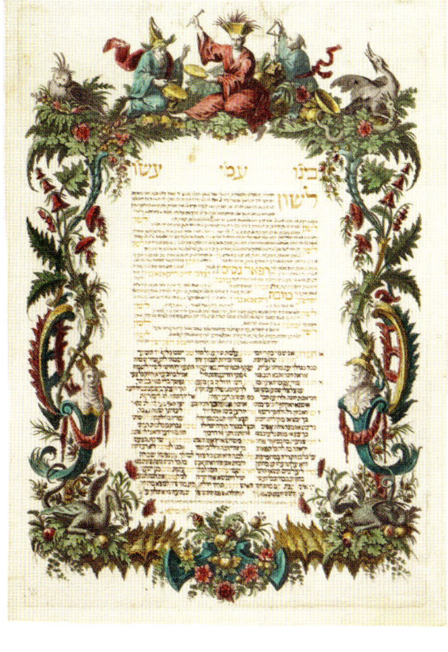

The Hebrew wedding poem, composed by friends and family of the bridal couple, was an integral part of this popular genre among both Christians and Jews in Italy in the seventeenth and eighteenth centuries. The form usually began with an honorific statement praising the bridal couple and their families and expressing good wishes. The central section was the poem itself, especially composed for the occasion. The form was often either sonnets or poems of multiple stanzas with regular allusions to the couple and emphasis given to their names through printing type. The last section was the salutation from and the signature of the author. While mostly found as printed documents, there are manuscript versions known as well. Both sorts exist in the Gross Family Collection. The introductory text about the couple and their families is larger than the text of the poem, an unusual phenomenon in such pages. From the richness of the page it is safe to assume that the Recanati family was a prominent one. Since both bride and groom have the same family name, it is likely that they were cousins, a not unusual circumstance in Sephardic society. This is a very nicely written wedding text and poem written inside a fine, elaborately designed etched border which has been brightly hand colored.

AC

8. *Megillah* of Esther (Scroll of Esther)

Italy, 1600–1690, with additional decoration from the eighteenth century
Manuscript on parchment, applied and watercolored printed decoration
22 × 156 cm
Biblioteca Palatina, Complesso Monumentale della Pilotta, Parma
Inv. Parm. 3345, De Rossi 888

Bibl.: De Rossi 1803, n. 888; Richler 2001.

This *megillah* offers an example of images being used eclectically outside their original context, with a decidedly unusual decoration that appears to draw on genre scenes of courtly life with no connection to the story of Esther or the events it describes. Here, we find knights and noble ladies engrossed in the arts of hunting, conversation, music and dance, as well as dining in company and taking walks, all against a stylized country scene punctuated with animals and fantastical figures such a turbaned man who finds himself face-to-face with an enormous butterfly.
Interestingly, the various figures are depicted in different scales, and were probably added in different periods after the text was set down. A number of the images are printed, and have been colored and glued to the parchment.

AC

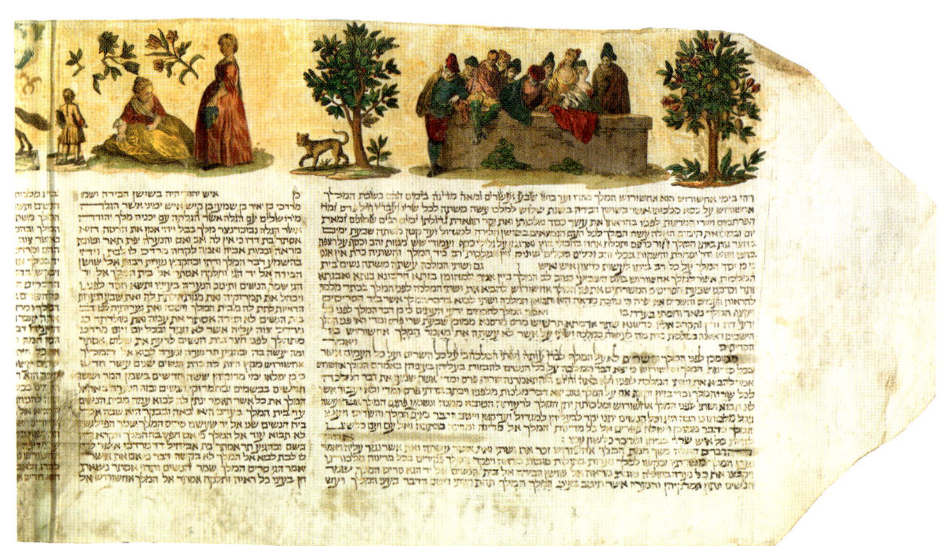

9. *Megillah* of Esther (Scroll of Esther)

Italy, eighteenth century
Manuscript on parchment with painted border
252 × 27 cm
Biblioteca Palatina, Complesso Monumentale della Pilotta, Parma
Inv. Parm. 3322, De Rossi 436

Bibl.: De Rossi 1803, no. 436; Tamani 1968, p. 90, no. 114; Richler 2001, p. 87.

This *megillah* was drafted freehand and colored by an inexperienced artist who drew inspiration from the engravings produced by Francesco Grisellini (1717–1787) for a *megillah* he, himself, produced in the mid-eighteenth century.
Grisellini's elegant arcades – supported by variegated columns on high pedestals and surmounted by an extravagant balustrade embellished with large paterae bearing impressive leafy branches and pairs of birds – are reproduced here in simplified form. Even the lines of the architectural elements are drawn freehand, without the use of precision instruments, and apparently without preparatory drawings. One possibility is that the artist traced the Grisellini drawings with a metal implement to leave a mark on the vellum that he could follow. It is also possible that the decoration was added by the owner of the scroll, as happened frequently; there is a name written in Hebrew in the lower edge of one of the drawings, but it has been almost entirely erased, with just the letter *aleph* still visible.
Interestingly, the scenes from the biblical story of Esther, which appear in rectangles at the base, are based not on the Grisellini version but on an older model, and reflect the scenic composition of the late-Baroque period (similar to the *megillah* in the U. Nahon Museum of Italian Jewish Art).
We can conclude, then, that the artist had access to more than one illustrated *megillah* as a model.

AC

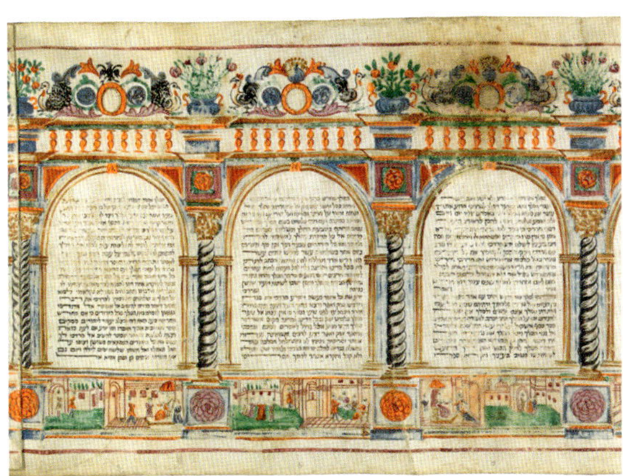

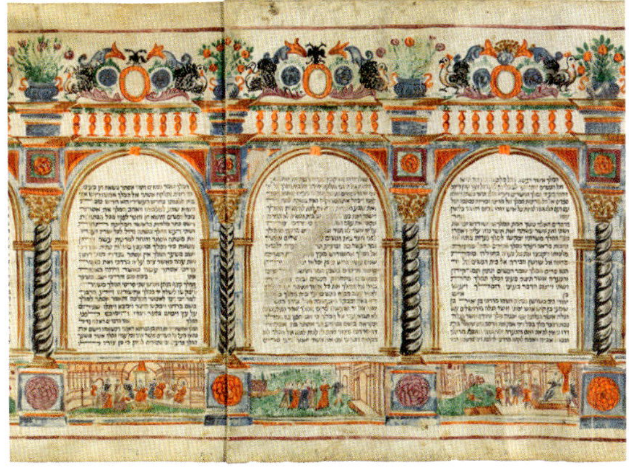

10. *Ketubah*, marriage contract

Ferrara, Friday 14 Shevat 5499 (1739)
Groom: Isaac son of Eliezer Ashkenazi
Bride: Fiora daughter of Yaakov Alfandari
Manuscript on parchment, watercolored and glued printed figures
71.6 × 49.9 cm
David and Cindy Sofer Collection, London

Bibl.: Colorni *et al.* 1984, p. 82; Sabar 2000, pp. 194–195.

The decoration of this *ketubah* is strongly influenced by the artistic tastes of the period. The text in Hebrew and Aramaic is clearly legible at the center of the manuscript. It is surrounded by a frame – painted in red and gilded – together with the key details of the contract: the year 5499 in the Jewish calendar, the equivalent of 1739; Ferrara, the location of the ceremony; and the names of the couple, Isaac son of Eliezer Ashkenazi and Fiora daughter of Yaakov Alfandari. The first witness was rabbi Yitzhak Lampronti, the author of the Talmudic encyclopedia *Pahad Yitzhak* The rest of the document is decorated against a sky-blue ground. At the sides rise two columns wrapped in a climbing vine, with a dame on the base of the right-hand column, and a knight directly opposite on the left-hand column.
At the top, in the center, there is a single, decorative inscription in Hebrew – "Good sign" – part of the traditional blessing offered to the bride and groom at their wedding. Below the inscription, we find the bride and groom. Around them, the vellum is decorated with allegorical figures. Their identities are not immediately obvious but they are probably pagan divinities: clearly identifiable are Hera, the female figure with the peacock, Diana, in her chariot pulled by dogs, and Apollo in his horse-drawn chariot. Completing the decoration at the foot are two young couples making merry with a flask of wine. The whole *ketubah* is decorated with vases of flowers and plant motifs, to emphasize the joyful nature of the union. The human figures have been cut out, glued to the parchment and watercolored.

SR

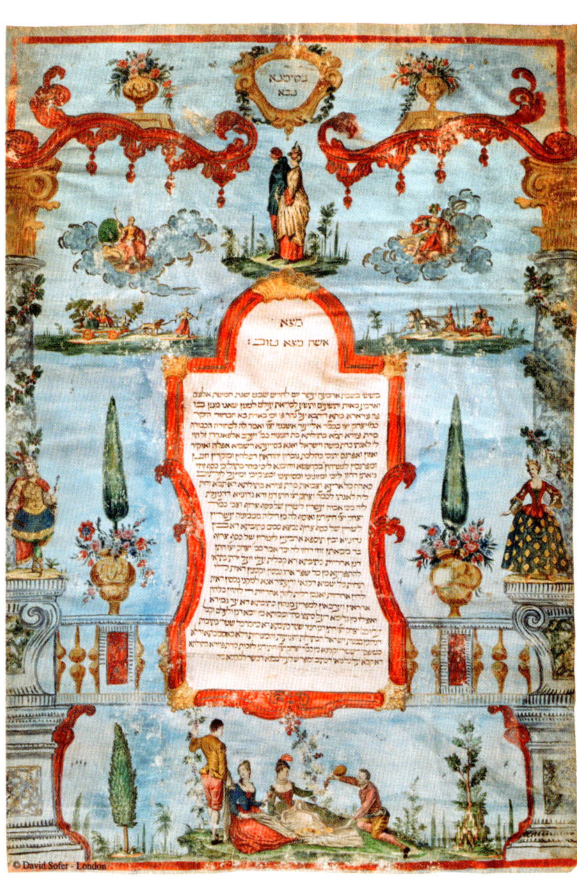

11. Leone da Modena,
L'Ester, tragedia tratta dalla Sacra Scrittura (Esther, a tragedy drawn from Holy Scripture)

Printed by Giacomo Sarzina
Venice, 1619
Print on paper
13,5 × 28 cm
Biblioteca Nazionale Centrale, Rome
inv. BNCR 34.3.A.20/1

Leone da Modena's (1571–1648) *Esther* is a vernacular tragedy in hendecasyllable verse. As the author informs his readers, a version of the story had been composed seventy years prior by Salomon Uschi, with the assistance of Leone's maternal uncle, Lazzaro di Grazian Levi. Leone took the tragedy and produced a new draft, which he dedicated to his pupil and benefactor, the Jewish writer Sara Copia Sullam. In the text, Leon also mentions another tragedy entitled *Rachel*, which he expected to finish in the near future. However, this second work was never completed, leaving *Esther* as the author's only dramatic work.

SR

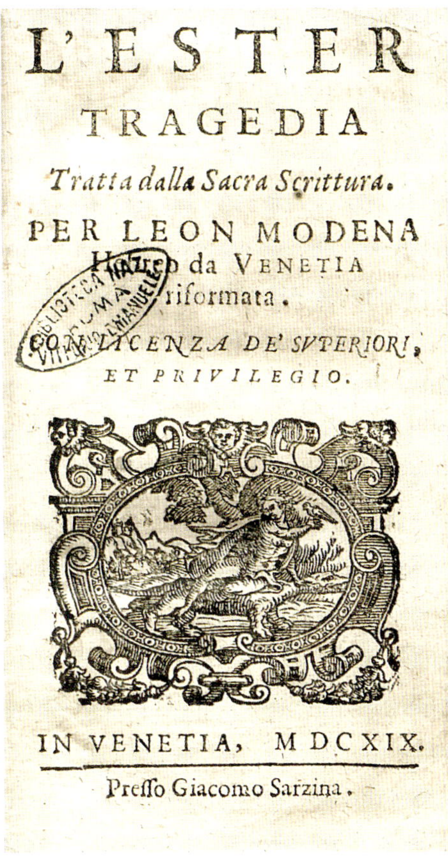
L'ESTER
TRAGEDIA
Tratta dalla Sacra Scrittura.
PER LEON MODENA
H[illegible] da VENETIA
riformata.
CON LICENZA DE' SVPERIORI,
ET PRIVILEGIO.
IN VENETIA, MDCXIX.
Preſſo Giacomo Sarzina.

12. Alessandro Magnasco, *Interior of a Synagogue*

1703
Oil on canvas
69 × 97 cm; with frame 80 × 100 cm
Uffizi Gallery, Florence
Inv. 1890, no. 5059

Alessandro Magnasco (1667–1749) was born in Genoa to Stefano Magnasco – also a painter – and studied under local artist Valerio Castello. Sometime around 1677, following the death of his father, he moved to Milan where he joined the workshop of Venetian artist Filippo Abbiati as an apprentice. He is recorded as being in Florence in 1703, working for the Grand Prince of Tuscany, Ferdinando de' Medici (1663–1713). *Interior of a Synagogue* is one of the works commissioned by Ferdinando, and can be identified in the inventory of his personal collection. It is part of a diptych, the other half being the *Quaker Meeting* – also housed at the Uffizi (Inv. 1890, no. 5992) – which gives some indication of the artist's interest in the contemporary religious debate. In this image, which depicts a synagogue, Magnasco sets the *bimah* (pulpit) at the heart of the composition, with the officiant draped in a prayer shawl, or *tallit*. Attending to the prayer on each side of the space are men and children. From the grated windows of the matroneum, a sort of gallery reserved for women, a number of female figures lean out to hear the prayer. This treatment of the subject would be followed by the *Synagogue* (1720–1725) in the Abbey of Seitenstetten, and another *Interior of a Synagogue* dating from 1725–1730, which is now in the Cleveland Museum of Art.

SR

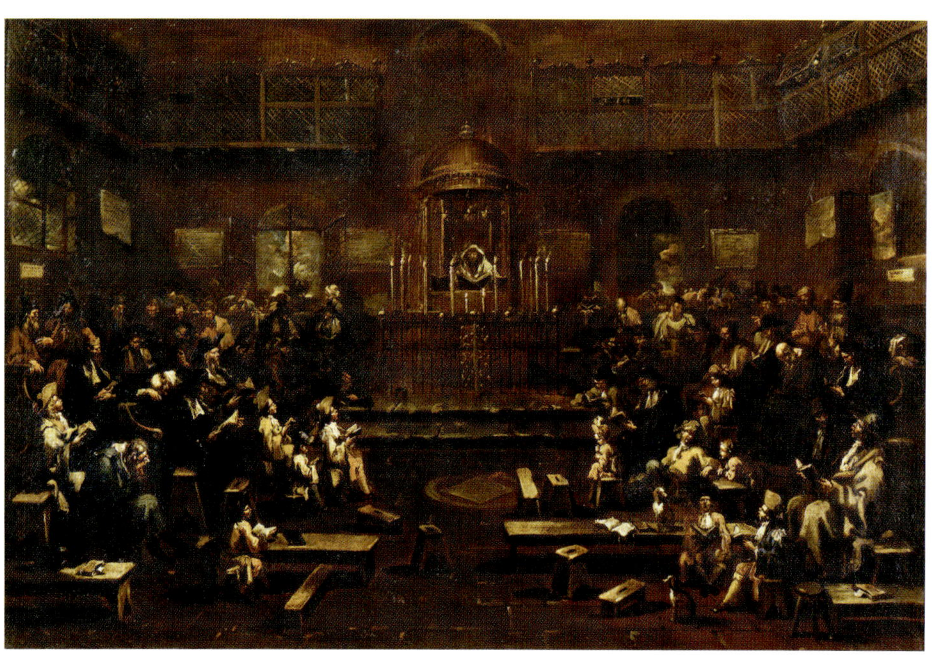

13. Painter active in the Venice Area, *The Circumcision*

Italy, eighteenth century
Oil on canvas
60 × 100 cm; with frame 72 x 112 cm
Alberto Di Castro Collection, Rome

This interior scene depicts one of the key rituals of Jewish life, the circumcision or *brit milah*. The Hebrew term literally means "covenant of circumcision," the covenant of faith between God and Abraham. Circumcision is performed by a skilled practitioner called a *mohel* on all Jewish boys at the age of eight days (or later, depending on the health of the child). In this painting, the *mohel* is seen performing the rite on the right-hand side of the scene.

SDS-RS

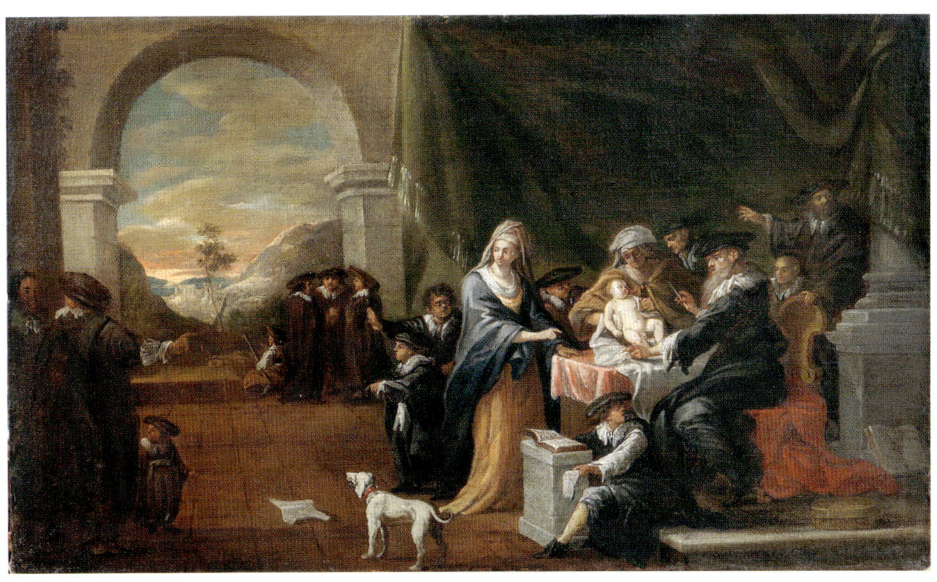

14. *Musaf Kippur*, Scuola Siciliana

Book of prayer with the additional prayers to be recited during Yom Kippur
Rome, 1863
Manuscript in paper, in Italian, decorated frontispiece. Cover made of brown leather with gold text and detailing
21.5 × 14.5 cm
Archivio Storico della Comunità Ebraica di Roma "Giancarlo Spizzichino," Rome

The text includes the additional prayers (*musaf*) of the feast days, in the rite of the Scuola Siciliana, practiced by those Roman Jews who had come from Sicily, most of whom had made their way to Rome after the expulsion of the Jews from the Spanish territories of southern Italy in the early sixteenth century. The date is calculated using the numerical value of the expression עננִי באמת ("Answer me in the truth," Psalm 69:14), in the last line of the frontispiece.

SDS

15. *Musaf Kippur*, Nedava (offering) made by Isacco G. Di S. Efrati to the Scuola Castigliana

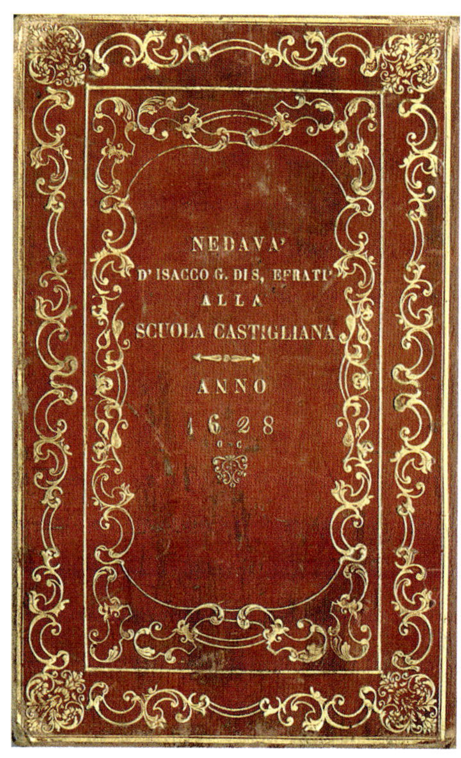

Book of prayer with the additional prayers to be recited during Yom Kippur. The booklet was donated by Isacco Efrati to the Scuola Castigliana (Sephardic rite)
Rome, 1678
Manuscript on paper, in Italian, decorated frontispiece. Cover made of brown leather with gold text and detailing
22.5 × 14.5 cm
Archivio Storico della Comunità Ebraica di Roma "Giancarlo Spizzichino," Rome

On the cover the year 1628 is stated, but the numerical value of the expression קרב לנו הגאולה ("our redemption draws near"), in the last line of the frontispiece, is 1678.
Worthy of note is the fact that neither the text nor the binding are in the seventeenth-century style. Having verified that the marriage contract of Isacco Giuseppe, son of Sabato Efrati, dates from 1859, it can be presumed that the seventeenth-century text was copied and re-bound in the nineteenth century.

SDS

16. *Shaar ha-Teshuvah* (Gate of Repentance) Book of Prayers of the Asmored Confraternity of the Scuola Castigliana

Edited and printed at the Bragadina printing house by Gad ben Shemuel Foà
Venice, 1775
Print on paper. Brown leather cover with gold text and detailing
20 × 13 cm

Archivio Storico della Comunità Ebraica di Roma "Giancarlo Spizzichino," Rome

The Asmored confraternity undertook to ensure the *minyan* – the presence of at least ten Jewish men – during the *selichot*, penitential prayers and hymns recited between midnight and dawn.

SR

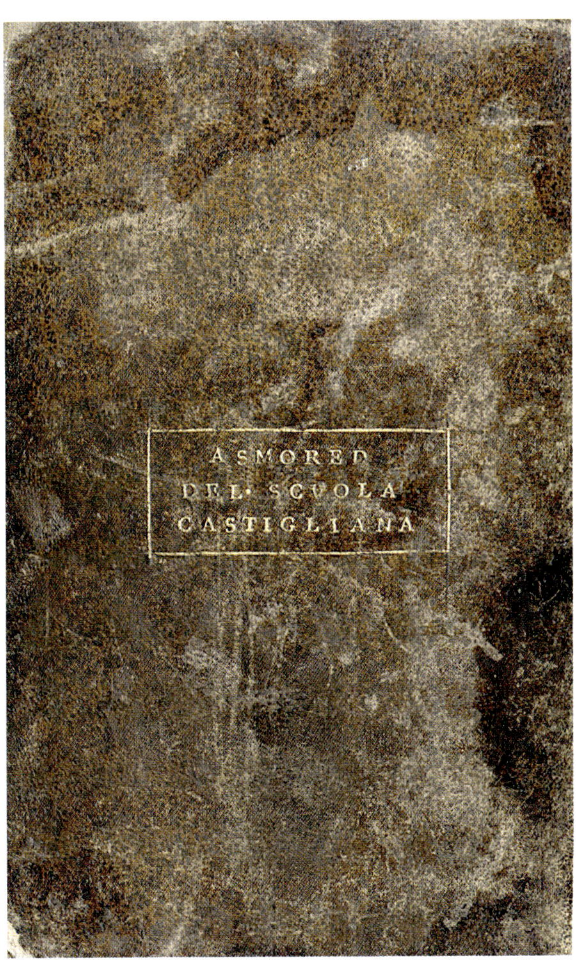

17. *Edict of the Cardinal Vicar of Rome*

Rome, Printing house of the Apostolic Camera
10 October 1702
Print on paper with handwritten inscription
26 × 37.5 cm
Gianfranco Moscati Collection, MEIS (National Museum of Italian Judaism and the Shoah), Ferrara

This edict, issued in 1702 by the Cardinal Vicar of Rome, forbade Christians from participating in the Jewish festival of Sukkot, which it refers to as the Feast "*delle Capannette*" (i.e., "of Huts"), on pain of a fine of 25 *scudi*. It refers back to the laws that enforced the segregation of the Jews, repeating the order to close all of the gates to the ghetto at night, and the ban prohibiting Christian citizens from participating in Jewish festivals. The discriminatory nature of this edict is a reminder that, despite the efforts of the authorities, relations between Christians and Jews did not cease with the establishment of the ghetto.

SR

GASPARO per la Miſericordia di Dio Veſcouo di Sabina della S.R.C. Card. di Carpegna della Santità di N.S. Vicario Generale &c.

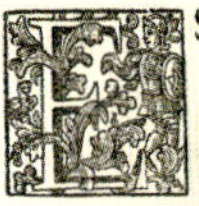SSENDO peruenuto à noſtra notizia, che molti Chriſtiani tanto huomini, come donne con ſcandaloſa curioſità, e ſouerchia domeſtichezza con gli Hebrei in materia anco toccante i loro riti, concorrano nelle loro Caſe in occaſione della feſta, che chiamano delle Caſelle; perciò per ouuiare à queſto inconueniente, inerendo all'Editti altre volte publicati, ordiniamo, e commandiamo à tutti, e ſingoli Hebrei commoranti nel Ghetto di Roma, che non ammettino alcun Chriſtiano, ò del vno, ò dell'altro ſeſſo nelle loro Caſe ſotto qualſiuoglia preteſto durante il tempo di detta feſta, mà ſolo per occaſione di neceſſario commercio vi trattino nelle Botteghe à piana terra, ſotto pena di ſcudi 25. da applicarſi ad vſi pij per qualſiuoglia contrauentione, e perſona, che ardiſſero d'introdurre contro queſta noſtra prohibitione, e da incorrerſi irremiſſibilmente anco per la prima volta, & altre à noi arbitrarie. Dichiarando, che la medeſima pena ſia impoſta à gli huomini, ò donne Chriſtiane, & à ciaſcheduno di eſſi, che traſgredirà queſto noſtro Editto, quale ſi debba eſtendere anco à quelli ch'entraranno nelle ſcuole di eſſi Hebrei in tempo delle loro feſte. E per leuare la facilità del concorſo nel tempo notturno, ordiniamo al Portinaro del detto Ghetto, che alle 24. hore ſerri tutte le Porte, e Portoncino di eſſo, ne quelle ſi aprano, ò intieramente, ò col ſolo ſportello durante detta feſta di notte tempo, ſe non per occaſione di mera neceſſità, ſotto pena della priuatione dell'offitio, e d'altre pene à noſtro arbitrio. Dat. Romæ ex Ædibus noſtris hac die 10. Octobris 1702.

G.Card. Vicario

N.A. Cuggiò Segr.

IN ROMA, Nella Stamperia della Reu. Cam. Apoſtolica 1702.

18. Del Monte Crown

Rome, 1625–1626
Embossed and pierced silver; paste gemstones
14.8 × 19.4 cm (inner Ø); 20 cm (outer Ø)
Museo Ebraico di Roma, Rome
Inv. 164

Bibl.: Di Castro 2010[b].

The Del Monte crown can be dated back to 1625–1626, although its creator is unknown. It is notable for its ornamentation, including paste stones and the arms of the Del Monte family, which figures two lions counter-rampant atop an Italian-style trimount. Three scrolls in the central band bear inscriptions in Hebrew, which together form the following text: "Sanctity to the Lord / to the Synagogue of the Quattro Capi; a donation of Yaakov Del Monte / may God spare his life / charges required by law / in year 5386 of the Jewish calendar / in honor of the God of Israel and of His Law."

SR

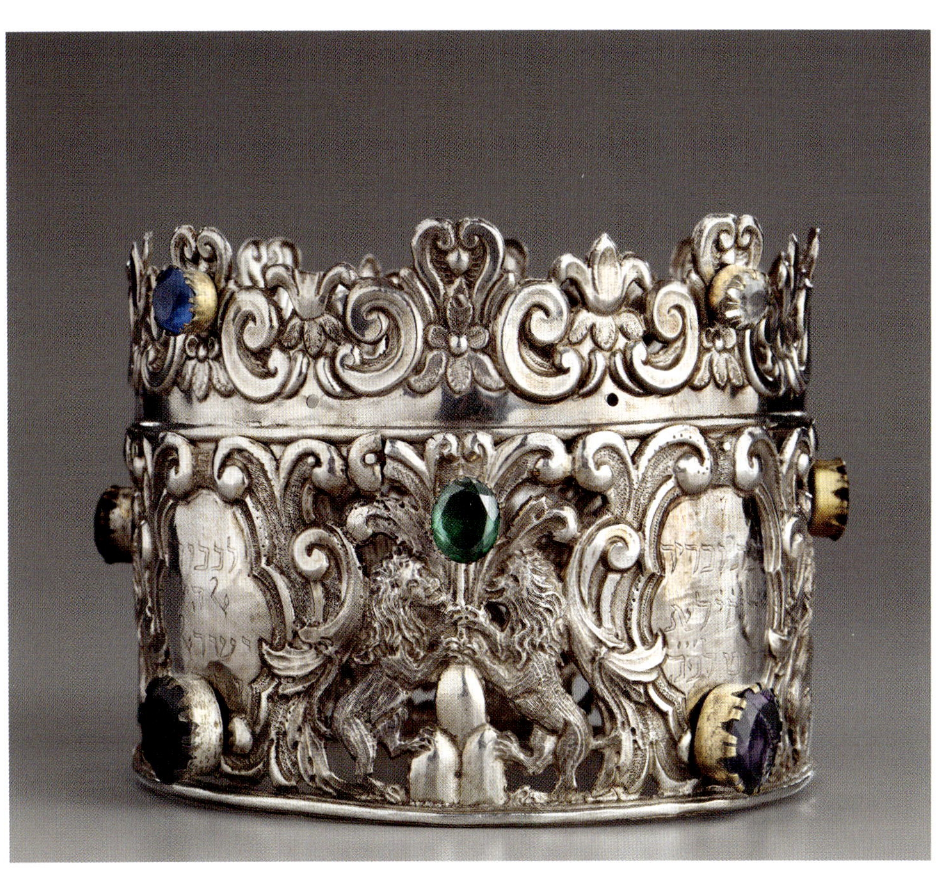

19. *Rimmonim* Efrati

Rome, 1727–1729
Embossed and chased silver
44.9 × Ø 14 cm
Museo Ebraico di Roma, Rome
Inv. 37

The term *rimmonim* is derived from the form of these ritual objects, which were first made to resemble a pomegranate (in Hebrew *rimmon*, pluralised as *rimmonim*). They are placed, as a form of ornamentation, on the wooden shafts that hold the Torah scroll. This pair of *rimmonim* are bulbous in shape, and cinched in the middle in a manner that is typical of eighteenth-century finials from Rome. They are decorated with plant-shaped motifs, and two orders of bells, one of which is made to resemble the little arils of the pomegranate. The donor's family arms are situated at the tip of the finials, and on one of the handles there is an inscription in Hebrew that reads, "Glory to God at the Scuola Castigliana. Offered by the elderly and honored Mordechai Efrati, for the life of his wife, his daughters and son-in-laws. Year 5491."

Adding to the ornamentation is the coat of arms of a Roman family, specifically the Ascarelli, in a variant that has three lions surrounding the tower rather than the two that are found on other objects linked to the family. These *rimmonim* were paired with a crown in the Museo Ebraico in Rome (Inv. 28).

SR

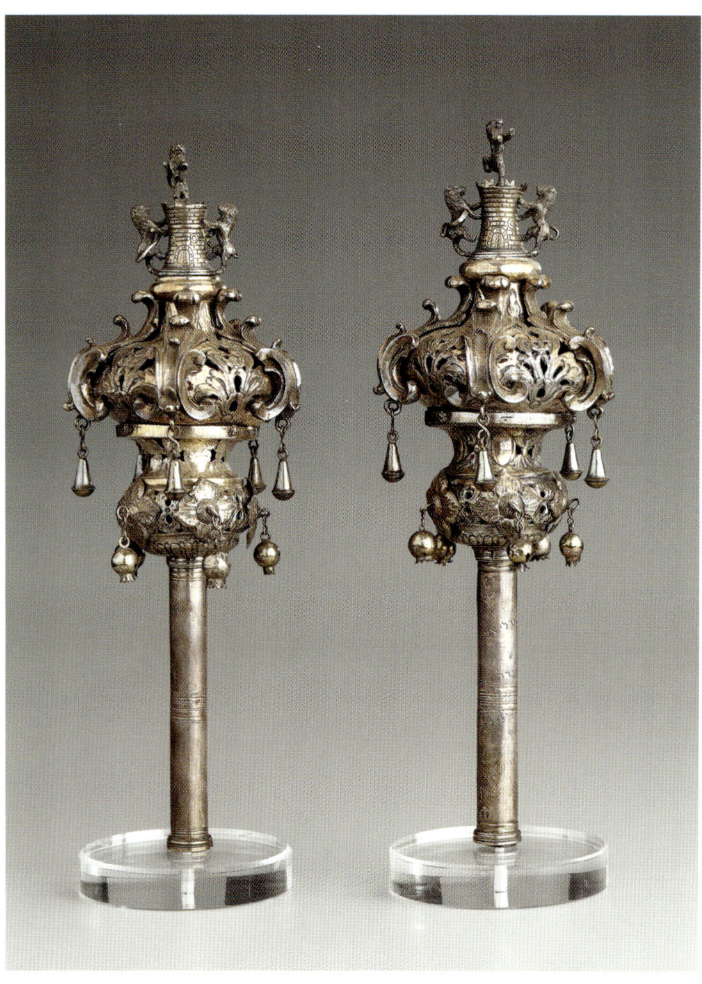

20. Offering record from the Synagogue of Carmagnola

Piedmont area
Eighteenth century
Manuscript on parchment, print on paper, with wooden frame and silk
63.5 × 39 cm
Archivio Ebraico Terracini, Turin
Inv. B.I.1

This object is a record of offerings that was used in the synagogue at Carmagnola, as attested by the inscription, which includes the Hebrew acronym קקק – *Kehilat Kodesh Carmagnola* ("holy congregation of Carmagnola"). The three panels each bear a parchment, which was used by the members of the community to record their commitment to donate money to the synagogue. The two side panels list the names of the benefactors in Hebrew. For each name, there is a box on the central panel in which a small hole would be made with a pin, indicating a pledge to donate to the community.

SR

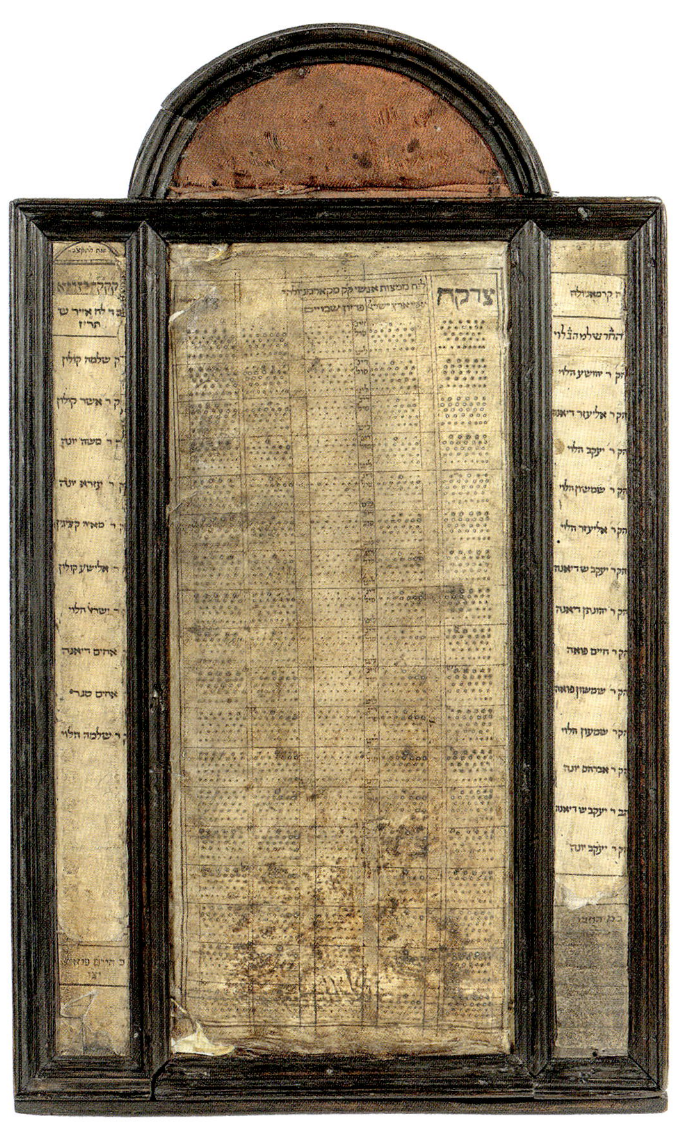

21. Temporary Decoration

Decorative panel produced by the Jewish "University" of Rome for the investiture of Pope Clement XII
Rome, 1730
Watercolor and ink on paper
52.5 × 73.8 cm
Archivio Storico della Comunità Ebraica di Roma "Giancarlo Spizzichino," Rome
Inv. 7

Bibl.: Caffiero 2000; Cancellieri 1802; O. Melasecchi, in Di Castro 2010[a], pp. 71–72.

Among the opportunities for public visibility afforded to Jews, who were otherwise segregated in the ghetto, some came in the form of forced participation in celebrations of the city's status and power. In Rome, the Jewish community contributed to the ceremony of the papal "*possesso*," in which the newly-elected pontiff paraded in triumph from his residences to the Vatican, and across Rome via the Quirinal Palace to the cathedral of San Giovanni in Laterano, where he would be invested as the Bishop of Rome. The celebration also formalized the new pope's assumption of his temporal power, and the entire population was invited to take part, with the city's Jewish community tasked with decorating the route between the Arch of Titus and the Colosseum. This practice enjoyed new impetus towards the end of the seventeenth century and the start of the eighteenth with an increase in the production of temporary structures and decorations made of wood, card and papier-mâché. In this panel, which was made for the investiture of Pope Clement XII in 1730, the decoration depicts the chariot of the sun followed by representations of the twelve hours and the night, with the motto "*Affert Diem, Tempus, et Hora.*" At the center is an inscription in both Hebrew and Latin, reading, "may all who love you be like the sun when it rises in its strength" (Judges 5:31).

SR

22. Temporary Decoration

Decorative panel produced by the Jewish "University" of Rome for the investiture of Pope Clement XIV
Rome, 1769
Watercolor and ink on paper
52.6 × 77.4 cm
Archivio Storico della Comunità Ebraica di Roma "Giancarlo Spizzichino," Rome
Inv. 18

Bibl.: Cancellieri 1802; Coccioli 1997, pp. 195–197; O. Melasecchi, in Di Castro 2010[a], p. 74.

This piece of temporary decoration was one of a series of fifty panels created for the "*possesso*" ceremony of Clement XIV. Inside a decorative lunette are a number of bees in flight above a group of copper utensils, vases and cymbals, which according to custom could be used to call them back. Above the bees is the motto: "*Congregatur sonitu*" ("gather together with the sound"). At the center is the quote, "You, his godly ones, sing to the Lord, give thanks at the mention of his holiness," which is erroneously identified on the panel as Psalm 30, verse 5 (it is actually verse 4).

SR

23. Temporary Decoration

Decorative panel produced by the Jewish "University" of Rome for the investiture of Pope Pius VI
Rome, 1775
Watercolor and ink on paper
52.5 × 76.5 cm
Archivio Storico della Comunità Ebraica di Roma "Giancarlo Spizzichino," Rome
Inv. 19

Bibl.: Cancellieri 1802; O. Melasecchi, in Di Castro 2010[a], p. 74; Milano 1954.

This is one of an incomplete series of 25 panels that the Jewish community commissioned for the investiture of Pope Pius VI (Giovanni Braschi) on November 30, 1775. A description of this series appears in a manuscript discovered by Attilio Milano in the collection of the Historical Archive of the Jewish Community of Rome, which it has been suggested was written by Tranquillo Del Monte, an intellectual noted for his work on the history of Rome's Jewish community. The same Del Monte was reimbursed for the costs of the celebrations for the "*possesso*" ceremony (ASCER Libro Mastro dell'Università dal 1745 fino a tutto il 1789. C cc. 111). The panel is decorated with a lunette, within which are two columns and the motto "*Ne aliquid mali ingrediatur*" ("let no evil be brought in"), an expression historically used at the house entrance, along with the figure of Herakles. It is to be assumed, therefore, that the two columns are included as the attributes of Herakles. The inscription in Latin and Hebrew reads, "Blessings crown the head of the righteous." The latin adjective "*Pii*" [righteous] is capitalized as an homage to the newly invested pope.

SR

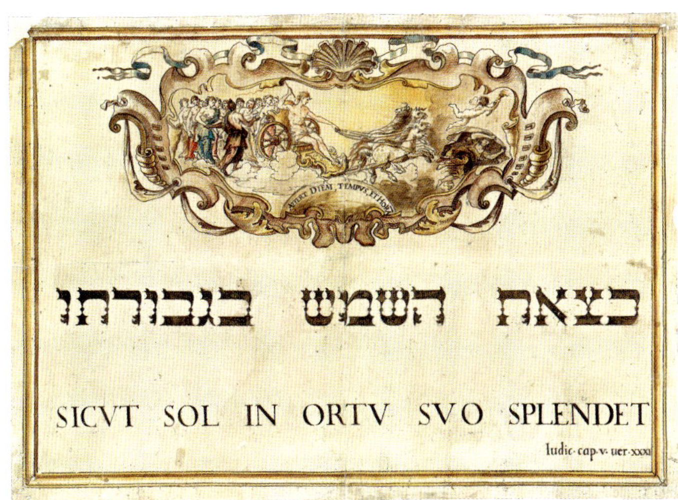
כצאת השמש בגבורתו
SICVT SOL IN ORTV SVO SPLENDET
Iudic·cap·v·uer·xxxi

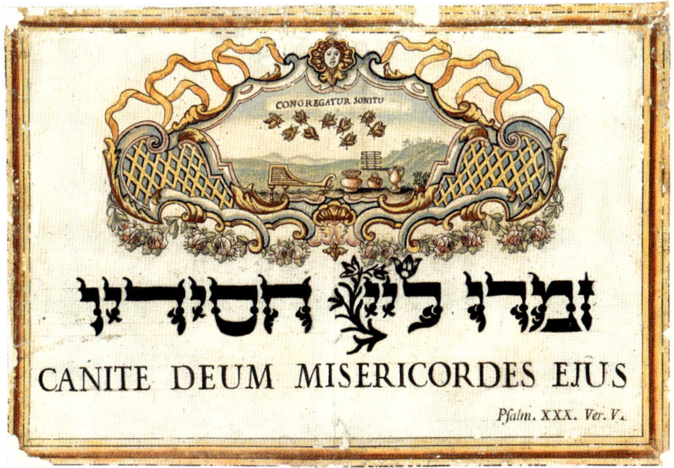
CONGREGATUR SONITU
זמרו ליי חסידיו
CANITE DEUM MISERICORDES EJUS
Pſalm. XXX. Ver. V.

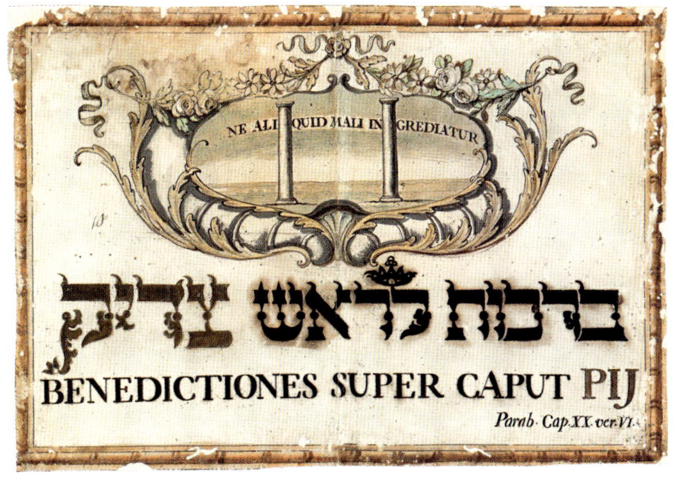
NE ALI QUID MALI IN GREDIATUR
ברכות לראש צדיק
BENEDICTIONES SUPER CAPUT PIJ
Parab. Cap. XX. ver. VI.

24. Silver binding of a Jewish holiday prayer book

Produced by Francesco Dassi
Rome, first half of the eighteenth century
Embossed and chased silver
18.30 × 13 cm
Private collection

Bil.: Fornari 1968 pp. 122, 130.

The silver binding was produced by Francesco Dassi, a Milanese silversmith who was active in Rome between 1732 and 1743. Engraved on the central shields are the arms of the Tagliacozzo family and "D.T.", the initials of the book's owner, Dario Tagliacozzo.

SDS

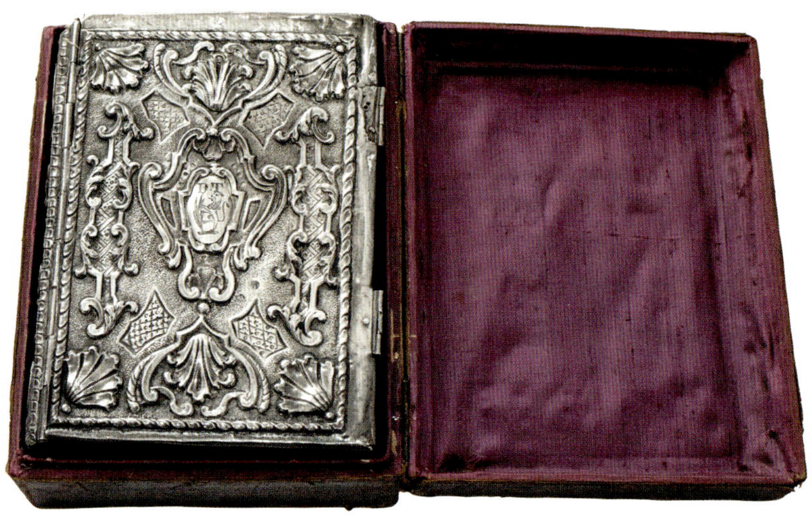

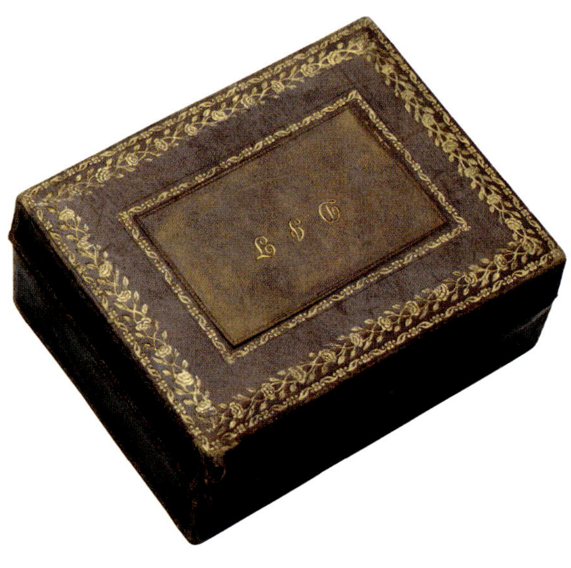

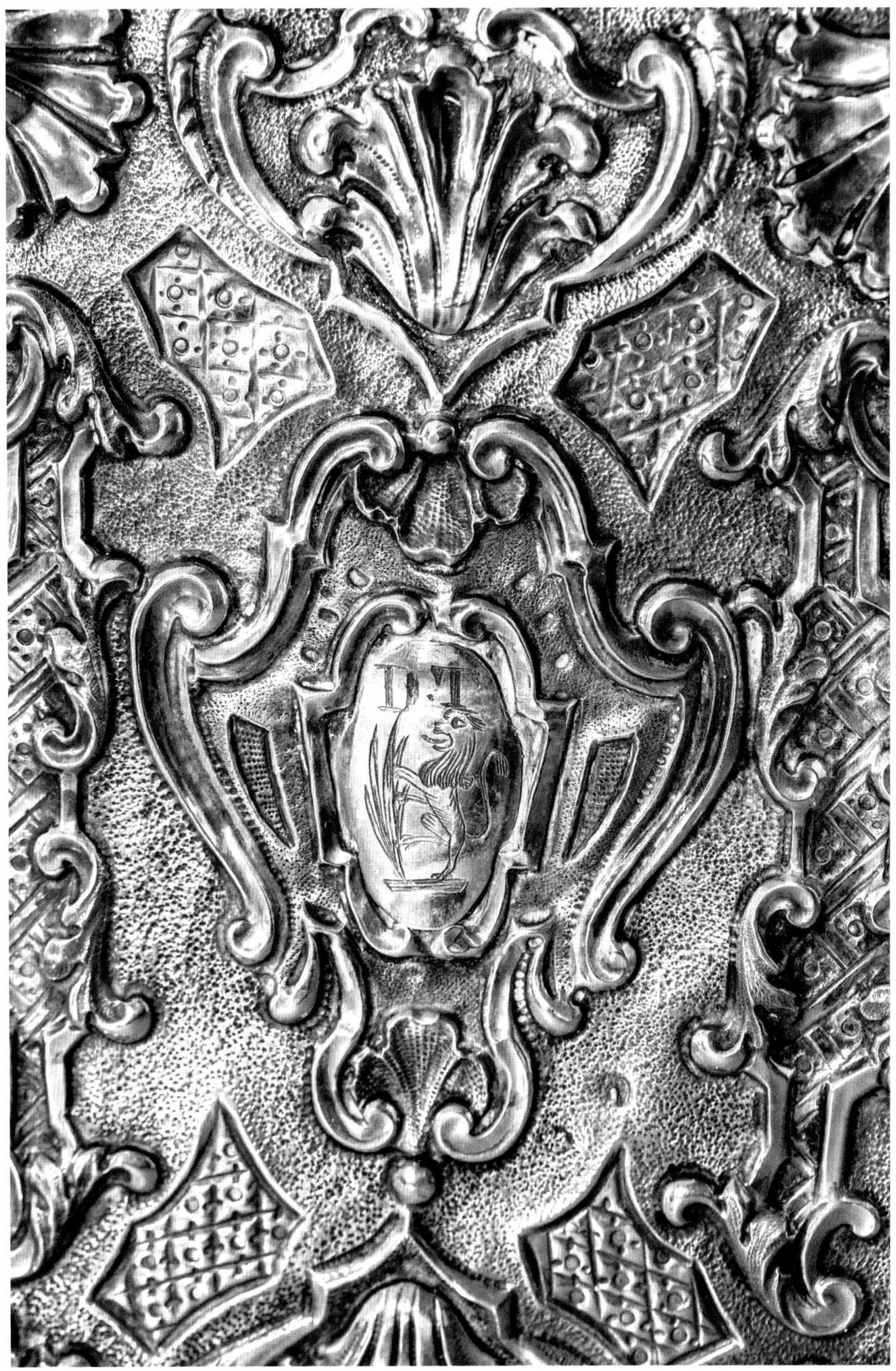
D.T

25. Di Castro *Mappah*

Rome, 1764–1765
Torah binder embroidered with silver thread and frizzled gold thread, brocaded damask, silk
56.7 × 184 cm
Museo Ebraico di Roma, Rome
Inv. 835 C (1942)

Bibl.: Davanzo, Poli, Melasecchi and Spagnoletto, 2016, pp. 222–223.

This *mappah* is composed of different pieces of fabric, which were attached to a silk support, evidence of a recent reuse of the embroidery. The side sections in brocaded, polychrome silk damask are an example of the traditional practice of reusing material to make liturgical objects for the synagogue. At the center of the *mappah* is the heraldic emblem of the Di Castro family, a palm tree, and their motto: "The righteous shall flourish like the palm tree" (Psalm 92:13).

SR

26. Della Torre *Mappah*

Rome, 1730–1731
Torah binder, velvet and gold thread, lampas
62 × 250 cm
Museo Ebraico di Roma, Rome
Inv. 471 B

Bibl.: Davanzo, Poli, Melasecchi and Spagnoletto 2016, pp. 176–177.

Even the most apparently sumptuous items could be made from different pieces of fabric, which could be combined and repurposed to serve in an entirely new context. The text embroidered on the velvet in gold thread and the embroidered family arms, which feature a tower flanked by two lions rampant, tell us that this *mappah* from the Museo Ebraico in Rome was donated by the Della Torre family to the Scola Tempio in 1730. To achieve the desired length, two irregular pieces of seventeenth-century silk lampas – featuring a pattern of minuscule flowers, pine cones and leaves on a gold background that is commonly found in formal clothing – were sewn to the velvet cloth. In spite of this, the overall effect is one of great elegance and opulence. After all, the misery and deprivations of the ghetto could not be allowed to impinge on the lavishness of the synagogues and their furnishings, or undermine the rituals and prayers, be they part of everyday worship or the solemnities of the Shabbat or feast days. As can be seen in the inscriptions, or texts embroidered on the fabric items, every silver or silk object was donated by a particular family.

AC

27. Zevi *Mappah*

Rome, 1732
Torah binder, grosgrain taffeta with silver thread, lampas
61 × 225 cm
Museo Ebraico di Roma, Rome
Inv. 469 B

Bibl.: Davanzo, Poli, Melasecchi and Spagnoletto, 2016, pp. 177–178.

Jewish tradition requires the active involvement of the community's female members in the making of liturgical objects in honor of the Lord and his Law. The production process must follow the instructions given in the Bible, which specify the design and materials to be used, including richly colored yarns and fabrics, gold thread and precious stones.
According to the Hebrew wording embroidered in silver thread to each side of the arms of the Zevi family (a crowned lion supporting a column surmounted by a crescent), this *mappah* was donated by Mordekhai and Moshe Zevi to the Scola Tempio on December 11, 1732.

SR

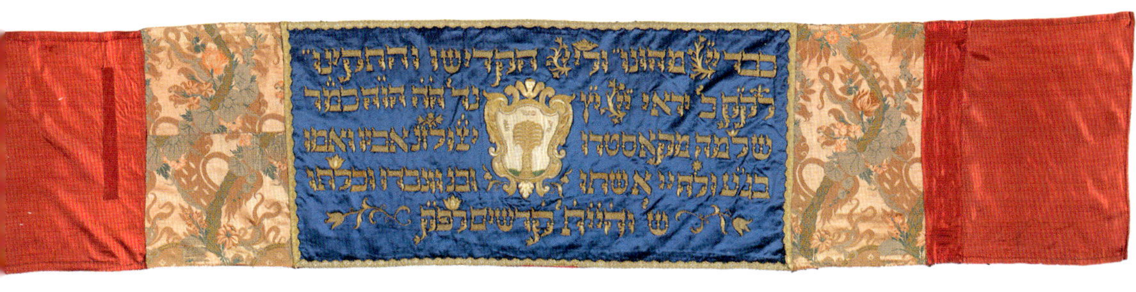

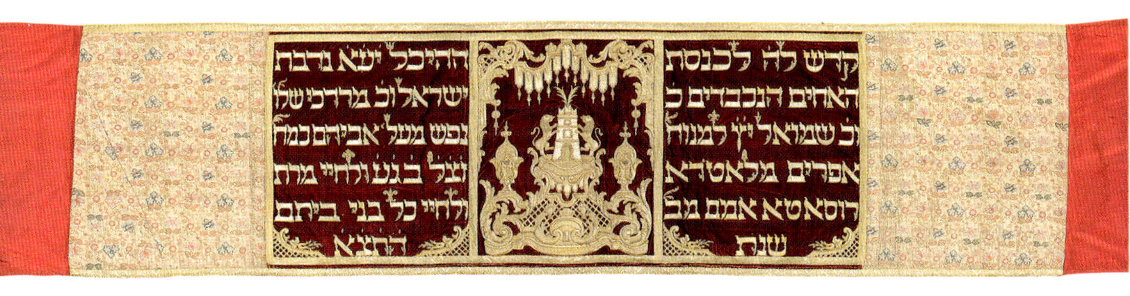
קדש לה׳ לכנסת
האחים הנכבדים כ
כ שמואל יצ״ו למנוח
אפרים מלאטרא
רוסאטא אמם מב
שנת
ההיכל יע״א מרבת
ישראל וכ מרדכי של
נפש מעל׳ אביהם כמה
נצ״ל בג״ע ולחיי מרת
לחיי כל בני ביתם
התצ״א

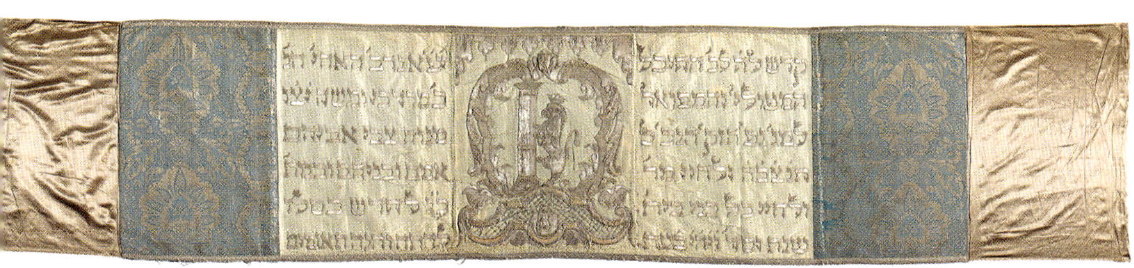

28. Leonardo Micheli, Sketch for temporary decoration

Mantua, 1771
Watercolor drawing on paper
Archivio della Comunità Ebraica di Mantova, Mantua
filza 162, *cart.* 01

This sketch by Leonardo Micheli, exhibited to the public for the first time, was probably produced on the occasion of the first visit to Mantua in 1771 by the Hapsburg archduke Ferdinand Karl. In decorations such as these we can read the eagerness of the city authorities to welcome the visiting sovereign – as he toured his domains – with great ceremony, setting out temporary constructions, decorations and other paraphernalia along his route through the city. The Jewish community was also involved, being charged with providing suitable decorations for their designated area of the city.

This preparatory sketch depicts a series of airy, ornamented arcades with a series of niches housing personifications of the rivers. Dominating the center of the image are the portraits of the rulers of the Hapsburg domains, Joseph II and Maria Theresa. Below these are portraits of the archduke and his young consort, surrounded by personifications of the virtues of "good government."

AC

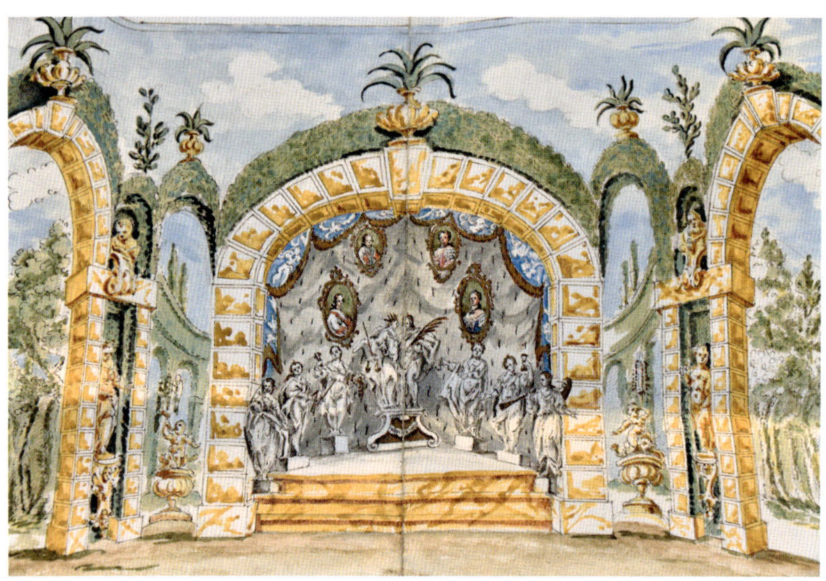

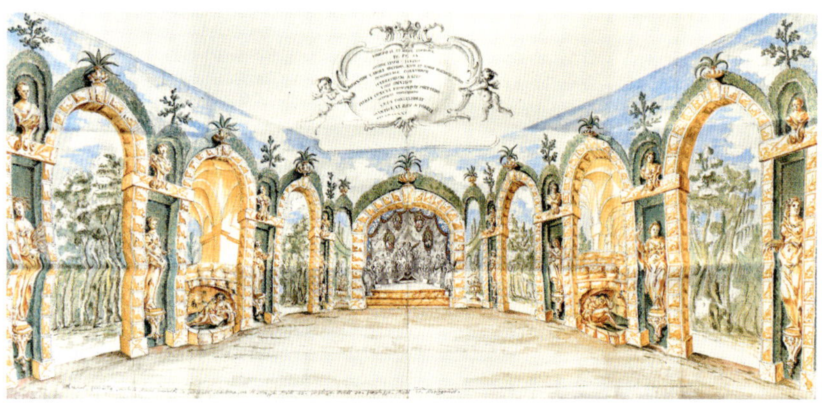

29. Medical diploma of Moyses Tilche

Padua, 1687
Manuscript, watercolor and gilt on parchment
24 × 17.5 cm
Gross Family Collection, Tel Aviv
Inv. IT.012.006

A lavishly illustrated and decorated medical diploma, this manuscript is one of a small number of such diplomas apparently by the same hand produced around this period. Such diplomas awarded to Jews are a great rarity. This one contains a portrait of the recipient, Moyses Tilche, as well as small portraits of Aristotle and Socrates. The pages are in an exquisite gold tooled leather binding with the original seal of the university largely intact. The only difference between the diploma for Jewish and non-Jewish students was the use of the term "*Anno Domini*" ("the year of our lord") for the Christians and the absence of that term for the Jews.

AC

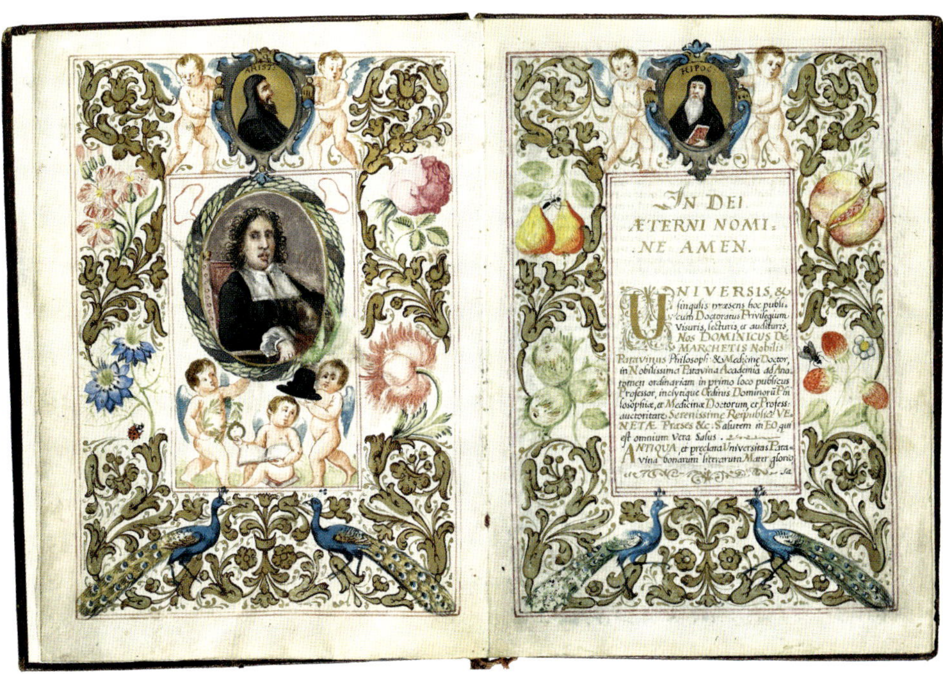

30. ***Manifesto by Sarra Copia Sullam, Jew In which she refutes and condemns the position denying the immortality of the soul fallaciously attributed to her by BALDASSARE BONIFACCIO***

Venice, 1621
Print on paper
195 × 150 × 12 cm
Fondazione Musei Civici di Venezia, Museo Correr Library, Venice
Inv. OP.CICOGNA 0752.12.2

Sara (or Sarra) Copio was born into one of the most important and wealthy Jewish families in Venice sometime around 1590. She would marry Jacob Sullam, taking his surname. A brilliant woman of great intelligence, she immersed herself in the study of literature, music, history, philosophy, astrology and ancient letters, also under the tutorship of Leone da Modena. Her home in the Venice ghetto became a literary salon, attracting numerous contemporary intellectuals, including a number of Christians. One of these was the Catholic writer and poet Baldassarre Bonifacio.
Sara maintained an intense correspondence with the Genoese intellectual Ansaldo Cebà, the author of the epic poem *La Reina Esther*, although of this exchange only Cebà's letters have survived, including his attempts to convince Sara to convert to Christianity.
A similar attempt was made, to no avail, by Baldassarre Bonifacio, who addressed Sara Copio Sullam directly in his 1621 text *Dell'immortalità dell'anima* ["On the immortality of the soul"]. Sullam's steadfast response came in the form of her celebrated Manifesto, in which she rejects the charge of impiety and asserts her faith in the immortality of the soul. Other than the Manifesto and a few poems, little remains of Sara Copio Sullam's writing, but she remains a key figure in Italian Jewish history.

SR

MANIFESTO
DI
SARRA COPIA
SVLAM HEBREA.
Nel quale è da lei riprouata, e deteſtata l'opinione negante l'Immortalità dell'Anima, falſamente attribuitale dal
SIG. BALDASSARE BONIFACCIO.
Con Licenza de'Superiori.

IN VENETIA, MDCXXI.
Appreſſo Antonio Pinelli.

A chi legge.

Oßo creder, benigni Lettori, che ſia per parerui coſa ſtrana, che il mio Nome non affatto ignoto in queſta Città, ne fuori, compariſca la prima volta alle ſtampe in materia aßai diuerſa da quella, che poteua forſe eſſer aſpettata dalla mia penna; mà l'altrui, o ſia ſtata malignità, ò ſimplicità, ò traſcuratezza, mi hà neceſſitata a quello, a che non ero per mouermi facilmente per qual ſi voglia occaſione, ancorche io mi ritroui qualche fatica da poter mandar alla luce, la quale, ſe io non fallo, potrebbe dal mondo eßer più volentieri veduta, e forſe più gradita di queſta; Dico che ſono ſtata aſtretta a comporre, e dar fuori frettoloſamente queſta breue ſcrittura, non con fine, ò penſiero alcuno di procacciarmi gloria, ma ſolo per defendermi da vna falſa calunnia datami dal Sig. Baldaſſarre Bonifaccio, il quale, in vn ſuo diſcorſo ſtampato vltimamente dell' Jmmortalità dell' Anima, dice affirmatiuamente che io nego queſt'infallibile verità, che l'Anima humana ſia immortale: coſa tanto lontana dalla mia opinione, quanto è lontano da ogni ſua ſcienza il poter ſapere l'interno de cuori; onde non douete prometterui nouità di penſieri, ne copia de dottrina;
A 2 prima

prima perche il mio fonte ne è scarso, massime hora che mi è molestissima la fatica degli studij, per esser a pena risorta da vna graue infirmità, che lungamente mi hà tenuta oppressa con pericolo di morte, dalla quale non per altro credo che la Diuina bontà sia sia compiaciuta preseruarmi, che perche io potessi liberar la mia fama da vna si graue macchia, che mi si era preparata; poiche la mia morte non haurebbe punto ritenuto l'Auersario dall'ambitiosa risolutione, per laquale quasi due anni si è affaticato: Poi perche non conueniua che io interponessi dilatione di tempo, ne longhe dicerie a ributtar l'offesa, per lo pericolo del danno che poteua risultarmene. E finalmente, perche il fatto stesso non richiedeua altra dottrina, che la sinceratione dell'animo mio, e di quel religioso affetto, che io deuo a Dio, & alla legge, che egli mi hà data, potendo nel resto ogni giudicioso intelletto per se stesso conoscere, in leggendo quel libro, quanto spropositamente l'Autore vada disfidando altri in cosa, alla quale a nessuno ò Hebreo, ò Christiano è lecito di contradire; Piacciaui dunque cortesissimi Lettori, di veder per semplice curiosità, questa mia necessaria difesa, e come giusti, e benigni giudici, assoluendo chi falsamente viene accusato, rimouete dalla vostra presenza il falso accusatore, e viuete lieti.

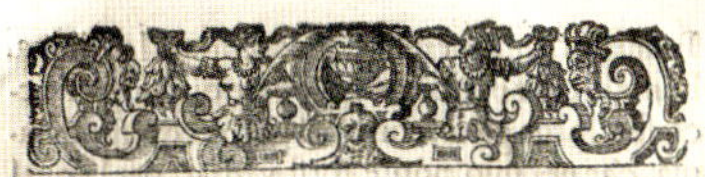

DEDICATIONE
Dell'Opera
AL SIGNOR SIMON COPIA suo dilettissimo Genitore.

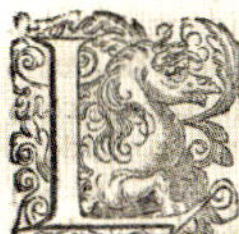

A Dedicatione di questa mia breue, ma necessaria fatica, non poteua conueneuolmente esser diretta, se non a chi hà fatto passaggio da questa mortal vita, accioche gl'effetti stessi corrispondessero a quel che nell'opera affermo di credere indubitatamente l'essere immortale dell'Anime; Onde a tè, Anima dilettissima, che desti l'essere a quel caro composto, da cui fui generata in questo mondo: a te dico mio suisceratissimo Genitore, che benche spogliato del caduco velo tra spirti viuenti dimori, e dimorerai in eterno, hò voluto io far questo picciolo dono;

Pri-

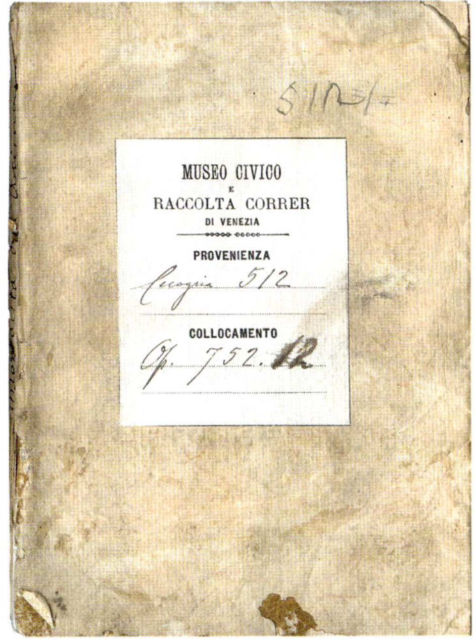

31. *Sukkah* decoration plaque

Engraved by Francesco Grisellini
Designed by Avraham Calimani
Venice, c. 1750
Engraving and watercolor on paper
35 × 46.5 cm
Gross Family Collection Trust, Tel Aviv
Inv. 038.011.008

This engraved sheet is perhaps one of the earliest printed examples extant of *sukkah* decoration, from the middle of the eighteenth century. The sheet was engraved in a baroque style by Francesco Grisellini (1717–1787), whose name is signed in Hebrew on the plate, and was then hand colored. Grisellini engraved images for a number of Jewish books and single sheets in the 1740s, including an Esther scroll and pages with biblical images.

The decoration sheet, designed by Avraham Calimani, encloses depictions of various events relating to the festival of Sukkot, as well as the figures of Moses and Aaron. Decorations for the *sukkah* were and are a regular feature of the Sukkot holiday.

The greatest number of surviving older examples is from Italy, both hand painted and printed. The image is dominated by an inscription from the book of Psalms (76:11): "Surely the wrath of man will give you thanks; the remnant of your furor will keep your feast."

AC

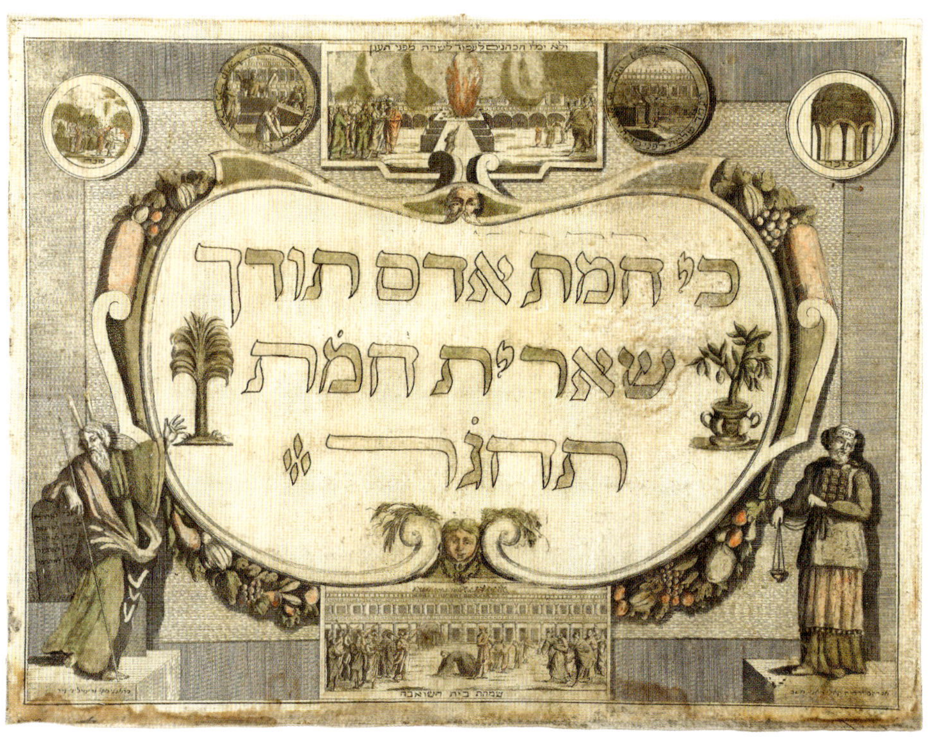

32. *Portrait of Rabbi Abraham Eliezer ha-Levi*

Trieste, early nineteenth century
Oil on canvas
55 × 41.5 cm
Alberto Di Castro Collection, Rome

A turbaned male figure, a conspicuous ring with a red stone on his little finger, holds a book with partially legible inscriptions in Hebrew on the spine and cover. It is the text on the cover that reveals the identity of the subject: "[Overseer of the] Torah and the divine service for the faithful among the chosen people/ Abraham Eliezer ha-Levi." On the spine, in golden Hebrew script, is written, "Grace for Abraham."
The figure in the portrait can only be rabbi Abraham Eliezer ha-Levi (Jerusalem, 1758 – Trieste, 1825). Abraham's grandfather, Netanel, was head of the rabbinical court of Modena and Padua at the start of the 18th century. His father, Zevi ben Netanel ha-Levi, moved to Palestine, where Abraham was born. In his youth, Abraham studied with rabbi Haiyym Yosef David Azulai, who was also known as "Hida." Having been sent to Italy to collect donations for religious institutions, he settled in Livorno, and in 1800, following the death of rabbi Nathan Tedeschi, he was called to take on the roles of leader of the rabbinical court and chief rabbi of Trieste.
His pupil David Luzzatto, also known as Shadal, remembered him as a learned man who fought on various fronts to preserve the traditional rites and orthodoxy of the faith, and who refused to adapt to western fashions, preferring to keep his long beard and cloak.

RS-SDS

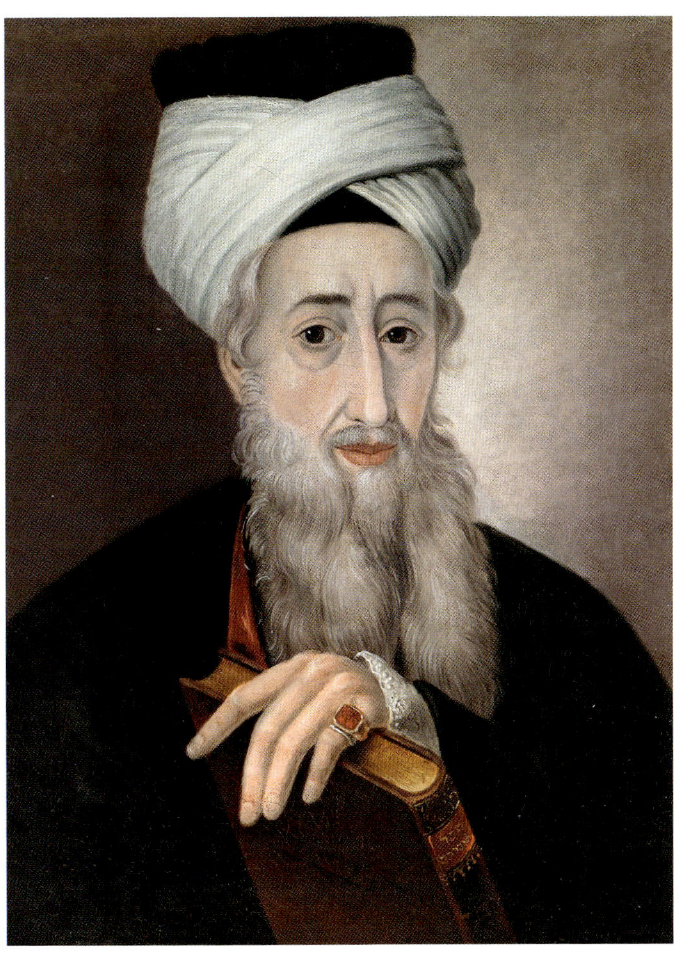

33. *Yad*

Produced in Livorno, 1800–1801
Torah pointer in carved red and gilded engraved metal
17 × 15 cm
Comunità Ebraica di Livorno, Museo Ebraico
Inv. 00554435

In recognition of the regal nature of the Sefer Torah, and to avoid it being touched by the reader, a special item was developed for following the text, a pointer known as a "yad," meaning "hand," from the shape of the part that made contact with the parchment.
Jewish merchants held a monopoly in the trade of coral in Livorno, and it is known that the local community made good use of it, to the point that it is typical of the ritual objects used by the city's Sephardic community.

SR

34. *Yad*

Produced in Livorno, first half of the nineteenth century
Torah pointer in carved red coral
12 × 15 cm
Comunità Ebraica di Livorno, Museo Ebraico
Inv. 00554435

This "yad" is inscribed along its length with a ribbon pattern embellished with small flowers. The end used to help the reader takes the traditional form of a hand, with a pointing index finger and the other fingers closed. At the other end, the handle is capped with an ornament in the form of a vase with flowers.

SR

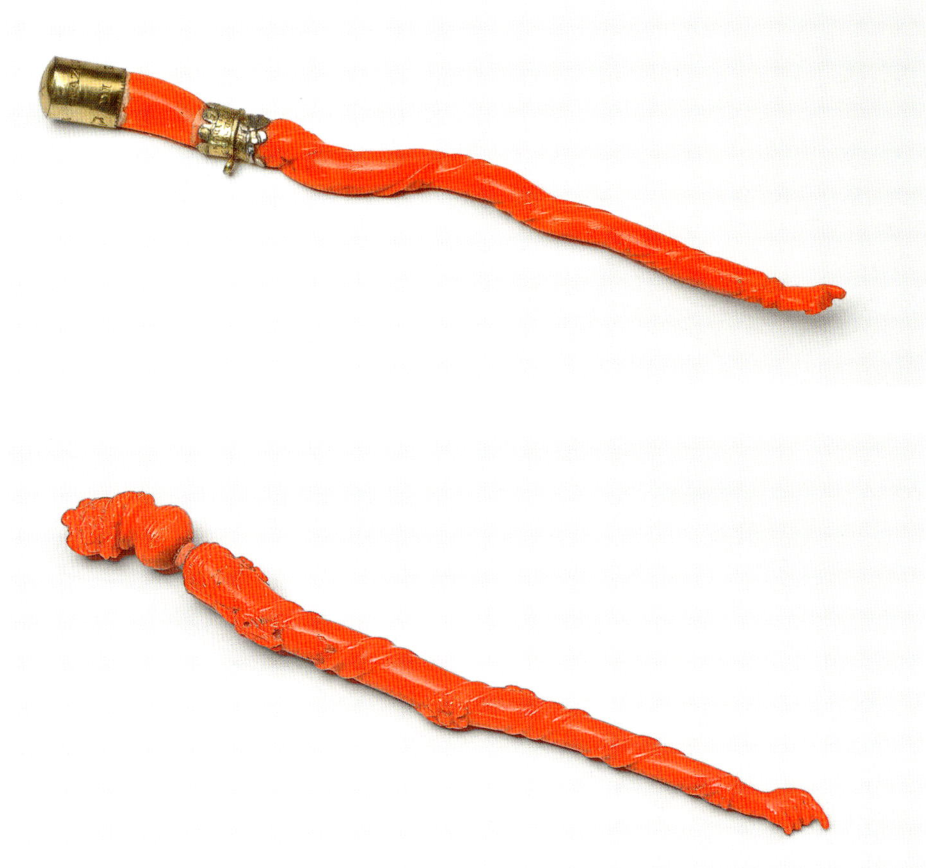

35. Ulvi Liegi,
Interior of the Synagogue in Livorno

Livorno, 1935
Oil on panel
27.5 × 50 cm; with frame 49.5 × 72 cm
Museo Civico "Giovanni Fattori," Livorno
Inv. 1957/1676; 1991/1121

Luigi Moisé Levi (1858–1939) was born in Livorno to a wealthy family, and studied at the Florence Academy of Fine Arts. Profoundly influenced by the Macchiaioli, he began painting under the name of Ulvi Liegi. In this work of 1935, he depicts the interior of the synagogue of Livorno during the morning prayer. The figures of the men with their *tallit* – prayer shawls – can be made out, as can the white and colored marble *tevah* – the pulpit – by Isidoro Baratta, which was inaugurated in 1745 and raised in the nineteenth century. From the original, late sixteenth-century nucleus, the synagogue had undergone constant expansion and embellishment, reflecting the community's growing prosperity. Following the earthquake of 1772, the architect Ignazio Fazzi was commissioned to restore and expand the building and the new space was solemnly inaugurated on September 20, 1789. The building was irreparably damaged by the bombardments of World War II and replaced by the new synagogue, which was inaugurated in 1962.

CFdU

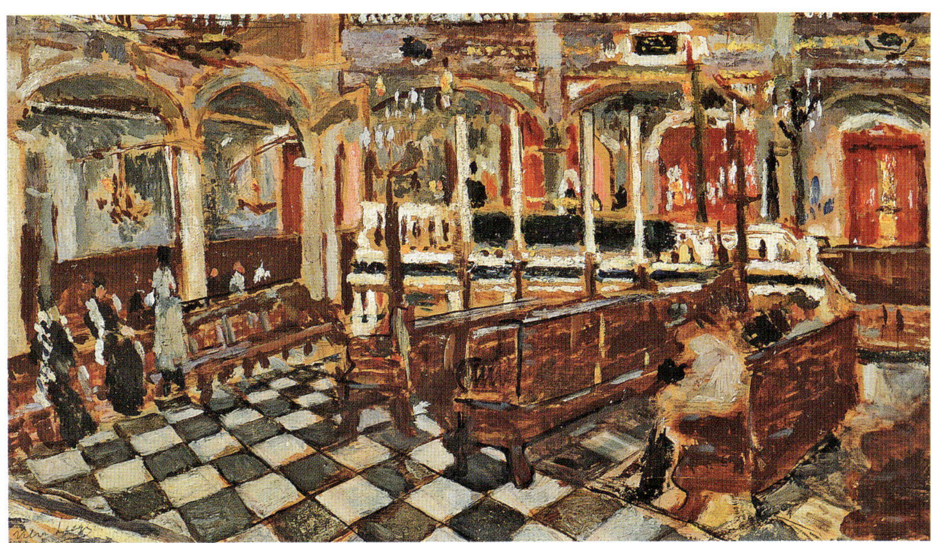

36. *Ketubah*, marriage contract

Livorno, 1803
Groom: Mordechai Di Segni
Bride: Yeosha Recanati
Manuscript on parchment, watercolor
41 × 53 cm
Comunità Ebraica di Livorno, Museo Ebraico

This contract of marriage was produced for the wedding of Mordechai Di Segni and Yeosha Recanati, which took place in Livorno on 1 Kislev 5564 (November 16, 1803). The document is embellished by watercolor decorations, with a sea (a subject rarely portrayed in marriage contracts) ploughed by sailing ships and a horse-drawn carriage with mythological figures.

SR

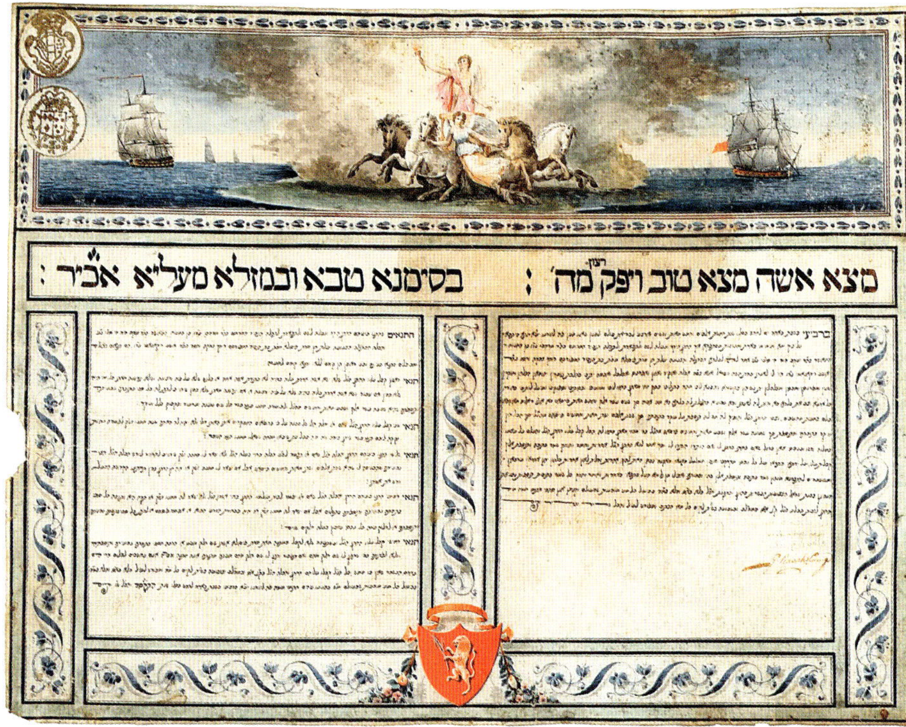
מצא אשה מצא טוב ויפק רצון מה׳ : בסימנא טבא ובמזלא מעליא אכי״ר :

37. *Sampler* in embroidered taffeta

Made by Eva Guttieres Pegna
Livorno, 1805
Silk taffeta embroidered with silk and silver threads
63 × 74 cm
Jewish Museum, Jewish Community of Livorno
Cod. 500189

In Jewish and non-Jewish schools alike, girls and young women would be taught what were deemed to be feminine skills and handicrafts, including needlework and embroidery. This *sampler* was made by Eva Guttieres Pegna on March 6, 1805. The ivory taffeta is embroidered with differently colored silks, using silver thread in satin stitch and stem stitch, and gold thread in long and short stitch. The *sampler* illustrates thirteen biblical scenes. Taking pride of place in the center is Moses showing the Tablets of the Law to the people. Beginning with Adam and Eve, the other scenes follow in sequence form right to left, like Hebrew script.

CFdU

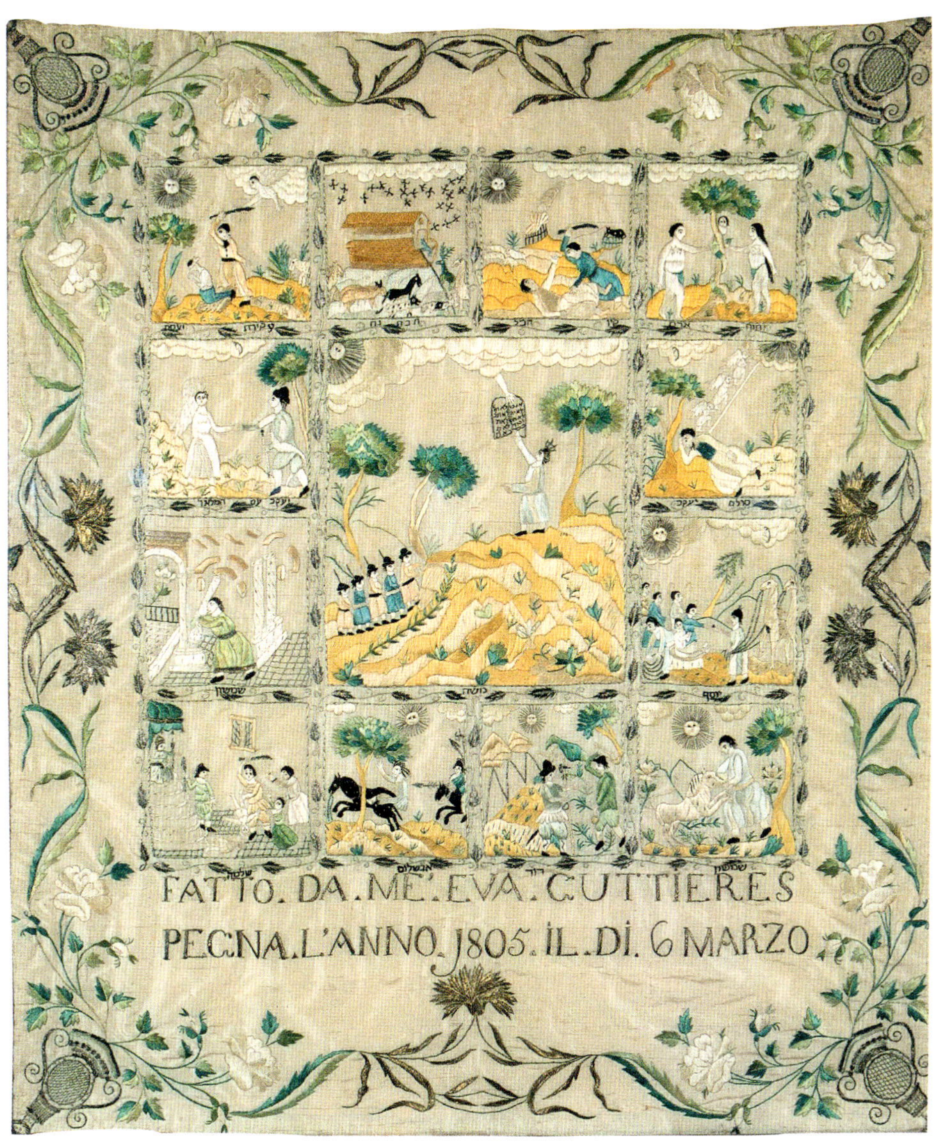

38. Moritz Daniel Oppenheim, *The Kidnapping of Edgardo Mortara*

1862
Oil on canvas
53 × 67 cm; with frame 79 × 93 cm
Private collection

German Jewish painter Moritz Daniel Oppenheim (1800–1882) lived in Frankfurt, Munich, Paris and Rome. Renowned for his representations of Bible stories and scenes of Jewish life, and for his portraits of the new German Jewish bourgeoisie, he was supported by the Rothschilds. The *Kidnapping of Edgardo Mortara* (1862), lost for around 150 years, was rediscovered in 2013 and is being exhibited to the public for the first time. The painting depicts Edgardo surrounded by a Franciscan, a Jesuit and a nun, who in reality were not the figures in attendance when the child was abducted on June 23, 1858. To the right are the women of the family, broken-hearted, while his father is leaning towards him as if out of a desire to protect him. There is a clear intention to highlight the clash between the Jewish identity of the family – represented by Edgardo's *tallit katan* (the fringed garment worn under his clothes), his father's *kippah* (skullcap) and the *mezuzah* (small box placed at the entrance to Jewish houses, containing a parchment with Deut. 6: 4-9 and 11: 13-21) – and the overwhelming power of the Church.

CFdU

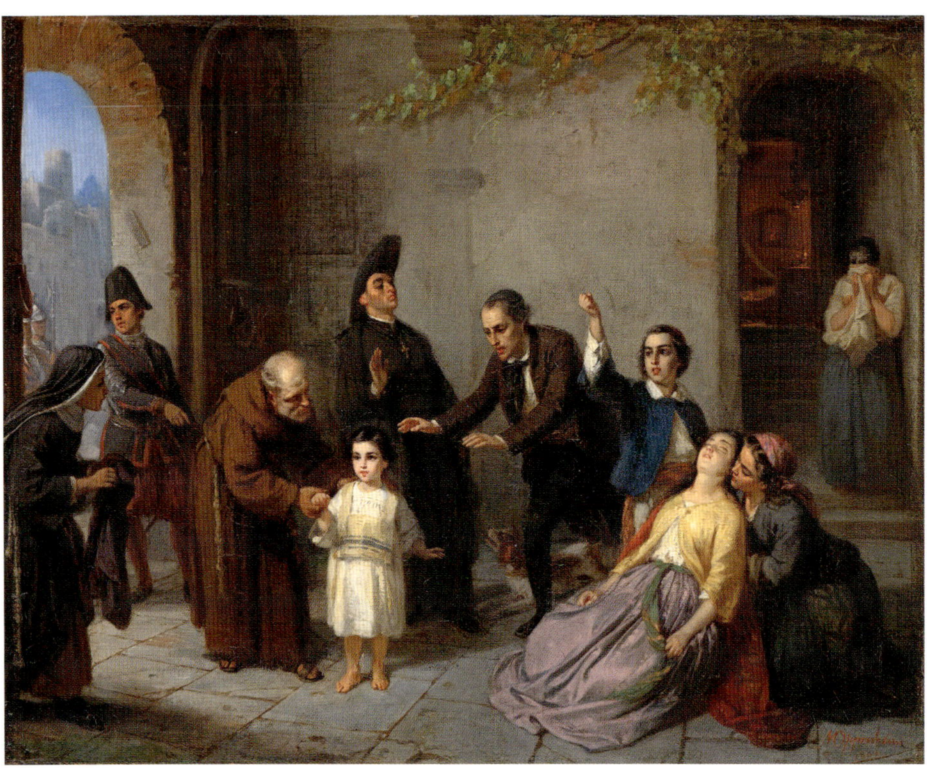

39. *Rome and public opinion in Europe regarding the Mortara affair. Records, documents, confutations. / Canonical and Natural Law, for Abbé Delacouture, former professor of theology*

Turin, Unione Tipografico-Editrice, 1859
Print on paper
Alberto Mortara Family Archive

This volume collects a series of documents on the Mortara affair, edited by the journalist David Rabbeno, although his name does not appear in the text (essay Mortara, p. 186). As testament to the international notoriety the case achieved, he includes the Italian translation of a pamphlet by the abbot André Vincent Delacouture (known in Italy for his translation of Manzoni's *Observations on Catholic Ethics*), published in France in 1858 with the title *Le Droit canon et le Droit naturel dans l'affaire Mortara* (Dentu, Paris). Delacouture, who had already written on the subject in three articles in the prestigious *Journal des Débats* (18, 20 and 29 October 1858), criticized the kidnapping of Edgardo, using erudite theological arguments to defend the principles of natural law (of the family) over those of canonical law.

CFdU

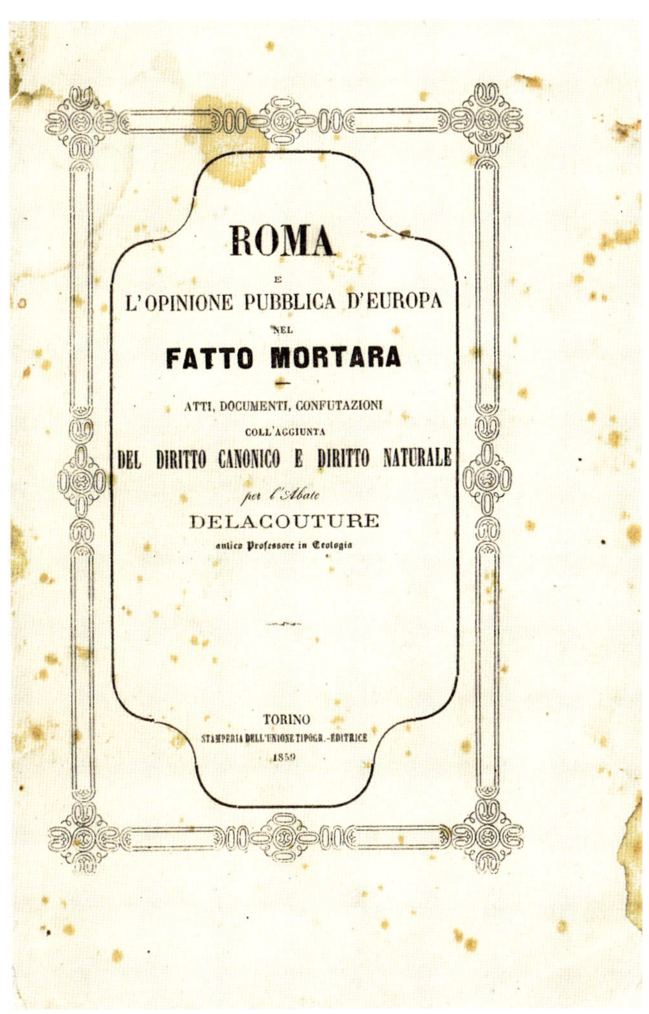

ROMA
E
L'OPINIONE PUBBLICA D'EUROPA
NEL
FATTO MORTARA
ATTI, DOCUMENTI, CONFUTAZIONI
COLL'AGGIUNTA
DEL DIRITTO CANONICO E DIRITTO NATURALE
per l'Abate
DELACOUTURE
antico Professore in Teologia

TORINO
STAMPERIA DELL'UNIONE TIPOGR.-EDITRICE
1859

40. Samuele Smiles, *He who helps himself, God shall help (Self-Help), or A history of those men who from nothing were able to raise themselves to the highest ranks in all branches of human activity*, edited by Cesare Donati

Milan, Fratelli Treves editori, 1890 (23rd ed.)
Print on paper
Alberto Mortara Family Archive

Samuel Smiles (1812–1904) was a Scottish author best known for his instructional volume *Self-Help*, which began as a collection of lectures on the subject of self-education and improvement of one's social, moral and economic conditions. The Italian translation was first published in 1865, with numerous editions following well into the twentieth century. This volume was gifted by Edgardo Mortara to his niece and nephews, as evidenced by the dedication dated "Modena, 9/7, 1891": "To my dearest niece and nephews, Vittorio, Margherita and Roberto – your devoted uncle Pio Edgardo." This gift can be seen as an evidence that as an adult Edgardo had managed to reestablish cordial relations with his family, in spite of the difference of religion and the many years of separation.

CFdU

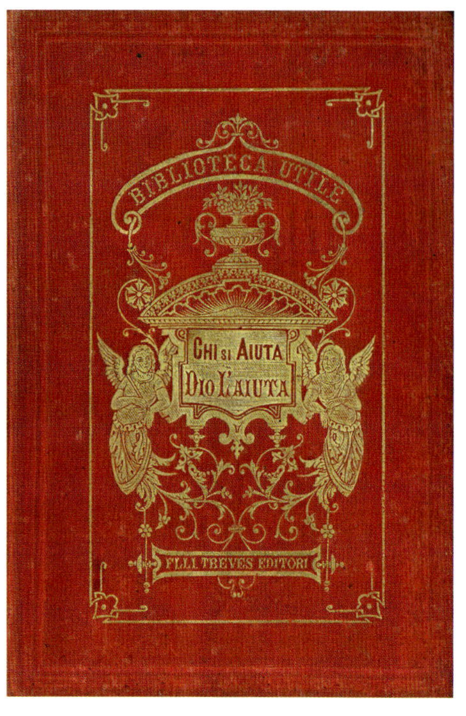

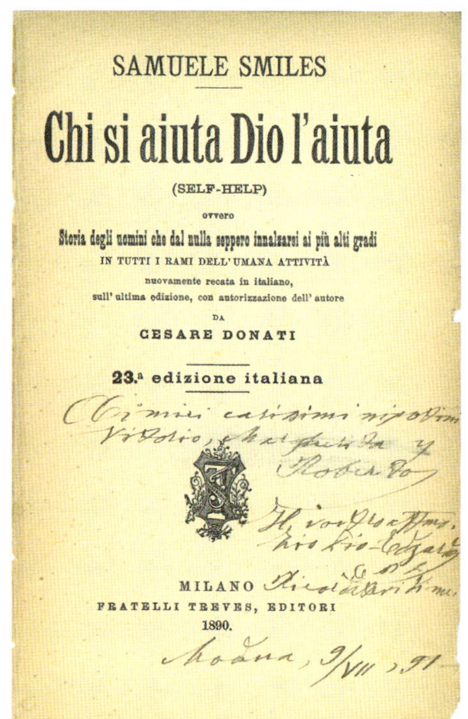
SAMUELE SMILES

Chi si aiuta Dio l'aiuta

(SELF-HELP)

ovvero

Storia degli uomini che dal nulla seppero innalzarsi ai più alti gradi
IN TUTTI I RAMI DELL'UMANA ATTIVITÀ

nuovamente recata in italiano,
sull'ultima edizione, con autorizzazione dell'autore

DA

CESARE DONATI

23.ª edizione italiana

MILANO
FRATELLI TREVES, EDITORI
1890.

41. Edict of the Cispadane Republic. Committee of the provisional Government of Modena and Reggio Emilia

Modena, April 6, 1797
In Modena for the heirs of Bartolomeo Soliani
Print on paper
44 × 31.5 cm
Gianfranco Moscati Collection, MEIS (National Museum of Italian Judaism and the Shoah), Ferrara

Founded in 1796, the Cispadane Republic comprised the cities of Bologna, Ferrara, Modena and Reggio Emilia, which had been liberated by the French army under the leadership of General Napoleon Bonaparte. With the birth of the Republic, the institution of the ghetto ceased and Jewish citizens acquired equal rights under the provisions set out in the constitution in 1797.

SR

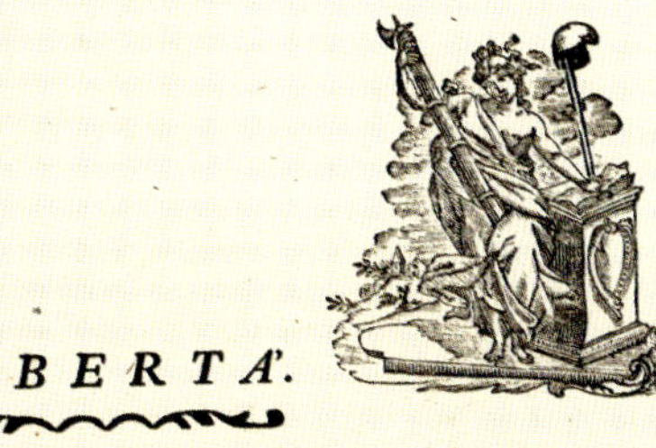

LIBERTA'. *EGUAGLIANZA.*

Modena 6. Aprile 1797., Anno I. della Repubblica Ciſpadana una, ed indiviſibile.

IL COMITATO DI GOVERNO PROVVISORIO
DI MODENA E REGGIO.

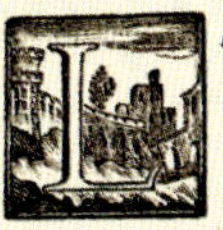

LA Coſtituzione Ciſpadana ſanzionata dal Popolo conſidera tutti gli Uomini viventi in Società come Fratelli, e preſcrive il riſpetto delle Proprietà, e delle Perſone, qualunque ſia il loro ſiſtema Religioſo. Rendendo giuſtizia alla Religione Cattolica ſegue in ciò i Precetti del ſuo Divino Autore, il quale fa riſplendere ſopra tutti lo ſteſſo Sole; quindi il Comitato di Governo ſi luſinga che queſto bravo Popolo ſaprà riſpingere qualunque principio d'intolleranza verſo la Nazione Ebrea, e ne vedrà con indifferenza gl' Individui curare i proprj Affari nelle diverſe parti della Città in quei pochi Giorni, che una volta ſi vedevano rinchiuſi entro certi Recinti. Già il Governo fino dal principio della noſtra Rigenerazione aveva abolite le Diſpoſizioni barbare ed inſane del così detto Codice Eſtenſe contro gli Ebrei. Sapranno eſſi contenerſi entro i limiti del dovere: Eſſi poſſono reclamare un diritto loro accordato dalla Coſtituzione.

VALDRIGHI Preſidente.
SALVIOLI.

NICCOLÒ BERNARBONI SEGRETARIO DEL COMITATO.

In MODENA, per gli Eredi di Bartolomeo Soliani.

42. Gabriele Castagnola,
King Charles Albert Signs the Emancipation of the Jews

1849
Print on paper
72 × 56 cm
Museo d'Arte e Storia Antica Ebraica, Casale Monferrato
Inv. 200

Charles Albert of Savoy (1798–1849) became King of Sardinia in 1831. A figure whose contribution is difficult to interpret, his name is forever linked to the *Statuto Albertino*, the constitution he conceded to the Kingdom, under popular pressure, on 4 March 1848. On March 23, 1849, following defeat at Novara, he abdicated in favor of his son, Victor Emanuel, and retired to Portugal.

In this etching by Gabriele Castagnola, the king is depicted standing with one hand resting on his sword hilt and the other on a document entitled *Diritti civili e politici agl'Israeliti il 29 marzo e il 19 giugno 1848* (Civil and political rights to the Israelites, March 29 and June 19, 1848), as though he has just signed it. The caption reads, "*Carlo Alberto ex Re di Sardegna, deceduto in Oporto li 28 Luglio 1849 ore 3 ¼ p.*" (Charles Albert, former King of Sardinia, deceased in Porto, July 28, 1849 at the hour of three and a quarter pm). The tone of the print is clearly celebratory, with the king presented as the liberator of the Jews. In truth, as can be discerned from the parliamentary debates of the time, Jewish emancipation was the product of a series of less than consistent measures, rather than a planned initiative on the part of the king.

CFdU

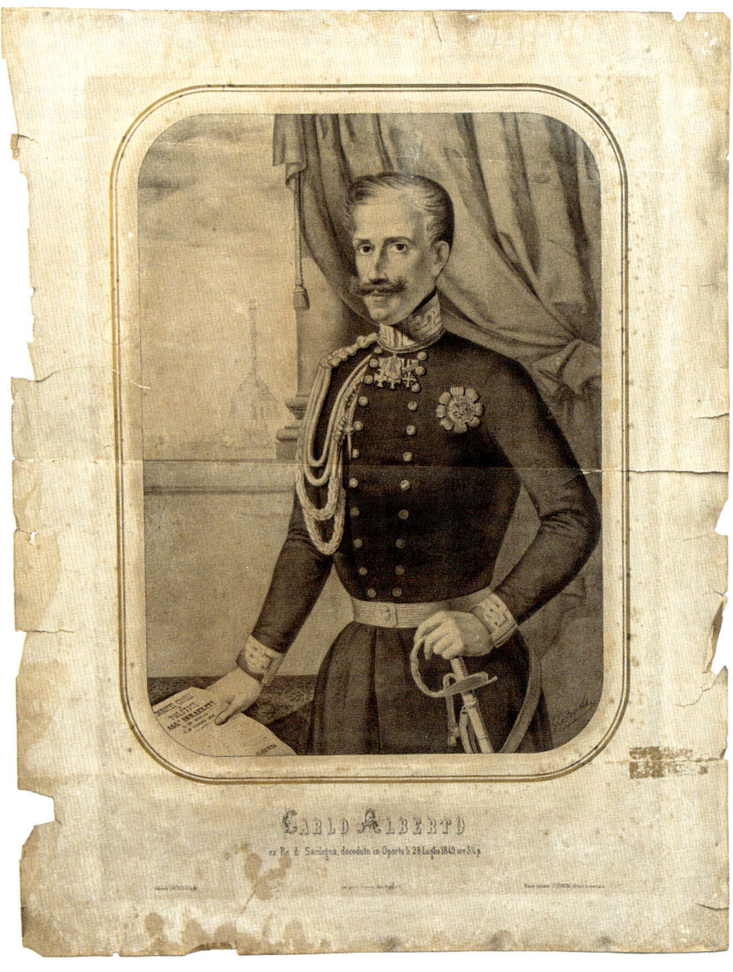

43. E.F. Sotteri, *Salomone Olper*

Second half of the nineteenth century
Print on paper
54 × 40 cm
Museo d'Arte e Storia Antica Ebraica,
Casale Monferrato
Inv. 102

This print is a portrait of Samuele Salomone Olper (1811–1877). The text at the bottom reads, "*Questi è / S. Salomone Olper / di Venezia / Rabbino Maggiore / fatto effigiare / Dai Giovani Israeliti Casalesi / alle sue virtù / Affezionatissimi*" (This is Chief Rabbi of Venice S. Salomone Olper, portrayed at the behest of the young Israelites of Casale, in admiration of his virtues). Olper studied at the Rabbinical College in Padua, where he also graduated from the university. Aligned with the ideals of Giuseppe Mazzini, he was a prominent figure in the Venice uprising of 1848–1849, becoming Secretary to the provisional government and being elected to the Assembly of Deputies for the Province of Venice, before being sent by Manin on a diplomatic mission to the Roman Republic. He was Chief Rabbi of Florence (1849–1853), of Casale (1857–1859) and, finally, of Turin, where he remained until his death. Here, he is portrayed without a head covering, which is not unusual for the time.
In addition to his services to his homeland, Olper is not remembered only as a patriot, but also for the reforms of worship he proposed, which provoked animated debate during the 1860s and fed into the discussion on whether to convene a national rabbinical council.

CFdU

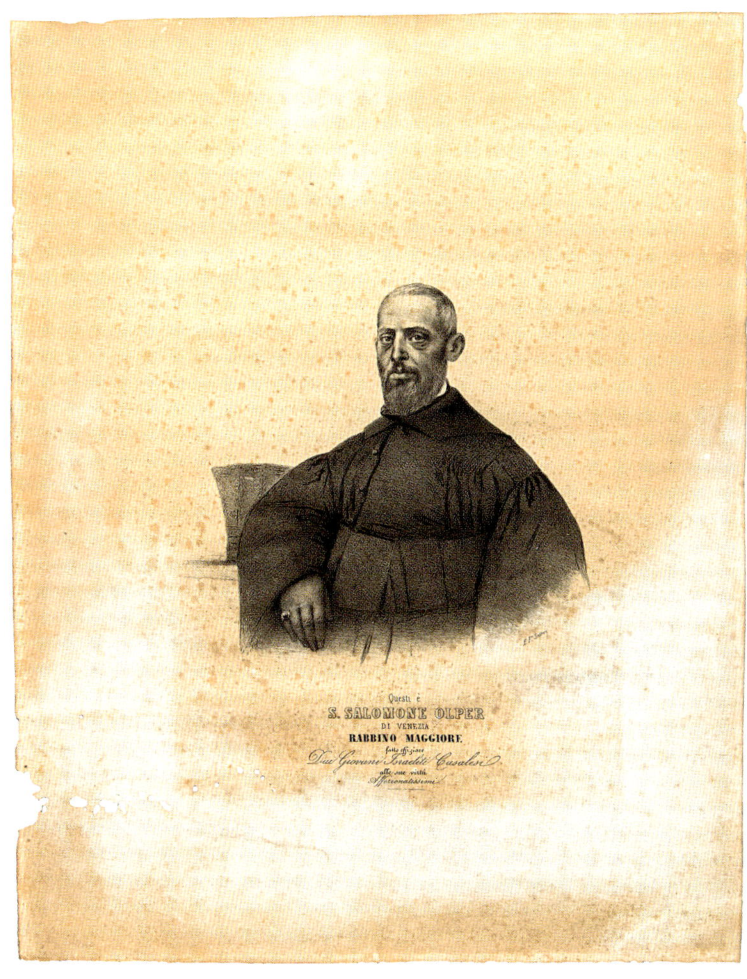

44. Royal Decree of March 29, 1848, granting full civil rights to all Israelites

Turin, 1848
Print on paper
21.5 × 31 cm
Archivio di Stato di Torino, Turin
Inv. Corte, Materie Ecclesiastiche, cat. 37, Ebrei, *mazzo* 10

Royal Decree no. 688 of March 29, 1848 is usually remembered as the document that conferred full equality in the eyes of the law to the Jews of Piedmont. In truth, it only granted them civil rights, giving rise to a hybrid legal status that was difficult either to manage or to justify. The document, signed by Charles Albert at his headquarters in Voghera (the war with Austria being in full swing) reads as follows: "*Gli Israeliti regnicoli godranno dalla data del presente di tutti i diritti civili e della facoltà di conseguire i gradi accademici, nulla innovato quanto all'esercizio del loro culto, ed alle scuole da essi dirette*" (The Israelites of the realm shall, from the present date, enjoy all civil rights and the faculty to attain academic qualifications, there being no change with regard to the exercise of their religion or to the schools directed by them). It would be another three months before full equality was reached: on June 19, the Senate approved Decree no. 735, known as the "Sineo Law," which stated, "*La differenza di culto non forma eccezione al godimento dei diritti civili e politici, ed all'ammissibilità alle cariche civili e militari*" (Difference of religion is not an impediment to the enjoyment of civil and political rights, or to admission to civil or military posts).

CFdU

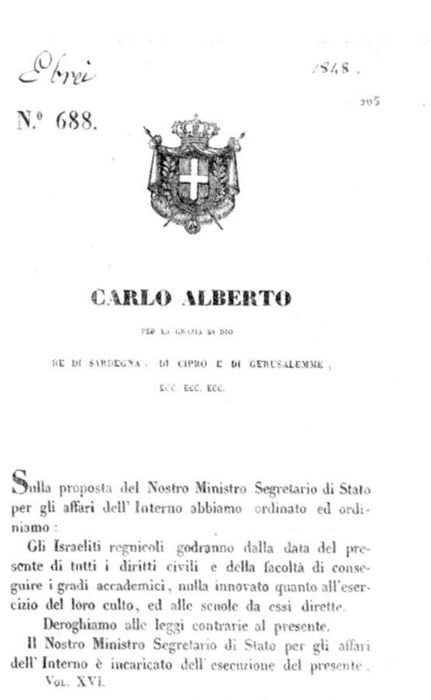

Ebrei 1848.

205

N.° 688.

CARLO ALBERTO

PER LA GRAZIA DI DIO

RE DI SARDEGNA, DI CIPRO E DI GERUSALEMME,

ECC. ECC. ECC.

Sulla proposta del Nostro Ministro Segretario di Stato per gli affari dell'Interno abbiamo ordinato ed ordiniamo:

Gli Israeliti regnicoli godranno dalla data del presente di tutti i diritti civili e della facoltà di conseguire i gradi accademici, nulla innovato quanto all'esercizio del loro culto, ed alle scuole da essi dirette.

Deroghiamo alle leggi contrarie al presente.

Il Nostro Ministro Segretario di Stato per gli affari dell'Interno è incaricato dell'esecuzione del presente,

Vol. XVI.

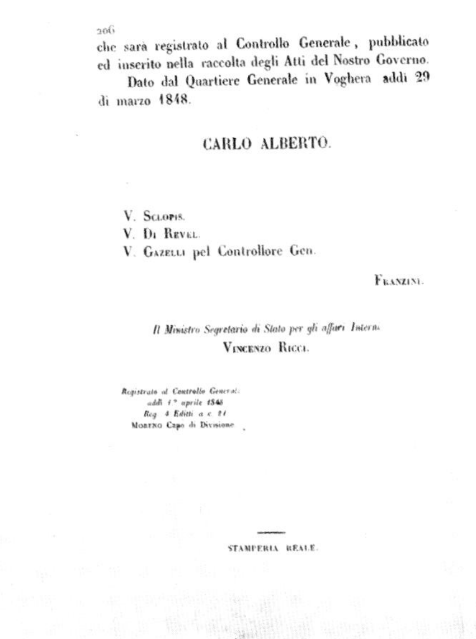

206

che sarà registrato al Controllo Generale, pubblicato ed inserito nella raccolta degli Atti del Nostro Governo.

Dato dal Quartiere Generale in Voghera addì 29 di marzo 1848.

CARLO ALBERTO.

V. Sclopis.
V. Di Revel.
V. Gazelli pel Controllore Gen.

Franzini.

Il Ministro Segretario di Stato per gli affari Interni
Vincenzo Ricci.

Registrato al Controllo General
addì 1° aprile 1848
Reg. 4 Editti a c. 21
Moreno Capo di Divisione

STAMPERIA REALE.

45. Giovanni Fattori, *The Battle of the Volturno*

1899–1900
Oil on canvas
59 × 100 cm; with frame 88 × 130 × 4 cm
Gallery of Modern Art in Palazzo Pitti,
Uffizi Gallery, Florence
Inv. 00158798

Giovanni Fattori (Livorno, 1825 – Florence, 1908) was one of the key figures in the group of technically innovative painters and patriots known as the Macchiaioli. He was the author of numerous military scenes, starting with his canvas of the *Battle of Magenta* – which was commissioned by the provisional government of Tuscany and which he finished in 1862 – but the majority of his work is concerned with depictions of rural landscapes. *The Battle of the Volturno* was painted in 1899–1900 and it is based on the first-hand account given by Gustavo Uzielli. A patron of the Macchiaioli and a friend of Fattori, Uzielli (1839–1911) had fought in the battle itself – a decisive turning point in Garibaldi's Expedition of the Thousand – and is portrayed on the left side of the canvas, legs spread, loading the canon under the arch of the Porta Capua. On the right, his arm raised to issue a command, is the general Aleksander Milbitz (1800–1883). The painting was part of Uzielli's private collection.

CFdU

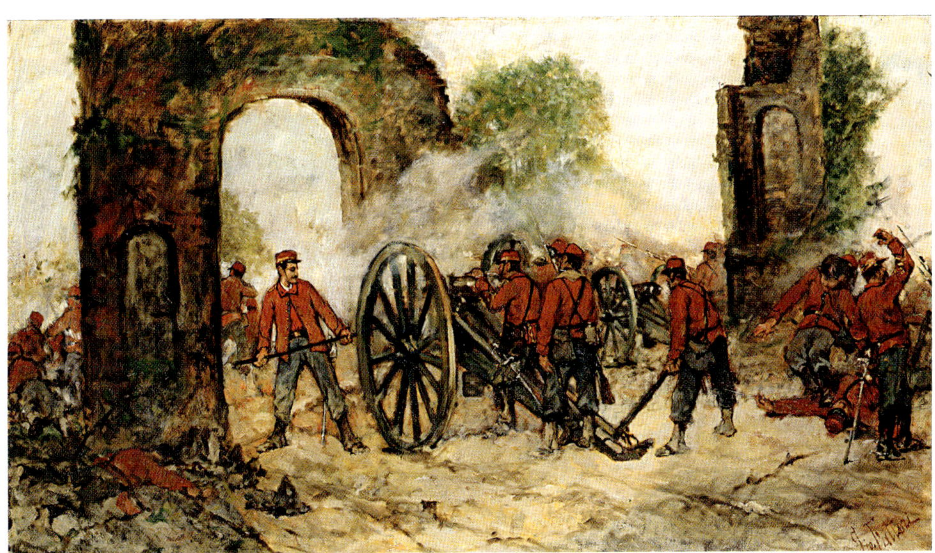

46. Giacomo Casa, *The Warrior*

1866
Oil on canvas
117 × 93 cm
Signed lower left, "G. Casa 1866"
Intesa Sanpaolo Collection
Inv. 003062

An alumnus of the Venice Academy of Fine Arts, Giacomo Casa (Conegliano, 1827 – Rome, 1887) subscribed wholeheartedly to the burgeoning Italian patriotism of his time and was involved in the 1848 Venice uprising. Between 1857 and 1859, he designed numerous interiors (Caffè delle Nazioni, Caffè Florian, Caffè Quadri and the Apollonian Rooms at the Fenice theatre), becoming well known for his orientalist style.

In this painting of 1866, the year Venice was annexed to the Kingdom of Italy, Casa represents the city as a courageous female warrior, who guides her people (with the pointed finger of her left hand) towards independence from foreign rule. The protagonist is painted in a manner that harks back to the Venetian masters of the sixteenth century, and takes her place in a long line of female allegories of the nation. With the green and red of her bodice offering an allusion to Italy, this warrior is not a flesh-and-blood woman but a symbol of a people in arms.

CFdU

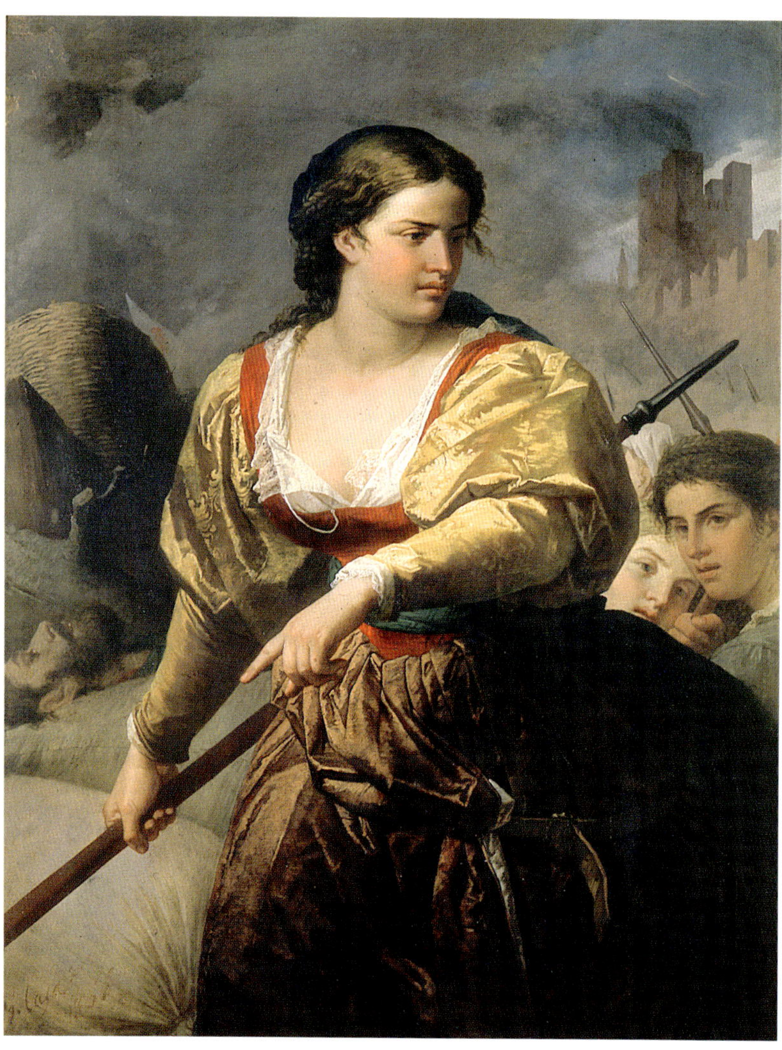

47. Candelabrum with the image of Giuseppe Garibaldi

Italy, nineteenth century
Silver
15 × 16 cm
Private collection

This silver candelabrum is decorated with an effigy of Giuseppe Garibaldi. It comes to us from a family who uses it during the holiday of Hannukah, which celebrates the victory of the Maccabees over the Seleucids in the second century BCE and the miracle of the lights. According to Jewish tradition, when the Maccabees regained control of the Temple, they wanted to resume their sacred practices. Among these was the tradition of lighting – each day – one of the lamps of the golden, seven-armed candelabrum or *menorah*, one of the Tabernacle's original furnishings (Exodus 25,31–40; 37,17–24). The lamps could only be filled with consecrated oil, of which – at this point in the story, following the revolt – there was only enough for a single day. Miraculously, the single flask they had kept the flame burning for eight days, the time required to purify more oil.

SR

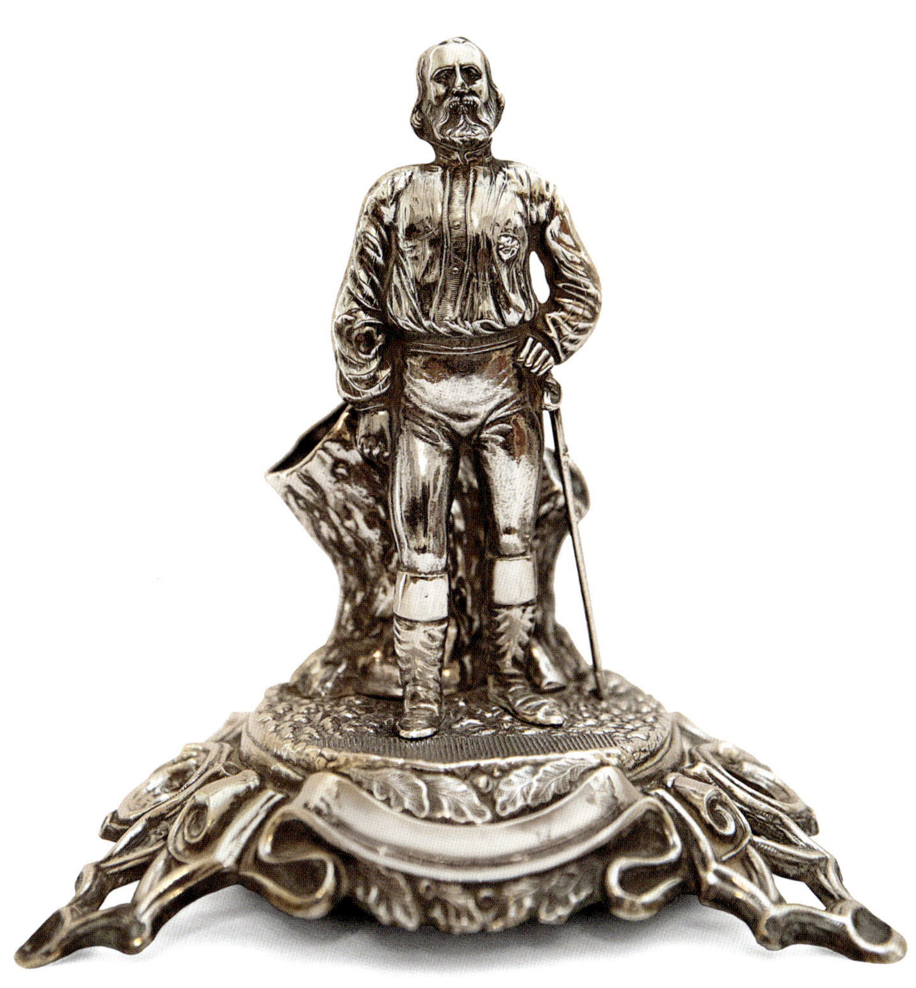

48. Serafino De Tivoli,
Portrait of Giuseppe Mazzini

Second half of the nineteenth century
Oil on canvas
70 × 100 cm
Domus Mazziniana, Pisa

Born in 1825 to a family of Jewish merchants who transferred to Florence in 1836, Serafino De Tivoli and his brother Felice began their art studies at a tender age. Together with other young Jews, including the painter Vito D'Ancona, De Tivoli fought with the Tuscan volunteers at the Battle of Curtatone and Montanara on 29 May 1848. With D'Ancona, and Telemaco Signorini, he became an active member of the patriotic group of painters known as the Macchiaioli. Following unification, De Tivoli separated from the group and moved first to Paris and then, in 1862, to London where he met Mazzini. Despite the success of the unification process, Mazzini had yet to be granted a place in the pantheon of Italian patriots, not least because he had always been an intransigent republican, and hostile to the House of Savoy. Little is known of this encounter, but it did produce this portrait. On the reverse is a note: "Giuseppe Mazzini/S De Tivoli/1 Long Acre WC/Vital De Tivoli/10 Gresham Park/Brixton SW."

CFdU

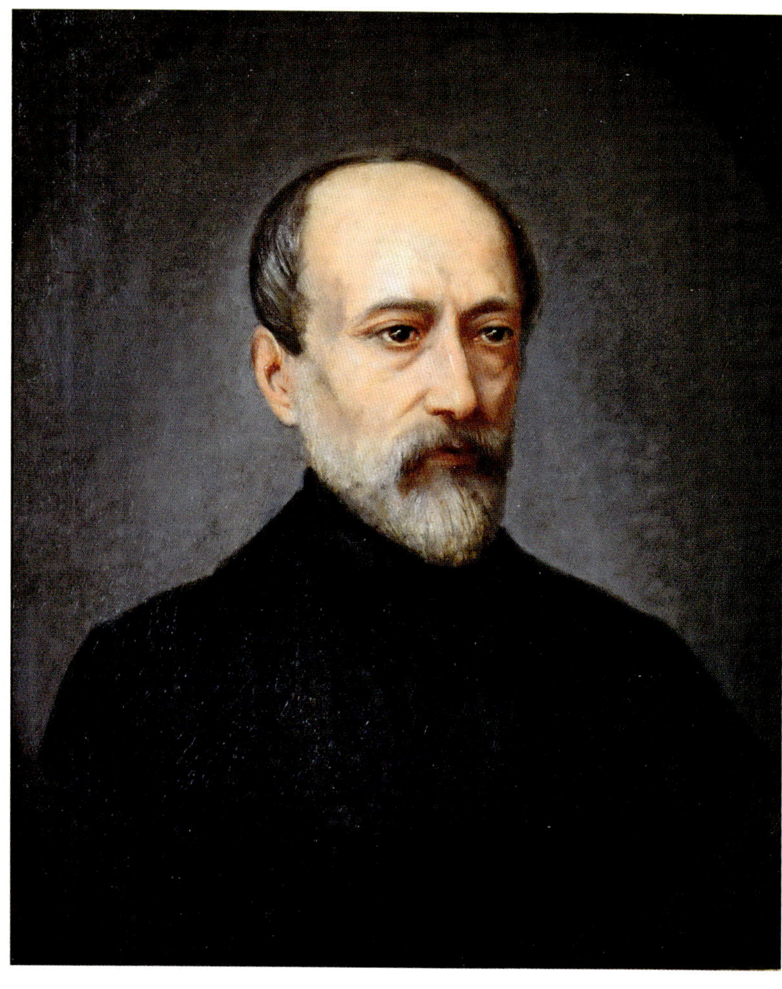

49. Album of prints of Gustave Doré's illustrations for the *Divine Comedy*, presented to the Rosselli-Nathan families by the Subalpine Democracy

1872
Print on paper
28.5 × 20 cm
Domus Mazziniana, Pisa

In 1861, the French painter, printmaker, caricaturist and illustrator Gustave Doré (Strasbourg, 1833 – Paris, 1883) published *L'Enfer*, comprising 75 plates of illustrations for Dante's *Divine Comedy*. The volume was a huge success and cemented the artist's status on the international stage. This album of prints was a gift: "*Alle famiglie Rosselli-Nathan che il Dante del XIX secolo Giuseppe Mazzini con pietà figliale ospitarono e affettuosamente confortarono nel lungo martirio della vita in segno d'imperitura riconoscenza l'Italia repubblicana dedica riverente*" (A token of the undying gratitude of Republican Italy to the Rosselli-Nathan families who, with filial devotion, gave lodging and affectionate consolation to the Dante of the nineteenth century, Giuseppe Mazzini, in the long martyrdom of his life. Humbly dedicated). Mazzini died on March 10, 1872 in the home of Janet Nathan Rosselli in Pisa. The death of the great "apostle" brought to a symbolic close the enduring support offered to his cause by many members of the family, but it also marked the start of their efforts to curate his memory, no easy task given the radical, republican ideals that underpinned his political enterprises and those of his followers. The dedication compares Mazzini to Dante, with whom he shared the status of exile.

CFdU

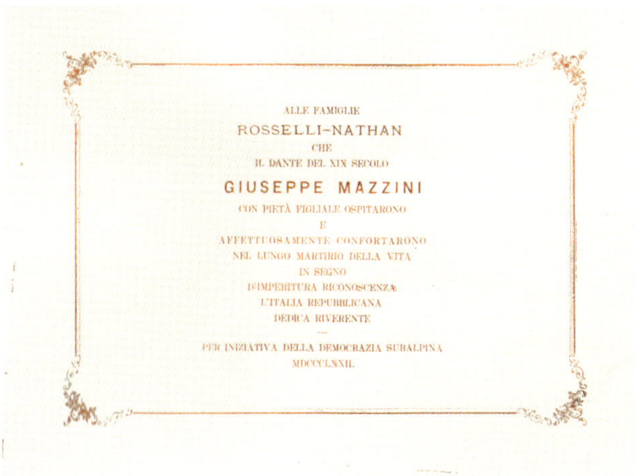

ALLE FAMIGLIE
ROSSELLI-NATHAN
CHE
IL DANTE DEL XIX SECOLO
GIUSEPPE MAZZINI
CON PIETÀ FIGLIALE OSPITARONO
E
AFFETTUOSAMENTE CONFORTARONO
NEL LUNGO MARTIRIO DELLA VITA
IN SEGNO
D'IMPERITURA RICONOSCENZA
L'ITALIA REPUBBLICANA
DEDICA RIVERENTE

PER INIZIATIVA DELLA DEMOCRAZIA SUBALPINA
MDCCCLXXII.

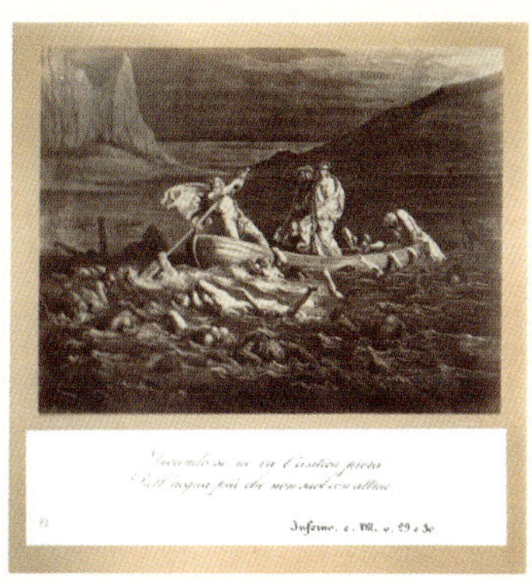

50. Album of signatures presented to the Nathan-Rosselli families on the occasion of the inauguration of the Monument to Mazzini in Genoa

1882
Print on paper
32 × 24.5 cm
Domus Mazziniana, Pisa

This album is a testimony to the close bond between Mazzini and the Nathan-Rosselli family. On each page is a black, decorative frame with portraits of (clockwise from upper-left) Carlo Cattaneo, Giuseppe Garibaldi, Giuseppe Mazzini and Aurelio Saffi. The dedication reads: "*Alla illustre famiglia Nathan / alla quale / va unita la solenne memoria di Giuseppe Mazzini / un / affettuoso pensiero degli Italiani / 22 giugno 1882*" (To the eminent Nathan family, who is inseparable from the solemn memory of Giuseppe Mazzini. With the fond thoughts of all Italians, June 22, 1882), followed by, "*Nel giorno dell'inaugurazione del monumento in Genova, all'Immortale pensatore, gli Italiani che qui segnano il loro nome, ricordando quanto faceste per l'Italia e Mazzini, vi esprimono il loro affetto e la loro riconoscenza. Salve!*" (On the day of the inauguration in Genoa of the monument to the immortal thinker, the Italians who have here signed their names acknowledge all you did for Italy and for Mazzini, and extend to you their affection and gratitude. Salve!). Below the text is the space for the signatures.
Mazzini met the Nathan-Rossellis in the early 1840s in London. Sara Levi Nathan (1819–1882) and various other members of the family would provide moral and financial support to Mazzini during his lifetime, but most of all, they would be the guardians of his memory after he died in the home of Janet Nathan Rosselli – Sara's daughter – on March 10, 1872.

CFdU

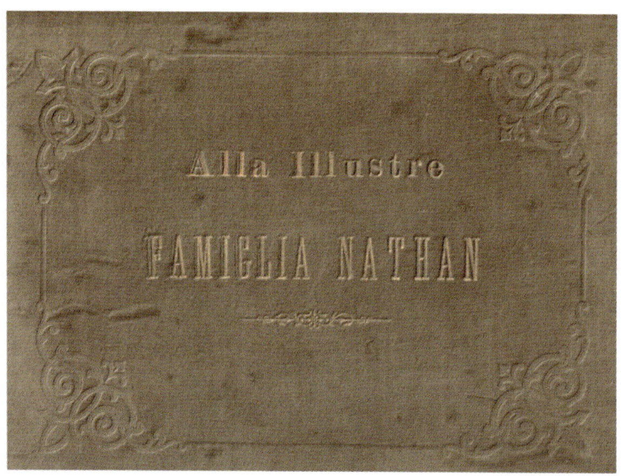

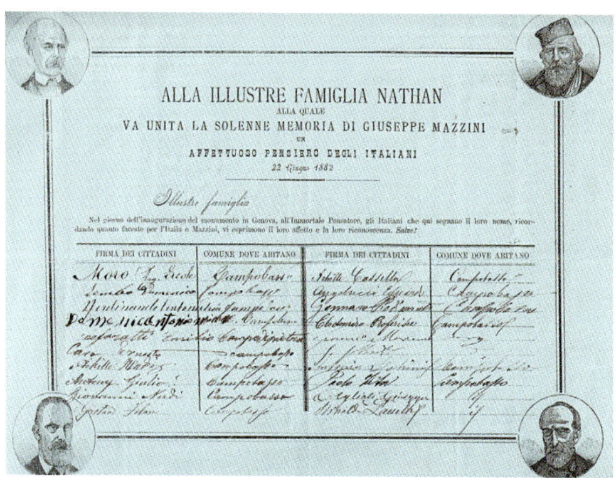

ALLA ILLUSTRE FAMIGLIA NATHAN
ALLA QUALE
VA UNITA LA SOLENNE MEMORIA DI GIUSEPPE MAZZINI
UN
AFFETTUOSO PENSIERO DEGLI ITALIANI
22 Giugno 1882

Illustre famiglia

Nel giorno dell'inaugurazione del monumento in Genova, all'Immortale Pensatore, gli Italiani che qui segnano il loro nome, ricordando quanto faceste per l'Italia e Mazzini, vi esprimono il loro affetto e la loro riconoscenza. *Salve!*

FIRMA DEI CITTADINI	COMUNE DOVE ABITANO	FIRMA DEI CITTADINI	COMUNE DOVE ABITANO

51. Portrait of Victor Emmanuel II

Italy, second half of the nineteenth century
(between 1850 and 1899)
Oil on canvas, wooden frame
76 × 58 cm; with frame 118 × 85 cm
Museo Storico e il Parco del Castello
di Miramare, Trieste

This half-length portrait depicts the king Victor Emmanuel II in full dress, decorated with the insignia of the orders of Sts Maurice and Lazarus and Our Lady of the Assumption.

The wooden frame, embellished with gilt decoration, is topped by a fastigium bearing the arms of the House of Savoy and a Latin inscription that identifies the royal sitter as Victor Emmanuel II, king of Italy. The work is part of a series of royal portraits that Ferdinand Maximilian Joseph assembled in one of the state rooms in his residence in Trieste, Miramare. The collection paid homage to contemporary rulers, in allusion to the fact that Maximilian had also risen to the rank of sovereign, becoming emperor of Mexico in 1864.

The inclusion of Victor Emmanuel II in the series is worthy of note, given the tension between Austria and the Kingdom of Italy at the time. Just a few years earlier, Maximilian, as viceroy of Lombardy-Venetia, was witness to the defeat of the Austrian army during the final phases of the Second Italian War of Independence.

AC

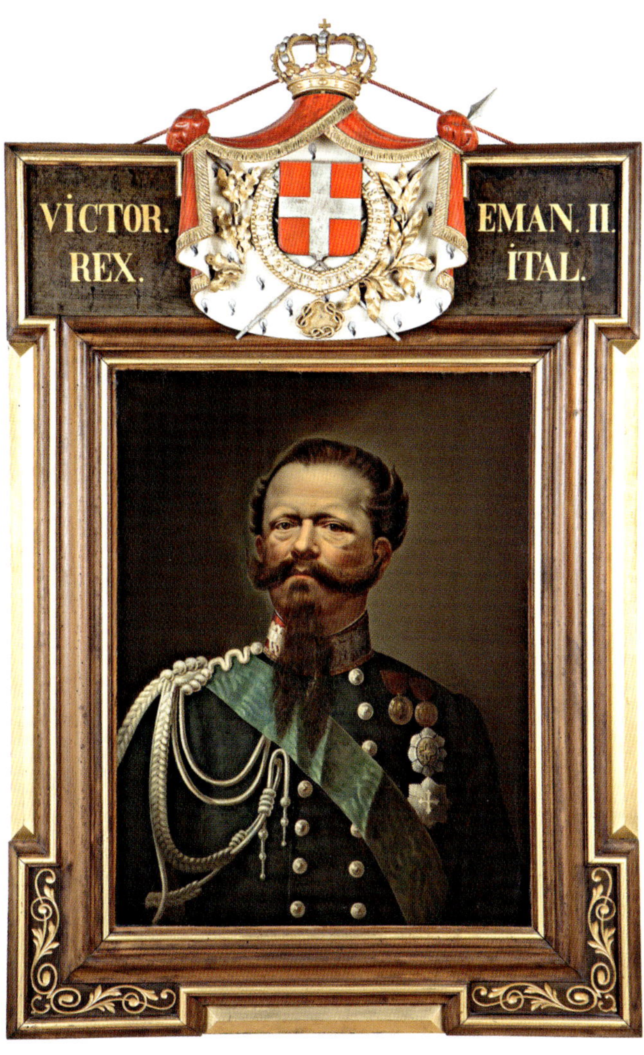

52. *Ketubah*, marriage contract

Busseto (Parma), 9 Nissan 5620 (1860)
Groom: Samuel Modena
Bride: Deborah Levi
Manuscript on parchment
61 × 46 cm
"Fausto Levi" Museum and Synagogue, Soragna

The design of this 1860 *ketubah* from Busseto is highly original. Clearly identifiable, alongside a number of traditional ornaments, are portraits of King Victor Emmanuel II (upper center), Cavour (to the left) and Garibaldi (to the right), with the king taking the place of honor in what amounts to a patriotic trinity. It was not entirely unheard of to include human figures in the ornamentation of a *ketubah*, but the choice of contemporary figures is undoubtedly unusual. It is no less than a declaration of "Italianness" – following a referendum, Parma had been annexed to the Kingdom of Sardinia in 1860 – that swept aside the dichotomy of private and public life to assert the identity of a family that was Jewish, but at the same time fully Italian. It is worth noting that civil marriages were not permitted under Piedmontese law. They would be introduced in unified Italy with the so-called "Pisanelli" Code, which took effect in 1866.

CFdU-AC

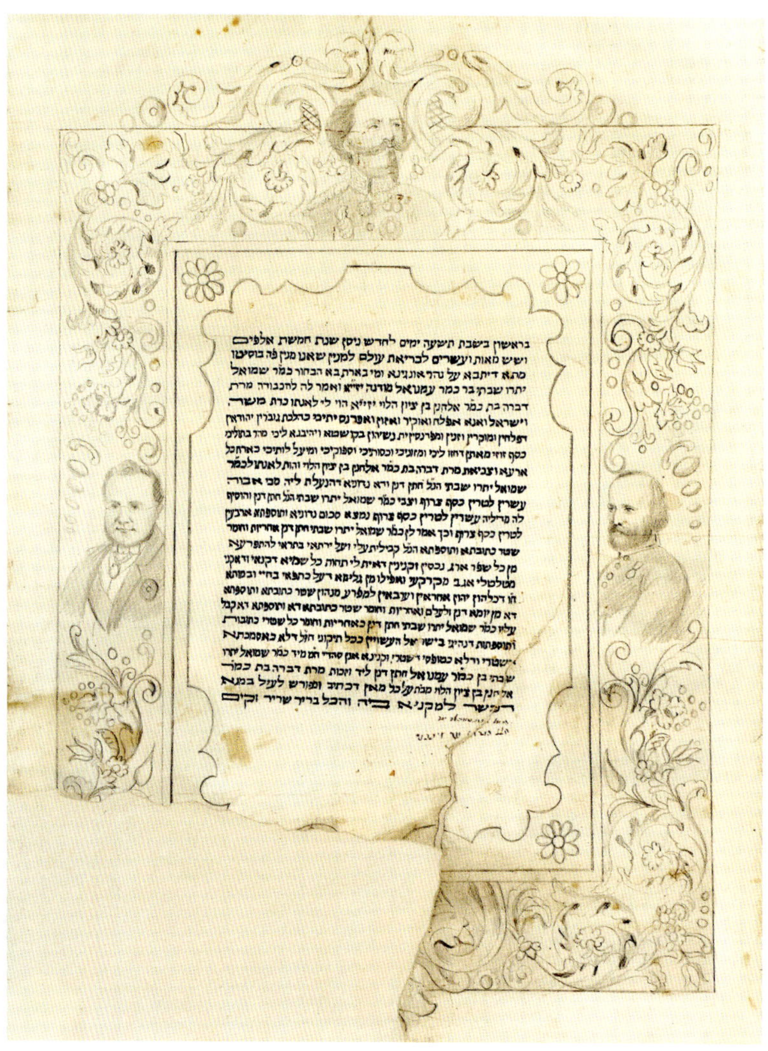

53. *Ketubah*, marriage contract

Rome, 21 Marcheshvan 5499 (1884)
Groom: Shalom son of Yosef Baruk Gai
Bride: Flaminia daughter of Mehalalel Di Nepi
Manuscript and watercolor on parchment
67 × 47 cm
Historical Archive of the Jewish Community of Rome "Giancarlo Spizzichino," Rome
Inv. Ascer 3

This *ketubah* was commissioned for the wedding of Shalom, son of Yosef Baruk Gai, and Flaminia, daughter of Mehalalel Di Nepi, which was celebrated in Rome on November 9, 1884. The decoration is not especially extravagant, but the choice of colors is significant. The frame and the floral motifs, against the white background, bring to mind the Italian *tricolore* flag. Created as the standard of the Cispadane Republic in 1797, the *tricolore* soon became symbol of the struggle to unite and liberate the peninsula. It was adopted by Charles Albert during the course of the First War of Independence, with the addition of the shield of the Savoy dynasty with its blue bordure, and it continued to be used in the Kingdom of Italy, even though it would not be legally enshrined as the official flag of Italy until the fascist period. In evoking the *tricolore* – a symbol of Italian identity in a Jewish document – in the decoration of this *ketubah*, the couple have chosen to express, publicly, how important both parts of their plural identity are to them.

CFdU

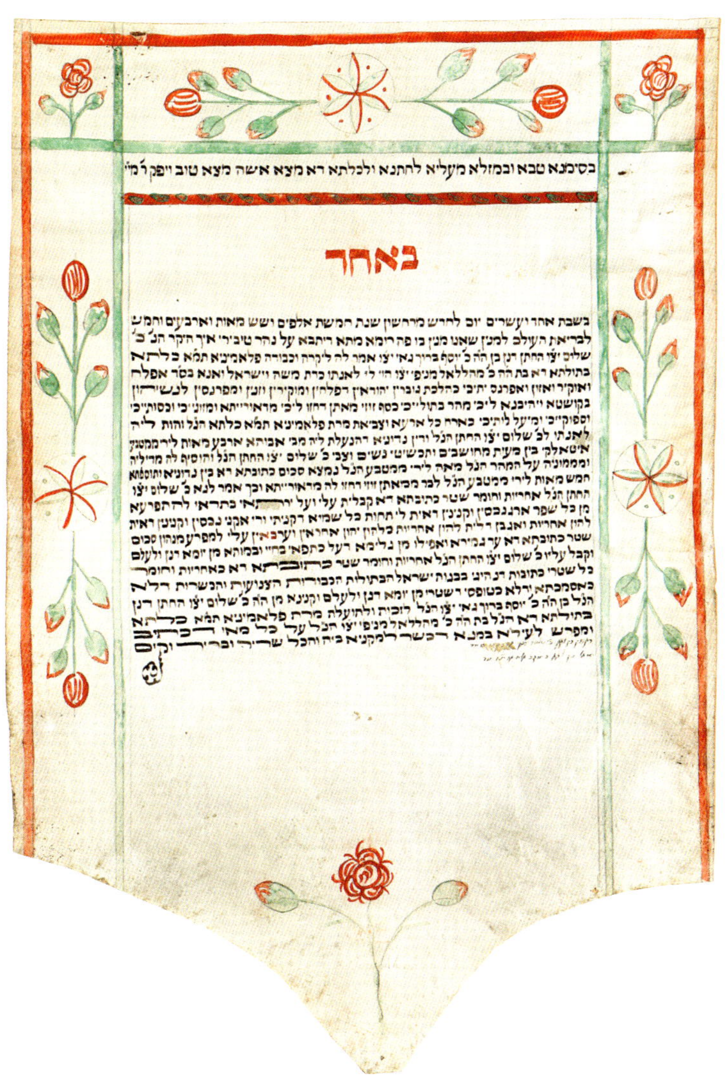

54. Aron ha-Kodesh, double-leaf door

Holy Ark
Piedmontese artist(s)
Late eighteenth – early nineteenth century
Carved, gilded and painted wood, with inserted mirrors
2.15 × 77 × 12 cm
Palazzo Madama - Museo Civico d'Arte Antica di Torino, Turin, on loan to Synagogue of the Comunità Ebraica di Torino
Inv. 1486/L

Bibl.: Mallé 1972, pp. 95–96.

This double-leaf door is the only remaining element of the housing of the Aron ha-Kodesh – the Holy Ark used to keep the Torah scrolls – in one of the synagogues in the Turin ghetto. It was donated to the city by the local Jewish "University" in 1884 to be conserved in the Civic Museum. Stylistic analysis and the manufacture of the nails and screws suggest that it was produced some time around the last decade of the eighteenth century and the first decade of the nineteenth. For instance, the doors are decorated with a form of gilded festoon that can be found on other furniture from that period. The upper panels – which are also gilded – depict two buildings (probably modeled on a church and baptistery), which symbolize the Temple of Jerusalem. The unit is framed at the sides by two pilasters, whose capitals are missing, and by panels of mirrored glass, which served to increase the sense of light within the synagogue.

SR

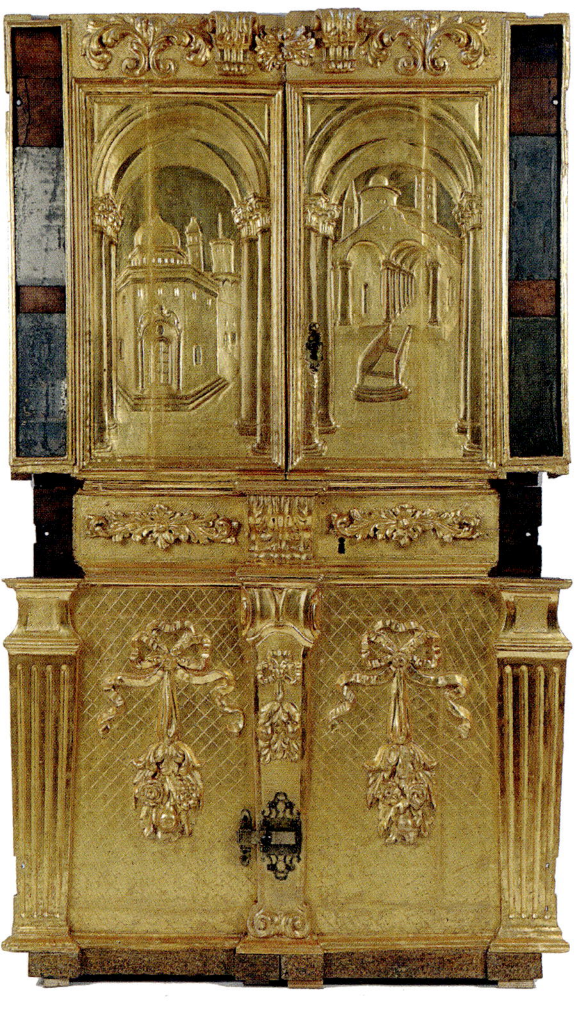

55. Lithograph of the Israelite Temple based on a drawing by Crescentino Caselli and published by Camilla and Bertolero

Turin, 1876
Lithograph print
52 × 22 cm
Archivio Storico della Città di Torino, Turin
Inv. *cart.* 71 *fasc.* 8 n. 20

In 1862, the Jewish "University" of Turin commissioned the architect Alessandro Antonelli to oversee the construction of a new great temple. Work began the following year, but encountered numerous problems, not least Antonelli's decision to dramatically rework the design. This, along with spiraling costs, prompted the decision to sell the structure to the city. In 1876, before approving the purchase, the city council requested a copy of the documentation relating to the building, so it could determine how much it would cost to complete. On 30 March of that year, the mayor, Felice Rignon, wrote to Antonelli asking him to send the "*disegno della facciata a sezione dell'opera quale dovrà essere ultimata*" (drawing of the facade in section in the manner in which it will be completed) (ASCT, Affari Lavori Pubblici, 1876, *cart.* 71, *fasc.* 8, n. 18). Antonelli sent him this lithograph, along with a letter of authentication.

SR

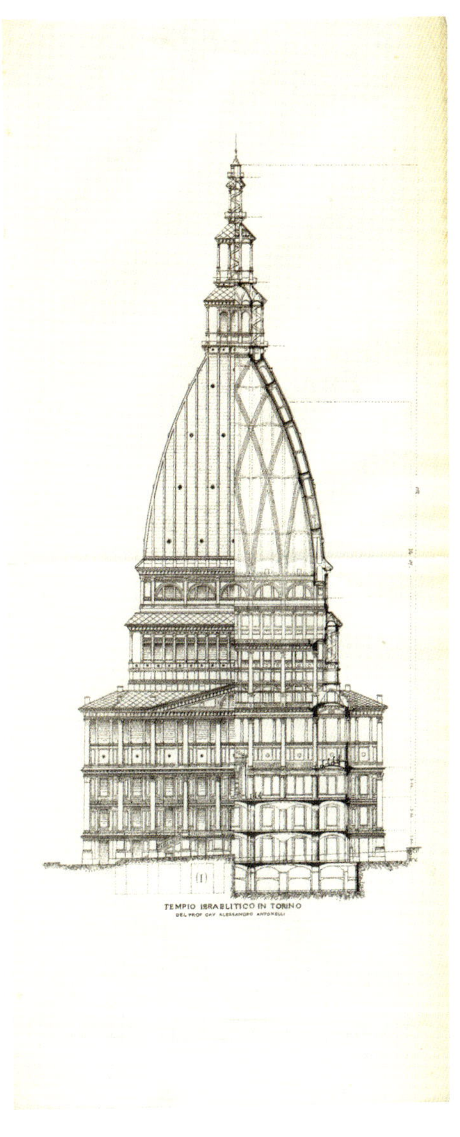

56. Declaration by Alessandro Antonelli

Turin, 1876
Manuscript on paper
41 × 27 cm
Archivio Storico della Città di Torino, Turin
Inv. Cart. 71 *fasc.* 8 no. 20.1

Antonelli's response to the mayor's letter reads as follows:
"Esteemed Mr. Mayor,
Eager to avoid any disruption or delay, I send you this lithograph, which has been printed with diligent precision by Camilla and Bertolero, and which I have recognized as valid and signed.
It is accurate with regard to the work carried out thus far, and to the work that is required to complete the Israelite temple, for which the municipal council has approved the generous contribution of 200 thousand lire.
I need not remind someone of your wisdom of the urgent need to ensure the resumption, at last, of the work required to bring this propitious, partially completed project to an acceptable state, such that it be safeguarded against any damage that may be caused by prolonged abandonment.
Maggiora, April 1, 1876
With my fullest regards,
Your most devoted servant
Professor Alessandro Antonelli"

SR

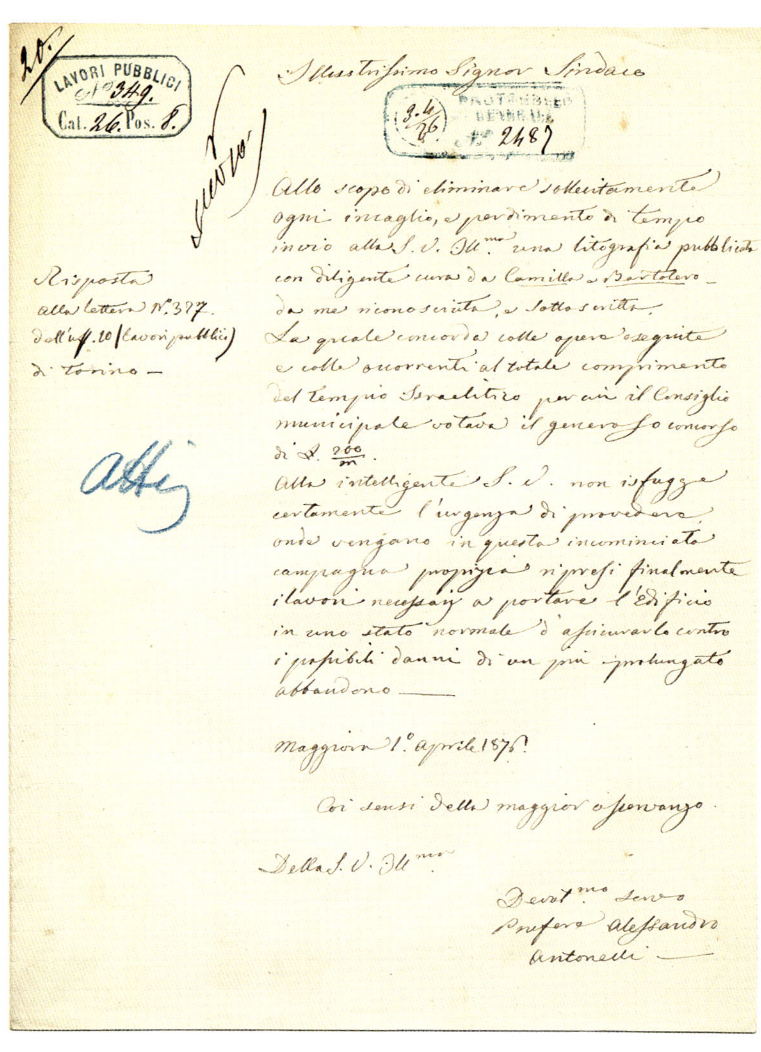

20.

LAVORI PUBBLICI N° 349. Cat. 26. Pos. 8.

3.4 / 76 N° 2487

Illustrissimo Signor Sindaco

Risposta alla lettera N. 377. dell'uff. 10 (lavori pubblici) di Torino —

Alle scopo di eliminare sollecitamente ogni incaglio, e perdimento di tempo invio alla S. V. Ill.ma una litografia pubblicata con diligente cura da Camilla e Bertolero — da me riconosciuta, e sottoscritta.
La quale concorda colle opere eseguite e colle occorrenti al totale compimento del tempio Israelitico per cui il Consiglio municipale votava il generoso concorso di L. 200/m.
Alla intelligente S. V. non isfuggirà certamente l'urgenza di provvedere onde vengano in questa incominciata campagna propizia ripresi finalmente i lavori necessarj a portare l'Edificio in uno stato normale ed assicurarlo contro i possibili danni di un più prolungato abbandono ——

Maggiora 1° aprile 1876.

Coi sensi della maggior osservanza

Della S. V. Ill.ma

Devot.mo Servo
Profess. Alessandro Antonelli —

57. Portrait bust of Sansone d'Ancona

Italy, nineteenth century
Sculpted marble
62 × 60 × (base) 25 cm
MEIS (National Museum of Italian Judaism and the Shoah), Ferrara

Sansone d'Ancona (1814–1924) was born in Pesaro in 1814. One of ten children, he was the brother of the celebrated painter Vito d'Ancona. In due course, d'Ancona moved to Tuscany, where his family on his mother's side (Ester Della Ripa, 1799–1862) had established themselves in the local banking sector. Having graduated with a degree in Mathematics from the University of Pisa, he began his career at the bank owned by his uncle, Laudadio Della Ripa, where from 1840 onwards his work focused increasingly on railway finance. The search of investors for the "*Strada Ferrata dell'Italia Centrale*" (linking Tuscany with Piacenza and Bologna) and the "*Leopolda*" line (linking Florence, Pisa and Livorno) would take him to Paris and London. At the same time, Sansone and his uncle Laudadio were active in the silk industry, and ushered in a number of innovative techniques in their own properties.

He would eventually dedicate himself to politics, aligning with moderate liberals from the political right such as Terenzio Mamiani, Luigi Carlo Farini and the Tuscans Bettino Ricasoli and Ubaldino Peruzzi. Despite opposition from antisemitic factions, in 1860 he became Minister of Finance in the provisional Tuscan government led by Bettino Ricasoli, and between 1861 and 1874 was one of the first Jewish deputies elected to the Chamber of Deputies, first of the Kingdom of Sardinia, and then of the Kingdom of Italy. From 1882 to his death in 1894, he held the title of Senator of the Realm. D'Ancona was actively involved in the affairs of Florence's Jewish community, including as a member of the commission charged with collecting subscriptions for the construction of the new Temple.

SR

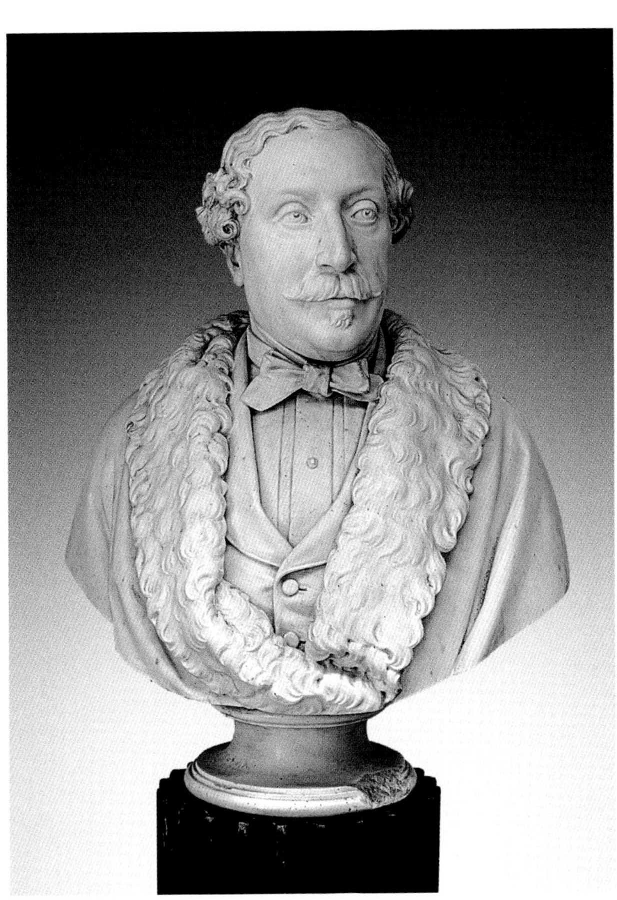

58. *Ricordi di Architettura* (periodical): Competition for an Israelite Temple to be built in Rome. Design selected for 1st prize, of the 1st degree. Costa & Armanni Architects

Rome, 1891
Print on paper
53.5 × 38 cm
MEIS (National Museum of Italian Judaism and the Shoah), Ferrara

In 1889, the Jewish community in Rome announced a competition to choose the design for a new "Monumental Temple" for the city. Two designs were awarded prizes, one by Attilio Murgia and one by Osvaldo Armanni and Vincenzo Costa. Ten years later, in 1899, Armanni and Costa were awarded the contract to build the temple. Their original design is characterized by a decidedly Orientalist quality, with a style that was heavily influenced by Babylonian architecture. The finished building, which was completed in 1904, was less archaized, and featured a large dome that brought to mind the forms of the Temple in Jerusalem.

SR

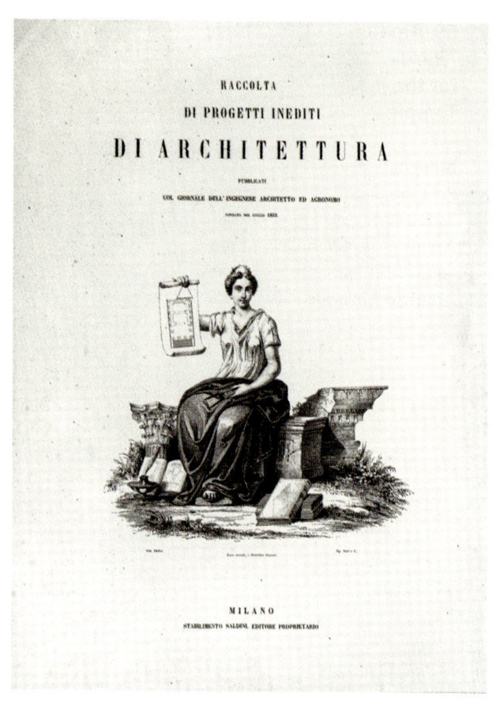

RACCOLTA
DI PROGETTI INEDITI
DI ARCHITETTURA
MILANO

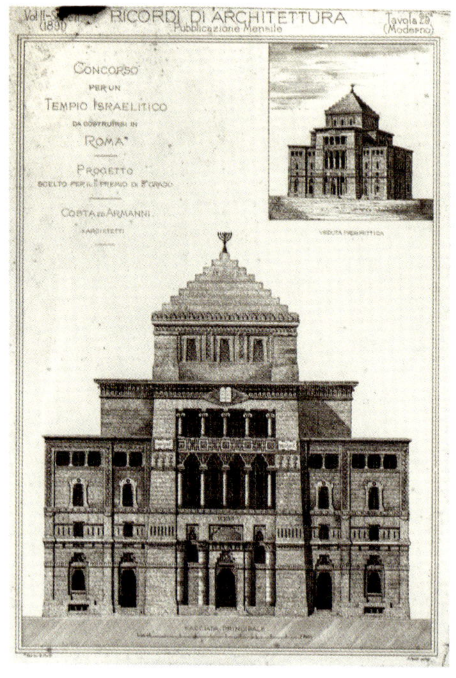

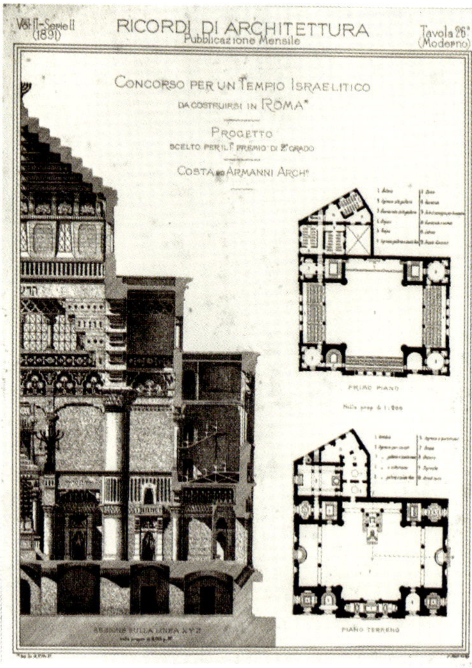

59. Amadio Di Segni, sheet music: "Baruk-Abbà", four-part choral arrangement for the inauguration of the new Jewish Temple in Rome

Bologna, Edizioni U. Cocchi, June 18, 1914
Print on paper
33 × 27 cm
Archivio Storico della Comunità Ebraica di Roma "Giancarlo Spizzichino," Rome
Archivio Musicale, b.3, *fasc.* 9

Amadio Di Segni (1837–1925) was born in Rome. Initially self-taught, he would go on to study music under G. Fenzi and complete his studies at the school of *maestro* Sangiorgi. He held the position of director of the temple choir in Rome and Marseille.
This volume contains Di Segni's arrangement of the *Baruch Haba* (Psalm 118:26), which he dedicated "as a sign of esteem and affection" to his friend Adolfo Piperno.

SR

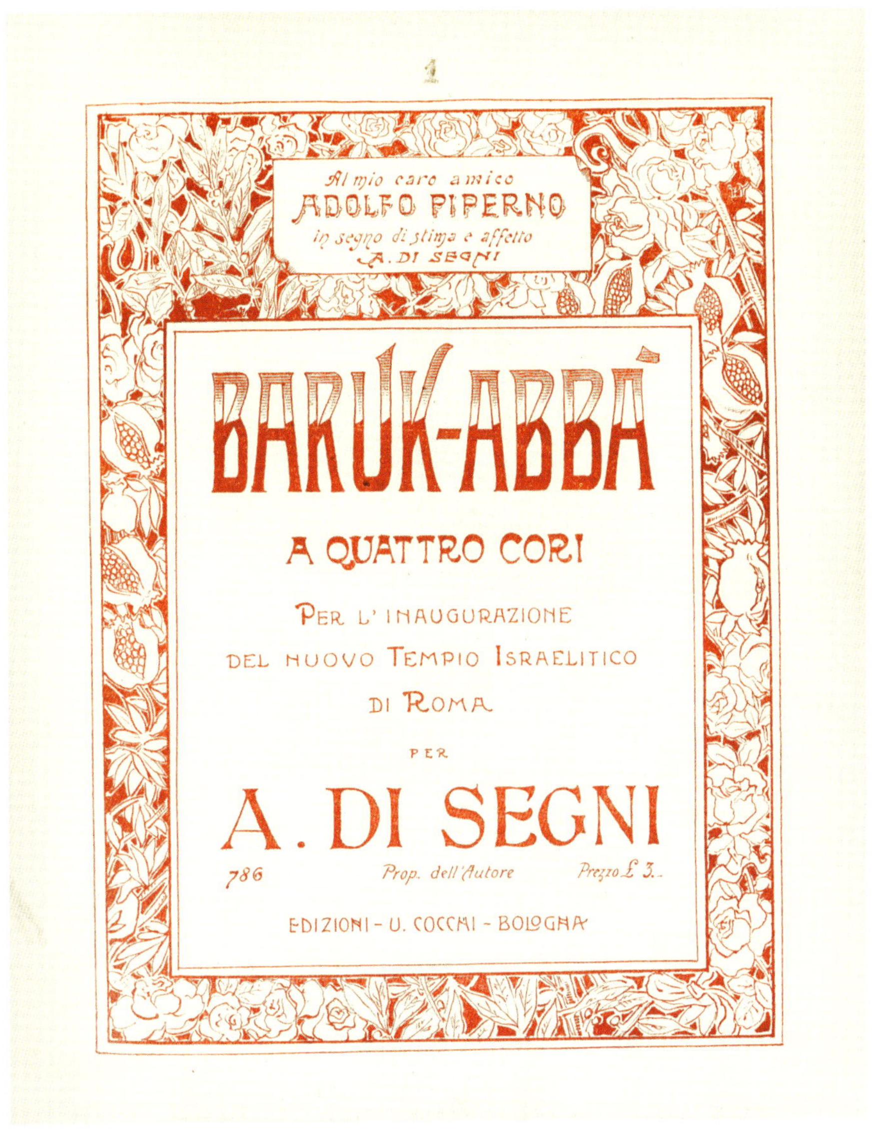

60. *Meghillah* belonging to the last Count Corinaldi, Adolfo

Greece, nineteenth century
Parchment, silver philigrane case
2.15 × 3.5 × 3.5 cm
Private collection

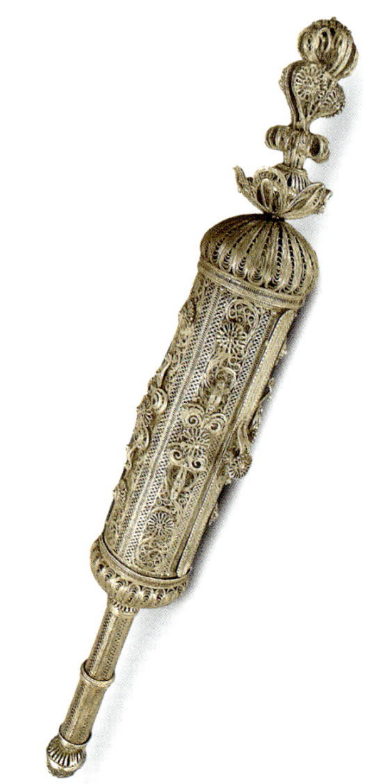

61. *Ketubah*, marriage contract

Original text: Northern Italy, eighteenth century
Later text: Padua, 10 Siwan 5599 (May 23, 1839)
Groom: Michele son of Isach Corinaldi
Bride: Benedetta Treves de Bonfili
Manuscript, watercolor and gilt on parchment
65 × 45 cm
Private collection

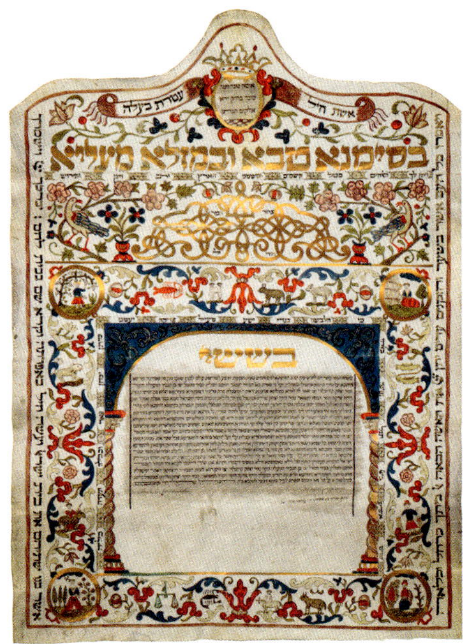

In 1839, Michele Corinaldi (1812–1874) son of Isach, a Law graduate and native of Pisa, married Benedetta Treves de Bonfili (1818–1881) and moved to the family home in Via delle Zitelle in Padua. Their union was formalized with a *ketubah*, a Jewish contract of marriage. In this case, the parchment is one that has been re-used, retaining the illustrations and decorative inscriptions of the eighteenth-century original, whereas the text of the original contract has been scraped off and replaced with that concerning the marriage of Michele Corinaldi and Benedetta Treves de Bonfili. Gilded family arms adorn the top of the parchment, while the floral border includes four gilded circles enclosing representations of the seasons. The signs of the zodiac are arranged around the four edges, and the text is flanked by two Solomonic columns.

RS-SR

62. *Biblical Wedding Scene*

Italy, mid-nineteenth century
Oil on canvas
70 × 85 × 8 cm (including frame)
Private collection

The main figure in this image, which depicts a biblical wedding scene, has been painted to resemble Benedetta Treves de Bonfili. Benedetta was born, probably in Padua, on October 7, 1818. The daughter of Isacco Treves de Bonfili and Enrichetta Consolo, she married Michele Corinaldi a few months before her twenty-first birthday, on May 23, 1839, as we know from the marriage contract or *ketubah*. Her dowry consisted of a wealthy amount, valued at a total of "100.000 florins in standard currency, which is to say, L 300.000 (three hundred thousand) Austrian Lire." The majority of this sum represented a number of properties, which were used by Michele although Benedetta would retain ownership. It is also said that the young bride was unable to sign the contract, because she was "currently suffering from a disease of the eyes, which prevented her from writing." This appears to be confirmed by family archive photographs, which suggest that rather than being a temporary affliction, the illness had left Benedetta blind. Her husband's political engagements took the couple first to Florence and then to Turin. She died in Padua on May 9, 1881 at the age of 63.

RS

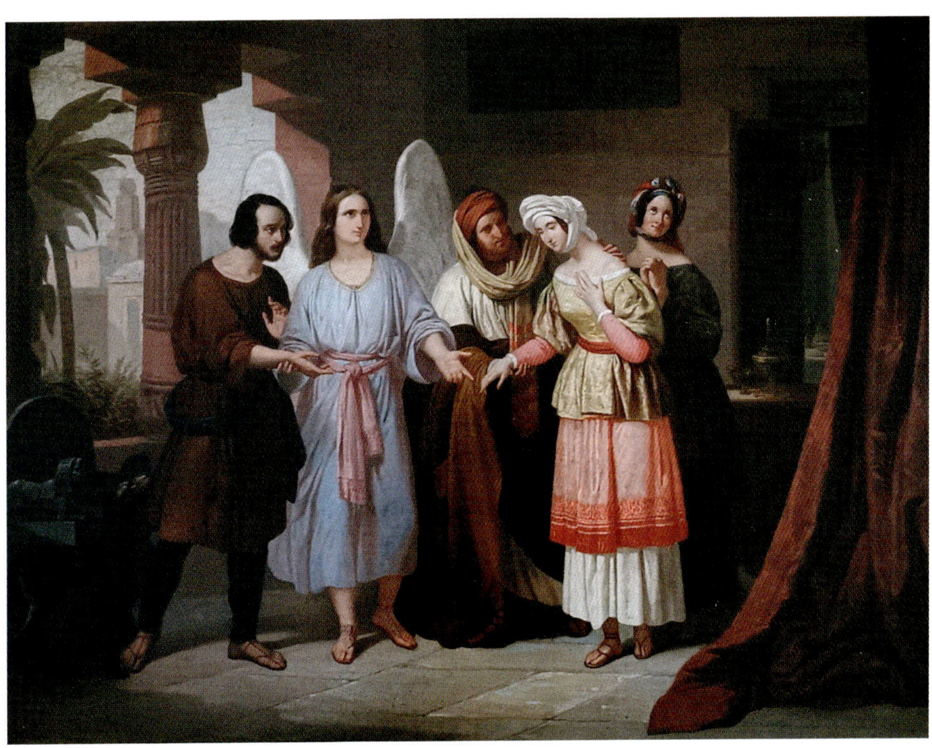

63. Photograph album with the arms of the Counts Corinaldi

Italy, second half of the nineteenth century
Cover made of velvet with passementerie and precious stones; interior in cardboard
27 × 22 × 4.5 cm
Private collection

Corinaldo is a walled, medieval town in the Province of Ancona. The presence of a Jewish community is recorded as far back as the early fifteenth century, although there is some evidence of an earlier presence. A sumptuously decorated Bible dating from 1396 has come down to us from Ferrara, having been made for a certain Benjamin ben Menachem of Corinaldo. This was probably the great-grandfather of the scribe Yaakov ben Yekutiel mi-Corinaldo, who was active in the Ferrara area around the end of the fifteenth century and the first decades of the sixteenth. The Corinaldi family remained in the Emilia area (particularly in Reggio Emilia and Scandiano) into the twentieth century. The sisters Olga, Bice and Alda Corinaldi were deported to Auschwitz, and died towards the end of February 1944. The surname is found in other regions, however, and is particularly common in Tuscany.
This velvet-bound album contains a collection of family photographs. It is embellished with the family's comital crown and a floral border, with gilded initials at the center.

RS

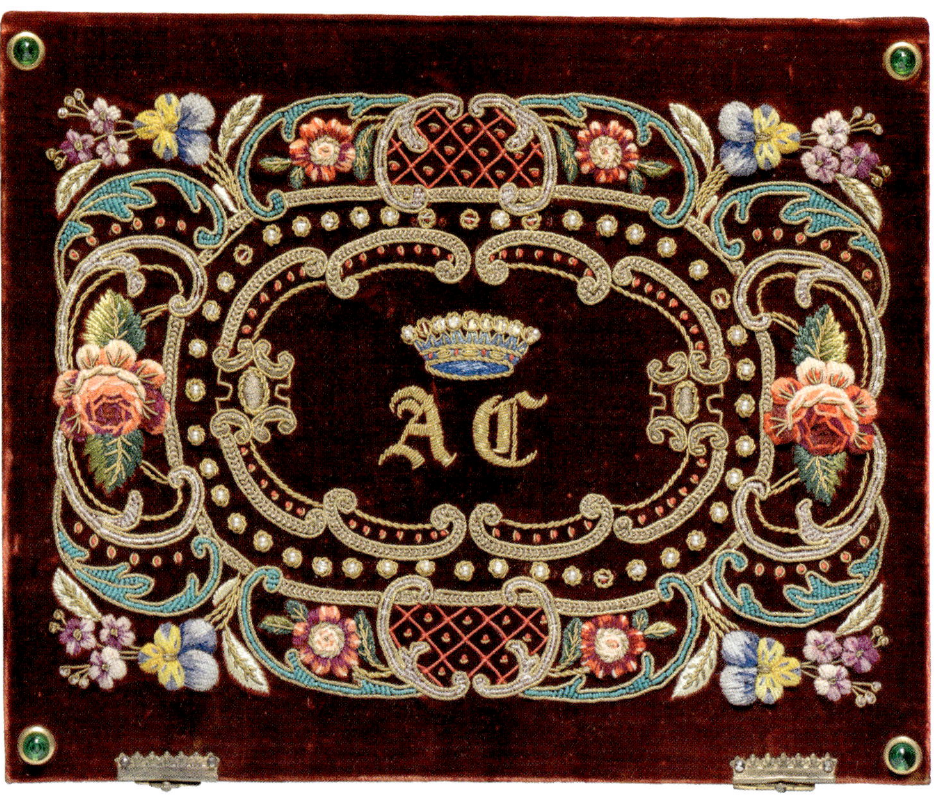

64. Drawing of the Corinaldi family arms and motto

Italy, 1862
Watercolor on paper
30 × 21 cm
Private collection

On April 21, 1862, even before his election to the Chamber of Deputies, Michele Corinaldi was granted the hereditary title of *Conte* by the king, Victor Emmanuel II. In contrast to the barony bestowed on the Treves de Bonfili by Napoleon (which was confirmed by Joseph II and renewed by Victor Emmanuel II), Corinaldi's title was awarded for political reasons in recognition of his contribution to the budding nation, and not for his business activities. The motto selected for the coat of arms is *Non fuorvierà*, "[he] shall not turn aside." This is derived from Deuteronomy, chapter 28, verses 13 and 14 – "The Lord will make you the head, not the tail. If you pay attention to the commands of the Lord your God that I give you this day and carefully follow them, you will always be at the top, never at the bottom. Do not turn aside from any of the commands I give you today, to the right or to the left, following other gods and serving them." This was an instruction answered in the motto with a pledge in the third person, which signifies both the family's sense of duty and its awareness of its identity.
The family title was annulled by Mussolini in 1938, but reconfirmed by the king following the fall of the Fascist regime.

RS

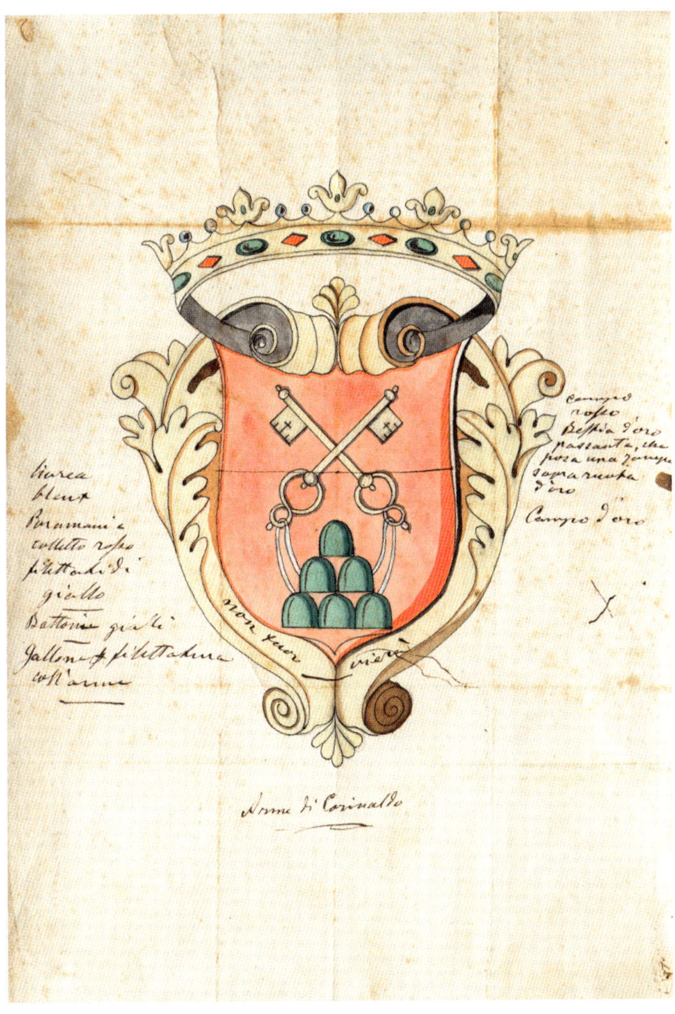

65. Print with a dedication by Victor Emmanuel II

Italy, 1862
Print on paper with dedication and signature by Victor Emmanuel II: carved, gilded wooden frame
65 × 50 × 10 cm (including frame)
Private collection

Bibl.: De Benedetti 2019.

The story of Michele Corinaldi's life is distinguished by his political endeavors and contribution to the unification of Italy. He had publicly declared his support for the Risorgimento cause in 1859, and was actively involved in supporting exiles. Careful not to step outside the bounds of the law, and protected by his wealth and status, Corinaldi was never arrested, but his life was made difficult, to the point that he felt forced to remove his family from Padua, moving first to Florence and then to Pisa. He stood as a Liberal candidate in the 1863 parliamentary elections, and was elected to represent the constituency of Leno, a small town midway between Brescia and Cremona. In the Parliament, Corinaldi "positioned himself to the right" – meaning what is now called the "historical right" – but "almost never spoke in the chamber." Despite standing again in Leno in 1865, and in Este in 1867, he was not re-elected. After his election to the parliament, he moved to Turin, where he made numerous official contacts, and in 1865 he applied for residency in the city. He later returned to Padua, where he died in 1874. This picture, with Victor Emmanuel II's personal dedication, is from the same year as the royal decree bestowing Corinaldi with the hereditary title of *Conte*.

RS

66. Feast day tablecloth, Pardo family

Veneto region, 1843
Taffeta embroidered with silk thread
76 × 113 cm
Private collection

Bibl.: D. Liscia Bemporad, in Mann 1990, p. 216.

It is presumed that this tablecloth was part of the trousseau assembled by the Ravenna family for the wedding of Tullio Ravenna, a Ferrara shopkeeper, and Eugenia Pardo, which was officiated in Verona by rabbi Isacco Pardo (1824–1892) on January 31, 1884.
It is embroidered with a floral border, with a basket of flowers and an inscription in Hebrew script at each corner. Starting from the upper right, these texts read: "Feast of unleavened bread," "Feast of Shavuot," "Feast of Sukkot", "Rosh haShanah (New Year)".
The following lines are embroidered in the centre of the tablecloth: "These are the Lord's appointed festivals, the sacred assemblies you are to proclaim at their appointed times" (Lev. 23:4); "She selects wool and flax and works with eager hands" (Prov. 31:13); "Pisila Levi Polacco, wife of Jehuda Haim De Chiaves, in the year 5603 [1843]." Nothing certain is known about how the tablecloth came into the hands of the Pardo family, although it was probably a gift from the embroiderer, whose grave has been identified in the Jewish cemetery in Verona.

SR

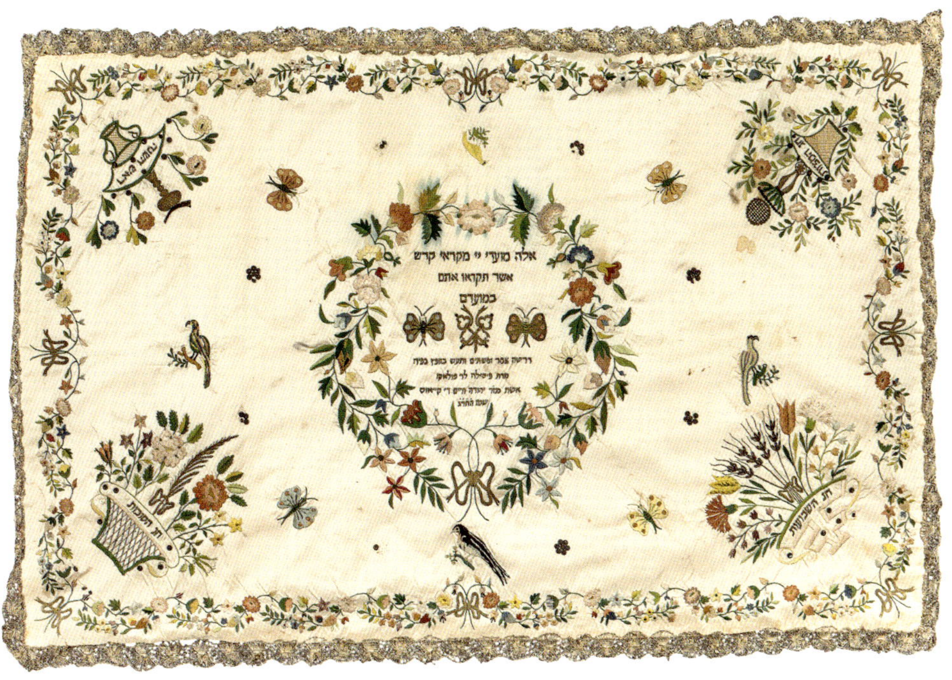

67. Portrait of Rabbi David Samuel Pardo

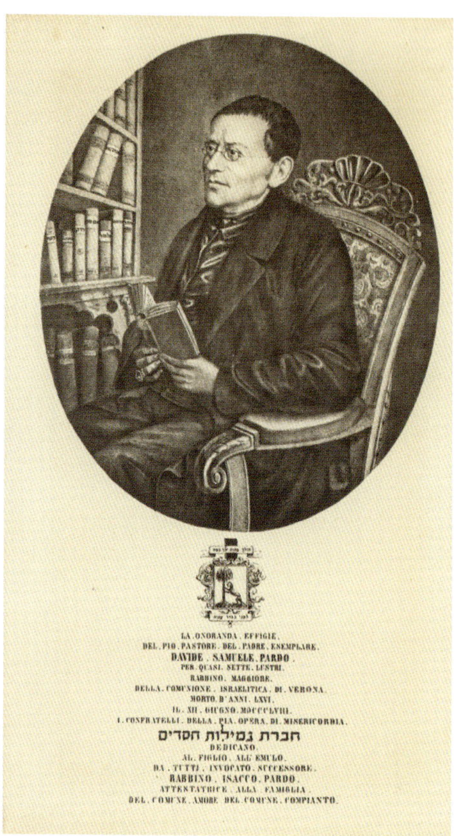

Verona, 1858
Engraving on paper
46 × 28 cm
Private collection

This posthumous engraving was executed very shortly after the death of rabbi David Samuel Pardo (Dubrovnik, 1792 – Verona, 1858). It was likely based on an oil portrait from the home of the Ravenna family, which was lost during World War II along with a portrait of the rabbi's wife, Enrichetta Valenzini.

The rabbi is shown sitting, in three-quarter view, with a bookcase behind him containing a mix of religious writings and community registries, such as the book of births, deaths and marriages. He wears a pair of spectacles, but no form of head covering.

The dedication includes the family arms, a leopard rampant depicted in profile against a palm tree. The same device appears in the documents of rabbi David Samuel Pardo and on his tombstone, but fell out of use among later generations of the family. The portrait is dedicated to his son and successor, rabbi Isacco Pardo, by the members of the Hevrat Gemilut Hasadim – the "Brotherhood of Good Works" – of the Jewish community of Verona.

In 1817, David Samuel Pardo, married Enrichetta Valenzini, with whom he would have four children. The scion of a family of rabbis and exegetes, he became chief rabbi of Livorno in 1820 and held the post for four years. In 1835, he moved to Verona, where he served as chief rabbi until his death in 1858. His son, Isacco, succeeded him, first as deputy rabbi, then as chief rabbi of Verona. David Samuel Pardo took a rigorous but moderate approach to the faith, based on tolerance, generosity and support for others. He was also very learned, and codified the coming-of-age rights for both young men and – a true first – young women. He left a sizable body of manuscripts on Jewish subjects, including sermons, poems, hymns and consolations. A passionate exegete, he published a number of interpretative works written both together with his father, Yaacov, and on his own. These include a multi-volume *Sefer Chasdei David* (1890) and a book of *Derashot* (sermons).

SDS

68. Siren letter by Cesare Lombroso for the Ravenna-Pardo wedding

Padua, March 15, 1855
Manuscript on paper
21 × 26,8 cm
Private collection, Ferrara

This letter was written by the renowned scientist Cesare Lombroso to mark the occasion of the wedding of Isacco Pardo and Bella – or "Bellina" – Gioconda. Isacco was born in Livorno in 1824. He was the son of the Sephardic rabbi and Ragusa (today Dubrovnik) native David Samuel Pardo, who held the position of chief rabbi first in Livorno and then in Verona. Following David Samuel's death in 1858, Isacco succeeded him as Chief Rabbi of Verona. In 1847, he was awarded the title of "Morènu ha-Rav" (our Master Rabbi) at the Rabbinical College of Padua. He died in Verona in 1892. Isacco Pardo's relationship with Cesare Lombroso is indicative of his open-minded attitude to innovative ideas.

SDS

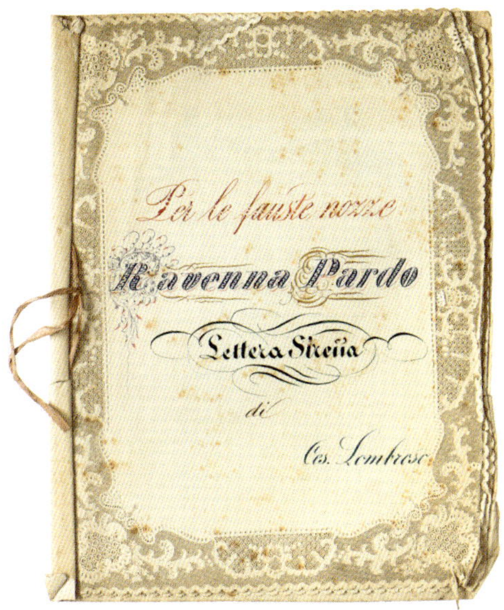
Per le fauste nozze
Ravenna Pardo
Lettera Sirena
di
Ces. Lombroso

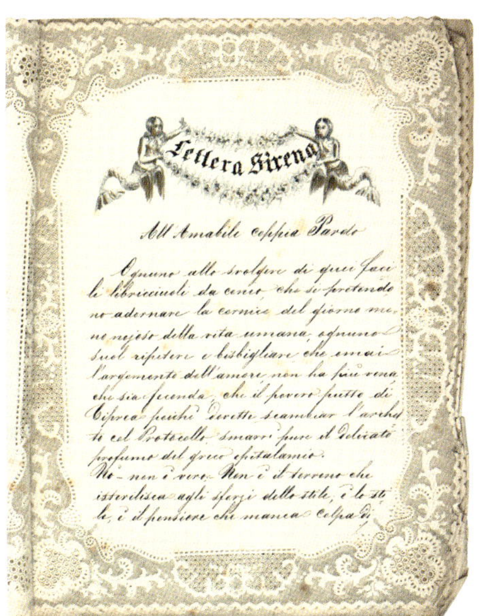
Lettera Sirena

All'Amabile coppia Pardo

Ognuno allo svolgere di quei fasci li libricciuoli da cenere che si pretendono adornare la cornice del giorno meno nojoso della vita umana, ognuno suol ripetere e bisbigliare che omai l'argomento dell'amore non ha più vena che sia feconda, che il povero putto di Ciprea poichè dovette scambiar l'archetto col Protocollo smarrì pure il delicato profumo del greco epitalamio.
No – non è vero. Non è il terreno che isterilisca agli sforzi dello stile, è lo stile, è il pensiero che manca. Colpa di

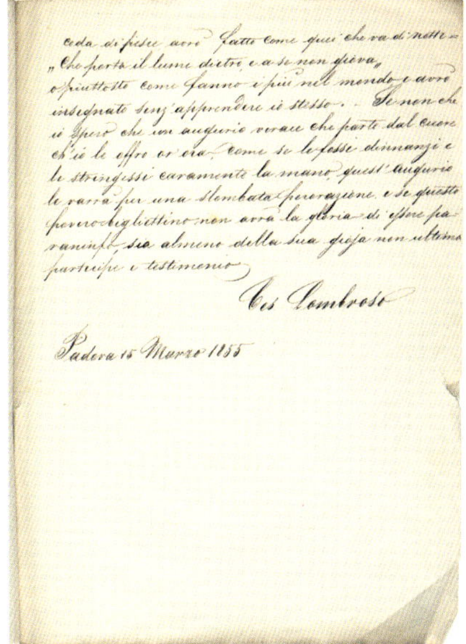
ceda di fisse avrò fatto come quei che va di notte – „Che porta il lume dietro, e a sè non giova„ o piuttosto come fanno i più nel mondo e avrò insegnato senz'apprendere io stesso. – Se non che io spero che un augurio verace che parte dal cuore ch'io le offro or ora, come se le fosse dinnanzi e le stringessi caramente la mano, quest'augurio le varrà per una slombata perorazione, e se questo povero bigliettino non avrà la gloria di essere paraninfo, sia almeno della sua gioja non ultimo partecipe e testimonio.

Ces. Lombroso

Padova 15 Marzo 1855

69. Degree in Engineering awarded to Dario Tagliacozzo Of the Royal School of Applied Engineering, Rome

1900
Printed and partly handwritten on paper
45 × 30.5 cm
MEIS (National Museum of Italian Judaism and the Shoah), Ferrara

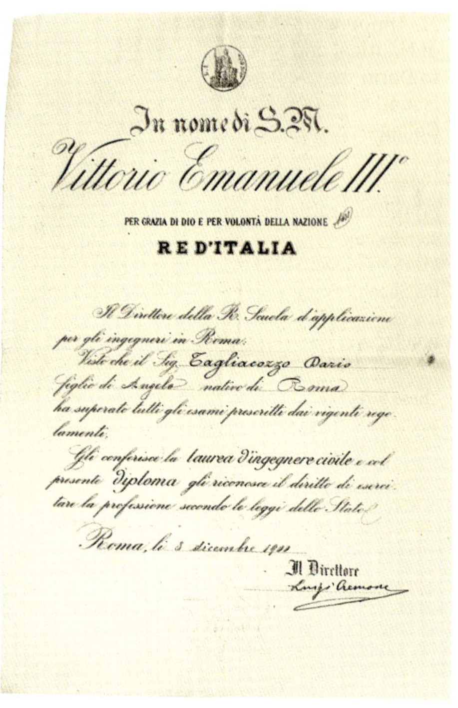

In nome di S.M.
Vittorio Emanuele III°
PER GRAZIA DI DIO E PER VOLONTÀ DELLA NAZIONE
RE D'ITALIA

Il Direttore della R. Scuola d'applicazione per gli ingegneri in Roma;
Visto che il Sig. Tagliacozzo Dario
figlio di Angelo nativo di Roma
ha superato tutti gli esami prescritti dai vigenti regolamenti;
Gli conferisce la laurea d'ingegnere civile e col presente diploma gli riconosce il diritto di esercitare la professione secondo le leggi dello Stato.

Roma, li 8 dicembre 1900
Il Direttore
Luigi Cremona

70. Decree appointing Dario Tagliacozzo to the position of Engineer Signed by Victor Emmanuel III, King of Italy

1902
Printed and partly handwritten on paper
27.5 × 40 cm
MEIS (National Museum of Italian Judaism and the Shoah), Ferrara

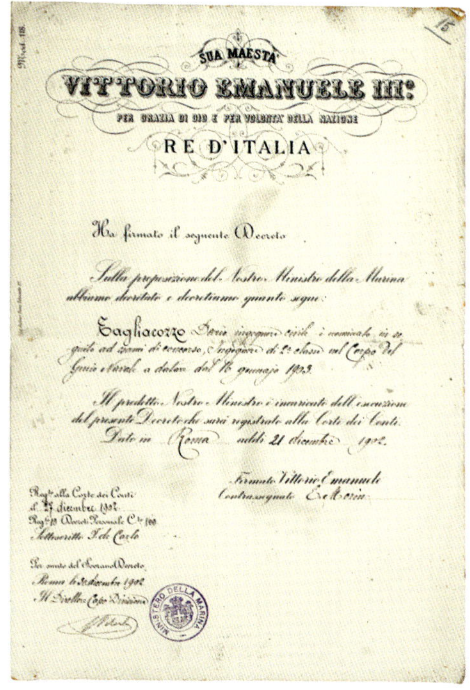

SUA MAESTA'
VITTORIO EMANUELE III°
PER GRAZIA DI DIO E PER VOLONTA' DELLA NAZIONE
RE D'ITALIA

Ha firmato il seguente Decreto

Sulla proposizione del Nostro Ministro della Marina abbiamo decretato e decretiamo quanto segue:

Tagliacozzo Dario ingegnere civile è nominato, in seguito ad esami di concorso, Ingegnere di 2ª classe nel Corpo del Genio Navale a datare dal 16 gennaio 1903.

Il predetto Nostro Ministro è incaricato dell'esecuzione del presente Decreto che sarà registrato alla Corte dei Conti.
Dato in Roma addì 21 dicembre 1902.

Firmato Vittorio Emanuele
Contrassegnato E. Morin

Regᵗᵒ alla Corte dei Conti
il 27 dicembre 1902
Regᵗᵒ 10 Decreti Personale C. 100
Sottoscritto F. de Carlo

Per copia conforme del Sovrano Decreto
Roma li 30 dicembre 1902
Il Direttore Capo Divisione

MINISTERO DELLA MARINA

71. Announcement of award of the title of Nautical and Mechanical Engineer to Dario Tagliacozzo Issued by the Directors of the Royal Naval College in Genoa

1904
Printed and partly handwritten on parchment
48 × 39 cm
MEIS (National Museum of Italian Judaism and the Shoah), Ferrara

Bibl.: Grenga, Pavoncello Piperno 2018.

These three documents testify to the rapid rise of Dario Tagliacozzo, and take us from his studies, via a competitive recruitment process, to a position in which he would serve his country at the highest level. With the outbreak of World War I, Tagliacozzo – by then, the chief inspector for the state railway and the naval engineering corps – was excused military service, as his contribution in other fields was deemed indispensable. A number of German steamships that happened to find themselves in Italian ports were requisitioned and turned over to the engineering department headed by Tagliacozzo, who succeeded in returning them to working order. A short time later, he was dispatched to England in the search for cargo vessels, which the Ministry needed to transport coal for the railways. For these efforts, he was made a knight of the Order of the Crown of Italy.

SDS

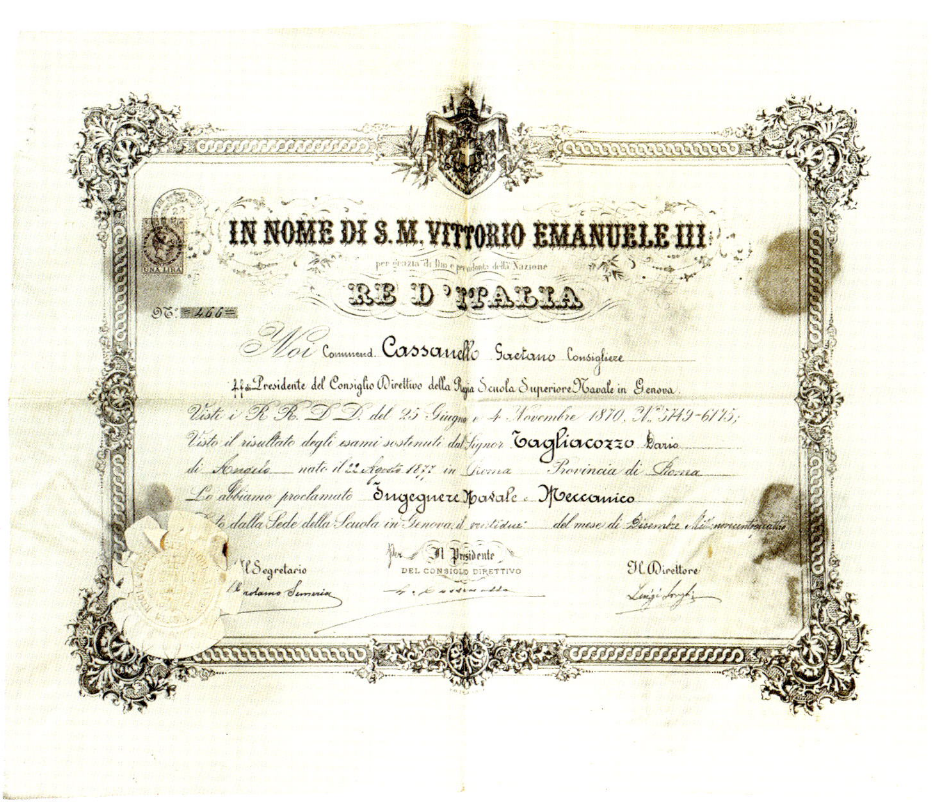

UNA LIRA

IN NOME DI S.M. VITTORIO EMANUELE III
per grazia di Dio e per volontà della Nazione
RE D'ITALIA

N.° =466=

Noi Commend. Cassanello Gaetano Consigliere
ff.di Presidente del Consiglio Direttivo della Regia Scuola Superiore Navale in Genova.
Visti i R.R. D.D. del 25 Giugno e 4 Novembre 1870, N.° 5749-6175;
Visto il risultato degli esami sostenuti dal Signor Tagliacozzo Dario
di Angelo nato il 22 Agosto 1877 in Roma Provincia di Roma
Lo abbiamo proclamato Ingegnere Navale e Meccanico
Dato dalla Sede della Scuola in Genova il ventidue del mese di Dicembre Millenovecentoquattro

Il Segretario
Per Il Presidente DEL CONSIGLIO DIRETTIVO
Il Direttore

72. Opera glasses with embroidered velvet sleeve, Tagliacozzo family

Italy, early twentieth century
Steel with mother-of-pearl decorations; embroidered velvet sleeve
10.5 × 8 cm
Private collection

These mother-of-pearl opera glasses date from the early twentieth century. The handle is inscribed with the name of the opticians where they were purchased – "A. Hirsch Ottico Roma" – whose address is listed in the 1896 *Calendario Generale del Regno d'Italia* ("General Calendar of the Kingdom of Italy") as number 402, Via del Corso.

The protective velvet pouch is decorated on each reticulated side with silk ribbons and gold thread, which form garlands and baskets of pink and pale green flowers.

A selection of invitations to theatrical events conserved in the family archive tell us that these glasses were used by Clelia Di Capua Tagliacozzo on her trips to the theatre with her husband, Dario Tagliacozzo.

SDS

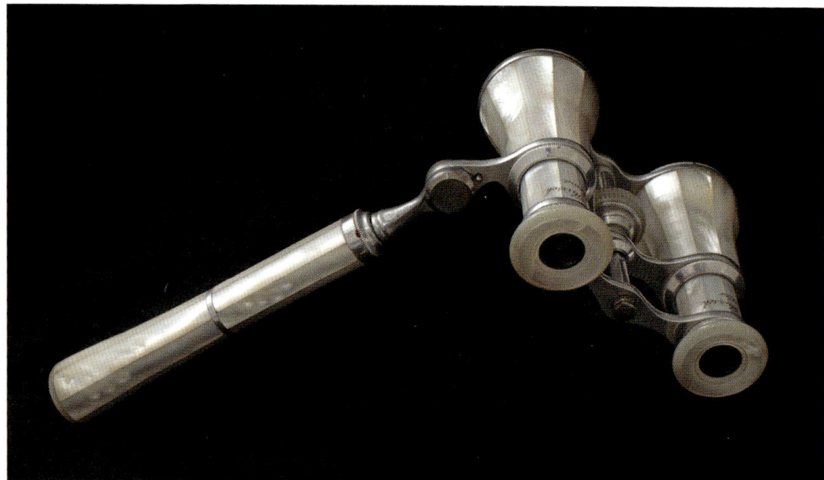

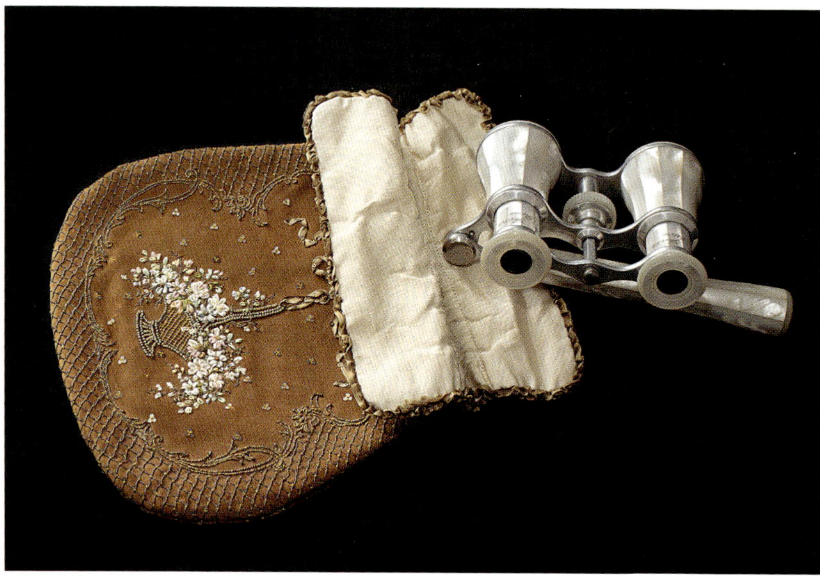

73. Parasol, Tagliacozzo family

Italy, early twentieth century
Embroidered cotton with lace inserts
81 × 95 cm
Private collection

This parasol is seen being used in photographs of the Tagliacozzo family from around 1907, the year in which Dario Tagliacozzo married his cousin Clelia Di Capua.

SDS

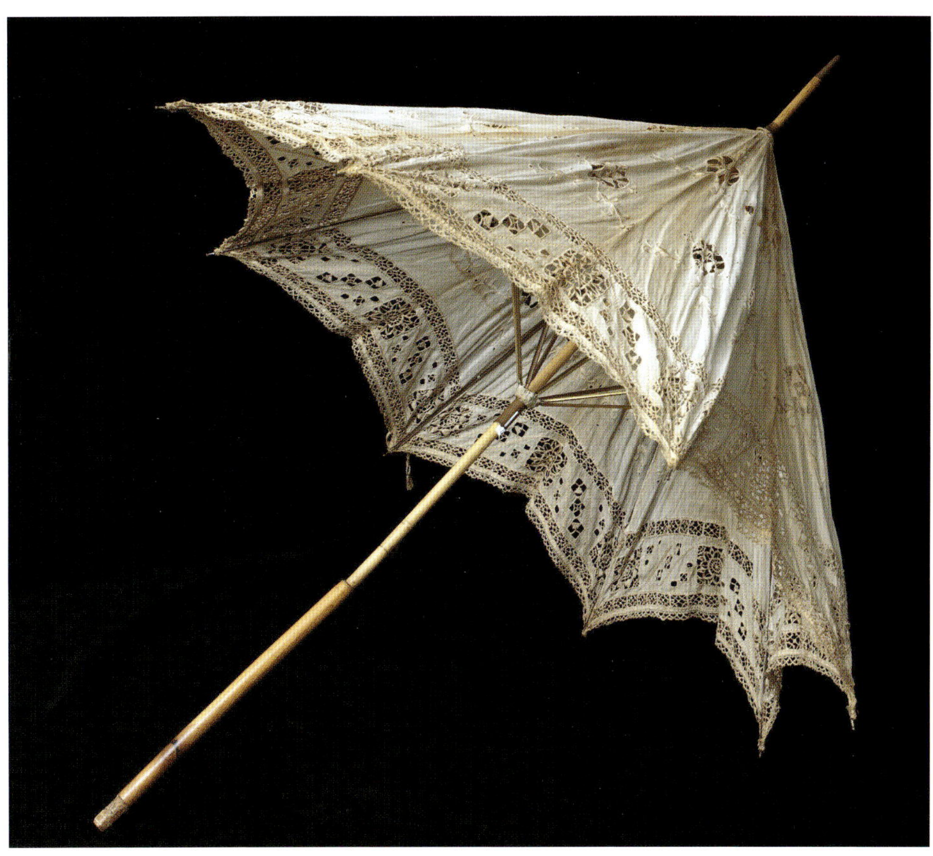

74. *LUX. Rivista mensile per il pensiero e per la vita ebraica*, year I, issue 1

Livorno, March 1904
Print on paper
Centro Bibliografico UCEI, Rome

The magazine *LUX* began as a cultural enterprise by two rabbis from Livorno, Arrigo Lattes (1879–1918) and Alfredo Sabato Toaff (1880–1963). The initiative did not meet with great success and publication ceased after just a few issues, but it remains an interesting experiment. The richly symbolic cover illustration is particularly significant. It is signed G. Micheli, probably Guglielmo Micheli (1866–1926), a typographer and lithographer from Livorno. On the left-hand side, from top to bottom, we find the inscription "*Ex Oriente Lux*", the star of David, and the tablets of the Law. The scene is typical of Orientalist evocations of a timeless Palestine, a point of anchorage for Jewish identity since the Biblical age. In its composition and aesthetics, the image is reminiscent of numerous, more famous illustrations by Efraim Lilien (1847–1925), an art nouveau artist and illustrator with links to the international Zionist movement.

CFdU

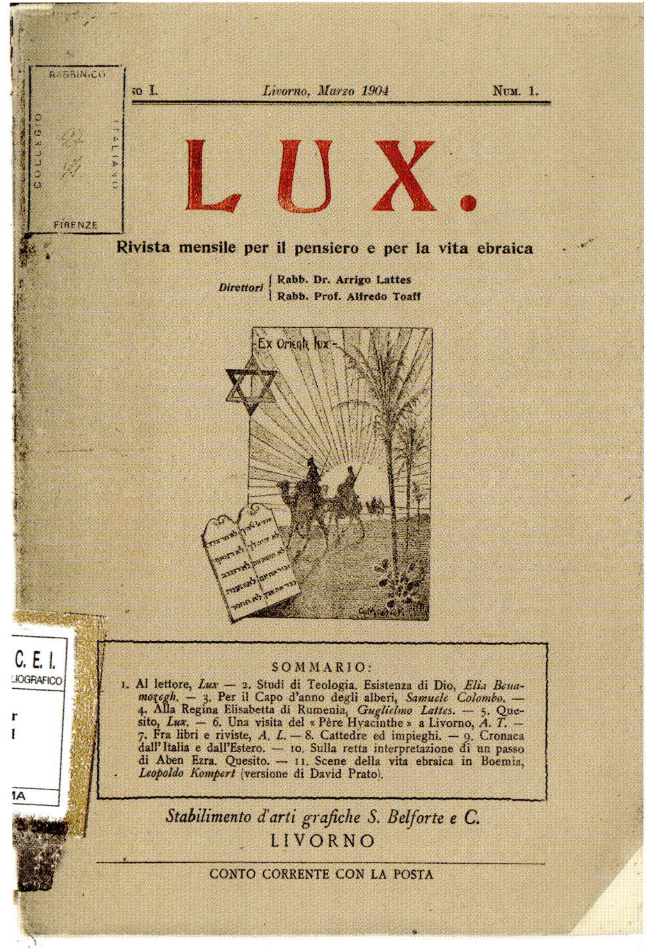

...no I. *Livorno, Marzo 1904* Num. 1.

LUX.

Rivista mensile per il pensiero e per la vita ebraica

Direttori { **Rabb. Dr. Arrigo Lattes**
Rabb. Prof. Alfredo Toaff

SOMMARIO:

1. Al lettore, *Lux* — 2. Studi di Teologia. Esistenza di Dio, *Elia Benamozegh.* — 3. Per il Capo d'anno degli alberi, *Samuele Colombo.* — 4. Alla Regina Elisabetta di Rumenia, *Guglielmo Lattes.* — 5. Quesito, *Lux.* — 6. Una visita del « Père Hyacinthe » a Livorno, *A. T.* — 7. Fra libri e riviste, *A. L.* — 8. Cattedre ed impieghi. — 9. Cronaca dall'Italia e dall'Estero. — 10. Sulla retta interpretazione di un passo di Aben Ezra. Quesito. — 11. Scene della vita ebraica in Boemia, *Leopoldo Kompert* (versione di David Prato).

Stabilimento d'arti grafiche S. Belforte e C.
LIVORNO

CONTO CORRENTE CON LA POSTA

75. *L'Idea Sionnista*

Modena, February 1908
Print on paper
32 × 21.5 cm
MEIS (National Museum of Italian Judaism and the Shoah), Ferrara

L'Idea Sionista. Rivista mensile del movimento sionista (The Zionist Idea. Monthly magazine of the Zionist movement) was founded in 1901 by Carlo Angelo Conigliani, Felice Ravenna, and Amedeo and Benvenuto Donati. Published in Modena, it stated in the first editorial: "To stand [...] side by side with our distant brothers, and improve their lot and ours: this is the only way to pre-empt and quash antisemitism; this is the ultimate goal of the new tendency that we call Zionism [...] which does not seek to provide us with a homeland, since we already have one that is noble and beautiful; [...] rather it must be a sacred defense of individual and social liberties" (I, 1). After Conigliani's death in 1901, the editorship was taken on by Benvenuto Donati, followed by Carlo Levi in 1904. In the same year, the styling of the banner was modified, and the title changed to *L'Idea Sionnista*. The cover reproduced here uses an illustration in the art nouveau style featuring an allegorical representation of the Zionist vision: a female figure in a statuesque pose holding a Star of David.

The cover was designed by Emma Goitein Dessau, who was born in Germany but grew up in Perugia. A painter from an early age, Emma had come into contact with Luigi Severini through her expertise in woodcuts. In this field, she designed numerous *ex-libris*, in addition to the cover of *L'Idea Sionnista*.

CFdU

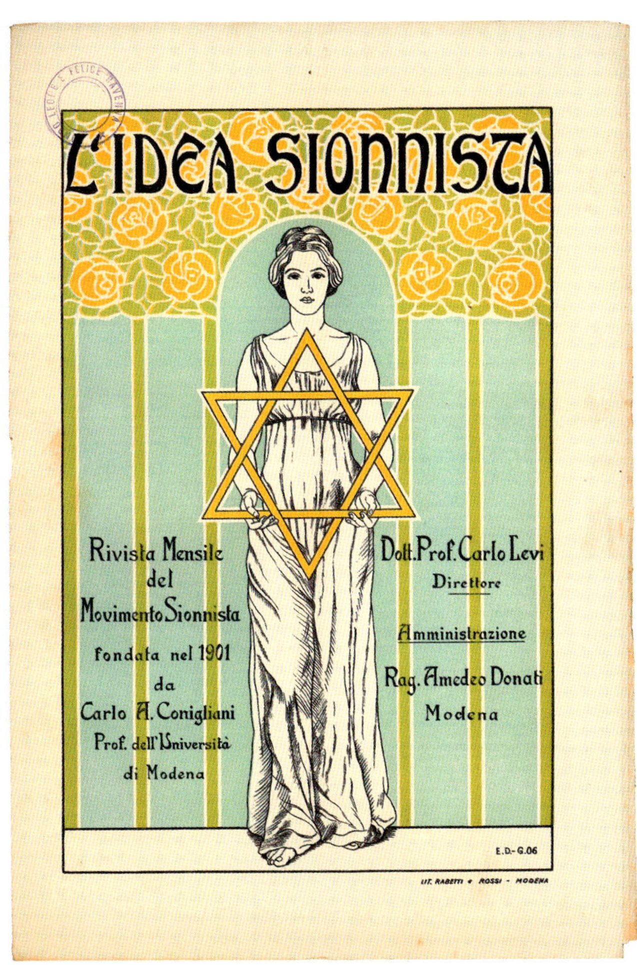

76. Receipt for a donation by Italian Zionists to the Zionist Congress made by the lawyer Felice Ravenna, president of the Italian Zionist Federation

Basel, July 22, 1902
In German
Print and handwritten text on paper
52 × 22 cm
Gianfranco Moscati Collection, MEIS (National Museum of Italian Judaism and the Shoah), Ferrara

This is a receipt for a donation of 261 Swiss francs, which was made by Felice Ravenna, a lawyer from Ferrara, on behalf of Italian "shekelisti" (from "shekel," the biblical currency from which the currency of modern Israel takes its name), who each supported the Zionist cause through the donation of a shekel.
The receipt is signed by Alexandre Marmorek, a Zionist from Galicia (Austrian Poland), who at that time was Secretary of the Action Committee of the Zionist Organization (later the World Zionist Organization). Article 1 of the Zionist Organization statute published by the Italian Zionist Federation in 1904 reads: "The Zionist Organization welcomes those Israelites who subscribe to the program of the Zionist Congress and make a payment of one shekel."
The only one of the events in Basel to involve the Italian Jews was that of 1898. Writing on the day after his appearance at the congress, Felice Ravenna asserted that, "for those Israelites for whom, in Poland, Russia, Romania, Galicia, Bohemia, in the very heart of Austria, the entitlement to life and property is no longer guaranteed, Zionism is a political and social movement; for us Italians, and for French and British Jews, it is a purely philanthropic and humanitarian movement" (*Il Corriere israelitico*, year 37, October 1898, p. 122). Theodor Herzl would show his appreciation for this donation, attending a meeting of Italian Zionists in Milan in 1902.

SDS

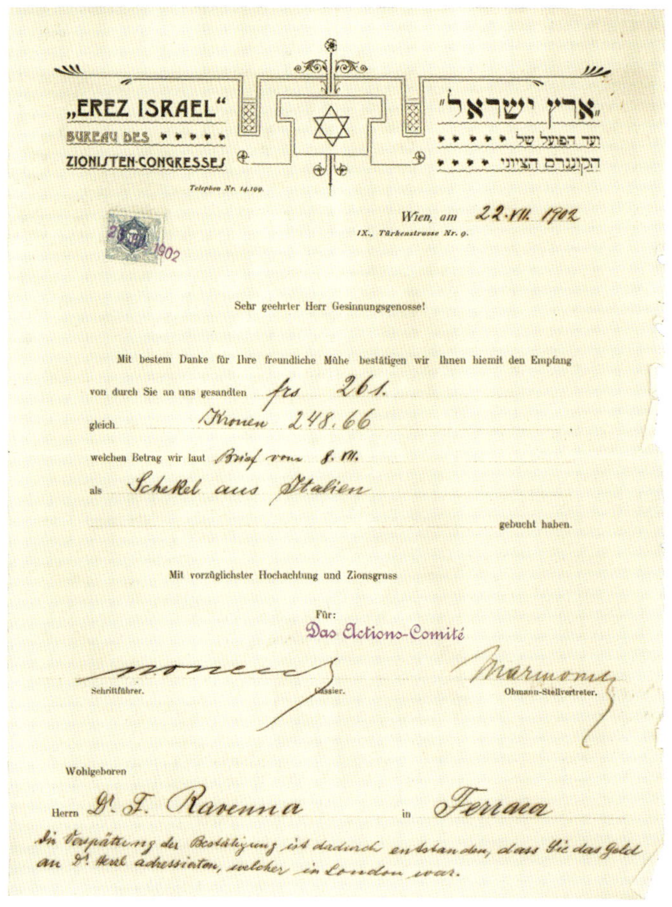

„EREZ ISRAEL"
BUREAU DES
ZIONISTEN-CONGRESSES

ארץ ישראל
ועד הפועל של
הקונגרס הציוני

Telephon Nr. 14.199.

Wien, am 22.VII. 1902
IX., Türkenstrasse Nr. 9.

Sehr geehrter Herr Gesinnungsgenosse!

Mit bestem Danke für Ihre freundliche Mühe bestätigen wir Ihnen hiemit den Empfang
von durch Sie an uns gesandten frs 261.
gleich Kronen 248.66
welchen Betrag wir laut Brief vom 8. VII.
als Schekel aus Italien
gebucht haben.

Mit vorzüglichster Hochachtung und Zionsgruss

Für:
Das Actions-Comité

Schriftführer. Cassier. Obmann-Stellvertreter.
Marmorek

Wohlgeboren
Herrn Dr. F. Ravenna in Ferrara

Die Verspätung der Bestätigung ist dadurch entstanden, dass Sie das Geld an Dr. Herzl adressierten, welcher in London war.

77. Dante Lattes, "Dr. Theodor Herzl," a commemorative address to the Zionist Circle of Trieste

Trieste, 1904
Includes an autobiography of Dr. Herzl
Published by the Zionist Circle of Trieste
Print on paper
22.5 × 15 cm
Gianfranco Moscati Collection, MEIS (National Museum of Italian Judaism and the Shoah), Ferrara

On July 12, 1904, nine days after the death of founder of the Zionist movement, Theodor Herzl, the Zionist Circle of Trieste commemorated his life with a tearful, and somewhat prophetically flavored address by Dante Lattes (Pitigliano, 1876 – Dolo, 1965). Soon afterwards, the address was published as the first pamphlet to be issued independently by the Library of the Trieste Circle. Lattes was educated at Elijah Benamozegh's Rabbinical College in Livorno, where he would qualify as a rabbi. In 1898, he moved to Trieste – at that time still part of the Austro-Hungarian Empire – to work for the periodical *Il Corriere Israelitico*. There, he also became a teacher and guiding figure at the Scola Vivante, a synagogue attended primarily by Jews of Corfiot descent. He remained in Trieste until the outbreak of the First World War. From the start, Lattes was an active contributor to the Zionist movement in Italy. In 1918, he took the role of secretary of the Italian Zionist Federation, later becoming president and maintaining relations with the Central Zionist Office in London for many years. In Lattes' eyes, the spiritual renewal of the Jews and the recovery of their moral and intellectual heritage could only come in tandem with the rebirth of the Jewish nation in the land of Israel. In 1916, he founded the monthly publication *L'Israel*, followed a few years later by *La Rassegna Mensile di Israel*, which is still in circulation. He also became a director of the Union of the Israelite Communities of Italy, but emigrated to Palestine in 1939, returning to Italy after the war. A prolific writer and translator, he is credited with introducing to Italy the writings of some of the founders of modern Zionism, such as Ahad Ha-Am, Leon Pinsker, Moses Hess, Chaim Nachman Bialik and Joseph Klausner, to name but a few. He was also the director of the Rabbinical College in Rome. Among the founding figures of the Italian Zionist movement, Lattes' few close friends included Felice Ravenna, Alfonso Pacifici, Riccardo Bachi and Riccardo Curiel. His pupils include Enzo Sereni, Attilio Milano, Guido Tedeschi, Giorgio Romano and Augusto Segre.

SDS

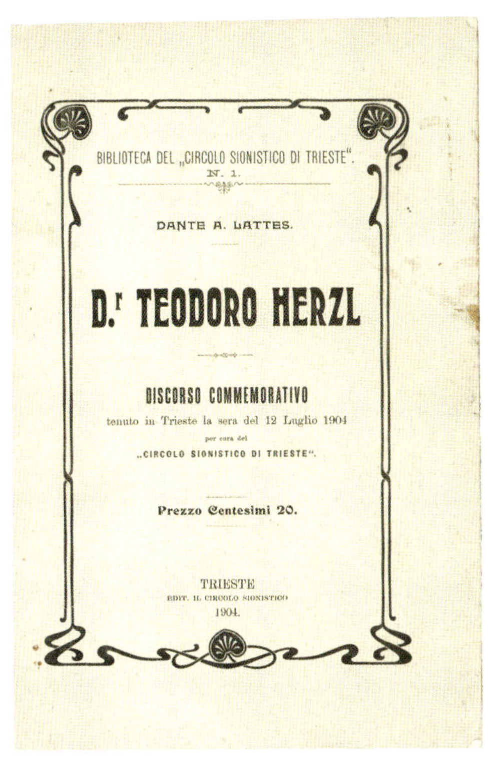
BIBLIOTECA DEL „CIRCOLO SIONISTICO DI TRIESTE".
N. 1.

DANTE A. LATTES.

D.r TEODORO HERZL

DISCORSO COMMEMORATIVO
tenuto in Trieste la sera del 12 Luglio 1904
per cura del
„CIRCOLO SIONISTICO DI TRIESTE".

Prezzo Centesimi 20.

TRIESTE
EDIT. IL CIRCOLO SIONISTICO
1904.

78. ***Israello Canto***

Venice, 1904
Print on paper
22.5 × 15 cm
Gianfranco Moscati Collection, MEIS (National Museum of Italian Judaism and the Shoah), Ferrara

About a month after the death of Theodor Herzl on July 3, 1904, a pamphlet published in an unusual format and characterized by elegant graphics appeared in Venice. It contained a composition in verse titled "Israel." The unknown author identified herself simply as "a Zionist"; an educated guess would suggest a member of the family of Angelo Sullam, who was one of the earliest proponents of the Zionist movement in Italy. The poem offers a very summary account of key events in Jewish history, up to and including the Dreyfus Affair and the constitution of the Zionist movement. The text is written in free verse, alternating between hendecasyllable and septenary meter without any apparent system. The booklet was printed on the presses of F. Garzia & C. 300 copies were printed, with the proceeds of any sales to go towards a subscription opened for the benefit of Herzl's children by the Special Committee on July 7, 1904.

SDS

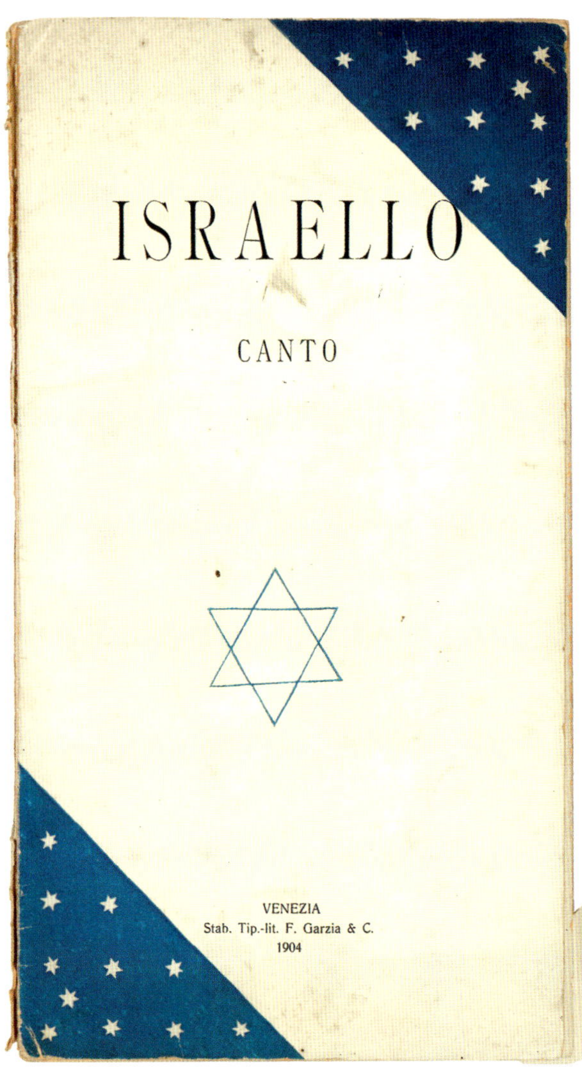

79. Letter from Max Nordau to Felice Ravenna

Paris, December 29, 1898
Manuscript on paper
28.5 × 21.8 cm
Gianfranco Moscati Collection, MEIS (National Museum of Italian Judaism and the Shoah), Ferrara

In this letter, written in French, Max Nordau – Hungarian sociologist and journalist, and friend and collaborator of Theodor Herzl, with whom he co-founded the Zionist Organization – congratulates the young lawyer Felice Ravenna of Ferrara for establishing an Italian Zionist organization, and goes on to offer the Italian group the support of the Parisian Zionists ahead of the upcoming congress in Basel (Nordau had moved to Paris from Budapest): "We are at the disposal of our brothers in Italy." Nordau and Ravenna had met at the second Zionist Congress in the summer of the same year.

SDS

Paris, le 29 Déc. 1898

Cher Monsieur,

Je vous félicite de votre bel idéalisme vif et de l'énergie que vous déployez pour créer une organisation sioniste en Italie.

Le Comité Central étant représenté dans votre patrie par Monsieur le Rabbin J. Sonnino, 30. Capella Vecchia, Naples, je vous engage vivement à vous mettre en rapport avec lui. Il faut évidemment que toutes les associations sionistes de l'Italie soient en contact réciproque constant.

Une édition française de la "Welt", quelque désirable qu'elle fut, serait trop coûteuse et nos moyens, hélas, sont des plus exigus. Nous sommes encore un mouvement de pauvres et devons compter avec les centimes.

Mais à partir du nouvel an il paraîtra à Paris une petite feuille purement sioniste en français naturellement, qui reproduira toutes les nouvelles positives publiées dans la "Welt". Nous comptons bien sur nos frères d'Italie pour faire vivre ce journal qui sera très bon marché. Avec 6 à 800 abonnés, dont 3 à 400 de l'Italie, on pourra se maintenir.

Très prochainement paraîtra également l'édition française des discours les plus importants prononcés à Bâle et nous en tiendrons à la disposition de nos frères d'Italie tant d'exemplaires qu'ils en demanderont.

Croyez à la haute considération de votre tout dévoué

Dr M. Nordau

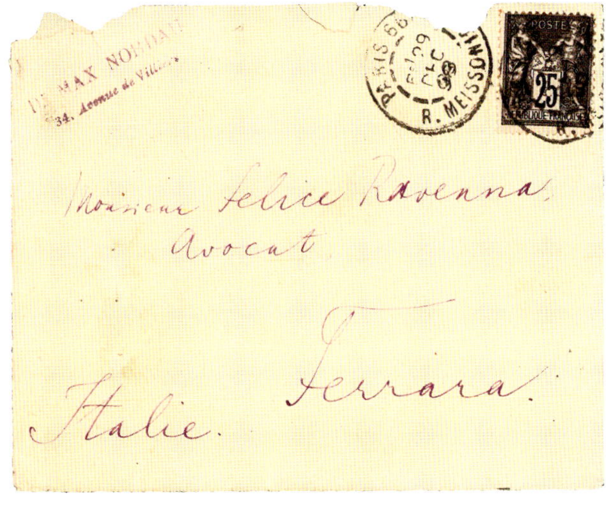

Dr MAX NORDAU
34, Avenue de Villiers

Monsieur Felice Ravenna,
Avocat
Ferrara.
Italie.

80. Trunk Belonging to Red Cross Nurse Matilde Levi Viterbo

Wood with steel inserts
31 × 70 × 30 cm
MEIS (National Museum of Italian Judaism and the Shoah), Ferrara

This trunk contains the uniform and equipment given to Matilde Levi (married name Viterbo, 1869–1959) as a Red Cross nurse in World War I. The contents are as follows: a white piqué uniform, two belts, a white canvas uniform, a white apron with the owner's name embroidered in red, five white belts, three white nurse's caps, two cotton mesh caps, a blue veil with a white band and red cross, a spare headband, two starched headbands, a white wimple, five headbands, six white canvas waist packs, scissors, tweezers, nail files, a tourniquet, two notebooks, three pencils, an eraser, a pencil sharpener, a blue silk bag with the Red Cross emblem, five pairs of white cotton stockings, a pair of white leather gloves, a pair of sleeve protectors, six white collars, eight red canvas crosses, a pillowcase embroidered with the initials "M. V.," a bed sheet, a hemp bag containing an iron, and a white-and-blue enameled metal bowl.

SR

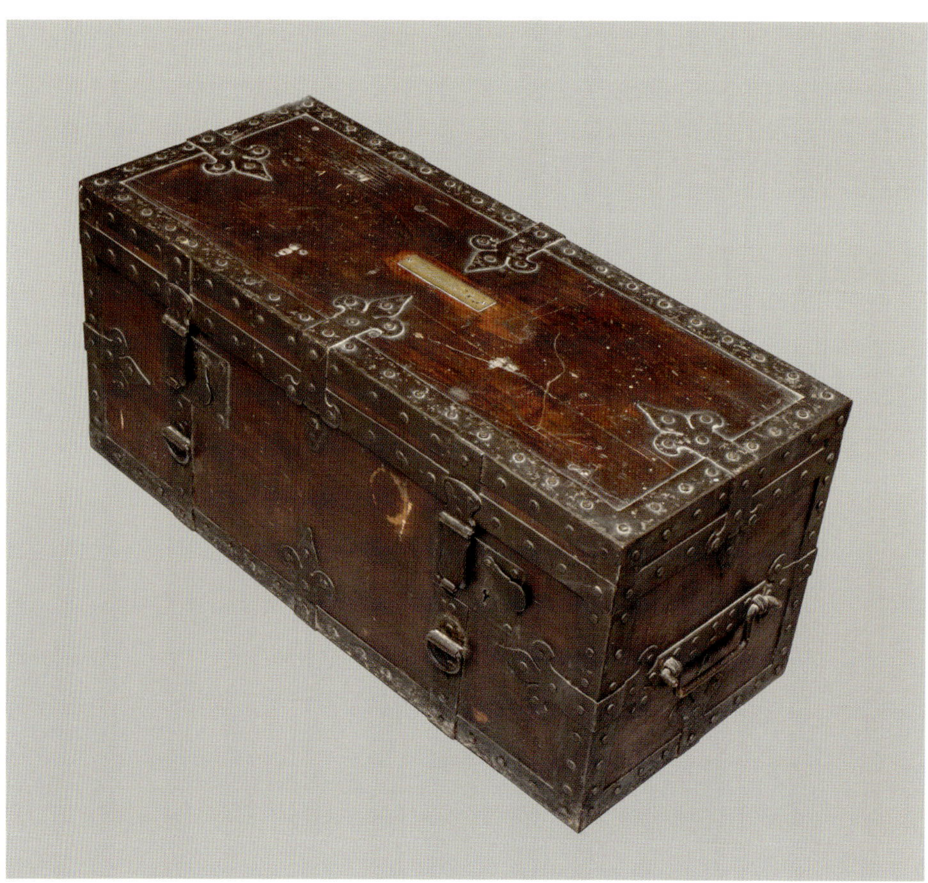

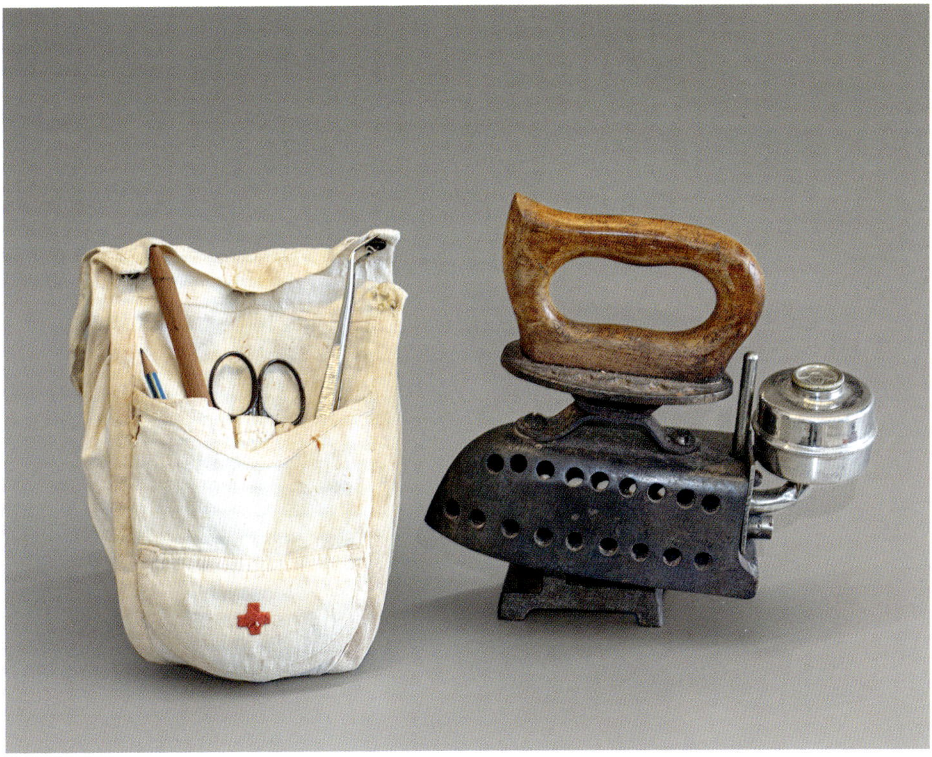

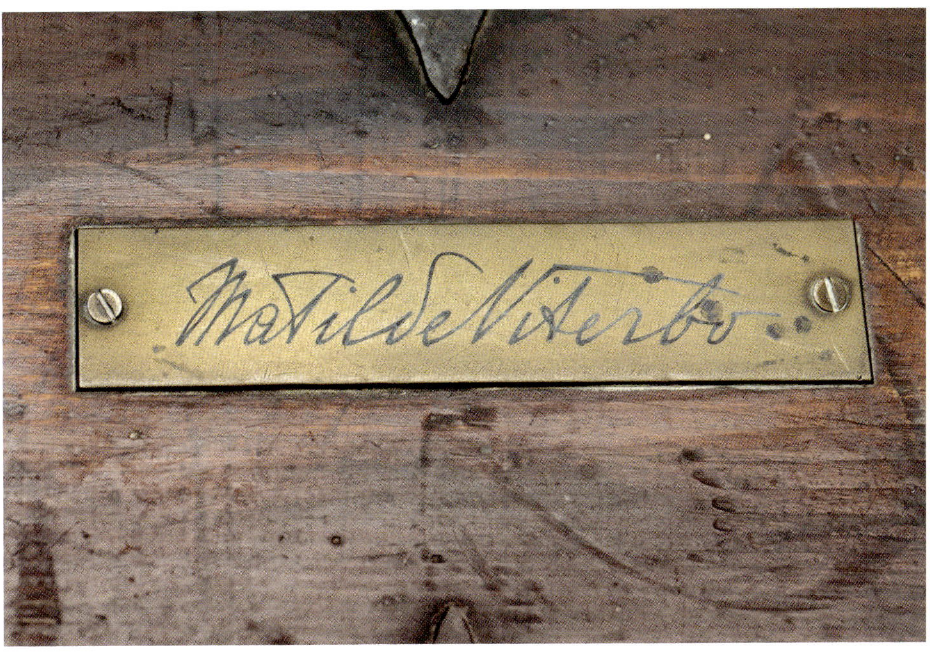
Matilde Viterbo

81. Giacomo Balla, *Portrait of Ernesto Nathan*

Rome, 1910
Oil on canvas
86 × 95 cm; with frame 88 × 97 × 3 cm
Inv. AM 566
Gallery of Modern Art, Rome
Inv. AM 566

In 1910, the mayor of Rome, Ernesto Nathan, sent a note to the painter Giacomo Balla: "*Caro Balla [...] dovrei regalare all'amministrazione un mio ritratto a olio mezzo busto, grandezza naturale ma non posso spendere più di 500 lire. Se lei credesse di incaricarsi di una faccia di così poco valore, è a sua disposizione, suo Nathan*" (Dear Balla [...] I am to present the administration with a portrait of myself. It is to be half-length, in oils, and life size, but I cannot spend more than 500 lire. If you feel you could take on such an unworthy visage, it is at your disposal. Yours, Nathan) (Balla 1984). The resulting portrait is composed in a rather unusual manner, with the mayor depicted sitting behind his desk, at work. It was shown in public for the first time at the 1911 Universal Exhibition in Rome.

Ernesto Nathan was born in London 1845 to Moses Meyer and Sara Levi, which placed him at the beating heart of the transnational Mazzinian network. Indeed, the family's political activities were fundamental to his education. Grand Master of the Grand Orient of Italy from 1896 to 1903, and again from 1917 to 1919, he served as mayor of Rome from 1907 to 1913 at the head of a coalition of radicals, left-leaning liberals, socialists and republicans.

CFdU

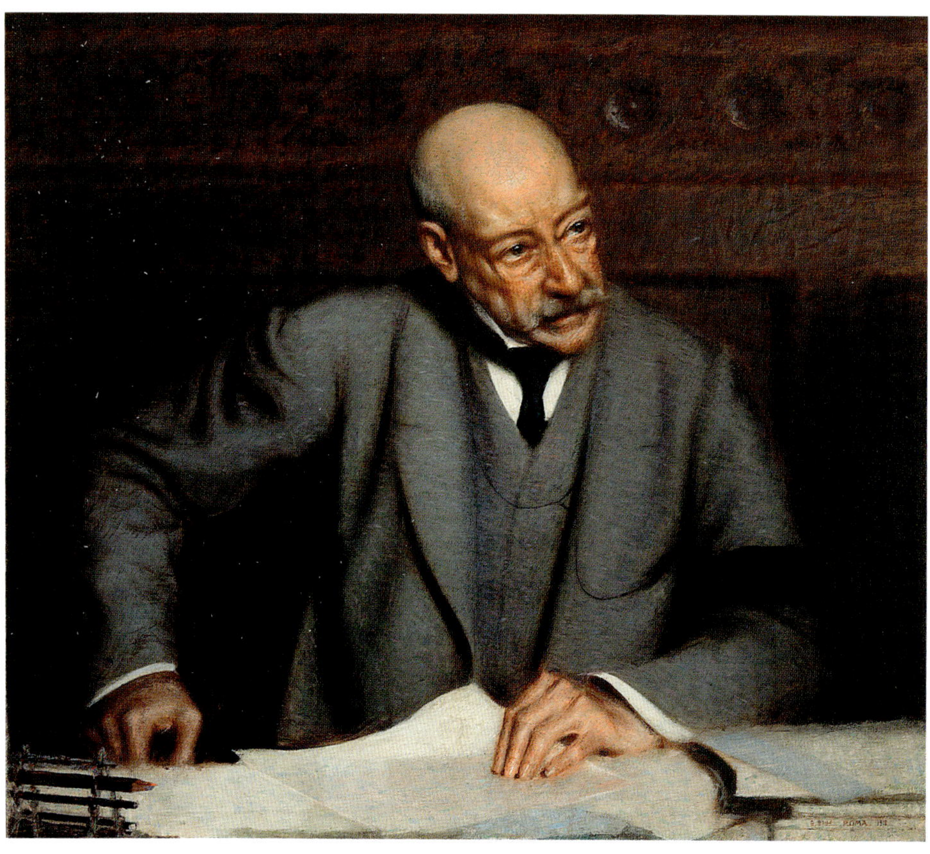

82. Vittorio Corcos, *Portrait of Giuseppe Garibaldi*

Paris, 1882
Oil on canvas
89.5 × 65.5 cm; with frame 110.5 × 85.5 cm
Civic Museum "Giovanni Fattori," Livorno
Inv. 1991/406

Vittorio Corcos (1859–1933) was born in Livorno and attended the Florence Academy of Fine Arts before continuing his studies in Naples and Paris. He returned to Italy in 1886 and converted to Catholicism in 1887. He quickly earned a name as a portraitist, and his list of subjects include many of the great figures of the age, from Giosuè Carducci to Kaiser Wilhelm II and Queen Margherita. In 1928, he was even commissioned to paint a portrait of Mussolini. "Who isn't familiar with Vittorio Corcos' work?" asked Ugo Ojetti, rhetorically, in the short obituary that appeared in the *Corriere della Sera* on November 18, 1933.

This portrait of Garibaldi is a celebratory piece that was completed, with the aid of a photograph, in 1882, shortly after the death of the great "hero of two worlds." Corcos gifted the painting to the city of Livorno, and it hung in the meeting room at the city hall. It depicts an elderly Garibaldi – instantly recognizable from his outfit of gray cloak, red shirt, and crimson, embroidered cap – with a meditative expression, as though deep in thought.

CFdU

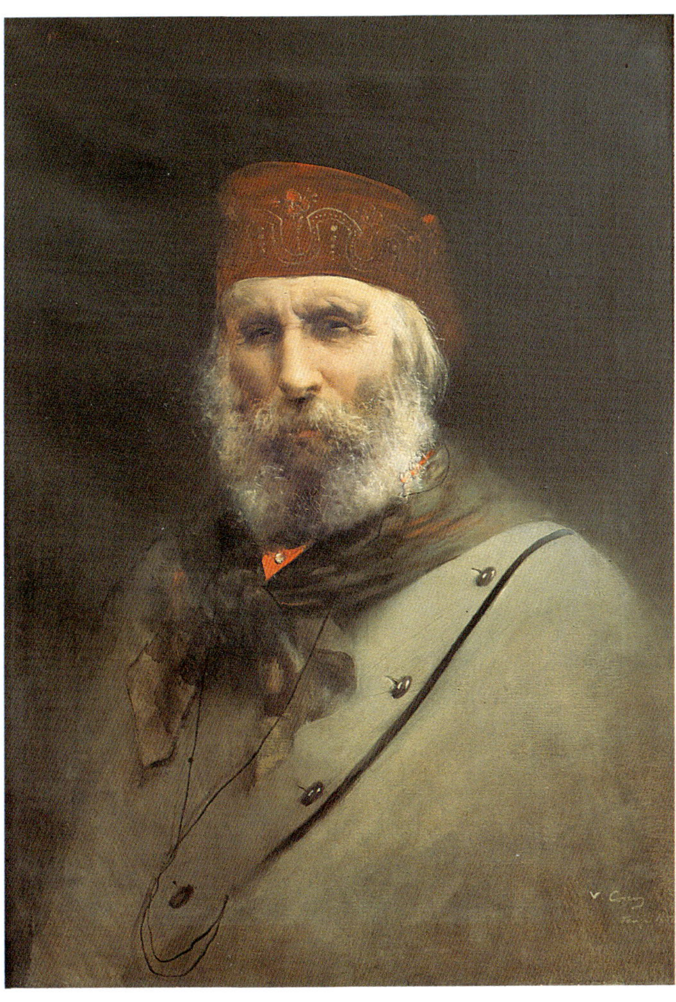

83. Alberto Pisa, *Self-Portrait*

1894
Oil on canvas
44 × 34 cm
Museo dell'Ottocento, Ferrara
Inv. 719

Alberto Pisa (1864–1930) was born in Ferrara to Abramo Pisa, the scion of a well-known Jewish banking family, and Malvina Anau. His artistic studies began under Gianfranco Domenichini at the Palazzo Diamanti School, before taking him to the Academies of Fine Art in Florence and Rome. During his time in Florence, he participated in the national exhibitions of painting. In 1886 he moved, first, to Paris, where he was able to see the works of the Impressionists, and then to London, where he remained for a significant period of time. During a moderately successful spell in England, he met the American artists James Abbott McNeill Whistler and John Singer Sargent, whose influence is discernible in his own work of those years. Pisa returned definitively to Italy in 1921, settling in Florence, where he died in 1930.

SR

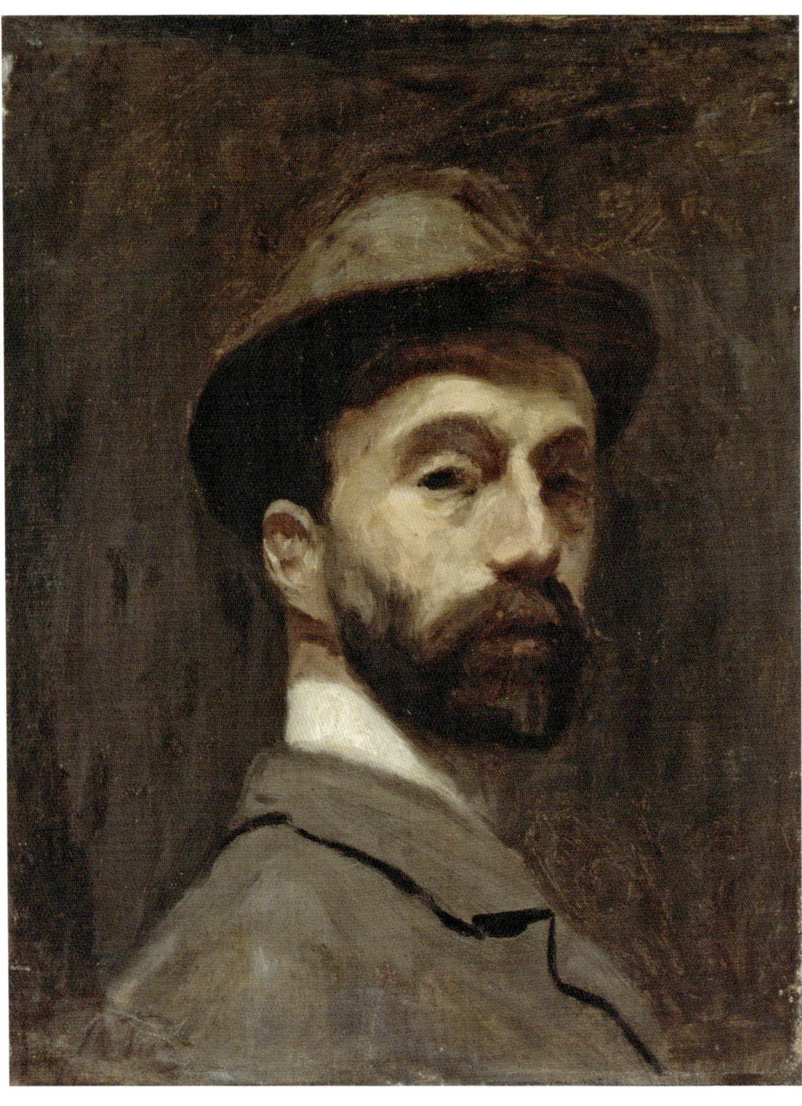

84. Portrait of a Jewish Girl from Rome

1913
Charcoal on paper
63 × 44 cm; with frame 82 × 63 cm
Alberto Di Castro Collection, Rome

Little is known about the girl portrayed in this painting, although the four labels on the reverse offer some information. Two of these are written by hand and indicate the title of the painting, "The Jewess." The other labels read as follows: The Jewess. £ 15 – 15/- Stewart Mamchael (?) 102 George Street – Edinburgh +65 Nettergate Dunde [hand-written]; Dundee Art Society Ed. The Jewess, Stewart Mamchael (?) 65 Nethergate Dundee £ 15 – 15--- Thos Murray & Son [hand-written]; MURRAY & SON; W.... BROWN & SON Removers & Storers.65, GEORGE ST., EDINBURGH. B3466.

RS-SDS

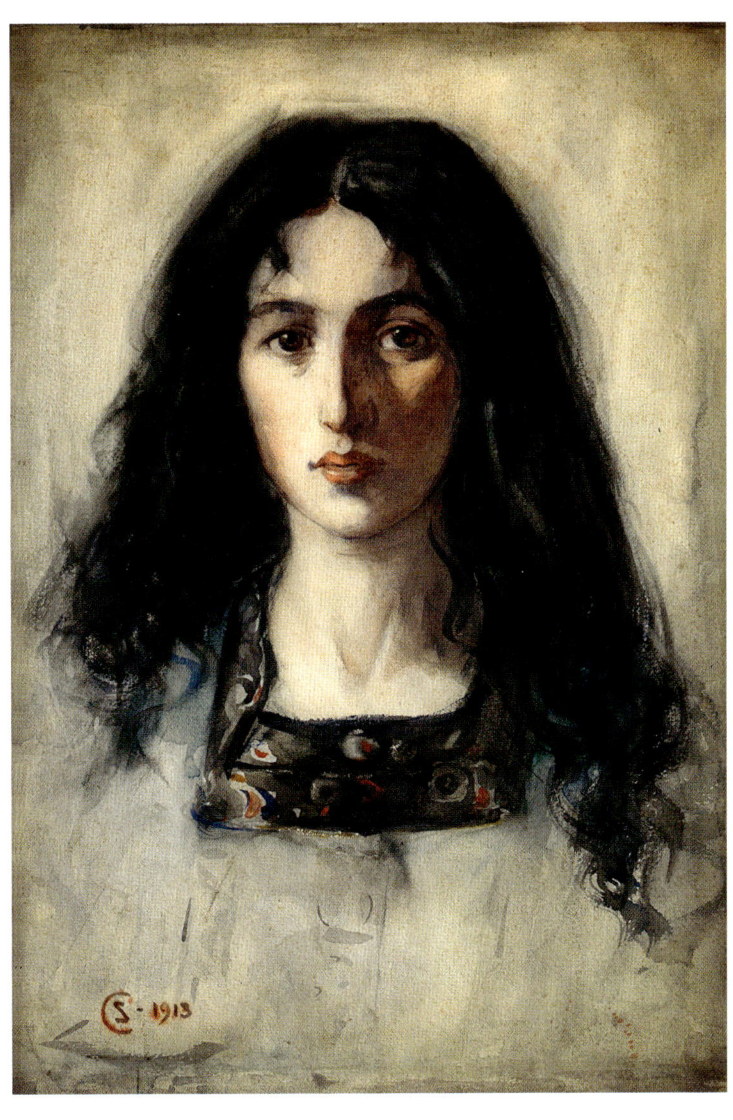

Bibliography

F.H. Adler 2005
F.H. Adler, "Why Mussolini turned on the Jews," in *Patterns of Prejudice*, 39, 2005, pp. 285–300.

F.H. Adler 2008
F.H. Adler, "Gli ebrei: borghesi, nemici, vittime del fascismo," in *Il Ponte*, 5, 2008, pp. 99–120.

I. Adler 1966
I. Adler, *La Pratique musicale savante dans quelques communautés juives en Europe aux XVII*[e] *et XVIII*[e] *siècles*, Paris - The Hague 1966.

I. Adler 1975
I. Adler, *Hebrew Writings Concerning Music in Manuscript and Printed Books from Geonic Times up to 1800*, RISM B/IX/2, Munich 1975.

I. Adler 1986
I. Adler, "Shelosha teqasim musiqaliim lehosha'na rabah baqehilat qasale monferato (1732, 1733, 1735)," in *Yuval: Studies of the Jewish Music Research Center*, vol. 5, *The Abraham Zvi Idelsohn Memorial Volume*, ed. by I. Adler, B. Bayer, E. Schleifer, Jerusalem 1986, pp. 51–137.

I. Adler 1987
I. Adler, "La pénétration de la musique savante dans les synagogues italiennes au XVIIe siècle : le cas particulier de Venise," in *Gli Ebrei e Venezia. Secoli XIV-XVIII*, proceedings of the international conference organized by the Istituto di storia della società e dello Stato veneziano della Fondazione Giorgio Cini (Venice, Isola di San Giorgio Maggiore, June 5–10, 1983), ed. by G. Cozzi, Milan 1987, pp. 527–535.

I. Adler 1989
I. Adler, *Hebrew Notated Manuscript Sources up to Circa 1840: A Descriptive and Thematic Catalogue With a Checklist of Printed Sources*, with the assistance of L. Shalem, RISM B/IX/1, Munich 1989.

I. Adler 1992
Hosha'nah Rabbah in Casale Monferrato, 1733. Musical ceremony for 3 voices, strings, oboes, trumpets and basso continuo by anonymous composers. Liturgical text and cantata "Dio, Clemenza e Rigore" (God, Defender and Accuser). Libretto by S.H. Jarach. Edited with realization of the basso continuo by I. Adler, Jerusalem 1992.

Airoldi 2015
S. Airoldi, "Practicies of Cultural Nationalism. Alfonso Pacifici and Jewish Renaissance in Italy (1910–1916)," in *Quest*, VIII, 2015.

Alemanno 1995
Y. Alemanno, *Hay ha-'olamim* ("The Immortal"), ed. by F. Lelli, Florence 1995.

***Alessandro Magnasco* 2015**
Alessandro Magnasco (1667-1749). Les années de la maturité d'un peintre anticonformiste / Alessandro Magnasco (1667-1749). Gli anni della maturità di un pittore anticonformista, exhibition catalogue (Paris, Galerie Canesso, November 25, 2015 – January 31, 2016; Genoa, Musei di Strada Nuova Palazzo Bianco, February 25 – June 5, 2016), Paris 2015.

Al Kalak, Pavan 2013
M. Al Kalak, I. Pavan, *Un'altra fede. Le case dei catecumeni nei territori estensi (1583-1938)*, Florence 2013.

Allegra 1996
L. Allegra, *Identità in bilico. Il ghetto ebraico di Torino nel Settecento*, Turin 1996.

Andreatta 2005
M. Andreatta, *Libri di preghiera della confraternita "Le sentinelle del mattino"*, Padua 2005.

Andreatta 2007
M. Andreatta, *Poesia religiosa ebraica di età barocca. L'innario della confraternita* Shomerim la-boqer *(Mantova 1612)*, Padua 2007.

Andreatta 2011
M. Andreatta, "The Printing of Devotion in Seventeenth-Century Italy: Prayer Books Printed for the Shomrim la-Boker Confraternities," in *The Hebrew Book in Early Modern Italy*, ed. by J. Hacker, A. Shear, Philadelphia 2011, pp. 156–170.

Andreatta 2014
M. Andreatta, *Raccontare per persuadere: conversione e narrazione in Via della Fede di Giulio Morosini*, in *Contributi di storia religiosa in*

onore di Pier Cesare Ioly Zorattini, ed. by M. del Bianco, M. Massenzio, Florence 2014, pp. 85–118.

Andreatta 2019
M. Andreatta, "The Baroque World of Moses Zacuto's Tofte Arukh," in *The Poet and the World: Studies in Honor of Wout van Bekkum*, ed. by E. Hollender, N. Katsumata, J. Yeshaya, Berlin 2019.

Angelozzi 1978
G. Angelozzi, *Le Confraternite Laicali. Un'esperienza cristiana tra Medioevo e Età Moderna*, Brescia 1978.

Anonymous [D. Rabbeno] 1859
Anonimo [D. Rabbeno], ed., *Roma e l'opinione pubblica d'Europa nel fatto Mortara. Atti, documenti, confutazioni. Il diritto canonico e il diritto naturale, per l'abate Delacouture, antico professore in teologia*, Turin 1859.

Aprile 2012
M. Aprile, *Grammatica storica delle parlate giudeo-italiane*, Galatina 2012.

Arian Levi, Disegni 1998
G. Arian Levi, G. Disegni, *Fuori dal ghetto. Il 1848 degli ebrei*, Rome 1998.

Aron Beller 2013
K. Aron Beller, "Outside the Ghetto: Jews and Christians in the Duchy of Modena," in *Journal of Early Modern History*, no. 17, 2013, pp. 245–271.

Ascarelli, Terracina 2004
G. Ascarelli, S.A. Terracina, "Un'architettura fra rappresentazione e tradizione," in G. Ascarelli, D. Di Castro, B. Migliau, M. Toscano, *Il Tempio Maggiore di Roma: nel centenario dell'inaugurazione della sinagoga 1904-2004*, Turin 2004.

Ascoli 1880
R. Ascoli, "In ricordo del fratello Leone Provenzal morto il 18 luglio 1880," in *Rivista massonica italiana*, XI, 1880, pp. 275–276.

Assézat 1858
J. Assézat, *Affaire Mortara : le droit du père*, Paris 1858.

Avineri 2011
S. Avineri, "Risorgimento and Zionism," in *Italy-Israel: The Last 150 Years*, Milan 2011.

Baldissin Molli, Sitran Rea, Veronese Ceseracciu 1998
G. Baldissin Molli, L. Sitran Rea, E. Veronese Ceseracciu, *Diplomi di laurea all'Università di Padova (1504-1806)*, Padua 1998.

Balla 1984
E. Balla, *Con Balla*, Milan 1984.

Bargoni 1976
A. Bargoni, *Maestri orafi e argentieri in Piemonte dal XVII al XIX secolo*, Turin 1976.

Barkai 1989
A. Barkai, *From Boycott to Annihilation: the Economic Struggle of German Jews, 1933-1943*, Hanover 1989.

Bartolocci 1675–1693
G. Bartolocci, *Bibliotheca Magna Rabbinica: De Scriptoribus, & Scriptis Rabbinicis ordine Alphabetico Hebraice, & Latine digestis*, Rome 1675-1693.

Benamozegh 1990
E. Benamozegh, *Israele e umanità. Studio del problema della religione universale* (1914), Genoa 1990.

Benayahu 1959
M. Benayahu, *Rabi Hayim Yosef David Azulai* [in Hebrew], Jerusalem 1959.

Benayahu 1971
M. Benayahu, *Copyright, Authorization and Imprimatur for Hebrew Books Printed in Venice* (in Hebrew), Jerusalem 1971.

Benayahu 1976
M. Benayahu, "Songs on the Occasion of the Graduation of the Physician Yehuda Matzliach Padova," in *Koroth*, VII, 1976, pp. 39–49.

Benayahu 1978
M. Benayahu, "R. Abraham ha-Cohen of Zante and the Group of Doctor-Poets in Padua" (in Hebrew), in *Ha-sifrut*, 26, 1978, pp. 108–140.

Benayahu 1998[a]
M. Benayahu, "Chevrat Shomerim la-boqer," in *Asufot*, 11, 1998, pp. 101–126.

Benayahu 1998[b]
M. Benayahu, "Sidre tefillah she-nidpesu be-Italyah le-chevrot Shomerim la-boqer mi-yissudam sel chakhamim be-Sa'loniqi," in *Asufot*, 11, 1998, pp. 87–99.

Bensoussan 2007
G. Bensoussan, *Il sionismo. Una storia politica e intellettuale (1860-1940)*, Turin 2007.

Berliner 1881
A. Berliner, *Luchot avanim* (*Hebräische Grabschriften in Italien, Erster Tail*), Frankfurt am Main 1881.

Berliner 1992
A. Berliner, *Storia degli Ebrei di Roma. Dall'antichità allo smantellamento del ghetto*, Milan 1992.

Bernstein 1935
S. Bernstein, "Luchot abanim, Part II," in *Hebrew Union College Annual*, X, 1935, pp. 483–552.

Bertini 1989
F. Bertini, *La massoneria in Toscana dall'età dei lumi alla Restaurazione*, in *Le origini della massoneria in Toscana (1730-1890)*, ed. by Z. Ciuffoletti, Foggia 1989, pp. 43–163.

Bettini 1894
P. Bettini, "Gli ebrei e la civiltà," in *Vita moderna*, III, 1894, pp. 90–91.

Bevan, Singer 1965
E.R. Bevan, C. Singer, *The Legacy of Israel*, vol. 10, Oxford 1965.

Biale 1988
D. Biale, *Power and Powerlessness in Jewish History*, New York 1988.

Biddau 2002
N. Biddau, *Gli spazi della parola. Sinagoghe in Piemonte*, Turin 2002.

Bidussa 1993
D. Bidussa, *Il sionismo politico*, Milan 1993.

Birnbaum, Katznelson 1995
P. Birnbaum, I. Katznelson, eds., *Paths of Emancipation: Jews, States and Citizenship*, Princeton 1995.

Black 1989
Ch. Black, *Italian Confraternities in the Sixteenth Century*, Cambridge (UK) 1989.

Bodian 1997
M. Bodian, *Hebrews of the Portuguese Nation. Conversos and Community in Early Modern Amsterdam*, Indianapolis 1997.

Boine 1993
A. Boine, *The Art of the Macchia and the Risorgimento. Representing Culture and Nationalism in Nineteenth-Century Italy*, Chicago-London 1993.

Bonfil 1985
R. Bonfil, "La Sinagoga in Italia come luogo di riunione e di preghiera," in *Il Centenario del Tempio Israelitico di Firenze*, proceedings of the conference, Firenze 1985.

Bonfil 1987[a]
R. Bonfil, "Cultura e mistica a Venezia nel Cinquecento," in *Gli Ebrei e Venezia. Secoli XIV-XVIII*, proceedings of the international conference organized by the Istituto di storia della società e dello Stato veneziano della Fondazione Giorgio Cini (Venice, Isola di San Giorgio Maggiore, 5–10 June 1983), ed. by G. Cozzi, Milan 1987, pp. 469–506.

Bonfil 1987[b]
R. Bonfil, "Halakhah, Kabbalah and Society: Some Insights into Rabbi Menahem Azariah da Fano's Inner World," in *Jewish Thought in the Seventeenth Century*, ed. by I. Twersky, B. Septimus, Cambridge (MA) 1987, pp. 39–61.

Bonfil 1991
R. Bonfil, *Gli ebrei in Italia nell'epoca del Rinascimento*, Florence 1991.

Bonfil 2012
R. Bonfil, *Rabbini e Comunità Ebraiche nell'Italia del Rinascimento*, Naples 2012.

Bonora 2014
E. Bonora, *Aspettando l'imperatore. I prinicipi italiani tra il papa e Carlo V*, Turin 2014.

Boralevi 1985
A. Boralevi, "La costruzione della Sinagoga di Firenze," in *Il Centenario del Tempio Israelitico di Firenze*, proceedings of the conference, Florence 1985.

Botti, Facchini, Zanini 2019
A. Botti, C. Facchini, P. Zanini, eds., "I modernisti, gli ebrei e l'ebraismo," in *Modernism*, monograph issue, 2019.

Botticini, Eckstein 2012
M. Botticini, Z. Eckstein, *I pochi eletti. Il ruolo dell'istruzione nella storia degli ebrei, 70-1492*, Milan 2012.

Boulouque 2018
C. Boulouque, "Elia Benamozegh's Printing Presses: Livornese Crossroads and the New Margins of Italian Jewish History," in *Italian Jewish Networks from the Seventeenth to the Twentieth Century: Bridging Europe and the Mediterranean*, ed. by F. Bregoli, C. Ferrara degli Uberti, G. Schwarz, Cham 2018, pp. 59–79.

Bregman 2003
D. Bregman, "Dimness and Clarity in Tofteh Aruch by Rabbi Moses Zacuto" (in Hebrew), in *Pe'amim*, 96, 2003, pp. 35–52.

Bregman 2012
D. Bregman, "A Few Words on Toftèh 'arùkh" (in Hebrew), in *Dechaq*, 2, 2012, pp. 333–376.

Bregman 2015
D. Bregman, "Hebrew Poems in the Valmadonna Broadside collection," in *The Writing on the Wall – A Catalogue of Judaica Broadsides from the Valmadonna Trust Library*, ed. by S. Liberman Mintz, S. Seidler-Feller, D. Wachtel, London - New York 2015, pp. 48–61.

Bregoli 2007–2008
F. Bregoli, "Hebrew Printing and Communication Networks between Livorno and North Africa, 1740–1789," in *Report of the Oxford Centre for Hebrew and Jewish Studies*, Oxford 2007–2008, pp. 51–59.

Bregoli 2014
F. Bregoli, *Mediterranean Enlightenment: Livornese Jews, Tuscan Culture, and Eighteenth-Century Reform*, Stanford 2014.

Briganti 2009
P. Briganti, *Il contributo militare degli ebrei italiani alla Grande Guerra 1915-1918*, Turin 2009.

Brown 1917
H. M. Brown, "Beginning of Intravenous Medication," in *Annals of Medical History*, I, 1917, pp. 177–197.

Budzioch 2016
D. Budzioch, "*Italian Origins of the Decorated Scrolls of Esther*," in *Jewish History Quarterly*, 1, 257, 2016, pp. 35–49.

Caffiero 1997
M. Caffiero, "Tra Chiesa e Stato. Gli ebrei italiani dall'età dei Lumi agli anni della Rivoluzione," in *Storia d'Italia. Annali 11. Gli ebrei in Italia 2. Dall'emancipazione a oggi*, ed. by C. Vivanti, Turin 1997, pp. 1089–1132.

Caffiero 2000
M. Caffiero, *Religione e Modernità*

in Italia (secoli XVII-XIX), Ghezzano 2000.

Caffiero 2004
M. Caffiero, *Battesimi forzati. Storie di ebrei, cristiani e convertiti nella Roma dei papi*, Rome 2004.

Caffiero 2008
M. Caffiero, ed., *Rubare le anime. Diario di Anna del Monte ebrea romana*, Rome 2008.

Caffiero 2012
M. Caffiero, *Legami pericolosi. Ebrei e cristiani tra eresia, libri proibiti e stregoneria*, Turin 2012.

Caffiero 2014
M. Caffiero, *Storia degli ebrei nell'Italia moderna. Dal Rinascimento alla Restaurazione*, Rome 2014.

Caffiero 2019
M. Caffiero, *Il grande mediatore. Tranquillo Vita Corcos, un rabbino nella Roma dei papi*, Rome 2019.

Calabi 2016
D. Calabi, *Venezia e il ghetto. Cinquecento anni del "recinto degli ebrei,"* Turin 2016.

Calabi *et al.* 1996
D. Calabi *et al.*, ed., *La città degli ebrei. Il ghetto di Venezia: architettura ed urbanistica*, Venice 1996.

Calimani 2016
R. Calimani, *Storia del ghetto di Venezia 1516-2016*, Milan 2016.

Campanini 1997
S. Campanini, "Peculium Abrae. La grammatica ebraico-latina di Avraham de Balmes," in *Annali di Ca' Foscari*, XXXVI, 3, 1997, pp. 5–49.

Cancellieri 1802
F. Cancellieri, *Storia de' solenni possessi de' Sommi Pontefici, detti anticamente processi o processioni, dopo la loro coronazione, dalla Basilica Vaticana alla Lateranense*, Rome 1802.

Canepa 1975
A.M. Canepa, *Emancipazione, integrazione e antisemitismo liberale: il caso Pasqualigo*, Rome 1975.

Cantoni 2005
A. Cantoni, "Israele italiano," in *Alberto Cantoni, L'umorismo nello specchio infranto*, ed. by Fabiana Barilli and Monica Bianchi, Mantua 2005, pp. 525–533.

Capuzzo 1999
E. Capuzzo, *Gli ebrei nella società italiana. Comunità e istituzioni tra Ottocento e Novecento*, Rome 1999.

Capuzzo 2004
E. Capuzzo, *Gli ebrei italiani dal Risorgimento alla scelta sionista*, Milan 2004.

Carioti 2005
A. Carioti, "Il nostro avo bambino rapito e plagiato da Pio IX," in *Corriere della sera*, June 17, 2005, p. 35.

D. Carpi 1972
D. Carpi, "Rabbi Yehuda Messer Leon and his Work as a Physician" (in Hebrew), in *Michael*, I, 1972, pp. 276–301.

D. Carpi 1974
D. Carpi, "Notes on the Life of Rabbi Judah Messer Leon," in *Studi sull'Ebraismo Italiano: in Memoria di Cecil Roth*, ed. by E. Toaff, Rome 1974, pp. 39–62.

D. Carpi 1986
D. Carpi, "Jews Who Received Medical Degrees from the University of Padua in the 16th and Early 17th Centuries" (in Hebrew), in *Scritti in Memoria di Nathan Cassuto*, Jerusalem 1986, pp. 62–91.

D. Carpi, Della Seta 1997
D. Carpi, S. Della Seta, "Il movimento sionistico," in *Storia d'Italia. Annali 11. Gli ebrei in Italia 2. Dall'emancipazione a oggi*, ed. by C. Vivanti, Turin 1997, pp. 1323–1368.

L. Carpi 1956
L. Carpi, "Il pensiero ebraico in un uomo del Risorgimento," in *R.M.I.*, XXII, July 1956, pp. 298–307.

Cassandro 1983
M. Cassandro, *Aspetti della storia economica e sociale degli ebrei di Livorno nel Seicento*, Milan 1983.

Cassen 2014
F. Cassen, "The Last Spanish Expulsion in Europe: Milan, 1565–1597," in *AJS Review*, 38, 01, 2014, pp. 59–88.

Cassen 2017
F. Cassen, *Marking the Jews in Renaissance Italy: Politics, Religion, and the Power of Symbols*, Cambridge 2017.

Cassuto 1988
D. Cassuto, "A Venetian Parokhet and its Design Origins," in *Jewish Art*, 1988, pp. 35–43.

Castelbolognesi 1966
G. Castelbolognesi, "Il Collegio Rabbinico di Padova al tempo di S.D. Luzzatto," in *R.M.I. Nel primo centenario della scomparsa di Samuel David Luzzatto*, Sept.-Oct. 1966, XXXII, no. 9–10, pp. 205–211.

Castelnuovo 1908
E. Castelnuovo, *I Moncalvo*, Milan 1908.

Castelvecchio 1861
R. Castelvecchio, *La famiglia ebrea*, a drama in four acts and a prologue, in *Florilegio drammatico*, file 409, Milan 1861.

Catalan 1991
T. Catalan, "L'emigrazione ebraica in Palestina attraverso il porto di Trieste (1908-1938)," in *Qualestoria*, 2–3, 1991, pp. 57–107.

Catalan 1996
T. Catalan, "I Morpurgo di Trieste. Una famiglia ebraica fra emancipazione ed integrazione (1848-1915)," in *Percorsi e modelli*

familiari in Italia tra '700 e '900, ed. by Filippo Mazzonis, Rome 1996, pp. 165–186.

Catalan 2000
T. Catalan, *La Comunità ebraica di Trieste (1781-1914). Politica, società e cultura*, Trieste 2000.

Catalan 2001
T. Catalan, "Presenza sociale ed economica degli ebrei nella Trieste asburgica tra Settecento e primo Novecento," in *Storia economica e sociale di Trieste*, vol. 1, *La Città dei gruppi 1719-1918*, ed. by R. Finzi, G. Panjek, Trieste 2001, pp. 483–518.

Catalan 2004
T. Catalan, "Mediazioni matrimoniali nell'ebraismo triestino nel corso dell'Ottocento," in *La mediazione matrimoniale. Il terzo (in)comodo in Europa fra Otto e Novecento*, ed. by B.P.F. Wanrooij, Fiesole-Rome 2004, pp. 127–156.

Catalan 2006
T. Catalan, "Ebrei italiani del Litorale austriaco nella rivoluzione del 1848," in *Quaderni Giuliani di Storia*, 1, 2006, pp. 73–100.

Catalan 2011
T. Catalan, "The Ambivalence of a Port-City. The Jews of Trieste from the 19th to the 20th Century," in *Quest. Issues in Contemporary Jewish History. Journal of Fondazione CDEC*, 2, 2011, pp. 69–98. url: www.quest-cdecjournal.it/focus.php?id=232.

Catalan 2012
T. Catalan, "Italian Jews and the 1848–49 Revolutions: Patriotism and Multiple Identities," in *The Risorgimento Revisited. Nationalism and Culture in Nineteenth-Century Italy*, ed. by L. Riall, S. Patriarca, New York 2012, pp. 214–231.

Catalan, Di Fant, Lelli, Tabor 2013
T. Catalan, A. Di Fant, F. Lelli, M. Tabor, eds., *Evraikì. Una diaspora mediterranea da Corfù a Trieste*, Trieste 2013.

Cavaglion 1988
A. Cavaglion, *Felice Momigliano (1866-1924). Una biografia*, Bologna-Naples 1988.

Cavour 1926
C. Cavour, *Il carteggio Cavour-Nigra dal 1858 al 1861*, vol. 1, Bologna 1926.

Cazzaniga 2014
G.M. Cazzaniga, "Presenze ebraiche nelle società segrete risorgimentali," in *Gli ebrei italiani dai vecchi stati all'Unità. Atti del convegno 9 novembre 2011, Museo ebraico di Bologna*, ed. by Franco Bonilauri and Vincenza Maugeri, Florence 2014, pp. 89–102.

Cessario 2018
R. Cessario, OP, "Non Possumus," in *First Things*, February 2018, www.firstthings.com/article/2018/02/non-possumus.

Cilluffo 2010
F. Cilluffo, *Il caso Mortara*, an opera in two acts, staged in New York, Dicapo Opera Theater, February 25, – March 7, 2010.

Ciscato 1901
A. Ciscato, *Gli Ebrei in Padova (1300-1800)*, Padua 1901.

Clermont-Tonnerre 1789
S. Clermont-Tonnerre, *Opinion relativement aux persecutions qui menacent les Juifs d'Alsace*, Versailles 1789.

Coccioli 1997
G. Coccioli, "Il possesso di Clemente XII," in *Corpus delle Feste a Roma. 2. Il Settecento e l'Ottocento*, ed. by M. Fagiolo, Roma 1997.

Cohen 1972
M. Cohen, "Leone da Modena's Riti: A Seventeenth-Century Plea for Social Toleration of Jews," in *Jewish Social Studies*, 34, 1972, pp. 287–321.

Cohen 1988
M. Cohen, ed. and trans., *The Autobiography of a Seventeenth-Century Venetian Rabbi: Leon Modena's Life of Judah*, Princeton 1988.

Colagrosso 1908
F. Colagrosso, *Un'usanza letteraria in gran voga nel Settecento*, Florence 1908.

Colombo 1966
Y. Colombo, "La polemica col Benamozegh," in *R.M.I., Nel primo centenario della scomparsa di Samuel David Luzzatto*, Sept.-Oct. 1966, XXXII, no. 9–10, pp. 179–204.

Colombo 1970
Y. Colombo, "Il congresso di Ferrara del 1863," in *R.M.I, Scritti in memoria di Attilio Milano*, July-Sept. 1970, XXXVI, no. 7–9, pp. 75–108.

Colorni *et al.* 1984
V. Colorni *et al.*, *Ketubbot italiane: antichi contratti nuziali ebraici miniati*, Milan 1984.

Connelly 2012
J. Connelly, *From Enemy to Brother. The Revolution in Catholic Teaching on the Jews, 1933-1965*, Cambridge (MA) - London 2012.

Consonni 2015
M. Consonni, *Split at the Root: Italian Jewish Identity between Anti-Zionism and Philo-Semitism 1961–1967, Research in Jewish Demography and Identity*, Brighton 2015, pp. 98–123.

Contessa 2013[a]
A. Contessa, "Jewish Book Collection and Patronage in Renaissance Italy," in *Proceedings for the Italia Judaica Jubilee Conference*, ed. by S. Simonshon, J. Shatzmiller, Leiden-Boston 2013, pp. 37–58.

Contessa 2013[b]
A. Contessa, *Towns of Silk and Silver. Architectural motifs in Italian Jewish Art*, Jerusalem 2013.

Contessa 2016
A. Contessa, *The Jewish Court of Venice. The heritage of Jewish Venice 500 years after the establishment of the first ghetto*, Jerusalem 2016.

Contessa 2017
A. Contessa, *Mantova e Gerusalemme. Arte e cultura nella città dei Gonzaga*, Florence 2017.

Conti 2003
F. Conti, *Storia della massoneria italiana. Dal Risorgimento al fascismo*, Bologna 2003.

Cooperman 1976
B. Cooperman, *Trade and Settlement: The Establishment and Early Development of the Jewish Communities in Leghorn and Pisa (1591–1626)*, PhD Dissertation, Harvard University, 1976.

Cooperman 2018
B. Cooperman, "The Early Modern Ghetto. A Study in Urban Real Estate," in *The Ghetto in Global History. 1500 to the Present*, ed. by W.Z. Goldman, J.W. Trotter, New York 2018, pp. 56–72.

Coryat 1611
T. Coryat, *Crudities*, I, London 1611 (reprint Glasgow 1905).

D'Antonio 2001
E. D'Antonio, "Aspetti della rigenerazione ebraica e del sionismo in Cesare Lombroso," in *Società e Storia*, XXIII, 2001, pp. 281–309.

D'Antonio 2012
E. D'Antonio, *La società udinese e gli ebrei fra la Restaurazione e l'età unitaria. Mondi cattolici, emancipazione e integrazione della minoranza ebraica a Udine 1830-1866/70*, Udine 2012.

Davanzo Poli, Melasecchi, Spagnoletto 2016
D. Davanzo Poli, O. Melasecchi, A. Spagnoletto, eds., *Antiche mappòt romane. Il prezioso archivio tessile del Museo Ebraico di Roma*, Rome 2016.

Dean 2008
M. Dean, *Robbing the Jews: The Confiscation of Jewish Property in the Holocaust, 1933–1945*, New York 2008.

De Angelis 2007
L. De Angelis, "Come un amore illecito. Sulla teshuvah di Zeno," in *Scrittori italiani di origine ebrea ieri e oggi: un approccio generazionale*, ed. by R. Speelman, M. Jansen, S. Gaiga, Utrecht 2007, pp. 13–26.

De Benedetti 2019
C. De Benedetti, *Non fuorvierà. Una storia di famiglia*, Livorno 2019.

Debenedetti 1971
G. Debenedetti, *Opere*, ed. by C. Garboli. Milan 1971.

Delacouture 1858
A.V. Delacouture, Abbé, *Le Droit canon et le droit naturel dans l'affaire Mortara*, Paris 1858 (Italian translation in *Roma e l'opinione pubblica d'Europa nel fatto Mortara. Atti, documenti, confutazioni. Il diritto canonico e il diritto naturale, per l'abate Delacouture, antico professore in teologia*, ed. by Anonymous [D. Rabbeno], Turin 1859, pp. 93–133).

Della Pergola 1976
S. Della Pergola, *Anatomia dell'ebraismo italiano. Caratteristiche demografiche, economiche, sociali, religiose e politiche di una minoranza*, Assisi-Rome 1976.

Della Pergola 1997
"La popolazione ebraica in Italia nel contesto ebraico globale," in *Storia d'Italia. Annals 11: Gli ebrei in Italia II. Dall'emancipazione a oggi*, Turin 1997, pp. 897–936.

De Rossi 1803
J.B. De Rossi, *Mss. codices hebraici Biblioth I. B. De Rossi*, Parma 1803.

Di Castro 1994
D. Di Castro, *Arte ebraica a Roma e nel Lazio*, Rome 1994.

Di Castro 2010[a]
D. Di Castro, *Et ecce gaudium. Gli ebrei romani e la cerimonia di insediamento dei pontefici*, Rome 2010.

Di Castro 2010[b]
D. Di Castro, *I tesori del Museo Ebraico di Roma. Guida alla visita e alle collezioni*, Rome 2010.

Di Fant 2002
A. Di Fant, *L'Affaire Dreyfus nella stampa cattolica italiana*, Trieste 2002.

Di Fant 2011
A. Di Fant, "Don Davide Albertario propagandista antiebraico. L'accusa di omicidio ritual," in *Antisemitismo e chiesa cattolica in Italia (XIX-XX sec.). Ricerche in corso e riflessioni storiografiche*, ed. by Cristiana Facchini, *Storicamente*, 7, no. 21, 2011.

Di Nepi 2013
S. Di Nepi, *Sopravvivere al ghetto. Per una storia sociale della comunità ebraica nella Roma del Cinquecento*, Rome 2013.

Di Nepi 2019
S. Di Nepi, "Jews in the Papal States between Western Sephardi Diasporas and Ghettos. A Trial in Ancona as a Case Study (1555–1562)," in *Religious Changes and Cultural Transformations in the Early Modern Western Sephardic Diasporas*, ed. by Y. Kaplan, Leiden 2019, pp. 291–322.

Di Porto 1999
B. Di Porto, "La 'Rivista Israelitica' di Parma. Primo periodico ebraico italiano," in *Materia Giudaica*, no. 5, 1999, pp. 33–44.

Di Porto 2000
B. Di Porto, "Il giornalismo ebraico in Italia. 'L'Educatore Israelita' (1853-1874)," in *Materia Giudaica*, no. 6, 2000, pp. 60–90.

Di Porto 2004
B. Di Porto, "'Il Corriere Israelitico': uno sguardo d'insieme," in *Materia Giudaica*, no. 1–2, 2004, pp. 249–263.

Di Segni 1986
Riccardi Di Segni, "Gli Studi Medici Jehuda Gonzago Ebreo Romano Del Primo Setecento," in Daniel Carpi *et.*

al., eds., *Scritti in Memoria di Nathan Cassuto*, Jerusalem 1986, pp. 248–264.

Dohm 1781-1783
C. W. von Dohm, *Übert die bürgerliche Verbesserung der Juden*, 2 vols, Berlin and Stettin 1781–1783.

Dolza 1990
D. Dolza, *Essere figlie di Lombroso. Due donne intellettuali tra '800 e '900*, Milan 1990.

Druker, Lerner 2018
J. Druker, L.S. Lerner, eds., "The New Italy and the Jews: From Massimo D'Azeglio to Primo Levi," in *Annali d'Italianistica*, 36, 2018.

Dubin 1999
L. Dubin, *The Port Jews of Habsburg Trieste: Absolutist Politics and Enlightenment Culture*, Stanford 1999.

Duneier 2016
M. Duneier, *The Invention of a Place, the History of an Idea*, New York 2016.

Dweck 2019
Y. Dweck, *Dissident Rabbi: The Life of Jacob Sasportas*, Princeton 2019.

Efron 2001
J. Efron, *Medicine and the German Jews: A History*, New Haven 2001.

***Epistolario* 1979**
Epistolario familiare. Carlo, Nello Rosselli e la madre, ed. by Z. Ciuffoletti, Milano 1979.

Esposito 1995
A. Esposito, *Un'altra Roma. Minoranze nazionali e comunità ebraiche tra Medioevo e Rinascimento*, Rome 1995.

Facchini 2010
C. Facchini, "Le metamorfosi di ostilità antica. Antisemitismo e cultura cattolica nella seconda metà dell'Ottocento," in *Annali di storia dell'esegesi*, 27/1, 2010, pp. 187–230.

Facchini 2011[a]
C. Facchini, "Antisemitismo delle passioni. La 'Palestra del clero' e il tema del deicidio," in *Antisemitismo e chiesa cattolica in Italia (xix-xx sec.). Ricerche in corso e riflessioni storiografiche*, ed. by C. Facchini, *Storicamente*, 7, 2011, pp. 1–30.

Facchini 2011[b]
C. Facchini, "The city, the ghetto and two books. Venice and Jewish early Modernity," in *Modernity and the Cities of the Jews*, ed. by C. Facchini, monograph issue of *Quest. Issues in contemporary Jewish History*, 2, pp. 2011, pp. 11–44.

Facchini 2013
C. Facchini, "Voci ebraiche sulla tolleranza religiosa. Pratiche e teorie nella Venezia barocca," in *Annali di storia dell'esegesi*, 30/2, 2013, pp. 393–419.

Facchini 2016
C. Facchini, "Luigi Luzzatti e la teoria della tolleranza religiosa. Per una storia del consumo pubblico delle scienze delle religioni," in *Annali di storia dell'esegesi*, 33/1, 2016, pp. 175–200.

Facchini 2019
C. Facchini, "Jesus the pharisee: Leon Modena, the historical Jesus, and Renaissance Venice," in *Journal for the Study of the Historical Jesus*, 17/1, 2019, pp. 81–101.

Facchini 2020
C. Facchini, "L'ostilità antiebraica nel mondo cattolico: percorso storiografico e politico," in *Annali di storia dell'esegesi*, 37/1, 2020.

Fahrmeir 2007
A. Fahrmeir, *Citizenship: The Rise and Fall of a Modern Concept*, New Haven 2007.

Fano 1607
J.S. Fano, *Mikveh Yisrael*, Venice 1607.

Farina, Pivato 2005
F. Farina, S. Pivato, eds., *Honor et Meritus. Diplomi di laurea dal XV al XX secolo*, Rimini 2005.

Farine 1973–1974
A. Farine, "Charity and Study Societies in Europe of the Sixteenth-Eighteenth Centuries," in *Jewish Quarterly Review*, 64, 1973–1974, pp. 16–47, 164–75.

Fasano Guarini 1978
E. Fasano Guarini, "Esenzioni e immigrazione a Livorno tra sedicesimo e diciassettesimo secolo," in *Atti del Convegno Livorno e il Mediterraneo nell'età medicea*, Livorno 1978, pp. 56–76.

Ferrara, Franzone 2011
P. Ferrara, G.Y. Franzone, "Fraternalismo e compagnonnage in ambito ebraico alla luce di alcuni documenti dei secoli XVII-XIX, con particolare riferimento al periodo 1814-1870," in *Le confraternite ebraiche. Talmud Torà e Ghemilut Chasadim: premesse storiche e attività agli inizi dell'epoca contemporanea*, Rome 2011, pp. 33–45.

Ferrara degli Uberti 2007
C. Ferrara degli Uberti, *La "Nazione Ebrea" di Livorno dai privilegi all'emancipazione (1814-1860)*, Florence 2007.

Ferrara degli Uberti 2012
C. Ferrara degli Uberti, *Fare gli ebrei italiani. Autorappresentazione di una minoranza (1861-1918)*, Bologna 2012.

Filippini 1997
J.P. Filippini, "La nazione ebrea di Livorno," in *Storia d'Italia: Annali 11; Gli ebrei in Italia*, vol. 2, *Dall'emancipazione a oggi*, ed. by C. Vivanti, Turin 1997, pp. 1047–1066.

Filippini 1998
J.P. Filippini, *Il porto di Livorno e la Toscana (1676–1814)*, 3 vols., Naples 1998.

Fink 2004
C. Fink, *Defending the Rights of Others: The Great Powers, the Jews, and International Minority Protections, 1878-1938*, New York 2004.

Finzi 2011
R. Finzi, *Il pregiudizio. Ebrei e questione ebraica in Marx, Lombroso, Croce*, Milan 2011.

Finzi, Panjek 2001
R. Finzi, G. Panjek, eds., "Storia economica e sociale di Trieste," vol. 1, *La Città dei gruppi 1719-1918*, Trieste 2001.

Fleischer 1975
E. Fleischer, *Hebrew Liturgical Poetry in the Middle Ages* (in Hebrew), Jerusalem 1975.

Foa 2014
A. Foa, *Andare per ghetti e giudecche*, Bologna 2014 (reprint Milan 2019).

Foà 1978
S. Foà, *Gli ebrei nel Risorgimento italiano*, Rome 1978.

Fontana 2001
R. Fontana, *Aimé Pallière. Un "cristiano" a servizio di Israele*, Milan 2001.

Fontana 2011
R. Fontana, "A noachide profile," in *European Judaism*, 11/2, 2011, pp. 106–115.

"Foreign Notes" 1887
"Foreign Notes and News," in *English Woman's Review: A Journal of Woman's Work*, November 15, 1887, p. 524.

Fornari 1968
S. Fornari, *Gli argenti romani*, Rome 1968.

Frances 1969
Y. Frances, *Kol shire Ya'aqov Franses (The poems of Jacob Frances [1615–1667])*, ed. by P. Naveh, Jerusalem 1969.

Frank 1992
M. Frank, *The Broken Staff. Judaism through Christian Eyes*, Cambridge-London 1992.

Frankel 1997
J. Frankel, *The Damascus Affair. "Ritual Murder", Politics, and the Jews in 1840*, Cambridge 1997.

Frattarelli Fischer 2008
L. Frattarelli Fischer, *Vivere fuori dal ghetto. Ebrei a Pisa e Livorno (secoli XVI-XVIII)*, Turin 2008.

Friedenwald 1921
H. Friedenwald, "The Jewish Medical Students of Former Days," in *Menorah Journal*, VII, 1921.

Friedenwald 1944
H. Friedenwald, *The Jews and Medicine*, Baltimore 1944.

D.A. Friedman 1942
D. A. Friedman, "Joseph Shelomoh Delmedigo," in *Medical Leaves*, IV, 1942, pp. 83–95.

Me. Friedman 1966
Me. Friedman, "Igerot be-parashat pulmus Hayyon" (in Hebrew), in *Sefunot*, X, 1966, pp. 583–621.

Mi. Friedman 1988
Mi. Friedman, "Transplanted Illustrations in Jewish Printed Books," in *Jewish Art*, XIV, 1988, pp. 44–55.

Frigessi 1999
D. Frigessi, "Cattaneo, Lombroso e la questione ebraica," in *Nel nome della razza. Il razzismo nella storia d'Italia 1870-1945*, ed. by A. Burgio, Bologna 1999, pp. 247–264.

Gaglia 1984
P. Gaglia, "L'arredo in argento," in *Ebrei a Torino. Ricerche per il centenario della sinagoga. 1884-1984*, ed. by Comunità Ebraica di Torino, Turin 1984, pp. 115–160.

Gaglia 1987
P. Gaglia, "Gli argenti: ornamenti del Sefer Torah e arredi del Tempio," in *Cultura ebraica in Emilia Romagna*, ed. by M. Bondoni, G. Busi, Rimini 1987, pp. 121–217.

***Gardens and Ghettos* 1989**
Gardens and Ghettos. The Art of the Jewish Life in Italy, exhibition catalogue (New York, Jewish Museum, Sept.-Dec. 1989), ed. by V.B. Mann, Berkeley - Los Angeles - Oxford 1989.

Gavi 1995
F. Gavi, "La disputa sull'ingresso del deputato della 'Nazione' ebrea nella comunità di Livorno, lettere e memorie," in *Nuovi Studi Livornesi*, III, 1995, pp. 251–271.

Germinario 2011
F. Germinario, *Argomenti per lo sterminio. L'antisemitismo e i suoi stereotipi nella cultura europea (1850-1920)*, Turin 2011.

Glasberg Gail 2016
D. Glasberg Gail, *Scientific Authority and Jewish Law in Early Modern Italy*, PhD Dissertation, Columbia University, 2016.

Gori 2006
O. Gori, "'Gazzette' segrete su Livorno per il Granduca Pietro Leopoldo," in *Fonti per la storia di Livorno fra Seicento e Settecento*, ed. by L. Frattarelli Fischer, C. Mangio, Livorno 2006, pp. 105–138.

Graf 1985
G. Graf, *Separation of Church and State. "Dina de-Malkhuta Dina" in Jewish Law, 1750-1848*, Tuscaloosa 1985.

Gramsci 1949
A. Gramsci, *Il Risorgimento*, Turin 1949.

Grass, Koselleck 2004
K. Martin Grass, R. Koselleck, "Emanzipation," in *Geschichtliche Grundbegriffe: historisches Lexikon zur politisch-sozialen Sprache in Deutschland*, 8 vols., ed. by O. Brunner, W. Conze, R. Koselleck, Stuttgart 2004, vol. 2, pp. 153–197.

Grawert 1973
R. Grawert, *Staat und Staatsangehörigkeit: Verfassungsgeschichtliche*

Untersuchung zur Entstehung der Staatsangehörigkeit, Berlin 1973.

Grazi 2015
A. Grazi, "*David Levi. A Child of the Nineteenth Century*, in *Portrait of Italian Jewish Life (1800s-1930s)*," in *Quest. Issues in Contemporary Jewish History*, ed. by T. Catalan, C. Facchini, 8, 2015 (http://www.quest-cdecjournal.it/focus.php?id=363).

Green 2010
A. Green, *Moses Montefiore: Jewish Liberator, Imperial Hero*, Cambridge (MA) 2010.

Greenberg 1960
S. Greenberg, *Jewish Educational Institutions*, in *The Jews: Their History, Culture and Religion*, ed. by L. Finkelstein, vol. 2, *1254-1287*, Philadelphia 1960.

Grégoire 1789
H. Grégoire, *Essay sur la régénération physique, morale et politique des Juifs*, Metz 1789 (Italian translation *La rigenerazione degli Ebrei*, Roma 2000).

Grenga, Pavoncello Piperno 2018
G. Grenga, C. Pavoncello Piperno, "Ingegnere Angelo Pace Tagliacozzo presidente dell'Ospedale Israelitico di Roma, 10 Febbraio 1847 - 26 Giugno 1926," in *La Rassegna Mensile di Israel*, 84, 1–2, 2018, p. 101.

Grossi 1965
C. Grossi, *Cantata Ebraïca in dialogo, voce sola e choro*, ed. by I. Adler, Tel Aviv 1965.

Guerrazzi 1846
F.D. Guerrazzi, *Documenti diversi*, II ed., 1846.

Guerrazzi 1899
F.D. Guerrazzi, *Note autobiografiche e poema di Francesco Domenico Guerrazzi*, Florence 1899.

Guetta 1998
A. Guetta, *Philosophie et Cabbale. Essai sur la pensée d'Élie Benamozegh*, Paris 1998.

Guetta 2014
A. Guetta, *Italian Jewry in the Early Modern Era*, Boston 2014.

Hamiel 1949–1950
Ch. Hamiel, "Tofteh 'Arukh me-et Mosheh Zacut," in *Sinai*, 25, 1949, pp. 304–19; 26, 1950, pp. 101–112.

Harrán 1989
D. Harrán, "Tradition and Innovation in Jewish Music of the Latter Renaissance," in *Journal of Musicology*, VII, 1989, pp. 107–130 (repr. in David B. Ruderman, ed., *Essential Papers on Jewish Culture in Renaissance and Baroque Italy*, New York 1992, pp. 474-501).

Harrán 1999
D. Harrán, *Salamone Rossi, Jewish Musician in Late Renaissance Mantua*, Oxford 1999.

Harrán 2003
D. Harrán, ed., *Salamone Rossi: Complete Works* (Corpus Mensurabilis Musicae, 100), vol. 13a–13b, Neuhausen-Stuttgart 2003.

Hertzberg 1959
A. Hertzberg, *The Zionist Idea: A Historical Analysis and Reader*, Philadelphia 1959.

Herzl 1896
T. Herzl, *Der Judenstaat*, Leipzig 1896 (Italian translation *Lo Stato Ebraico*, Lanciano 1918; new edition Jerusalem 2015).

Herzl 1960
T. Herzl, *Diaries*, Gloucester (MA) 1960.

Hess 1862
M. Hess, *Rom und Jerusalem, die Letzte Nationalitätsfrage*, Leipzig 1862 (Italian translation *Roma e Gerusalemme. L'ultima questione nazionale*, Naples 2002).

Holquist 2001
P. Holquist, "To Count, to Extract and to Exterminate: Population Statistics and Population Politics in Late Imperial and Soviet Russia," in *A State of Nations: Empire and Nation-Making in the Age of Lenin and Stalin*, ed. by R.G. Suny, T. Martin, New York 2001, pp. 111–144.

Horowitz 1982
E.S. Horowitz, *Jewish Confraternities in Seventeenth-Century Verona: A Study in the Social History of Piety*, PhD Dissertation, Yale University, 1982.

Horowitz 1984
E.S. Horowitz, "R. Isaac ben Gershom Treves in Venice," in *Kiryat Sefer*, 59, 1984, pp. 252–257.

Horowitz 1985
E.S. Horowitz, "A Jewish Youth Confraternity in Seventeenth-Century Italy," in *Italia*, 5, 1–2, 1985, pp. 36–97.

Horowitz 1987
E.S. Horowitz, "Jewish Confraternal Piety in the Veneto in the Sixteenth and Seventeenth Centuries," in *Gli Ebrei e Venezia. Secoli XIV-XVIII*, proceedings of the international conference organized by the Istituto di storia della società e dello Stato veneziano della Fondazione Giorgio Cini (Venice, Isola di San Giorgio Maggiore, June 5–10, 1983), ed. by G. Cozzi, Milan 1987, pp. 301–313.

Horowitz 1989[a]
E.S. Horowitz, "Coffee, Coffee Houses, and the Nocturnal Rituals of Early Modern Jewry," in *AJS Review*, 14, 1, 1989, pp. 17–46.

Horowitz 1989[b]
E.S. Horowitz, "The Eve of the Circumcision: A Chapter in the History of Jewish Nightlife," in *Journal of Social History*, 23, 1, 1989, pp. 45–69.

Horowitz 1993
E.S. Horowitz, "'Yeshiva' and 'Hevra': Educational Control and Confraternal Organization in Sixteenth-Century Italy," in *Shlomo Simonsohn Jubilee Volume: Studies in the History of the Jews in the Middle Ages and*

Renaissance Period, ed. by D. Carpi *et al.*, Tel Aviv 1993, pp. 123–147.

Horowitz 2000[a]
E.S. Horowitz, "Jewish Confraternal Piety in Sixteenth-Century Ferrara: Continuity and Change," in *The Politics of Ritual Kinship: Confraternities and Social Order in Early Modern Italy*, ed. by N. Terpstra, Cambridge 2000, pp. 150–171.

Horowitz 2000[b]
E.S. Horowitz, "La confraternita dei Solerti – Hevrat Nizharim. Religiosità ebraica delle confraternite nella Bologna del XVI secolo," in *La cultura ebraica a Bologna tra Medioevo e Rinascimento*, proceedings of the international conference (Bologna, April 9, 2000), ed. by M. Perani, Florence 2000, pp. 175–187.

Horowitz 2001
E.S. Horowitz, "Processions, Piety, and Jewish Confraternities," in *The Jews of Early Modern Venice*, ed. by R.C. Davis, B. Ravid, Baltimore-London 2001, pp. 231–248.

Hyman 1998
P. Hyman, *The Jews of Modern France*, Berkeley - Los Angeles - London 1998.

Idel 1987
M. Idel, "On Mishmarot and Messianism in Jerusalem in the 16th-17th Centuries" (in Hebrew), in *Shalem*, 5, 1987, pp. 83–94.

"Il fatto" 1858
"Il fatto di Bologna," in *L'Educatore Israelita*, 6, no. 19, 1858, p. 312.

"Il piccolo neofita" 1858
"Il piccolo neofita Edgardo Mortara," in *La Civiltà Cattolica*, series 3, vol. 12, October 30, 1858, pp. 385–416.

"I nostri ideali" 1901
"I nostri ideali," in *L'Idea Sionista*, I, 1, January 31, 1901, pp. 1–2.

Invernizio 1887
C. Invernizio, *L'orfana del ghetto*, Milan 1887.

Ioly Zorattini 1980–1999
P.C. Ioly Zorattini, ed., *Processi del S. Uffizio di Venezia contro ebrei e giudaizzanti*, Florence 1980–1999.

Ioly Zorattini 1987
P.C. Ioly Zorattini, ed., *Processi del S. Uffizio di Venezia contro Ebrei e Giudaizzanti (1579-1586)*, Florence 1987.

Ioly Zorattini 2001
P.C. Ioly Zorattini, "La tipografia del 'Kaf Nachat' di Iedidia Salomon Gabbai a Livorno," in *La formazione storica della alterità. Studi di storia della tolleranza nell'età moderna offerti a Antonio Rotondò*, promoted by H. Méchoulan, R.H. Popkin, G. Ricuperati, L. Simonutti, 3 vols., Florence 2001, vol. 2, pp. 495–515.

Ioly Zorattini 2001–2002
P.C. Ioly Zorattini, "Ancora sui Giudaizzanti portoghesi di Ancona (1556): condanna e riconciliazione," in *Zakhor. Rivista di storia degli Ebrei d'Italia*, V, 2001–2002, pp. 39–51.

Ioly Zorattini 2010
P.C. Ioly Zorattini, "Ebrei in Italia," in *Dizionario storico dell'Inquisizione*, 4 vols., ed. by A. Prosperi, with the collaboration of V. Lavenia and J. Tedeschi, Pisa 2010, vol. 2, pp. 523–527.

Ioly Zorattini 2012
P.C. Ioly Zorattini, "La prima anagrafe del ghetto di Ferrara," in *Studi sul mondo sefardita in memoria di Aron Leoni*, ed. by P.C. Ioly Zorattini, M. Luzzati, M. Sarfatti, Florence 2012, pp. 151–185.

Ioly Zorattini 2013
P.C. Ioly Zorattini, "Gracia Nasci alias Beatriz Mendes de Luna, la Señora," in *Archivio Veneto*, s. 6, no. 6, 2013, pp. 113–134.

Isastia 2010
A.M. Isastia, *Storia di una famiglia del Risorgimento: Sarina, Giuseppe, Ernesto Nathan*, Turin 2010.

Israel 1998
J. Israel, *European Jewry in the Age of Mercantilism, 1550–1750*, 3rd ed., London 1998 (Italian edition *Gli ebrei d'Europa nell'età moderna, 1550-1750*, Bologna 1991).

Israel 2002
J. Israel, *Diaspora within a Diaspora: Jews, Crypto-Jews and the World of Maritime Empires (1540–1740)*, Leiden-Boston 2002.

Jesi 2007
F. Jesi, *L'accusa del sangue. La macchina mitologica antisemita*, 2nd ed., Turin 2007.

Jussi 1860
F. Jussi, *Difesa del padre Pier Gaetano Feletti, imputato come Inquisitore del Santo Uffizio del ratto del fanciullo Edgardo Mortara davanti al Tribunale Civile e Criminale di Prima Istanza in Bologna*, Bologna 1860.

Kaplan 2000
Y. Kaplan, *An Alternative Path to Modernity. The Sephardi Diaspora in Western Europe*, Leiden 2000.

Karp, Sutcliffe 2011
J. Karp, A. Sutcliffe, *Philosemitism in History*, Cambridge 2011.

Karwacka Codini, Sbrilli 1995
E. Karwacka Codini, M. Sbrilli, "La sinagoga di Livorno: una storia di oltre tre secoli," in *Le tre sinagoghe: Edifici di culto e vita ebraica a Livorno dal Seicento al Novecento*, ed. by M. Luzzati, Turin 1995, pp. 47–82.

Katan, Gerber 2009
Y. Katan, D. Gerber, eds., *Shiltei haGibborim*, Jerusalem 2009.

D.E. Katz 2017
D.E. Katz, *The Jewish Ghetto and the Visual Imagination of Early Modern Venice*, Cambridge 2017.

J. Katz 1964
J. Katz, "The Term Jewish Emancipation: Its Origins and Historical Impact," in *Studies*

in Nineteenth-Century Jewish Intellectual History, ed. by A. Altmann, Cambridge (MA) 1964.

J. Katz 1967
J. Katz, "Freemasons and Jews," in *The Jewish Journal of Sociology*, IX, 1967, pp.137–148.

J. Katz 1970
J. Katz, *Jews and Freemasons in Europe, 1823–1939*, Cambridge (MA) 1970.

Kaufmann 1900
D. Kaufmann, "Die Vertreibung der Marranen aus Venedig im Jahre 1550," in *Jewish Quarterly Review*, V.S., XIII, 1900, pp. 520–532.

Kertzer 1996
D. Kertzer, *Prigioniero del Papa re*, Milan 1996 (English translation *The Kidnapping of Edgardo Mortara*, New York 1997).

Kertzer 2005
D. Kertzer, *Prigioniero del papa re. Il rapimento di Edgardo Mortara nel Vaticano di Pio IX*, Milan 2005.

Kertzer 2018
D. Kertzer, "Edgardo Mortara's Doctored Memoir of a Vatican Kidnapping," in *The Atlantic*, April 15, 2018.

Kertzer 2019
D. Kertzer, "The Enduring Controversy over the Mortara Case," in *Studies in Christian-Jewish Relations (SCJR)*, 14, no. 1, 2019, pp. 1–10.

Kiron 1992
A. Kiron, *Sabato Morais Collection*, Library at the Herbert D. Katz Center for Advanced Judaic Studies, University of Pennsylvania, 1992, ARC MS 8, http://dla.library.upenn.edu/dla/ead/detail.html?id=EAD_upenn_cajs_ARCMS8USUSUSPUCJS (accessed on January 1, 2020).

Kisch 1949
B. Kisch, "Cervo Conigliano: A Jewish Graduate of Padua in 1743," in *Journal of the History of Medicine*, IV, 1949, pp. 450–459.

Klausner 1966
J. Klausner, "Il carattere, le credenze, le idee," in *R.M.I., Nel primo centenario della scomparsa di Samuel David Luzzatto*, Sept.-Oct. 1966, vol. 32, no. 9–10, pp. 64–102.

Korn 1957
B.W. Korn, *The American Reaction to the Mortara Case: 1858-1859*, Cincinnati 1957.

Kravitz 2017
M. Kravitz, ed., *Amar ha-Gaon. Shi'urei Rabbenu 'Ovadya Sforno*, Beith Shemesh 2017.

"L'adesione" 1918
"L'adesione del Governo Italiano ad un Centro nazionale ebraico in Palestina," in *Israel*, May 23, 1918.

Langham 2004
R. Langham, "The Reaction in England to the Kidnapping of Edgardo Mortara," in *Jewish Historical Studies*, 39, 2004, pp. 79–101.

A. Lattes, Toaff 1909
A. Lattes, A. Toaff, *Gli studi ebraici a Livorno nel secolo XVIII: Malahi Accoen (1700-1771)*, Livorno 1909.

A.Y. Lattes 2012–2013
A.Y. Lattes, "La concezione della morte e dell'oltretomba nel dramma Tofte 'Aruk di Rabbi Mošeh Zacuto," in *Materia giudaica*, 17–18, 2012–2013, pp. 149–154.

A.Y. Lattes, Perani 2010-2011
A.Y. Lattes, M. Perani, "Un poema per la rifondazione della 'Compagnia di mezzanotte' nella Lugo ebraica di metà Settecento," in *Materia giudaica*, 15–16, 2010–2011, pp. 439–456.

G. Lattes 1901
G. Lattes, *Vita e opere di Elia Benamozegh*, Livorno 1901.

Lehmann 2014
M. Lehmann, *Emissaries from the Holy Land: The Sephardic Diaspora and the Practice of Pan-Judaism in the Eighteenth Century*, Stanford 2014.

Leibowitz 1936
N. Leibowitz, ed., *Seridim*, Jerusalem 1936.

Lenz 2014
M.A. Lenz, *Genie und Blut. Rassendenken in der italienischen Philologie des neunzehnten Jahrhunderts*, Paderborn 2014.

Leoni 1991
A. Di Leone Leoni, "Due personaggi della 'Nation Portughesa' di Ferrara: un martire e un avventuriero," in *La Rassegna Mensile di Israel*, LVII, 1991, pp. 407–448.

Leoni 2000
A. Di Leone Leoni, "Gli Ebrei a Ferrara nel XVI secolo," in *Storia di Ferrara*, Ferrara 2000, pp. 278–311.

Leoni 2011
A. Di Leone Leoni, *La Nazione ebraica spagnola e portoghese di Ferrara (1492-1559). I suoi rapporti col governo ducale e la popolazione locale e i suoi legami con le Nazioni Portoghesi di Ancona, Pesaro e Venezia*, 2 vols., ed. by L. Graziani Secchieri, Florence 2011.

A. Levi 1931
A. Levi, "Amici Israeliti di Giuseppe Mazzini," in *La Rassegna Mensile di Israel*, V, no. 12, 1931, pp. 587–612.

G. Levi 1996
G. Levi, "Comportements, ressources, procès : avant la 'révolution' de la consommation," in *Jeux d'echelles. La microanalyse à l'expérience*, ed. by J. Revel, Paris 1996, pp. 187–208.

Y.Y. Levi 2013
Y.Y. Levi, *Kos tanchumin we-qinot acherot*, ed. by A. Rathaus, Jerusalem 2013.

Levis Sullam 2007
S. Levis Sullam, "Arnaldo Momigliano e la 'nazionalizzazione parallela'. Autobiografia, religione, storia," in *Passato e Presente*, LXX, 2007, pp. 59–82.

Levis Sullam 2010[a]
S. Levis Sullam, *L'apostolo a brandelli. L'eredità di Mazzini tra Risorgimento e fascismo*, Roma-Bari 2010.

Levis Sullam 2010[b]
S. Levis Sullam, "Critici e nemici dell'emancipazione degli ebrei," in *Storia della Shoah in Italia. Vicende, memorie, rappresentazioni*, ed. by M. Flores, S. Levis Sullam, M.A. Matard Bonucci, E. Traverso, vol. 1, Turin 2010, pp. 37–61.

Levis Sullam 2017
S. Levis Sullam, "Uncovering the Italian Muscle Jew from Zionist Gymnastic to Fascist Boxing," in *Quest*, VIII, 2017, pp. 29–45.

Levy 1988
Sh. Levy, "Tofteh 'arukh: machazeh masa' 'ivri moderni me-ha-me'ah y"z," in *Bamah*, 113–114, 1988, pp. 114–124.

Levy 1989
Sh. Levy, "Hellish Hebrew Theatre: The Spiritual Quest of Tofteh Aruch," in *Maske und Kothurn*, 35, 1, 1989, pp. 45–58.

Liberman Mintz, Seidler-Feller, Wachtel 2015
S. Liberman Mintz, S. Seidler-Feller, D. Wachtel, eds., *The Writing on the Wall: A Catalogue of Judaica Broadsides from the Valmadonna Trust Library*, London - New York 2015.

Lindemann, Levy 2010
A. Lindemann, R. Levy, eds., *Antisemitism: A History*, Oxford 2010.

Liscia Bemporad 1989
D. Liscia Bemporad, "Jewish Ceremonial Art in the Era of the Ghetto," in *Gardens and Ghettos. The art of the Jewish life in Italy*, ed. by V.B. Mann, exhibition catalogue (New York, Jewish Museum, Sept.–Dec. 1989), Berkley - Los Angeles - Oxford 1989, pp. 110–135.

Liscia Bemporad 1996
D. Liscia Bemporad, "Argenti veneziani nelle sinagoghe italiane," in *Contributo per la storia dell'oreficeria, argenteria e gioielleria*, ed. by P. Pazzi, Venice 1996, pp. 204–206.

Liscia Bemporad 1997
D. Liscia Bemporad, "Gli arredi (secc. XVI-XIX)," in *La Sinagoga di Pisa. Dalle origini al restauro ottocentesco di Marco Treves*, ed. by M. Luzzati, Florence 1997, pp. 69–82.

Liscia Bemporad 2007
D. Liscia Bemporad, "Ricamatrici ebree nell'Italia dei ghetti," in *Italia judaica. Donne nella storia degli ebrei d'Italia*, proceedings of the 9th international conference (Lucca, June 6–9, 2005), ed. by M. Luzzati, C. Galasso, Florence 2007, pp. 295–304.

Liscia Bemporad 2015
D. Liscia Bemporad, "Gli arredi cerimoniali della sinagoga," in *La Comunità ebraica di Napoli, 1864/2014. Centocinquant'anni di storia*, ed. by G. Lacerenza, Naples 2015, pp. 178–188.

Liscia Bemporad 2018
D. Liscia Bemporad, ed., *Preziose Dediche. Arte cerimoniale ebraica a Livorno*, Livorno 2018.

Lombroso 1867
C. Lombroso, *Sulla mortalità degli Ebrei in Italia nel decennio 1855-1864*, Milan 1867.

Lombroso 1871
C. Lombroso, *L'uomo bianco e l'uomo di colore. Letture su l'origine e la varietà delle razze umane*, Padua 1871.

Lombroso 1894
C. Lombroso, *L'antisemitismo e le scienze moderne*, Turin-Rome 1894.

Luzzati 1986
M. Luzzati, "Privilegio e identità nella storia degli ebrei livornesi," in *Studi Livornesi*, 1, 1986, pp. 37–42.

Luzzati 1990
M. Luzzati, ed., *Ebrei di Livorno tra due censimenti (1841-1938). Memoria familiare e identità*, Livorno 1990.

A. Luzzatto 2000
A. Luzzatto, *La Comunità ebraica di Venezia e il suo antico cimitero*, 2 vols., Milan 2000.

M.Ch. Luzzatto 1945
M.Ch. Luzzatto, *Sefer ha-shirim*, ed. by S. Ginzburg, B. Klar, Jerusalem 1945.

S. Luzzatto 2013
S. Luzzatto, *Scritti politici e filosofici di un ebreo scettico nella Venezia del Seicento*, ed. by G. Veltri, Milan 2013.

S. Luzzatto 2019
S. Luzzatto, *Discourse on the State of the Jews*, ed. by G. Veltri, A. Lissa, bilingual edition, Berlin 2019.

Luzzatto Voghera 1998
G. Luzzatto Voghera, *Il prezzo dell'eguaglianza. Il dibattito sull'emancipazione degli ebrei in Italia (1781-1848)*, Milan 1998.

Luzzatto Voghera 2005
G. Luzzatto Voghera, "Dante Lattes," in *Dizionario Biografico degli Italiani*, vol. 64, Rome 2005.

Mahler 1944
R. Mahler, *Jewish Emancipation. A Selection of Documents*, New York 1944.

Maifreda 2000
G. Maifreda, *Gli ebrei e l'economia milanese. L'Ottocento*, Milan 2000.

Maifreda 2014
G. Maifreda, *I denari dell'Inquisitore. Affari e giustizia di fede nell'Italia moderna*, Turin 2014.

Malkiel 2001
D. Malkiel, "The Ghetto Republic," in *The Jews of Early Modern Venice*, ed. by Robert C. Davis and Benjamin Ravid, Baltimore-London 2001, pp. 117–142.

Malkiel 2013
D. Malkiel, *Poems in Marble: Inscriptions from the Jewish Cemeteries of Padua, 1529–1862*, Jerusalem 2013 (texts).

Malkiel 2014
D. Malkiel, *Stones Speak - Hebrew Tombstones from Padua, 1529–1862*, Leiden-Boston 2014 (historical-critical analysis).

Mallé 1972
L. Mallé, *Museo Civico d'Arte Antica di Torino. Mobili e arredi lignei. Arazzi e bozzetti per arazzi*, Turin 1972.

Mancini 2015
M. Mancini, OP, "Pier Gaetano Feletti e l'affare Mortara," in *Dominikaner und Juden / Dominicans and Jews: Personen, Konflikte und Perspektiven vom 13. bis zum 20. Jahrhundert / Personalities, Conflicts, and Perspectives from the 13th to the 20th Century*, ed. by Elias H. Füllenbach OP and Gianfranco Miletto, Berlin/ Munich/Boston 2015, pp. 421–437.

Mangio 1995
C. Mangio, "La riforma municipale a Livorno," in *L'ordine di Santo Stefano e la nobiltà toscana nelle riforme municipali settecentesche*, Pisa 1995, pp. 85–120.

Mann 1990
V.B. Mann, ed., *I TAL YA'. Duemila anni di arte e vita ebraica in Italia*, Milan 1990.

Marconcini 2016
S. Marconcini, *Per amor del cielo. Farsi cristiani a Firenze tra Seicento e Settecento*, Florence 2016.

Marcou Baruch 2009
J. Marcou Baruch, *Un ebreo garibaldino*, Pisa 2009.

Marrus, Paxton 1995
M. Marrus, R.O. Paxton, *Vichy France and the Jews*, 2nd ed., Stanford 1995.

Martina 1971
G. Martina, "La fine del potere temporale nella coscienza religiosa e nella cultura dell'epoca, in Italia," in *Archivum Historiae Pontificiae*, 9, 1971, pp. 309–376.

Martina 1986
G. Martina, *Pio IX: 1851-1866*, Rome 1986.

Mascilli Migliorini 1997
L. Mascilli Migliorini, "L'età delle riforme," in F. Diaz, L. Mascilli Migliorini, C. Mangio, *Il Granducato di Toscana: I Lorena dalla Reggenza agli anni rivoluzionari*, Turin 1997, pp. 249–421.

Massariello Merzagora 1977
G. Massariello Merzagora, *Giudeo-Italiano. Dialetti italiani parlati dagli Ebrei d'Italia*, Pisa 1977.

Matvejevitch 1971
P. Matvejevitch, *La poésie de circonstance. Etude des formes de l'engagement poétique*, Paris 1971.

Matvejevitch, Levin 1973
P. Matvejevitch, I. Levin, *The lamentation over the Dead* (in Hebrew), Tel Aviv 1973.

Mayer 2010
M. Mayer, "'Die französische Regierung packt die Judenfrage ohne Umschweife an'. Vichy-Frankreich, deutsche Besatzungsmacht und der Beginn der 'Judenpolitik' im Sommer/ Herbst 1940," in *Vierteljahreshefte für zeitgeschichte*, 58, 3, 2010, pp. 329–362.

Melasecchi, Spagnoletto 2019
O. Melasecchi, A. Spagnoletto, eds., *Antiche ketubbòt romane. I contratti nuziali della Comunità Ebraica di Roma*, Rome 2019.

Mendelssohn 1991
E. Mendelssohn, *The Popes' Jewish Doctors. 492-1655 CE*, Lauderhill 1991.

Mendes-Flohr, Reinharz 2011
P. Mendes-Flohr, J. Reinharz, eds., *The Jew in the Modern World: A Documentary History*, 3rd ed., New York 2011.

Menken 1859
A.I. Menken, "To the Sons of Israel," in *The Israelite*, Cincinnati, January 28, 1859, p. 236.

Meroz 1987
R. Meroz, "The Circle of R. Moshe ben Makhir and Its Regulations" (in Hebrew), in *Pe'amim*, 31, 1987, pp. 40–61.

Meroz 2003
R. Meroz, "Rabbi Moses Zacuto's Allusions in Tofteh Aruch" (in Hebrew), in *Pe'amim*, 96, 2003, pp. 107–119.

Messori 2005
V. Messori, *"Io, il bambino ebreo rapito da Pio IX". Il memoriale inedito del protagonista del "caso Mortara"*, Milan 2005.

Messori 2017
V. Messori, *Kidnapped by the Vatican? The Unpublished Memoirs of Edgardo Mortara, trans. by Michael J. Miller, intr. by Roy Schoeman*, San Francisco 2017.

Miccoli 1997
G. Miccoli, "Santa Sede, questione ebraica e antisemitismo tra Otto e Novecento," in *Storia d'Italia. Annali 11. Gli ebrei in Italia 2. Dall'emancipazione a oggi*, ed. by C. Vivanti, Turin 1997, pp. 1369–1564.

Milano 1938
A. Milano, "Un secolo di stampa periodica ebraica in Italia," in *La Rassegna Mensile di Israel*, 12, 7–9, 1938, pp. 96–136.

Milano 1954
A. Milano, "Omaggi della comunità

di Roma per l'elezione di Pio VI," in *La Rassegna Mensile di Israel*, 20, 1954.

Milano 1958
A. Milano, "Le confraternite pie del Ghetto di Roma," in *La Rassegna Mensile di Israele*, 24, 3–4, 1958, pp. 107–120, 166–180.

Milano 1963
A. Milano, *Storia degli ebrei in Italia*, Turin 1963.

Milano 1966
A. Milano, "Il Purìm in un ignorato poemetto del Seicento," in *Rassegna Mensile d'Israel*, XXXII, 1966, pp. 67–87.

Milano 1988
A. Milano, *Il ghetto di Roma*, Rome 1988.

Millo 1998
A. Millo, *Storia di una borghesia. La famiglia Vivante a Trieste dall'emporio alla guerra mondiale*, Gorizia 1998.

Minerbi 1970
S.I. Minerbi, *L'Italie et la Palestine 1914-1920*, Paris 1970.

Minerbi 1978
S.I. Minerbi, *Raffaele Cantoni*, Roma 1978.

Minerbi 1992
S.I. Minerbi, *Un ebreo fra D'Annunzio e il sionismo: Raffaele Cantoni*, Rome 1992.

Minervini 1994
L. Minervini, "*Gli usi linguistici degli ebrei spagnoli in Italia*," in *Medioevo Romanzo*, XIX, 1–2, 1994, pp. 133–192.

Miniati 2008
M. Miniati, *Le "emancipate". Le donne ebree in Italia nel XIX e XX secolo*, Rome 2008.

Miniati 2017
M. Miniati, "Donne in guerra: il contributo femminile ebraico nella Prima Guerra Mondiale," in *Gli ebrei italiani nella Grande Guerra (1915-1918)*, ed. by C. Quareni, V. Maugeri, Florence 2017, pp. 127–147.

Mirsky 1987
D. Mirsky, *The Life and Work of Ephraim Luzzatto*, Hoboken (NJ) 1987.

A. Modena, Morpurgo 1967
A. Modena, E. Morpurgo, *Medici e chirurghi ebrei dottorati e licenziati nell'Università di Padova dal 1617 al 1816*, Bologna 1967.

L. Modena 1637
L. Modena (da), *Historia de' riti Hebraici*, Paris 1637.

L. Modena 1932
L. Modena (da), *The Divan of Leo de Modena*, ed. by S. Bernstein, Philadelphia 1932.

Moïse 1858
P. Moïse (M. P.), "Tribute of Condolence," in *The Jewish Messenger*, New York, December 24, 1858 - 17 Tebeth 5619, p. 1.

Molinari 1991
M. Molinari, *Ebrei in Italia: un problema di identità (1870-1938)*, Florence 1991.

Momigliano 1933
A. Momigliano, "Recensione a Cecil Roth, Gli Ebrei a Venezia," in *Nuova Italia*, April 22, 1933.

Momigliano 1987
A. Momigliano, *Pagine ebraiche*, ed. by S. Berti, Turin 1987.

Monaco 2013
C.S. Monaco, *The Rise of Modern Jewish Politics: Extraordinary Movement*, New York 2013.

Montaldo 2018
S. Montaldo, "Le début de la pensée raciste de Lombroso (1861-1870)," in *La Pensée de la race en Italie. Du romantisme au fascisme*, ed. by A. Aramini, E. Bovo, Besançon 2018, pp. 87–100.

Moos 1860
H.M. Moos, *Mortara: or, the Pope and His Inquisitors; a Drama, Together with Choice Poems*, Cincinnati 1860.

Morosini 1683
G. Morosini, *Derekh emunah. Via della fede mostrata a'gli ebrei*, Rome 1683.

Morpurgo 2010
A. Morpurgo, "Le architetture israelitiche," in *Attilio Muggia. Una storia per gli ingegneri*, ed. by M.B. Bettazzi, P. Lipparini, Bologna 2010, pp. 131–139.

Morselli, Maestri 2017
M.C. Morselli, G. Maestri, *Elia Benamozegh nostro contemporaneo*, Genoa 2017.

E. Mortara 2015
E. Mortara, *Writing for Justice: Victor Séjour, the Kidnapping of Edgardo Mortara, and the Age of Transatlantic Emancipations*, Hanover (NH) 2015.

E. Mortara 2018
E. Mortara, "Cronache e performances, 1858-1860: il caso Mortara nei diari e documenti ebraico-italiani dell'epoca," in *The New Italy and the Jews: From Massimo D'Azeglio to Primo Levi*, ed. by J. Druker, L.S. Lerner, *Annali d'Italianistica*, 36, 2018, pp. 193–215.

M. Mortara n.d. [1873]
M. Mortara, *Della nazionalità e delle aspirazioni messianiche degli Ebrei. A proposito della questione sollevata dall'onor. Deputato Pasqualigo*, Rome n.d. [1873].

Mossetti 1984
C. Mossetti, "La schedatura dei manufatti tessili in alcune considerazioni di carattere metodologico," in *Ebrei a Torino. Ricerche per il centenario della sinagoga. 1884-1984*, ed. by Comunità Ebraica di Torino, Turin, pp. 163–164.

Myers, Ruderman 1998
D.N. Myers, D.B. Ruderman, eds., *The Jewish Past Revisited: Reflections on Modern Jewish Historians*, New Haven 1998.

Nahon 1960
U. Nahon, "Le lettere di Teodoro Herzl a Felice Ravenna," in *R.M.I.*, XXVI, 1960, pp. 235–256.

Nani 2006
M. Nani, *Ai confini della nazione. Stampa e razzismo nell'Italia di fine Ottocento*, Rome 2006.

Nascimbeni 2014
A. Nascimbeni, *Medici Ebrei e la Cultura Ebraica a Ferrara*, Ferrara 2014.

Nashman-Fraiman 2006
S. Nashman-Fraiman, "Joy and Gladness, Happy Festivals for the House of Yehudah: A Unique Parokhet from Alessandra della Paglia," in *Ars Judaica*, 2006, pp. 151–162.

Nevins, Levine 2015–2016
M. Nevins, J. Levine, "A Face in the Crowd: Vesalius' Jewish Friend," in *Koroth*, XXIII, 2015–2016, pp. 237–256.

Nider 2010
V. Nider, "José Penso e l'accademia sefardita 'de los Sitibundos' di Livorno nella diffusione di un genere oratorio fra Italia e Spagna: traduzione e imitazione nelle Ideas Posibles (1692)," in *Studi Secenteschi*, LI, 2010, pp. 153–197.

Nirenberg 2013
D. Nirenberg, *Anti-Judaism. The Western Tradition*, New York 2013.

Orsucci Granata 2017
P. Orsucci Granata, *Moisè va alla guerra. Rabbini militari, soldati ebrei e comunità israelitiche nel primo conflitto mondiale*, Livorno 2017.

Ortalli 2001
F. Ortalli, *"Per salute delle anime e delli corpi". Scuole Piccole a Venezia nel tardo Medioevo*, Venice 2001.

Orvieto 1915
A. Orvieto, "Povera gente," in *Il Vessillo Israelitico*, July 15, 1915, pp. 371–372.

Pacifici 1953
A. Pacifici, "Aimé Pallière. Ricordi e riflessioni," in *La Rassegna Mensile di Israel*, XIX, 3, 1953, pp. 99–106.

Pagis 1973
D. Pagis, "Hamtza'at ha-ya'mbus ha-'ivri u-temurot ba-metriqah ha-'ivrit be-Italyah," in *Ha-sifrut*, 4, 1973, pp. 651–712.

Pagis 1975
D. Pagis, "Liturgical Poetry in the 17th Century Italy: A Hebrew Manuscript," in *Kiryat Sefer*, 50, 1975, pp. 288–312.

Pagis 1976
D. Pagis, *Change and Tradition in the Secular Poetry: Spain and Italy* (in Hebrew), Jerusalem 1976.

Pagis 1986
D. Pagis, *A Secret Sealed- Hebrew Baroque Emblem-Riddles from Italy and Holland* (in Hebrew), Jerusalem 1986.

Pagis 1991
D. Pagis, *Hebrew Poetry of the Middle Ages and the Renaissance*, Berkeley - Los Angeles - Oxford 1991.

Pancorbo 2019
F.J. Pancorbo, *Joseph Penso de Vega. Profil cultural y literario*, Florence 2019.

Parente 1983
F. Parente, "Il confronto ideologico tra l'ebraismo e la chiesa in Italia," in *Italia Judaica*, proceedings of the 1st international conference (Bari, May 18–22, 1981), Rome 1983, pp. 303–381.

Pavan 2008
I. Pavan, "L'impossibile rigenerazione. Ostilità antiebraiche nell'Italia liberale (1873-1913)," in *Storia e problemi contemporanei*, XX, 2008, pp. 34–67.

Pavan 2013
I. Pavan, "Fascism, Antisemitism and Racism. An ongoing debate," in *Telos*, 164, 2013, pp. 45–62.

Perlove 1989
S. Perlove, "Guercino's 'Esther Before Ahasuerus' and Cardinal Lorenzo Magalotti, Bishop of Ferrara," in *Artibus et Historiae*, 10, 19, 1989, pp. 133–147.

Pertici 2015
R. Pertici, "'Religioni libere entro lo Stato sovrano.' Libertà religiosa e separatismo nel pensiero di Luigi Luzzatti," in *Luigi Luzzatti Presidente del Consiglio*, ed. by P.L. Ballini, P. Pecorari, Venice 2015, pp. 171–257.

Pines 1961
J. Pines, "Des médecins juifs au service de la Papauté du XIIe au XVIIe siècle," in *Le Scalpel*, CXIV, 1961, pp. 462–470.

Pinkus 1988
B. Pinkus, *The Jews of the Soviet Union: The History of a National Minority*, Cambridge (UK) 1988.

Pirandello 1994
L. Pirandello, "Un goj," in *Novelle per un anno*, ed. by Pietro Gibellini. Florence 1994, pp. 465–471.

***Pirkei Avot* 1706**
Pirkei Avot estos son los Perakim los quales se dizen los Sabatoth que ay entre pesah y sebuhoth cada Sabath uno, En Venezia MDCCVI, Na Stamparia Bragadina, Venice 1706.

Poggi 1978
G. Poggi, *La vicenda dello stato moderno: profilo sociologico*, Bologna 1978.

Poliakov 2013
L. Poliakov, *Storia dell'antisemitismo*, Milan 2013.

Polonsky 2010
A. Polonsky, *The Jews in Poland and Russia*, 3 vols., Oxford 2010.

Procaccia, Teodonio 2007
M. Procaccia, M. Teodonio, *Sonetti giudaico-romaneschi, sonetti romaneschi, prove e versioni*, unabridged edition, Florence 2007.

Provenzali 1988–1989
M. Provenzali, *Shut Rabbenu Mosheh Provenzalo* [*sic*] (Responsi del nostro Maestro Mosheh Provenzalo), vol. 1, ed. by A.Y. Janni, Jerusalem 1988–1989.

Pullan 1971
B. Pullan, *Rich and Poor in Renaissance Venice: The Social Institutions of a Catholic State, to 1620,* Oxford 1971.

Pulzer 1986
P. Pulzer, "The Beginning of the End," in *Die Juden im Nationalsozialistischen Deutschland, 1933–1943*, ed. by A. Paucker, Tübingen 1986, pp. 17–27.

Pulzer 1988
P. Pulzer, *The Rise of Political Antisemitism in Germany and Austria*, revised edition, Cambridge (MA) 1988.

Rabinowitz 1983
I. Rabinowitz, *The Book of the Honeycomb's Flow by Judah Messer Leon: A Critical Edition and Translation*, Ithaca 1983.

Rathaus 2001
A. Rathaus, "Poesia, preghiera, midrash. Il verdetto di R. Netanel Trabotto sul piyut contemporaneo," in *La Rassegna Mensile di Israel*, 67, 1–2, 2001, pp. 129–150.

Rathaus 2012
A. Rathaus, "I dottori e le Muse: pratica poetica fra i rabbini medici italiani nel XVII e XVIII secolo," in *Medici rabbini. Momenti di storia della medicina ebraica*, ed. by M. Silvera, Rome 2012, pp. 105–121.

Ravid 1978
B. Ravid, *Ecomomics and Toleration in Seventeenth Century Venice: The Background and Context of the Discorso of Simone Luzzatto*, Jerusalem 1978.

Ravid 1991
B. Ravid, "A Tale of Three Cities and Their 'Raison d'État': Ancona, Venice, Livorno, and the Competition for Jewish Merchants in the Sixteenth Century," in *Mediterranean Historical Review*, VI, 1991, pp. 138–162.

Ravid 2008
B. Ravid, "How 'Other' Really Was the Jewish Other? Evidence from Venice," in *Acculturation and its Discontents: The Italian Jewish Experience Between Exclusion and Inclusion*, ed. by R. Weinstein, D.N. Myers *et al.*, Toronto 2008, pp. 19–55.

Ravid 2018
B. Ravid, "Ghetto. Etymology, Original Definition, Reality, and Diffusion," in *The Ghetto in Global History. 1500 to the Present*, ed. by W.Z. Goldman and J.W. Trotter, 22–37, New York 2018, pp. 22–37.

Reichman 2008
E. Reichman, "The Anatomy of Halakhah," in *Beracha Le'Avraham*, ed. by Y. Steinberg, Jerusalem 2008, pp. 69–97.

Reichman 2017
E. Reichman, "The Valmadonna Trust Broadside Collection and a Virtual Reunion of the Jewish Medical Students of Padua," in *Verapo Yerapei: Journal of Torah and Medicine of the Albert Einstein College of Medicine Synagogue*, VII, 2017, pp. 55–76.

Reichman 2019
E. Reichman, "The Yeshiva Medical School: The Evolution of Educational Programs Combining Jewish Studies and Medical Training," in *Tradition*, LI, 2019, pp. 41–56.

Reichman in press
E. Reichman, "Confessions of a Would-Be Forger: The Medical Diploma of Tobias Cohn (Tuvia HaRofeh) and Other Jewish Medical Graduates of the University of Padua," in *Ma'ase Tuviya (Venice, 1708): Tuviya Cohen on Medicine and Science*, ed. by K. Collins, S. Kottek, Jerusalem, in press.

Richler 2001
B. Richler, ed., *Hebrew manuscripts in the Biblioteca Palatina in Parma: Catalogue*, paleographic and codicological descriptions by Beit-Arié, Jerusalem 2001.

Rigano 2017
G. Rigano, "Identità nazionale e identità religiosa. Comunità di confine nella Grande Guerra: il caso di Trieste e Fiume," in *Gli ebrei italiani nella Grande Guerra (1915-1918)*, ed. by C. Quareni, V. Maugeri, Florence, 2017, pp. 85–102.

Righini 1901
E. Righini, *Antisemitismo e semitismo nell'Italia politica moderna*, Milan-Palermo 1901.

Rignano 1847
I. Rignano, *Sulla attuale posizione degli Israeliti in Toscana. Brevi cenni*, Florence 1847.

Rivlin 1989
B. Rivlin, "Taqqanot 'Chevrat ha-nizharim' be-Bolonyah mi-shenat sh"z," in *Asufot*, 3, 1989, pp. 357–396.

Rivlin 1991
B. Rivlin, *'Arevim zeh la-zeh ba-geto ha-italqi. Havurot gama"ch 1516-1789*, Jerusalem 1991.

Robinson 1981
I. Robinson, "Messianic Prayer Vigils in Jerusalem in the Early Sixteenth Century," in *Jewish Quarterly Review*, 72, 1, 1981, pp. 32–42.

Romani 2018
R. Romani, *Sensibilities of the Risorgimento. Reason and Passions in Political Thought*, Leiden 2018.

Rosselli 2001
A. Rosselli, *Memorie*, ed. by M. Calloni, Bologna 2001.

Roth 1930
C. Roth, "The Medieval University and the Jew," in *Menorah Journal*, XIX, 1930, pp. 128–141.

Roth 1953
C. Roth, "The Qualification of Jewish Physicians in the Middle Ages," in Speculum, XXVIII, 1953, pp. 834–43.

Roth 1967
C. Roth, "Stemmi di famiglie ebraiche italiane," in D. Carpi, A. Milano, A. Rofé, *Scritti in memoria di Leone Carpi*, Jerusalem 1967, pp. 165–184.

Rovighi 1999
A. Rovighi, *I militari di origine ebraica nel primo secolo di vita dello Stato italiano*, presentation by E. Pino, introduction by A. Levi, Rome 1999.

Ruderman 1995
D. Ruderman, *Jewish Thought and Scientific Discovery in Early Modern Europe*, New Haven-London 1995.

Ruderman 2010
D. Ruderman, *Early Modern Jewry. A new Cultural History*, Princenton 2010.

Rürup 1975
R. Rürup, "Emanzipation: Anmerkungen zur Begriffsgeschichte," in Id., *Emanzipation und Antisemitismus*, Göttingen 1975, pp. 126–132.

Rürup 1986
R. Rürup, "Das Ende des Emanzipation: Die antijüdische Politik in Deutschland von der "Machtergreifung" bis zum Zweiten Weltkrieg," in *Die Juden im Nationalsozialistischen Deutschland*, 1933–1943, ed. by A. Paucker, Tübingen 1986, pp. 97–114.

Rusconi 1986
R. Rusconi, *Confraternite, compagnie e devozioni, in Storia d'Italia. Annals, 9: La Chiesa e il potere politico dal Medioevo all'età contemporanea*, ed. by G. Chittolini, G. Miccoli, Turin, 1986, pp. 469–506.

Sabar 2000
S. Sabar, *Ketubbah: The Art of the Jewish Marriage Contract*, New York 2000.

Sabar 2012
S. Sabar, "A New Discovery: The Earliest Illustrated Esther Scroll by Shalom Italia," in *Ars Judaica*, VIII, 2012, pp. 121–122.

Sarfatti 2000
M. Sarfatti, *Gli ebrei nell'Italia fascista*, Turin 2000.

Scalise 1997
D. Scalise, *Il caso Mortara*, Milan 1997.

Ch. Schirmann 1934
Ch. Schirmann, *Mivchar ha-shirah ha-'ivrit be-Italiah*, Berlin 1934.

J. Schirmann 1979
J. Schirmann, *Studies in the History of Hebrew Poetry and Drama* (in Hebrew), 2 vols., Jerusalem 1979.

Scholem 1973
G. Scholem, *Sabbatai Sevi: The Mystical Messiah*, trans. by R.J.Z. Werblowsky, Princeton (NJ) 1973.

Scholem 1980
G. Scholem, *La kabbalah e il suo simbolismo*, Turin 1980.

D.V. Segre 1984
D.V. Segre, "Risorgimento italiano - Risorgimento ebraico," in *Garibaldi, Mazzini e il Risorgimento nel risveglio dell'Asia e dell'Africa*, Milan 1984.

D.V. Segre 1998
D.V. Segre, "L'emancipazione degli ebrei in Italia," in *Integrazione e identità. L'esperienza ebraica in Germania e in Italia dall'Illuminismo al fascismo*, ed. by M. Toscano, Milan 1998, pp. 84–113.

R. Segre 1996
R. Segre, "La controriforma: espulsioni, conversioni, isolamento," in *Storia d'Italia. Annali 11. Gli ebrei in Italia 1. Dall'alto Medioevo all'età dei ghetti*, ed. by C. Vivanti, Turin 1996, pp. 709–778.

Séjour 1860
V. Séjour, *La Tireuse de cartes (Drame, en cinq actes et un prologue, en prose. Par Victor Séjour)*, Paris 1860.

Sephiha 1984
H.V. Sephiha, "Quelques œuvres judéo-espagnoles editées à Livourne," in *La Rassegna Mensile di Israel*, L, 1984, pp. 743–765.

Sereni 1935
E. Sereni, "L'assedio del ghetto di Roma del 1793 nelle memorie di un contemporaneo," in *La Rassegna Mensile di Israel*, 2–3, 1935, pp. 101–125 (republished in *Scritti in memoria di Enzo Sereni. Saggi sull'ebraismo italiano*, ed. by D. Carpi, A. Milano, U. Nahon, Jerusalem 1970, pp. 168–198).

Sergi 1894
G. Sergi, "L'antisemitismo," in *Educazione e istruzione*, I, 1894, pp. 109–112.

Sermoneta 1989[a]
G. Sermoneta, "La cultura ebraica a Roma nel secolo XVIII alla luce di nuovi documenti" (in Hebrew), in *Italia Judaica, Gli ebrei in Italia dalla segregazione alla prima emancipazione*, proceedings of the 3rd international conference (Tel Aviv, June 15–20, 1986), Rome 1989, pp. 69–96.

Sermoneta 1989[b]
G. Sermoneta, ed., *Ratto della Signora Anna del Monte trattenuta a' Catecumini tredici giorni dalli 6 fino alli 19 maggio anno 1749*, Rome 1989.

Seroussi 2002
E. Seroussi, "Livorno: A Crossroads in the History of Sephardic religious music," in *The Mediterranean and the Jews. Society, Culture and Economy in Early Modern Times*, ed. by

E. Horowitz, M. Orfali, Ramat Gan 2002, pp. 131–154; 158–306.

Servi 1864
F. Servi, "Religione e patria," in *L'Educatore Israelita*, 12, 1864, pp. 75–78, 106–110, 133–136, 271–275, 297–301, 328–333.

Servi 1865[a]
F. Servi, "Religione e patria," in *L'Educatore Israelita*, 13, 1865, pp. 71-74, 113-117.

Servi 1865[b]
F. Servi, "Studi statistici," in *L'Educatore Israelita*, XIII, 1865, pp. 364–366.

Servi 1866
F. Servi, "Statistica degl'Israeliti Italiani - Anno III," in *L'Educatore Israelita*, XIV, 1866, pp. 363–364.

Servi 1903
F. Servi, "Popolazione israelitica in alcune città italiane," in *Il Vessillo Israelitico*, LI, August, 1903, p. 251.

Settimi 2017
P. Settimi, *L'ultimo traduttore. Jacob Alpron tra yiddish e italiano*, Saonara 2017.

Shasha, Massry 2002
S. M. Shasha, S. G. Massry, "The Medical School of Padua and its Jewish Graduates" (in Hebrew), in *Harefuah*, CXLI, 2002, pp. 388–394.

Shatzky 1950
J. Shatzky, "On Jewish Medical Students of Padua," in *Journal of the History of Medicine*, V, Autumn 1950, pp. 444–447.

Shulvass 1944
M.A. Shulvass, *Roma we-Yerushalaym. Toledot ha-yachas shel yehude Italyah le-Eretz Yisra'el*, Jerusalem 1944.

Siegmund 1996
S. Siegmund, "La vita nei ghetti," in *Storia d'Italia. Annali 11. Gli ebrei in Italia 1. Dall'alto Medioevo all'età dei ghetti*, ed. by C. Vivanti, Turin 1996, pp. 845–892.

Siegmund 2006
S. Siegmund, *The Medici State and the Ghetto of Florence. The Construction of an Early Modern Jewish Community*, Stanford 2006.

Silva 2008
G. da Silva, *L'affaire Mortara et l'antisémitisme chrétien*, Paris 2008.

Silvera 2012
M. Silvera, ed., *Medici rabbini. Momenti di Storia della Medicina Ebraica*, Rome 2012.

Simonsohn 1959–1960
Sh. Simonsohn, "Pinqase ha-qehillah be-Werona," in *Kiryat Sefer*, 35, 1–2, 1959–1960, pp. 127–136, 250–268.

Simonsohn 1977
Sh. Simonsohn, *History of the Jews in the Duchy of Mantua*, Jerusalem 1977.

Sofia 2006
F. Sofia, "Gli ebrei risorgimentali fra tradizione biblica, libera muratoria e nazione," in *Storia d'Italia. Annali 21: La Massoneria*, ed. by Gian Mario Cazzaniga, Turin 2006, pp. 244–265.

Sofia 2008
F. Sofia, "Il tema del confronto e dell'inclusione. Il Sinedrio napoleonico," in *Le religioni e il mondo moderno*, ed. by G. Filoramo, *II. Ebraismo*, ed. by D. Bidussa, Turin 2008, pp. 103–124.

Sofia 2010
F. Sofia, "La nazione degli ebrei risorgimentali," in *La Rassegna Mensile di Israel*, LXXVI, 2010, pp. 95–112.

Sofia 2011
F. Sofia, "Il Vangelo eterno svelato: David Levi e la massoneria," in *Massoneria e Unità d'Italia. La Libera Muratoria e la costruzione della nazione*, ed. by F. Conti, M. Novarino, Bologna 2011, pp. 203–211.

Sonne 1936
I. Sonne, "Al devar ha-chevrah 'Chadashim la-beqarim' be-Mantovah," in *Zion*, 1, 1936, p. 94.

Sonnino 1912
G. Sonnino, *Storia della tipografia ebraica in Livorno con introduzione e catalogo di opere e di autori*, Turin 1912.

Sorkin 2001
D. Sorkin, "Port Jews and the Three Regions of Emancipation," in *Port Jews: Jewish Communities in Cosmopolitan Maritime Trading Centres*, 1550–1950, ed. by D. Cesarani, London-Portland 2001, pp. 31–46.

Sorkin 2019
D. Sorkin, *Jewish Emancipation: A History Across Five Centuries*, Princeton 2019.

Spagnolo 2005
F. Spagnolo, "Musiche in contatto. Le fonti delle tradizioni musicali ebraiche in Italia," in *EM. Annuario degli Archivi di Etnomusicologia. Accademia Nazionale di Santa Cecilia*, 2005, pp. 83–107.

Spagnolo 2007
F. Spagnolo, *The Musical Traditions of the Jews in Piedmont (Italy)*, PhD Dissertation, The Hebrew University of Jerusalem, 2007.

Spagnolo 2018
F. Spagnolo, "Sounds of Emancipation: Politics, Identity, and Music in 19th-Century Italian Synagogues," in *The New Italy and the Jews from Massimo D'Azeglio to Primo Levi*, ed. by J. Druker and L.S. Lerner, *Annali d'Italianistica*, 36, 2018, pp. 115–140.

Stefani 2004
P. Stefani, *L'antigiudaismo. Storia di un'idea*, Rome-Bari 2004.

Stow 1977
K.R. Stow, *Catholic Thought and the Papa Jewry Policy*, New York 1977.

Stow 2001
K.R. Stow, *Theatre of Acculturation. The Roman Ghetto in the Sixteenth Century*, Seattle 2001.

Stuczynski 2010
C.B. Stuczynski, "Marranesimo," in *Dizionario storico dell'Inquisizione*, ed. by A. Prosperi, with the collaboration of V. Lalvenia, J. Tedeschi, Pisa 2010, II, pp. 989–997.

Sutcliffe 2003
A. Sutcliffe, *Judaism and the Enlightenment*, Cambridge 2003.

Tamani 1968
G. Tamani, "Elenco dei manoscritti ebraici miniati e decorati della 'Palatina' di Parma," in *La Bibliofilia*, LXX, 1968.

Tamani 2003
G. Tamani, "La Tipografia Marrana di Ferrara (1552-1555)," in *L'interculturalità dell'ebraismo*, proceedings of the international conference (Bertinoro-Ravenna, May 26–28, 2003), ed. by M. Perani, Ravenna 2003, pp. 287–298.

Tamani 2005
G. Tamani, ed., *Libri ebraici dei secoli XVI-XIX nella Biblioteca Universitaria di Padova*, Padua 2005.

Taradel 2002
R. Taradel, *L'accusa del sangue. Storia politica di un mito antisemita*, Milan 2002.

Taradel, Raggi 2000
R. Taradel, B. Raggi, *La segregazione amichevole, "La Civiltà Cattolica" e la questione ebraica, 1850-1945*, foreword by R. Di Segni, Rome 2000.

Terracini 1948
U. Terracini, "Introduzione," in *Il centenario dal Parlamento, 8 maggio 1848 - 8 maggio 1948*, Rome 1948, p. 9.

Tesi-Passerini 1879
C. Tesi-Passerini, *Pio Nono e il suo tempo*, vol. 2, Florence 1879.

Tirosh-Rothschild 1991
H. Tirosh-Rothschild, *Between Worlds: The Life and Thought of Rabbi David ben Judah Messer Leon*, Albany 1991.

Tishby 1974
I. Tishby, "The Confrontation between Lurianic Kabbalah and Cordoverian Kabbalah in the Writings and Life of Rabbi Aaron Berechiah of Modena" (in Hebrew), in *Zion*, 39, 1–2, 1974, pp. 8–85.

A. Toaff 1933
A. Toaff, "Vita artistico-letteraria degli Ebrei a Livorno nel '700," in *La Rassegna Mensile di Israel*, VII-VIII, 1933, pp. 370–378.

A. Toaff 1937
A. Toaff, "Il Collegio Rabbinico di Livorno," in *La Rassegna Mensile di Israel*, XII, 1937, pp. 184–195.

A. Toaff 1955
A. Toaff, "Cenni storici sulla comunità ebraica e sulla sinagoga di Livorno," in *La Rassegna Mensile di Israel*, XXI, 1955, pp. 355–430.

A. Toaff 1962[a]
A. Toaff, "Moshé Aharon Rachamim Piazza: Rabbino-predicatore, poeta, cabbalista livornese del secolo XVIII," in *Scritti in memoria di Federico Luzzatto*, ed. by A. Milano, G. Romano, Rome 1962, pp. 3–15.

A. Toaff 1962[b]
A. Toaff, *Una sinagoga che non è più*, Livorno 1962.

R. Toaff 1990
R. Toaff, *La Nazione Ebrea a Livorno e a Pisa (1591–1700)*, Florence 1990.

Todeschini 2016
G. Todeschini, *La banca e il ghetto. Una storia italiana (secoli XIV-XVI)*, Rome-Bari 2016.

Todeschini 2018
G. Todeschini, *Gli ebrei nell'Italia medievale*, Rome 2018.

Todeschini, Ioli Zorattini 1991
G. Todeschini, P.C. Ioli Zorattini, eds., *Il Mondo Ebraico*, Pordenone 1991.

Toscano 1998
M. Toscano, "Risorgimento ed ebrei: alcune riflessioni sulla 'nazionalizzazione parallela,'" in *R.M.I.*, XLIV, 1998, pp. 59–70.

Toscano 2003
M. Toscano, *Ebraismo e antisemitismo in Italia. Dal 1848 alla guerra dei sei giorni*, Milan 2003.

Toscano 2005
M. Toscano, "Religione, patriottismo, sionismo: il rabbinato militare nell'Italia della Grande Guerra (1915-1918)," in *Zakhor*, VIII, 2005, pp. 77–133.

Toscano 2010
M. Toscano, "Gli ebrei nell'Italia unita: tra storia e storiografia," in *R.M.I.*, LXXVI, 2010, pp. 1–18.

Toscano 2016
M. Toscano, "Gli ebrei italiani, la guerra e l'intervento. Un dibattito tra italianità, religione e sionismo," in *L'Italia neutrale 1914-1915*, ed. by G. Orsina, A. Ungari, Rome 2016, pp. 217–229.

Toscano 2017
M. Toscano, "Il movimento 'Pro causa ebraica' tra filantropia e politica (1915-1918). Note e problemi di ricerca," in *Gli ebrei italiani nella Grande Guerra (1915-1918)*, ed. by C. Quareni, V. Maugeri, Florence 2017, pp. 57–69.

Toscano 2019
M. Toscano, *Ebrei e ebraismo nell'Italia del Novecento*, Milan 2019.

Tribunale 1860
Tribunale Civile e Criminale di Prima Istanza in Bologna, *Bologna. Nella Causa di Separazione violenta del fanciullo Edgardo Mortara […] Contro Feretti Frate Pier Gaetano […]*, Archivio di Stato di Bologna, 1860.

Trivellato 2009
F. Trivellato, *The Familiarity of Strangers: The Sephardic Diaspora, Livorno, and Cross-Cultural Trade in the Early Modern Period*, New Haven 2009.

Trivellato 2016
F. Trivellato, *Il commercio interculturale. La diaspora sefardita, Livorno e i traffici globali in età moderna*, Rome 2016.

Troìa 2013
P. Troìa, "Musicisti e canti sinagogali a Roma tra il 1814 e il 1914. Una ricerca nell'Archivio Storico della Comunità Ebraica di Roma," in *Ebrei a Roma tra Risorgimento ed emancipazione, 1814–1914*, ed. by C. Procaccia, Rome 2013, pp. 163–232.

Turner 2019
P. Turner, "Considering the Baptism of Edgardo Mortara in the Context of Catholic Teachings and Rituals Then and Now," in *Studies in Christian-Jewish Relations (SCJR)*, 14, no. 1, 2019, pp. 1–9.

***Tutti i colori* 2019**
Tutti i colori dell'Italia ebraica. Tessuti preziosi dal Tempio di Gerusalemme al prêt-à-porter, exhibition catalogue (Florence, Uffizi Gallery, June 27 – October 27, 2019), ed. by D. Liscia Bemporad, O. Melasecchi, Florence 2019.

Uhry 2002
A. Uhry, *Edgardo Mine*, play performed at the Hartford Stage, Hartford CT 2002.

Uzielli 1909
G. Uzielli, "Dai ricordi di uno studente garibaldino (1859-1860)," in *Il Risorgimento Italiano*, 2, 1909, pp. 915–951.

Veca 2019
I. Veca, *Il mito di Pio IX. Storia di un papa liberale e nazionale*, Rome 2019.

Vian 2012
G. Vian, *Il modernismo. La Chiesa cattolica e il conflitto con la modernità*, Rome 2012.

Vio 2004
G. Vio, *Le scuole piccole nella Venezia dei dogi. Note d'archivio per la storia delle confraternite veneziane*, Costabissara 2004.

Vita Finzi 1989
P. Vita Finzi, *Giorni lontani*, foreword by R. De Felice, Bologna 1989.

Vital 1980
D. Vital, *The Origins of Zionism*, Oxford 1980.

Vital 2001
D. Vital, *A People Apart: A Political History of the Jews of Europe 1789-1939*, Oxford 2001.

Vogelstein, Rieger 1895–1896
H. Vogelstein, P. Rieger, *Geschichte der Juden in Rom*, 2 vols., Berlin 1895–1896.

Volkov 2006
S. Volkov, *Germans, Jews, and Antisemites. Trials in Emancipation*, Cambridge - New York 2006.

Volli 1960[a]
G. Volli, "Il caso Mortara nell'opinione pubblica e nella politica del tempo," in *Bollettino del Museo del Risorgimento*, 5, 2, 1960, pp. 1087–1152 (new edition Bologna 1961).

Volli 1960[b]
G. Volli, "Il caso Mortara nel primo centenario," in *La Rassegna Mensile di Israel*, Rome 1960 (Facsimile reprint as *Il caso Mortara. Il bambino rapito da Pio IX*, foreword by Ugo Volli, Florence 2016).

Walfish 1993
B.D. Walfish, *Esther in Medieval Garb. Jewish Interpretation of the Book of Esther in the Middle Ages*, New York 1993.

Walk 1981
J. Walk, ed., *Das Sonderrecht für die Juden im NS-Staat: Eine Sammlung der gesetzlichen Maßnahmen und Richtlinien-Inhalt und Bedeutung*, Heidelberg 1981.

Weber 1997–1998
A. Weber, "Ark and Curtain: Monuments for a Jewish Nation in Exile," in *The Real and Ideal Jerusalem in Jewish, Christian and Islamic Art*, ed. by A. Cohen-Mushlin, B. Kühnel, *Jewish Art*, 23/24, 1997–1998, pp. 89–99.

Weinstein 2007
R. Weinstein, "Feminine Religiosity in Jewish-Italian Context during the Early Modern Period: Preliminary Observations," in *Italia judaica.Donne nella storia degli ebrei d'Italia*, proceedings of the 9th international conference (Lucca, June 6–9, 2005), ed. by Michele Luzzati, Cristina Galasso, 2007, pp. 147–170.

Wirth 1927
L. Wirth, "The Ghetto," in *The American Journal of Sociology*, 33, 1, 1927, pp. 57–71.

Wirth 1928
L. Wirth, *The Ghetto*, Chicago-London 1928.

Wyrwa 2014
U. Wyrwa, "Osservatore Cattolico and Davide Albertario: Catholic Public Relations and Antisemitic Propaganda in Milan," in *Sites of European Antisemitism in the Age of Mass Politics 1880-1918*, ed. by R. Nemes, D. Unowsky, Waltham (MA) 2014, pp. 61–75, 283–290.

Wyrwa 2016
U. Wyrwa, "The Language of Antisemitism in the Catholic Newspapers Il Veneto Cattolico - La Difesa in Late Nineteenth Century Venice," in *Church History and Religious Culture*, 96, 2016, pp. 346–369.

Yaari 1950
A. Yaari, *Sheluche Eretz Yisrael: Toledot ha-shelichut me-ha-Aretz la-golah*, Jerusalem 1950.

Yaniv 2009
B. Yaniv, *Ma'ase Rokem. Textile Cerimonial Objects in the Askenazi, Sephardi and Italian Synagogue*, Jerusalem 2009.

Yerushalmi 1971
Y.H. Yerushalmi, *From Spanish Court to Italian Ghetto. A Study in Seventeenth-Century Marranism and Jewish Apologetics*, New York - London 1971.

Yerushalmi 2011
Y.H. Yerushalmi, *Zakhor*, Florence 2011.

Zacuto 1715
M. Zacuto, *Tofteh 'arukh*, Venice 1715.

Zacuto 1744
M. Zacuto, *Sefer tofteh 'arukh... we-Sefer eden 'arukh*, Venice 1744.

Zacuto 2016
M. Zacuto, *"L'inferno allestito" (Toftèh 'arùkh). Poema di un rabbino del Seicento sull'oltretomba dei malvagi*, ed. by M. Andreatta, Milan 2016.

Zardin 1987
D. Zardin, "Le confraternite in Italia settentrionale fra XV e XVIII secolo," in *Società e storia*, 35, 1987, pp. 81–137.

Photo Credits

Archivio della Comunità Ebraica di Mantova
Archivio di Stato di Torino
Archivio eredi famiglia Alberto Mortara
Archivio Fondazione CDEC di Milano
Archivio Fotografico della Fondazione Torino Musei 2010
© Archivio GBB / Archivi Alinari
Archivio Patrimonio Artistico Intesa Sanpaolo
Archivio Storico della Città di Torino
Archivio Storico della Comunità Ebraica di Roma "Giancarlo Spizzichino"
Dody Bassani, Mantova
© 2020 Biblioteca Correr - Fondazione Musei Civici di Venezia
Biblioteca Nazionale Centrale di Roma
Biblioteca Queriniana, Brescia
Dario Canova, Casale Monferrato
Marco Caselli Nirmal, Ferrara
Centro Bibliografico UCEI, Roma
Comunità Ebraica di Casale Monferrato
Comunità Ebraica di Livorno, Museo Ebraico
DeA Picture Library, concesso in licenza ad Alinari
P. Della Corte - Savio Benefator
Pino Dell'Aquila, Torino
Alberto Di Castro, Roma
Federico Disegni, Torino
Foto Araldo De Luca © Museo Ebraico di Roma
Foto Massimo Listri © Museo Ebraico di Roma
© 2020 Foto Scala, Firenze
Luca Gavagna, Le Immagini s.a.s., Ferrara
Gross Family Collection, Tel Aviv
Gross Family Collection Trust, Tel Aviv
Jay and Jeanie Schottenstein Family Collection of Judaica
© Look and Learn / Bridgeman Images
Ministero per i Beni e le Attività Culturali e del Turismo - Biblioteca Palatina, Parma
Ministero per i Beni e le Attività Culturali e del Turismo - Gallerie degli Uffizi, Firenze
Museo Civico Giovanni Fattori, Livorno
Museo dell'Ottocento, Ferrara
Museo Ebraico di Roma
U. Nahon Museum of Italian Jewish Art, Gerusalemme
National Library of Israel
Angelo Piattelli, Gerusalemme
Paolo Robino, Torino
© Roma-Sovrintendenza Capitolina ai Beni Culturali
Segretariato Generale della Presidenza della Repubblica - Foto Giuseppe Schiavinotto, Roma
Sinagoga e Museo Ebraico "Fausto Levi" di Soragna
© SZ Photo / Bridgeman Images

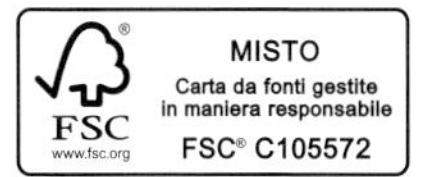

Cover
Sebastiano Ricci, *Esther before Ahasuerus*, details (cat. 1)

Brand Design
Teikna, Claudia Neri

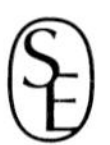

Silvana Editoriale

Direction
Dario Cimorelli

Art Director
Giacomo Merli

Editorial Coordinator
Sergio Di Stefano

Copy Editor
Paola Rossi

Layout
Annamaria Ardizzi

Translations
Sarah Elizabeth Cree
Gordon Fisher
Karen Tomatis

Production Coordinator
Antonio Micelli

Editorial Assistants
Ondina Granato, Giulia Mercanti

Photo Editors
Alessandra Olivari, Silvia Sala

Press Office
Lidia Masolini, press@silvanaeditoriale.it

Available through ARTBOOK | D.A.P.
155 Sixth Avenue, 2nd Floor, New York, N.Y. 10013
Tel: (212) 627-1999 Fax: (212) 627-9484

Silvana Editoriale S.p.A.
via dei Lavoratori, 78
20092 Cinisello Balsamo, Milano
tel. 02 453 951 01
fax 02 453 951 51
www.silvanaeditoriale.it

Reproductions, printing and binding in Italy
Printed by Modulgrafica Forlivese S.p.A., Forlì
July 2020